TO THE MEMORY OF A MOTHER WHOSE PIETY AND
WHOLESOME TEACHINGS HAVE BEEN OUR CONSTANT
INSPIRATION, THIS BOOK IS GRATEFULLY DEDICATED.

"BEHOLD I STAND AT THE DOOR AND KNOCK"

BEAUTIFUL BIBLE STORIES

By

Rev. Charles P. Roney, D. D.

Rev. Wilfred G. Rice, *Collaborator*

INSPIRATIONAL, ENTERTAINING, FASCINATING,
EDUCATIONAL, CHARACTER-BUILDING

History • Romance • Adventure • Tragedy
Intrigue • Action • Bravery
Thrills • Loyalty
Faith

Designed to stimulate a greater interest
in the Bible through the arrangement of
extensive References, Suggestions for
Study, and Test Questions

THE JOHN A. HERTEL CO.

CHICAGO, ILLINOIS

To this edition have been added full-color paintings from selected subjects

By

FRANK MCDONOUGH

with interpretations

AUTHOR'S PREFACE

When the publishers of this book asked that I undertake to write a series of narratives which might be fittingly called "Beautiful Bible Stories" in which the essential events of the Bible would be related in a manner adapted to this generation, acquainted to some extent at least with modern science, history, and biblical criticism; and in which the stories of the Bible would be given to the world in such fascinating and dramatic language that the Bible would become even more inspiring to people who believe in it and love it, and compellingly attractive to doubters; I accepted the task with modesty and humble reliance upon the Divine Spirit for aid.

The work was undertaken with a realization that the Bible, though the most popular Book of the world, is to most people a "closed Book." It has been our constant aim, therefore, to so simplify the Holy Scriptures that their teachings might be easily understood by children, young people, and adults; to place within the grasp of all ages and classes the saving and character-building truths of the Holy Book. We have sought to make the history, romance, adventure, tragedy, bravery, loyalty, and faith exemplified in biblical history entertaining, inspirational, educational.

This book has been written with the purpose of acquainting its readers with the history lying back of all religious truth. We have undertaken to do this by giving a simple and understandable account of the principal events contained in the Bible. "Beautiful Bible Stories" is not a paraphrase of the Bible, but it is a series of narratives covering the main events of the Bible. Without entering the field of controversy or sectarian dogmatism, it briefly summarizes the principal teachings of these events.

It is inevitable, of course, that everything covered in the Bible could not be included in a book of this character. There are some incidents, and much teaching-material, which are not even mentioned. We have undertaken, however, to present in vivid and attractive style the dramatic pageant of the life which runs through the Bible from its earliest pages to the ascension of the Lord Jesus Christ.

During the period of composition the question has been often asked, "Is Beautiful Bible Stories being written for grown people or for children?" This question is answered by another question, "Was the Bible written for grown people or for children?" It was written, of course, for both. This book has been written for both. We have tried to relate the incidents of the Bible in such a way that mature and advanced minds will feel their fascination; and yet at the same time reproduce the Bible's incomparable pictures of human life and of God's manifestations of power in language simple enough for every child to readily understand and to grasp their truths.

In writing this book we have been constantly overshadowed by a firm and unshaken belief in the inerrant inspiration of the Holy Bible and in the supernatural work of God in the development of this system of truth. Many of the events related can be explained only on the basis of supernatural intervention by a personal Deity, and this fact has been fully recognized. The supremacy of God in the creation of all things, in the absolute control of all natural phenomena, in the outcome of human history, and in directing world-events for the accomplishment of his own purposes in man's redemption, is kept constantly before the reader.

We began our task with many misgivings, and have carried it to its present conclusion with gratitude to God for health and strength and Divine guidance. Our fondest hope is that this book may bring to those who read it an inspiration and happiness equal to that found by us in writing it.

CHARLES PATRICK RONEY.

Chicago, Ill.
September 1940

PREFACE TO SECOND EDITION

The author of "Beautiful Bible Stories" is profoundly grateful for the popular reception and extensive use given to the first edition; 25,000 copies were sold within a little over one year after it was placed on the market. After a long delay, due to the lack of available paper caused by World War II, this second edition is sent forth with our continued prayers for increased benedictions upon its users. Six matchless colored paintings have been included in the new edition which will add greatly to its beauty and value.

Chicago, Ill.
June 1948

TABLE OF CONTENTS

PART ONE

Stories from the Creation to the Call of Abraham

PART TWO

Stories from the Call of Abraham to Israel's Migration to Egypt

PART THREE

Stories of Israel in Egypt to the Birth of Moses

PART FOUR

From the Birth of Moses to the Call of Joshua

8

CONTENTS 9

PART FIVE

From the Appointment of Joshua to the Three Hundred Years Struggle

PART SIX

From the Three Hundred Years Struggle to the Beginning of the Monarchy

PART SEVEN

From the Beginning of the Monarchy to the End of the United Kingdom

PART EIGHT

Stories of the Northern Kingdom

PART NINE

Stories of the Kingdom of Judah

PART TEN

Stories of Judah in Captivity

PART ELEVEN

Stories of the Life of Christ

SONGS

INDEX TO ILLUSTRATIONS

(*indicates full page)

STORY 1

THE WONDERFUL STORY OF CREATION

GENESIS 1:1-31; 2:1-7,
18-25

Away back, many thousands and thousands of years ago, in the beginning of all things, there were no cities, no towns, or villages, as we now see them; there were no homes, no farms, no trees, no green fields, no cattle, no sheep or lambs, and no birds. There were no seas, no lakes, no rivers, no streams of any kind. Why at one time, there was no ground, no sky, no sun, no moon, or stars. There was neither day nor night; there were no people, neither men or women, boys or girls. There was nothing—nothing of all that we see now.

Today the existence of this world in all its beauty and grandeur, of the great planets and myriads of stars in the vast expanse of the universe, are actualities before our eyes, realities to the five senses of human beings throughout the world. Men and women, boys and girls, everywhere, hunger to know something of the mystery and origin of these things. For thousands of years there have been many speculations as to how the world came into being. We know by intuition that it had a commencement; and our instinct and reason revolt at the suggestion that it sprang into existence by chance, or was formed by spontaneous emanations from a source not yet discovered by science.

THE CREATION OF LIGHT

People are always asking: Has the world always existed? If not, how did it begin? Did the sun make itself? If not, what brought it into existence? What is the source of the great planetary systems of the universe? Was this source created? If so, by whom?

There is a GOOD BOOK which we call the Bible in which we find the only satisfactory answers to these, and scores of other similar, questions. The opening statement of that Divinely inspired Book is:

"In the beginning God created the heaven and the earth."

For there existed before the world was, one great Being whom we call God: uncreated, self-existent, all-sufficient, and eternal; who always was and always will be. In his infinite purpose he planned the creation of man in his own image and likeness; and he wished to provide for man a suitable place to live—a place with rivers and lakes and great seas to sail over, with mountains and forests and green fields, with animals and birds and living creatures for his use, a world with great unlimited material resources for man's exploitation. And so before creating man, God first brought into existence the earth as his home; the sun, moon, other great planets, and millions of stars—all for man's benefit.

Into the primal chaos, described as empty, dark and formless, God brought into being by his word all that exists in the natural world. In six stages which are defined as "days" there occurred first the creation of light, the creation of the "firmament" dividing the upper waters, the formation of earth and seas, with the earth producing vegetation; the creation of the sun, the moon, and the stars; followed by the creation of the creatures that inhabit the waters and the air, and the creation of all the creatures that inhabit the land; including man as his top-most act of creative genius. These stages of creation called "days" were not periods of twenty-four hours each as we know them, for there was no sun to regulate time; and with the Lord:

"A day is as a thousand years, and a thousand years as a day."

The first words of the Lord God in the process of creation were:

"Let there be light, and there was light."

Thus began a gradual process for making the world a place where flowers and fruits could grow, where animal life could exist, and where man could live happily. With the coming of light, the first stage of creation ended.

During the second period of creation God caused the waters of the chaotic expanse of the universe to break asunder, thus forming the arch of sky which He called the heaven. Then as the world began to take form, its surface covered with vast waters, He caused the waters to come together in vast oceans, commanded the land to rise up in great continents and islands, and ordered the formation of great lakes and rivers throughout the land. He called the water Sea, and the dry land Earth, and the third creative period ended with the command that the earth produce vegetation, trees, and growths of every kind.

During the fourth period of Creation the Lord ordered the sun and moon and stars to come into being and to assume their proper relation to the earth, and the dark clouds and mist which covered the whole face of the earth were rolled away. The sun began to shine by day, and the moon and stars by night. The countless worlds which revolve through space were thus brought into existence, and assigned to their functions in relation to the earth, by the voice of Omnipotence.

God then commanded the waters of the sea to bring forth fishes, both small and great, and ordered that the air be filled with winged creatures; this was the work of the fifth period of creation. On the sixth day He commanded that the earth be filled with animals and creeping things. The whole land became inhabited with living creatures which roamed in the forests, grazed upon the plains, and moved about everywhere. Every form of animal life was germinated by the power of God.

Now that a state of chaos had given place to order, and the earth had been provided with vegetation and animal life, the world was ready for the creation of man. Then God said: "Let us make man in our image, after our likeness: and let them have dominion over the fish of the sea, and over the fowl of the air, and over the cattle, and over all the earth, and over every creeping thing that creepeth upon the earth."

"So God created man in his own image, in the image of God created he him; male and female created he them." This creation was separate and distinct from all previous creations. It took place as the climax and completion of the creative work of God. The physical elements in the creation of man came from the earth, but the life that flowed into Adam's body was the "breath of God." Thus man became the offspring of God in respect to intelligence, moral nature, and immortality. He was endowed with creative genius, and with the power of dominion. Invested with God-like attributes he was placed in this beautiful world and given authority over all its creatures and latent powers.

Man was commanded to "multiply and to replenish the earth." He was endued with the power to sing hymns, to offer prayers, and to commune with God. He was gifted with intelligence, the power of thought, and with a benevolent disposition; to these endowments were added the passion of love, the faculties of understanding and reasoning, and the power of choice which is called free-will. He was placed upon the earth as its tenant, and as a steward of the Creator. His chief end was to glorify God and to carry out the Divine will in his creation. He was in a state of innocence, and though occupying a position a little lower than the angels of heaven, he was permitted to share with them the intimate and perpetual fellowship of God. Man was to declare the glory of God in language more eloquent than the voice of the heavens, to utter his benevolence in ways more brilliant than the emanations of light, and to magnify His name in powers and deeds far superior to all previous manifestations of the creative energy. Having been endowed with creative genius by which he can induce combinations of material forces and produce new forms of material power, he is to use these for God's glory.

In whatever circumstance man may be placed today, he should always remember that the world and all that it contains, as well as all the hidden potentialities of the universe, were created by God for the welfare and happiness of all mankind. It was for man that:

"God spake, and on the new dressed earth
Soft smiled the glowing sun,
Then full of joy He sprang aloft,
His heavenly course to run."

All nature tells us that God is, that He is supremely great, and that His chief concern is the security and happiness of His greatest creation.

SUGGESTIONS FOR STUDY
Biblical Index to Helpful References

God The Creator of All Things. (Ps. 148: 3-10; Isa. 44:24; Acts 14:15, 17:24.)

God The Creator of Heavenly Bodies. (Ps. 8:3; 136:7-9.)

God The Creator of Sea Animals. (Ps. 104:26.)

Christ's Association with God in Creation. (Jno. 1:1, 10; Eph. 3:9.)

The Creation of Man by God. (Ps. 100:3; Mal. 2:10; Deut. 4:32.)

Man Created in The Image of God. (Eccl. 7:29; Acts 17:26, 29; 1 Cor. 11:7.)

The Element of Faith in Creation. (Ps. 33:6; Heb. 11:3.)

Man Given Dominion over The World. (Ps. 8:5-8; 1 Cor. 15:27.)

Questions

1. Where do we find answers to questions concerning the origin of the world?

2. How many periods were employed by God in creation?

3. Were these "days" of twenty-four hours?

4. What did God create during the first period? The second? The third? The fourth? The fifth? The sixth?

5. In what way did the creation of man differ from all other creations?

6. What was the chief purpose of God's creation of man?

STORY 2

SIN ENTERS THE GARDEN OF EDEN

GENESIS 2:8-17; 3:1-24

After God created man and gave him dominion over all the earth He placed him in the beautiful garden known as E'den. Here the Lord provided for all the temporal requirements of man amid the most splendid beauties of nature. In the scenic glory of E'den there flowed a beautiful river with four parting streams, encompassing a tract in which all manner of fruit-bearing trees flourished. Man was ordered to labor, caring for the garden and developing its vast resources. Work was divinely appointed, given as a token of dignity, prescribed as a means of sustenance, health, and happiness, and established as the proper order of life upon the earth. Certain moral restrictions were placed around man, and there was one particular tree in the midst of the garden whose fruit he was forbidden to eat. This restriction was not unreasonable, and should not have been irksome; its object was to preserve man in his innocence and happiness, and to prevent a break in the delightful relations between him and his Creator.

The location of the Garden of E'den is unknown, and it is utterly impossible to ascertain its site. Every vestige of it was probably swept away by the deluge about which we shall tell you in a later chapter.

While it was true that all the animals which God had created were placed under the dominion of man, and that he found delight and joy in many of them, none was found suitable to become a companion in the propagation of the race. God therefore caused a deep sleep to come upon man, whom He now called Ad'am, and took from his side a rib from which He made the woman Eve. She was blood of his blood and bone of his bone, and by nature fully prepared to become a help-meet, the mother of the race. Between them there was to be happy companionship, moral sympathy, community of earthly enjoyments, and perfect conjugal affection.

It was there in the Garden of E'den, during the period of man's innocence and moral purity, that God established the holy ordinance of marriage, and gave the command for the propagation of the race. To Ad'am, Eve was given by God as a wife, "the twain to become one flesh." She was to be protected, nourished, and loved by Ad'am, and to be his companion in intellectual, moral, economic, and religious progress. She was placed under the same moral restrictions as Ad'am, enjoyed the same spiritual intimacy with God, and was equal to man in every respect except physical prowess, and in her subordinate position in the marriage relationship. The same laws of conjugal faithfulness and moral conduct applied to both alike, and any violation of moral uprightness on the part of either was subject to the same punishment.

For a time Ad'am and Eve lived very happily together amid the flowers and fruits and lovely scenery of nature in the Garden prepared for them, having all that was needful for their comfort and happiness in life. There were frequent hours of intimate communion with God, with no taint of impurity upon either the man or his wife.

One day, however, as Eve was enjoying the delights of her surroundings and the fruits of the Garden, temptation came to her. The fallen angel Sa'tan, an enemy of God and of all that is right and holy, approached her in the form of a serpent and questioned her about the restrictions which God had placed upon her concerning the fruit of the tree in the midst of the Garden. When Eve told Sa'tan that the penalty of death had been placed against eating the fruit of this tree, he naively suggested that God had lied in this matter. He then declared that not only would she not die if she ate of the fruit, but that she would become as God.

Through craftiness and cunning words Sa'tan projected into Eve's heart a spirit of doubt and unbelief, and thus laid the foundation for her disobedience to God which soon followed.

By this subtility and alluring false promises Sa'tan engendered in the heart of Eve a feeling of curiosity, a state of dissatisfaction with the purity and happiness which she then enjoyed, and such resentment against the restrictions which God had placed upon her, that she was overcome with an inordinate desire to eat of the forbidden fruit. Led on by unbelief, curiosity, and rebellion against restraint, she ate of the fruit and gave some of it to her husband, who also disobeyed God in eating it.

Soon after they had eaten of the fruit, when its rich and tempting color had faded, and its delightful taste turned into bitterness, Ad'am and Eve became painfully aware of their plight. Then came unbearable moments of despair and sad recollections; with the smitten conscience of sin they discovered something shameful about their appearance which they did not wish the Lord to see. Covering themselves with fig leaves, they sought to hide from the presence of God in the foliage of the Garden.

Their efforts to cover the shame of wrong doing were without avail; instead of becoming wise and Divine, as promised by Sa'tan, they now found themselves foolish and mortal. Their covering for sin was unworthy and futile, and it was impossible for them to escape the all-seeing eye of God. When caused to face God in their unhappy dilemma Eve confessed that she had yielded to the enchanting allurements of Sa'tan, and that she and Ad'am had eaten of the fruit of the forbidden tree. They were driven from the Garden, the curse of irksomeness was placed upon the required labor of Ad'am, great pain in child-bearing was pronounced upon Eve, and the blight of mortality was placed upon both of them.

Though the judgments placed upon them by God were grievous and mortal, they were mitigated by the gracious promise that the seed of the woman should bruise the serpent's head. This promise was fulfilled when the Sav'ior, born of woman, came into the world bringing redemption from sin and from the power of Sa'tan.

By doing what God had told them not to do, Ad'am and Eve lost their intimate fellowship with God, the happy surroundings of their days of innocence, and many of the good things which God had given them. What is more, they lost these blessings not for themselves alone, but for

THE VOICE OF THE LORD GOD

all their descendants as well. That is what is meant by Adamic, or Original Sin, or Natural Depravity, for the sin which entered human life in the trangression of Ad'am and Eve became the heritage of all people. However, the promise of redemption given in the pronouncement of the curse of God upon them for their sin also embraces the entire human race, and in the realization of the blessings of that promise an even greater Paradise is provided for all mankind.

Thus we have the tragic story of the entrance of sin into the world, and of its blighting curse upon all the world and all humanity. Had Eve never eaten of the forbidden fruit, and had Ad'am remained obedient to the laws of God, the earth would never have been blighted by evil, nor would humanity have known suffering and death. Instead, the Garden of E'den would have been extended until the entire earth had become a Paradise, and God would have continued to dwell with His people in the most intimate and happy relationship.

Over against this tragic story we must always seek a correct view of the new and living way into a holier Paradise provided in Christ:

"A Friend who will gather the outcasts,
And shelter the homeless poor;
A Friend who will feed the hungry
With bread from the heavenly store."

SUGGESTIONS FOR STUDY

Biblical Index to Helpful References

Eve's Temptation Through the Serpent. (2 Cor. 11:3; 1 Tim. 2:14.)

The Sense of Sin Makes Afraid. (1 Jno. 3:20.)

Sin Separates from God. (Isa. 59:2; Ps. 34:21.)

Sin Produces Spiritual Death. (Eph. 2:1; Col. 2:13; Rom. 6:23.)

Sin a Universal Curse on the Race. (Isa. 64:6, 7; Rom. 3:23.)

The Error of Trying to Cover Sin. (Prov. 28:13; Ps. 32:3, 5; 1 Jno. 1:8, 10.)

The Promise of a Savior to be Born of Woman. (Isa. 8:6, 7; 7:14; Rom. 16:20; Heb. 2:14-18.)

Questions

1. Where did God place man after he created him?

2. In what way did he make for him a companion?

3. Did Eve enjoy equal rank with Adam?

4. What steps did Satan take in tempting Eve?

5. In what way did Adam and Eve try to hide from God?

6. What penalties were inflicted upon them for their disobedience?

7. What promise of redemption was given?

8. In what way has that promise been fulfilled?

THE BIRTH OF CAIN AND ABEL

GENESIS 4:1-24

Driven from the Garden of E'den under the curse of God, Ad'am and Eve went out into the world to set up another home and to work for a livelihood. In the course of time their home was blessed by a first-born son, and Eve called him Cain.

The next birth recorded is that of A'bel, whose name has been taken to mean either "vanity" or "short-lived." The name could therefore indicate either the pride with which he was accepted, or the untimely death soon to overtake him at the hands of his brother.

As the two boys grew into manhood they were taught to work. They were not allowed to grow up in idleness and sloth, but were instructed and trained for the active duties of life. A'bel became a keeper of sheep, while Cain chose to work in the fields, raising grains and fruits. Each followed his chosen vocation industriously, achieving prosperity.

When Ad'am and Eve lived in the Garden of E'den they enjoyed close personal fellowship with God, carrying on intimate conversations with Him. When the barrier of sin separated them from God they were required to build an altar of heaped up stones on which they offered blood sacrifices in atonement for their sins. Before the altar they made their confessions and prayers to God, and asked God to bless them.

Cain and A'bel were taught to make such offerings to God. They grew into manhood with a sense of their obligations for worship, and were faithful in practicing formal sacrifices on the altar. Each of them brought to the Lord offerings from the fruits of labor, presenting them in formal worship.

Just as there were differences in the offerings presented to God upon the altar of sacrifice, so there were fundamental differences in the meaning of the offerings, and in the spirit in which they were given. Cain brought of the fruits and grains which he had grown, but did not take the time or trouble to select the best. A'bel brought of the firstlings and best of his flock, which he killed and burned on the altar as a blood offering to the Lord. His offering conformed to the religious instructions received from his father, both in regard to the form and substance of the offering, and in the motive and spirit with which it was made. Cain's offering was un-

CAIN'S PUNISHMENT

acceptable to God, not only because of his failure to provide the right sort of sacrifice and to conform to the manner prescribed by God, but because his heart was not right before the Lord.

God was well pleased with A'bel's offering and gave tokens of its acceptance because it was made in obedience to Divine law, was an offering of faith, and clearly indicated reliance upon Divine grace for the forgiveness of sin. He rejected the offering of Cain, who exhibited the spirit of sin in his heart by becoming angry with God instead of confessing his wrong and asking forgiveness. He therefore stealthily fell upon his brother while he was in the fields caring for his flocks. So Cain slew A'bel, and so the first child born into this world became the first murderer.

Soon afterwards the Lord apprehended Cain and inquired of him: "Where is A'bel thy brother?" Cain sought to evade the question by asking, "Am I my brother's keeper?" Then the Lord declared that A'bel's blood was like a voice crying to Him out of the ground. For this evil deed Cain was cursed as a vagabond to wander over the earth, a continual exile without a home.

God placed a mark upon Cain, and sent him away with the announcement that anyone who harmed him should be punished. Cain and his wife went into a distant land, and there his children were born. He built a city which he named after his first son, whom he had called E'noch. Included in the curse of God against him was that the land should no longer yield its fruit to his efforts, and he was therefore obliged to turn to industrial occupations for a livelihood. Bitterest of all his sufferings must have been the constant image of his murdered brother in his conscience, and the hours of remorse and anguish as the blood of his own mother's son clung to his hands.

Not one item of moral goodness is recorded of Cain's descendants. They became leaders in arts and crafts, advanced in wordly wisdom and material prosperity, and spread abroad in the land. Seven successive generations are mentioned in the Bible, but there is no indication that any of them ever worshipped God or performed any religious or moral deed worthy of record. La'mech, the fifth in the line of Cain's descendants, was the first polygamist, also a murderer. In the remorse of conscience he said:

> "Adah and Zillah, hear my voice!
> Ye wives of Lamech, hearken unto my speech:
> For I have slain a man to my wounding,
> And a young man to my hurt.
> If Cain hath been avenged sevenfold,
> Truly Lamech, seventy-and-sevenfold."

In the sixth generation they introduced refinements into the system of society. Ja'bel stabilized the occupations of the shepherd and the herdsman. Tu'bal Cain promoted the use of scientific tools, and Ja'bal excelled in music and poetry. The Cainite line excelled in worldly ambition, in wealth and luxury, and in material knowledge. Their moral and spiritual decline, however, led to their complete extinction in the deluge which soon came upon the world.

SUGGESTIONS FOR STUDY
Biblical Index to Helpful References

Children to Be Regarded as Gifts from God. (Gen. 33:5; Ps. 127:3; Isa. 8:18.)

The Blessings of Work. (Prov. 10:4; 13:4.)

The Best to Be Sacrificed to God. (Num. 18:17; Prov. 3:9.)

Abel's Offering an Act of Faith. (Heb. 11:4.)

The Evil of Envy. (Jas. 3: 16; Acts 7:9; Mark 15:10.)

The Source of Murder. (Matt. 15:19; 1 Jno. 3:15.)

Questions

1. What was the name of the first son of Adam and Eve?

2. What was the name of their second son?

3. In what occupations did they engage?

4. What kind of offering did Abel make to God?

5. What kind of offering did Cain make?

6. Why was Abel's offering accepted and Cain's rejected by God?

7. What did Cain do because of his envy toward Abel?

8. How did he try to evade his guilt when caused to face God?

9. What punishment did God impose on Cain?

10. What were the differences in the character of the descendants of Cain and Abel?

STORY 4

SETH AND HIS DESCENDANTS

GENESIS 4:25-26; 5:3-20

After their son A'bel had been slain by his brother Cain, and Ad'am and Eve had been deprived of Cain as a result of the curse of God upon him, a third son was born to them. He was called Seth, which means "compensation" or "substitute." At the time of his birth his mother exclaimed: "God hath given me another."

Little is known of Seth except there sprang from his lineage E'noch and No'ah, the two most notable characters of the next few centuries, and that he was head of the Messianic line through which Je'sus came into the world. Ad'am reached the great age of 937 years, and many sons and daughters were born to him and Eve. These children increased in the same manner, as did their descendants, and since people of that era often lived for eight or nine centuries the population was greatly increased.

For a period of more than a thousand years the history of the human race was overshadowed with a pale of silence and oblivion. The multiplied thousands who lived during that period had ideas, emotions, and habits common to all humanity, sustained relations to one another and to the universe much the same as those who live today, and owed supreme allegiance and obedience to God. New discoveries were made, great deeds were wrought, communications received from God, and the race moved forward in material progress. The Divine record, however, mentions only the fact that the people increased in wickedness until God so greatly repented their creation that He brought upon the world a deluge which destroyed every living creature except those who were preserved in the Ark which Noah prepared under His direction. As God looked down upon the world He saw that every imagination of man was continually evil, though there were no doubt some good men whom the knowledge of God kept alive on the earth throughout that dark period. Only one man, however, was sufficiently distinguished for righteousness and true spiritual religion to gain recognition in the sacred annals. His name was E'noch, the subject of our next chapter.

One of the things which greatly accelerated the increase of wickedness during this period was the abuse of the marriage ordinance. As noted in a previous chapter, the descendants of Cain were grossly materialistic, immoral, and wicked. On the other hand, Seth and his descendants represented the lineage of righteousness. Though few in this line were sufficiently notable to be included in the Biblical record, they preserved the knowledge of God in the world. By Divine grace they were enabled to live pure and upright lives notwithstanding the natural depravity of the human heart and the engrossing wickedness of their companions. There was in their hearts an abiding consciousness of God's presence, a sense of intimate fellowship with the Infinite, the appropriation of spiritual provisions more real than the closest human relationship. They were the living witnesses of God in the world's darkest period.

Certain members of the Sethite line ignored the moral and religious barriers between the families, and took wives from among the Cainites. This fact is stated in the passage: "The sons of God saw the daughters of man that they were fair; and they took them wives of all which they chose." To interpret this passage as referring to the marriage of angels with mortal women violates the truth revealed through Divine inspiration. The meaning is simply that the moral requirements in the marriage relation were discarded. The separation Divinely ordered between the Sethites and the Cainites was set aside, thereby permitting the sons of the Sethites to marry the daughters of the Cainites. This situation led to an indescribable state of spiritual decline and wickedness, involving both lines of the human family in the curse of the approaching deluge. Of all the descendants of Seth then living on the earth only No'ah and his family were saved.

SUGGESTIONS FOR STUDY

Biblical Index to Helpful References

A New Testament Description of Man's Depravity. (Rom. 1:18-32.)

The Deceitfulness and Evil of the Human Heart. (Jer. 17:9; Heb. 3:13.)

The Sin of Abusing the Marriage Ordinance. (2 Cor. 6:14; Deut. 7:3; 1 Ki. 11: 1-8.)

Seth, the Head of the Messianic Line. (Luke 3:38.)

Questions

1. What was the name of the third son of Adam and Eve?

2. What does this name mean?

3. For how many years in man's early history was there nothing concerning his progress written in the Bible? during that time?

4. What probable things was he doing

5. What general moral tendency is noted in the Bible?

6. What is meant by "The sons of God married the daughters of men"?

7. Why was it wrong for members of the "Sethite" line to marry members of the "Cainite" line?

8. What moral condition prevailed as a result of these inter-marriages?

STORY 5

ENOCH GOES TO HEAVEN
WITHOUT DYING

GENESIS 5:21-32   In the midst of the almost universal wickedness that existed before the deluge when men were evil without any admixture of goodness whatever, there lived a man who was distinguished for his pious and continuous walk with God over a period of three hundred years. He pleased God, and God communed with him from day to day. At the end of his earthly journey he had the further distinction of passing immediately into the heavens above, without undergoing death. His body was translated, and both body and soul were carried into the presence of God.

The name of this man was E'noch, not the E'noch who was a son of Cain, but a man of the family of Seth. He was of the eighth generation

GAZA

from Ad'am and was the great-grandfather of No'ah. In spite of the inherent depravity of sin, notwithstanding the wickedness of his companions and the violent evils of the age, E'noch walked with God. His character was above reproach, his conduct was blameless, and his soul was pure. He was a bright and shining star in the midst of the darkest night in world history, and a sun of righteousness during the storm of violent wickedness.

After walking with God here on earth, E'noch was called one day to continue his walk with God in heaven. As a supernatural manifestation of the immortality of man to a generation which had completely forgotten God, and which had no faith in the future life, the glorious and instantaneous transition of this good man was a compelling message. He left behind him the testimony that he pleased God, and that by faith he was translated.

E'noch had a son whose name was Me-thu'se-lah, and who is famed for attaining the greatest age of all time. He lived to be nine hundred and sixty-nine years of age, and though the usual lifetime of men of that period ranged from six to nine hundred years, we do not have the record of any other man who reached so great an age. It is a sad commentary on the man who lived longest of all that nothing else worthy of note is said about him, except that he was the father of La'mech. In the course of years La'mech became the father of No'ah, the hero of faith in preserving the human family from complete destruction in the flood, and through whom the Messianic line from Seth was saved.

SUGGESTIONS FOR STUDY

Biblical Index to Helpful References

Enoch, a Man of Faith. (Heb. 11:5.)

Enoch, a Preacher of Righteousness. (Jude 14, 15.)

Man's Duty and Privilege of Walking with God. (Mic. 6:8; Mal. 2:6; Ps. 84:11.)

The Source of Divine Help in Walking with God. (Ps. 119:105; Jno.12:35.)

Another Biblical Example of Translation. (2 Ki. 2:11.)

Questions

1. To which lineage of the human race did Enoch belong?

2. What age was he when he began to walk with God?

3. How long did he walk with God?

4. Describe "walking with God"?

5. How did his life on earth end?

6. Has any one else ever gone to heaven without dying?

7. Was Enoch justified by "works" or by "faith" resulting in good works?

STORY 6

THE SHIP THAT SAVED MANKIND

GENESIS 6, 7, 8, 9:1-17

In the midst of the universal wickedness of mankind and the gross immorality which caused God to order the destruction of the race and of all animal life upon the earth, there was found one good man. Of him alone could it truly be said that he walked with God, enjoyed constant communication with God, and always did what was right in the midst of a perverse and wicked generation. The name of the man was No'ah, who was of the Sethite line, and an immediate descendant of E'noch.

No'ah retained the integrity of his soul when all the world around him was impure. Sinful companions and degenerate times were to him no excuse for faltering goodness; the darkness of the age merely enhanced the lustre of his rectitude. His goodness was genuine, unique, and stalwart. He was heaven's representative upon earth, the world's hero, and the preserver of the human race.

The piety of No'ah was characterized by justice and moral perfection; by holy communion with God, and by unfaltering faith and fervor. It did not waver before the rude winds of sin which swept the whole world into destruction, nor was it weakened by the persecution and sufferings of perilous times. It was kept bright and constant in its flame by the inward grace of God.

No'ah was the mouthpiece of God to the world of his age; because of his genuine goodness God entrusted to him the purposes of heaven in respect to the future. By the anointing of the Spirit of God his pure soul was made the vocalizing agency for God's message to humanity, and he was, indeed, a preacher of righteousness.

In his communications with God it was revealed to No'ah that the time had come when all the people on earth were to be destroyed because of their wickedness. A great flood was to sweep over the whole earth, drowning every living creature. No'ah and his family, however, were to be spared because he alone had walked uprightly before the Lord.

God then told No'ah how he was to save his life and that of his family, and the means by which the lives of two animals of every kind and specie, a male and a female, should be preserved for the future habitation of the world. No'ah was then directed to build a very large ship as large as many of the sea-going steamers of today, very long and very wide, containing three separate stories, and covered with a water-proof roof. The dimensions of the craft, the materials to be used, and the methods of construction were all prescribed by God. God was the architect, but No'ah was the builder; the plan of safety was of Divine origin, but human cooperation was required. The very elements which were to be used for the destruction of the wicked were to bear up in perfect safety this wondrous craft for the security of the righteous.

BUILDING THE ARK

The building of the Ark required a long time and involved a great deal of arduous labor. No'ah and his three sons, Shem, Ham, and Jā'pheth, were one hundred and twenty years in carrying to completion this gigantic undertaking, in which utter self-abandonment to God's will was required. Self-denial and whole-hearted obedience, enormous expense and long hours of hard labor were involved in this Divine assignment, but No'ah faithfully met every requirement, and the rude carpenter's name graces the roster of the heroes of faith in sacred history.

Presently the Ark was completed, and the prophecies of the noble patriarch began to be fulfilled. Two animals of every kind, male and female, and a larger number of the domestic animals which were used for food, together with large supplies of grain and other food were placed in the Ark by No'ah. He and his wife, his sons and their wives, entered the Ark and closed the doors. The rains came with ever increasing violence, day by day the waters poured out of the overcast clouds until it seemed as though great oceans had been lifted into the sky, pouring their contents down upon the earth. Forty days and forty nights passed without cessation of the downpour; in every valley and on every plain the torrents swept into ruin everything before them until all the land was submerged. The waters rose higher and higher, covering the hills and the mountains. While millions of human beings joined every living creature of the earth in a watery grave, the great boat in which No'ah and his family abode in perfect security glided over the waters.

For one hundred and fifty days the waters covered the entire face of the earth. Then the rains ceased, the winds began to blow, and the waters gradually receded toward the rivers, and lakes, and oceans. God's judgments had been accomplished: the human race had been destroyed, with the exception of No'ah and his family, and animal life had been exterminated.

For many months after the waters began to go down, No'ah and his family remained in the Ark. One day No'ah opened the window which he had made in the Ark and sent out a raven. This bird, being capable of long flights without stopping, flew round and round until the waters had gone down from some high point, and never returned. No'ah then sent out a dove, but it failed to find a place to rest, and soon flew back to the Ark. After another week the dove was sent out again, and this time it returned with a leaf from an olive tree, indicating that the waters had sufficiently abated to permit vegetation to grow upon the land. After waiting another seven days No'ah sent forth the dove for the third time, and this time it did not return.

It was now evident that much of the land near the Ark was dry, and on investigation No'ah discovered that the land all around was dry. God then directed that he and his family leave the Ark, liberating all the animals which they had preserved. It is said that the mountain on which the Ark rested was Mt. Ar'a-rat, in the heart of the elevated plateau between the Black and Caspian Sea where rise the Ti'gris and Eu-phrā'tes rivers. The mean elevation of this district is 5000 feet above sea level, and Mt. Ar'a-rat reaches a height of 17,750 feet. South of this mountainous region lies the land of ancient Bab-y-lo'ni-a and Mes-o-po-ta'mia, where the descendants of No'ah later settled.

When No'ah came out of the Ark his first step was to render thanks unto God. He erected an altar of heaped up stones and made blood offerings upon it. These offerings were accepted by God, who then made a solemn covenant with No'ah. In this covenant God declared that he would not again destroy man and beast by a deluge, and as a sign of this promise He placed in the heavens what we call the rainbow. This token stands as a reminder to humanity that the seasons will come and go in regular order, that there shall always be planting time and harvest season, and that as long as time shall last God shall never bring upon the world so great a destruction.

The covenant which God made with No'ah included other important matters. Provision was made for the continuity and perpetuity of human life upon the earth through the institution of marriage, for the sustenance of mankind through the fruitfulness of the earth, for the protection of human life from man's inhumanity to man, and for the perpetuation of religious knowledge to all the unborn posterity.

No'ah lived for three hundred and fifty years after the deluge, his sons reared large families, and the populating of the world was begun anew.

There was, however, a tragic sin in the life of this noble patriarch after the effects of the flood had passed away, and before his final blessing upon his children and their descendants.

He resumed his former vocation of farming, and turned to the cultivation of a vineyard. One sorry day he began to make wine, and was presently tempted into over-indulgence. Though not at first intending to prostrate himself beneath the power of strong drink, he was gradually led on by the gratification which it offered, finally losing all control of himself and becoming intoxicated.

This sin of drunkenness by No'ah was the occasion of a great wrong by his son Ham which brought him and his descendants under a severe curse from God.

SUGGESTIONS FOR STUDY

Biblical Index to Helpful References

Noah, a Man of Faith. (Heb. 11:7.)

Noah, a Man of Righteousness. (2 Pet. 2:5.)

Noah's Name Associated with Other Great Men. (Ezek. 14:14.)

Noah, an Ancestor of Jesus. (Luke 3:36.)

The Deluge Caused by Universal Sin. (Matt. 24:38-39; Luke 17:26-27.)

Questions

1. To which branch of the human family did Noah belong?

2. Describe the character and life of Noah.

3. Where did he get the dimensions for the Ark?

4. How long was he in building the Ark?

5. What religious work did he do besides the building of the Ark?

6. How long did the rains continue?

7. How long were the waters in subsiding?

8. Where did the ark settle down on land?

9. How high is Mt. Ararat?

10. What was Noah's first act after coming out of the ark?

THE UNFINISHED TOWER OF BABEL

GENESIS 11:1-9

When God restored the human race through the three sons of No'ah He clearly revealed the intention of distributing the race over all the world, a process that would form many different nationalities. Before the flood all the people had lived in a small section of the world where the Ti'gris and Eu-phrā'tes rivers flowed. No one had crossed the mountains on the east or the great desert on the west.

After the Flood the families which sprang from Shem, Ham, and Jā'-pheth began to move into other lands, some crossing the mountains to the east and to the north, some going further south in the great plains along the two rivers, and others going down into what is now called Africa. In this way the populations of the world began to settle in other parts of Asia, in various parts of eastern Europe, and in northern Africa.

Presently the families which had drifted into the plains of the two great rivers desired to rule all the rest of the world. Having learned to make brick from the soil of the land, the people began to build houses and cities of this material. In their ambition to rule all the people around them they sought to build a great city, and planned the erection of a tower that would reach far up into the heavens.

By building this great tower the people hoped to make a name for themselves, to raise up a monument to their own glory. It was the expression of human ambition in evil form. Their own greatness and fame were the principal objectives in this gigantic enterprise, and it was promoted without regard to the will and honor of God. It was the outward expression of their thirst for universal dominion, a desire which has been the curse of many subsequent nations. It sought the unity of the race upon the false basis of centralized autocracy, whereas the plan of God was to promote this unity by means of variety in human governments, with human rights being shared by all.

In their unrestrained ambition they designed a tower whose top should reach to heaven; in their pride they presumed to take the place of God, casting off His rule. The desire to pierce the heavens above was a symbol of their determination to acknowledge no power above themselves.

Nim'rod, the mighty hunter and ruler of men, conceived the ambitious plan and gathered about him a few like-minded men. They began to build the tower with bricks, erecting story upon story, and ascending higher and higher into the heavens. Great throngs of laborers were employed in a work that prospered until God intervened in a strange manner. God brought upon the people a confusion of tongues, so that the various groups of workmen spoke in different tongues. When the instructions of the overseers could not be understood by the laborers, who in turn could not work together intelligently, disorder and chaos reigned. The leaders were obliged to give up in despair, and the great tower was never completed. The city in which the tower was undertaken was known as Bā'bel, which means "confusion"; later it was called Bab'y-lon, one of the world's greatest cities.

THE TOWER OF BABEL

As a result of the confusion of speech many of the people removed to other parts of the world, families and groups speaking the same tongue going together and forming great nations. Some traveled north and built the city of Nin'e-veh, which later became the capital of the As-syr'i-ans. Another company went to the west and settled by the river Nile, where the great empire of E'gypt was developed. Others moved north-west to the shores of the Mediterranean Sea, where the cities of Tyre and Si'don were founded. Here there was gradually established the great maritime nation of Phoe-ni'ci-a from which settlers crossed the seas to Europe.

What became of this tower nobody knows, although tradition relates that it was demolished by lightning, with terrible tempests. One Jewish writer says that fire came down from heaven and split the tower through to its foundations.

In the course of the world's history many "towers of Babel" have been erected in mythical and philosophical systems of religion, and all these, like the first tower of Babel, produce confusion, and shall be brought to nought. Jesus Christ and his system of truth provide the only God-appointed way of access to God.

> "O, sons of earth! attempt ye still to rise,
> By mountains piled on mountains, to the skies!
> Heaven still with laughter the vain toil surveys,
> And buries madmen in the heaps they raise."

SUGGESTIONS FOR STUDY

Biblical Index to Helpful References

Nimrod, the Builder of Babel. (Gen. 10: 8-10.)

The Curse of Sinful Ambitions. (Isa. 5:8.)

Satan—a Fallen Angel Because of Sinful Ambition. (Isa. 14:13, 14.)

Warnings Against Envious Ambitions. (1 Tim. 3:6.)

Satan's Delusive Offer for Acquiring Worldly Glory. (Matt. 4:8-10.)

Confusion of Tongues to Be Overcome by Christianity. (Acts 8:14; 1 Cor. 14:1-16.)

Man-made Religions to Be Frustrated. (1 Cor. 10:20; 1 Ki. 18:27-29.)

Questions

1. Name the three sons of Noah.
2. Where did they settle after the flood?
3. Who led in the building of the tower of Babel?
4. What was the reason for building this tower?

5. Why was it never completed?

6. What resulted from the "confusion of tongues"?

7. In what countries did the dispersed peoples settle?

STORY 8

THE DIVINE CALL OF ABRAHAM

GENESIS 12:1-20   On the plains of the great Ti′gris and Eu-
phrā′tes rivers, to the south of Mt. Ar′a-rat where No′ah and his sons came
out of the Ark, and not far from the site of the unfinished tower of Bā′bel,
there stood the city called Ur of the Chal-dees′. There lived in this city
the family of Te′rah, who was a direct descendant of Shem. Among the
sons of this family was a man named Ab′ram, afterward called A′brā-häm.

Ab′ram was chosen by God to found the nation later known as Is′ra-el,
a people who, in the main trend of history, should worship the one God
of heaven and earth, to whom the revealed Word of God should be committed, and through whom a Sav′ior should be provided for the entire
race. Beginning with the story of his call by God and his long journey
to the land of Ca′naan, the remainder of the Old Testament Scriptures is
confined almost entirely to the history of that race. The references to
other nations which sprang from the descendants of the three sons of
No′ah are purely incidental, relating to matters in which these nations
played some part in the history of Is′ra-el. It was not the purpose of the
Bible to trace the development of the kingdoms of this world, but rather
to unfold the spiritual dealings of God with man, and to make known
the plan of human redemption.

The people who lived in Ur were not as a rule worshipers of the true
God. They made gods of the sun and moon, and bowed in prayer before
idols made of wood and stone. Although his father was an idolater,
Ab′ram worshiped God. He sought in every way to know and do His
will, led an upright life in the midst of idolatry and wickedness, and
sought to guide his neighbors in the way of truth. The Lord talked with
Ab′ram from time to time, and one day directed him to remove from Ur
to a land which He would afterwards show him.

Ab′ram told his father and the entire family of the message which he
had received from God, and they were so greatly impressed by his
earnestness and deep religious convictions that they went with him on
the journey to Ca′naan. After traveling several hundred miles in a
northwesterly direction they came to Hā′ran, where they established a
home. This city was located in what was then known as A′ram, or

Mes-o-po-ta'mia, and was about five hundred miles northeast of the land which the Lord later gave to Ab'ram.

After living in Hā'ran for a time Ab'ram's father Te'rah, died, and was buried in this city. Ab'ram's brother Hā'ran, who was the father of Lot, had died before they left the city of Ur. Ab'ram and Na'hor, who was another brother, prospered in the land of Mes-o-po-ta'mia; their herds of sheep and cattle were greatly increased, and they had gathered many servants. Na'hor and his wife were blessed with several children, but Ab'ram and Sa'rai remained childless.

The Lord appeared to Ab'ram in Hā'ran and directed him once again to take his family and all his possessions and resume the journey to the distant land of promise. God then blessed Ab'ram, assuring him that his family would become a great people; the entire land would be given to his descendants, from whom there was to spring a great nation. Though the blessing was given to Ab'ram, all the families of the earth were to be blessed through his future generations.

ABRAHAM ADVISES SARAH

Ab'ram did not grasp the full meaning of these promises, nor did he know the course which was to bring him at last to the promised land, but he promptly obeyed the voice of God. Accompanied by his nephew Lot and all the servants gathered in Hā'ran, Ab'ram started at once on the long journey. Over the plains, and hills, and mountains they journeyed with all their possessions, not knowing where the journey would lead, but safely guided by Divine Providence.

Ab'ram's journey began at his native city of Ur, going up the river Eu-phrā'tes more than five hundred miles to the mountainous region of Mes-o-po-ta'mia, and then turning southwest from Hā'ran, with lofty ranges of mountains on the west, and the great desert to the east. The travelers crossed many rivers and hills, passing through narrow valleys for another five hundred miles until they entered the narrow strip of country between the Mediterranean Sea and the Jordan river. This country was then known as Ca'naan, now called Pal'es-tine, and is appropriately named the Holy Land because of its historic identity with true religion and the birth of the Sav'ior.

Upon reaching the land of Ca'naan, Ab'ram passed well into the center of the territory, setting up his tent under an oak tree on a plain not far from the city of She'chem. Here the Lord appeared to him and renewed the promise to give this land to him and to his descendants. Ab'ram built an altar, offered sacrifices unto the Lord, and worshiped Him. He then removed to a mountain east of Bethel, to the south of She'chem, and once again built an altar and worshiped God. He loved the Lord, believed His promises, and faithfully served Him wherever he stopped, even when surrounded by heathens.

SUGGESTIONS FOR STUDY
Biblical Index to Helpful References

Abraham's Choice by Elective Grace. (Josh. 24:3; Isa. 51:2.)

Abraham, a Man of Preeminent Faith. (Acts 7:2-4; Heb. 2:8-18.)

Abraham Called the Friend of God. (2 Chron. 20:7.)

Questions

1. Where was Abraham's original home?

2. What was his father's name?

3. What was his father's religion?

4. What Divine call did Abraham receive in Ur?

5. To what place did he and his father's family remove?

6. How far was Haran from Ur?

7. What Divine call came to Abraham in Ur?

8. Who accompanied him on his journey to an unknown land?

9. Who was Lot?

10. Where did Abraham first stop in Canaan?

11. How far was this from Haran?

12. What was his first act?

STORY 9

THE PARTING OF LOT AND ABRAM

GENESIS 13:1-18   Ab'ram and Lot were prosperous before they went down into E'gypt, and when they returned to Ca'naan they were rich in cattle, silver, and gold. In the vicinity of Bethel, where Ab'ram again built an altar and worshiped God, the shepherds of these two kinsmen searched the hill country for sufficient pasturage to feed their greatly increased flocks and herds. Some of the land was occupied by herdsmen of the native people, so the servants of Ab'ram and Lot found difficulty in securing grass for their sheep and cattle. Quarrels and contention arose between the two groups of herdsmen, and when Ab'ram learned of the unhappy situation he said to Lot:

"Let there be no strife, I pray thee, between me and thee, and between my herdmen and thy herdmen; for we be brethren. Is not the whole land before thee? Separate thyself, I pray thee, from me: if thou wilt take the left hand, then I will go to the right; or if thou depart to the right hand, then I will go to the left."

In these generous words Ab'ram displayed the spirit of true meekness and recognized the obligations of kinship. Rather than permit another to be injured he was willing to yield his own rights and privileges, even to suffer loss. The grasping, assertive spirit so common among other men in similar circumstances was wholly lacking; his conduct was marked by generosity and self-denial, and by a spirit of true humility. As the elder, more prominent of the partners, and as Lot's uncle and benefactor he had the right to choose his part of the country first, but he yielded the privilege to Lot. He could have claimed the entire country for himself, or selected the best parts of it, but he deferred to Lot's preference, taking the land which Lot had refused.

From the vantage point afforded by the high hills around Bethel, where Ab'ram and Lot now resided, one could look eastward toward the Jor'-dan, beholding a beautiful plain, fertile and covered with luxuriant vegetation. Beyond the plain and within the immediate vicinity of the Jor'dan, perhaps on what now constitutes a part of the bed of the northern end of the Dead Sea, stood the wealthy and wicked cities of Sod'om and Go-mor'-rah. The fame of this area for beauty and fertility was comparable to

THE DAUGHTERS OF LOT

that of the Garden of Ed'en or the valley of the Nile in E'gypt. No crust of salt, volcanic action, or curse from God had yet blasted its verdure, or wrecked the civilization of the early Phoenician settlements which had developed into these two great cities. All that here takes place was before the Lord had destroyed the cities of Sod'om and Go-mor'rah, and the country was wholly unlike the present barren waste.

Lot was attracted by the fertility of this plain, and impressed also by the commercial advantages offered by the two great cities. Disregarding the moral contamination and spiritual disaster that might result from contact with immoral neighbors, he chose the plains for himself. Going down from the mountains where God was known and worshiped, Lot took all his possessions and "pitched his tent toward Sod'om." He did not settle within either of the wicked cities at first, but gradually moved closer and closer, becoming more and more involved in their low standards of morality and gross paganism.

The choice proved to be very unfortunate for Lot, though he had only himself to blame. It was a choice determined solely by material gain and worldly advantages, guided entirely by worldly wisdom, and devoid of all spiritual sensitivity. The dangers to his moral and spiritual welfare were completely overlooked in his inordinate desire for riches and fame. He purchased worldly prosperity at a fearful cost; for it nourished his selfishness and pride, exposed him to the contagion of evil associates, and ·deprived him of the benefits of religious ordinances.

Lot no doubt thought that he was doing a clever thing in apparently taking advantage of his uncle, but his fancied shrewdness resulted in his own undoing. Instead of overreaching Ab'ram, he overreached himself; in the lust for worldly gains he suffered immeasurable spiritual loss. No doubt his worldly goods were increased, but in the sight of God he became a spiritual pauper.

There was no altar to the true God in Sod'om, and Lot was too much embarrassed by the sinfulness of his surroundings to erect one. Though Lot may have been vexed in his better moments by the vileness of the people of Sod'om and Go-mor'rah, he failed to protest against the proud luxury and idleness which vaunted itself on every side. He appears to have avoided the grosser immoralities of Sod'om, but his wife and a number of his children became fatally entangled. Some of his daughters married men of Sod'om, and in their lack of faith declined to leave the city when its destruction was announced by the messengers of God. Lot's wife lost her life during the flight from the city because she paused to look back upon the worldliness to which her heart had become attached. Lot and his two daughters who escaped the destruction of Sod'om and Go-mor'rah were later guilty of shameful deeds which brought disgrace to his name and a curse upon his descendants.

SUGGESTIONS FOR STUDY

Biblical Index to Helpful References

The Source of Strife and Quarrels. (Prov. 28:25; Jas. 4:1.)

Undue Love of the World Incompatible with Spirituality. (1 Jno. 2:15, 16.)

Close Associations with the Wicked Contrary to Will of God. (Jas. 4:4.)

The Gain of the World at the Loss of the Soul. (Matt. 16:26.)

The Pride, Self-conceit, and Idleness of Sodom. (Ezek. 16:49.)

The Blessings of Meekness. (Isa. 29:19; Ps. 149:4.)

Questions

1. What was the occasion of strife between the shepherds of Lot and of Abraham?

2. What proposal did Abraham make?

3. Why was this generous and unselfish?

4. Why did Lot choose the plains of Sodom?

5. For what was Sodom and Gomorrah noted?

6. What was wrong in the choice made by Lot?

7. How did his choice affect the future of his family?

GOD'S WONDERFUL PROMISE TO ABRAM

GENESIS 15:1-21

After Ab'ram had been blessed by Mel-chiz'e-dek, and had given to this priest of God a tenth of all his possessions, the Lord appeared to him in a special vision. Of the many remarkable conversations between God and His servant Ab'ram the most wonderful now took place. The opening words were spoken by God: "Fear not, Ab'ram: I am thy shield, and thy exceeding great reward."

Ab'ram then laid bare his heart before the Lord, complaining that no blessing which the Lord might bestow upon him could make up for the fact that he had no child of his own through whom the promises which God had already made could be fulfilled. Up to this time Ab'ram and Sa'rai had not been blessed with children, and the only heir of Ab'ram's household was a servant named E-li-e'zer, who was a foreigner from Da-mas'cus. Under these conditions it was hard for Ab'ram to see how the Lord could keep His promise of making a great nation of his descendants. Because he truly loved the Lord, and had perfect faith in His power and justice, Ab'ram was willing to trust himself completely to His mercy.

The Lord then told Ab'ram that he should have a son of his very own, through whom His promises should be fulfilled. That night He took Ab'ram out of his tent and told him to gaze at the countless stars in the heavens. Then he was told that the number and glory of his descendants should be like unto the multitudes of bright, shining stars upon which his eyes looked in wonder, and which no man could count. Before this meeting with God, Ab'ram had been told that his offspring should be as innumerable as the

SARAH DOUBTS THE PROMISE

sands of the sea and the dust of the ground. From now on, whether Ab'ram looked down toward the ground, or out upon the shores of the sea, or up into the heavens he would always be reminded of the vast number of descendants to be given him by the Lord.

Although Ab'ram and his wife had reached so great an age that it seemed impossible for God to perform the miracle of giving them a son, Ab'ram did not lose hope. Believing with all his heart that God would do what seemed to be impossible in order to keep His promise, Ab'ram accepted the word of God without question. His faith rose into heroic vigor, and for it he was accounted righteous before the Lord.

The Lord took Ab'ram into full confidence concerning the future of his offspring; in symbolic language He revealed the future slavery of the children of Is'ra-el in E'gypt, their return to the land of Ca'naan, and their growth into the great nation through which the Sav'ior should be given to the world. All the promises which God had given before were now summarized and made binding in a holy covenant. Included in this covenant were the following promises: the gift of a son, the future greatness of the people descended from him, and final possession of the promised land. In return for these blessings Ab'ram promised to serve God faithfully for all his days upon earth. Of Ab'ram in that hour it may be said:

"Majesty, combined with meekness,
Righteousness and peace unite,
To ensure those blessed conquests,
His possession and full right;
Ride triumphant,
Decked in robes of purest light."

SUGGESTIONS FOR STUDY
Biblical Index to Helpful References

God's Reasurrances to His Servants. (1 Sam. 15:10; Dan. 10:12; Luke 1:13, 30.)

God the Shield of His People. (Deut. 33:29; Ps. 33:20; 115:9-11.)

God's Promise to Give Canaan to Abraham's Seed When He Had No Heir. (Acts 7:5.)

God's Promise to Make of Abraham's Descendants an Innumerable Host. (Gen. 22:17; 26:4; Deut. 1:10; Jer. 33:22; Rom. 4:17.)

Israel's Sojourn in Egypt. (Ex. 12:40; Ps. 105:23-45; Acts 7:6, 7.)

Questions

1. What complaint did Abram make to God?

2. What promise did God then make to Abraham?

3. Why did this promise involve the miraculous?

4. List the promises included in God's covenant with Abraham.

5. What three figures are used to illustrate the number of Abraham's descendants?

6. Where was Israel to spend a long time in slavery before inheriting Canaan?

STORY 11

ISHMAEL'S BIRTH AND THE VISIT OF ANGELS TO ABRAHAM

GENESIS 16, 17, 18:1-15

As Ab'ram grew older without seeing the fulfillment of God's promise to give him a son he became very impatient, and was greatly disturbed by the thought of dying without leaving descendants. Instead of asking the will of God, as he had done before, Ab'ram talked the matter over with his wife Sa'rai, who was now well advanced in years beyond the usual period of childbearing, and who felt very deeply her disappointment in not having a son. Her heart, like that of Ab'ram, had grown sore with hope deferred. They did not doubt God, but instead of awaiting His appointed time and way they sought means of their own for securing a son. They rebelled, not against God, but against a providence which seemed unbearable.

Ab'ram and Sa'rai then took advantage of a custom that was often used in their time. Men frequently had more than one wife, and wives taken after the first were known as concubines. It often happened that when a man and his wife had been childless for many years the wife herself would suggest that a concubine bear children for her, and this is what Sa'rai did. There was in the household an Egyptian woman named Ha'gar, who was Sa'rai's maid. At Sa'rai's request Ab'ram took her as a concubine, and she gave birth to a son whom they named Ish'ma-el.

In passing judgment upon this act of Ab'ram and Sa'rai, one should not be too severe. Their faith was great, but it wavered under the heavy trials placed upon it; in their human weakness Ab'ram and Sa'rai fell short of absolute perfection. They did not think it unwise or wrong to aid God in carrying out a promise which was impossible to fulfill in the usual course of nature, and therefore, did what seemed best under the circumstances. Their deed, however, brought great unhappiness to their home, and resulted in trials that were even harder to bear.

By the raising of Ha'gar from a bondservant to the position of a wife, her relation to Ab'ram's family was greatly changed. Even before her son was born she became proud and self-satisfied, despising the very person who had made it possible for her to rise. Sa'rai, who had suggested

HAGAR IN THE DESERT

the entire matter, was now filled with envy for the honor which Ha'gar would soon enjoy as the mother of Ab'ram's son, and felt more keenly than ever the disappointment of her own childlessness. She complained bitterly to her husband, blaming him for her unhappiness. Ab-ram refused to quarrel with her, merely telling her to do as she wished with Ha'gar. The jealousy between Sa'rai and Ha'gar increased day by day, and Sa'rai began to treat her former maid harshly, no doubt making life miserable for the entire household.

At last Ha'gar decided to flee into the wilderness rather than endure the ill treatment of Sa'-rai. Forgetting that she had been chosen to bear a son for Ab'ram, Ha'gar fled from the unhappy home and started back toward her native land. As she stopped by a fountain of water on the roadside an angel of God appeared to her, addressing her by name and asking why she was there, and where she was going. These questions were asked not merely to learn what the angel already knew, but to show God's care for Ha'gar and His interest in the solving of her problems. When Ha'gar told the angel of her wish to escape from Sa'rai, she was ordered to return to Ab'ram's home and do whatever Sa'rai commanded her. She was also told that God knew all about her troubles, and would protect and prosper her. The angel told her that she would bear a son who should be called Ish'ma-el, meaning "God hath heard." He was to be strong and fierce, the founder of a tribe that no one could overcome.

The visit of the angel was seen by Ha'gar as a special providence of God, and she accepted his message as the voice of God. She believed all that he told her, and the place where the angel appeared to her was afterwards called: "The well of the Living One who sees me."

Ha'gar returned to the home of Ab'ram, and hereafter showed proper respect for Sa'rai. In due time she gave birth to a son, whom she named Ish'ma-el as commanded by the heavenly messenger. From Ish'ma-el there descended a people who became noted for their numbers and strength, and of whom we shall learn more in later chapters. Thus did God permit an alien in the house of faith to rise from the lowly place of a bondservant. As a wife of the man whose name was soon changed to mean "Father of a multitude," she had a part in founding one of the largest groups of the human family.

For thirteen years after the birth of Ishmael Ha'gar remains in Ab'-ram's home, caring for her son, and helping her mistress Sa'rai. They were filled with doubts and fears for Ab'ram and Sa'rai, but they remained faithful to God; making no further effort to interfere with God's fulfillment of the promise for a son of their very own. God then appears to his servant, talks with him face to face, and again assures him that Sa'rai shall give birth to a son who shall be the true heir to the promised heritage of Canaan. The covenant was renewed and enlarged,

ANGELS VISIT ABRAHAM

with the rite of circumcision prescribed for Ab'ram and all male children descending from him. His name was changed from Ab'ram to A'bra-ham, which means "father of a multitude." The name of his wife Sa'rai was changed to Sa'rah, which means "princess."

Soon after this third renewal of the covenant with God, A'bra-ham was sitting at the door of his tent in true Oriental fashion, resting from the heat of the day; ready to greet any passing traveller, and to invite strangers of respectable appearance to pause and share a meal with him. When three men of striking countenance and superior bearing approached the tent, A'bra-ham hastened to meet them, bowed courteously and invited them to tarry with him for dinner. His urgent invitation was accepted, and a bounteous meal was prepared for them by Sa'rah.

The courteous behavior of A'bra-ham toward these strangers, his humble bearing toward persons whose superiority evidently impressed him, his gracious hospitality, and the reverent manner in which he listened to them, all gave proof of his lovable and deeply religious nature. With noble humility he claimed no merit for his kindly service, with true courtesy and forethought he made the distinguished guests feel at ease in his home, and in a deeply religious spirit he thanked the Lord for this opportunity of doing a good deed.

At this time A'bra-ham did not know that the three passing strangers were heavenly messengers. One of them appears to have been the Lord in the form of a man, probably the "Angel Je-ho'vah," which was a name for the Lord in His earthly appearances during ancient times. This leader of the group talked freely with A'bra-ham, speaking with him further about God's promise to send the promised heir to him and Sa'rah.

When Sa'rah overheard the words of the heavenly guest concerning the promise of God that she should become the mother of a son, though advanced in age and greatly lessened in strength, Sa'rah simply could not believe what she heard. She burst into laughter, not from a spirit of wickedness or impiety, but from sheer astonishment. Such a happening was so contrary to the usual laws of nature that she could not see how it could possibly take place.

The time had come when Sa'rah should become a party to the covenant of God, and this may have been the reason for the angelic visitor to speak as he did where Sa'rah could overhear the conversation. She must be told of the miracle that was soon to take place in her life, and her doubts must be overcome. It was not enough that she be told of the miracle by her husband; God himself must make known to her the wonderful prospects, and her unbelief and fear must be overcome by a message direct from the heavens.

In range of Sa'rah's hearing, and especially for her benefit, the angel of the Lord therefore said to A'bra-ham: "Is anything too hard for the Lord?" In such words he called attention to the Almighty God with whom all things are possible, and Sa'rah's doubts and fears were transformed into victorious faith.

In later history Sa'rah was praised as a model for womanly virtue and subjection. Her name appears in the notable list of the heroes and heroines of faith. She found favor with God, and all her unbelief was removed from her faithful heart. In due time the promised son was born, and Sa'rah became the mother of Is'ra-el, and of kings, princes, and nations.

SUGGESTIONS FOR STUDY

Biblical Index to Helpful References

Entertaining Angels Unaware. (Heb. 13:2; Matt. 25:35.)

The Duty of Hospitality. (1 Tim. 3:2; 1 Pet. 4:9.)

Sarah Included in the Covenant Promises. (Rom. 9:9; Heb. 11:11, 19.)

Sarah's Respect and Obedience to Abraham. (1 Pet. 3:.6)

Nothing Too Hard for God. ** (Jer. 32:17, 27; Matt. 19:26; Ps. 118:23.)

All Nations Blessed in Abraham. (Gal. 3:8.)

Sarah's Childlessness. (Gen. 11:30.)

Other circumstances similar to Sarai's actions. (Gen. 30:3, 4, 9, 10.)

The sin of jealousy and strife. (Prov. 6:34; 10:12; Jas. 3:16.)

Angel Ministrations. (Heb. 1:14; Acts 12:7.)

The Prophecy Concerning Ishmael Fulfilled. (Gen. 21:20; 25:18.)

Questions

1. How did Abraham entertain angels unaware?

2. What did the angels tell Abraham?

3. How did Sarah behave when she overheard the promise of the angels?

4. How did the angels overcome her doubts?

5. Did Sarah also believe the promise for a son?

6. What expedient did Abraham and Sarai adopt for securing a son?

7. Was this a common practice in those days?

8. What domestic complications arose in Abraham's home?

9. As a result of this strife what did Hagar try to do?

10. How was she prevented, and what did the angel tell her to do?

11. What promise was given concerning her unborn son?

12. What was the name given to her son when he was born?

13. How were the promises concerning him fulfilled?

STORY 12

THE RAIN OF FIRE ON SODOM AND GOMORRAH

GENESIS 18:16-33;
19:1-38   This chapter takes us back to the wicked cities
of the plains of Jor'dan, and to Lot and his family. During the years
that had passed since Ab'ram saved the king of Sod'om and many of his
people from conquest by the king of E'lam the city had fallen deeper
and deeper into sin. Lot had chosen to remain in Sod'om, and his family
had become entangled in the evils of this unrighteous city.

Having finished their mission to A'bra-ham and his wife, the three
angelic visitors started on the journey to Sod'om, accompanied for part
of the way by A'bra-ham. Presently the leader of the group lingered in
conversation with A'bra-ham, while the others continued the march
toward Sod'om. The latter two angels had been sent to Sod'om to announce its approaching destruction under the judgment of God. Remembering the faith of A'bra-ham and his kindly interest in Lot and his family, the Lord said: "Shall I hide from A'bra-ham what I am going to do?"
So close had been the relation between God and A'bra-ham that he was
called "the friend of God." To such a friend the Lord was willing to
reveal His purpose concerning the overthrow of a city in which there flourished the worst forms of immorality known in the history of the world.

The Lord therefore took his friend into full confidence, telling him
that the time of judgment had come, and that the sins of Sod'om must
be punished. A'bra-ham then offered an earnest prayer in the hope of
sparing Sod'om. He said to the Lord: "If there can be found as many
as fifty righteous people in the city, wilt thou not spare it for the sake
of these fifty?"

When the Lord agreed to spare the city if fifty righteous people could
be found there, A'bra-ham pleaded: "Peradventure there shall lack five
of the fifty righteous: wilt thou destroy all the city for lack of five?"
After the Lord agreed to this condition A'bra-ham succeeded in having the
required number of righteous people reduced, first to forty, then to thirty,
then to twenty, and finally to ten. Beyond this number A'bra-ham did
not dare to go, but was content with the Lord's assurance that the city

would not be destroyed if there could be found only ten who were righteous.

In spite of the heroic efforts of A'bra-ham to save the city, not even ten righteous people could be found, and the judgment of God was duly carried out.

The two angels who had left A'bra-ham and the Lord in conversation went on into the city of Sod'om, walking through the city on a tour of observation, and trying to find at least ten good men and women. Instead of finding the good people whose presence would have saved the city from destruction, the angels were forced to look upon the worst forms of wickedness and vice. No matter where they looked, they could find nothing but pride, luxury, and self-indulgence; everywhere the people gave themselves up to worldly pleasures and disgraceful conduct of the worst kind. Finally they came to the house of Lot and found him sitting at the gate of Sod'om, where he acted as a magistrate. True to the training which he had received from his uncle A'bra-ham, and mindful of the customs of hospitality, Lot rose up and greeted the strangers courteously. He welcomed them to his home, treated them with kindness, and made them a feast.

The people of Sod'om had seen the angels as they went about the streets of the city, but did not know that they were angels because they were in the appearance of men. Attracted by the superior bearing of the two strangers within their city, some of the most depraved people looked upon them with evil intentions. They stealthily watched the angels as they entered the house of Lot, planning to seize them at the first opportunity. Finally they demanded that Lot bring out his guests and let them be mistreated by the mob. When Lot refused their demands they turned upon him with jeers and scorn, accusing him of taking too much authority for one who was only a sojourner within their city, and threatening to break down the door and take the two visitors by force.

The Sod'om-ites were bold unashamed in their evil intentions, and no arguments or resistance which Lot could offer would prevent them from carrying out their wicked purposes. They rushed the door which Lot had closed and attacked him violently. Now the angels had made their special visit to Lot because he had kept himself free from the more vicious sins of Sod'om; though he had done wrong by associating with wicked neighbors, he was still counted among the righteous. He was grieved by the evils of Sod'om, and had often rebuked the people for their disgraceful

ABRAHAM SEES SODOM IN FLAMES

deeds. The Lord therefore wished to spare him from the terrible disaster that was soon to fall upon Sod'om.

When Lot's life was in danger by the attack of the people who sought the strangers in his home the two angels opened the door and drew him to safety. The angels then caused the angry mob to be smitten with blindness, and the confusion became so great that the Sod'om-ites could not even find the door of Lot's house.

The heavenly messengers then informed Lot that the Lord was preparing to rain fire and brimstone upon Sod'om and Go'mor'rah, bringing utter destruction to both cities, and they suggested that he take all his kinsmen and property out of the city at once. When Lot brought the news to his sons-in-law they scoffed at his warning, refusing to heed the call of God for safety.

Lot was then told to take his wife and the two daughters who still lived in his home and to flee to the surrounding mountains. Instead of obeying at once, Lot permitted business matters and selfish interests to delay his going. The love of such worldly things as gold and silver seemed more important at the moment than the safety of his family. The angels therefore seized him by the hand and led the family out on the road toward the mountains.

As Lot and his family fled from Sod'om he became fearful that he could not reach a place of safety in the mountains. He then pleaded with the angel who was guiding him to spare the little town to the northeast that was later called Zo'ar, and to allow him to reside there with his family. When the Lord agreed to this request Lot and his wife and two daughters turned their steps toward the little town.

Lot's wife could not bear the thought of giving up all that they had left behind in Sod'om. Her heart clung to her home, her worldly possessions, and her former companions. She halted in their flight to look back longingly upon the city, her heart filled with memories of the life she had found so happy. As she stood there, lost in revery, smoke and ashes began to spread all over the plain, and suddenly she was petrified with fear. Standing erect and motionless, gazing toward Sod'om, her body was turned into a pillar of salt,—an everlasting monument of warning against turning back when one is on the road to salvation.

The Lord then caused a rain of fire to fall upon Sod'om and Go-mor'rah; destroying also the neighboring towns of Ad'mah and Ze'bo-im; only the little town of Zo'ar escaped the calamity.

From his mountain home nearby the faithful A'bra-ham looked out upon the plains below. The once fertile and smiling lands were now a flaming furnace, and the former prosperous and wealthy cities had become a vast heap of charred ruins. The idle luxury of the day before had been turned into utter desolation. The heart of A'bra-ham was stirred deeply, but he humbly acknowledged the righteousness of God in all His ways.

In the meantime Lot and his two daughters had feared for their lives in Zo'ar, and had fled to the mountains of Mo'ab to the east, where they took shelter in a cave. Here took place the most shameful incident of Lot's career, and his name passed from the pages of sacred history. When his two daughters realized that all the descendants of their father had perished in the flames of Sod'om, they took what seemed to be the only means of preserving their father's line. They made Lot drunk with wine, induced him to commit the crime of incest, and gave birth to the sons from whom there sprang the Mo'ab-ites and Am'mon-ites. We shall learn more about them in later chapters.

SUGGESTIONS FOR STUDY

Biblical Index to Helpful References

The Secret of the Lord with His Faithful Servants. (Ps. 25:14; Job 29:4; Prov. 3:32.)

The Wickedness of Sodom and Gomorrah. (2 Pet. 2:6; Luke 17:29; Jude 7.)

Examples of Intercession. (2 Sam. 24:17; Ex. 32:31, 32; Rom. 10:1; Jno. 17:9.)

Lot's Vexation at the Wickedness of Sodom. (2 Pet. 2:7, 8.)

Smiting Wicked People with Blindness. (2 Ki. 6:18; Acts 13:11.)

Separation of the Good from the Bad for the Destruction of Evil. (Num. 16:21, 45.)

The Lord's Devastation of Lands of Wickedness. (Ps. 107:34; Deut. 29:23.)

Lot's Wife a Pillar of Salt. (Luke 17:32.)

Moabites and Ammonites Descendants of Lot's Two Sons. (Deut. 2:9, 19.)

Questions

1. After the visit of the angels to Abraham where did two of them go?

2. What was their mission to Sodom?

3. When the angel that talked with Abraham told him of Sodom's doom what did he do?

4. Tell of his pleadings for Sodom and of the response of God.

5. What were the moral conditions of Sodom?

6. In whose home did the angels stop?

7. What attack was made upon these angels by men of Sodom?

8. What happened to these men?

9. What did the angels tell Lot and his family to do?

10. What did Lot's wife do and what happened to her?

11. Where did Lot and his two daughters hide?

12. Of what sin were they guilty?

STORY 13

THE BIRTH OF ISAAC

GENESIS 20, 21:1-8   Soon after the destruction of Sod'om and the other cities of the Jor'dan plain A'bra-ham removed from that part of the land and settled in a place called Ge'rar, in the southwestern part of Ca'naan near the great sea. This land was occupied by a strong, war-like people known as Phi-lis'tines, and their king was named A-bim'e-lech. Although it had been twenty-four years since A'bra-ham had misrepresented his wife as his sister in order to protect her from the king of E'gypt, the reproach which he suffered on that occasion should have remained fresh in his memory. Out of fear of A-bim'e-lech, however, A'bra-ham was guilty once again of the same deception.

Just as the deception planned by A'bra-ham had failed once before, so it failed again. A-bim'e-lech had decided to take Sa'rah as one of his wives, but before he was able to carry out this plan the Lord appeared unto him in a dream, warning him not to take Sa'rah because she was the wife of A'bra-ham. A-bim'e-lech then called A'bra-ham into his presence, bestowed rich presents and grants of land, and asked that the prophet of God pray for him. Both A'bra-ham and Sa'rah stood severely reproached before God, in which state they humbly accepted the thanks of the heathen king and made their home within his country.

In answer to a special prayer of intercession by A'bra-ham the Lord healed A-bim'e-lech and his family of a serious ailment, and blessed them with many children. A-bim'e-lech then bestowed still greater favors upon A'bra-ham, who was also blessed more and more by the Lord until he became very prosperous and highly regarded in the land of Ge'rar.

Some months after A'bra-ham's removal to this part of Ca'naan the promised son was born to Sa'rah, and he was called I'saac as previously directed by the angel of God. His birth was regarded by all as no ordinary work of nature, but as the direct result of God's mercy. It was also accepted as a mark of Divine preference, and as a prophecy of the future greatness of A'bra-ham's descendants. The miraculous birth was also the reward of faith, for A'bra-ham and Sa'rah had believed in God against all human hope. Although their faith had been severely tried by long waiting and natural difficulties, it was fully rewarded in God's good time and in His own marvelous way. It was the beginning of a Divine supernatural agency which would continue to operate throughout the history of the chosen people of God. He was not only the child of the Covenant, but the supernatural element in his birth was a sign of the Divine in the development and fulfillment of the Covenant of Redemption for man.

Greatest of all, the miraculous birth of I'saac was prophetic of a still greater supernatural birth which was to take place in the future A-bra-ham'ic family. It foretold the miracle by which God would bring "His first-begotten" into the world. As in the case of I'saac, the birth of Jesus was announced long before it took place, the name was given prior to the birth, and the birth occurred at a time appointed by God. In both cases the beginning of a greater Is'ra-el in the world was marked by a miraculous birth.

Sa'rah's visitation recalls that of Ma'ry, the mother of Je'sus, though there were differences. Sa'rah gave birth when she was old and the natural faculties of child-bearing were dead, while Ma'ry was little more than a child herself. Sa'rah's child was to be the father of natural Is'ra-el; the Son of Ma'ry was to be the founder of spiritual Is'ra-el.

The birth of I'saac was the occasion for the first cradle hymn of history, the song of Sa'rah being the first of its kind in literature. It was a hymn of wonder and joy in supreme acknowledgment of the gift of God, and a song in which her relatives and friends heartily joined in singing. It was a song of the greatness that was to come for her son, and of the hope for countless descendants.

SUGGESTIONS FOR STUDY

Biblical Index to Helpful References

Abraham's Fear and Deception. (Gen. 12:13, 15; 26:7.)

God's Reproof of Kings for the Sake of His Servants. (Ps. 105:14.)

Isaac a Child of Promise. (Gal. 4:28.)

Isaac the Heir to the Covenant Promise Given to Abraham. (Rom. 9:7, 8; Heb. 11:18; Gal. 4:30.)

Questions

1. Where did Abraham reside after the destruction of Sodom?

2. What deception did he again practice?

3. What nation lived in that region?

4. What was the name of their king?

5. What did he propose in respect to Sarah?

6. How was he prevented from carrying out his intentions?

7. What blessings came to Abimelech in answer to Abraham's prayer?

8. What miracle baby was born to Sarah?

9. How old was she at the time? How old was Abraham?

STORY 14

ISHMAEL AND HAGAR SENT AWAY

GENESIS 21:9-21

The coming of I'saac into the home of A'bra-ham and Sa'rah was not without moments of trial and sorrow. There was already in the household of A'bra-ham, as previously related, a son of Ha'gar, the Egyptian maid. The boy was greatly loved by his father A'bra-ham, who had grown to think of him almost as the Divinely promised heir. Twelve years before the birth of I'saac there had been a serious quarrel between Sa'rah and Ha'gar, and only the intervention of God had restored Ha'gar and her son to the household. Now that Sa'rah had a son of her own the old jealousy would be revived, with each mother looking with suspicion and envy upon the other concerning the future of the two boys. Since Ish'ma-el was twelve years old when I'saac was born, Ha'gar would naturally expect him to be his father's heir.

When I'saac was about three years old, according to a custom of that age, a great festival was held in honor of his becoming weaned. For the first time the child was permitted to eat the food which was to form his regular diet from that time on. Neighbors and friends were invited to join in the festivities, and it was an occasion of great joy and happiness.

Ish'ma-el was now about fifteen years old, and for the past three years had looked upon I'saac with growing suspicion and envy, taunting the younger son with bitter, sarcastic remarks. He seems to have been a rough, unruly lad who scorned the quiet, gentle habits of I'saac, and his conduct toward his half-brother was rude, indiscreet, and vulgar. On this occasion he was probably jealous of the honor being paid to I'saac in the festivities.

Sa'rah felt that Ish'ma-el's unbecoming attitude toward her son was not only the expression of his own envy, but was the result of Ha'gar's influence and training. Her pent up envy now burst forth in sharp anger. She went to A'bra-ham and demanded that Ha'gar and Ish'ma-el be sent away, saying that she did not wish her son to be reared with this rough lad.

Sa'rah realized that Ish'ma-el's jeers and ill-mannered mocking had a deeper meaning than mere impoliteness in speech. She felt that his attitude was connected with the birthright, and that he would use violence

ISHMAEL THE ARCHER

if necessary to defend what he thought was his rightful heritage. Her quick temper may have led her to call for the removal of a rival to her son's succession and title to his father's inheritance, but in her words the way was opened for the Lord to overcome evil with good, hence she may unknowingly have uttered a Divine decree. Whatever her motives may have been, it is clear that the Lord was on her side. She no doubt feared that A'braham's fondness for his first-born son might lead him to seek some way of depriving I'saac of the heritage which had been Divinely announced as his.

The request of Sa'rah presented A'bra-ham with a very difficult problem. He therefore sought guidance from the Lord, and was told to do as Sa'rah had asked. The Lord advised him that it would be better for both I'saac and Ish'ma-el, for Ha'gar and her son to be sent away, and promised that He would bless Ish'ma-el, making a great people of his descendants.

The next morning A'bra-ham provided food and a bottle of water for Ha'gar and Ish'ma-el and sent them away, thinking, no doubt, that they would go to Ha'gar's native land of E'gypt. Ha'gar became lost, however, and wandered in the desert south of Ge'rar until the water given her for the journey was all gone. The sufferings of Ha'gar and Ish'ma-el were severe, for Divine Providence sought to cure them of their wilfulness, and to prepare Ish'ma-el for a great future. Though punished, they were not forsaken by the Lord; though exiled from A'bra-ham's home, they were destined to make a way for themselves in the world, and though deprived of their membership in the family of Is'ra-el they were Divinely chosen to be the head of another great branch of the human race.

Lost in the desert, both she and her boy perishing from thirst, Ha'gar despaired. With only the hot, burning sands for a bed, and with no canopy over them except the open skies from which there blazed down upon them a consuming heat, Ha'gar placed her son under a little bush and turned away to let him die. Her act was not cruel or heartless, she simply could not bear to see her son die.

It was in that hour of despair that the angel of the Lord appeared to her. The angel comforted her with the assurance that her cries had been heard by the Lord, who would deliver them from danger, and who would make a great nation of Ish'ma-el's descendants. Then her eyes were opened by the Lord, and she saw a refreshing spring of water gushing forth in the midst of the desert.

Ha'gar remained in the desert country, where she reared her son to full manhood. Ish'ma-el learned to shoot the bow and arrow with great skill, a talent that was useful in his wild, nomadic life in the desert. He was known as a wild man, and his children resembled him in their love of roaming the desert and being their own masters. Twelve sons were born to him, and each of them became the head of a roving tribe of people later known as A-ra'bi-ans.

SUGGESTIONS FOR STUDY

Biblical Index to Helpful References

Ishmael's Jealousy Toward Isaac. (Gal. 4:29-31.)

Descendants of Ishmael. (Gen. 25:12-18.)

Ishmael Becomes a Nomad and Head of a Great Nation. (Gen. 17:20; 25:12-18.)

The Evils and Consequences of Envy. (1 Jno. 3:12; Jas. 3:16; Job. 5:2.)

Questions

1. How old was Ishmael when Isaac was born?

2. How old was he when Isaac was given the feast of weaning?

3. In what manner did Ishmael treat Isaac?

4. What appears to have been the natural disposition of Ishmael?

5. What appears to have been the natural disposition of Isaac?

6. What demand did Sarah make of Abraham regarding Hagar and Ishmael?

7. What did Abraham do in respect to her request?

8. Tell of Hagar's despair in the wilderness and of the visit of an angel.

9. Where did Hagar and Ishmael live?

10. Where did Hagar secure a wife for Ishmael?

11. How many sons did Ishmael have?

12. Who are the descendants of Ishmael and where do they live today?

ABRAHAM ORDERED TO SACRIFICE ISAAC

GENESIS 22:1-19   In the days of A'bra-ham the central idea in
worship was the offering of sacrifices. The custom had prevailed in the
period before A'bra-ham, and was continued for hundreds of years after
him. In keeping what they regarded as the chief duty of worship, the
people erected altars and made offerings unto the Lord. The sacrifices
consisted of such domestic animals as sheep, goats, and cattle, which were
slain and burnt upon altars built of either stone or earth, and were dedicated to God. The offering of these animals was an expression of thanks
for the blessings of life, and the blood was accepted as a full pardon for
sin. In making such offerings the worshiper acknowledged his complete
dependence upon God, confessed his wholehearted surrender to Him, and
pledged himself to a life of obedience.

A'bra-ham had been very faithful in making offerings to God; when
he moved from one place to another the first thing he did was to build
an altar for sacrifices. Many of the heathen people of the world, or those
who worshiped false gods, also made sacrifices, and some of them even
offered their own children. In the hope of pleasing their gods these cruel
people would bind their children to the altar and slay them, or cast them
to wild animals to be torn and devoured. Those who worshipped the
true God never followed this custom, for they knew that it was wrong
to do such things. Instead of harming their children, whom the Lord had
given them to love and protect, they considered it a religious duty to guard
them from all danger.

It was, therefore, a great shock to A'bra-ham, and a severe trial of his
faith, when one day he was ordered by the Lord to offer his son I'saac
on the altar as a burnt sacrifice. A'bra-ham was then living at Be'er-she'ba,
which was near the southwestern border of the land of Ca'naan, and
about fifty miles from the mountainous regions of Beth'el, where he had
formerly made his home. The Lord told him to take I'saac back into the
hill country, where he should offer him as a burnt sacrifice on the mountain which was then known as Mo-ri'ah. To make such a journey would

take nearly three days of the slow travel that could be made at that time.

With his heart filled with sorrow and despair, but still loyal and obedient to the voice of his God, A'bra-ham prepared at once for the journey. He arose early in the morning, saddled an ass, which was the animal used for travel in those days, split the wood for the burnt offering, and took two of his young men with him as servants. With his son I'saac and the two servants he then travelled in a northeasterly direction, searching for the place where God would direct him to make the sacrifice.

For nearly three days A'bra-ham and his companions walked over the hills and across the valleys, up many steep and rugged paths, sleeping at night under the trees in the open forests of that country. It must have been a sad, solemn journey for A'bra-ham, with bitter thoughts to fill his mind every step of the way. No doubt he thought most often of I'saac, the son and true heir whom God had given after long years of waiting. He knew that the death of I'saac would destroy all hope of the many descendants whom the Lord had promised, yet he seems not for a moment to have thought of disobeying God's command.

A'bra-ham loved the Lord with all his heart, and there was no earthly possession that he would not quickly and happily yield to Him. He had faithfully given a tenth part of all his increase, and often much more. He had always taken the best of his sheep or cattle for burnt offerings unto the Lord. He firmly believed in God's word, trusted fully in His mercy, grace, and love, and had done without question whatever the Lord had asked. But never before had he been asked to give as a burnt offering his own son, the child he loved above everything else in the world, and through whom all the families of the earth were to be blessed. What greater trial could come to any man?

A'bra-ham had a firm and conquering faith in the power of God. He had passed through many trials before, and his faith had always won. It had been hard to leave his father's home in Mes-o-po-ta'mia, to sojourn in E'gypt, and to bear the separation from Lot. His faith had been tried by the ruin of Sod'om and Go-mor'rah, which he had tried to save for the sake of the few righteous people who lived in these cities. There had been great trials in the long years of waiting for the birth of I'saac, and the parting with Ha'gar and Ish'ma-el had filled him with sorrow. By these and many other trials his faith had been severely tested, yet never had failed. But now he must face a trial far greater than all the others combined. Could he trust God even now?

Yes, he had faith to believe that even though his son should be slain and the body burned into ashes, God was able to give the child back to him from the dead. How this could be done was more than A'bra-ham could understand, for the ways of God are too wonderful to be known by even the best of men. And yet, though A'bra-ham could not understand the ways of God, there was one thing he could do. He could believe in God's mercy and power, and obey the command, knowing that He would do no wrong. To A'bra-ham:

> "Providence was dark in its permissions; yet
> One day when all is known,
> The universe of reason shall acknowledge
> How just and good were they."

As the weary travelers passed on into the third day, there suddenly appeared in the sky a bright cloud pointing out the place where the burnt

ABRAHAM OFFERS ISAAC

offering was to be made. The glory of God shone from the top of a high hill, as if to say to A'bra-ham, "There I am, and there I wait for thee." This was a prophecy of the She-ki'nah, or miraculous light, which later was to hover over the altar of the temple on this very spot. The light of God's glorious acceptance of the faith and obedience of his servant, and of the giving back of his precious son shone upon the place where the altar was to be built.

A'bra-ham said to his two young servants, "Remain here at the foot of this mountain while I'saac and I go up to the top for worship, and presently we will return." In these words he may have spoken more than he understood, yet he fully believed that God would provide a way by which I'saac would return with him, and still the offering could be made.

The wood for the fire which was to consume the offering was placed upon I'saac, while A'bra-ham carried a knife and some glowing sticks from the fire which they had kindled at the foot of the hill.

As the two walked up the mountainside I'saac turned to his father and said, "Behold the fire and the wood, but where is the lamb for a burnt offering?" In reply to this heart-rending question of his son, A'bra-ham uttered one of the most comforting statements to be found in all the Bible. He said: "God will provide himself a lamb for a burnt offering." Once again faith had moved him to speak more than he understood, making a prophecy that was soon to come true in a marvelous way, and which foretold the sacrifice of the Lord Je'sus for the world's sin.

When A'bra-ham and I'saac reached the top of the mountain where the sacrifice was to be made, they proceeded at once to build an altar. A'bra-ham then tied the hands and feet of I'saac and placed him on the wood which had been laid upon the altar. He took a knife in his hand, raised up his arm to strike the fatal blow into the heart of his son, and was in the very act of offering him as a burnt sacrifice unto God.

Suddenly an angel spoke to him out of the heavens, saying: "A'bra-ham, A'bra-ham; do not lay thy hands upon the lad, and do not harm him in any way: for now I know that thou fearest God, because thou hast not withheld thy son, thine only son from me."

What joy and relief these words brought to the father's heart! He had been permitted to go just far enough to test his faith and obedience, and now God restrained his hand from an act of murder. A'bra-ham was spared the actual deed of slaying and burning his son because he had proved himself ready to do so if God really demanded it.

Then A'bra-ham looked behind him and saw a young ram caught by its horns in a thicket. He quickly released I'saac, seized the ram, and offered it upon the altar prepared for the sacrifice of his own son.

The Lord then renewed the covenant which he had previously made with A'bra-ham, and which had been repeated a number of times in the course of his life. The covenant was now strengthened by God's solemn promise, and it was declared that all people should be saved through the descendants of A'bra-ham. In the willingness of A'bra-ham to sacrifice I'saac we are reminded of a love that was even greater. God spared the son of A'bra-ham, but freely gave His own Son to die for man's salvation. The rescue of I'saac was a prophecy of the resurrection of the Sav'ior, and of His return to glory. All of these truths may not have been grasped by A'bra-ham, but centuries later the Lord said: "A'bra-ham rejoiced to see my day, and he saw it, and was glad."

A'bra-ham and I'saac then went down the mountain together, returning to the young servants just as A'bra-ham had declared that they would.

I'saac continued to be a faithful son. Gentle and gracious by nature, he remained obedient to the laws and duties of his father's religion. When he was fully grown in body, mind, and spirit he became the honored and worthy successor of his father. Of his career we shall learn in future chapters.

SUGGESTIONS FOR STUDY

Biblical Index to Helpful References

The Worship of God in Sacrifices. (Gen. 4:3; 8:20; 31:54; 35:14.)

The Trial of Faith. (1 Pet. 1:17; Heb. 11:17.)

Abraham's Faith Evidenced in Works. (James 2:21.)

The Temple Later Built on Mt. Moriah. (2 Chr. 3:1.)

All Nations to Be Blessed Through Abraham's Descendants. (Acts. 3:25.)

God Spared Not His Only Son in Sacrifice for Man's Redemption. (Rom. 8:32.)

Isaac Bearing His Cross, Jesus Bearing His Cross. (John 19:17.)

Questions

1. What was the central idea in worship in ancient times?

2. Was Abraham always faithful in offering sacrifices to God?

3. What strange command came to Abraham concerning Isaac?

4. Where was this sacrifice to be made? How far from Abraham's home?

5. Explain this trial of Abraham's faith.

6. Tell of Abraham's obedience to the command of God.

7. When asked about the sacrifice by Isaac what did Abraham say?

8. In what way was this saying fulfilled?

9. What sacrifice for our sins did this incident typify?

THE DEATH AND BURIAL OF SARAH

GENESIS 23

After I'saac had been spared by the Lord on the altar of burnt offering, A'bra-ham and his family moved once again to the hill country of Ca'naan. Here A'bra-ham settled at He'bron, where he had lived forty years before. He'bron was the oldest city and the first place that might be called civilized in that land. It had been built by descendants of Heth, who was a son of Ham, seven years before the building of Zo'an, the oldest capital of E'gypt.

Soon there came great sorrow to A'bra-ham, and the shadow of death fell upon his home. Death came at last to Sa'rah, the beloved wife of A'bra-ham, and the mother of his son I'saac. Married to A'bra-ham when they both were young, Sa'rah had gone with him on many long, danger-ous journeys, had been a faith-ful companion to him during years of hardship and disap-pointment, and had rejoiced with him at the birth of I'saac. She had lived to the ripe old age of one hundred and twenty-seven years, having been spared to raise her only son until he reached the age of thirty-seven.

The death of one who had been dear to him for so many years was a great shock to A'bra-ham. He was a stern, stout-hearted man, one who had borne many trials without com-plaint, and who had yielded only to the will of God, but now he bowed his head in bitter grief. But he wept not as those who have no hope; the blinding tears of grief opened the eyes

ABRAHAM'S WIFE

of his soul to see more clearly into the world beyond. With a firm belief in the future life, A'bra-ham was comforted by the thought that Sa'rah's spirit had passed into a state of perfect happiness, and that soon he would follow.

A'bra-ham wished to provide an honorable burial for the body of Sa'rah, and to make sure that her grave would not be disturbed. For this reason he thought it wise to purchase a large plot of ground for a family cemetery. The Lord had promised the entire land of Ca'naan to A'bra-ham and his descendants, but the region in which he lived at this time was still held by people who were called the Hit'tites.

There was a large tract of land which belonged to a man named E'phron, and on which there was a cave well-suited for a burial place. A'bra-ham proposed to buy this land, and to pay whatever price the owner might ask. Because of the high regard which the Hit'tites had for A'bra-ham and out of respect for his noble character and righteousness, E'phron offered to give him the land without cost. A'bra-ham appreciated the kind offer, but insisted upon paying the full market price of four hundred shekels in silver.

Thus we have the first record of the transfer of property by legal title, the first instance of the purchase of land for a burial place, the first account of the use of silver as money, and the first family burying ground known in history.

The field of Mach-pe'lah and the cave bearing the same name became the permanent property of A'bra-ham and his family. Here A'bra-ham himself was later buried, as were Ja'cob, Jo'seph, and many later patriarchs.

SUGGESTIONS FOR STUDY

Biblical Index to Helpful References

Abraham a Sojourner in Canaan. (Gen. 17:8; Heb. 11:9, 13; 1 Chr. 29:15.)

Mourning for the Dead. (2 Sam. 13:31; Joel 2:13; 2 Sam. 14.2; Num. 20:29.)

Machpelah as a Burying Place for Generations. (Gen. 25:9, 10; 47:28-31; 49:29-33; 50:12, 13.)

Questions

1. Where was Abraham living when Sarah died?

2. How old a town was Hebron?

3. How old was Sarah when she died?

4. Tell of Abraham's grief at the death of Sarah.

5. Why was it necessary that Abraham buy a burying place for Sarah?

6. What was the name of the field purchased by Abraham?

7. Did it become a permanent burying place for Abraham's descendants?

STORY 17

A WIFE IS CHOSEN FOR ISAAC

GENESIS 24   The death of Sa'rah left an unhappy vacancy in A'bra-ham's family. For three years the man of God lived in deep, heart-felt mourning. He found the home very sad without the presence of Sa'rah, and he watched with anxiety the loneliness of his son I'saac. The chief interest in A'bra-ham's life was to provide for the happiness and security of I'saac, through whom the family was to be carried on according to the will of God.

I'saac was now forty years old, about the usual age when men of those days began to think seriously of marriage. It was then the custom for parents to arrange the marriage of their children.

In carrying out his duty as a parent A'bra-ham was both loving and careful, for he intended to find I'saac a wife whom the Lord approved. The people of the land in which they were now living worshiped idols, and were guilty of some of the worst sins. They were all descendants of Ham, but had divided into various tribes, which were known as the Hit'-tites, Per'iz-zites, Ca'naan-ites, and similar names. Since few, if any of them, worshiped the true God, A'bra-ham did not feel it right for I'saac to take a wife from such heathen people. The Lord had already made it plain that the chosen nation of which A'bra-ham was the head should be descended from Shem, and had warned A'bra-ham not to allow any descendants of Ham or Ja'pheth to come into his family. His chief duty, therefore, in choosing a wife for I'saac was to carry out the will of God in this respect.

For this reason A'bra-ham decided to send one of his most trusted servants back to the land of his kinsmen to find a wife for I'saac. When he and Lot had moved from Ha'ran in Mes-o-po-ta'mia down to the land of Ca'naan, his brothers had remained in Mes-o-po-ta'mia. They had prospered, and had reared large families, and news of these facts had been brought to A'bra-ham. He was certain that somewhere among his kinsmen there was the chosen wife for I'saac, a woman of outstanding character and deep religious feeling; to find her, he put his trust in the Lord.

The task of searching for the woman and bringing her back to the home of A'bra-ham was placed upon E-li-e'zer, who had been a faithful steward

REBEKAH AT THE WELL

of the household for nearly sixty years. To him was given the duty of making the long journey of about four hundred miles back to the region between the two great rivers, the Ti'gris and the Eu-phra'tes, far to the north and east of Ca'-naan. Here he was to trust in Divine Providence for discovering the woman whom God had chosen to become the wife of I'saac, and for securing her consent, and that of her parents, for the marriage.

In facing so difficult a mission, E-li-e'zer was naturally disturbed by the thought of failure. His fears, however, were overcome by the spirit of faith in God shown by A'bra-ham, and by the promise that if he should fail, he would not be held responsible or judged harshly by his master. It appears that A'bra-ham never had the slightest doubt of success, and that he sent his servant away in perfect faith that he would return in due time with a wife for his son.

In making ready for the long journey, and for whatever might happen during it, E-li-e'zer took ten camels, a number of servants, and enough supplies to provide food for many weeks of travel. He also took presents to be given to the bride, and gifts for her parents, for these were required by the customs of those days.

Having entered the land of Mes-o-po-ta'mia, and arrived in the vicinity of the region where Na'hor, one of A'bra-ham's brothers, made his home, E-li-e'zer stopped at a well to give water to his camels. Knowing that this was the time of evening when the women usually went to the wells to draw water, the faithful servant of A'bra-ham turned to the Lord in prayer. He prayed for the success of his mission, and for certain signs by which the woman who was to become the wife of I'saac might be pointed out to him. He asked that the maiden upon whom his choice should fall should come to the well, grant his request for a drink of water, and offer to draw water for the camels. The fulfilment of these signs would show that God approved the choice of the woman, and would prove that one so kind and thoughtful toward a stranger was well suited to become the wife of I'saac.

Before the prayer was finished, there came to the well a beautiful maiden whose name was Re-bek'ah, a daughter of Be-thu'el. When E-li-e'zer asked her for some water she quickly lifted a jar from her shoulder, placed one hand under it, and tilted it for him to drink. She then offered to draw water for the camels, and did not pause until she had done so.

E-li-e'zer was delighted by the kindliness and dignity of the beautiful young woman, and felt in his heart that his prayer was already answered. He thought it best, however, not to tell her of his mission until he was absolutely certain that she was the woman chosen by the Lord. He gave her an earring and two bracelets of gold as a token of gratitude for her kindness, and then opened the way for an offer of hospitality in her father's home. Re-bek'ah assured him that there was room for him and his companions in her father's house, and that provisions could be found there for feeding the camels.

E-li-e'zer then told Re-bek'ah that he was a servant of her uncle A'bra-ham, who was now a prosperous herdsman in the land Ca'naan. Now certain that he had been led by the hand of Providence, E-li-e'zer bowed his head in a prayer of gratitude. Meanwhile Re-bek'ah ran to her father's house and told her family about the stranger, and the things which he had told her. Her brother La'ban went out to meet E-li-e'zer, whom he addressed as a servant of the Lord, and urged him to come into the house. E-li-e'zer and the servants which he had brought with him on the mission were shown all the courtesies of Oriental hospitality.

E-li-e'zer refused to join the feast until he had explained his errand to the hosts. First he told them of his master's prosperity, and of the blessings which God had granted him, pointing out the fact that A'bra-ham had only one son to inherit his entire estate. He then praised the nobility and piety of both A'bra-ham and I'saac, explaining the many advantages that would be enjoyed by the woman who became the wife of I'saac. He also described the instructions which A'bra-ham had given him for the task of finding a wife for I'saac, and the Providential guidance which had led him to the choice of Re-bek'ah. Finally, he asked that the parents give their consent for Re-bek'ah to become the wife of I'saac, and that he be permitted to return to Ca'naan with her.

When La'ban, who was Re-bek'ah's brother, and Be-thu'el, her father, heard how A'bra-ham had sent his servant up to Ha'ran to find a wife for I'saac, and how E-li-e'zer had seen the will of God in the choice of Re-bek'ah, they both exclaimed, "Surely this comes from the Lord. Here is Re-bek'ah, take her, and let her be the wife of your master's son."

Early the next morning E-li-e'zer prepared at once for the journey back to Ca'naan, but Re-bek'ah's family felt that they could not let her go away so soon. They asked that E-li-e'zer tarry with them, and that the return trip be delayed for ten days. A'bra-ham's servant felt, however, that his master's business required haste, and insisted that it was God's will that he go at once. His mission had been carried out, so the woman chosen by the Lord to become I'saac's wife must be taken to him without further delay. When Re-bek'ah was consulted about the matter she said, "I will go at once."

E-li-e'zer then took his departure as he had planned, taking Re-bek'ah with him, and followed by the good wishes, blessings, and prayers of the entire household. Be-thu'el bestowed upon Re-bek'ah certain goods according to the customs of those days, and gave her the maid who had watched over her from infancy. Her name was Deb'o-rah, and she remained a faithful servant of Re-bek'ah until her death many years later.

While all these events were taking place in Mes-o-po-ta'mia, I'saac remained in Ca'naan, hoping and praying for the success of E-li-e'zer's mission. He went out to the well where the Angel Je-ho'vah had comforted Ha'gar, for A'bra-ham was now living once more in southwestern Ca'naan near Be'er-she'ba. Here I'saac recalled how many times the Lord had blessed his father's family, and here he entreated the Lord concerning his own marriage.

We are not told how long I'saac remained lost in meditation, nor what thoughts filled his mind, but we do know that while his eyes were still lifted up toward heaven, there suddenly appeared in the distance E-li-e'zer's caravan of camels. When Re-bek'ah was told that the man coming out to meet the caravan was I'saac, she followed the custom of the day by covering her face with a veil. I'saac loved her from the first moment, and in due time the marriage ordained by the Lord was carried out. As a token of love and respect I'saac placed Re-bek'ah in the tent which Sa'rah had occupied until her death, thus proving that he was comforted for his mother's death.

Such is the story of this beautiful, romantic marriage, a marriage not unlike many which take place today among certain peoples of the East, except that it was directed in every detail by the Lord. It was a marriage made possible by faith in God: faith on the part of A'bra-ham and his loyal servant E-li-e'zer, on the part of I'saac, and on the part of Re-bek'ah. The prompt, cheerful response of Re-bek'ah, and the good spirit which she showed in the course of so many strange events can be explained in no other way than to credit her with perfect faith in the Lord.

This was truly a marriage in the Lord. It was pervaded by a spirit of reverence toward God as the founder of the institution, and by a desire for his blessings. The motives of all concerned were pure and sincere, and supreme regard was given to the will of God. A spirit of prayer precipitated every movement, and the Lord's indication of his own choice of a bride was accepted by I'saac as a gracious Providence.

Although there were taints of idolatry in Te'rah's family and in the households of some of his descendants, there were also striking examples of loyalty to the true God worshiped by A'bra-ham, and Re-bek'ah may be counted as one of those who was most faithful. We shall learn more of this sublime truth in future chapters.

SUGGESTIONS FOR STUDY

Biblical Index to Helpful References

God's Promise of Material Blessings for the Righteous. (Ps. 112:1-3.)

Law Again God's Children Marrying Idolaters. (Exo. 34:16; Deut. 6:13.)

Abraham's Kindred Lived in (Haran) Mesopotamia. (Gen. 11:31.)

Angels Sent to Guide the Lord's Servants. (Exo. 23:20, 23; Heb. 1:14.)

The Lord's Guidance and Blessings for Those Who Commit Their Way Unto Him. (Ps. 37:5; Prov. 16:3; 1 Pet. 5:7.)

Marriage a Divine Institution (Gen. 1:27, 28; Rom. 7:2, 3; Prov. 5:18.)

Pledges of Faithfulness Commended. (Jer. 4:2; Eccl. 5:2.)

God's Forwardness in Answering Prayer. Isa. 65:24; Dan. 9:23.)

Questions

1. How old was Isaac when his father sought for him a wife?

2. Why did Abraham not wish Isaac to marry a woman in Canaan?

3. Where did Abraham send to secure a wife for Isaac?

4. Tell of Eliezer's experience at the well of Bethuel?

5. What was the name of the maiden pointed out to him in answer to prayer?

6. How was Isaac employing his time during this period?

7. Tell of the meeting of Isaac and Rebekah, and of their marriage?

STORY 18

THE CLOSING YEARS, DEATH, AND BURIAL OF ABRAHAM

GENESIS 25:1-10

A'bra-ham lived for thirty-eight years after the death of Sa'rah, or thirty-five years after the marriage of I'saac and Re-bek'ah, thus reaching the great age of one hundred and seventy-five years. His good health, which had been restored prior to the birth of I'saac, was preserved to the end of life, while his strength of body and mind enabled him to survive the loss of his beloved wife.

After the marriage of I'saac and his removal from his father's house, A'bra-ham sought to overcome his loneliness by taking another wife. He married Ke-tu'rah, who gave birth to six sons. They became the founders of families which grew into strong tribal nations outside of Ca'naan, which was the promised land for the descendants of I'saac. We shall learn some-

ON THE BORDER OF EDOM

thing of their relation to Is'ra-el in future history.

A'bra-ham remained active and successful in all the cares and responsibilities of life right up to the end. Provision was made for the settlement of his sons by Ke-tu'rah outside the land Divinely promised to I'saac and his descendants, and care was taken to see that all the rights and privileges which belonged to I'saac as the first-born son should be safeguarded. He was a strong, able-bodied man even in extreme old age, and his mind and senses remained clear and active to the last. Before passing into the higher life he put his house in order, both in matters of worldly importance, and in those which relate to spiritual welfare.

Ab'ra-ham's body was laid to rest in the family cemetery which he had purchased for the burial of Sa'rah. There was a notable funeral, in which his family and great company of servants gathered to pay honor and reverence to his memory. All jealousy and bad feeling between Ish'ma-el and I'saac was forgotten in the presence of death, and they united in sorrow at the burial of their father. It is often true that, a time of great sorrow brings together those who have been separated by misunderstandings.

The Bible tells us that "A'bra-ham was gathered to his people." These words do not refer to his burial, for his kinsmen were buried in far distant Mes-o-po-ta'mia, while A'bra-ham was laid to rest in the cave of Machpe'lah near He'bron. What it does mean is that his spirit passed into a continued personal existence after death, that his soul passed at once into the happy life to which all the saints who died before had gone. Thus ended the earthly sojourn of a noble patriarch, and thus began his heavenly citizenship in the glory of "the city whose builder and maker is God, for which he looked."

SUGGESTIONS FOR STUDY
Biblical Index to Helpful References

Keturah Called "Concubine" of Abraham. (1 Chron. 1:32.)

Descendants of Abraham by Keturah. (1 Chron. 1:32, 33.)

God's Promise to Abraham for Ripe Old Age. (Gen. 15:15.)

Extension of Life Attributed to God's Favor. (Ps. 118:17, 18; Isa. 54:7, 8.)

The Death of Saints "a Gathering Unto Their Fathers." (Num. 20:26; Deut. 32:50.)

Questions

1. How long did Abraham live after the death of Sarah? After the marriage of Isaac and Rebekah?

2. To whom was he later married? How many sons were born to this second marriage?

3. Where did he arrange for the settlement of these sons?

4. How old was Abraham when he died?

5. Where was his body buried? Describe the funeral.

6. What note of special interest about Isaac and Ishmael at the funeral?

7. What is meant by the statement, "Abraham was gathered to his people"?

STORY 19

THE BIRTH OF THE FIRST TWINS IN HISTORY

GENESIS 25:19-28   The life of I'saac, who took the place of A'bra-ham in the Covenant promise concerning the land of Ca'naan, the founding of a great nation, and the coming of the Mes-si'ah, was not unlike that of his father in the trial of faith. While the other sons of A'bra-ham had many children, I'saac remained childless, though it had been promised that his descendants should be like the stars of heaven. His mother Sa'rah was barren for nearly half a century, and now his wife Re-bek'ah had entered the twentieth year of marriage without bearing a child.

Unlike his father, I'saac did not stoop to unworthy means of overcoming the trying situation in his home. Instead, he prayed to the Lord without ceasing, constantly asking that a son and heir should be given to him. Re-bek'ah joined him in such prayers, earnestly asking the Lord to bless them with a son to carry on the line through which all the families of the earth were to be blessed.

After twenty years of prayer and patient waiting their hopes were answered; Re-bek'ah knew that the promise would soon be fulfilled. And yet Re-bek'ah was made uneasy by certain vague, foreboding thoughts. Worried by such a state of mind, she turned to the Lord for guidance, and was told that she would become the mother of twin sons. It was also revealed that two great nations should spring from these sons, one of whom should be stronger than the other, and that the elder son and his descendants should serve the younger. Such strange thoughts in the mind of Re-bek'ah, and the revelations of God in answer to her prayer, had a strong influence upon her, no doubt accounting for her preference of the younger of the two sons after their birth.

When the two sons were born the fears of Re-bek'ah were fully justified. The first of the two was abnormal in appearance, very red and hairy, while his brother was perfectly normal. The elder child was called E'sau, which means "hairy," or "rough," while the younger was called Ja'cob, which means "to trip" or "a supplanter."

As the boys grew older the traits of character which were to divide them and their descendants became very clear. E'sau inherited from his mother a bold, active disposition, but one which lacked her nobility of spirit; from I'saac there came a liking for open spaces, and a fondness for good living. Ja'cob inherited from I'saac a quiet, thoughtful nature, and from Re-bek'ah a talent for sly, sharp dealing. In E'sau there were the elements of manly courage, great energy, and practical genius which tended to make him hasty and hard to manage. In Ja'cob there were the traits of timidity, gentleness, and cunning which led to the dangers of being too crafty for his own good in life.

E'sau became a great hunter, and one who excelled in all of the rough, vigorous sports of the age. He took for granted the position of his father's favorite son, and acted as though he had already inherited the estates of his father. In the meantime Ja'cob gave his time to the gentle occupation of caring for the sheep, and was always ready to help around the

IN THE SHEPHERD'S FIELD

home. He was the favorite of his mother, and was under her influence during the formative years of childhood and youth.

When the two sons reached the age of maturity I'saac showed a strong preference for E'sau, to whom he intended to leave his property and family heritage. If I'saac knew of the Divine revelation to Re-bek'ah which declared that Ja'cob was to be the chosen son, he seems to have regarded it as only a wish of Re-bek'ah, and not as the voice of God.

I'saac seems also to have felt that E'sau, who was strong, bold, and active, was better fitted than Ja'cob to take possession of the land of Ca'-naan for the descendants of A'bra-ham. The rights which belonged to a first-born son, the physical powers of E'sau, and I'saac's personal wishes were all in favor of E'sau as the natural heir to his property.

Re-bek'ah, on the other hand, preferred Ja'cob, feeling that his sharpness of mind, his love for domestic peace and prosperity, and the choice of God which had been announced before his birth overcame the natural preference of I'saac for E'sau.

The strong preferences on the part of I'saac and Re-bek'ah became the source of much unhappiness in the domestic life of the family, and gave rise to the jealousy and bitterness which often broke out between the two sons. Happiness and justice in the home were forgotten, and the future relations of the two sons and their descendants were turned into hatred, disputes, and warfare. Later chapters in these narratives tell the story of the sad results of these unfortunate circumstances.

SUGGESTIONS FOR STUDY

Biblical Index to Helpful References

Childlessness Cured by the Lord. (Ps. 113:9.)

Children a Heritage of the Lord. (Ps. 127:3.)

The Divine Choice of the Younger Son to

Be Heir to the Abrahamic Promise. (Rom. 9:10-13.)

Conflicts Between Descendants of Esau and of Isaac. (Num. 20:14-21.)

Descendants of Isaac Forbidden to Take Lands of Esau's Descendants. (Deut. 2:4-6.)

Questions

1. What trial of faith was suffered by Isaac for twenty years?

2. What course did Isaac and Rebekah pursue to overcome her childlessness?

3. What did the Lord reveal to Rebekah concerning her anticipated child-birth?

4. What were the differences in the physical appearances and temperamental characteristics of Esau and Jacob?

5. In what occupations did Esau and Jacob engage?

6. Which son was preferred by Jacob? By Rebekah? Why?

7. What unfortunate circumstances resulted from these preferences?

Story 20

ESAU SELLS HIS BIRTHRIGHT TO JACOB

GENESIS 25:29-34

In the course of events in the home of I'saac and Re-bek'ah, and in the strained relations between their twin sons, a small thing gave rise to circumstances which clearly foretold the separate character and destiny of each son.

E'sau, the wild, roving lover of outdoor life, had just returned from a long, hard day of pursuing game in forest and field. He was very tired and hungry, and for the moment his ravenous appetite outweighed all other thoughts. His brother Ja'cob, whose quiet, domestic habits had given him practical experience in home comforts, had just prepared a bowl of red pottage made of different grains and lentils beaten in a mortar and boiled into a gruel. This was a favorite dish among the Oriental people of that day, and its odor brought the pangs of hunger in the exhausted, fainting E'sau to the breaking point.

He begged his brother Ja'cob to give this bowl of pottage to him. Under the circumstances such a kindness would have been a natural expression of brotherly sympathy and love, but Ja'cob refused the request. Taking advantage of his brother's great hunger, and of his weakness at that moment, Ja'cob offered to give him the food which he requested in exchange for his birthright. It was really a cruel, unworthy thing to ask, even though Ja'cob may have had just reasons for believing that he was entitled to the rights and privileges of the firstborn.

Ja'cob's conduct was also irreverent and sacrilegious, for the birthright dealt with religious privileges which should not have been sought by driving a hard bargain, or by any kind of trickery or scheming. To think of the birthright as something which could be bought or sold was altogether wrong, and to offer a mess of pottage for it was a shameful act.

The rights of the firstborn included a double share in the property left by the father, leadership of the family, and the right to act as priest in family worship. In the case of Ja'cob and E'sau it also gave the honor of being the head of the chosen people who were later known as the children of Is'ra-el, and the right to occupy the land of Ca'naan.

Ja'cob's desire for the birthright was probably caused by what his mother had told him about the place he was to hold according to God's promise, and one cannot blame him for such a desire. He did wrong, however, in trying to gain the birthright before the Lord was ready to give it to him, and in the cruel bargain which he forced upon E'sau when his brother was too weak to protect his own interests. His deed showed that he did not trust in the Lord to carry out the promise as He thought best. The use of unworthy means to gain an honorable end cannot be justified in the sight of God.

The conduct of E'sau was also disgraceful. When he heard the shrewd offer of Ja'cob, he agreed to it without argument, and even spoke slightingly of his birthright. If he had been honorable enough to deserve the birthright, he would have preferred a crust of bread and a cup of water to the more satisfying food for which he was willing to give so much. He acted without any regard for his spiritual welfare, giving up all prospects of a great future inheritance for the sake of one good meal while he was hungry. The blessings promised to the descendants of A'bra-ham, the honor of being the head of God's chosen people, and all the property and wealth that would come to the one who held the birthright were exchanged for a mess of pottage.

Ja'cob afterwards suffered much because of his wrong-doing on this occasion, and E'sau lost forever all that he had sold so cheaply. Of these consequences we shall learn in future chapters.

SUGGESTIONS FOR STUDY

Biblical Index to Helpful References

Another Circumstance Where a Pot of Pottage Proved Dangerous. (2 Ki. 4:38-41.)

Inheritance of the First-born. (Deut. 21:15-17.)

Other Exceptions Where the Birthright Was Forfeited. (1 Chron. 5:1, 2; 1 Ki. 2:15-20.)

The Irreligiousness of Esau's Act. (Heb. 12:16.)

Esau's Wrong Act Irreparable. (Heb. 12:17; Jer. 49:8-10.)

Questions

1. What was one of the favorite dishes of Esau?

2. Why did he urgently request Jacob to give him a dish of this gruel?

3. What did Jacob demand of Esau in exchange for a mess of pottage?

4. What special privileges were involved in the "birthright"?

5. How did Esau show his unworthy character in selling his birthright?

6. What was wrong in the manner in which Jacob bought Esau's birthright?

STORY 21

THE CRAFTY SCHEME OF REBEKAH AND JACOB TO GAIN THE BLESSING INTENDED FOR ESAU

GENESIS 27, 28:1-9

E'sau's lack of respect for the covenant which God had made with A'bra-ham, and for his parents' wishes was shown in his marriage. During his hunting trips he had become well acquainted with the Hit'tites, a heathen people of Ca'naan who were under the curse of God for worshiping idols. When he was forty years old he took two wives in this heathen land. Such a deed brought great sorrow to his father and mother, for it was a disgrace to the family name. From these unholy marriages there sprang a people known in later history as the E'dom-ites, who were always enemies of God's chosen people.

In spite of his disobedience and scorn for true religion, E'sau remained the favorite son of the patient, long-suffering I'saac. As the strength of I'saac began to fade and his eyesight to grow dim, he felt that he should prepare for the death which might come at any moment. He was now one hundred and thirty-seven years old, his half-brother Ish'ma-el had been dead for fourteen years, and he was now so feeble that even his family thought that death was near. Although he did not die until forty-three years later, he thought it wise to arrange for the division of his property. In those days it was the custom for a father to make what is now called a will by giving his blessing to the sons who were to inherit his belongings. In these blessings the father would tell what each son was to inherit, and once a blessing had been given it could not be changed.

E'sau's unholy marriages to the two Hit'tite women had taken place thirty-seven years before, but he had remained in the household of I'saac during all these years, and his father had gradually forgiven his disobedience. And so I'saac planned to bestow upon E'sau, his elder son and favorite, the blessing which belonged to the first-born son, in spite of the fact that E'sau had sold his birthright to Ja'cob many years before, and had proven himself unworthy of the heritage.

One day as I'saac sat in his house, no doubt tired and worried by his

ISAAC SENDS ESAU TO HUNT

feeble state of health, and believing that he might soon be called from this world, he said to E'sau: "I am failing in strength, and my eyes are dim; I do not know how soon I may die. Before I die let me bestow upon you, my elder son, the blessings of the first-born. I wish you to inherit this land, and to become the head of the nation through which all the families of the earth are to be blessed. Before I give this blessing, however, take thy bow and quiver and go out into the fields. Kill a deer, and bring me the venison which I love so well."

It was the duty of E'sau to remind his father that the rights of the first-born had been sold long ago to Ja'cob, and he should have admitted his unworthiness to carry on the family from which the Mes-si'ah was to come. Instead of acting honestly in this matter, E'sau was moved by the spirit of irreverence and boldness which had marked his entire life. That is why he obeyed his father's request, not so much in the spirit of a dutiful son as in the hope of gaining the blessing which he had sold to Ja'cob for a mess of pottage.

Re-bek'ah overheard the words between I'saac and E'sau, and knew that whoever brought the dish of venison to her husband would receive the blessing which belonged to the firstborn. She also knew that E'sau had sold his birthright to Ja'cob, but she remembered the promise of God that the heritage should be given to Ja'cob, and that E'sau was morally and spiritually unfit to carry out the deeds which God had named in His covenant with A'bra-ham. She felt that in some way I'saac should be thwarted in his plans, and that the blessing intended for E'sau should be given to her favorite son.

In a desperate attempt to win the birthright for Ja'cob, Re-bek'ah used a cunning scheme. The scheme was unworthy of the high purposes desired, but Divine Providence permitted it for the sake of carrying on the chosen race of God. It is true that she tricked I'saac into doing what was right, but it is always wrong to deceive; both she and Ja'cob paid dearly for their acts of deception. The evil in their deeds did not cease to be evil merely because God was able to bring some good out of a wicked action.

Re-bek'ah called Ja'cob and told him to go out among the flocks and kill two young goats, explaining that she would cook the meat into a savory dish which I'saac would think was venison, and that Ja'cob should take the meat to his father and receive the blessing intended for E'sau. Ja'cob was afraid that his father would discover the trickery, even though he was almost blind, for E'sau was a very hairy man, and his clothing had the strong odor of the huntsman. Re-bek'ah then declared that she could overcome all danger by having Ja'cob wear clothes which belonged to E'sau, and by covering his hands and neck with goat skins to give the appearance of human hair.

Ja'cob finally gave in to his mother's will, and agreed to do as he had been told. The scheme was carried out perfectly, just as Re-bek'ah had predicted. In the course of the meal which he served to I'saac, Ja'cob not only represented himself as E'sau, but actually lied to his father in the name of the Lord. Tricked into believing that he was speaking with E'sau, who was still searching for venison to bring his father, I'saac pronounced upon Ja'cob the blessings of the firstborn. Among these blessings were: the promise of future security in the land of Ca'naan, prosperity and increase of both goods and family, the leadership of the chosen people of God, and supremacy over his brother and all his kinsmen.

Before these blessings were fully enjoyed by Ja'cob he had to travel a long, hard road of trial and suffering, had to be cured of his craftiness and deceit, and had to have his name changed from that of Ja'cob, the supplanter, to Is'ra-el, the contender with God. Of these events we shall learn in future chapters.

As soon as I'saac had given the blessing Ja'cob hurried out of the room. Presently E'sau returned from the hunting field, cooked the venison, and came to his father to receive the blessing which belonged to him. I'saac was then forced to admit that he had just finished a meal provided by one whom he thought to be his elder son. E'sau was overcome with disappointment and sorrow, and pleaded with his father to give him a blessing. It was too late to receive the blessing of the firstborn, for once it was given it could not be changed.

Realizing that he had now been twice supplanted by his brother Ja'cob, E'sau now begged his father to give him whatever blessing that could still be given. I'saac then promised that E'sau and his descendants should enjoy great prosperity and fame, and should be successful in war. With these blessings, however, there would be burden of servitude to his brother. Sometimes his descendants would triumph over the house of Ja'cob, but would then be forced again into serving them.

Although E'sau wept bitterly in his disappointment, there was no repentance in his heart for the sins which had brought him so great a loss.

JACOB DECEIVES ISAAC

At no time was there a word of humility or an admission of sin; all that E'sau desired was revenge. In a fit of anger he vowed to kill Ja'cob at the first opportunity. He wept, not for the sins of selling his birthright and entering marriages forbidden in the covenant with A'bra-ham, but for the loss of the blessing.

Re-bek'ah became so alarmed by E'sau's threats against the life of Ja'cob that she decided to send her younger son to her brother's home in Mes-o-po-ta'mia until E'sau's anger had become less violent. She pretended to I'saac that her reason for sending Ja'cob away was to prevent him from repeating the error of E'sau in marrying among the women of Ca'naan. Hurried plans were made for Ja'cob's journey, and he went away with the blessings of his father and the anxious prayers of his mother. Re-bek'ah had thought that his visit would be brief, but she did not live to see his return twenty years later. Everyone who had taken part in the crafty schemes of Re-bek'ah and Ja'cob suffered greatly for the sins they had committed. Though the Lord overruled the entire affair for the accomplishment of His purposes and the glory of His name, sorrow and suffering came to all who had done wrong.

SUGGESTIONS FOR STUDY

Biblical Index to Helpful References

Limits of Man's Life Set by God. (Job 14:5; Ps. 139:16; Matt. 6:27.)

The Dew of Hermon Used as Tokens of Divine Blessings. (Ps. 133:3; Deut. 33: 13, 28.)

The Evil of Practicing Deception. (Prov. 24:28; Ps. 5:6; Jer. 9:7-9.)

The Enormity of Jacob's Sin in Lying. (John 8:44; 2 John 2:21; Rev. 21:8.)

Hatred Between Esau and Jacob. (Gen. 32:3-11.)

Conflicts Between Descendants of Esau and of Isaac. (2 Ki. 8:20; 14:7.)

Abraham's Blessing of Jacob and Esau an Act of Faith. (Heb. 11:20.)

Questions

1. In what manner did Esau violate the laws of God in his marriage?

2. Upon which of his sons did Isaac wish to bestow the heritage of the firstborn?

3. Why was he unworthy to receive this blessing?

4. What did Isaac ask of Esau before giving his last blessing?

5. How did Rebekah plan to have this blessing given to Jacob instead of Esau?

6. Was this scheme of Rebekah and Jacob right? Why not?

7. How did God over-rule the scheme for his own will and glory?

8. Did Abraham bestow upon Esau any blessing? Explain the meaning of it.

9. How did Esau feel toward Jacob?

10. What did Rebekah do to prevent his carrying out his threats?

JACOB DREAMS OF THE STAIRWAY TO HEAVEN

GENESIS 28:10-22

Ja'cob had led a happy life in his father's home, and had enjoyed many favors because of his mother's love for him. That is why it was a great trial for him to become a wanderer, facing unknown dangers in a world that was strange to him. The journey to La'ban's home in Mes-o-po-ta'mia was a long, hard trip, filled with many perils.

Still he must go out and face with courage the hardships that would come to him for many years. With staff in hand, and carrying a few necessities for the long journey, he took leave of his parents and started on the strange roads to a land far to the north. Leaving Be'er-she'ba, which lay on the border of the desert in the extreme southwestern part of the land, Ja'cob walked over the hills, through the valleys, and across the plains in a northerly direction. After several days of travel had wearied him, he paused one evening at a spot in the mountains not far from Beth'el, about fifty miles from his home at Be'er-she'ba.

As Ja'cob rested his weary body upon the bare ground and looked at the countless stars overhead, many solemn thoughts filled his mind. A feeling of guilt rested heavily upon his heart, and the loneliness of having to bear the results of wrong-doing without a mother's sympathy and good advice filled his soul with fear and worry. With the passing of the light and cheer of the sun a gloomy darkness descended upon him. As he fell into slumber his last thought was upon the need for protection and guidance from the Lord. He now realized that if the blessings promised in the covenant with A'bra-ham were ever to be fulfilled in him they must come through the forgiving and redeeming love of God, and not by trickery or cunning fraud.

There came to Ja'cob a wonderful dream, a spiritual vision from God. Suddenly the heavens above him were radiant with the glory of God; he saw a stairway leading from the ground near where he slept up into the heavens where God was dwelling, and angels were going up and coming down the stairs. Carried away by the dream, Ja'cob opened his whole mind and heart to its message. The Lord seemed to be speaking to him from the top of the stairway, renewing in every detail the covenant which He had made with A'bra-ham.

The Lord told Ja'cob that the whole land of Ca'naan should belong to his descendants, who could no more be counted than the dust of the ground. It was promised that in his children all the families of the earth should be blessed, and Ja'cob was assured that the Lord would guide and protect him in the journey just ahead. It was also promised that in due time he should be permitted to return to the land of Ca'naan, and that the property left him by his father I'saac would come to him as soon as he was worthy to receive it.

When Ja'cob awoke the next morning he exclaimed with unspeakable joy, "Surely the Lord is in this place, and I knew it not. I thought that God had completely forsaken me, but now He has appeared before

JACOB'S DREAM

my very eyes. Since He has promised to give me bread to eat, to protect me wherever I go, and to bring me back safely to my father's house, I will worship Him alone. Of all that the Lord shall give me in worldly things I will surely return one-tenth unto Him." Ja'cob then anointed a stone as an altar, and lifted up his heart to God in worship.

While thinking about the meaning of the wonderful vision Ja'cob realized that the great distance which sin had put between him and the Lord was now wiped out by God's mercy. There was now an open way of communication between God and man, and over it the angels of mercy came down to bless the earth, then returned to heaven bearing the prayers and thankful praises of the saints. The vision also taught him that the light of heaven brings comfort and assurance to even the darkest ways of life.

How fitting was this mid-night vision to the peculiar needs of Ja'cob at the moment! To his sense of loneliness caused by the loss of parental comradeship, God said "I will be with thee." To his feeling of poverty and homelessness, the Lord said "I will give thee all this land as an inheritance." To his despairing hopelessness for the future the promise was given "Thou shalt spread abroad to the east and to the west."

This experience of Ja'cob on the lonely plateau near Beth'el was a turning point in his life; it was a changed man who continued the journey into Mes-o-po-ta'mia. Having now been taught by the Lord through heartfelt experience, his worldly and crafty nature was turned into higher channels. It is true that Ja'cob made further mistakes in the future, and that his life was far from perfect, but he was made a much better man by the vision.

Ja'cob then walked on toward the east. Crossing the rugged mountain slopes to the Jor'dan valley, he waded across the river. Then he moved on over high plateaus and across the valleys until he reached the land from which his mother had come many, many years before. Here he lived for more than twenty years, and our next story will tell some of his experiences during that time.

SUGGESTIONS FOR STUDY

Biblical Index to Helpful References

Abraham's Worship at Bethel. (Gen. 12: 8; 13:3.)

Abraham's Payment of Tithes. (Gen. 14: 20.)

Great Blessings Often Followed by Severe Trials. (Matt. 3:4.)

God's Repeated Pledges to Make of Abraham's Descendants a Great Nation. (Gen. 12:2, 3; 22:18; 26.4; Num. 23:10.)

God's Revelations in Dreams. (Num. 12: 6; Gen. 37:5-10; 1 Ki. 3:3-14; Matt. 1: 20-25.)

Another Vision Similar to Jacob's. (Isa. 6: 1-8.)

Making and Keeping Vows. (Eccl. 5:4-6; Deut. 23:21; Ps. 132:1-5.)

Questions

1. To what land was Jacob sent by his mother? Why?

2. What added to Jacob's loneliness as he journeyed away from home?

3. Where did he stop to spend the night?

4. What happened as he slept?

5. What promises did the Lord make to Jacob in that night-vision?

6. What promises did Jacob make when he awoke?

7. What influence did this experience have on Jacob's future life?

STORY 23

JACOB'S TWENTY YEARS IN MESOPOTAMIA

GENESIS 29, 30, 31 On the way from Beth'el to Mes-o-po-ta'mia
Ja'cob passed through many trials and dangers, and must have grown very
tired. But on he marched, feeling less weary now that he had cast his
burdens upon the Lord, and greatly encouraged by the blessings which had
been promised him. Having put himself in the hands of Divine Providence, he knew that God would lead him safely to the home of La'ban.

At last he paused to rest for a moment by a well some distance from the
town of Ha'ran, where his grandfather A'bra-ham had once lived, and
where many of his kindred still made their homes. Here he began to talk
with some of the shepherds who had come to water their sheep, and
learned that they knew La'ban, who was Re-bek'ah's brother. When
Ja'cob politely inquired about the health and prosperity of his uncle, he
was told that La'ban was well, and that his daughter Ra'chel was now
coming toward them with her father's sheep.

From the first moment that he saw her, Ja'cob was carried away by the
beauty and grace of Ra'chel. After removing the stone from the top of
the well, and drawing water for her sheep, he told her that he was the son
of her aunt Re-bek'ah. Overjoyed by the sight of his lovely cousin, Ja'cob
embraced her most tenderly.

Ra'chel then went home and told her father of the meeting with Ja'cob,
and La'ban went out to invite his nephew to come and stay at his home.
Ja'cob was unwilling to accept the food and shelter of his uncle without
giving something in return, and for this reason he helped in the care of the
sheep, and did his part in the work that made La'ban prosperous. After
thirty days had passed, La'ban offered to give wages to Ja'cob if he would
stay.

There were two daughters in the household of La'ban, the elder named
Le'ah, and the younger Ra'chel. The eyes of Leah were dull and without
charm, while those of Ra'chel were brilliant and attractive; Ra'chel, moreover, was truly beautiful. Ja'cob had been attracted to Ra'chel from the
moment that he first saw her at the well, and this feeling had grown even

stronger during the month that he had spent in her father's home.

It was a custom in that country for a young man to make some payment to the parents of the woman whom he had chosen as a wife. Since Ja'cob had no money or property to give La'ban, he offered to work seven years to gain Ra'chel as his wife. It must have been hard for Ja'cob, who was the son of a wealthy man back in Ca'naan, and to whom great riches had been promised, to have nothing but his own labor to offer for the hand of the woman he loved. For seven long, weary years he must work like a slave, given courage only by the hope of some day having Ra'chel as his wife. As we read in the Bible: "And Ja'cob served seven years for Ra'chel; and they seemed unto him but a few days, for the love he had to her."

When the seven years had passed, La'ban made Ja'cob the victim of one of the most selfish plots in history. In place of Ra'chel, for whom Ja'cob had toiled so long and earnestly, La'ban gave him Le'ah, the elder daughter of little charm. When Ja'cob complained of the deception he was told by La'ban that a custom of that country required an elder daughter to be given in marriage before her younger sister. In order to keep the services of one who had proved himself so useful, La'ban promised to give Ra'chel to Ja'cob in marriage if he would serve another seven years.

The shrewd plan of La'ban to bind Ja'cob for a longer term of service

RACHEL AND LEAH

succeeded. The crafty Ja'cob who had taken advantage of his brother to gain the rights of the first born was now overcome by a shrewdness more clever than his own. Ja'cob had not hesitated to turn his father's blindness to his own advantage, but now he was deceived into taking another for the bride whom he desired. Ja'cob was paid in his own coin; having deceived others, he was now himself deceived.

Ja'cob accepted his lot in patience and humility, and agreed to the suggestion of La'ban. After a week had passed he was given Ra'chel in marriage, though he must still serve her father for seven years. The fact that he had two wives was not to his discredit, for in those days men took as many wives as they could afford to keep. It is said that he loved Ra'chel and hated Le'ah, but this only means that he loved Ra'chel much more than her sister. Both of the daughters of La'ban were good wives to Ja'cob, sharing with him all the joys and sorrows of life.

During the next few years Le'ah became the mother of four sons, who were called in turn Reu'ben, Sim'e-on, Le'vi, and Ju'dah; Ra'chel, meanwhile, had no children. For this reason Ra'chel followed a custom of the times in giving Ja'cob her maid Bil'hah to bear children for her. Bil'hah became the mother of two sons, who were named Dan and Naph'ta-li. Then Le'ah gave Ja'cob her maid Zil'pah, and she bore him two more sons, who were called Gad and Ash'er. Later two more sons and a daughter were born to Le'ah, and their names were Is'sa-char, Zeb'ul-un, and Di'nah. In the course of years God answered the earnest prayers of Ra'chel, and she became the mother of a son who was called Jo'seph.

Thus there were born to Ja'cob eleven sons while he was in Mes-o-po-ta'mia, and after his return to Ca'naan Ra'chel gave birth to Ben'ja-min, making twelve in all. Each one of these sons became a prince, and was the founder of a tribe in the nation that was later known as Is'ra-el.

After Ja'cob had served La'ban seven years in return for the hand of Ra'chel in marriage, making a total of fourteen years of service, he told La'ban that he would like to go back to his native land with his wives and children. La'ban did not want Ja'cob to leave, for his services had been worth a great deal. He therefore asked Ja'cob to stay with him as a partner, promising him a certain share in the increase of the sheep and cattle.

Under this agreement Ja'cob soon gained in property much faster than did his father-in-law. The terms of the agreement were changed several times by La'ban, who had become very jealous of Ja'cob's success, but each time the Lord blessed Ja'cob more than He did La'ban.

For six years Ja'cob and La'ban remained partners, but they became less and less friendly as time went on. There were bitter quarrels over the share that each was to have in the increased flocks and herds, and many times each felt that the other was cheating him. At last Ja'cob made up his mind that he would live no longer in such an unhappy household.

Rather than have another quarrel with La'ban, Ja'cob decided to leave without telling him. He gathered his sheep and cattle, packed up all his goods that were easily movable, and took his wives and children on the journey back to Ca'naan. La'ban pursued him, trying to force him to return. He was then warned by the Lord in a dream not to harm Ja'cob in any way, and after a covenant of peace had been made between La'ban and his son-in-law, Ja'cob was allowed to continue his journey to Ca'naan.

The solemn covenant of peace that was made between La'ban and Ja'cob on the east side of Jor'dan at a place later called Gil'e-ad was binding upon all future generations, and there was never war between the descendants of La'ban and Ja'cob. The final parting was friendly enough for men who had been enemies until the Lord put peace in their hearts. Ja'cob said, "The Lord watch between me and thee, when we are absent one from another." These words are now called "The Miz'pah Benediction."

SUGGESTIONS FOR STUDY
Biblical Index to Helpful References

Jacob's Flight Into Syria and Service for a Wife. (Hos. 12:12; Deut. 26:5.)

The Ancient Custom of a Week of Festivities in Confirmation of Weddings. (Judges 14:12.)

The Unquenchableness of True Conjugal Love. (Songs 8:7.)

Jacob Reaped in Like Kind to the Sin Against His Father. (Num. 32:23; Gal. 6: 7, 8.)

Divine Methods of Retribution. (Deut. 32:21; Isa. 65:11, 12; Micah 2:1-3.)

The Right Way to Seek Deliverance from Reproach of Childlessness. (Gen. 25:22; 1 Sam. 1:11.)

Jacob's Desire to Return to Canaan Based on Faith in Abrahamic Covenant. (Heb. 11: 13, 16.)

Questions

1. Tell of the providential way in which Jacob was led to the home of Laban.

2. What relation was Laban to Jacob?

3. What was Laban's daughter's name with whom Jacob fell in love?

4. How long did Jacob work for Laban that he might have Rachel as a wife?

5. What deception did Laban play on Jacob?

6. How much longer did he then work for Rachel?

7. Did he have to wait these seven years before marrying her?

8. What expedient did Rachel adopt because of her childlessness?

9. Why did Leah later do the same thing?

10. Name the sons of each of Jacob's wives.

11. How long did Jacob work for Laban as a partner? Why did he leave?

STORY 24

JACOB WRESTLES WITH AN ANGEL

GENESIS 32, 33

After the treaty of peace had been made between Ja'cob and La'ban, and La'ban had turned back toward his own land, Ja'cob continued his journey toward Ca'naan. He entered the land east of the Jor'dan river which was later known as Gil'e-ad, and encamped near the river Jab'bok. Although he had now escaped the anger of his father-in-law, he was by no means free from danger. Other trials were ahead, and Ja'cob was filled with worry and fear. Most of all he feared the anger of his brother E'sau, from whom he had stolen both the birthright and blessing which belonged to him.

During Ja'cob's absence from the land of Ca'naan, E'sau had taken another wife. This woman was a member of the family of Ish'ma-el, the half-brother of his father, and he had married her in the hope of regaining his former place in the blessings which had been promised in the covenant with A'bra-ham. E'sau had prospered, and was now the head of a great people. Each of his three wives had given birth to many children, and the number of his servants had increased greatly.

While Ja'cob was moved to the heart by fears of E'sau, he was visited by a host of angels from heaven. They told him that his only hope of safety was the mercy of God, but that all the forces of heaven would come to his rescue if needed. The visit of the angels was not enough to quiet the fears of Ja'cob. Hoping to escape by his own shrewdness, he first tried to make peace with E'sau. Messengers were sent to tell his brother that Ja'cob was already sending fine gifts to make up for the wrongs which he had done to E'sau in the past. These messengers, however, came back with the news that E'sau was coming to meet Ja'cob with four hundred armed men, evidently seeking revenge upon his brother.

Ja'cob then felt that he was in great danger, and feared that E'sau would not only take all his possessions, but also take the life of his wives and children. For this reason he divided his household into two parts, placing those who were dearest to him in the positions of greatest safety.

After putting his wives and children where they were most likely to be safe, and scattering his flocks and herds so that only half of them could be seized in any event, Ja'cob sent many sheep and cattle as a peace-offering

JACOB WRESTLES WITH AN ANGEL

to E'sau. This was done in the hope of delaying E'sau's arrival at the place where Ja'cob and his household were encamped, and was intended as a gesture to cool the wrath of his brother.

Now that he had done everything in his power to protect his family from E'sau, Ja'cob turned to the Lord in earnest prayer. Appealing to Him as the God who had a covenant with A'bra-ham and I'saac, he admitted his own unworthiness, but asked that the Lord deliver him from E'sau out of sheer mercy.

Having done all that he could to protect his family and to make his brother less angry, and having sought help from the Lord in prayer, Ja'cob went to a quiet place where his thoughts would not be disturbed. Suddenly he was seized by a mysterious person who first appeared in the form of a man, was then called an angel, and was still later spoken of as God. All night long Ja'cob wrestled with the stranger, but as the morning began to dawn the struggle ended. The angel touched the hollow of Ja'cob's thigh, making him lame. Ja'cob now realized that he could no longer count upon his own strength, and saw that there are times when the Lord alone can help. Though wounded in the struggle, he still had courage and persistence; he clung to the angel, and refused to let him go until he blessed him.

The angel then asked, "What is thy name?" When Ja'cob gave his name the angel told him that he should no longer be called Ja'cob, but his name should be changed to Is'ra-el, which means "prince." The angel explained the change by saying, "For as a prince hast thou power with God and with men, and hast prevailed." From this point on in the Bible Ja'cob is known as Is'ra-el, and his descendants were called Is'ra-el-ites.

After blessing Ja'cob the stranger disappeared as mysteriously as he had come. Ja'cob then declared that he had seen God face to face, and had been assured that his life would be saved. A new triumph had come into the life of Ja'cob. He had "tripped" his brother E'sau, and for this reason had long lived in fear of his brother's anger. He has now been "tripped" himself by the Angel Je-hov'ah, but has learned to trust not in his own strength, but in the Lord. Nevermore is he to be called Ja'cob, "the supplanter," but from now on shall be known as Is'ra-el, the prince of God

As Ja'cob left the place where he had wrestled with the angel he saw his brother E'sau coming to meet him with a band of four hundred armed men. Knowing that God would take care of him, yet still humble, he walked forward to meet E'sau. First, he bowed his body almost to the ground, then moved a little nearer, and bowed again. Seven times he bowed to his brother, and then E'sau rushed up to him with open arms. The brothers kissed one another, and were so happy to be friends once more that they wept for joy. Ja'cob's wives and children were then brought forward to meet E'sau, who rejoiced in the blessings which had come to his brother during the twenty years that they had been separated.

Ja'cob then insisted that E'sau keep the gifts which had been sent to him as a peace-offering. At first E'sau refused, but finally agreed to keep them as a token of their renewed friendship. E'sau offered to send some of his servants to help Ja'cob and his family in caring for his many sheep and cattle, or in getting ready for their journey to the heart of Ca'naan. Ja'cob declined the offer with thanks, and the two brothers separated, never to meet again until they stood together at the grave of their father.

After camping for several days at a place afterwards known as Suc'coth, near the river Jab'bok, Ja'cob and his company journeyed westward across the river Jor'dan, settling at last in the hill country near the town of She'chem. Here he paid one hundred pieces of silver for a plot of land owned by a man named Ha'mor. Here, too, he built an altar which he named "The Altar of The Mighty One" in honor of the Lord. It was on this very spot that A'bra-ham had built the first altar in the land of Ca'naan one hundred and eighty-five years before.

SUGGESTIONS FOR STUDY

Biblical Index to Helpful References

Esau's Method of Living. (Gen. 27:40.)

The Encampment of Angels About God's Children. (Ps. 34:7, 8; 91:11-16.)

Safety in Relying on the Spoken Promises of God. (Ps. 62:11, 12.)

Jacob's Prevailing Power Through Prayer. (Hos. 12:4, 5.)

The Duty of Striving in Prayer. (Luke 22:44; Rom. 15:30.)

Divine Help Comes When Weakness Leads to Complete Surrender to God. (2 Cor. 12:10; Heb. 13:5.)

God's Children Wrestlers by Divine Calling. (Eph. 6:12; 2 Tim. 2:3.)

Questions

1. Tell of the treaty of peace between Jacob and Laban.

2. During the twenty years of Jacob's absence what had happened in the life of Esau?

3. Why did Jacob fear Esau?

4. What did he do to try to placate his anger?

5. To whom did he turn in the hour of greatest fear?

6. Who came to Jacob and wrestled with him all night?

7. What happened toward day-break?

8. What new name was given to Jacob? What is its meaning?

9. What happened when Jacob and Esau finally met?

10. Where did Jacob settle?

JOSEPH IS SOLD INTO SLAVERY

GENESIS 37:1-36

After Ja'cob had attended his father's funeral, he and his sons and their shepherds settled at He'bron, where they continued to raise sheep and cattle. Their flocks and herds had increased so greatly that it was difficult to find enough pasture land to feed them, and it was necessary to let them graze over large tracts of land.

Ten of Ja'cob's sons had been born during the early years of his exile in Mes-o-po-ta'mia, and had now become full-grown men. Jo'seph, the son of his beloved wife Ra'chel, was much younger, and Ben'ja-min, who was born in Ca'naan at the time when Ra'chel died, was a small child.

Ja'cob was especially fond of Jo'seph for several reasons. He was the son of his old age, having been born when Ja'cob was ninety years old, and was the child of Ra'chel, whom Ja'cob loved more than Le'ah. He was also a child of prayer, for Ja'cob and Ra'chel had prayed for many years that a child be given them.

Jo'seph was very different from his half-brothers, who were much older. He was quiet and thoughtful, well behaved, and polite. His brothers were rough and ill-mannered, often disobedient, and careless in the duties of worship. When they were at work in the fields, or busy caring for their father's sheep, they would often say things or do things which Jo'seph knew were wrong, and which he felt should be told to his father. He was not a tale-bearer, but rather an obedient son who did not want his father's good name to suffer from the evil deeds of his brothers.

Because he was very fond of Jo'seph, and because he thought that so good a son deserved a reward, Ja'cob showed him many favors. They spent much time together, and both father and son came to love one another more deeply every day. As a sign of his fondness for Jo'seph, Ja'cob made him a long coat of many colors, very much like those worn by princes. The boy was very proud of this coat, wearing it on special occasions, and when sent on long journeys by his father.

Partly because of the good conduct which Jo'seph showed at all times, and partly because he was their father's favorite son, the older brothers became very jealous of him. They were also angered by the dreams which Jo'seph was unwise enough to tell them. It was only natural that a boy with a quick mind and a lively imagination should dream of glorious days to come in the future, but his brothers could not understand his dreams and hopes.

There were two dreams in particular which added to the envy and hatred of Jo'seph's brothers. In the first, he dreamed that he and his brothers were binding sheaves of wheat in the field, and that his sheaf suddenly stood upright, while the sheaves of his brothers bowed before it. In the other dream, he saw the sun, moon, and eleven stars also bowed before him.

His brothers thought that Jo'seph was telling them these dreams because he expected some day to rule over them. They disliked him very much for having such hopes, and for even suggesting that he might become the head of his father's household.

When Jo'seph told his father of the second dream, Ja'cob scolded him, and said, "Do you think that I and your brothers will one day bow before you as if you were a king?" In spite of this rebuke from his father, Jo'seph did not lose hope, and it seems that Ja'cob himself wondered if the dream might not well come true some day. The way that his brothers later treated Jo'seph makes one think that they, too, must have believed that he was likely to rule over them.

Some days after Jo'seph had told his father and brothers about his dreams, his ten older brothers were sent into the land near She'chem with a flock of sheep. This was a distance of about fifty miles from He'bron, and near the place where Ja'cob had purchased a plot of ground from Ha'mor.

Wishing to send a message to his sons, and to find out if all was well with them, Ja'cob told Jo'seph to go on an errand to his brothers at She'-chem. Although it was a long journey for a boy of Jo'seph's age to make alone, and in spite of the knowledge that he would not be kindly received by his brothers, Jo'seph promptly and cheerfully did what his father told him. While Jo'seph and his father were thinking of their welfare, the older brothers were plotting how to do away with Jo'seph. All they were waiting for was a chance to deal with him where Ja'cob could not hinder them, and the chance was now about to come.

When Jo'seph reached the pasture land near She'chem where his brothers had been sent, he found that they were no longer there. While looking for them he met a stranger, and asked if he knew where his brothers had gone with their sheep. The stranger told him that they had gone to Do'than, which was about fifteen miles farther north. Jo'seph had already been walking over hills and valleys for two or three days, and must have been very tired from the fifty-mile journey, but he started off at once toward Do'than.

As Jo'seph drew near to the fields where his brothers were letting their sheep graze, they saw him from the distance, and knew who he was by the bright colors of the coat which he wore. They began to say to one another, "Look, that dreamer is coming!" Then they began to plot among themselves what they might do to dispose of him. One of the brothers suggested that they slay him and put his body into an open well in the field, then they could tell Ja'cob that he had been killed and eaten by a wild animal.

The envy of these wicked brothers had grown into such bitter hatred that they now did not stop even at the thought of murder. Because they knew that their brother was better than they were, they were willing to commit the awful crime of murder in order to keep him from the honors which they were certain would come to him.

But Reu'ben, who was the oldest of the brothers, and who did not hate Jo'seph as much as the others did, suggested that instead of killing him

JOSEPH SOLD INTO SLAVERY

by their own hands they might throw him into an open well. He said this in the hope of saving Jo'seph, for he intended to come back to the pit when the other brothers were gone and rescue him.

Jo'seph had probably brought his brothers some good things to eat from his father's house. He came to them in a friendly spirit, gave them the message from Ja'cob, and began to unpack the food and provisions which he had brought them. At once they seized him, cast him into a pit nearby, and deliberately sat down to eat their dinner while Jo'seph begged to be rescued from the pit.

As they sat about on the grass eating their dinner, there suddenly appeared in the distance a caravan of Ish'ma-el-ites. These people were going from Gil'e-ad to E'gypt with spices, fragrant balms, and myrrh to sell. They also dealt in slaves, and would frequently sell to the E-gyp'-tians young men and women to become servants in their homes. An older brother named Ju'dah then suggested that instead of leaving Jo'seph in the pit they might sell him to these slave-traders. In this way they would be rid of him forever, and at the same time might avoid the great sin of murder. No doubt Ju'dah was also thinking of the money that they would receive from the traders, for slaves were worth a great deal of money.

In the meantime Reu'ben had finished his dinner, and had gone away to look after the sheep. So the other nine brothers lifted Jo'seph from the pit and sold him to the Ish'ma-el-ites for twenty pieces of silver, which was the usual price for a slave boy. They also kept the coat of many colors which their father had given Jo'seph. The Ish'ma-el-ites took Jo'seph into E'gypt, where they sold him to a man named Pot'i-phar as a household servant. What happened to Jo'seph in E'gypt will be told in future stories.

When Reu'ben had finished caring for the sheep, he went to the pit into which Jo'seph had been thrown, and was very much alarmed when he found it empty. He rushed to his brothers greatly excited and said, "The child is gone, and now what am I to do?" The other brothers may have suspected that Reu'ben had intended to rescue Jo'seph, and for this reason had not told him that the younger brother had been sold as a slave. But now that he was gone they must think of some story to tell their father. They took Jo'seph's beautiful coat of many colors, dipped it in the blood of a young goat which they killed for this purpose, and carried the stained coat back to their father.

When they reached home they showed the coat to Ja'cob and said, "We found this coat out in the hill country. You can tell whether or not it belonged to Jo'seph." Ja'cob knew that it was the coat which he had given his favorite son, and declared that some wild animal must have killed him. Since the brothers had hoped that their father would believe this to be true, they said nothing to change his mind.

Ja'cob's sorrow seemed to be greater than he could bear, and he gave up all hope of ever being happy again. Now that his favorite son appeared to have lost his life, Ja'cob could not blame himself enough for having sent him on a dangerous journey without anyone to go with him. The older brothers added one more sin to those already committed by pretending to mourn with their father in his grief, and the comfort which they tried to bring him was as false as their hearts.

For twenty years Ja'cob carried this great sorrow in his heart, thinking all the time that his favorite son Jo'seph was dead; while the ten brothers of Jo'seph were forced to suffer the tortures of remorse in the secret cogitations of their own guilty hearts. In the meantime, the domestic life of the chosen family was seriously disrupted by the faithlessness and indiscretions of Ju'dah. Leaving the family where God was known and honored he made friends with the Ca'naan-ites; and positively disobeying the command of God married an idolatrous woman of Ca'naan.

SUGGESTIONS FOR STUDY

Biblical Index to Helpful References

Jacob Pondered Joseph's Dream as Mary Pondered the Angelic Message About Her Son. (Luke 2:19.)

Joseph's Brothers Sold Him for Envy. (Acts 7:9; Ps. 105:17.)

Their Crime Similar to That of Cain's, Murder in Heart. (Matt. 5:23; 1 John 3: 15.)

Arabian Merchants Noted for Precious Balms. (Jer. 8:22; 46:11.)

The Price of a Slave Under Twenty. (Lev. 27:5.) Above twenty. (Exo. 21:32.)

Joseph Sold as a Slave Naked; Later Arrayed in Pomp. (Isa. 20:4; Gen. 41:42.)

Questions

1. What was the vocation of Jacob and his sons?

2. How many of his sons were old enough to care for sheep?

3. Which of his sons did Jacob seem to love most and why?

4. Relate two dreams which Joseph told to his brothers?

5. What kind of boy was Joseph?

6. How did his ten older brothers feel toward him and why?

7. How far away was it that Joseph was

sent on an errand to his brothers?

8. What did they propose to do when they saw him coming?

9. Which of his brothers wished to try to save the life of Joseph?

10. Which one proposed that he be sold to slave dealers?

11. How much did they receive for him?

12. How did they cover up their crime in reporting to their father?

13. How did Jacob feel about his missing son?

STORY 26

JOSEPH IN POTIPHAR'S HOUSE

GENESIS 39

Our story now turns back to the life of Jo'seph. When last we heard of him, he was being taken to E'gypt by a band of Ish'ma-el-ite slave-traders who had bought him from his hard-hearted brothers, and his father Ja'cob was mourning him as dead.

When the slave-traders came to E'gypt, Jo'seph was sold as a household servant to a man named Pot'i-phar, who was a high officer in the army of Pha'raoh. Even though he was still a slave, Jo'seph did not give up hope that some day his dreams would come true.

In place of the hills and mountains of Ca'naan, Jo'seph now looked out upon the great plains of the river Nile; instead of living in a crude tent in the wilderness, he now enjoyed the comforts of a splendid home in a rich city. Looking out upon the beautiful temples of E'gypt, the pyramids, and the Sphinx, Jo'seph must have longed for the day when he could take an active part in the affairs of this great country.

Jo'seph was a handsome young man, pleasant and cheerful by nature, and blessed with a quick mind and upright heart. He was also honest and loyal, and always ready and willing to do his duty. He did his work so well in the house of Pot'i-phar that he soon won the complete trust of his master, and was rapidly promoted to positions of greater honor. At length Pot'i-phar made Jo'seph his chief steward, giving him charge of his entire household. Though Pot'i-phar did not worship the God of Jo'seph, he was greatly impressed by the good character and true faith of his servant. It is said in the Bible that Pot'i-phar saw that the Lord was with Jo'seph, making him prosper in all that he did.

While Jo'seph was mourned by his father in Ca'naan as dead, he now prospered in E'gypt under Pot'i-phar. Honoring God, he was now being honored by the Lord he worshiped; having served faithfully over a few things, he was now made ruler over many; having learned to manage Pot'i-phar's house, he was now being prepared to rule over all the land of E'gypt.

The same noble qualities which won for Jo'seph the admiration of Pot'i-phar were also the means of subjecting him to severe temptation. Pot'i-phar's wife was attracted by his magnetic personality and manliness, and sought to lure him into a friendship which he thought wrong. Jo'seph wished to maintain the integrity of his character and good opinion of his master, and was careful not to do anything to violate the trust imposed in him.

The mightiest fortress in Jo'seph's character was the fear of God. He acknowledged the supreme authority of high heaven in all matters of human conduct. Though the dagger of temptation pierced his heart, his uncompromising devotion to the principle of right prevented any fatal wound. Under severe trial he said, "How can I do this in the presence of my God?" Having set God in complete control of his affections he could not be moved by the most violent attacks of satan.

Angered by Jo'seph's refusal to do that which he thought wrong, Pot'i-phar's wife made false charges against him and had him cast into prison.

In the gloom and hardships of life in prison Jo'seph was made happy by the knowledge that he had done nothing which deserved such punish-ment. His conscience was clear, and the Lord continued His blessings upon him. Jo'seph became a favorite of the keeper of the prison, and was soon put in charge of the other prisoners; he was trusted and hon-ored in prison just as he had been in the house of his master. The walls of an E-gyp'tian dungeon could not hide his good character, nor could the iron bars prevent the Lord from visiting His servant.

Jo'seph had been chosen by the Lord to rule over the land of E'gypt. The trials which had come to him were sent only to strengthen him in the faith, and make him a better servant of God in the hour of victory. We shall learn in the next story how he was called from prison to the palace of one of the greatest kingdoms of history.

SUGGESTIONS FOR STUDY

Biblical Index to Helpful References

The Lord's Promise to Honor Those That Honor Him. (1 Sam. 2:30; Ps. 1:1, 3.)

God's Warnings Against Evil Temptresses. (Prov. 6:24-35; Matt. 5:28.)

Victory Over Temptation by Devotion to God. (Ps. 16:8.)

Joseph's Sufferings in Prison Overcome by God's Presence. (Ps. 105:18-21.)

Paul's Rejoicing and Victory Under Simi-lar Conditions. (Acts 16:25-35.)

Questions

1. Into whose house was Joseph sold as a slave?

2. Describe the personality and character of Joseph?

3. How did Potiphar feel toward him?

4. Who made false charges against Joseph for which he was imprisoned?

5. What was the secret of Joseph's power to resist temptation?

6. What honors came to Joseph in prison?

STORY 27

JOSEPH RISES FROM PRISON TO THE KING'S PALACE

GENESIS 40, 41

It seems probable that Pot'i-phar realized that Jo'seph was forced to remain in prison for two years as a result of the false charges preferred against him by Pot'i-phar's wife. But his quiet, trustworthy manner, his gentle, friendly behavior, and his patience under unjust punishment won for him the confidence of all the prisoners with whom he was associated. Among these prisoners were two former servants of Pha'raoh, a butler and a baker. They were placed under the care of Jo'seph, and in the course of time he was called upon to explain for each of them a dream which greatly worried them.

The interpretations which Jo'seph gave came to pass within three days: the baker was hanged, and the butler was released and given his former position in the king's court. Jo'seph requested the butler to use his good offices for his release, but two years passed before he even mentioned to the king the name of his friend and benefactor. In the meantime Jo'seph did not despair, but clung to the belief that God would save him in his own time and manner.

It was then that things began to happen in his favor. Pha'raoh had two strange dreams, both of which were similar, and which seemed to carry the same meaning. When the king awoke in the morning, he was very much disturbed in mind by these dreams. He felt that they were very important, and was eager to know just what they meant. All the magicians and wise men of E'gypt were called in to help the king, but none of them could explain his dreams. Though naturally trying as hard as they could to give the meaning of the dreams, they were puzzled as deeply as Pha'raoh by the visions which had come to him in the night.

Pha'raoh was unable to hide his troubled feelings from his servants, and his chief butler soon realized that something must be done to solve the problem. Suddenly he remembered how Jo'seph had explained his dream and that of the chief baker when they were in prison two years before, so he said to Pha'raoh, "There is in prison a young man, a He'brew, who possesses the wisdom of God by which the most difficult dreams may be made known."

JOSEPH TELLS PHARAOH'S DREAM

The king made haste to send for Jo'seph, asking him to come to the palace at once. It was the custom in those days for men in prison to let their beards grow as a sign of sorrow, but Jo'seph quickly removed his beard when he heard that the king wished to see him. After changing his prison garments for clothes provided by the king's servants, he was brought before Pha'raoh.

When Jo'seph stood before him, Pha'raoh told him at once that he had been greatly troubled by two dreams which his magicians and wise men had not been able to explain. Pha'raoh also said that he had learned of Jo'seph's ability to interpret dreams, but Jo'seph replied, "It is not in me: God shall give Pha'raoh an answer of peace." Pha'raoh then told his two strange dreams to Jo'seph.

"In my dream," declared Pha'raoh, "I stood upon the bank of the river: and, behold, there came up out of the river seven cows, fat and well favoured; and they fed in a meadow. And, behold, seven other cows came up after them, poor and very ill favoured and lean, such as I never saw in all the land of E'gypt for badness: and the lean and the ill favoured cows did eat up the first seven fat cows, but after eating every one of them they were still as thin as ever."

"After falling asleep again," Pha'raoh went on to say, "I saw seven ears of corn growing on one stalk, and each ear was full and good. Then I saw another stalk with seven poor and worthless ears upon it. The seven poor ears devoured those that were good, but were afterwards poor as ever."

Jo'seph then told Pha'raoh that the two dreams had the same meaning. The Lord was telling him that a time of great prosperity for the land of E'gypt was to be followed by an equal period of famine and suffering. Jo'seph said, "The seven fat and well favoured cows, and the seven full ears of corn, mean that for seven years there will be good harvests and great prosperity in E'gypt. The seven thin cows and the seven withered ears of corn mean that the years of plenty will be followed by seven years of famine. Unless the good crops are used wisely, and the surplus carefully stored up in each city, the whole country will be in danger of starving to death."

Having explained the dreams to Pha'raoh so clearly that everyone could see the Lord was speaking through him, Jo'seph gave still further good advice. He suggested that Pha'raoh choose some man of great wisdom and proven ability to take charge of the work of storing up surplus food during the seven good years. It was a very difficult task, but unless it was done, and done well, there would be no hope of saving the people of E'gypt from starvation during the seven years of famine. That is why it was so important to find a man wise enough to direct the storing up of food in all the cities of E'gypt. Besides gathering the surplus food, it was necessary to distribute it in such a way that each city would have enough for its own needs, and to store the food where it would not spoil or be damaged. The one who took charge of this work would also have to direct a great many assistants, telling each one what he must do, and then making sure that the work had been properly done. Seldom in history has a greater burden been placed upon any one man.

Without waiting for Jo'seph's predictions to come true, or doubting in the least the words which had been spoken, Pha'raoh decided to act at once. The first step was the choosing of a leader to carry out the plan of storing up food for the years of famine that were to come, and here the king made a very wise choice, indeed. To Pha'raoh, there was only one man in his kingdom who could do the work which Jo'seph had suggested, and that man was Jo'seph himself. The king was deeply impressed by the faith of the He'brew prophet, and believed that he must be under the direct guidance of the Lord. A man of strong, upright character was needed for the task, and in this respect Jo'seph had proved himself second to none.

Pha'raoh said to his servants, "Can we find such a one as this is, a man in whom the Spirit of God is?" The courtiers made no reply, probably because they were jealous of one who was a foreigner, but the king at once appointed Jo'seph to the office. To remove any further jealousy, Pha'raoh gave him the E-gyp'tian title Zaph'e-nath-pa-ne'ah, which means "God speaks." He also gave Jo'seph a signet ring as a token of his office as grand vizier of E'gypt, provided him with the fine linen garments which were worn by only the highest officials, placed around his neck the gold chain which was the mark of prominent citizens, and caused him to ride in the chariot next to that of the king in a great public procession. The people of E'gypt bowed before him, honoring him as the ruler second only to the king. Thus was Jo'seph advanced from a forgotten prisoner to one who held a place of honor in the royal palace. We shall learn how well he carried out his duties in the next story.

SUGGESTIONS FOR STUDY

Biblical Index to Helpful References

God Often Speaks to Men in Dreams. (Job. 33:14, 15; Num. 12:6.)

Dreams of Agitation in the Heart. (Dan. 2:1; Matt. 27:19.)

Qualities for Advancement in Rulership. (2 Ki. 23:3, 4; Ps. 72:2-4.)

Victory of Truth Over Unjust Imprisonment. (2 Tim. 2:9.)

Double Warnings in the Two Similar Dreams. (1 Ki. 11:9; Job 33:14; Ps. 62:11.)

King's Hearts in the Hands of God, Whether They Will It or Not. (Prov. 21:1; Ezra 6:22.)

Wisdom of God Confounding Man's Wisdom. (Rom. 8:28.)

Acknowledgment of Israel's God by Heathen Kings. (Gen. 20:3-7; 21:22, 23; 26:28, 29.)

Another Prophet Who Predicted a Famine. (2 Ki. 8:1.)

Another Prisoner Promoted for His Righteousness and Wisdom. (Dan. 2:48.)

Joseph's Advancement Caused by God. (Ps. 105:19-22; Acts 7:10.)

Questions

1. How did Joseph fare in prison? Why?

2. Tell of the dreams of the butler and baker in jail with Joseph?

3. What interpretation did Joseph give to each? Did what he said come true?

4. What request did he make of the butler?

5. How long before the butler told Pharaoh of Joseph?

6. Relate the two strange dreams of Pharaoh?

7. Why did he send for Joseph to interpret these dreams?

8. What did Joseph say they meant?

9. What advice did Joseph give to Pharaoh for meeting the calamity of famine?

10. Whom did Pharaoh appoint ruler over the land? Why?

JOSEPH SAVES EGYPT FROM STARVING

GENESIS 41:46-57

No greater change has come to any man than that which Jo'seph knew in E'gypt. The fetters of iron which bound his feet were exchanged for a golden chain around his neck, and the coarse prison clothes for the fine linen worn by the nobility. The gloomy dungeon was forgotten as he dwelt in the royal palace, and all disgrace was removed when he rode next to the king in a public procession. He had been in prison through no fault of his own, but now had become master of all that the king possessed.

Pha'raoh added still another blessing by giving him a wife from one of the most noble families of the land, and so Jo'seph was married to the daughter of the high priest of the temple in the capital city of E'gypt. In the course of time two sons were born of this marriage, and were brought up in the faith of their father.

Many people would have been puffed up with pride by so wonderful a change, but Jo'seph was too busy to waste time in self-admiration. Instead, he went to work at once on the task which the king had given him. His first step was to make a thorough study of the country, finding out how much food was needed, and how much could be raised during the seven years of abundant crops. To the law which required the people to give one tenth of all their produce to the government, he added the rule that they place one fifth in storage for the years of famine which were to come. The people were also forbidden to waste food, and all that they

THE GLORY OF JOSEPH

did not need was purchased by the government and stored up for future needs.

Jo'seph was wise enough to foresee the evil days that were coming, and to prepare for them before it was too late. In times of abundant harvest and prosperity he made sure that the nation would not suffer when crops were poor and times were hard. He was honored by the king, and proved his right to such honor by enriching the nation. By his careful management he saved the lives of the E-gypt'ians, provided food for even their cattle and live-stock, and maintained the glory of their nation.

Jo'seph's work during the seven years of famine was even more brilliant than in the time of prosperity. Instead of giving the people food without charge, he kept up their courage and dignity by mak:ng it possible for them to pay for what they needed. All the people had been required to save their money when times were good, and when their savings were spent he gave them work to do. In this way even the most needy were able to earn their food, and no one was forced to become a beggar.

Truly, Jo'seph was the savior of E'gypt and of many surrounding nations. Had he not ruled with such wisdom, E'gypt and its neighbors would have perished during the seven long years of famine. Faith in God was the chief reason for his success in this great undertaking. It is true that Jo'seph was a man of great ability, blessed with a brilliant mind and good judgment, and willing to work long and hard at whatever duties which came his way. All these good qualities, however, would not have been enough to bring him success if he had not been guided by the Lord. Because Jo'seph was a good man, willing always to do what the Lord told him without fear or complaint, his name is truly great.

SUGGESTIONS FOR STUDY

Biblical Index to Helpful References

The Signet Ring an Emblem of High Office. (Esther 3:10; 8:2.)

The Gold Chain About His Neck a Token of Chief Ruler. (Dan. 5:7.)

Joseph Ruler Over Egypt. (Acts 7:10.)

Seven Years of Drouth. (Ps. 105:16.)

The Temple at On Called Aven. (Ezek. 30:17.) Bethshemesh. (Jer. 43:13.)

Questions

1. Describe the difference in the state of Joseph?

2. Whose daughter did Joseph marry?

3. What names were given his two sons?

4. What measures did Joseph take to preserve the produce of the years of plenty?

5. What additional tax was assessed against the people and why?

6. What wise measures did he employ in distributing food during the famine?

7. Besides being a wise ruler, what other reason is given for his success?

STORY 29

JOSEPH'S BROTHERS COME TO EGYPT TO BUY GRAIN

GENESIS 42

The seven years of famine brought suffering to many countries. In E'gypt, the wise plan of Jo'seph had kept the people from starvation, but other lands were not so fortunate. They had not received the warnings given to Pha'raoh in his dreams and explained by Jo'seph, so none of them had prepared for the famine. When their supply of food gave out, as it did in a very short time, they were forced to go to E'gypt and purchase grain from the huge storehouses which Jo'seph had built.

The land of Ca'naan was two hundred miles from E'gypt, and between the two countries there were vast deserts and wilderness, making travel very difficult. In some way, however, Ja'cob and his family learned that there was plenty of food in E'gypt, and that Pha'raoh was willing to sell some of it to people of other nations.

More than twenty years had passed since the brothers of Jo'seph had sold him to the Ish'ma-el-ite slave-dealers, and they had no idea what had become of him. Ja'cob, of course, had lived through all these years thinking that Jo'seph was dead, for the elder brothers had never told him the true story. No news had come to them of Jo'seph's early hardships and suffering in E'gypt, nor of the great honors he had later been given by Pha'raoh; as far as they knew, he might well be dead.

One might think that Jo'seph would have sent a message to let his father know that all was well with him, or would have tried to find out how things were going with his family back in Ca'naan. Jo'seph thought it best, however, to say nothing. For one thing, he did not wish his father to know how cruelly he had been treated by the elder brothers; for another, he had perfect faith that the Lord would permit no harm to come to his father's household.

No doubt Jo'seph often thought of his father and brothers, but never with hatred toward those who had wronged him. For nearly a quarter of a century the memory of his early dreams lingered in his mind, and he still believed that they would come true. Instead of talking about them, or complaining because they were not as yet fulfilled, he kept them secret in his heart, patiently waiting for the Lord to bless him when the time had come.

When famine swept over the land of Ca'naan, bringing hunger and starvation to the people, Ja'cob and his family were soon in great danger. All of Ja'cob's wealth was in gold, silver, and live-stock; without food for his household and grain for his cattle, the money would do him no good. He therefore sent his ten sons down into E'gypt to buy corn, so that both the people and animals might have food.

It was a great blow to the sons of Ja'cob to be sent into E'gypt, where they knew that Jo'seph had been carried to be sold as a slave. Every step of the two hundred mile journey must have been filled with memories of the great wrong which they had done, but they must either go to E'gypt or starve. Of course, they did not know what had happened to Jo'seph there, but a guilty conscience made them dread even the thought of meeting him.

Upon reaching the land of E'gypt they were sent to the high officer who had charge of all the grain. Without his permission, no grain could be taken from E'gypt. Little did the brothers think that this mighty ruler was the boy they had sold into slavery! They feared that they might meet him among the slaves of that country, but never dreamed of seeing him as a ruler second only to the king. For this reason it was easy for Jo'seph to keep them from knowing who he was.

When the brothers were brought before Jo'seph, they bowed so low that their faces almost touched the ground, for this was the manner in which common people showed respect to a great ruler. Jo'seph wore the costly robes of his office,

JOSEPH'S BRETHREN

spoke the E-gyp'tian language perfectly, and acted with all the dignity of a nobleman. It is no wonder that even his own brothers did not know him as he stood before them. Jo'seph, however, knew them at once, for they had changed very little since he last had seen them. Because he loved his brothers in spite of what they had done to him, it was hard for Jo'seph to treat them as though they were strangers, but this he did.

Jo'seph had dreamed of the day when his brothers should bow before him, and they had been very angry when he told them the dream, but now it had come true. They had mocked him, making light of his prophetic dreams, but now they bowed before him in all humility. It was not yet the proper time to tell them who he was, so he patiently continued to let them think that he was an E-gyp'tian.

Speaking roughly to them, Jo'seph forced his brothers to tell him from whence they came. When they said that they had come from the land of Ca'naan to buy food, he pretended not to believe them, and declared that they were spies who had come to plan an attack upon his country. By these words Jo'seph hoped to lead his brothers into telling him all about his father without their suspecting that he was their long lost brother.

The plan of Jo'seph was successful, for the brothers said: "Thy servants are twelve brethren, the sons of one man in the land of Ca'naan; and, behold, the youngest is this day with our father, and one is not." Having learned that his father was living, Jo'seph continued to test his brothers by demanding that all but one of them be left with him in E'gypt while the other went back to Ca'naan to bring their youngest brother before him. Jo'seph then warned them that their only hope of escaping death was for the youngest brother to come back with the one who should go to fetch him.

This demand brought both sorrow and fear to the hearts of Jo'seph's brothers. To do what he asked might cause their father's death, for Ja'cob had found comfort for the supposed loss of Jo'seph only in his fondness for Ben'ja-min. They also were unwilling to run the risk of being held in E'gypt while one of their number returned to their father's house for the youngest son whom Ja'cob loved so dearly. When they refused to do what Jo'seph had asked, they were put in prison. For three days they remained prisoners, while Jo'seph searched his mind for some way of carrying out the will of God without harm to his brothers.

On the third day, Jo'seph visited his brothers in prison and offered them an easier way to prove that they were not spies. He said to them: "This do, and live; for I fear God: If ye be true men, let one of your brethren be bound in the house of your prison: go ye, carry corn for the famine of your houses: But bring your youngest brother unto me; so shall your words be verified, and ye shall not die." The fact that an E-gyp'tian officer, as they supposed him to be, believed in the true God filled the brothers with shame for all their evil deeds.

It was natural for them to use their own language while discussing the offer which Jo'seph had now made them; since he had questioned them with the aid of an interpreter, they took it for granted that he would not know what they were saying. He, therefore, heard them confess to one another that they were now being justly punished for the cruel wrong they had done their brother twenty-three years before. They had paid no attention to Jo'seph's cries of distress when they cast him into the pit, so now they had no right to complain if they were shown no mercy.

Then Jo'seph bound Sim'e-on as a prisoner before their very eyes. This was to remind them that he would be put to death as a spy if they failed to return from the land of Ca'naan with Ben'ja-min, their youngest brother. The servants of Jo'seph then filled the grain sacks which his brothers had brought to E'gypt, and in the top of each sack placed the money which had been paid for the grain. The brothers went away with mingled feelings. They were happy to have the grain which was so greatly needed in Ca'naan, and thankful that they were now freed from prison, but it was sad to think of Sim'e-on having to remain a prisoner until they returned to E'gypt.

They did not know that their money had been returned until they stopped at an inn to spend the night. One of the sacks was opened to get some grain, and then the brothers were amazed to find money in the mouth of the sack. Instead of being happy to learn that the grain had cost them nothing, they were very much alarmed by the discovery. It had been hard enough to bear the suspicion and rough treatment which they were shown by the E-gyp'tian ruler, but they were even more frightened by his strange act of returning their money. It did not occur to them that he might have meant nothing but kindness in so doing, and they wondered what further punishment the Lord was preparing for them. They dared not return to E'gypt and give back the money, for this time they, too, might be held in prison as spies, so all they could do was to hope for the best, and hasten to the land of their father.

When they reached the land of Ca'naan, they told Ja'cob of all that had happened to them in E'gypt. Then all the sacks of grain were opened, and in each one was found the money which had been paid for the grain. Once again the brothers were frightened, and even Ja'cob could find no way of explaining the strange return of their money; he, too, felt that it was a sign of bad news in the future.

Ja'cob was overcome by the demand that Ben'ja-min, his beloved youngest son, be taken to E'gypt. He still thought that Jo'seph had been slain by a wild animal twenty-three years before, he knew that Sim'e-on was now in an E-gyp'tian prison, perhaps doomed to die, and now he was called upon to give up the son who had brought him comfort during many trials. The thought was more than he could bear, so he declared that it would be better if they all died of hunger. After the older brothers had failed to overcome the fears of Ja'cob, or to persuade him to let Ben'-ja-min go down into E'gypt, it was agreed to do nothing about the matter for the time being. In our next story we shall learn how Ja'cob was forced to send Ben'ja-min to E'gypt, and how wonderfully the Lord blessed Ja'cob and his sons.

SUGGESTIONS FOR STUDY

Biblical Index to Helpful References

News of Plenty in Egypt Brought to Jacob. (Acts 7:12.)

Joseph's Dream Fulfilled in the Bowing Before Him of His Brethren. (Gen. 37:7.)

The Pretense That Their Brother Was Dead. (Gen. 37:30; 44:20.)

Conscience of Sin Caused by Affliction. (Job 36:8-10.)

Reaping What One Sows. (Matt. 7:2.)

Questions

1. Did the famine in Egypt reach other lands?

2. Did the Egyptians have corn enough to sell to other countries?

3. What did Jacob do when starvation faced him and his family?

4. How long had it been since Joseph's brothers sold him to be a slave?

5. Did they or their father know what had become of Joseph?

6. When they went to Joseph to buy corn how did he treat them at first?

7. Did they know it was Joseph?

8. What did he propose at first?

9. What was his second proposition?

10. What did all this call to the mind of Joseph's brothers?

11. Which one of Jacob's sons was left a prisoner in Egypt?

12. What did these nine brothers discover in their sacks of corn later?

13. How had Joseph's dreams been fulfilled by his brothers?

14. How did Jacob feel about sending Benjamin down to Egypt?

STORY 30

JOSEPH FORGIVES HIS BROTHERS

GENESIS 43, 44, 45   It was not long before the grain which the sons of Ja'cob had purchased in E'gypt was used up. In addition to the sixty-six members of his own household, Jo'seph had to provide food for the families of his many servants. The famine still brought suffering and starvation to the land of Ca'naan, and it was only a matter of time before Ja'cob and his family would have nothing to eat.

Ja'cob had declared that he would rather die than send his youngest son Ben'ja-min to E'gypt, but now it seemed that death would come to Ja'cob and his sons in the land of Ca'naan unless food could be brought in from E'gypt. For this reason Ja'cob finally decided to risk the life of his favorite son by sending him to E'gypt for the food which was so greatly needed.

When Ju'dah offered to give his life if Ben'jamin did not return safely from E'gypt, Ja'cob decided to send his nine remaining elder sons with Ben'ja-min to make a second purchase of grain in E'gypt. He told his sons to take with them twice the sum of money needed to pay for the grain which they sought, as well as the money which had been hidden in their sacks when they made their first purchase. As a special gift for the ruler of the E-gyp'tian supplies, Ja'cob sent balm, honey, spices, and nuts, for the famine had not destroyed these crops.

The sons of Ja'cob again reached the land of E'gypt in safety, and were brought before Jo'seph for questioning. As they bowed down before him, Jo'seph saw that one of them was a stranger to him; since he was much younger than his brothers, Jo'seph knew that he must be Ben'ja-min. The sight of the brother he had waited so long to see brought tears of joy to the eyes of Jo'seph, and his heart was filled to overflowing with happiness. Not wishing the others to see that he was overcome by his feelings, he went to his own room to wash away the tears of joy.

Jo'seph then told his chief steward to take these He'brews into his own house, and ordered him to prepare a meal at which they were to be his guests of honor. Nor was Sim'e-on forgotten, for Jo'seph ordered him to be released from prison and sent to join his brothers. To be treated with such great honor made the brothers suspicious; they were afraid that they might be accused of stealing the money which had been secretly placed in their sacks of grain when they left E'gypt after their first visit.

They knew, of course, that the money had come to them without their having done anything wrong, but still they feared that the E-gyp'tian ruler was scheming to do them harm. The real reason for such thoughts was the guilty conscience which they had for the wrong they had done Jo'seph some twenty years before. They still did not know that the E-gyp'tian ruler was their brother, but since they had done a wrong which they could never forget, they looked upon any strange events as a possible means of punishment for their sins.

Before going in to the banquet hall, they paused to talk with the steward, and told him the true story of how they had found the money hidden in their sacks of grain after they had made a day's journey on their way home. They also told him that their father had sent the money back, and that they were ready to pay for the grain to be purchased on this visit. The steward declared that they could not possibly be blamed for having the money in their sacks, and said to them, "The Lord God of heaven, the God of your fathers, brought to you this treasure."

The sons of Ja'cob were both alarmed and encouraged to hear an E-gyp'tian steward speak so kindly of the God of the He'brews. It was good to hear that the true God was known in the household of an E-gyp'-tian ruler, yet they feared that one who knew their God might also know their sins against Him.

The steward and all the servants who assisted him were very kind to the brothers, washing their feet according to the Oriental custom, and making them feel welcome in every way. Jo'seph had a table prepared for them as the guests of honor, while he sat at his own table, and the E-gyp'tian officials who dined with them were given a place to themselves. Because of the different customs and religious beliefs of each race, it was not permissible for E-gyp'tians and He'brews to eat at the same table.

In arranging his guests about the table, Jo'seph began with the eldest of the brothers, and placed them all in regular order according to their ages. This act greatly puzzled the sons of Ja'cob, for they could not understand how he knew the order in which they were born. In serving them, he took pains to favor Ben'ja-min, giving him five times as much as any other in each course of the banquet. All these things amazed the brothers, who could see no possible reason for such kindness to them.

The occasion was also a great trial for Jo'seph, and he found it very hard to pretend to be a stranger when his own brothers sat at his table as guests. Wishing to put them at ease, he began to ask questions about the health of their father, and continued to show special kindness to Ben'ja-min. The evening passed cheerfully enough for all, and Jo'seph was still unknown to his brothers.

When the meal was over, Jo'seph ordered his steward to fill the sacks of his brothers with grain, and to place the money which had been paid in the top of each sack. Jo'seph had failed in his wish to reveal himself to his brothers in the banquet hall. Everything which he had done should have given his brothers a clue to his identity, but it never occurred to them that he was their long lost brother. Jo'seph now resolved to take some other means of letting them know who he was.

He, therefore, followed a plan which may seem cruel, but which was the best possible way of revealing himself to his brothers. The steward was told to put in Ben'ja-min's sack of grain a valuable silver drinking cup which belonged to Jo'seph, and which had been used during the dinner which his brothers had attended as guests of honor. The next morning found the sons of Ja'cob well on the road back to Ca'naan, but before they had gone far from the home of Jo'seph the steward was ordered to take them prisoners, and to accuse them of stealing the cup.

The steward soon overtook the brothers, and declared that they had stolen his master's silver cup. Their happiness over the release of Sim'e-on from prison, and the permission to return to Ca'naan with their brother Ben'ja-min, in addition to the supply of grain which they had bought, was suddenly turned into deepest sorrow. They naturally denied their guilt, and were so sure that they had done no wrong that they offered to let the one who might be proved to have stolen the cup to be put to death, while all his brothers should become slaves of the E-gyp'tian ruler for life. It was then agreed that their sacks should be searched by the E-gyp'tians.

The sacks were then spread out upon the ground and carefully searched. The E-gyp'tians began their search with the sack of the eldest brother, and gradually examined the others until ten of the brothers had been found to be innocent. By this time the sons of Ja'cob felt that they would soon be free to continue their homeward journey, but their hopes were suddenly crushed. When the sack of Ben'ja-min was searched, the E-gyp'tians found at once the silver cup which belonged to Jo'seph. The brothers felt sure that Ben'ja-min had not stolen it, but when it was found

THE CUP FOUND

in his possession there was nothing for them to say. It was hard to think that blame for the crime should fall upon the very son whom they had pledged to return to their father.

The brothers were taken back to Jo'seph to answer for the crime which seemed to have been committed, and to face whatever punishment that he might order. Jo'seph spoke to them very sternly, saying, "What a wicked, ungrateful thing you have done to me! Didn't you know that I would find out who took the cup?" Ju'dah then spoke for his brothers, admitting that he could see no way of explaining how the cup came to be in Ben'ja-min's sack. He said, "We are your slaves, all of us, and we shall each of us serve the penalty of him in whose sack the cup was found."

Jo'seph would not hear of this arrangement, and declared, "The man who stole the cup shall be my servant, but the rest of you must go back to your father's home at once."

Questions naturally come to our minds over the severe treatment which Jo'seph gave his brothers. Why was it necessary for him to be so stern, to accuse Ben'ja-min of a crime he had not committed, and to threaten to keep him as a slave?

The answer is, that only by such harsh treatment could the conscience of his brothers be stirred to the depths; by this way alone could they be brought to genuine repentance for their crime against Jo'seph. He had forgiven them in his heart long ago, but knew that they must be brought to the lowest depths of sorrow before their souls could be healed. They had been terribly distressed by the fear of being punished, and had felt the hand of God upon them, but such feelings were not enough to save them.

Before revealing himself to his brothers, and openly forgiving them, Jo'seph wished to see a clear proof of their repentance and change of heart. Would they desert Ben'ja-min when he was about to be made a slave, and return to their father without him? Would they treat this son of Ra'chel as they had once treated her elder son? Were their hearts still full of envy and hatred toward a favorite son of their aged father? All of these questions must be answered to the satisfaction of Jo'seph before he could treat them as his brothers again. Proof that they were worthy to receive the blessings yet to be given them must be found, so Jo'seph took these harsh, apparently unfair methods to prove their sincerity.

The test succeeded in every possible way, and the brothers endured the trial in a manner which did them credit. Ju'dah, who spoke for the entire group, came forward with a tender, heart-stirring, and eloquent appeal for a true understanding of their position. He boldly declared that he and all his brothers were determined to cling to Ben'ja-min, and that they were willing to pay the full penalty required for the crime with which he was charged.

The plea which Ju'dah made on this momentous occasion is truly one of the masterpieces of the He'brew language. He did not insist upon the innocence of Ben'ja-min, nor did he confess his guilt; but he did make a humble confession of his own iniquity. Without giving a description of the crime against Jo'seph, he admitted that he and his brothers had been guilty of great sins in their lives, and that the Lord had now called them to account.

In his pleadings for Ben'ja-min's release, Ju'dah spoke with words that came from the heart, and with a sincerity which no one could doubt. He gave a true and moving description of the trials which had come to his father's family, and told with great feeling all that had taken place between his brothers and the E-gyp'tian ruler during their two visits. He held himself strictly to the truth, but spoke with such fervor that his appeal could not be denied.

Ju'dah remained humble and respectful in manner as he pleaded with the E-gyp'tian ruler, but his words were not lacking in force. He said, "Oh, my master, I beg you to hear my plea. Do not let your anger be aroused against your servant, for I know that you are like unto Pha'raoh in power. When you inquired of us, we told you truthfully that we have a father who is now a very old man, feeble in strength, and on the verge of the grave; we also said that there is a younger brother who is very dear to his father's heart, his only full brother being dead. When you told us that we must bring him down to E'gypt that you might look upon his face, we truthfully explained that such a demand would break our father's heart. But we have prevailed upon our father to grant your request, because he and his household are facing starvation, and have no other way of securing food."

Then Ju'dah went on with these passionate words, "Our father said to us, 'You know that my own most beloved wife Ra'chel bore me two sons, and that one of them went out on an errand for me and returned not, and that for all I know he was torn to pieces by wild beasts. If you take this son also from me, and mischief befall him, you will bring down my gray hairs with sorrow to the grave.' If I return to my father and the lad is not with me, he will die; and we, your servants, will have been the cause of our father's death. I, myself, became surety to my father for the return of the lad. I now wish to take his place as a slave, and earnestly ask that you let him go back to his father."

When Ju'dah had finished speaking, Jo'seph could no longer hold his feelings in check. His heart was melted into compassion for a father who had lost one son whom he thought to be dead, and who now trembled in the fear of losing another son, dearer to him now than the first. Now Jo'seph knew that his brothers had sincerely repented for their crime against him, and that they might safely be trusted with Ben'ja-min.

Suppressing his emotion for a moment, Jo'seph ordered that all his E-gyp'tian officers should leave the room at once, as he wished to be alone with his eleven brothers. His feelings were too deep to be exposed even to his most trusted officers. What was about to take place concerned the sons of Ja'cob alone, and all the world must be shut out.

Jo'seph knew that when he revealed himself to his brothers as the one they had sold to the Ish'ma-el-ite slave-dealers, they would at once confess their crime. He did not wish the E-gyp'tians to know about this, for they would not readily forgive such a crime against their ruler, even though it had taken place many years before.

When the room was cleared of all outsiders, Jo'seph turned to his brothers and said, "I am Jo'seph." He wept as he said this, trembling and overcome by the depth of his feelings. The brothers sat dumbfounded and terrified by this announcement, not one of them being able to speak. Again Jo'seph said, "I am your brother Jo'seph." And then he asked tenderly, "Is my father alive?"

Jo'seph then asked his brothers to draw near, and talked with them in a gentle, tender way. He might have said to them, "You are murderers, and I am a prince in spite of you. My position and power make it easy for me to have revenge upon you. My glory is your shame, and you are now in peril of your lives." But Jo'seph did not speak in this manner. Instead, he assured his brothers of pardon, and love, and future protection under his own hand. He said, "Do not be grieved or angry with yourselves because you sold me into bondage. God sent me before you into this land, and has made me the friend of Pha'raoh and ruler over his country that I might preserve life. It is God's plan that I should save not only the lives of E'gypt, but also the lives of my own family now in Ca'naan."

Jo'seph went on to explain to his brothers that the famine would continue for five years more, and that in every country except E'gypt, where the Lord had enabled him to store up food enough to meet the calamity, there would be continued suffering and starvation. He told them that he had made ready a place for the covenant family of Is'ra-el to dwell, and that his father's entire household should be brought to E'gypt at once.

Tenderly embracing Ben'ja-min and kissing all the others a fond farewell, Jo'seph sent his brothers, with servants and wagons, for his father.

SUGGESTIONS FOR STUDY

Biblical Index to Helpful References

The Terror of Conscious Hidden Guilt. (Ps. 32:3, 4; 39:2, 3.)

No Fear Where Perfect Love Rules. (1 John 4:18.)

Intercession for Mercy to Others. (Num. 16:20-22; 2 Sam. 24:17; Acts 20:32.)

Christ's Intercession for Us. (Rom. 8:34.)

Judah, the Spokesman for Israel. (Deut. 33:7; Ps. 78:67, 68.)

The Christ of Judah Our Spokesman. (Heb. 7:14.)

Banqueting With Our New Testament Joseph. (Ps. 23:5.)

The Duty of Forgiving Offenses. (Lev. 19:18; Prov. 20:22; Rom. 12:17, 19.)

Questions

1. What compelled Jacob to send again to Egypt for grain?

2. Who offered to become surety for the return of Benjamin?

3. How did Joseph treat his brother on this second visit?

4. What partiality did he show toward Benjamin?

5. Describe his suppressed emotions as he sat among his brethren?

6. What apparently cruel course did he take to make his brothers truly sorry for their old sin against him?

7. Describe the eloquent plea for Benjamin made by Judah?

8. Tell of Joseph's making known himself to his brothers?

9. What Divine explanation did Joseph offer for what had happened to him?

10. What proposal did Joseph make in respect to his father's family?

Story 31

THE REMOVAL OF JACOB AND HIS FAMILY TO EGYPT

GENESIS 45:16-28; 46;
47:1-12

The news that Jo'seph was a brother of the men who had come down from Ca'naan to buy grain spread rapidly among the officers of Pha'raoh and finally was brought to the great king himself. Instead of being angry with Jo'seph for inviting his father's household to come to E'gypt without first asking the king's permission, Pha'raoh and all his officers were very happy to hear the news. When the king learned that Jo'seph intended to have his father and all his family come to E'gypt to make their home, he sent an official invitation to Ja'cob to come at once, assuring him that his family would be given the choicest part of E'gypt for their future home.

It is true that Jo'seph had been given charge of all the affairs of E'gypt, and therefore had the right to ask his father to come there to live, but Pha'raoh graciously showed his approval by adding an invitation in the name of the king. What is more, he helped a great deal in making the hard journey more comfortable for Ja'cob and the members of his family. By his command wagons were sent to aid in moving Ja'cob's household goods, and Jo'seph was ordered to see that provisions were supplied for the journey. In addition to providing the bare necessities of food and transportation, certain luxuries were given by Pha'raoh in order that Ja'cob's family might see how well the brothers had been treated. New clothes were given them, and to Ben'ja-min there was given five new robes and three hundred pieces of silver. Choice articles of food and other valuable presents were sent to Ja'cob as a mark of the king's good will toward him.

All these kind acts by Pha'raoh proved to Ja'cob and his sons that Jo'seph was very highly regarded in E'gypt, and that both the king and people were grateful to him for saving their nation from the famine. Before letting his brothers go back to the land of Ca'naan, Jo'seph warned them not to quarrel with one another on the way. He told them not to let any feelings of anger or jealousy arise among them, and to be especially careful not to harm Ben'ja-min because he had been shown greater favor than the other brothers. After these warnings had been given, Jo'seph ordered his brothers to hasten to their father's house, and to bring him back to the land of E'gypt without delay.

The eleven sons of Ja'cob made the long trip back home as quickly as possible. Safe at last in their own home, they sat down with their father and told him about all the strange and trying things which had happened to them during this visit. First they told him of the friendly way in which the E-gyp'tian ruler had made them his guests of honor at a banquet, and of all the acts of kindness which his servants had shown them. Then they told their father of the strange manner in which Ben'ja-min was accused of stealing the silver cup which belonged to E-gyp'tian officer.

This brought them to the point where they must explain who the E-gyp'tian ruler really was. The officer who had kept Sim'e-on in prison as a spy at the time of their first visit, and who had insisted that Ben'ja-min be brought to E'gypt before the much-needed supplies could be bought, was none other than Ja'cob's beloved son Jo'seph. The son he had mourned as dead for nearly twenty-five years was not only alive and well, but was governor of all the land of E'gypt!

In telling their father this wonderful news they were obliged to go into the disgraceful story of how they had treated their brother so many years before. With tears of repentance, and with their heads bowed in shame, they admitted that they had sold Jo'seph to a band of slave-dealers, and had led Ja'cob to believe that his favorite son had been slain by a wild animal.

The tenderness with which Jo'seph had heard his brothers admit their sin, and the kindly spirit with which he had forgiven them and become friends with them again, was related to their father. They also told Ja'cob of his son's glory and power in E'gypt, of his wonderful way of seeing the hand of God in all that took place, and how he had warned them that the terrible famine would continue for five more years. Nor did the brothers forget to tell their father of the gracious manner in which they had been entertained by Jo'seph, or of the request of both Jo'seph and the E-gyp'tian king that Ja'cob and all his family come at once to dwell in E'gypt.

The family of Jacob then sat in comfort within their tent, awaiting the word of the master concerning the great news which had just come to him. As the ten sons humbly confessed their guilt before their father, Ja'cob was moved by strong feelings; as they told him the wonderful news

JACOB AND HIS FAMILY GOING TO EGYPT

that Jo'seph was alive, and had sent for him to come at once into the land in which he was now a ruler, second only to the king, the old man was completely overcome. The news that his beloved son was alive seemed too much to believe, and the cruel behavior of his ten sons was too heavy a burden to bear. Ja'cob fainted, falling helpless at the feet of his sons.

When Ja'cob had recovered from the shock, and had seen the wagons which had been provided for his journey to E'gypt, he no longer doubted the good news which his sons had brought him concerning Jo'seph, but cried out with great joy, "It is enough; Jo'seph my son is yet alive: I will go and see him before I die." So happy was he to know that his beloved son was alive and well, that he declared that he was willing to die if only he might see Jo'seph once again.

The sixty-six members of Ja'cob's household, together with the large number of servants in his employ, started toward the land in which Ja'cob's descendants were destined to live for the next two hundred and fifteen years, and where they were to grow into a great people numbering nearly three million souls. Here they were to learn the arts and trades of the greatest nation of their time, and to be prepared both in mind and spirit for a glorious return to the land which they were now leaving.

When they reached Be'er-she'ba, a town on the southern border of the country just before crossing into the wilderness and deserts lying between Ca'naan and E'gypt, there was a pause for sacrifices unto the God of I'saac. Here both A'bra-ham and I'saac had lived at different times in their lives, and the place was filled with memories of these noble ancestors of Ja'cob. Before leaving the land which had been promised to his descendants, Ja'cob sought to know the will of God. He felt sure that the right course was being followed, and that Jo'seph would do all that he had promised, but before making so dangerous a journey into a foreign land he thought it wise to seek guidance from the Lord.

While Ja'cob and his sons were engaged in this act of worship, the Lord appeared to Ja'cob in a wonderful vision. He revealed Himself to Ja'cob as the Almighty, who was able to keep all His promises, and to bring Ja'cob in perfect safety through all the trials and hardships of the journey. The Lord said to Ja'cob, "Fear not to go down into E'gypt; for I will there make of thee a great nation. I will go down with thee into E'gypt, and I will also surely bring thee up again." In these words the Lord renewed His promise to make a great nation of the descendants of Ja'cob, and in due time to bring them back to the land of Ca'naan.

Upon reaching the borders of E'gypt, Ja'cob and his large company halted their march for a short time. Ja'cob then sent his son Ju'dah, who had shown his ability as a leader on other occasions, to inform Jo'seph of their arrival, and to ask him what course they should follow in entering the new land. E'gypt was a strong, well organized kingdom, and a group of wandering shepherds could not safely pass through the land without proper ceremony and official protection. Authority and directions were given for them to pass directly to the land of Go'shen, which was the finest pasture land in all E'gypt.

Jo'seph at once ordered his official chariot made ready, and quickly drove out to meet his father. Ja'cob and his beloved son fell into the arms of one another, embraced most tenderly, and for a long time shed tears of happiness. For the first time since he had sent the lad of seventeen upon a long and dangerous journey to Do'than with a message for his brothers, Ja'cob now looked upon the face of his favorite son. So happy was he that he expressed a desire to pass on at once to the happy land beyond this life, but it was God's will that he should live for another seventeen years.

Then Jo'seph knew that he must make plans for introducing his family to Pha'raoh. This was done by choosing five of his brothers to represent the family before the king. The number five was a favorite of the E-gyp'tians, so in choosing this number of his brothers as representatives, Jo'seph did much to win the favor of the E-gyp'tian court toward his family.

The wisdom and foresight of Jo'seph in keeping his people from mingling with the E-gyp'tians either through marriage or religious customs was then shown in a remarkable way. He told Pha'raoh that his father and all his household were shepherds, and that the family had followed this calling for many generations; he also told the brothers who were to appear before the king to make it clear that this was their chosen occupation. For this reason also he selected for their home the land of Go'shen, which was so well adapted to the raising of sheep and cattle, and in this way made sure that his family would be kept separate from the E-gyp'tians no matter how long they might stay in the foreign land.

The plans of Jo'seph were carried out perfectly in every way. The five brothers who represented his family appeared before Pha'raoh, and were treated with great honor. They asked no favors because of the high position which their brother held in the land, nor did they show any feelings of envy because of his grandeur. They told the king that they had come as pilgrims and sojourners in the land, and that they asked no other favor than that of carrying on their life as shepherds and cattle-raisers. Pha'-raoh granted their wishes, and gave them permission to make their home in the land of Go'shen. To Jo'seph he said, "As to promoting your brethren, it does not appear to suit their calling or wishes. I leave it to you to make them happy in their own way. Appoint those who are best qualified to be chief of my herdsmen." —

As a special honor, Jo'seph then arranged to have his father presented to the E-gyp'tian king. When the time for this meeting arrived, Pha'raoh was deeply impressed by the great age and strong religious character of Ja'cob. He politely inquired about the age of his visitor, not from mere curiosity or in a trifling manner, but because he was genuinely interested in the fine old man who stood before him.

Ja'cob was greatly moved by the sight of a king who had been so kind to him, and who had come to the rescue of his family during the terrible famine. With proper respect to the king, and in a spirit of deep gratitude, Ja'cob spoke as a prophet of the Lord in giving a special blessing upon Pha'raoh. He prayed to the God of Heaven for the blessings to be given to the king. Speaking most humbly of the years of sorrow and trial which he had known, Ja'cob gave thanks to the Lord for all the blessings which had come to him during the closing years of his life.

SUGGESTIONS FOR STUDY

Biblical Index to Helpful References

Migration to Egypt the Fulfillment of Prophecy. (Gen. 15:13; Ps. 105:23; Acts 7:6.)

Joseph Ordained a Savior of Israel. (Ps. 81:5, 6.)

Egyptian Sojourn the Making of a Great Nation. (Deut. 26:5; Isa. 52:4.)

God's Providential Sovereignty Over Nations. (Deut. 32:8.)

The Number That Went Down to Egypt. (Acts 7:14.)

The Sacred Number Five Among Egyptians. (Gen. 41:34; 43:34; 45:22.)

Questions

1. How did Pharaoh and his officers receive the news of the coming of Jacob and his family?

2. What provisions did Pharaoh make for the removal of Jacob to Egypt?

3. How did Jacob feel and act when told that his son Joseph was alive?

4. How many were there in the family of Jacob that went down into Egypt?

5. Were there any others beside the family, and if so, who were they?

6. What events took place at Beersheba on the way?

7. On reaching the borders of Egypt why did Jacob and his family halt?

8. Tell of Jacob's introduction to Pharaoh.

9. What wise course did Joseph take to keep Jacob's family from mingling with the Egyptians?

10. What favors did Jacob bestow upon Pharaoh when introduced to him?

STORY 32

THE CLOSING YEARS AND DEATH OF JACOB

GENESIS 47:27-31,
48, 49
After the settlement of his father's family in
the land of Go'shen Jo'seph had little time for visiting them. In spite
of all the duties which he must perform to help the nation through the
distress caused by the famine, he took pains to see that every possible aid
was given his own people.

In managing the affairs of E'gypt during the years of famine, Jo'seph
acted with great wisdom. His policy was to supply the needs of the people by selling them grain, not by giving it to them without charge, and
thus encouraging idleness until the public peace was endangered. Sometimes he found it necessary to purchase the lands of the people for the

JOSEPH PRESENTS HIS FATHER TO PHARAOH

king, and to let the people cultivate them on shares. In this way the people received the food they needed without going into debt or becoming beggars.

Jo'seph overlooked nothing that would make the famine easier to bear. Special care was taken to protect the religious leaders of the nation, the supply of food was so wisely handled that no one went hungry, and E'gypt remained strong and wealthy even in the midst of famine. Hard work and loyalty among the people brought generous rewards, and Jo'seph was not only trusted and honored by the king, but was greatly loved by the people.

After the famine of seven years had passed, the people began to prosper again. Their lands were now held by the government, but the people were far from being slaves. One fifth of what they produced was paid to government as rental for the lands, but there was no other charge.

Ja'cob lived seventeen years after the removal of his family to E'gypt, surviving the famine by twelve years. Seventeen years he had provided for Jo'seph in his youth, and for the same number of years he was provided for by Jo'seph in his old age. Among his greatest joys was that of watching his household grow and prosper.

The family of Ja'cob lived apart from the E-gyp'tians, who regarded them as people of little account, and who therefore shut them out of society and politics. Such treatment by the E-gyp'tians was really a great blessing, for it kept the children of Is'ra-el from mingling with people who worshiped idols, and who did many things that were not to their credit.

Saved from hardship and starvation during the years of famine, settled in a fertile land most suitable for raising sheep and cattle, and free to live in their own way, the Is'ra-el-ites were prepared by the Lord for the wonderful prosperity that was soon to be granted them. The foundations for the future greatness of Is'ra-el as a nation were truly laid during the years of sojourn in E'gypt.

When Ja'cob felt that the hour of his death was near at hand, he set his house in order for his departure to the land of the saints. He sent for Jo'seph, and made him promise not to bury his body in E'gypt, but in the grave of his fathers in Ca'naan. Thus, in his last words, he proved his faith concerning the Promised Land, warned his people against planning to stay in E'gypt forever, and reminded them that they would finally go back to the land of Ca'naan.

JACOB'S LAST MOMENTS

In his weakened condition, Ja'cob did not fail to carry out a very solemn duty. Jo'seph's two sons must be made members of the family which God had promised A'bra-ham to bless. The sons of Jo'seph had an E-gyp'tian mother, and had not been born in the Promised Land. It was therefore very important that a blessing should be given them by one whom the Lord had chosen to carry on the promise made to A'bra-ham, and surely no one was more worthy to give it than the man whose name had been changed from "Ja'cob" to "Is'ra-el."

Jo'seph brought his two sons before Ja'cob to receive the blessing, and to be adopted into his father's family. Ma-nas'seh, as the older of the two, was placed at the right, while E'phra-im was placed at the left. When Ja'cob stretched forth his arms to bless them, however, he crossed his arms, placing his right hand on the head of E'phra-im, and his left on that of Ma-nas'seh. This meant that the blessing of the firstborn was being given to the younger son.

Thinking that his father's dimness of sight had led him to make what seemed to be a mistake, Jo'seph told his father that he had chosen the wrong son for the chief blessing. But Ja'cob insisted that he was doing what he intended. He said, "The greater blessing shall rest upon E'phra-im; his descendants shall be stronger and more numerous. A double portion is to be bestowed upon Jo'seph, and two shares of the Promised Land are to be given him. Both E'phra-im and Ma-nas'seh are to be the heads of tribes."

Thus the two sons of Jo'seph who belonged to E'gypt by birth, and who might have advanced to the highest ranks in that nation, were now numbered among the children of Is'ra-el. The prophecies which Ja'cob uttered in his dying words all came true, and the descendants of E'phra-im and Ma-nas'seh were among the strongest tribes of Is'ra-el in the land of Ca'naan two hundred years later.

Ja'cob then called his sons to his bedside, and gave his blessing to each one of them in turn. His bodily powers were fast failing, but the strength of his faith in God grew brighter as his eyes dimmed. He believed that God would be with his descendants, bringing them at last up from E'gypt to the land of promise.

As the things of this world faded from his sight, the glories of the world beyond became more clear, and he was filled with the spirit of true prophecy. He told each son what the history of his descendants would be, and very clearly described the characteristics of each tribe of Is'ra-el. The choice of the tribe of Ju'dah for the honor of carrying on the line through which the Mes-si'ah was to be born was positively announced from the death bed of Ja'cob.

With his life work finished, his last blessing and prophetic message spoken, and his last prayer ended, Ja'cob quietly fell asleep in the Lord.

SUGGESTIONS FOR STUDY
Biblical Index to Helpful References

God's Promise to Make of Jacob's Descendants a Great Nation. (Gen. 28:13-19.)

The Imposition of Hands in Divine Blessing. (Num. 27:18, 23; Acts 6:6; 8:17.)

Ephraim and Manasseh Made Heads of Tribes. (Deut. 33:13-17; Josh. 14:4.)

Ephraim Greater Than Manasseh. (Num.

1:33-35.)

Jacob's Faith in His Dying Moments. (Heb. 11:21.)

God's Presence with His People in Death. (Ps. 23:4; Isa. 43:2.)

The Hope of Happiness in the Next Life. (Ps. 17:4; 1 Thess. 4:14-17.)

Questions

1. Did Joseph visit his people often? Why not?

2. What care did Joseph take to see to the comfort of his people?

3. How long did Jacob live after removing to Egypt? How old was he at death?

4. What advantages came to Israel in living apart from the Egyptians?

5. Before dying, what did Jacob do in respect to Joseph's two sons?

6. Which was the older, Manasseh or Ephraim?

7. To which one was the superior blessing promised?

8. Did Ephraim and Manasseh become the heads of tribes in Israel?

9. What was Jacob's last act before dying?

10. Tell of Jacob's peaceful and confident dying moments.

STORY 33

ISRAEL'S SLAVERY IN EGYPT AND THE BIRTH OF MOSES

EXODUS 1, 2:1-10

Following the brief story of the death of Jo'seph, the history of Is'ra-el is passed over in silence for a period of one hundred and forty-five years. During this century and a half important changes took place among the royal families which ruled E'gypt, and control of the government passed from the hands of the Shepherd Kings, who were not members of the original E-gyp'tian royalty, back to native E-gyp'tian rulers. The Shepherd Kings had treated the He'brews with great kindness, but the E-gyp'tian rulers who followed looked upon them with suspicion and jealousy.

In the Covenant promise made to A'bra-ham, the founder of the He'brew people, God had told him that for four hundred and thirty years his descendants should be under the rule of foreign people, and that in the closing years of this period they would be treated very harshly. Two hundred and fifteen years of this time passed before Ja'cob and his family went down into E'gypt. During this time A'bra-ham, his son I'saac, and then Ja'cob and his family, had lived much of the time in Ca'naan, not as owners of the land, but as wandering strangers.

The land of Ca'naan was largely occupied by various tribes which were all known under the general name of Ca'naan-ites. God had promised A'bra-ham that his descendants should be like the stars of the heavens and the sands of the sea in numbers. Up to the time of the removal of Ja'cob to the land of E'gypt the immediate family of the chosen race had increased to only seventy, including Jo'seph and his family. As a result of God's will in keeping them separate from the E-gyp'tians, and in giving them a land of great fertility, the passing of two hundred years had left the family greatly increased in both numbers and prosperity.

Jo'seph had been ruler in E'gypt for ten years before the removal of Ja'cob and his family to that land, being forty years old at the time, and he ruled for seventy years after the settling of his father and brothers in the land of Go'shen. These were years of good fortune for the children of Is'ra-el, and their numbers increased very rapidly. They remained in the land of E'gypt for one hundred and forty-five years after the death of Jo'seph, and for at least half a century of that period continued to enjoy the kindest of treatment from the E-gyp'tian rulers. The hardships and oppression which followed began shortly before the opening of our next story.

During the years of kind treatment by the rulers of E'gypt, and while they were being increased in numbers and wealth, the children of Is'ra-el had been faithful in serving the one true God, and had kept themselves almost entirely free from the idol worship practiced in E'gypt. They lived far away from most of the E-gyp'tians, and were careful not to mingle with them in either marriage or religion. Thus the customs and worship of the Is'ra-el-ites was kept pure, and

JOCHEBED

they soon became a large and powerful band of united people. The tribal life of each of Ja'cob's eleven sons, and of the two sons of Jo'seph, was carefully preserved, and each group was determined to do its part in making Is'ra-el a great nation. They all looked forward to the time when they might return to the land of Ca'naan, where they would be free to prosper as the Lord had promised. In these worthy hopes and ambitions the children of Is'ra-el were misunderstood by the E-gyp'tians, who were greatly alarmed by their growth and power, but who were still unwilling to let them leave the country.

So different were the He'brews from the native E-gyp'tians, and so rapid had been the growth and progress of these chosen people of God, that the new line of kings became fearful that they would revolt against

E'gypt. They looked upon the Is'ra-el-ites as a group of strangers who stubbornly clung to their own customs, and who were too proud to become members of the E-gyp'tian empire. "What would happen," they began to ask, "if E'gypt should become involved in a foreign war?" They also said among themselves, "Suppose these rich and powerful Jews were to unite with our enemies, then our country might be overcome by a revolution."

The Pha'raoh who was then on the throne made up his mind that he would crush the spirit of the Jews so thoroughly that there would be no danger of their taking part in a revolt. He decided to make slaves of the He'brews, forcing them to work without wages upon various government projects. Taskmasters were appointed to see that the slaves were driven as hard as possible at their work. The purpose of this cruel treatment was to weaken the He'brews, and in this way to reduce their numbers.

The kings of E'gypt had always been noted for their interest in erecting great public buildings and monuments. The gigantic pyramids, which are among the wonders of the world today, had been built by the hard labor of countless slaves. The huge stones for the pyramid were quarried and shaped by the slaves, carried on floats down the river Nile, and hoisted into position by some wonderful engineering method which is unknown today. Magnificent temples, exceeding in size and beauty many of the finest buildings of this age, had been erected in The'bes, Kar'nak, and Mem'phis.

The Pha'raoh who decided to make slaves of the Is'ra-el-ites also erected many new temples, built great treasure houses and palaces, and ordered the construction of vast tombs for the dead. In addition to these great works, the king must be credited with the building of many roads, a system of canals, and vast embankments in the valley of the Nile.

In carrying out this extensive programme of public works, Pha'raoh drafted the He'brews as laborers. He placed over them hard taskmasters, who not only forced them to spend long hours in back-breaking work, but abused and insulted them. The lives of the He'brews were filled with sorrow and suffering; through no fault of their own they had become slaves of the lowest class.

The E-gyp'tians imposed taxes which they knew the He'brews would be unable to pay, and then seized their property as a penalty for not paying the taxes. The unhappy children of Is'ra-el were treated harshly in every possible way, and they were no longer permitted to live according to their own customs. Special efforts were made to destroy their family life, which had been the chief reason for their remarkable growth and strength. To prevent further increase in their numbers the midwives, or nurses who cared for mothers and young children, were ordered to see that all male He'brew children did not live after birth. When the mid-wives, who worshiped the true God, failed to carry out this cruel demand, it was ordered that all male children born to the He'brews should be thrown into the river Nile at once.

And yet, the more cruel the king of E'gypt became in his effort to destroy the He'brews, the stronger became their faith and courage. All through history members of the Jewish race have been hated and perse-cuted by people who were jealous of their success, but no tyrant has ever been able to destroy them. Through all the inhuman persecution which they received from Pha'raoh, the He'brews knew that the Lord was with them, and that He would surely find some way of delivering them from all their troubles.

Even the wicked order of the king to drown all the boys born to the He'brews could not prevent the Lord from raising up a savior for His chosen people when the proper time had come. Among the hundreds of devout families in Is'ra-el at the time there was one most noted for faith in the Lord. The head of this family was named Am'ram, the son of Ko'hath, who was one of the descendants of Ja'cob's son Le'vi. His wife's name was Joch'e-bed, and she was also of noble lineage through her descent from Le'vi. Two children had been born to them before the king had ordered the death of all male children born to the He'brews; one of them was a boy named Aa'ron, and the other was a very lovely girl called Mir'i-am. We shall learn much of the life and work of these two children in future stories.

In the midst of Pha'raoh's bitter persecution of the He'brews Joch'e-bed gave birth to her second son. The nurse who cared for her was gracious and God-fearing, and therefore failed to report this birth to the officers who were charged with drowning all boy babies. Joch'e-bed and her good husband managed to hide the child in their home for three months, but as time went on they feared that he would be discovered by the cruel E-gyp'tians. The mother was not only moved by natural love for a child, but by a divinely given feeling that her new-born son was intended for an important mission among her people.

After keeping the child safely hidden in her home for three months,

Joch'e-bed began to search for some way of making sure that he would never be taken from her by the E-gyp'tian officers. As long as the child was kept at home there was always the danger that some unfriendly neighbor or E-gyp'tian spy would discover him, and then the innocent child would be drowned in the river Nile. One day the thought came to her that the daughter of the king came down to the river every day to bathe, and at once there flashed into her mind a way of giving the baby a home in which he would never be in danger. At once she decided to trust in the beauty of the child to win the favor of the king's daughter. The time had come when she had done everything in her power to save the child; from now on his welfare must lie in the hands of the Lord.

The mother then took some reeds which grew near the river bank and wove them into a little basket, just the right size to hold her baby, then she coated it so carefully with pitch that no water could come in. When the basket, which is sometimes called an "ark," was ready for the purpose which she had in mind, she tenderly placed her baby in it, and hid it carefully in the bulrushes which grew in the marshes near the banks of

MOSES AND PHARAOH'S DAUGHTER

the river. Her daughter Mir'i-am, who was now twelve years old, was put on watch nearby to see that no harm came to the child, and to tell her mother what the king's daughter had done when she saw the baby.

Mir'i-am did not have to wait long for the answer to her mother's prayer for the safety of the little boy. When Pha'raoh's daughter and a number of her maids came down to the river, guided by the Lord to the place where the child still floated on the waters in his basket, the princess saw the basket almost at once. When she lifted the cover from the ark of bulrushes and saw the beautiful child within, she was greatly touched by the sight, and said, "This is one of the He'brews' children." The child began to cry, and her heart went out to it with compassion and love. While she stood telling her maids about finding the baby, and wondering what she should do with it, little Mir'i-am rushed up to her. Pretending not to know anything about the baby, she said, "Shall I go and call for thee a nurse of the He'brew women, that she may nurse the child for thee?"

The kindly offer of Mir'i-am was quickly accepted by Pha'raoh's daughter, and the little girl hurried home to tell her mother the wonderful news. Joch'e-bed was filled with joy by the opportunity of caring for her son in the home of the king who had sworn to destroy the He'brews. Not knowing that Joch'e-bed was the mother of the child found by the river, Pha'raoh's daughter agreed to pay her the customary wages for taking care of the child.

It was hard to pretend that she did not even know the child which she had born, but Joch'e-bed knew that his safety depended upon her ability to care for him without revealing the fact that he was her own son. She therefore entered the royal palace at once, and patiently acted as nurse to the child which Pha'raoh's daughter had adopted.

The E-gyp'tian princess gave the child every comfort and attention which great wealth could supply, and in many ways tried to act as a good mother to him. It was Joch'e-bed, however, who took advantage of her position as a hired nurse to bring up her son in the faith and wisdom of his own people. And yet, even when telling him of the customs and duties which were most sacred among the He'brews, she was careful never to let the child know that she was his mother.

When it came time to give the baby a name the daughter of Pha'raoh called him Mo'ses, which means "drawn out" in the E-gyp'tian language. This name was given because the princess had literally drawn him out of the waters upon which the basket was floating when she found him.

Just as the infant Mo'ses had been saved from drowning by the Lord's guidance upon two different occasions, so he was saved from the slavery of his people by being raised in the palace of the king. Had he been found by the E-gyp'tian officers in his parents' home, he would have been thrown into the river Nile; had Pha'raoh's daughter not found him when she did, he soon would have been drowned in the same river when the basket in which he floated finally sank.

It was truly a miracle which saved Mo'ses from the waters of the Nile, and it was a miracle equally great which preserved him from the evils and idolatry of the E-gyp'tians by letting him be brought up under the care of his God-fearing mother. The Lord also made it possible for him to enjoy all the advantages of education which the adopted son of an E-gyp'tian princess could gain through wealth and high position. Thus the very king who sought to destroy Is'ra-el was led by the providence of God to be the means of training the child who would soon become the deliverer of the people held in bondage.

SUGGESTIONS FOR STUDY

Biblical Index to Helpful References

The Growth and Prosperity of Israel in Egypt. (Ps. 105:24; Acts 7:17.)

Evil Treatment of Israel by Egyptians. (Gen. 15:13; Num. 20:15; Deut. 26:6.)

Counsel Against the Lord's People Comes to Nought. (Prov. 16:25; 21:30; Isa. 8: 9-10.)

Moses Saved by Divine Appointment. (Acts 7:19-21.)

Obedience to God Against the Orders of Kings. (Dan. 3:16, 18; 6:13; Acts 5:29.)

God Honors Those Who Serve Him Under Trial. (Prov. 11:18; Eccl. 8:12; Isa. 3:10.)

Jochebed's Faith in Hiding Her Baby. (Heb. 11:23.)

Questions

1. How long a period of silence respecting Israel have we after the death of Joseph?

2. For how many years did the kings of Egypt show kindness to the Israelites?

3. What happened that brought about a change in this treatment?

4. What was to be the total number of years from Abraham to the occupation of Canaan by his descendants?

5. How many of these years passed before Israel entered Egypt?

6. What was the total number of years Israel spent in Egypt?

7. Why did the new rulers of Egypt try to crush the Israelites?

8. Describe some of the cruelties suffered by the Israelites?

9. What did Amram and his wife Jochebed do to prevent their new baby boy from being drowned in the Nile?

10. Did they have any older children? What were their names?

11. Tell of Jochebed's hiding her baby.

12. Who found it and adopted it? What name did she give the boy?

13. How did Jochebed manage to become the nurse of Moses?

STORY 34

THE YOUTH, TRAINING, AND MANHOOD OF MOSES

EXODUS 2:11-25

For forty years Mo'ses remained in the palace of Pha'raoh, enjoying all the luxury and advantages afforded by the court of one of the richest and most powerful rulers in all history. As an adopted son of the E-gyp'tian princess he was given the advantages of the best education which could be had in any land. It is said of Mo'ses, "He was instructed in all the wisdom of the E-gyp'tians, and was mighty in his words and works." We also know that he was proficient in mathematics, natural philosophy, engineering, warfare, grammar, and medicine. From such training he was well prepared to hold a place of honor among the greatest nobles and princes, and to turn at last to the great mission of his life.

His nurse, who was really his own mother, continued to care for him until he was no longer a child. She taught him to worship the true God of the He'brews, and told him about all the customs of his people. No doubt she also secretly told him of the wonderful way in which the Lord had caused him to be saved from death, and laid upon his heart the burdens and hardships of his own people.

During all these years of royal advantages Mo'ses never forgot the sufferings of his own people held in bondage. The luxury and gaiety of his own surroundings did not close his eyes to the poverty and hardships of his brethren, nor could he enjoy his life of ease and comfort while the children of Is'ra-el remained so miserable. His unselfish love for the down-trodden people, and his patient hope for an improvement in their condition became so strong that he decided to take some definite step toward helping them.

One day while he was quietly passing among the workmen on one of the government projects, probably an embankment near the river Nile, he saw one of the E-gyp'tian taskmasters striking a He'brew laborer with a whip. As he watched his own kindred straining under unbearable burdens, and saw how they were mistreated by the cruel overseer, his blood boiled with righteous indignation. Looking around and seeing that no other E-gyp'tians were near, he struck the taskmaster so fierce a blow that it killed him. He then secretly covered the body in the sand, and went on his way.

This act of the young prince was not known to any of the E-gyp'tians, but the He'brew whom Mo'ses had protected whispered the news to other workmen, and they in turn told their brethren, until the deed was finally known to most of the He'brews. The next day Mo'ses visited the workmen again, and this time saw one of the He'brews strike another during a quarrel. At once he went up to them in the hope of settling their differences, and rebuked the one who seemed to be in the wrong. He had intended merely to show them that even though they were slaves, they still were kindred, and should try to deal patiently with one another.

The friendly act of Mo'ses was resented by the two He'brews, and the one who had been the aggressor in the quarrel said to him, "Who made you a prince and a judge over us? Do you intend to kill me as you killed that E-gyp'tian?" This placed Mo'ses in a very difficult position. His own people feared him because he had slain the E-gyp'tian while trying to protect one of them, and now they resented his friendly effort to promote peace and good will among them. He had been right in his sympathy for them, and was justified in using force to protect the man whom the taskmaster was treating so cruelly, but in killing the E-gyp'tian he had committed a serious crime against the government.

The life of Mo'ses was now in danger. If news that he had murdered one of the E-gyp'tian officers reached Pha'raoh, he would probably be put to death as a criminal. Fearing for his own life, and knowing that once his sympathy for the oppressed and hated He'brews became known to the king there would no longer be any hope of delivering them, he fled from the country at once. He went across the desert to the east of E'gypt into A-ra'bi-a, and into the part of the peninsula that was known as Mid'i-an. He was compelled to remain in hiding, for Pha'raoh was greatly angered when he learned of the death of the E-gyp'tian overseer. The king felt that his hospitality had been abused, and that a member of his own household had turned against him in order to help the He'brews; it was ordered, therefore, that the young prince be captured and put to death.

While hiding in Mid'i-an, Mo'ses lingered by the side of a well and gave serious thought to his problems. He had suddenly found it necessary to forsake the ease and comfort of the E-gyp'tian palace, and to give

Destruction of Sodom *by Jean Baptiste Corot*
METROPOLITAN MUSEUM OF ART : NEW YORK

The Sacrifice of Abraham
by Jacopo Chimenti da Empoli
UFFIZI PALACE : FLORENCE

Jacob's Dream *by Domenico Feti*
DETROIT INSTITUTE OF ARTS : DETROIT

Isaac Blessing Jacob *by Gerbrand van den Eeckhout*
METROPOLITAN MUSEUM OF ART : NEW YORK

Joseph Sold by His Brethren *by Antonio del Castillo*

Moses Saved from the Waters of the Nile *by Orazio Gentileschi*   THREE LIONS
THE PRADO : MADRID

Brazen Serpent
by Anthony van Dyck
THE PRADO : MADRID

up the kindness of the princess who had adopted him.

Now in the country known as Mid'i-an there lived a noble priest who owned large flocks of sheep and other valuable properties. He had seven daughters who cared for his flocks, and who often brought them for water to the well where Mo'ses was resting. There were also in that vicinity certain shepherds who were unfriendly toward the young women, and who often molested them when they came to the well to draw water for their sheep.

While Mo'ses was sitting by the well lost in deep thought, the seven daughters of the Mid'-i-an-ite priest came to water their flocks. Then the ill-mannered shepherds came and started to drive away the flocks that were being watered. Mo'ses

MOSES SLAYS AN EGYPTIAN

saw the unkind treatment of the women, and knew that someone ought to help them. Realizing that he was now a wanderer because he had once tried to help others in a matter which they thought did not concern him, he must have been strongly tempted not to interfere, but he could not bear to see the women so ill treated. He rebuked the shepherds, drove them away, and then drew water for the flocks of sheep which belonged to the priest of Mid'i-an.

When the young women returned to their father's house they told him of the kindness which had been shown them by one whom they took to be an E-gyp'tian. The priest, whose name was Je'thro, reproached his daughters for not inviting the man to come to their home as a guest. The daughters then returned to the well and asked Mo'ses to come to their father's house. He was glad to accept the invitation, and before long decided to enter the priest's household as a shepherd. The next forty years of Mo'ses' life were spent in the land of Mid'i-an. The Mid'i-an-ites were descendants of one of A'bra-ham's sons by his wife Ke-tu'rah, and were of She'met-ic blood, but were not members of the race blessed in the Covenant which God made with A'bra-ham.

Soon after entering the employ of Je'thro, Mo'ses fell in love with Zip'po-rah, who was a daughter of the Mid'i-an-ite priest. She was given to him in marriage by Je'thro, and a son was born to them. Mo'ses continued to look after the sheep for his father-in-law, and remained in the household for forty years. During that time he spent many hours every day out on the plains and hills with the sheep, communing in his heart with God, and never forgetting his hope some day to deliver the He'brews from bondage in E'gypt.

Strange were the ways in which God prepared Mo'ses to deliver his people. First, his life had been saved by an E-gyp'tian princess, and his early years had been spent under the care and instruction of his own mother, who had providentially been permitted to attend him as a nurse. Then came the period when he enjoyed all the advantages open to a member of the E-gyp'tian royalty. Next came the forty years of exile from E'gypt, during which time he married a daughter of the Mid'i-an-ite priest, and communed with God while caring for the sheep in the desert regions of A-ra'bi-a. Then came the call of God to begin the work for which he had been trained for eighty years, and this will be the subject of our next story.

SUGGESTIONS FOR STUDY

Biblical Index to Helpful References

Concern of Moses for His Oppressed People. (Acts 7:23-29.)

Moses Forsaking the House of Pharaoh an Act of Faith. (Heb. 11:24-27.)

Giving Up Worldly Honor for the Service of God. (Ps. 84:10.)

The True Spirit of Love for Kindred. (Rom. 9:2-5; 10:1.)

God's Providential Care of His Chosen Servants. (2 Cor. 9:8; Phil. 4:19.)

Providential Guidance in Finding a Wife. (Gen. 24:11; 29:10.)

Questions

1. How long did Moses live in the palace of Pharaoh?

2. Why did he leave?

3. When he observed an Egyptian taskmaster abusing an Israelite, what did he do?

4. When he saw two Israelites fighting, what did he do?

5. How did these Israelites treat his interference?

6. When he knew that it was known that he had killed an Egyptian, what did he do?

7. What happened as he was meditating at a well in Midian?

8. Where did he live for forty years? What occupation did he follow?

9. What more important engagement did he have during these forty years?

10. To whom was he married?

STORY 35

GOD SPEAKS TO MOSES FROM A BURNING BUSH

EXODUS 3; 4:1-17

All through the forty years which Mo'ses spent in Mid'i-an caring for the sheep of his father-in-law the burdens of the Is'ra-el-ites were made heavier and heavier. Their daily tasks were greatly increased, brutal methods were taken to check their increase in numbers, and life was made miserable for them in every possible way. They did not know whether Mo'ses was living or dead, and probably never expected to hear of him again.

Death had come to the Pha'raoh who was on the throne at the time when Mo'ses had fled from E'gypt, but another king, also called by the title of Pha'raoh, had taken his place. The Is'ra-el-ites had hoped that the change in monarchs would bring some relief from their burdens, but the new king seemed to be more cruel than any who had come before him. Under the new trials and sufferings the He'brews became much more earnest in their prayers to God for deliverance, and in this way their religious life was brought into a deeper understanding of their complete dependence upon God.

One day Mo'ses led his sheep far out into the desert regions of A-ra'bi-a to the level plain at the foot of Mount Ho'reb, which is sometimes called Mount Si'nai. While the sheep were grazing, a very startling experience came to Mo'ses. While his heart burned with love and compassion for his oppressed brethren back in E'gypt, and while he was thinking of their increased burdens under the cruel new king, a strange sight came to his eyes.

A bush on the plain was aflame with a brilliant and dazzling fire, yet it was not burned or consumed. Mo'ses stood before the strange sight lost in wonder and amazement, unable to take his eyes from such a miracle. And so he said to himself, "I will now turn aside and see this great sight, why the bush is not burnt." Suddenly a voice came from the burning bush, saying, "Mo'ses, Mo'ses." He humbly replied, "Here am I." Then the voice said to him, "Draw not closer; put off thy sandals, for the ground whereon thou standest is holy ground."

THE BURNING BUSH

As Mo'ses stood in silence and awe, the voice spoke again from the burning bush: "I am the God of thy father, the God of A'bra-ham, the God of I'saac, and the God of Ja'cob." After Mo'ses had covered his face as a sign of respect, the voice continued: "I have seen the affliction of my people in E'gypt, and have come to deliver them. I shall take them to Ca'naan, the good land flowing with milk and honey, the land which I promised them long ago."

The voice from heaven then described the cruel treatment which the children of Is'ra-el had suffered in E'gypt, and spoke of the wonderful land in Ca'naan which God would give them for their own as soon as they drove out the heathen nations which then held the land. Mo'ses was told that this voice had come to him as a sign from heaven, and that he should tell Pha'raoh that the Lord had sent him to deliver the He'brews from the land of E'gypt. By this command Mo'ses was called by the Lord to become the leader of Is'ra-el at once.

Although the one thing in the world which Mo'ses desired above all was the deliverance of his people from bondage in E'gypt, he felt that he was unable to serve as the leader in such an undertaking. With all humility he answered the summons from the burning bush in these modest words, "Who am I, that I should go unto Pha'raoh, and that I should bring the children of Is'ra-el out of E'gypt?"

It was only natural for Mo'ses to think of the fact that he was still sought by the E-gyp'tian authorities for the killing of an overseer so many years before, of the fact that for forty years he had been out of touch with events in E'gypt, and of his own lack of experience in serving as the leader of a great people. For these reasons he was most reluctant to accept the divine commission now thrust upon him.

If Mo'ses had been a proud, conceited man, he no doubt would have said, "Who am I not?"; but as a man who trusted only in the Lord, he said, "Who am I?" In reply to the modest question of Mo'ses, the Lord assured him that He would be with him, and that as a token of His presence Mo'ses should worship on this mountain when he brought Is'ra-el out of E'gypt.

Then Mo'ses remembered the treatment his people had received when he had slain the cruel taskmaster so many years before. It also occurred to him that perhaps the Is'ra-el-ites would not follow a leader who had spent forty years in the king's palace while they were forced into the hardest kind of labor, and who had now been absent from the country for forty years. He knew that his people must be broken in spirit by the years of bondage, and must have lost all hope of being delivered from their troubles. Honestly facing these difficulties, Mo'ses asked the Lord, "Who shall I say sent me, what is his name?" To this question God replied, "Tell them that I AM THAT I AM sent you, that is my name."

This name for the God of Is'ra-el means a great deal; though it cannot be fully understood by man, it helps us to learn something about the nature of God. It means, in part, that God is eternal, without beginning or end; independent, unchangeable, and all-powerful; that he is the great and only ruler of everything that has been, or ever shall be created. Mo'ses did not fully understand the words of God, but he knew that they cast a blessing upon his mission to Is'ra-el. He knew that he could begin his work of deliverance in the name of God, a name which has power to free slaves, and to inspire men to the most courageous deeds.

After telling Mo'ses the great name by which he was to be known in the mission to the Is'ra-el-ites, God commanded him to call together the elders of Is'ra-el and tell them of the divine plan which had been arranged for their freedom. God also commanded Mo'ses to ask Pha'raoh to free the He'brews from their bondage. A word of warning, however, went with this final command. The Lord said, "I am sure that the king of E'gypt will not let you go; but I will stretch out my hand and smite E'gypt with all my wonders, and after that he will let your people go."

In spite of all these wonderful promises from God, Mo'ses still felt himself unable to carry out the mission with success, so the Lord gave him two special signs of encouragement. First, He told him to throw his shepherd's staff upon the ground, and when he did so, it was suddenly turned into a serpent. Then the Lord told him to pick it up by the tail, and as soon as he touched it, it became a shepherd's staff once again.

The second sign took place when Mo'ses was directed to put his hand into his bosom. When Mo'ses withdrew his hand, it was turned white by the dread disease of leprosy. Once again he was ordered to place his hand in his bosom, but this time it was completely healed when he withdrew it.

Still worried about his ability to make a successful appeal to Pha'raoh on the behalf of his people, Mo'ses complained that he was a very poor speaker. He declared that he had an impediment of speech which would make it impossible for him to address Pha'raoh with any hope of success. The Lord then rebuked him for his unbelief, and for the suggestion that someone else be sent in his place; Mo'ses was told that his brother Aa'ron would speak for him in all the interviews with Pha'raoh.

While these conversations were going on between the Lord and Mo'ses, the heart of Aa'ron was moved to go out toward the wilderness east of E'gypt. Here he was led by the Lord to meet Mo'ses, and to become an assistant in the great work to which his brother had been called. Mo'ses then accepted the call of God, returned to the house of his father-in-law and arranged to leave at once for E'gypt; taking his wife and son.

SUGGESTIONS FOR STUDY

Biblical Index to Helpful References

God's Pre-arranged Plan for Israel's Deliverance from Egypt. (Gen. 15:14, 16.)

Horeb Called the Mount of God. (Exo. 18:5; 1 Ki. 19:8.)

The Angel-Jehovah in the Burning Bush. (Deut. 33:16; Acts 7:30-35.)

Reverence in the Presence of God. (Josh. 5:15; Isa. 6:1-8; 1 Ki. 19:13.)

Modesty in Assuming Grave Responsibilities. (1 Sam. 9:21; 18:18; Jer. 1:6.)

Divine Utterance Given to God's Servants. (Isa. 50:4; 51:16; Matt. 10:19.)

Moses and Aaron Sent to Deliver Israel. (Ps. 105:26.)

The Righteous Honored by Their Enemies. (Prov. 16:7; Ps. 106:46.)

The Eternal Name of God. (Ps. 90:2; 135:13; Isa. 43:8; John 8:58.)

Questions

1. While Moses was in Midian what was happening to Israel in Egypt?

2. Did the Israelites ever expect to see Moses again?

3. Where was Moses when he saw the burning bush?

4. What about the burning bush was unusual?

5. As Moses approached it, what was said to him?

6. What call came to him from the burning bush?

7. How did Moses feel about accepting such a call? Why?

8. What name did God give by which he was to be known afterwards?

9. What does this name signify?

10. Who was selected by God to be Moses' assistant?

MOSES BEGINS THE WORK OF DELIVERING ISRAEL FROM EGYPT

EXODUS 4:18-31; 5; 6;
7:1-13

Before taking his family on the perilous journey to E'gypt, Mo'ses asked the consent of his father-in-law. Without meaning actually to deceive Je'thro, Mo'ses thought it best to tell him nothing about the vision which he had, or the divine appointment to become the leader of his people in casting off their bondage in E'gypt. Even though he did not think it wise to share his wonderful secret with Je'thro, Mo'ses was truly grateful to his father-in-law for taking him into his home when he was a wanderer, for hiring him to look after his sheep for forty years, and for giving him one of his daughters in marriage. Je'thro took the news of the departure in good spirit, and said to Mo'ses, "Go in peace." He was very fond of his son-in-law, and knew that he would not go away unless he had some very good reason.

Mo'ses took his wife and sons, and started out in the wilderness for the long journey back to the home of his kindred. In the course of the journey God reminded Mo'ses that he had neglected an important duty while he was living in Mid'i-an. For some reason he had failed to have one of his sons circumcised as required of the chosen people of God. When this neglect was called to his mind by the Lord, and the rite duly performed, Mo'ses sent the boy and his mother back to the home of Je'thro. The Lord directed Aa'ron to go out into the wilderness to meet his brother Mo'ses, and the two brothers journeyed on into E'gypt to perform the great work to which they had been called.

The elders of Is'ra-el were then called together, and Mo'ses told them of the call which he had received from God. They accepted him as their leader, and news of his mission spread rapidly among the Is'ra-el-ites. At first there was great rejoicing among the people, and they treated Mo'ses and Aa'ron with deep respect and affection. Then Mo'ses and Aa'ron went directly to Pha'raoh, the king of E'gypt, told him that they were messengers sent by the Lord, and asked that all the He'brew people be allowed to make a three days' journey into the wilderness outside the borders of E'gypt so that they might worship their God in a special feast.

MOSES AND AARON BEFORE THE PEOPLE

This reasonable request was bluntly refused by Pha'raoh. The proud king of E'gypt said, "Who is the Lord that I should obey his voice? I know not the Lord, neither will I let Is'ra-el go." He had no respect for the God of Is'ra-el, and no mercy toward the people who worshiped Him; his answer shows that he did not believe that God could help the people of Is'ra-el. Thus the servants of God were scorned and insulted, and the wicked king of E'gypt sought to make himself a god superior to the God of Is'ra-el.

Hardened in heart, darkened in mind, and filled with a cruel, selfish spirit, Pha'raoh mocked the suggestion that his great host of slaves should be permitted to leave their work long enough to worship their God. At once he ordered his officers and taskmasters to increase the burdens of the children of Is'ra-el, and to make their work more difficult to do.

At this particular time the He'brew slaves were employed in making brick for the great temples being erected in E'gypt. In the process of moulding bricks out of clay they used straw, which was cut in fine strands to hold the bricks together. Up to this time the straw had been gathered by other workmen, but Pha'raoh now ordered that the He'brews go out into the fields and gather their own straw, and that they must make just as many bricks as they had been making before. This increase in their burdens filled the He'brews with despair, and in their disappointment and anger they turned upon Mo'ses and Aa'ron, blaming them for the new hardships inflicted by the E-gyp'tians.

Mo'ses and Aa'ron were overwhelmed with discouragement, and complained to the Lord because of their failure in the first approach to Pha'-raoh, and because of his cruel treatment of their brethren. They had been sent by the Lord, and expected immediate success; when these hopes were disappointed, they felt that it was useless to carry on their work. In the hour of bitter sorrow, however, the Lord renewed with them the promise and covenant which He had made with A'bra-ham, I'saac, and Ja'cob. He told them plainly that Pha'raoh would finally be forced to let the children of Is'ra-el go in freedom by the judgments brought upon him and his people. To His faithful servants the Lord said:

"Watch, though so long be the twilight delaying,
Let the first sunbeam arise on thee praying;
Fear not, for greater is God by thy side,
Than armies of Satan against thee allied."

God told Mo'ses that the apparent failure of his first attempt to persuade Pha'raoh to let the people go did not mean that his entire mission would fail. The Lord was simply waiting for the best possible time to show His power over the wicked king, and to visit the E-gyp'tians with such terrible judgments that they would be glad to let the children of Is'ra-el return to the land promised to their fathers.

Although Mo'ses had been chosen by the Lord to lead Is'ra-el from E'gypt to the Promised Land, he knew nothing of the secret plans of God, nor of the length of time that was to pass before the departure from E'gypt. He expected the Lord to perform some miracle by which Pha'-raoh would consent at once to the freedom which the children of Is'ra-el desired. Instead of this prompt deliverance, however, there was a trying period of many months of sorrow and disappointment before Mo'ses was given the honor of leading the Is'ra-el-ites on the journey to Ca'naan. The Lord sought to build up the faith of His noble servant, and to prepare him for all the trials which lay ahead. The leader of the children of Is′ra-el must be made fearless in carrying out his duty, but must also be taught to trust only in the Lord.

Mo′ses knew that Pha′raoh was one of the most powerful kings upon earth, but he was soon to learn that the Lord is mightier than any earthly king. He knew that Is′ra-el was weak, but soon he was to learn that their strength was in God. All the trials and problems of his task were safely placed in the hands of God, to whom he must look for victory.

"For who that leans on His right arm
    Was ever yet forsaken?
What righteous cause can suffer harm
    If He its part has taken."

The Lord said to Mo′ses, "I will make thee a god before Pha′raoh, and Aa′ron shall be thy prophet." By this He meant that Mo′ses was to be God's messenger to the wicked king, to show the E-gyp′tians how their cruel treatment of the Is′ra-el-ites was to be punished by the God of Is′ra-el and to release all the powers of God against Pha′raoh until the proud king was willing to let the Is′ra-el-ites leave his country.

GOD COMFORTS MOSES

After strengthening his servant against the discouragements which had almost broken his spirit, and assuring him of his presence and power in the long road ahead, the Lord then told Mo′ses to appear before Pha′raoh again. On this appearance Mo′ses was instructed by the Lord to show that Divine power was aiding him. Mo′ses, therefore, told Aa′ron to cast down his staff before Pha′raoh, and the staff was turned into a serpent; when Aa′ron picked it up again, however, it was changed back into a staff.

Pha'raoh then called upon his sorcerers and magicians to imitate what Aa'ron had done. The sorcerers and magicians were men who practiced artful tricks of magic in the name of religion. They were able to give the appearance of turning a staff into a serpent, perhaps by concealing snakes which they had tamed in their clothes, and then releasing them by some sleight of hand trick. But the serpent formed by Aa'ron's staff ran after the E-gyp'tian snakes, and ate them all up.

This miracle should have convinced Pha'raoh that Mo'ses and Aa'ron were truly messengers from God, and that they spoke with Divine authority, but his skeptical mind refused to yield. He rejected the message from God, and denied the request of Mo'ses and Aa'ron that Is'ra-el be allowed to go three days' journey into the wilderness to worship their God. His effort

"To steal the livery of the court of heaven
To serve the devil in"

had failed, but his proud, stubborn spirit would not give in to God. The plagues which followed were brought upon Pha'raoh and the E-gyp'tians because the king would not yield to the reasonable request of Mo'ses and Aa'ron. We shall learn of the plagues in stories which follow.

SUGGESTIONS FOR STUDY

Biblical Index to Helpful References

The Law of Circumcision. (Gen. 17:10; Josh. 5:2.)

Deceitfulness of a Sinful Heart. (Ps. 12: 1-2; Prov. 28:26; Jer. 17:9.)

Hardening the Heart Against God. (Deut. 2:30; Josh. 11:20.)

Persistence in Sin Hardens the Heart. (Ps. 10:4; Jer. 5:23-24.)

The Doom of Those Who Harden the Heart. (Ps. 81:12; Prov. 29:1; Rom. 1:24.)

Failures of Heathen Magicians. (Gen. 41: 1-8; Dan. 1:20.)

Punishment for Haughty Contempt Against God. (Job 21:15; Dan. 3:15.)

Questions

1. Why did Moses return to his father-in-law before going to Egypt?

2. What rite was performed on the way to Egypt?

3. Did Moses' wife continue with him to Egypt?

4. How did Pharaoh treat Moses' request to take Israel out for the worship of God?

5. What reply did Moses make to Pharaoh's refusal?

6. What kind of work were the Israelites doing at the time?

7. How did Pharaoh make their work more irksome?

8. How was Moses and Aaron encouraged by the Lord?

STORY 37

EGYPT PLAGUED BY RIVERS OF BLOOD, HORDES OF FROGS, MYRIADS OF LICE, AND SWARMS OF FLIES

EXODUS 7:14-25; 8:1-32 The Lord then told Mo'ses to go out and meet Pha'raoh as he was walking near the river Nile, and to perform a miracle by which the river would become a raging torrent of blood. Mo'ses and Aa'ron had presented the message of God to Pha'raoh, but had failed to gain his consent by any appeals to his pity or sense of justice; the time had now come when the stubborn king must be punished.

Going down to the river Nile at a place where he could be seen by Pha'raoh, Aa'ron waved his staff over the waters, and they were suddenly turned into blood. Before the king's very eyes the great river which was the pride of all E'gypt, the source of great wealth and prosperity, and the object of superstitious reverence as the birthplace of the gods of E'gypt, was suddenly transformed into a stream of blood.

On the banks of the river were splendid crops of wheat and barley, and groves of sycamore and palm trees cast their welcome shade over many beautiful parks and paths. The richly scented flowers of the sacred lotus floated on the surface of the river. The waters abounded in fish, some of them valued highly for food, while others were regarded with superstitious fear or wonder. The waters of the Nile were considered safe for drinking, and were widely used for domestic purposes.

What a terrible blow it was to have these waters instantly changed into a disgusting stream of blood! The fish died, and soon an unbearable odor rose from the river. At the same time the waters of the canals and lakes throughout the country were also turned into blood. For seven days this terrible condition prevailed. Wherever the people turned in search of water their eyes fell upon blood, nothing but blood. Surely they must have felt that the God of Is'ra-el had power!

The blighting of this great river was also a terrible blow to the industry and commerce of the country. The Nile was the chief strength of E'gypt's trade, and it would be impossible to carry on commerce in a river which was now filled with blood. The nation which had grown wealthy from the forced labor of its thousands of slaves was now on the point of ruin because its great river was unfit for use. And yet, desperate as the people were, the king refused to help them by yielding to the will of God.

The Lord then directed Mo'ses to appear before Pha'raoh the third time, and to say to him, "If you still refuse to submit to God, then He will send a worse plague upon the land." The wicked king gave no heed to this warning, possibly because his magicians had been able to perform a trick in which water was apparently turned into blood.

Mo'ses again directed Aa'ron to wave his staff, and suddenly great numbers of frogs came out of the waters of the land and infested the whole country. The houses of the people and the palace of the king were soon made loathsome by these slimy, croaking creatures. There was no way to escape or resist these afflictive and pestilent "marsh-leapers."

Pha'raoh had been contemptuous and unrepentant under the first plague; the sign of God's power in the torrents of blood which flowed throughout the land seems to have left him unmoved. But now that his own home was made miserable by the frogs, which infested even his bed-chamber and dining room, his stubborn resolution began to weaken. He had no way of protecting himself from these contemptible creatures; they were more numerous and irresistible than any army of soldiers invading the land of E'gypt. His pride was humbled, and he was forced to give in before the army of pests sent by the Lord. He sent for Mo'ses, and asked his aid in freeing the country from the ugly creatures which seemed to have taken possession of it. Mo'ses asked when the king wished him to intercede with God to remove the frogs, and was told to make his prayer on the following day. The prayer of Mo'ses was granted at once; all the frogs died, and had to be piled up in great heaps all over the land.

The apparent repentance of Pha'raoh was short-lived and deceitful. He had promised that if the plague of frogs was

THE PLAGUE OF FLIES

removed he would let the children of Is'ra-el go out into the wilderness to worship God in their own way. As soon as all the frogs were dead, however, Pha'raoh took back his promise, and refused to let the Is'ra-el-ites go out into the wilderness.

A third plague came upon the land without any warning whatever. Mo'ses told Aa'ron to wave his rod over the dust of the earth, and the whole land became infested with lice. They covered both man and beast, and the very dust of the ground became a bed for these annoying insects. The magicians of E'gypt tried to do the same, but were unable to turn the dust of the ground into lice. They then told the king that the miracle just performed by Mo'ses and Aa'ron must have been caused by the finger of God, but Pha'raoh would not take the advice of his own servants.

It is not quite clear whether these three plagues also affected the Is'ra-el-ites in the land of Go'shen, but we are plainly told that they were spared from the plagues which followed. This was an exception to the usual method of Divine Providence in dealing with the world, for as a rule both good and evil persons suffer alike in the calamities of nature. All people are subject to the laws by which the Lord instructs His children, and good conduct does not always save one from a part in the judgments which fall at times upon the world.

The punishments which the Lord permits are intended to turn sinners into saints, and to transform saints into even more heavenly beings. It is true, however, that good character often shields one from misfortune, and that those who love the Lord are saved from the trials which come to those who are too proud to call upon His name. In the further plagues upon E'gypt God showed the wicked king that He was able to protect His own people, and that the sufferings brought upon Pha'raoh and his country for refusing to let the children of Is'ra-el go out into the wilderness should not afflict the He'brews.

After Pha'raoh had refused to take the advice of his magicians concerning the plague of lice, the Lord directed Mo'ses to tell the king that a further refusal would be punished by a great plague of flies. The proud king still refused to heed the warnings of Mo'ses and Aa'ron, and the whole land swarmed with insects whose sharp bites caused bitter suffering.

These four plagues were increasingly severe; each one worse than the one that had come before. With his house swarming with these insects, and his own body and those of his servants bitten all over by them, Pha'-raoh could endure the torture no longer. He called for Mo'ses and

Aa'ron, and offered a partial agreement to their request. They were told that the children of Is'ra-el might sacrifice unto their God, provided they would do so in E'gypt.

This offer was promptly declined by Mo'ses, for it was no time to make a compromise. He explained to Pha'raoh that if the Is'ra-el-ites made their sacrifices according to their own customs the E-gyp'tians would be offended, and would think it their duty to punish the Is'ra-el-ites for killing animals which they regarded as sacred. God's claims upon Is'ra-el were supreme, and as obedient and loyal children, they could not accept any policy which would compromise His honor, or the dignity of the services to be rendered.

Pha'raoh probably offered to Mo'ses the use of the magnificent temples of E'gypt for the worship which the Is'ra-el-ites wished to render unto their God. The use of these buildings, however, which were dedicated to false gods, would have been a compromise with idolatry. Mo'ses preferred to go out into the wilderness to find a place where Is'ra-el could worship the Lord in the manner which He had ordered.

Then Pha'raoh said, "Very well, if you will only entreat the Lord that these troublesome flies be removed from the land, then you may take Is'ra-el a little way into the wilderness for worship; but do not go very far." Mo'ses prayed to the Lord, and the flies were removed, every one of them. Once again Pha'raoh's repentance was false, and as soon as the flies had been removed, he gave orders that the children of Is'ra-el should not be permitted to leave the land. He had repeatedly hardened his heart, and rejected God's will, until it was now impossible for him to yield.

SUGGESTIONS FOR STUDY

Biblical Index to Helpful References

Plagues of Egypt Sent by God. (Ps. 78: 43-51; 105:27-36.)

Certainty of Divine Retribution on Evil

Doers. (2 Thess. 2:8-10; Matt. 8:12.)

(See Biblical Index on preceding chapter.)

Questions

1. Describe the plague of the river Nile and other waters.

2. In what ways did this plague injure Egypt?

3. Describe the plague of frogs.

4. How did this plague torture the Egyptians?

5. Why did Pharaoh ask for the removal of this plague?

6. Describe the plague of lice.

7. What did the magicians of Egypt say of the plague of lice?

8. Tell of the plague of flies.

9. What partial offer did Pharaoh offer to Moses? Why did Moses reject it?

10. In what way did these plagues reflect on the religion of Egypt?

STORY 38

PHARAOH'S OBSTINACY PUNISHED BY MORE SEVERE PLAGUES
CATTLE DIE, BOILS BREAK OUT, TERRIBLE STORMS

EXODUS 9

It was the duty of the king of E'gypt to give the children of Is'ra-el complete freedom, but he treated this solemn obligation with increasing contempt. Mo'ses and Aa'ron had shown themselves to be very generous, and had proved beyond question that they were servants of God, but still he scorned them. Four plagues had visited the land, each one more severe than any other calamity which had ever befallen E'gypt, but the king remained obstinate and insolent toward God.

The solemn promises to let Is'ra-el go were forgotten as soon as God

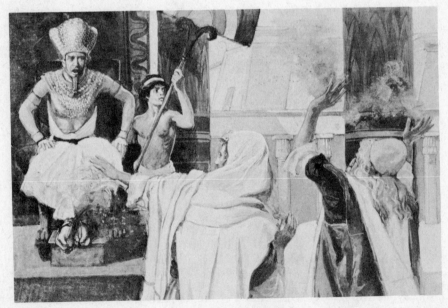

THE PLAGUE OF BOILS

removed the afflictions. During the fear and suffering brought on by each plague Pha'raoh pretended deep repentance for his sins, but when the danger seemed past, committed even greater sins. The righteous judgments of God had forced Pha'raoh to acknowledge His supremacy, but when these judgments were lifted, he became more defiant than ever.

God's mercy was abused by Pha'raoh; instead of leading him to repentance, it seemed only to make him worse. When the rod of justice ceased to strike, he rebelled again. As soon as one voice of Divine judgment was stilled, he seemed to think that there would be no others.

But the Lord God of heaven continued his appeals and warnings, and made it clear to Pha'raoh that he was trifling with Divine justice. The wrath of God could not be halted by false promises and pretended repentance.

AARON

Mo'ses was directed by the Lord to appear again before Pha'raoh, and this time he was to tell the king that an even worse plague would come if he still refused to let Is'ra-el go into the wilderness to worship their God. The next calamity to be sent by God would strike the domestic animals of the E-gyp'tians, bringing death to thousands of cattle, sheep, horses, and camels.

On the day after Mo'ses had spoken to Pha'raoh a deadly disease fell upon all the animals of the E-gyp'tians, and in one day they were dead. The whole land became one gruesome plain covered with the dead bodies of animals. Thousands of oxen, which were regarded as sacred by the E-gyp'tians, lay lifeless upon the ground; the horses, asses, and camels which were used for transportation were also dead, as were the sheep and cattle which provided the E-gyp'tians with food. Surely such terrible calamities would bring the stubborn king to his knees!

This plague, however, had only the effect of hardening Pha'raoh's heart the more. He made a special visit to the land of Go'shen, where the Is'ra-el-ites lived, and found that none of their live-stock had been harmed by the plague. It angered him greatly to find that the despised He'brews had not been touched by the judgment which had cost him so much, and he became more determined than ever not to yield to the command of God.

Then the Lord directed Mo'ses and Aa'ron to take up ashes from the furnace, and to cast them into the heavens. As the ashes floated toward the ground a plague of boils began to afflict all the people of E'gypt, including the king. Even the magicians were so afflicted by the plague that they were unable to stand before the king.

The sixth plague upon the E-gyp'tians threatened all human life. It caused great sores and intense suffering, often resulting in death. It was by far the worst pestilence so far visited upon the people of E'gypt. It was also brought on in a manner designed to show the purpose of God in all the plagues. For years the Is'ra-el-ites had been forced to labor in the brick-kilns under the unbearable heat of the furnaces; when Mo'ses brought on this plague, the ashes of these very furnaces became a sign and promise of the affliction to smite the cruel E-gyp'tians. The very work-shops in which the He'brew slaves had toiled in preparing materials for the great temples of E'gypt became the source of ruin for the slave-masters.

No one in the land, except the Is'ra-el-ites in Go'shen, was spared from the terrible scourge of boils. But still the heart of Pha'raoh remained proud and unyielding, and he became more obstinate and wilful than ever in his rejection of God. His pride was not yet humbled, nor his cruel spirit conquered; he still refused to grant the request of Mo'ses and Aa'ron.

After the sixth plague had failed to move Pha'raoh to repentance, the Lord sent Mo'ses with another message for the king. This time Mo'ses reminded him that all these judgments had come from God, that they had followed in quick succession, and that the king had sealed his own doom by repeated failure to obey the clear command of God. During

these punishments there had
been many opportunities for the
king to repent, and to let the
children of Is'ra-el go, but he
had only hardened his heart the
more. The Lord was, therefore,
about to bring such great afflictions upon the people of E'gypt
that they would have no other
choice than to free the He'-
brews.

The seventh plague was announced to Pha'raoh as a destructive hailstorm covering the
whole land. So terrible was the
storm to be that it would bring
violent death to any animals
which had escaped the disease
of a previous plague, and to any
human beings who might be
caught in it. Under its terrific

THE PLAGUE OF HAIL

force all vegetation would be
destroyed, and the trees of both orchard and forest would be stripped of
their branches.

But in this threatened destruction a special offer of mercy was made
to any E-gyp'tians who had become convinced of the avenging power of
God. Mo'ses told Pha'raoh to send warning of the approaching hail
storm to all workmen in the fields, and to other servants whose duties
might expose them to the storm. This request was made so that all who
believed in God might take shelter in their homes.

On the day following this warning by Mo'ses, he and Aa'ron stretched
forth their hands toward the heavens in prayer. Then Mo'ses raised up
his staff, and from the heavens there poured down upon the land the
terrible wrath of an avenging God. The same heavens which had sent
a destroying flood upon the world in the time of No'ah, and had rained
fire upon the wicked cities of Sod'om and Go-mor'rah, now poured out
great streams of both upon the land of E'gypt. It was a terrific, awesome
sight, with hail and water and fire all pouring forth from the clouds above.

The E-gyp'tians were especially terrified by the sight, for in that country rain was almost unknown, and what few thunderstorms there were seldom did harm. Fire was regarded as a god, and was worshiped in many heathen ways. The plague was miraculous in every respect, and called the E-gyp'tians to repentance with the voice of God.

This plague was especially harmful to the wealth and commerce of the country. The gardens which yielded vast supplies of fruits and flowers, and upon which the E-gyp'tians bestowed such great care, were swept into ruin. Dates, grapes, and pomegranates; olives, figs, and various kinds of melons,—all the pride and support of the land—were completely destroyed. The barley crop, which was now ready for harvest, and the fine fields of flax, were smitten and ruined. E'gypt's commerce in grains and flax, which was the principal source of her wealth, was now wrecked, and her manufacture of fine linens was stopped.

As the floods of hail and fire and rain poured out upon the land, as thunder roared through the heavens and lightning flashed a trail of death through the country, Pha'raoh was stricken with terror. He sent for Mo'ses and Aa'ron, and said to them: "I have sinned this time: the Lord is righteous, and I and my people are wicked. Entreat the Lord, for it is enough, that there be no more mighty thunderings and hail; and I will let you go, and ye shall stay no longer." This was a noble confession and plea, if only it had been sincere. Had Pha'raoh spoken the truth in these words it would have meant that his pride, stubbornness, and contempt for God were all gone. The wicked king, however, was more concerned with removing the calamities which his sins had brought upon the land than he was with the welfare of his soul, and with the pardon of his sins.

SUGGESTIONS FOR STUDY

Biblical Index to Helpful References

The Lord's Use of Fire and Hail and Storms for Judgment. (Ps. 148:8; Job. 38: 22-23; Ps. 18:13.)

Egypt's Fame for Flax and Linens. (1 Ki. 10:28; Prov. 7:16; Ezek. 27:7.)

Questions

1. Did Pharaoh keep his promises to let Israel go? Why not?

2. Describe the plague which fell upon the animals of Egypt?

3. Did these plagues effect the Israelites in Goshen?

4. How did this fact affect Pharaoh?

5. What was the sixth plague, and what serious threat was involved?

6. What was used in bringing on this plague? How did this reflect on Egypt?

7. Tell of the plague of hail and fire and storms.

8. What exception was made to the Egyptians in this plague?

9. How did this plague inflict special punishment on the country?

STORY 39

DIVINE REASONS FOR THE PLAGUES OF EGYPT; THE LAND INFESTED WITH LOCUSTS, AND WITH A GREAT DARKNESS

EXODUS 10

The Lord knew that Pha'raoh was not speaking the truth when he promised to let the Is'ra-el-ites go, but He told Mo'ses to deal kindly with any acts which seemed to show repentance on the part of the king. He had already shown great mercy and forgiveness toward Pha'raoh, and did not let him pay the penalty for his evil ways until the last possible offer of mercy had been scorned.

The soul of man is so constituted that the continued rejection of the mercies of God leaves it less ready to yield to them. The abuse of Divine grace has a hardening effect upon man's moral nature. Pha'raoh had paid no attention to repeated offers of mercy, and had not learned wisdom from continued acts of Divine justice. But he was not yet wholly forsaken by God, and still further opportunities were given him to prove that his repentance was genuine.

Mo'ses and Aa'ron had called upon him before and after each plague, and had shown mercy toward him whenever it was asked. Under the influence of these repeated acts of grace the heart of the king must either melt into genuine repentance or harden into an even more obstinate state. To say that God hardened Pha'raoh's heart means only that the Lord continued to test the king until it was clear that he definitely preferred the ways of evil to those of good. The Lord did not force Pha'raoh to choose either course, He merely left him in freedom to follow the desires of his own heart

"Till, like a frozen mass, his heart was chilled,
Its upward movement stayed, and conscience stilled."

Mo'ses was generous and forbearing toward the wicked king in his confessions of guilt, in his acknowledgment of the righteousness of God, and in his request for pardon. Nevertheless, Mo'ses reminded the king that he had little confidence in the truth of his words, and fearlessly told him that his repentance was not real. He promised, however, to ask the Lord to put an end to the rain and hail and lightning. Mo'ses then went

MOSES DEPARTS FROM PHARAOH

outside the city, raised his hands toward heaven in a prayer to God, and the terrible storm ceased at once.

Once again Pha'raoh failed to keep his promise. He took back his permission for the Is'ra-el-ites to leave E'gypt, and turned against the Lord as wickedly as before.

Now that the seventh plague had failed to produce any real change in the attitude of Pha'raoh toward the requests of Mo'ses and Aa'ron, the Lord sent his servants to deliver a strong message to the king, and to announce that a much greater plague was coming.

In the message to be delivered to Pha'raoh this time, the Lord set forth His purpose in visiting the land of E'gypt with such terrible proof of His supreme power. He wished to make clear to the king and to all future generations that the power of God rules all the elements of nature. The rivers, the dust of the ground, the atmosphere, the thunder and lightning and hail, the waters of the earth, and the fire had all served His supreme power in the previous plagues.

The Lord God of heaven intended also to prove to Pha'raoh and all succeeding generations that He was able to overcome Sa'tan and all his agencies in the world. The magicians were the cunning instruments of the devil in E'gypt, but they had been completely thwarted by the plagues inflicted upon Pha'raoh and his people. God is able to deliver man from the power of Sa'tan, overcome his evil designs in the world, and destroy all wicked works.

A further purpose of God in these continued plagues was to show His power, over all false religions and heathen worship in this great nation. The E-gyp'tians believed that the Nile was the birthplace of gods, but from this river had come the plague of water turned into blood, and the frogs which had infested the land. To the E-gyp'tians the frog was a sacred object of worship, but now the ugly creatures had plagued the entire country. Many domestic animals had been worshiped by the E-gyp'tians, but now they had been suddenly destroyed by a great plague.

Having explained the purposes of God in sending the plagues, Mo'ses then told Pha'raoh that unless he released the Is'ra-el-ites at once the Lord would send a mighty army of locusts to devour every herb and plant left from the previous plagues. Some of the servants of the king were now fully convinced of the supreme power of God, and of the authority of His servants, Mo'ses and Aa'ron, so they advised the king to let the Is'ra-el-ites depart.

Pha'raoh then proposed to Mo'ses that the men of the He'brews go out into the wilderness to worship as requested, but that the women and children be left behind in E'gypt. Mo'ses fearlessly refused to accept this condition, and told Pha'raoh that unless he permitted the He'brews to leave the land with their wives and children and servants, and with all their flocks and herds, he must suffer again for disobedience to the known will of God.

Upon the refusal of Pha'raoh to grant this request, Mo'ses waved his hand over the land of E'gypt. The whole country was suddenly overrun with great hordes of locusts, which swept before them all the plants and trees which had escaped the plague of hail. The locusts had always been dreaded by the E-gyp'tians, and in this plague they came upon the land in countless numbers. The wheat and rye was just budding forth when the hail and rain swept over the land, and was, therefore, not destroyed. But in the plague of locusts these two important sources of food for the people were completely ruined, and the whole country became a barren, desolate plain.

Once again Pha'raoh was smitten with terror, and once again he pretended deep repentance. This time he called for Mo'ses and said to him: "I have sinned against the Lord your God, and against you. Forgive, I pray thee, my sin only this once; and entreat the Lord that he will take away from me this death." Again it was a desire to have the punishment removed, rather than sincere regret for his sins, which caused Pha'raoh to ask for mercy. He asked for pardon, but not for purity, and the one cannot be had from God without the other.

Mo'ses went out from the presence of Pha'raoh, and prayed unto the Lord. At once a mighty wind swept the locusts from the land, but Pha'-raoh hardened his heart once again, and refused to let the Is'ra-el-ites go. Then, without any further warning, the Lord sent upon E'gypt a season of intense darkness covering the whole land. It was so dark that the E-gyp'tians could not see one another, nor could they even leave their homes.

This plague struck at the very heart of E-gyp'tian idolatry, for they wor-shiped the sun under the name of Osiris. To have the chief of their gods fail them was a curse which filled the hearts of the E-gyp'tians with ter-

THE PLAGUE OF LOCUSTS

ror. We are not told what natural forces were used in performing this miracle, but we do know that there was light in the houses of the Is'ra-el-ites in the land of Go'shen. They did not have to sit in darkness, as did the E-gyp'tians, but were free to go and come as they chose.

How alarming and unbearable must have been those three days of dense and perpetual darkness! The tradition of the Jews that the devil and his angels were given a wider range and greater liberty for working mischief than usual during those three dreadful days is probably true. "God cast upon them the fierceness of his anger: Wrath, and indignation, and trouble; A band of angels of evil."

In spite of the stern judgments brought upon him, Pha'raoh would not give in to the Lord's will. He continued to defy the servants of God, and sought again to make a compromise that would enable him to keep the wealth brought to him by the enslaved He'brews. Calling for Mo'ses, he told him that all the Is'ra-el-ites might go into the wilderness to worship, provided that they did not go very far, and that they should leave all their herds and flocks in E'gypt. By keeping the property of the He'brews, who had not suffered any loss during the plagues, there would be a supply of food for the hungry E-gyp'tians, and the Isra-el-ites would finally have to return to their bondage.

But this selfish offer was rejected as promptly as all others made by Pha'raoh. The king became angry, and drove Mo'ses from his presence with the threat that if he ever saw his face again he would have him slain. Mo'ses then went among the people of God to prepare for their departure from E'gypt following the plague that was soon to come.

SUGGESTIONS FOR STUDY

Biblical Index to Helpful References

Other Examples of False Repentance. (1 Sam. 15:24-30; 1 Ki. 21:27-29; Matt. 27:3-5.)

Locusts Used for Terrible Judgments Against Sin. (Joel 1:1-4.)

(See Biblical Index on three preceding chapters.)

Questions

1. What natural result followed Pharaoh's false claims of repentance?

2. Did God continue to give him opportunities to let Israel go?

3. What special message did Moses deliver to Pharaoh before the next plague?

4. Tell of the plague of locusts.

5. Tell of the plague of darkness.

6. Why did this plague strike such a blow to the religion of Egypt?

7. What proposal was not made by Pharaoh?

8. Why was it rejected by Moses?

STORY 40

ISRAEL FREED BY THE FINAL PLAGUE UPON EGYPT

EXODUS 11, 12

After Pha'raoh had made his threat against the life of Mo'ses, the prophet of God lingered for a short time with the king in order to tell him what course the Lord would now follow. During these tragic moments in the presence of the great king, the Lord spoke secretly to Mo'ses. He said that this was to be the last meeting between Pha'raoh and Mo'ses, and that He would visit the land with a final plague which would force the cruel king to let the Is'ra-el-ites leave his country.

Mo'ses said to Pha'raoh: "The Lord's mercy has now reached its limit. For weeks and months He has been patient, showing mercy time after time. True, He has brought nine calamities of increasing severity upon the land, but has offered to show mercy whenever you obey His command and let Is'ra-el depart. While His patience with you has been exhausted, He still has further means of punishment. There shall be one more curse sent upon the land which shall bring you to your knees. About midnight, within a few days, the Lord will send the angel of death throughout the land of E'gypt, and the oldest child in every home shall suddenly die; there shall also be taken the oldest of all the cattle and sheep and other animals still left from previous plagues."

The last plague upon E'gypt was to be so terrible that not even the hard-hearted Pha'raoh could fail to be moved by it. Without being ill, the oldest child in every family and in every home was to be taken by death. The Pha'raohs of E'gypt had slain the male children of Is'rael during a long period of persecution, and now the Lord was to cause the death of the firstborn in every E-gyp'tian home. This fatal blow was to reach every family, the highest as well as the lowest. The royal prince who expected to take Pha'raoh's place upon the throne was doomed to sudden death, and the oldest child in the home of the lowest peasant was to suffer the same fate. From the palace to the dungeon, from the splendid home of the rich to the tent of the poorest of the land—through every family in E'gypt this plague was to travel; and at the stroke of midnight all through the land death would come to every firstborn child.

Mo'ses then went on to say to Pha'raoh, "But against the children of Is'ra-el shall not a dog move his tongue, against man or beast; that ye may know that the Lord doth put a difference between the E-gyp'tians and Is'ra-el." God's chosen people were to be sheltered by the protecting wings of the great God of heaven and of earth. The pestilence which was to walk through the darkness of the night should not come near them. While the oldest child of the wicked lay still in death, all the children of the good would be unharmed. At the time when the lamentations of the E-gyp'tians were rending the midnight air of the whole country, the hearts of the righteous would be filled with peace, hope, and joy.

But Pha'raoh remained stubborn and unrelenting, and Mo'ses left him to carry out the instructions of God in preparing all Is'ra-el for the great tragedy that was to befall the E-gyp'tians, and for the birth of an Is'ra-el-itish nation. The children of Is'ra-el had been spared from the nine previous calamities inflicted upon the people of E'gypt, but there were certain Divine instructions which they must carefully follow if they were to escape this final plague. Is'ra-el was facing an extremely important crisis, a supreme moment in the history of their formation as a free, united people, and great issues depended upon the promptness and wisdom with which they obeyed the Lord's command.

Mo'ses was given full directions by the Lord concerning the things to be done by the people in this crisis. Careful instructions were given for the preparations to be made for their departure, and the plan and conditions necessary for their deliverance from the death plague soon to sweep over the land were fully outlined.

During the course of the nine plagues sent upon E'gypt, and during the increased hardships which Pha'raoh forced upon the Is'ra-el-ites, a great many of the E-gyp'tians had lost sympathy with the king to a large extent, and some of them had begun to look with favor upon the Is'ra-el-ites. The special care which God had shown for Is'ra-el convinced many of the people that the He'brews were a chosen race, and Mo'ses had become a great religious hero in the eyes of many. The E-gyp'tians had also grown weary of their own sufferings brought on by the stubborn conduct of the king, and there was great indignation over his continued persecution of the people whom he hated to his own ruin.

Partly from sympathy for the oppressed He'brews, and partly in the hope of winning their favor and that of their God, the E-gyp'tians brought them many valuable presents. They brought them gold and silver and

THE SIGN ON THE DOOR

jewels, and all manner of other precious things. God's favor was now upon Is'ra-el in a most remarkable manner, while a stream of grace from heaven flowed through the land:

"It did through wild and rock-bound valleys run,
Like glittering dew drops in the morning sun."

Mo'ses and Aa'ron then went among the children of Is'ra-el in the land of Go'shen and told them what to do to escape the plague of death. Every householder was to take a lamb, less than one year old and without blemish; after keeping it in the house for four days they were to kill it, and then to sprinkle the blood upon the upper door posts. This was to be a sacrificial offering to God, and for this reason the lamb to be offered must not be lame or blind or sick, or imperfect in any way.

Just as the angel of death would strike every home in E'gypt at the same hour, so every family of Is'ra-el was to offer the sacrificial lamb at the same hour. The blood was to be sprinkled upon the door posts with a spray of hyssop (a lowly herb which grew in rocky places) as a sign of faith and humility. When the angel of death saw the blood upon the door posts of a home, he would pass over that house, thus sparing a family the life of its firstborn.

The Pass'o-ver lamb was to be eaten with unleavened bread and bitter herbs, tokens of the bitterness from which Is'ra-el was to be redeemed, and of the sincerity of their faith and obedience. In preparing for their departure from E'gypt their hearts must be pure and upright, in perfect harmony with the law of God.

In eating the flesh of the Pass'o-ver lamb the Is'ra-el-ites were to be fully dressed and ready for a hasty flight. They were required to wear clothing strong enough for hard work and travel in the wilderness, to wear stout shoes or sandals, and to hold in their hands the staff which they used for guiding their flocks and herds. All their belongings were to be packed and ready for quick removal, and the sheep and cattle were to be gathered so that they could be driven away at once on the journey out of E'gypt.

Mo'ses also instructed the elders of Is'ra-el to establish an annual feast to be observed by all future generations as a memorial of the wonderful deliverance from E'gypt. The feast was to be called "The Pass'o-ver," and we shall learn more about it other stories.

Mo'ses had not told Pha'raoh just when the last dreadful plague was to strike the land of E'gypt, but had merely said that it would come at midnight. Days had passed since his last warning to the wicked king, so before long Pha'raoh began to think that the terrible hour would not come. Soon all E'gypt began to feel safe; weeks went by, and still there was no sign from heaven.

Then, on the night of the 14th of the month called Ni'san, a sudden cry of anguish filled the land at midnight. The angel of death swept over the land, smiting every family of E'gypt. The words which Mo'ses had spoken to Pha'raoh had now all come true, for not a single home escaped.

> " 'Twas dark—that dreary witching hour of night,
> When restless spirits stole in mortal sight,
> And grim spectres stalked their dreary round."

The whole land rose up in one mighty shout for the deliverance of Is'ra-el at once, for the people feared still greater calamities if Pha'raoh still defied the Lord. So Pha'raoh sent for Mo'ses and Aa'ron, and in the darkness of this night of grief told them to take all the Is'ra-el-ites out of the land at once. With the Is'ra-el-ites went their wives and children, their flocks and herds and all other possessions, and Pha'raoh advised the E-gyp'tians to supply them with whatever they might need for the journey.

Under the direction of Mo'ses the Is'ra-el-ites had been thoroughly organized by families and by tribes. Six hundred thousand men capable of bearing arms marched out of the land, and with the old men, women, and children, the number reached to nearly three millions. The children of Is'ra-el carried with them enormous quantities of food and worldly goods, treasures of gold, silver, and jewels, and drove before them great flocks of sheep and herds of cattle.

At last the children of Is'ra-el were free from the land of bondage, released by order of the king after ten successive plagues had crushed his proud, hard-hearted spirit. From the seventy souls which had migrated to this land two hundred and fifteen years before, there had now sprung up a mighty host of nearly three millions. They were now strong in numbers, skilled in the arts and science of civilization, and increased in wisdom and experience to the point where they could safely begin their national history as the chosen people of God.

Although forty years of hardship took place before they finally settled in the land of Ca'naan, they were free at last from E'gypt, never to return. Long years of discipline and vital instruction from the Lord lay ahead before they would be fully prepared to set up all the national institutions of a great people, but they were on their way.

"Already she is on her august way,
And marching to her final goal."

SUGGESTIONS FOR STUDY

Biblical Index to Helpful References

The Feast of the Passover. (Exo. 23:15; Lev. 23:5-8; Josh. 5:10-11; Ezra 6:19-20.)

Rules for Observing the Passover. (Deut. 16:1-8.)

Christ Our Passover. (1 Cor. 5:7.)

Other Examples of Men Made Great by the Lord. (2 Sam. 7:9; Esth. 9:4.)

Pestilences Sent by the Lord as Judgments. (Lev. 26:25; Num. 14:12; 2 Sam. 24:13-15.)

Sacrificial Offerings "Without Blemish." (Lev. 22:19-21; Mal. 1:8, 14.)

Christ Our Passover "Without Blemish." (Heb. 9:14; 1 Pet. 1:19.)

The Lord's Judgment Against False Gods. (Num. 33:4; Isa. 19:1; Jer. 43:12.)

Deliverance for Those Who Have the "Mark of the Lord." (Ezek. 9:6; Rev. 9:4.)

The First-born of Egypt Smitten. (Ps. 135: 8; 136:10.)

Questions

1. What did Moses tell Pharaoh as to the last plague?

2. What did he say in respect to the deliverance of Israel?

3. How were the people of Egypt beginning to feel toward Pharaoh?

4. How did they feel toward the Israelites?

5. What special favors did they bestow upon the Israelites?

6. What provision were the Israelites required to make for deliverance from the death angel?

7. What kind of lamb were they to take? Why?

8. What annual festival was set up to celebrate this deliverance?

9. Explain the rules for its observance?

10. Following the death of the first-born in Egypt what did the people demand?

11. Were the people of Israel allowed to leave Egypt?

STORY 41

THE MIRACULOUS DIVIDING OF THE RED SEA FOR ISRAEL'S PASSAGE

EXODUS 13, 14

After leaving E'gypt, the great host of Is'ra-el-ites journeyed in an easterly direction to a place called Suc'coth, where they pitched their tents. Here the Lord directed Mo'ses to remind the people of the gratitude which they owed to the One who had so miraculously delivered them from bondage in E'gypt. Ceremonies and duties in keeping with their new freedom were now announced by the Divinely appointed leader.

The Is'ra-el-ites were told that the eldest child in every family should be dedicated to God in a special manner, and that ever afterwards the first child born to a newly married couple should be set apart to God. In this way God established in Is'ra-el a perpetual memorial of His saving of the firstborn of the Is'ra-el-ites on the night when the eldest child in every E-gyp'tian family was taken by death. That eventful night would be kept alive in the memory of the chosen people of God forever. This requirement also taught the Is'ra-el-ites that the best of their earthly possessions were to be consecrated to the service of God; in offering sacrifices to Him, the people were to give the very best of whatever they had. In making this dedication of the firstborn to the Lord, a sacrifice of a lamb was to be offered as a reminder to Is'ra-el of the way in which their eldest children had been spared from the angel of death in E'gypt.

Then Mo'ses repeated the orders which he had already given in E'gypt for the establishment of the Pass'o-ver as a ceremony to be kept for all time, and warned the Is'ra-el-ites not to overlook this duty after they were settled in the land of Ca'naan. It would be impossible for them to keep the Pass'o-ver during their prolonged journey through the wilderness, but it must be renewed in Ca'naan. The people were told to explain to their children the meaning of the Pass'o-ver Feast, and to do everything in their power to keep alive in the memory of future generations their wonderful deliverance from bondage in E'gypt. Among all the children of Is'ra-el the observance of the Pass'o-ver was to mark their national birthday.

Following a brief rest at the place called Suc'coth, the Is'ra-el-ites resumed their journey toward Ca'naan. The most direct route over which they might travel was a caravan road around the northern end of an arm of the Red Sea, where there is now the Suez Canal. By taking this route they could have reached the southwest border of Ca'naan within five or six days. This route, however, would have led them through the territory held at that time by the warlike Phi-lis'tines, and it would have been impossible for Mo'ses to engage in battle while the He'brew warriors were accompanied by their wives and children, and encumbered with vast herds of cattle and flocks of sheep and large quantities of goods. The Lord also wished them to spend a year in the wilderness, where Mo'ses would be given special instructions for setting up the laws and religious rites of the nation, and for proclaiming the Divine laws which they were to observe in the promised land.

For these reasons the Lord directed Mo'ses to take a rather difficult and hazardous route in a southwesterly direction through the uncharted wilderness. For some two or three days the Is'ra-el-ites moved along in an uncertain course. Fully organized into five great groups arranged according to families and tribes, but without any definite idea as to where they were going, they reached the shores of an arm of the Red Sea. They were in the midst of a broken, mountainous desert, facing the Sea at a point where it was several miles wide and much too deep to be forded. They did not know where they were going, but the Lord had guided them by a pillar of cloud by day and a pillar of fire by night.

While the Is'ra-el-ites were making the journey, things back in E'gypt had taken a sudden change against them. No sooner were these thousands of former slaves out of E'gypt than the wicked, greedy king began to think about what he had lost. He was very sorry that he had given permission for the He'brews to leave, and sent out spies to find them. It was soon reported that the Is'ra-el-ites were lost and entangled in the wilderness.

Determined to regain the slaves whose services had been so valuable to him, Pha'raoh organized a great force to pursue and capture them. He called for his own chariot, and for six hundred chariots of his army; with many squadrons of horsemen, and with thousands of his bravest soldiers to assist in the pursuit, Pha'raoh set out to capture the people whom God had delivered.

Soon the Is'ra-el-ites heard the rumblings of the chariot wheels as they

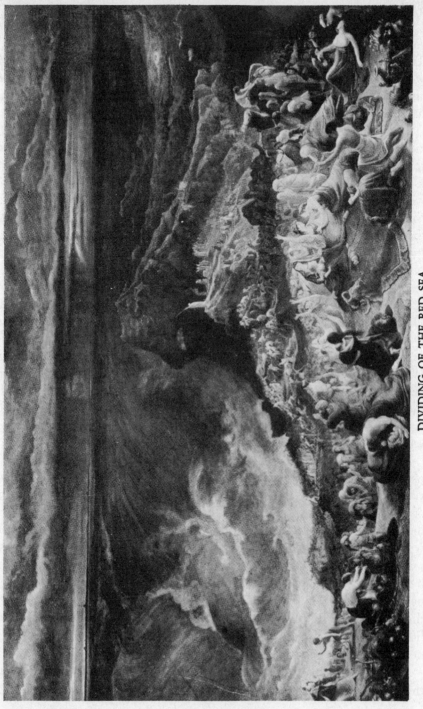

DIVIDING OF THE RED SEA

rolled through the wilderness, and the thundering of the horses' hoofs. They knew that the heart of Pha'raoh was filled with hatred, and that he would stop not even at murder to force them back into his service. They also knew that whether they returned to E'gypt or not, so many of them would be killed or wounded that their nation would be greatly weakened.

The situation of the great company of Is'ra-el-ites was desperate. On either side of them huge mountains, too steep to climb; in front of them rolled the great billows of the Red Sea, while close behind them the angry E-gyp'tian king urged on his mighty army. The Is'ra-el-ites were without weapons or military training; their enemies were too strong to meet in battle; they could not level the mountains or span the sea. Lost in despair they could only bemoan their fate and complain against Mo'ses for bringing them into this dreadful predicament. They cried, "Why hast thou brought us out here into the wilderness to die? We should have preferred to remain in bondage in E'gypt."

But God was on the side of the oppressed and distracted Is'ra-el-ites. He had led them into this perilous position, but He knew all the time how He would deliver them from it. Pha'raoh's greed and power must be so thoroughly shattered that he would never trouble them again. Is'ra-el must be taught once again that God is able to solve any problem, and that for a long time to come they would have to rely upon Him. In their fear and panic the Is'ra-el-ites forgot the past mercies of the Lord, and could see nothing but their foes; in their unbelief they saw graves where there were none, but God had not forsaken them.

Mo'ses prayed to the Lord in this emergency, and said to the children of Is'ra-el, "Calm your fears; be rid of your worries, for God shall deliver you." The Lord told him to lead the Is'ra-el-ites right down to the edge of the Red Sea, and then to say to them, "Go forward." As Mo'ses lifted his staff toward the great, surging waters a miracle took place. The waters were suddenly divided, leaving a dry, safe highway entirely across the sea, and forming high walls of water on either side. All night long the host of Is'ra-el walked in safety through the highway which the Lord had made in the sea, and their flocks and herds were not afraid to make the crossing. The pillar of fire which had guided the Is'ra-el-ites was lifted by the Lord and placed behind them, providing light for their journey, and bringing confusion to the enemies who pursued them.

Pha'raoh and his great army recklessly followed the Is'ra-el-ites into the great highway across the Red Sea. Here the heavy wheels of their chariots sank deep into the sand, and the E-gyp'tian forces were hindered in many other ways. As the dawn of a new day found the last of the Is'ra-el-ites climbing to safety on the other side of the sea, Mo'ses saw that the entire host of Pha'raoh was in the great lane which God had prepared for the escape of His chosen people. Mo'ses then lifted his staff toward the E-gyp'tians, and the mighty walls of water came rushing down upon them, drowning Pha'raoh and all his warriors.

During the confusion which fell upon the E-gyp'tians just before their destruction, some of them cried out, "Let us fly from the face of the Is'ra-el-ites! The Lord is fighting for them, and against us!" But their cry came too late. The hour was at hand for the Lord to complete the deliv-

THE EXODUS FROM EGYPT

erance of Is'ra-el by the destruction of her enemies. Safe and secure at last, all Is'ra-el gazed upon the terrible spectacle of destruction.

"She saw avenging wrath in heaven above—
A gathering tempest—clouds of blighting woe—
Teeming destruction on the vanquish'd foe."

Following the mighty deliverance of Is'ra-el and the miraculous destruction of her foes, Mo'ses composed a beautiful poem which all Is'ra-el sang in praise of God. It is truly a wonderful poem, rich in color and power, and filled with beauty in every line. Stroke follows stroke with breathless haste, and future events are foretold in the same glorious fashion as deeds which had already made history.

"I will sing unto Je-ho'vah, for He hath triumphed gloriously:
The horse and his rider hath He thrown into the sea.

Je-ho'vah is my strength and song,
And He is become my salvation:
He is my God, and I will praise Him:

Je-ho'vah is a man of war: Je-ho'vah is his name.

Pha'raoh's chariots and his host hath He cast into the sea;

And his chosen captains are sunk in the Red Sea.

The depths covered them,
They went down into the depths like a stone.

Thy right hand, O Je-ho'vah, is glorious in power,
Thy right hand, O Je-ho'vah, dasheth in pieces the enemy.

And in the greatness of thine excellency Thou overthrowest them that
    rise up against Thee:
Thou sendest forth thy wrath, it consumeth them as stubble.

And with the blast of thy nostrils the water were piled up,
The floods stood upright as a heap;
The deeps were congealed in the heart of the Sea.

The enemy said,
I will pursue, I will overtake, I will divide the spoil;
My desire shall be satisfied upon them;
I will draw my sword, my hand shall destroy them.

Thou didst blow with thy wind, the sea covered them:
They sank as lead in the mighty waters.

Who is like unto thee, O Je-ho'vah, among the gods?
Who is like Thee, glorious in holiness,
Fearful in praises, doing wonders?

Thou stretchest out they right hand,
The earth swallowed them.

Thou in Thy loving kindness hast led the people that Thou hast
    redeemed:
Thou hast guided them in Thy strength to Thy holy habitation.

The peoples have heard, they tremble:
Pangs have taken hold on the inhabitants of Phi-lis'ti-a.

Then were the chiefs of E'dom dismayed;
The mighty men of Mo'ab, trembling taketh hold upon them:
All the inhabitants of Ca'naan are melted away.

Terror and dread falleth upon them:
By the greatness of thine arm they are as still as stone;
Till thy people pass over that thou hast purchased.

Thou wilt bring them in, and plant them in the mountains of Thine
    inheritance,

The place, O Je-ho'vah, which Thou hast made for Thee to dwell in,

The Sanctuary, O Lord, which Thy hands have established,

Je-ho'vah shall reign forever and ever."

Truly, this song was put into the mouth of Mo'ses by the spirit of God. It was not only sung to the glory of God, but was composed and revealed unto Mo'ses by the Lord. Its grandeur and beauty surpass by far the greatest compositions of the mind of man. Its contents are descriptive, historical, and prophetic. The song speaks with equal beauty of Divine vengeance and grace, and of the deliverance of the righteous through the destruction of the wicked. It has lived through the centuries, will abide to the end of time upon earth, and will be among the most glorious hymns of heaven. The redeemed of the Lord shall sing together around the great white throne the "Song of Mo'ses and the Lamb."

> "Hark, how the adoring hosts above
> With songs surround the throne,
> Ten thousand thousand are their tongues,
> But all their hearts are one."

SUGGESTIONS FOR STUDY

Biblical Index to Helpful References

The Law Governing Consecration of First Born. (Lev. 27:26-28; Num. 3:13; 8:17.)

Rules for Observing the Passover. (Deut. 16:1-12.)

The Duty of Faithfully Teaching God's Laws. (Deut. 6:20; Josh. 4:6-7.)

The Removal of Joseph's Body from Egypt. (Gen. 50:25; Josh. 24:32.)

The Lord's Guidance of Israel by Pillar of Fire. (Neh. 9:12, 19; Ps. 78:14.)

Appearances of Desertion by God. (Ps. 71:11.)

God's Wonderful "Fear Not." (Isa. 41:10, 13, 14.)

The Lord's Fight for His People. Neh. 4:20; Isa. 31:4.)

God's Power Over the Sea. (Ps. 66:6.)

Questions

1. Where did the Israelites first stop after leaving Egypt?

2. What directions did Moses give in references to the first born child?

3. What was the most direct route for Israel to Canaan?

4. Why did they not take this route?

5. In what direction did they travel?

6. What distressing situation did they soon face?

7. How did the Israelites feel about their situation?

8. What did Moses first do? What did he mean by "stand still"?

9. What miracle was performed for Israel's passage beyond the Red Sea?

10. What happened to Pharaoh and his army?

11. Tell of the celebration of the Israelites after this deliverance?

STORY 42

TRIALS AND MURMURINGS IN THE WILDERNESS; THE BREAD FROM HEAVEN

EXODUS 15:23-37; 16

Following the great triumph over their enemies in the miraculous crossing of the Red Sea there was a season of rejoicing in the camp of Is'ra-el. Led by Mir'i-am, the sweet singer, all the children of Is'ra-el joined in singing the Song of Mo'ses. Then they journeyed in a southeasterly direction alông the rugged coast line of the sea. Still guided by the pillar of cloud by day and the pillar of fire by night, they turned into the interior of the A-ra'bi-an Peninsula, which was a great desert, toward the place where Mo'ses had seen the flaming bush that was not burned.

After travelling for three days they came to a place where there were springs of water, but they soon found that the water was too bitter to drink. Once again the Is'ra-el-ites forgot the mercies and power of God, and began to murmur against Mo'ses because of the bitterness of the water. Then the Lord directed Mo'ses to find a certain shrub and to throw it into the water. As soon as this was done the water became pure and good to drink, and Mo'ses assured the people that all would go well with them if they would only trust in the Lord and obey His commandments.

From Ma'rah, which was the name they gave to the place of bitter waters, the children of Is'ra-el journeyed to a place called E'lim. This was a beautiful valley about one mile long, with twelve fountains of water and seventy palm trees. Here they encamped for several months before resuming their journey. Although the waters were sweet and healthful, and there was an abundance of grass for their cattle, it was the duty of the He'brews to journey on toward their promised home in Ca'naan.

"E'lim! sweet foretaste of rest and blessing,
   Soon must be left for the lengthening way;
But it is well that Thy pilgrims should gather
   Courage and strength for the wearisome way."

As they travelled deeper into the desert of the A-ra'bi-an Peninsula they came into what was known as the wilderness of Sin, between E'lim and Mt. Si'nai. It was now two months since they had left E'gypt, and the small food supplies which they had been able to bring with them were nearly gone. The sheep and cattle which they had brought out of E'gypt had to be kept for making offerings to God, and for future increase in their new home. And so the three million people began to wonder where they were to secure food. Fear and panic spread among them, for their future in this vast wilderness seemed hopeless. They remembered that even during the bondage and hardships suffered in E'gypt they had never been forced to go hungry.

GATHERING THE MANNA

In their desperation the people murmured against Mo'ses and Aa'ron, the two noble servants of God who had just led them so miraculously out of slavery in E'gypt. The whole company of Is'ra-el, including the elders and the appointed leaders of the twelve tribes, joined in this complaint. In the face of the wonderful events of the past three months these murmurings of Is'ra-el were unreasonable, ungrateful, and actually wicked. The people complained about things which never happened, and even longed to return to their old life of bondage in E'gypt.

The Lord knew that these complaints against His servants were in reality complaints against Him, yet He looked with tender mercy upon the sad condition of the people. He therefore told Mo'ses of His purpose to supply Is'ra-el with meat in the evening and bread in the morning, declaring that He would send down like rain from heaven all the food which the Is'ra-el-ites needed. These promises of God were announced to the entire company of Is'ra-el by the elders and leaders of each tribe.

The people were called to worship, and in the evening as they looked toward the wilderness on the east the glory of the Lord shone in the clouds. As the sun sank in the horizon the Lord caused great flocks of quails to come up to their camp, so that the ground was covered with them. The quails were then used to supply the people with meat.

When the people arose on the next morning and looked out upon the wilderness around them, they saw that the ground everywhere was covered with small, round particles, white like frost, and sparkling in the dew like diamonds. Amazed at the strange sight, they cried aloud, "Manna! Manna!" which means, "What is it?"

Mo'ses explained to them that this was the bread which the Lord had promised to send like rain from heaven, and that they were to go out and gather just enough of it to last them for one day. This wonderful supply of food was to be given by the Lord on every morning except the Sab'bath, so on the sixth day of each week the people were to gather a double supply.

The people gathered the manna as directed by Mo'ses, and prepared it for their meals in various ways. It was a fine, nourishing food, with a taste like that of wafers and honey. Whenever one of them disobeyed the Lord's command and took more than he needed, it would spoil before it could be eaten. Those who failed to gather a double portion on the sixth day of the week found that there was no manna to be had on the Sab'bath; for their disobedience they had to go without food for one day.

Both the manner in which God supplied this food and the nature of the food itself were miraculous. The manna was not produced by any natural means, and it was wholly independent of climate, weather, or any other worldly condition. It was supplied in the same miraculous way during the entire forty years of Is'ra-el's sojourn in the wilderness, and fell upon them in the same manner at every encampment in various parts of the desert.

God sent the manna as a free gift of Divine grace, but the people had to use their own strength in gathering it, and their own skill in finding ways of preparing it. God fed them, but they had to work to satisfy their hunger. The manna had to be gathered quickly, for it was melted by the heat of the rising sun; if the people failed to gather enough, they went hungry; if they took more than their proper share, it spoiled. The gathering of the manna was a daily duty, and those who became indolent or careless were forced to do without food.

The laws of God had to be followed in gathering the manna. From the time of Creation the seventh day of the week had been a holy day, and man had been commanded to do no manual work on this day. For this reason no manna was provided on the Sab'bath, and those who searched for it were properly punished by going hungry. The double portion gathered on the sixth day did not spoil, as it would have done had it been gathered on any other day. The Lord still has a way of making worthless that for which men labor on the day which He has set aside for worship.

The failure of the Is'ra-el-ites to obey this order was a sign of their lack of reverence for the One who had so wonderfully helped them, and it showed a wicked nature which brought down upon itself a fitting punishment. Mo'ses ordered Aa'ron to keep a pot of the manna as a memorial of God's wonderful providence in feeding Is'ra-el during the long sojourn of forty years in the wilderness. Later this pot of manna was placed in the sacred Ark about which we shall learn in other stories. It was a valuable reminder to future generations of God's power to provide for His people in dire need.

SUGGESTIONS FOR STUDY

Biblical Index to Helpful References

Discouragement Resulting from Trials. (Num. 21:4; Neh. 4:10.)

The Sin of Murmuring. (Ps. 77:3; Prov. 19:3; Jno. 6:43; 1 Cor. 10:10.)

Death Desired in the Face of Trials. (Num. 11:15; 1 Ki. 19:4; Job 3:20, 21; 7:15.)

The Lord's Ears Open to Cries of His People. (Ps. 34:15; 94:9; Isa. 65:24; Jas. 5:4.)

Manna Given by God. (Num. 11:6-9; Deut. 8:3, 16; Neh. 9:20; Ps. 78:24.)

Sample of Manna Preserved in Ark of Covenant. (Heb. 9:4.)

Cessation of Manna. (Josh. 5:12.)

Jesus, the Manna for Spiritual Food. (John 6:31, 32; 49; Rev. 2:17.)

Sabbath Violation Denounced. (Ex. 31:14; Num. 15:32-36; Neh. 13:15.)

Questions

1. Why did Israel murmur at a place later called Marah?

2. How did Moses remove the cause of their complaints?

3. Where did Israel next stop? For what was this place noted?

4. What next caused Israel to murmur against Moses and Aaron?

5. In what way did God supply them with food?

6. How much manna were the Israelites allowed to gather each day?

7. What happened, if they gathered more than allowed?

8. How much were they directed to gather on the sixth day of the week? Why?

9. How long did God continue to supply manna from heaven?

10. Explain the New Testament fulfillment of the manna symbolic meaning?

STORY 43

WATER DRAWN FROM A ROCK; PRAYER BRINGS VICTORY IN BATTLE

EXODUS 17

After leaving their encampment in the wilderness of Sin, the Is'ra-el-ites journeyed in the direction of Mount Si'nai. They halted for a short time at places called Doph'kah and A'lush, and finally pitched their tents at a place called Reph'i-dim, which was near Mt. Ho'reb and Mt. Si'nai.

The region called Reph'i-dim was without water; although the Is'ra-el-ites were being supplied with food from heaven, they were suffering intensely with thirst. They began to murmur again; knowing that Mo'ses had been aided by the Lord many times before in serving them, they said to him, "Give us water that we may drink."

In reply to the prayer of Mo'ses, the Lord said to him, "Behold, I will stand before thee there upon the rock in Ho'reb; and thou shalt smite the rock, and there shall come water out of it, that the people may drink."

Facing the multitude of thirsty men and women, whose little children were crying for water, and whose sheep and cattle were panting with thirst, Mo'ses asked them to gather before the rock called Ho'reb. He struck the rock as the Lord had commanded, and suddenly there burst forth from the mountain of stone a stream of fresh water which ran like a river through the encampment of the Is'ra-el-ites. Both people and cattle had water in abundance, and the stream continued to flow as long as they remained in the valley.

Living in A-ra'bi-a at that time was a large and fierce tribe of wanderers known as the Am'a-lek-ites. They were descendants of E'sau, about whom we learned in a previous story.

When the Am'a-lek-ites learned that the descendants of Ja'cob who were now called the Is'ra-el-ites had encamped in the wilderness near Mount Si'nai, they made a crafty attack upon the weakest point in the defenses of their ancient enemy.

Mo'ses chose from all the Is'ra-el-ites a noble and courageous young man named Josh'u-a as the military leader for this battle. He also called out the men who were most likely to be good soldiers, and sent them into battle against the invading enemies. While the battle was raging, Mo'ses stationed himself on a high mountain in order to watch the movements of his army, and at the same time to lift his heart in prayer to the Lord. On either side of him stood his loyal assistants: Aa'ron, his brother and trusted adviser in many previous trying hours, and Hur, the good friend who was the husband of his sister Mir'i-am.

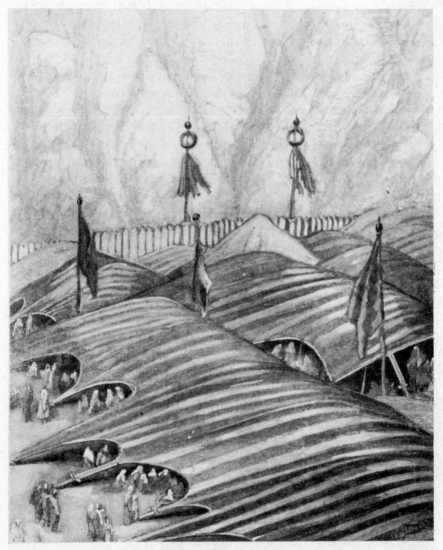

THE CAMP AT SINAI

As the conflict grew more fierce, Mo'ses lifted his hands toward heaven in prayer. This attitude could no doubt be seen by Josh'u-a, and would give the young general new courage in the face of apparent defeat. At last Mo'ses became too weary to hold up his hands, and he sank down exhausted upon a stone. Then Aa'ron and Hur came to his aid, helped him to rise again, and held up his hands as he prayed.

Through the prayers of Mo'ses the armies of Is'ra-el were given new strength, and Josh'u-a was able to lead them in victory over the Am'a-lek-ites. The intercession of the man of God had stretched its hands out to heaven, and the dark portentous clouds of destruction had been quickly scattered; for human hands linked to Divinity become as strong as God. "More things are wrought by prayer than this world dreams of."

The children of Is'ra-el were taught many important lessons by this first experience of war after leaving E'gypt. They learned to trust in the Lord when they were attacked by enemies, and to put their hopes before the Lord in earnest prayer. When the prayer of Mo'ses was interrupted, the enemy gained the advantage; when his prayer was renewed, the Is'ra-el-ites won the battle.

After the great victory over the Am'a-lek-ites special thanks were offered to God, with sacrifices which represented the gratitude of all the people of Is'ra-el. Mo'ses was instructed to make a permanent record of the event for the encouragement of future generations who might be attacked by savage enemies.

SUGGESTIONS FOR STUDY

Biblical Index to Helpful References

Sufferings Caused by Unbelief. (2 Ki. 7:2; Ps. 78:17-19; Matt. 13:58.)

The Lord's Power to Turn Rock into Water. (Num. 20:11; Jgs. 15:19; Ps. 114:8.)

Faith Testings. (Gen. 22:2; Josh. 6:3; Jgs. 7:7; Matt. 9:28-30.)

Added Power in Prayer When Supported by One or More. (Matt. 18:19.)

Strength in Weakness. (1 Cor. 1:27; 2 Cor. 12:9.)

Memorials to Special Favors. (Josh. 4:7; 24:27.)

Questions

1. For what reason did the Israelites complain at Rephidim?

2. What miracle did Moses perform for the supply of water?

3. Where was Rephidim and why notable at the time?

4. How long did Israel encamp in this vicinity?

5. Did the water supply continue?

6. What war-like tribe attacked the Israelites while encamped here?

7. Who was chosen lead in the battle against them?

8. What was the outcome of the battle?

9. How did the Israelites celebrate this victory?

STORY 44

GOD SPEAKS FROM A FIERY MOUNTAIN; THE TEN COMMANDMENTS

EXODUS 19, 20

Soon after Je'thro's visit the children of Is'-ra-el traveled a short distance to the level plain which faced Mount Si'nai. It was on this plain that Mo'ses had received his final call to return to E'gypt to deliver Is'ra-el. It was now three months since the Is'ra-el-ites had left E'gypt. They encamped before the great mountain for a whole year, and some of the greatest messages from God in the history of Is'ra-el were given to Mo'ses during this period. The moral code for the government of the nation was spoken and written by the Lord, rules for the domestic, social, and religious life of the people were revealed to Mo'ses, and full instructions were given for the elaborate system of worship and priestly sacrifices. The Tabernacle was erected, its furnishings provided, a portable altar was built, and many other important customs were founded.

The Mosaic Law was given from the high granite mountain called Si'nai. The mountain consists of three lofty peaks: the one on the northeast being called Ho'reb, the southwestern peak called Mount St. Cath'-er-ine, and the highest of all being known as Mt. Si'nai.

When the Is'ra-el-ites encamped before this mountain the Lord spoke secretly to Mo'ses, calling to mind the miraculous deliverance of Is'ra-el from E'gypt, and giving a new promise of love and grace if the people would only obey His voice and live according to His laws. The Lord said, "Is'ra-el shall be a peculiar treasure unto me above all people; for all the earth is mine." The children of Is'ra-el were to be fenced in, preserved in their own manner of living, and kept apart from others until the Mes-si'-ah reigned. Truly they might have sung!

"We are a garden walled around,
Chosen and made peculiar ground;
A little spot enclosed by grace
Out of the world's wide wilderness."

Mo'ses called together the elders of Is'ra-el, and they in turn summoned all the people to hear the special message which God proclaimed to them.

MOSES COMES DOWN FROM THE MOUNTAIN

The people replied, "All that the Lord hath spoken we will do." Then Mo'ses informed the Lord of the hearty response of the people. But the great laws which God was now ready to give the Is'ra-el-ites were so important that He would not reveal them through any human being, not even through the mouth of one so good and loyal as Mo'ses.

The Lord therefore told Mo'ses to have the people gather in a great assembly before Mount Si'nai, saying that He would appear in the midst of the mountain in fire and smoke. It was also promised that the Lord would declare His divine laws so clearly that all the people might hear them with their own ears, and see with their own eyes the majesty and power of their God.

Special preparations were required of the people before this great revelation of God could be given. They were told to wash their bodies and
their clothing, to separate their hearts from all sin, to dedicate themselves
to God with renewed consecration, and to stand before the mountain in
a humble, reverent attitude. They were also warned not to risk death
by coming too near the mountain.

On the third day after these orders had been given, and when all the
people stood in readiness, there came a great rumbling in the midst of
the mountain, like the sounding of many trumpets. The whole face of
the mountain suddenly became a cloud of fire and smoke, and lightning
flashed from it with a great crash of thunder while the entire mountain
trembled. Then a mighty voice spoke from the midst of the cloud of fire.

From the top of Mount Si'nai the Lord told Mo'ses, in the hearing of
all the people, to come up to the top of the mountain. Through the
blazing fire and smoke which covered the high mountain of God, Mo'ses
bravely climbed until he was in the presence of God. He was then told
to return to the people, and to warn the priests and all the people that
no one must come near the mountain while it was aflame with the presence of God, and while He was uttering the words of His divine laws.

Mo'ses returned from the top of Mount Si'nai while the people stood
lost in wonder and awe on the plain below. They were cautioned that
God was about to speak, and that under the penalty of immediate death
they must not touch the foot of the mountain, or go beyond the bounds
already set forth.

Then there resounded from the top of the mountain words which all
could hear and understand. The Lord said:

"I am the Lord thy God, which have brought thee out of the land of
E'gypt, and out of the house of bondage." There followed this solemn
announcement the giving of that code of spiritual and moral laws which
we know today as "THE TEN COMMANDMENTS." These laws were
spoken by the voice of God from the top of Mount Si'nai. Three million
Is'ra-el-ites heard them word for word, just as we have them today, except
that they were spoken in the language of the He'brews. The translation
given in the Bible is absolutely true to the meaning of the original words
spoken by God himself.

The Ten Commandments spoken on this momentous occasion, and in
the most remarkable manner of any communications ever given to man
by God, stand out above all other revelations of the Old Testament scrip-

tures. They mark the only direct utterance ever made by God to man since the Fall in the Garden of E'den. They are as follows:

I. Thou shalt have no other gods before me.

II. Thou shalt not make unto thee any graven image, or any likeness of anything that is in heaven above, or that is in the earth beneath, or that is in the water under the earth: Thou shalt not bow down thyself to them, nor serve them: for I the Lord thy God am a jealous God, visiting the iniquity of the fathers upon the children unto the third and fourth generation of them that hate me; and showing mercy unto thousands of them that love me, and keep my commandments.

III. Thou shalt not take the name of the Lord thy God in vain; for the Lord will not hold him guiltless that taketh his name in vain.

IV. Remember the Sabbath Day, to keep it holy. Six days shalt thou labor, and do all thy work: But the seventh day is the Sabbath of the Lord thy God: in it thou shalt not do any work, thou, nor thy son, nor thy daughter, thy man servant, nor thy maid servant, nor thy cattle, nor thy stranger that is within thy gates: For in six days the Lord made heaven and earth, the sea, and all that in them is, and rested the seventh day: wherefore the Lord blessed the Sabbath Day, and hallowed it.

V. Honor thy father and thy mother: that thy days may be long upon the land which the Lord thy God giveth thee.

VI. Thou shalt not kill.

VII. Thou shalt not commit adultery.

VIII. Thou shalt not steal.

IX. Thou shalt not bear false witness against thy neighbor.

X. Thou shalt not covet thy neighbor's house, thou shalt not covet thy neighbor's wife, nor his man servant, nor his maid servant, nor his ox, nor his ass, nor any thing that is thy neighbor's.

These Ten Commandments were later inscribed on two stone tablets, the first four on one tablet, and the remaining six on the other. The first group concerns our duties to God; the second our duties to others. They may be easily remembered by the use of a key-word for each, as follows:

Duties to God, respecting: 1. God's Being. 2. God's Worship. 3. God's Name. 4. God's Day.

Duties to others, respecting: 5. Parents. 6. Human Life. 7. Moral Purity. 8. Property Rights. 9. Truthfulness. 10. Covetousness.

They are all comprehended in the Two Great Commandments: Love God with all the Heart; Love thy neighbor as thyself.

The people listened carefully to the announcement of these commandments, kept a reverent and prayerful attitude, and greatly appreciated the direct message from God, but were all nearly overcome with fright and terror. For this reason they said to Mo'ses, "Speak thou with us, and we will hear: but let not God speak with us, lest we die." They asked that he talk with God for them, and that whatever God had to say to them should be said through Mo'ses.

Inspired by the Lord, Mo'ses then told the Is'ra-el-ites that they were to fear God with the awe of true religion, but that they should not be frightened by His presence in any miraculous appearance, nor by His voice when the commandments were given.

Special attention was called to the Lord's command against worshiping idols, and the Is'ra-el-ites were warned again not to make unto themselves gods of silver and of gold. Directions were also given for the offering of burnt sacrifices, and for other forms of worship.

SUGGESTIONS FOR STUDY

Biblical Index to Helpful References

The Mount of God in Smoke. (Ps. 68:8; 144:5-6.)

The Majesty of God. (1 Chr. 29:11; Job 37:22; Ps. 29:4; 93:1-5.)

The Intimacy of Moses with God. (Ex. 24:2; 25:22; 31:18; 33:9.)

Required Preparations for Hearing God. (Lev. 20:26; Ps. 24:3-5; 2 Tim. 2:21.)

Peril in Refusing to Hear God. (Eccl. 5:1; Heb. 12:25; 2 Pet. 3:17.)

Happiness Secured by Keeping the Commandments. (Prov. 3:13-27; 1 Tim. 4:8; 6:6.)

The Commandments to Be Faithfully Taught. (Deut. 5:17-21; 6:3-25; Josh. 8:32.)

Man's Need of a Mediator. (Num. 16:48; Deut. 5:5, 27; 9:18-26.)

Questions

1. From what place were God's commandments spoken by God himself?

2. How was his majesty manifested at the time?

3. What were the children of Israel commanded to do in preparation for this great event?

4. Before speaking to the people what did God ask Moses to do?

5. Repeat the Ten Commandments given by God.

6. What particular command did Moses urge on the people?

MOSES IN THE MOUNT WITH GOD; THE TEN COMMANDMENTS WRITTEN ON TABLETS OF STONE; AARON MAKES A GOLDEN CALF

EXODUS 24:12-18, 31,
32, 34   The Ten Commandments which form the
principles upon which the Mosaic laws were based were first spoken by
the Lord to all Is'ra-el, and then were written by God himself on two
tablets of stone. In this form they were kept by the Is'ra-el-ites for many
centuries.

God said to Mo'ses, "Come up to me in the mount, and be there: and
I will give thee tablets of stone, and a law, and commandments which
I have written; that thou mayest teach them."

Mo'ses then told the children of Is'ra-el that he was going up to the
top of Mount Si'nai, where God would .talk with him at length, and
would give him the laws by which they were to be governed. He also
told the people that they were to remain obedient to God under the care
of Aa'ron and Hur, who were to take his place while he was absent from
them. Mo'ses took with him his servant Josh'u-a, who remained on the
side of the mountain while Mo'ses went to the top for communion with
God.

The top of Mount Si'nai was still covered with the fiery cloud and with
billows of smoke, showing the presence and glory of God. Mo'ses entered
the cloud, and held intimate converse with God for forty days and nights.
He walked among the flames and smoke without being harmed, and went
without food for forty days and nights without loosing strength. He was
in deep communion with God, listening carefully to the instructions
which the Lord gave him, and probably putting into written form the
laws which he afterwards read to the people of Is'ra-el. It was a prolonged season of prayer and meditation, and of holy communion with
the Lord God. For the entire period of forty days his intimate converse
with God was free from interruption. There was nothing to disturb or
distract him from the great experience of talking with God.

During this long period of converse with God, Mo'ses was given the two tablets of stone on which it is said that the Ten Commandments had been written by the finger of God. These tablets were to be taken back to Is'ra-el and kept for the instruction of future generations.

But forty days and nights was a long time for Is'ra-el to wait for the return of their great leader. They no doubt thought that God had taken him as He had E'noch many centuries before, and that he would never return to them. They had looked upon him as one who spoke with the authority of God, so now that no one else seemed capable of taking his place they felt that they must have some symbol of God's presence with them.

The Is'ra-el-ites did not intend to forsake the God who had brought them out of the land of E'gypt, who had provided for them so graciously thus far in their journey, and who had recently spoken to them from Mount Si'nai, but they did want some visible object to remind them of the presence of the Lord.

They went to Aa'ron and said, "Make us a god that we may worship,

MOSES HALTS THE PEOPLE

and that will go up before us." Aa'ron thought it best to do what the people asked. He did not have the courage to deny the request of the Is'ra-el-ites for a god like those which they had seen in E'gypt, and so he took the first step in a course which led the people into a disgraceful state of idol-worship. It was his intention to hold them to their faith and loyalty to the true God, but he did not realize that they would soon worship the idol itself, instead of the God which it was supposed to represent.

Aa'ron said to the people, "Break off the gold from your ear rings and bring this to me, and other jewels of gold." Then he took the gold furnished by the Is'ra-el-ites, melted it in the fire, and carved for them a golden calf which resembled some of the idols worshiped by the E-gyp'-tians. One of the chief gods of the E-gyp'tians was a sacred bull, and the people often used little golden images of a bull in their heathen worship.

In the hope of preventing the people from turning away from the true God during their worship around the golden calf, Aa'ron built an altar near the idol, and proclaimed a day of special worship unto the Lord. But once the first step toward idolatry had been taken, the people could not be controlled. Memories of the riotous worship they had seen in E'gypt filled them with sinful thoughts, and they began to dance around the golden calf shouting, "These are thy gods, O Is'ra-el, that brought thee out of the land of E'gypt."

Both Is'ra-el and Aa'ron were guilty of sins against the Lord. Already they had broken the first of the commandments spoken by the Lord just a short time before from the fiery top of Mount Si'nai. The golden idol had for the moment taken the place of God in the hearts of His chosen people, and the forbidden worship had led them on to other shameful sins.

When Mo'ses came down from Mount Si'nai with the two tablets of stone upon which God had written the Ten Commandments, and saw the Is'ra-el-ites bowing down before an idol, his anger was so great that he hurled the tablets to the ground and broke them. Aa'ron tried to excuse himself for what had happened, but was severely blamed and rebuked by Mo'ses. His excuses were weak and false, and did not deceive the man of God. He said that the people had forced him to make the image, that he had cast the gold into the fire and the calf had come out, so that the blame for all this mischief rested upon the Is'ra-el-ites. But Mo'ses said, "Thou hast brought this great sin upon Is'ra-el."

The people were also sternly rebuked for the sins which they had committed, and a severe punishment was inflicted upon them. God had seen the idolatry of Is'ra-el, and had heard their cries of worship for the golden calf. He, therefore, told Mo'ses that He intended to destroy the entire nation, and to make of Mo'ses' descendants the chosen nation for which Is'ra-el had been intended. But Mo'ses set the welfare of the nation above the glory of his own family, and pleaded with God to spare the Is'ra-el-ites. God was moved by this prayer, and agreed to pardon Is'ra-el after suitable punishment.

ON MT. SINAI

Mo'ses took the golden calf, burned it in the fire, ground it into a fine powder, and sprinkled the powder upon water. The Is'ra-el-ites were then forced to drink the water filled with golden particles: token of the bitterness of their sin.

Then Mo'ses entered the camps of Is'ra-el and gave this solemn command: "Who is on the Lord's side, and not on the side of this idol? Let him come and stand by my side." One whole tribe, the descendants of Le'vi, came forward at once. Mo'ses said to them, "Take your swords, go through the camp, and slay every man his brother, and companion, and neighbor." As a result of this order about three thousand of the wicked Is'ra-el-ites were slain.

After this terrible punishment had been inflicted, Mo'ses ordered a special sacrifice for those who had repented from their sins, and then he made one of the most wonderful prayers ever offered by man. He offered to take the place of Is'ra-el, and to suffer the punishment which his people deserved. God heard this prayer with favor, and granted forgiveness. The people were called to renewed consecration to God, and continued their journey under His blessings.

God then directed Mo'ses to prepare two tablets of stone similar to those which he had broken in his anger against Is'ra-el, and to come up into the mountain again to receive another copy of the Ten Commandments. Mo'ses obeyed the order, and went alone to the top of the mountain to commune with God. The Ten Commandments were written by the Lord on the two tablets of stone prepared by Mo'ses, and other important laws were revealed.

Mo'ses remained on Mount Si'nai for another forty days and nights, and once again was kept in good health by the Lord during a fast which lasted for the same period. God's promise of continued blessings upon Is'ra-el was made even more clear than it had been during the previous season of converse. More elaborate and advanced rules for the government of Is'ra-el were given which Mo'ses put into permanent written form.

When Mo'ses returned to the camp of Is'ra-el with the two tablets of stone upon which God had written the Ten Commandments, his face was so radiant with the glory of God that the people were afraid of him. For this reason he had to cover his face with a veil when the elders of Is'ra-el came to him to hear the message which he brought from God. Before long this glory passed away, and Mo'ses was no longer hindered in his dealings with Is'ra-el.

SUGGESTIONS FOR STUDY
Biblical Index to Helpful References

Manifestations of God's Glory. (Ex. 40:34; 1 Ki. 8:11; Ps. 8:1; 2 Cor. 3:18.)

Noted "Forty-Day Periods." (Gen. 7:12; 8:6; 50:3; Num. 13:25; Deut. 9:25; 1 Ki. 19:8; Luke 4:2.)

Tables of the Law Preserved. (Deut. 10:5; 1 Ki. 8:9; Heb. 9:4.)

The Sin of Instability. (Ps. 106:13; 2 Ki. 17:33; 1 Chron. 12:33; Heb. 13:9.)

The Sin of Conniving with Error. (Ps. 50:18; Prov. 17:15; 24:24.)

The Golden Calf a Warning Against Idolatry. (Deut. 9:16; Neh. 9:18; Ps. 106:19; Acts 7:41.)

The Evil of Excessive Revelry. (Jgs. 9:27; 16:25; 1 Sam. 25:36; 1 Pet. 4:3.)

Questions

1. After orally giving the Ten Commandments what command did God give Moses?

2. What condition still existed on top of Sinai?

3. How long did Moses remain in the Mount with God?

4. How was he engaged during that long period?

5. What did the Israelites think when he remained away so long?

6. What did they ask Aaron to do for them?

7. What kind of an image did he make?

8. In his efforts to prevent idolatry what else did Aaron make?

9. Was this effort successful?

10. Besides worshipping the golden calf, what other wrongs did the Israelites engage in?

11. How did Moses feel when he returned from the mountain and saw the idol?

12. What challenge did he make to the people?

13. Which tribe responded unanimously?

14. How were the unrepentant punished?

STORY 46

THE BUILDING OF THE FIRST
HOUSE OF WORSHIP

EXODUS 25-27; 30-31;
35-38; 40

Among all the provisions which God made for the safety and welfare of Is'ra-el in the wilderness, He was careful to include full instructions regarding Divine worship. The first of His commandments was that they should worship God, and Him alone; the second commandment forbade the making of graven images of any kind for worship, or the setting up of any god whatsoever.

The first great sin committed by the Is'ra-el-ites after the Lord had given Moses the Ten Commandments was the breaking of the first two commandments. Evidently the Is'ra-el-ites needed more instruction, so when Mo'ses was called to the top of Mount Si'nai for the second forty-day season with God he was told to build a house of worship for Is'ra-el. Complete details were given by the Lord concerning the size and shape of the building, the materials to be used, the furnishings to be placed within it, the outer court to be provided, and the altar to be placed before the entrance.

Thus the command to worship God, the set time for worship, the type of building to be erected for worship, and the forms of services to be rendered, all came directly from the Lord.

The plans which God gave to Mo'ses for building a house of worship were intended to remove the temptation to bow down before idols. The Lord would provide for them a building which would remind them of His presence in Is'ra-el, and which at the same time would lead them away from the worship of graven images. He had taught them that the true God is a spirit, that He cannot be seen by the eyes of men, and that no graven image can give a true picture of the Divine. These truths would be kept before the people at all times in the building and furnishing of a house of worship.

The Is'ra-el-ites were living in tents at the time when the house of worship was built, and they were constantly moving from place to place. It was, therefore, necessary for the house of worship to be made somewhat like a tent, so that it could easily be taken down and carried as often as the Is'ra-el-ites moved to another encampment. For this reason the building was called a tabernacle. It was to be the best tent in all the camp of Is'ra-el, made of the finest materials, furnished with the most costly equipment, and made as beautiful as possible. It must also be planned to meet the purposes of worship in the most adequate and complete manner.

The Lord directed that the tabernacle be placed in the very center of the camp of the Is'ra-el-ites. The various tribes of Is'ra-el were to be arranged in an orderly manner, with their tents going back from the four sides of the court around the tabernacle, and forming a great square with the house of God exactly in the middle.

The open court in which the tabernacle occupied the central spot was one hundred and fifty feet long and seventy-five feet wide. It was enclosed with curtains of fine linen, in brilliant colors, hanging upon posts of brass or copper. These posts were held in place by cords fastened to tent pins driven into the earth, and the height of the enclosure was between seven and eight feet. This court was always placed with its ends facing east and west, and its sides north and south, with an entrance in the center of the east side. Midway between the two sides, and about midway between the eastern entrance of the court and the east gate to the tabernacle, there stood a special altar for burnt sacrifices.

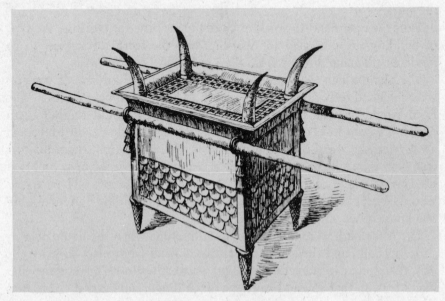

THE PORTABLE ALTAR

The tabernacle itself was a half-tent, half-wooden structure, about forty-five feet long, fifteen feet wide, and fifteen feet high. It was divided into two rooms by a veil which hung down from the roof. The larger room was at the east end, and was thirty feet long, while the other room was fifteen feet long.

The walls of the tabernacle were made of specially prepared boards which stood upright on silver bases, and were completely covered on each side with gold. The east end had no wall of boards, but could be closed by a curtain. The roof was made of four layers of curtains, the inner one forming a beautiful ceiling. The three other curtains were made of ram skins to keep out the rain and the sunshine.

The larger room of the tabernacle was called the Holy Place. On the right, as one came in from the opening at the east end, there was a table overlaid with gold, and upon the table were twelve loaves of bread. Each loaf of bread was placed there by one of the twelve tribes of Is'ra-el as a sign of complete consecration to the Lord. On the left stood the golden lampstand with seven branches, and on each branch there was a brilliant light. At the west end of the Holy Place, near the veil which separated this room from the smaller one, was the small golden altar of incense. Here offerings of incense were burned as a symbol of love to the Lord.

The smaller room on the west end of the tabernacle was called the Holy of Holies. It was within this room that the presence of God was shown in a brilliant halo called the She-ki'nah. The room was furnished with nothing but a wooden chest overlaid with plates of gold and lined with gold, and called the Ark of the Covenant. The lid to this chest was made of solid gold, and had on it two golden ornaments called cherubim. The two stone tablets on which God had written the Ten Command-ments were kept in the chest, and later there was added a pot of manna and Aa'ron's wonderful rod which budded. Only the High Priest was allowed to enter this room, and even he could come in only once a year.

The cost of the materials used in making and furnishing the tabernacle was met by voluntary gifts from the Is'ra-el-ites. As soon as Mo'ses called the people together and told them what a wonderful building the taber-nacle would be, there was a quick, whole-hearted response from all the people. The elders of Is'ra-el informed the people what was needed to carry out the plans which God had revealed to Mo'ses, and they gladly brought in their gifts.

There was no need to urge the Is'ra-el-ites to do their duty in providing

THE ARK OF THE COVENANT

the materials that were to be used in making the tabernacle. God had graciously forgiven them for their idoltary, and now wished them to build for Him a house in which there would be a constant reminder of His presence. Such a sacred cause was reason enough to the Is′ra-el-ites for making generous gifts.

The gifts of the people differed according to their means and skill. Some gave gold and silver, some gave badger skins, while the women spun fine linens, and made beautifully decorated curtains. The rich did not try to excuse themselves by mentioning other demands upon their wealth, nor did the poor refuse to help because they had only a little to give.

In many instances there was voluntary labor in the work of construction. Both men and women used their strength and skill in preparing the materials, or in the actual work of building the tabernacle. Gifts of love, and services of love filled the hearts of Is′ra-el; truly could they sing:

"But what or who are we, alas!
That we in giving are so free?
Thine own before our offering was,
And all we have, we have from thee."

The total cost of the tabernacle would be about two million dollars. The value of the gold and silver and brass, or copper, exceeded one million dollars. The finest, most expensive workmanship was used in making boards for the walls, and in preparation of the fine linens and curtains. The altar and the interior furnishings were made from the very best materials by workmen of the greatest skill.

One might ask how the He′brews could afford such enormous expenditures for the house of God, and from what source did they secure such quantities of precious metals. The answer lies in the fact that when these three million people left E'gypt they took with them great quantities of gold, silver, and other valuables in the form of ornaments and jewelry. They also brought quantities of flax for spinning fine linen, and the women were skilled in making the finest quality of linens and curtains. The fine woods which they used could be obtained from various parts of the A-ra'bi-an Peninsula, and skins could easily be had from their own flocks of sheep and herds of cattle. The fact remains, however, that the giving of all these valuable articles and services speaks well for the liberality and willingness to serve of the ancient Is'ra-el-ites.

One might also ask why so much gold and other precious metals was used. First, to impress upon Is'ra-el the majesty and glory of the true God, whose presence among them was represented by the tabernacle. They needed to learn at the very beginning of their national life that the best must be given to God, that the place built for His worship must be superior in every respect to their own homes, and that true love to the Lord is best shown by unselfishness and generosity. The Lord also wished to prevent them from having any occasion for pride, envy, or jealousy over their treasures. By giving the best that they had to the Lord's service, the people had no reason to be jealous of one another's possessions.

SUGGESTIONS FOR STUDY

Biblical Index to Helpful References

Sacredness of the Tabernacle. (Lev. 8:10; 16:16; Num. 1:51.)

Israel Required to Make Free-will Offerings for Support of Tabernacle. (Num. 15:3; Deut. 12:6; 2 Chr. 31:14.)

The Tabernacle Set Up at Shiloh in Canaan. (Josh. 18:1.)

Tabernacle Located at Gibeon. (1 Chr. 21:29.)

Tabernacle Removed to Jerusalem. (2 Chr. 1:3, 4.)

Tabernacle Superseded by Temple at Jerusalem. (1 Ki. 8:4; 2 Chr. 5:5.)

A New Tabernacle with Christ as High Priest. (Heb. 9:11.)

Questions

1. What two commandments did the Israelites break in making the golden calf?

2. What did God then propose so they would have a visible sign of His presence?

3. Why was the tabernacle to be a movable tent?

4. Who supplied Moses with the specifications for the tabernacle?

5. What kind of materials were to be used?

6. Describe the tabernacle.

7. Describe the furniture to be placed in each apartment.

8. How was the cost of the tabernacle provided?

9. How much did the tabernacle cost? How much was the precious metals worth?

10. Why such costly expenditures for a movable house of God?

STORY 47

AARON APPOINTED HIGH PRIEST;
HIS GARMENTS OF GOLD

EXODUS 28

After giving Mo'ses full directions for building a place of worship, the Lord gave further instructions concerning the services to be held in the tabernacle. The first requirement for these services was that there should be a High Priest, who would represent both the Lord and the people as a mediator, and who would have charge of all the ministrations within the house of God and its court. The High Priest was to have the assistance of other priests in carrying on the tabernacle services.

The Lord himself chose Aa'ron as High Priest, and directed that his sons be appointed to assist him. It was His order that the office of High Priest should be continued in Aa'ron's family, and that the eldest son of each successive generation should be appointed to this office. The Lord also directed that all the male descendants, from one generation to another, were to be priests. Thus the priesthood of Is'ra-el was to remain in Aa'ron's family, and was to be limited strictly to his descendants. The appointment of any man outside the Aa'ron-ic family to the priesthood was to be unlawful, and death was the penalty for any person who attempted to fill this office without being properly anointed.

Divine directions were given for an elaborate and impressive ceremony by which Aa'ron should be inducted into his office of High Priest, and for the dedication of his sons to the work of the priesthood. Aa'ron was to be gorgeously arrayed in specially prepared garments and bedecked with certain jewels as a sign of his office. Divine instructions were given in regard to all these details. His sons were also to have specially prepared garments and distinctive marks of office, and these were all prescribed by the Lord.

The distinguishing garments and jewels which were to be prepared for Aa'ron were: a breastplate, an ephod, a robe, a girdle, a turban, two onyx stones, and twelve precious stones embedded in the breastplate. Underneath these garments he wore a close fitting coat of white linen.

For the sons of Aa'ron, the priestly garments consisted of coats of white linen, bonnets of similar material, a mitre, a girdle, and fine linen breeches. These were all prepared, as the Lord directed, from the finest materials and by the most skilled workmen of Is'ra-el.

Aa'ron's robe was an upper garment made of one piece entirely woven without the use of a needle, with an opening at the top well hemmed to prevent rending; with arm-holes, but without sleeves, and blue in color. The fringe at the bottom was richly decorated with artificial pomegranates of blue and purple and scarlet, and little golden bells placed between each pair of pomegranates.

This robe distinguished the wearer as one whose duty was to preserve and declare God's truth. Made of one piece, it symbolized the unity of God's revelations, one in spirit and beauty and authority; God's word is all truth, not partly true and partly false, partly human and partly Divine, or partly beautiful and partly unseemly. The color, which was the same as the lofty firmanent of the heavens, indicated that the truth of God is the highest, purest, and only eternal revelation given to man.

The ornaments on the fringe of Aa'ron's robe also had an important meaning. Pomegranates, with their pleasant odor, their sweet, refreshing juice, and the richness of their delicate meat, symbolized the refresh-

AARON CHOSEN AS HIGH PRIEST

ing, strengthening power of the word of God as the spiritual food of His children.

The golden bells, ever tinkling as the High Priest performed the duties of his sacred office, proclaimed to the people that he had found access to God in their behalf, and that his ministries were pleasing to Him.

The ephod worn by Aa'ron was an ornate upper garment with one part falling over his shoulders in front and covering his breast, and the other falling behind and covering his back. It was made of the same material as the inner curtain and draperies of the Holy of Holies in the tabernacle, blue, purple, scarlet, and finely twined linen, interwoven with gold threads cut from plates of pure gold. It was tied around the waist with an embroidered girdle made of the same material.

Upon each of the shoulder pieces of the ephod was an onyx stone set in borders of gold, and on these stones were engraved the names of the twelve heads of the tribes of Is'ra-el. The names of the six elder sons of Ja'cob were on one of these stones, and the names of the six younger sons were engraved on the other.

This article of dress for the High Priest, expensive, gorgeous, and brilliant, indicated the beauty and glory of the priestly services in the tabernacle; while the names of the heads of the twelve tribes of Is'ra-el carried upon the shoulders pointed out the High Priest as the only one who could speak for the nation with God. Since gold is the emblem of regal power, the golden garments of Aa'ron were a sign that he was the head of the nation in all religious matters.

The breastplate was joined to the ephod by chains of gold. It was a highly decorated woven square about ten inches each way, and was worn over the breast. It was made of the same material as the ephod, but was made somewhat in the form of a pouch. It was adorned with twelve precious stones, arranged in three perpendicular rows of four each. Engraved on these sparkling jewels were the names of the tribes of Is'ra-el, one name on each.

The twelve precious stones, representing each of the twelve tribes of Is'ra-el, were symbolic of the different traits of each one. In the first row were: the Emerald, of brilliant green, on which was the name of Zeb'u-lun; the Diamond, transparent or reddish yellow, bearing the name of Ash'er; the Amethyst, violet-blue, engraved with the name of Ben'jamin; and the Jasper, dark red, representing Gad.

In the second row were: the Topaz, golden tinged, engraved with the name of Ju'dah; the Sapphire, sky-blue, on which was placed the name of Sim'e-on; the Agate, of divers colors and transparent, bearing the name of Ma-nas'seh; and the Beryl, sea-green, on which the name of Naph'ta-li appeared.

In the third row were: the Sardius, carnelian or blood-red, engraved with the name of Is'sa-char; the Carbuncle, of fine ruby color, on which the name of Reu'ben appeared; the Ligure, orange and transparent, representing E'phra-im; and the

THE ALTAR OF INCENSE

Chrysolite, golden colored, on which the name of Dan was inscribed.

This beautifully jewelled breastplate indicated the truth that the intercession of the High Priest must rest upon a foundation of purity, righteousness, and holiness; and these precious stones typified the purity and glory of Is'ra-el under the saving grace of God.

In the pouch formed by the front and back of the breastplate were placed what was called the U'rim and Thum'mim. No description is given, and whether these words represented material objects, or simply the He'brew terms for "lights and perfections," is not known. They seem to have been a sign to Is'ra-el of God's solemn promise to send information for every need in answer to the prayer of the High Priest.

Worn over his heart, this article of dress reminded both Aa'ron and the people of the loving care which he must always have for the nation, of the fact that he represented the people before God, and of the duty of faithfully reporting the will of God to Is'ra-el at all times.

The turban or Mi'tre worn by Aa'ron on his head was made of fine linen, with a gold band encircling the front on which was inscribed "Holiness to the Lord." Crowned with this diadem symbolic of purity and majesty, the High Priest was constantly reminded of his complete consecration to God, and the people were reminded of the holiness which they must always seek.

Thus we see that even the splendid garments worn by the High Priest had a spiritual meaning in keeping with the purposes of God in founding the whole priestly system of ancient Is'ra-el.

How wonderfully do all these sublime provisions made for the High Priest of Is'ra-el point to our great High Priest at the right hand of God, who:

> "Exalted high at God's right hand,
> And Lord of all below;
> Through Him is pardoning love dispensed,
> And boundless blessings flow."

The tabernacle having been completed, the High Priest and his assistants having been provided with suitable garments, Aa'ron and his sons were set apart to their offices by a special service of consecration. They were washed thoroughly, and then anointed with holy oil; this was a symbol of peace, indicating the grace imparted to them by the Lord, and through them to all Is'ra-el. There was also the offering of burnt sacrifices to the Lord, and the sprinkling of blood upon the priests, signs which pointed to the nature of the ministry to which Aa'ron and his sons had been divinely appointed.

All these rites and ceremonies clearly signify the absolute necessity for thorough sanctification of heart and life for worshippers of God:

> "No spot or wrinkle on their holy brow,
> No film upon their robes of dazzling white,
> Most beautiful, most glorious; every saint
> HOLY in individual HOLINESS."

SUGGESTIONS FOR STUDY

Biblical Index to Helpful References

Aaron a Brother and Assistant of Moses. (Ex. 4:14; 5:20; 7:1, 12; Num. 12:1.)

High Priests Confined to Descendants of Aaron. (Lev. 21:10; Zech. 3:1.)

Christ Our High Priest. (Heb. 2:17; 4:14, 15; 6:20; 7:26; 8:1.)

Garments of the High Priest. (Lev. 8:7; Num. 20:26; Ezek. 44:17.)

Consecration to Special Services for the Lord. (Lev. 8:12; Num. 3:3; Acts 6:6; 13:3.)

Ornaments of High Priest Symbolisms. (Ps. 132:16; Isa. 61:10; Zech. 3:4.)

Questions

1. Who was chosen at the first High Priest of Israel?

2. To whose descendants was the High Priest confined?

3. Describe the gorgeous robe of the High Priest.

4. What was the distinguishing significance of this robe?

5. What was the significance of the names engraved on the ephod?

6. Name and give the significance of the twelve stones in the breastplate.

7. Who is the High Priest under the gospel dispensation?

8. Describe the consecration of the High Priest to his office.

THE MOSAIC SYSTEM OF SACRIFICES AND OFFERINGS

LEVITICUS 1-9

With the setting up of the tabernacle a new order of worship for Is'ra-el was established. Up to this time Mo'ses alone had been the one through whom God spoke to the people, and who served as their spokesman to God. Now God dwelt among His people in an unseen and mysterious manner, but in a very real sense, in the Holy of Holies. Now there was also provided a means of reaching the Lord every day through the system of sacrificial offerings and ministries of the priesthood, and the people might secure pardon for their sins by offering the sacrifices of repentance.

Just as the moral law had been issued through Mo'ses from Mount Si'nai, so the laws of worship for the system of sacrifices and ceremonies were given from the tabernacle. Both were given with equal solemnity, and both were equally binding upon the Is-ra-el-ites.

In giving Is-ra'el this code of sacrifices, God provided a way by which His people could always reach him. From the beginning there had been a feeling in the heart of mankind that some sort of sacrificial offering was needed in the worship of God. This feeling grew out of a sense of sin and need, and the knowledge of obligation to God. It was to meet this sense of sin and need, and to provide for Is'ra-el the sacrifices which foreshadowed the atonement made for all believers by Je'sus Christ, that God gave the Mo-sa'ic, or Aa'ron-ic, system of offerings.

The Divine way for man's approach to God has always been by sacrifice. The objects of the sacrifices appointed for ancient Is'ra-el were the following: to provide a satisfactory way for man to lay his problems before the Lord, to awaken and maintain reverence for God, to secure greater consecration and obedience, and to open a new channel for the expression of man's feelings toward his Maker.

In the Divinely given ritual for the He'brews there were three principal classes of sacrifices: the burnt offering, the sin offering, and the peace offering. In addition, there were several sacrifices of less importance, including the meat offering, the trespass offering, the peace offering, and consecrations of various kinds. These were usually offered in connection with other sacrifices.

The first of these sacrifices, both in the order in which they were given, and in importance, was the burnt offering. Its chief purpose was to make atonement for sin, and thereby to keep open man's channel of communication with God.

The animal to be offered in making this sacrifice must be chosen from the best of the flocks or herds, and must be absolutely free from any flaws or defects. It was entirely consumed by the fire, with no part being withheld from God.

In presenting this offering the donor must act entirely of his own free will; there was no element of extortion or force by the Lord. The one who made the offering placed his hands on the head of the animal as it was presented to the priest; this was to show that his guilt was to be transferred to the animal which he gave as a sacrifice for his sins. He was required to slay the animal himself, calling attention to the fact that his own sins were the reason for making the offering. The entire procedure of the sacrifice took place in the open, and in a reverent, orderly manner.

In many respects the Sin Offering was similar to the Burnt Sacrifice. The animals used and the requirements for perfection and cleanliness were the same, and the purpose in both sacrifices was that of removing sin. One difference appears in the fact that the Burnt Offering was made for the entire assembly of Is'ra-el, and for sins in general, although it was sometimes offered by individuals; while the Sin Offering was almost always made by an individual for his own benefit.

The Sin Offering was also frequently made by a priest for his own sins, and in such cases the entire offering was burned; while in offering it for others only a part of the animal was burned, the remainder being given to the priests for food.

This offering covered every kind of sin: sins of which the donor was conscious, and for which he made a direct confession; and sins which had been committed through ignorance, or without knowing that they were wrong. The sacrifice was an example of the hatefulness of sin in the sight of God, and required the one who made it to prove his repentance by looking upon sin with the same loathing. Through this offering sin was blotted out, and the eating of a part of the animal by the priest was a symbol of God's complete reconciliation with the sinner.

In the Peace Offering, the donor brought to the priest some animal which had been selected because it was the best which he had. The sacrifice could be a bullock, a ram, a lamb, or a dove. Certain portions were offered to God in burnt sacrifices, while the remainder was eaten by the donor and the priest in a meal of thanksgiving and fellowship. Sometimes friends and relatives of the one who made the sacrifice were invited to take part in the feast. This offering was observed after the Burnt Sacrifice and the Sin Offering, and could not properly be celebrated until peace had been made between God and man.

There were elements of both confession and consecration in this offering. A portion of the animal was burnt unto the Lord, the blood was sprinkled upon the burnt offering, the donor placed his hands upon the head of the animal and slew it

THE SPRING OF MOSES

himself, as in the previous offerings. The outstanding features of this sacrifice, however, were thanksgiving, fellowship, and friendship; and the donor came to the altar in a spirit of joy and spiritual delight.

The idea of fellowship was at the very center of the entire procedure, for in this sacrificial meal the donor enjoyed fellowship with God, with the anointed priest of God, and shared these blessed fellowships with his family and friends. It was a social meal in which there was holy communion with God, and blessed fellowship with one another.

It is the right of God to say where and how He shall be worshiped. For one to look with scorn upon the ancient forms of sacrifice prescribed by the Lord is a sin unworthy of human intelligence, showing disgraceful ignorance and wilful misunderstanding. The entire system of sacrificial offerings was provided by the Lord to meet Is'ra-el's great need of atonement for sin.

The tabernacle was the only proper place for Is'ra-el to worship God. The Great Altar was the only place of sacrificial worship, and on this holy place there burned a constant fire as the sign of God's willingness ever to forgive the sins of those who look to Him alone for salvation. It stood between the door of the tabernacle and the symbol of the presence of God in the Holy of Holies, pointing to the Cross of Je'sus, without which no man may find shelter in His loving arms.

Every detail of the sacrificial system of Is'ra-el was fulfilled in Christ. The offering of animal sacrifices, and the work of the priests in this respect have been set aside by the Gospel teachings of Christ, but the great spiritual truths taught by these offerings can never cease; they have full power upon us today in our relation and worship toward God through Christ the Lord.

> "He who would be cleansed from every sin
> Must to God's holy altar bring
> The whole of life—its joys, its tears,
> Its hopes, its loves, its powers, its years;
> The will, and every cherished thing."

SUGGESTIONS FOR STUDY

Biblical Index to Helpful References

The Use of Blood Sacrifices for Access to God. (Ex. 30:10; Lev. 17:1-10; Heb. 9:7.)

Salvation Provided Through the Blood of Christ. (Heb. 9:14; 1 Pet. 1:18, 19; Matt. 26:28; Rom. 5:9.)

Importance of the Burnt Offering. (Num. 28:3; 29:6; Josh. 8:31; 1 Chr. 16:40.)

Importance of Sin Offering. (Num. 6:11; 8:8; Heb. 9:13; 10:10.)

Importance of Peace Offering. (Num. 6:14; 7:17; 10:10.)

Questions

1. What is the authority back of the sacrificial system of the Mosaic Law?

2. What feeling in the heart of man demands sacrifice to God?

3. What has always been the basis of atonement for man's sins?

4. Name the three more important sacrifices in the Mosaic system.

5. Explain to character and meaning of the Burnt Offering.

6. Explain the character and meaning of the Sin Offering.

7. Explain the character and meaning of the Peace Offering.

8. To whom do all these sacrifical offerings point?

9. Did Christ fulfill the Sacrificial rites of the Mosaic system?

10. In what way does his offering for us become effective?

11. What offering should we make to him?

THE SIN OF IMPIETY IN DIVINE WORSHIP; ITS PUNISHMENT

LEVITICUS 10

Not long after the tabernacle was erected, and the priests had begun the daily services ordered by Mo'ses, two sons of Aa'ron committed a great sin against the laws of worship. The Lord had directed that the fragrant gum used for incense be lighted from the fire which He had kindled on the Great Altar. Instead of following these instructions, however, two priests named Na'dab and A-bi'hu took coals of fire from some other place to set the incense in flames.

This act of the two young men who had so recently been consecrated as priests was unforgivable. It profaned their sacred office, disobeyed the clear command of God, and showed inexcusable carelessness. The fire from the Great Altar was to be used because it had been lighted by the Lord, because it had been consecrated by the blood of atoning sacrifices, and because it had been especially blessed by the Lord.

It appears that the sinful act of the two young priests was the result of their own sinful indulgence. In the recklessness and folly of youth, they had taken too much wine, and then had tried to take their part in Divine worship with their minds beclouded by the evil drink.

For this act of sacrilege the two young men were suddenly smitten with death. As they stood beside the holy altar of incense the fire of God struck them, and they dropped dead by the altar. Their clothing was unharmed, there was no scorch of fire, but they were dead.

Their punishment was both sudden and severe, but was fully justified by the terrible sin which they had committed. Na'dab and A-bi'hu had dared to offer fire which was forbidden by the Lord, and so they were punished by a fire which took their lives. They had burned their own fire in preference to that which God had commanded to be used in Divine worship, and were justly consumed by the fire which they had failed to use.

When Mo'ses was told of their act, and of the sudden punishment inflicted, he declared, "This is the token of the holiness of God's house; His worship must be holy." He refused to allow Aa'ron or his two other sons to touch the dead bodies, but called for two distant relatives to remove them. The usual mourning for the dead was also forbidden, for the two unworthy priests had been slain for sin against the Lord.

Surely this striking episode, which took place at the very beginning of the new system of worship, and within the doors of the place which had been appointed for it, was a stern lesson in the need for sobriety, thoughtfulness, and strict obedience to every detail in the code of worship which God had given. Carelessness in the worship of God has within it an explosive fire which is sure to fall upon all who are guilty of it. The Divine command which should be written in letters of fire before every worshiper of God is, "Be not rash with thy mouth, for God is in heaven and thou upon earth: therefore let thy words be few."

Our worship should always be filled with deep emotion and outpourings of the spirit, but care must be taken to preserve true reverence; there is no place in true religion for presumptuous, undignified acts of our own. Whatever services we render unto God must be performed in the way and in the spirit prescribed by God.

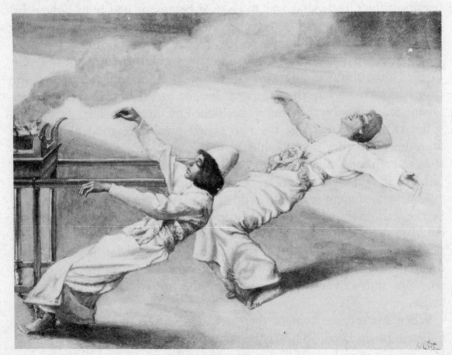

TWO WICKED PRIESTS DIE

"No sacred lore, howe'er profound,
Nor all the long and varied round
Of sacred rites, can bliss procure
For worthless man, in heart impure.

Altho' a man with zeal and skill
Should all external rites fulfil,
He reaps no fruit of all his toil
If sin his inner man should soil.

E'en he his all in alms who spends,
With heart defiled, secures no meed;
The disposition, not the deed,
Has value—on it all depends."

The dreadful sin of Na'dab and A-bi'hu, and the sudden punishment of death inflicted upon them by the Lord, struck their father a hard blow. He felt that God had been insulted, that Is'ra-el had been disgraced, and that his own honor had been dragged into shame. But he restrained himself from making any comment on what had happened, or complaining to the Lord. He bowed in complete obedience to God's will, and held his peace before all that Mo'ses had to say. Beautiful, indeed, was the spirit of Aa'ron under so terrible a misfortune. Unable to eat the portion assigned to the priests in a Peace Offering brought at that time, he quietly accepted the rebuke of Mo'ses, and bore with silence the deep sorrow in his heart.

The Lord then made use of the tragic occasion to lay down strict rules concerning the use of wine by the priests. Mo'ses was directed to say, "Let no priest drink wine or strong drink of any kind before entering upon the sacred duties of his office." Severe warnings were given against any form of intemperance which would tend to becloud the mind, defile the body, or in any way make the priest unfit for the solemn duties of his office.

These words of Mo'ses have a message for those who seek to worship God today. Everything which makes it impossible for one to worship God in the way that He has commanded must be strictly avoided. The spiritual sight must be kept clear, the heart and conscience pure and undefiled, the eye single, and the mind free from all distracting thoughts when we come before God in worship.

Throughout the history of religion, both during the period of Ju'da-ism and under the new era brought by the gospel of Christ, divine worship holds the central place. Spiritual worship and the proper observance of appointed hours of worship must be kept up, or else everything connected with the life of religion will go wrong. The Christian who does not keep his priestly garments unspotted, who fails to free himself from all that leads to carelessness and irreverence in worship, and who neglects the Divinely-given laws of worship, will become fruitless and without joy in his religious life. We need to give the best that we have to His worship today:

Take my soul and body's powers; take my memory, mind and will;
All my goods and all my hours; all I know and all I feel;
All I think, or speak, or do,—take my heart, but make it new.

Now, O God, Thine own I am; now I give Thee back Thine own;
Freedom, friends, and health and fame, consecrate to Thee alone;
Thine I live, thrice happy I! Happier still if Thine to die."

After this event was over, and the bodies of the two unfaithful priests had been buried outside the camp of Is'ra-el, Aa'ron and his other two sons, whose names were E-le-a'zar and Ith'a-mar, continued to carry on the services and sacrifices of the Lord's house. They were very careful, indeed, to perform them in exactly the place, manner, time, and spirit which God had commanded.

SUGGESTIONS FOR STUDY

Biblical Index to Helpful References

Righteousness in Worship. (I Pet. 2:5; Ps. 4:5; Mal. 3:3.)

A Good Rule for Worshippers in the House of God. (Eccl. 5:2.)

The Only Kind of Intoxication Allowed in Spiritual Worship. (Isa. 9:9, 10.)

Sacrilege in Worship Denounced. (Num. 18:32; Rom. 2:22; 1 Cor. 11:22.)

Other Examples of Sacrilege. (1 Sam. 2:17; 2 Ki. 21:7; 2 Chr. 24:7.)

The Warnings of God Against Strong Drink. (Prov. 20:1; Num. 6:3; Deut. 29:6.)

Questions

1. In what way did Nadab and Abihu violate the laws of worship?

2. What appears to have been the reason for their recklessness?

3. How were they punished for their sin?

4. What great lesson does this teach?

5. What effect did this terrible sin of his sons have on Aaron?

6. What place does worship hold in the Christian's life?

7. What strict rules should be observed in our worship?

STORY 50

THE GREAT DAY OF ATONEMENT
AND THE SCAPEGOAT

LEVITICUS 16

One of the natural results of the sin of Na'dab and A-bi'hu, and of the severe penalty inflicted upon them, was to put in the mind of Aa'ron a feeling of dread, lest he, too, should err in the ministries of his office. For this reason the Lord soon appeared to Mo'ses with full instructions for the High Priest to carry out on the one day of each year in which he was permitted to enter the Holy of Holies in the tabernacle. That day was called the Great Day of A-tone'ment, and became the most solemn day in the Jewish calendar.

The sacrificial system of Mo'ses reached its highest point in the worship which took place on the Great Day of A-tone'ment. It was an annual day for Is'ra-el to make atonement for all the sins of the past year which might have escaped notice in the regular daily sacrifices. It was the day on which the entire nation received pardon for such sins, and the sacrifices and ceremonies then performed marked the climax of all the others.

The first observance of the Day of A-tone'ment took place soon after the tragic death of Na'dab and A-bi'hu for impiety, and was held on the tenth day of the seventh month in the He'brew year. It was at the critical period in Is'ra-el's history when the chosen nation was being firmly established, and when the Mo-sa'ic system of rites and ceremonies was being completed. It was also just before the Is'ra-el-ites departed from Si'nai for the journey to Ka'desh-Bar'ne-a, where they were to be severely tested as to their readiness to enter at once into the Promised Land.

The sacrifices of the Great Day of A-tone'ment were made by Aa'ron alone, and in this respect they were different from the daily sacrifices, which could be offered by any of the priests. As the High Priest, Aa'ron had to perform all the rites and ceremonies of the day without any help from the other priests. The refueling of the fire on the Great Altar within the courts of the tabernacle, the filling of the lamps within the Holy Place, the lighting and burning of the incense, and all the daily offices required, were performed by the High Priest.

The appointed sacrifices for that day were a Sin Offering and a Burnt

Offering. A bullock and two young goats, each one perfect in every respect, were furnished from the public treasury of the whole house of Is'ra-el. Before going out to make these offerings, Aa'ron washed himself thoroughly, and dressed in the priestly garments specially designed for this particular day.

On the Great Day of A-tone'ment the High Priest wore fine white linen breeches next to his body, a fine linen coat, clean and white; a white linen girdle, and a linen mitre for his head. These garments were symbolic of perfect righteousness and complete purity. On this occasion the splendid golden garments which the High Priest ordinarily wore as a sign of his office were laid aside for the plain, simple garments of holiness. The mitre with a plate of pure gold around the brow, the wonderful breastplate studded with twelve precious stones, the ephod with its onyx stones and tinkling bells of gold—all these were put away on the solemn day of A-tone'ment.

First in the order of the sacrifices was that of a young bullock which was offered in atonement for the sins of the High Priest and his family. Aa'ron slew the bullock, and let its blood flow into a vessel used for that purpose while he entered the Holy of Holies, carrying a censer of burning coals in his right hand, and a platter of fragrant incense in his left.

THE SCAPEGOAT

The burning coals were placed at once in front of the Ark of the Cov'e-nant, and were sprinkled with finely ground incense until the tabernacle was filled with a silvery cloud of smoke, symbolic of praise and prayer.

Aa'ron then returned for the vessel of blood, and sprinkled some of it upon the Mercy Seat as an atonement for his own sins and those of the priests who assisted him. This act of worship was performed seven times as a token of completeness.

When Aa'ron stood once again before the Great Altar in the court of the tabernacle, he was presented with two young goats which were just alike in appearance, and size, and value. These were placed by the altar with their backs toward the assembled people, and their faces toward the sanctuary of the Lord.

Two lots of the same size, shape, and material were placed in an urn; on one was written, "For the Lord," while the other said, "To be sent away." After lifting this urn toward the people and shaking it, Aa'ron drew out the lots and placed one on the head of each goat. He then tied a piece of scarlet cloth around the neck of the goat which had been chosen for the Lord, and a similar cloth was tied on the horns of the one which was to be sent away.

The goat on which the lot "for the Lord" had been placed was given as a sin offering for the people. This sacrifice was made in the same manner as the offering of the bullock. The blood was carried by the High Priest alone into the Holy of Holies, and was sprinkled upon the Mercy Seat as an atonement for the sins of all Is'ra-el. By various ceremonies the tabernacle and all its furnishings were newly sanctified. Thus full atonement was made for the sins of all the people, and by ceremonial rites they were dedicated anew to the service of the Lord.

Then the High Priest turned again to the Great Altar where there still remained the goat on which the lot "to be sent away" had fallen. This goat, which was given the name "scapegoat," was then turned to face the assembled people, waiting for their sins to be laid upon him. Then it was sent into the wilderness, to a land "not inhabited."

Before the goat was sent away, however, the priest laid his hand on its head and made the following prayer:

"O Lord, the house of Is'ra-el, thy people, have trespassed, rebelled, and sinned before thee. I beseech thee, O Lord, forgive their trespasses and sins which they have committed, that they may be clean from all their sins before the Lord."

The "scapegoat" was then led away to some distant place in the wilderness, so far away that it could never find the way back, and was turned loose to wander wherever it pleased.

In the sacrifice of the first goat there was blood atonement for sin, while the second goat was an example of the results of the atonement. Through the mercy and grace of God the sins of the people were carried away into the wilderness, never to return to the people from whom they had been separated, indicating full and perfect remission of sins. Having completed these ceremonies Aa'ron removed the white garments designed for the Great Day of Atonement, donned his regular priestly robe, and made burnt offerings for the people in token of gratitude and renewed consecration.

Instructions were then given by Moses for continuing the Great Day of A-tone'ment, and rules for its annual observance were announced. It was to be observed by the entire nation, whether in their own land or among foreign people, and was set apart as a Sab'bath of rest. All worldly pursuits were to be laid aside during the sacred observances, and the whole thought of the people was to be centered upon the sacrifices, ceremonies, and rites of that Great Day. It was also required that the day be observed with deep sorrow, humble confession of sin, and genuine repentance toward God. This Annual Feast Day was faithfully observed by Is'ra-el to the time when its symbols of Atonement were wonderfully fulfilled by the Lord Jesus in his death on Calvary.

SUGGESTIONS FOR STUDY

Biblical Index to Helpful References

Appointment and Significance of the Day of Atonement. (Ex. 30:10; Lev. 23:27; Num. 29:7; Heb. 9:7.)

Christ Our Atonement. (Rom. 5:6; Rev. 5:9.)

The Holiness of Jesus as Our High Priest. (Heb. 7:26.)

"No Remission of Sin Without Shedding of Blood." (Heb. 9:22.)

God's Complete Separation of Our Sins From Us. (Ps. 103:12; Micah. 7:19; Jer. 31:34; 50:20.)

Sacrifices Offered in the Wrong Spirit of no Avail. (Micah. 6:6-8.)

Questions

1. What was the most solemn day in the Jewish Calendar?

2. For whom were the sacrifices made on the Day of the Atonement?

3. Who alone administered all the rites of that day?

4. What sacrifices were made on the Day of the Atonement?

5. Explain the difference in the garments of the High Priest on this day.

6. In the scape goat offering how many goats were used?

7. How did the High Priest determine which was to be offered and which was to be sent away in the wilderness?

8. What was done with the scapegoat?

9. What did this signify?

STORY 51

THE JOURNEY OF ISRAEL FROM SINAI TO KADESH-BARNEA

NUMBERS 10, 11, 12

Silver trumpets had been provided by Mo'ses for the priests to use in calling together the Is'ra-el-ites for an assembly of any kind. When all was in readiness for them to start on their journey from Si'nai, the sound of the trumpets summoned the people to the line of march.

The pillar of cloud which always rested over the tabernacle by day was lifted by the Lord. Mo'ses directed the Le'vites to take down the tabernacle, and to pack the various pieces so that they could easily be carried. The two golden staves prepared for carrying the Ark of the Cov'e-nant were passed through the rings of gold on each side, and certain priests were appointed to carry it before the host of Is'ra-el. The pillar of cloud which served as the Divine guide for Is'ra-el during their journeys in the wilderness then hovered over the Ark, going forward with it as the sacred chest was carried along. Whenever the pillar of cloud by day or pillar of fire by night ceased to go forward, there the Is'ra-el-ites paused and pitched their tents for encampment.

After three days the pillar of cloud halted, and the Is'ra-el-ites encamped for a month at a place which was later called Kib-roth-Hat-ta'a-vah. Here some of the people fell into their old habit of murmuring. They complained about the hardships of travel in the wilderness, about the weather, and about the conditions under which they lived, just as many people do today. For this ungrateful spirit the Lord sent fire into the camps of Is'ra-el, and many of the people lost their lives.

Some days later a number of the less worthy Is'ra-el-ites gathered in groups to complain of their hardships, and began to talk of revolting from the leadership of Mo'ses. Although they were being fed with manna from heaven, a delicious and nourishing food, they were not satisfied.

Fish was abundant and cheap in E'gypt, cucumbers flourished, and melons were one of the chief crops. Another favorite food in E'gypt was the sort of onion called leeks, besides a very highly flavored onion greatly prized by the E-gyp'tians, and the garlic which was the choicest appetizer of that land. So greatly did the Is'ra-el-ites crave these foods of E'gypt that they spoke with scorn of the manna which God provided.

The cries and complaints of the Is'ra-el-ites distressed Mo'ses, and he felt that the management of such a multitude of unruly people was more than he could endure. He sought help from God, and was told to select seventy elders from the tribes of Is'ra-el to help him. This left Mo'ses free to give most of his time to matters of great importance.

In the land of A-ra'bi-a, where they were now encamped, there were many wild birds called quails. They migrated in great numbers from place to place, flying very close to the ground. The Lord caused a great wind to blow a huge flock of quails into the place where Is'ra-el was encamped, and there were so many of them that they covered the ground for miles around. Many of the Is'ra-el-ites were so greedy for the new food that they ate too much, and some of them died.

The sickness caused by the natural effects of their gluttony was regarded as a plague sent by the Lord, and as a punishment for the complaining spirit of the Is'ra-el-ites. The section of the encampment where the people were smitten with fire was called Tab'e-rah, meaning "The place of burning," and the entire encampment was called Kib-roth-Hat-ta'a-vah, which means "graves of greediness."

The Is'ra-el-ites then journeyed a short distance further east, encamping at Ha-ze'roth for a brief period. During the encampment in this place Mir'i-am and Aa'ron were guilty of a great offense. They united in speaking against Mo'ses, the divinely chosen and anointed leader of the nation. Envious of his position and power, jealous of the authority with which he ruled all Is'ra-el, and hoping to gain equal rank with him, they formed a plot against Mo'ses. Aa'ron had been made the head of the nation in religious matters, and Mir'i-am was distinguished as a prophetess, but both were lower in rank than Mo'ses, and did not enjoy the same close communion with God. For these reasons they were envious of the superior office and ability of their brother.

This deadly poison of unholy ambition spoiled all the sweetness and beauty of virtues possessed by two honored servants of God. Their envy was like a fountain from which there flowed a stream of hatred and evil. They tried to injure Mo'ses by saying wicked, untrue things about him, but this brought harm only to themselves.

The excuse which they used for slandering their brother was that after the death of his wife Zip-po'rah, he had married a Cush'ite woman. She was probably one of those who had been converted to the He'brew religion, and had come out of E'gypt with Is'ra-el at the time of the Exodus.

Mo'ses was very much hurt by the unfriendly action of his own brother and sister, but suffered the attack in meekness and silence, making no effort to defend himself. But the Lord took notice of what Aa'ron and Mir'i-am had said.

The Lord spoke to Mir'i-am, Aa'ron, and Mo'ses, telling them to come at once to the tabernacle for trial before Him. He then upheld Mo'ses, and told the others that their brother had been chosen to receive the great messages from God because of his perfect faith and honesty. Mir'i-am and Aa'ron were sternly rebuked for daring to tell false tales about their brother.

So wicked did the Lord regard this deed that He caused the pillar of cloud, which was the symbol of His presence, to vanish for the moment.

Mir'i-am was suddenly smitten with leprosy, a terrible disease which was regarded as a stroke from the hand of God. Her foul tongue was justly punished with a foul face; while Mo'ses was forced to hide his face with a veil because of the glory of God, she was forced to hide hers in shame. She had been the leader in the plot against Mo'ses, and was, therefore, punished more severely. Aa'ron's punishment consisted in performing his priestly duty of examining Mir'-i-am's leprosy, and keeping her away from the house of God.

As a result of his humiliation in the punishment of Mir'i-am, Aa'ron humbly confessed to Mo'ses his sin and that of his sister, admitted that they had acted foolishly, and begged his brother to pray for the healing

MIRIAM A LEPER

of Mir'i-am. He cried, "Let her not be as one dead," for leprosy is nothing short of a living death in its torturing pain and corrupting power over the body. No persons who were afflicted with this terrible disease were allowed to go near the house of God.

The gracious, forgiving spirit of Mo'ses was then revealed in his earnest prayer to God for the healing of his sister. Instead of resentment in his heart, there was forgiveness and mercy. His prayer was earnest and persistent, and was answered immediately, but seven days passed before Mir'i-am was completely healed. This was done to give her sufficient time to meditate upon her sin, and for the instruction of Aa'ron and all Is'ra-el. What wonders are wrought through fervent prayer!

Having been unduly delayed at Ha-ze'roth by the plot of Mir'i-am and Aa'ron, and the punishment inflicted upon them by the Lord, the Is'ra-el-ites then journeyed to Ka'desh-Bar'ne-a, on the southwest borders of the land of Ca'naan. They were now within sight of the Promised Land, and the reasons for their failure to enter the divinely promised heritage at once will be related in our next story.

SUGGESTIONS FOR STUDY

Biblical Index to Helpful References

Trumpets Used in War. (Josh. 6:4; Ezek. 33:3.)

Trumpets Used in Worship. (Lev. 25:9; 1 Chr. 1:34; 2 Chr. 5:12.)

Pillar of Cloud and of Fire. (Ex. 13:21; Deut. 1:33; 31:15; Ps. 78:14.)

Divine Leadership. (Deut. 8:2; 32:12;

Ps. 77:20; Isa. 63:14.)

The Evil of Complaining. (Job 10:1; Ps. 55:2; 77:3; 142:2.)

The Evil of Carnality. (Ps. 78:18; Rom. 7:23.)

Unholy Ambitions. (2 Sam. 15:1, 2, 4; 1 Ki. 1:5; Luke 22:24.)*

Questions

1. How were the Israelites summoned for departure from Sinai?

2. What sacred furniture was carried in the front of the march?

3. What Divine sign was given for their guidance?

4. When the pillar of cloud ceased moving what did Israel do?

5. For what did the Israelites complain on their journey?

6. What kind of meat did the Lord provide?

7. What happened to those who surfeited themselves?

8. What conspiracy was formed by Miriam and Aaron?

9. How was Miriam punished?

10. How was Aaron punished?

11. What happened when Moses prayed for Miriam?

12. Was Miriam ever given distinction after this?

STORY 52

ISRAEL AT KADESH-BARNEA; SPIES ARE SENT INTO CANAAN

NUMBERS 13, 14;
DEUTERONOMY 1
The children of Is'ra-el had now arrived at the border of the Promised Land, and there seemed to be no reason why they should not enter it and take possession at once. God himself had declared that it was a good land, He had promised to guide them to it, and this promise had now been fulfilled. He was present with them in the majestic pillar of cloud by day and of fire by night, He had miraculously provided for all their needs thus far on the journey, He had assured them that He would drive out the heathen nations of Ca'naan and give the Is'ra-el-ites possession of the land, and His order when they arrived at Ka'desh-Barnea was, "Go up and possess the land."

But the hearts of the people were filled with fear and unbelief. They felt it necessary to take certain precautions which the Lord had not included in His plan for the immediate occupation of Ca'naan. Their answer to God's command that they "go up at once" was, "Let us send men before us, that they may search out the land for us." Mo'ses was deceived as to the real purpose of this request; thinking that it was a wise precaution which would be followed by whole-hearted obedience to the command of God, he yielded to the advice of the people. Without suspecting the mixture of unbelief and cowardice which prompted this request, he conferred with God about it. Although such a course seems not to have been in the plan of God for Is'ra-el, He permitted it in order to teach the people a lesson. God will sometimes let man have his own way and lean upon his own understanding so that he will find out the utter folly of his fancied wisdom.

It would have been better for Is'ra-el if the sending of spies had never been suggested, if they had walked by faith instead of seeking to go by sight.

After securing permission from God to send men into Ca'naan to explore the land, Mo'ses proceeded to appoint and instruct those who were to go on this mission. He chose twelve men, one from each tribe of Is'ra-el; all of these men had proved their courage and wisdom by noble deeds in the past. They were sent out to make a careful study of the entire land of Ca'naan, paying attention to its fertility, the measures which were taken to protect its towns, and the number and strength of the people. The report which they were to bring back was to be proved by samples of the fruit which they had found in the land.

For forty days the spies traveled through the land of Ca'naan, from the southern border where they entered the country, over the fruitful hills of the interior, along the coast facing the Med'i-ter-ra'ne-an Sea, and into the most distant towns of the northern border.

They visited many villages and towns of the country, finding some of them walled and strongly fortified. Special attention was given by the spies to He'bron, a town which was older than Zo'an, the most ancient city of E'gypt. Three generations of Is'ra-el-ite ancestors had been buried near He'bron—Ab'ra-ham and Sa'rah, I'saac and Re-bek'ah, and Ja'cob and Le'ah. Here lived at the time of this visit three tribes of people who were giants in stature, and who were fierce and warlike by nature.

As the twelve men surveyed the land of Ca'naan, they found that much of it was fertile, yielding the finest grains, fruits, and grass. Among the things they found were: grapes, olives, figs, pomegranates, apricots, dates, apples, quinces, various kinds of berries, almonds, walnuts, oranges, lemons, bananas, pears, and other fruits. Some of these were in great abundance.

The vast forests of the country were filled with wild animals, many of which could be used for food. The whole country was alive with bees, so quantities of the finest honey could be found everywhere. It was, indeed, a "land flowing with rich foods and honey."

In the valley of Esh'col, which was about two miles north of He'bron, and was

THE GRAPES OF CANAAN

noted for its grapes of superior size and quality, they gathered some fruit to take back to their people at Ka'desh. Here they found great clusters of grapes, some weighing from twenty to forty-five pounds. They carried some of these back home with them, and the largest were so heavy that they had to be hung on poles and carried over the shoulders of two men.

And so the twelve spies had two different reports to make when they returned to Ka'desh. Ten of them said, "It is a good land, a land of plentiful grass, of superb fruits, of glorious valleys and plains and hills and mountains, a land greatly to be desired; but it is held by fierce enemies which we cannot overcome." To them, the strong cities could not be taken, nor the giant warriors defeated in battle. They said, "The land is so fertile and fruitful that it is filled with warlike tribes which constantly destroy one another, and we shall be destroyed along with the weakest of them."

This report was filled with the spirit of cowardice and unbelief. The ten spies who made it forgot the strength of the 600,000 soldiers of Is'ra-el, and the supreme power of their God. There was no place in their faltering hearts for the memory of how Pha'raoh's army had been destroyed in the Red Sea, of Josh'u-a's victory over the Am'a-lek-ites, or of the continued presence of God with them in all their difficulties.

Ca'leb and Josh'u-a made a different report than the other spies. They said, "All that these men have said about the excellence of the land is true, and it is also true that there are strong cities and fierce warriors to be overcome, but we are well able to take the land." They admitted that there were giants in the land, but chided the ten faint-hearted spies for regarding the Is'ra-el-ites as mere "grasshoppers" before them. "Why," they said, "anointed with the power of God, and with the unseen hosts of heaven to fight on our side, we shall be the "giants," and the people of Ca'naan will be the "grasshoppers.""

In a stirring appeal to the Is'ra-el-ites, Ca'leb said, "Let us go up at once, and possess the land." He urged quick, bold action, insisting that all Is'ra-el act together with the assurance of faith in their hearts. His hope of victory was based upon the certainty of God's promises, and the knowledge of His all-conquering power.

What a striking contrast between moral courage and moral cowardice is presented in the reports and conducts of these two groups! Overcome by moral cowardice, the ten spies trembled with fear before facing the enemy, exaggerated the strength of their foes, minimized their own abilities, and were willing to give up without striking a blow. Ca'leb and Josh'u-a, on the other hand, had the courage to face self-denial and hardship boldly, and to declare their faith in the power of right.

The results of the timid report made by the unbelieving explorers of Ca'naan were most distressing. The people of Is'ra-el were made fearful and angry, and expressed their dismay in a great tumult of shouting and lament. Rioting broke out in the camps of Is'ra-el, and the people were further distracted from peace and quiet by rumors and plots of every nature. In a fit of unjust murmuring against Mo'ses and Aa'ron, they cried that it would have been better to perish in E'gypt or in the wilderness than to die with their wives and children at the hands of the Ca'-naan-ites.

The wild, unreasoning crowds even went so far as to blaspheme the name of God, and to accuse Him of deceit in bringing them out of the land of E'gypt. With daring impudence and base ingratitude they turned against their great Benefactor and His servants.

Mo'ses and Aa'ron were much grieved by the disgraceful conduct of the Is'ra-el-ites, but remained calm and patient. They tried to urge the people to refrain from such foolish actions, and to obey the command of God; they finally threw themselves prostrate before the people in prayer to God.

Josh'u-a and Ca'leb sought again to calm the fears of the people, and for their faithfulness were threatened with death by stoning. These devoted leaders tried to convince the Is'ra-el-ites that in following the directions of God they would be assured of His presence and power, and of certain victory over the inhabitants of the land of Ca'naan. All their efforts, however, were in vain.

In His righteous indignation over the blasphemy and lack of faith of Is'ra-el, and because they continued to be rebellious, the Lord declared to Mo'ses that He would destroy the whole nation by a plague, and would raise up another people for the occupation of Ca'naan from the family of Mo'ses alone. But Mo'ses thought more of Is'ra-el than of his own honor and glory, and pleaded with God to spare the people. He declared that the heathens back in E'gypt and those in Ca'naan would say in scorn that God was not able to establish His people in the land which He had promised to give them.

The earnest request of Mo'ses was granted by the Lord, but with certain conditions. The children of Is'ra-el were to wander in the wilderness for forty years before occupying the Promised Land, the 600,000 men over the age of twenty who had refused to enter Ca'naan when the Lord commanded should die without ever entering it, and the land would finally be given to the new generation to be born in the wilderness. Only Josh'u-a and Ca'leb were to be spared from this divine decree.

The people's sins of rebellion and blasphemy were pardoned in answer to the prayers of Mo'ses, but the privilege of occupying the Promised Land was denied for all time to those who had refused it after hearing the report of the spies. God's covenant with Is'ra-el was preserved, but its blessings in respect to Ca'naan were reserved for a new generation. Is'ra-el was turned away from the very doors of the Promised Land, and for forty years lived a wandering life in the wilderness of the A-ra'bi-an Peninsula. We shall learn more about this in our next story.

SUGGESTIONS FOR STUDY

Biblical Index to Helpful References

God's Yielding to Excessive Demands Though Not for Man's Good. (1 Sam. 8:5-22.)

Other Occasions of the Use of Spies. (Josh. 2:1; 2 Ki. 6:23; Luke 20:20.)

The Lord's Chastisements for Disobedience. (Deut. 8:5; Ps. 107:39, 40.)

Hebron Noted for Abraham's Sojourn. (Gen. 13:18.)

Hebron Noted as Burial Place of Sarai and Others. (Gen. 23:2, 17-20; 25:9; 49:31; 50:13.)

Hebron, Place Where David Began His Reign. (2 Sam. 2:1.)

Hebron Occupied by Giant-like Peoples. (Josh. 15:13, 14; 21:11.)

Joshua a Man of Courage and Bravery. (Ex. 17:9; 24:13; 33:11.)

Caleb a Man of Courage and Renown. (Num. 26:65; Josh. 14:6-14; 15:14.)

Canaan a Rich and Fruitful Land. (Ex. 3:8; Deut. 8:7-9; Jer. 2:7.)

Faintheartedness the Cause of Disaster. (Lev. 26:36-38; Deut. 20:8.)

Moral Cowardice a Great Sin. (Josh. 7:5; Jgs. 7:3; Jno. 6:66.)

The Sin of Stubbornness. (Ex. 32:9; Deut. 21:20; Zech. 7:11; Acts 7:51.)

Questions

1. What reasons favored Israel's immediate entrance into Canaan?

2. Why did the Israelites ask for spies to be sent into Canaan?

3. In what way was Moses deceived by their request?

4. How many were appointed as spies? What kind of men were they?

5. Name some of the places visited? What importance was attached to Hebron?

6. How long were the spies in Canaan?

7. Tell of the character of the country. Its fruitfulness. Its products.

8. What type of cities did they find? What kind of inhabitants?

9. Tell of the report made by ten of the spies.

10. Who made a different report, and what was it?

11. Which report was accepted? What judgment did God utter against them?

12. In what way did the Israelites then again disobey God?

STORY 53

ISRAEL'S THIRTY-EIGHT YEARS OF WANDERING IN THE WILDERNESS

NUMBERS 15, 16, 17

After Mo'ses told the Is'ra-el-ites that they were doomed to forty years of wandering in the wilderness, and that nearly all of them would die before the chosen race would finally occupy the Promised Land, they rebelled against the decree, and proposed to go at once into Ca'naan. They uttered words of confession for their sin, but with no evidence of genuine repentance; even while confessing their sins they persisted in them. They were determined to do exactly what God had told them not to do. When He said, "Go up into Ca'naan," they replied, "We will return to E'gypt." When He said, "Return to the wilderness," they said, "We will now go over into Ca'naan."

In reply to their proposal to enter Ca'naan, Mo'ses told them that the Lord would not go with them; that if they persisted in this fool-hardy course, the Am'a-lek-ites and Ca'naan-ites would defeat them with great slaughter. But they stubbornly insisted on making war against the heathen tribes of Ca'naan, even though Mo'ses would not go with them, and the Ark of the Cov'e-nant remained in camp. They were disgracefully beaten; many were slain, and the others returned to weep before the Lord.

After this unhappy event, the Is'ra-el-ites remained in Ka'desh for many days. Then they journeyed, as the Lord had commanded, into the wilderness toward the Red Sea. For nearly thirty-eight years they wandered over the deserts of the A-ra'bi-an Peninsula. Little worthy of record took place during this dark period in Is'ra-el's history. Some new regulations were given by Mo'ses, and the laws already given were enforced. It was no doubt for the benefit of the younger generation that these special messages from God were revealed by Mo'ses, and it also served as a proof of the continuance of the Lord's covenant with those who would later occupy the Promised Land.

Among the happenings recorded during these thirty-eight years is the violation of the Sab'bath by a man who gathered wood on that day, and who was punished by stoning. We are not told just when this took place, but we know that the Sab'bath had been set apart by the Lord after the six days of Creation, and that it had been consecrated in the religion of Is'ra-el.

The Sab'bath was consecrated to God, dedicated to His honor, and its violation was a direct reproach upon Him. It was also a memorial of Is'ra-el's deliverance from E'gypt, so those who violated the Sab'bath were guilty of sin in the eyes of both God and man. In setting apart the Sab'-bath day, the Lord intended to serve the well-being of His people by providing a season for rest and spiritual culture.

The punishment of the man who violated the Sab'bath took place in an orderly and legal manner. He was arrested in the very act of doing wrong, was brought before the elders for trial, was held in custody until the manner of his execution was determined by Divine instructions, and was then slain as directed by the Lord.

It is evident that the entire procedure was intended as a solemn warning to Is'ra-el against violating the Lord's day by doing anything which was forbidden in the Law. The Sab'bath was made for man, and man cannot do without it. Worship for the soul and rest for the body are two of the deepest needs of humanity. The Sab'bath was made holy for the glory of God, and any violation of it dishonors Him.

Another incident mentioned in the record of these thirty-eight years in the wilderness was the rebellion which Ko'rah led against Mo'ses and Aa'ron.

Ko'rah was a member of the tribe of Le'vi, a distant relative of Mo'ses and Aa'ron, and a Le-vit'i-cal officer who took part in the services at the tabernacle. He stirred up a rebellion against Mo'ses as the leader of the people, and against Aa'ron as the High Priest. Ko'rah was joined by Da'than and A-bi'ram, two prominent members of the tribe of Reu'ben, and another man from this tribe, whose name was On, seems to have dropped out after a short time.

The three leaders of the revolt were presently joined by two hundred and fifty princes of other tribes. The rebels declared that Mo'ses and Aa'ron had forced their way into the positions which they held, that they were harsh and overbearing toward the people, and that they were practicing deceit and fraud in the name of the Lord. It was further declared by the plotters that there should be no civil head over Is'ra-el, and that the order of the priesthood should be overthrown.

At heart, however, Ko'rah wished to be a priest, and his rebellion grew out of jealousy and selfish ambitions; though claiming to represent the people, he had no real interest in their welfare. His crime was all the more grievous because of the position which he held. As a Le'vite, he was set apart from the general congregation of Is'ra-el; his office was one of honor and responsibility. He performed certain holy duties in the tabernacle services, stood before the congregation to minister unto them, and was given a place of distinction by the Lord. For all these reasons his rebellion was inexcusable.

When the news of Ko'rah's rebellion was brought to Mo'ses he went at once to God in prayer, seeking to compose his own spirit, and to secure Divine help in meeting this trying hour. Then he made a bold, but fair, proposal for settling the demands made by Ko'rah and his followers. He directed that Ko'rah and all his company take censers in hand and march before the tabernacle on the following day. The censers were to be filled with the coals of fire and incense which under the laws of Is'ra-el could be carried only by the priests. If Ko'rah and his companions were justified in their demands, then their services would be accepted by the Lord; if

THE FIRE OF ATONEMENT

they were in the wrong, then a proper punishment would be inflicted by God.

On the next day Ko'rah and his company gathered before the tabernacle for the test appointed by Mo'ses, but Da'than and A-bi'ram were not present. They had left the day before, while Mo'ses was speaking to Ko'rah. In so doing, they defied the authority of Mo'ses as the Divinely appointed leader of Is'ra-el, and reviled him in a most insulting manner. Then Mo'ses was moved by righteous indignation, and prayed that the Lord would justify him by bringing a just penalty upon the evil-doers. Suddenly the ground gave way under the plotters as they stood in the door of their tent, and they were instantly buried alive.

Then Mo'ses prayed for the judgment of God concerning Ko'rah and the two hundred and fifty princes who followed him. As they marched before the tabernacle with burning incense in the sacred vessels, a miraculous fire from the Lord suddenly consumed them all. In order that Aa'ron might be found innocent before the people, Mo'ses had ordered him to march with Ko'rah and his company. But the consuming fire which destroyed the rebels did not harm the anointed High Priest of God.

By this stern judgment upon the rebels, the Lord made clear the upright character of Mo'ses and Aa'ron. He then directed Mo'ses to have the priest E-le-a'zar take the censers from the burning hands of the men who had been consumed, and to beat them into broad plates for a covering of the altar. This was a perpetual sign to Is'ra-el that no one outside the family of Aa'ron should ever assume the office of the priesthood.

On the day after this incident there was another revolt among the people, and complaints were made that Mo'ses had slain Ko'rah and his followers. For this uprising the Lord sent a plague upon the people, and it was only through the intervention of Mo'ses and Aa'ron that multitudes were not taken by death.

Soon after these events came the miracle in which Aa'ron's rod budded, blossomed, and bore ripened almonds. This took place as a token of the Divine choice of Aa'ron to be the High Priest, and his sons to assist in the priestly duties. Mo'ses directed each of the princes of the twelve tribes to place the staff of his tribe in the tabernacle, and Aa'ron was told to place his staff with the others. Then Mo'ses announced that the Lord would visit him in the sanctuary, and would make plain His choice for the priesthood. On the next morning Mo'ses entered the tabernacle and saw a very strange sight. Aa'ron's rod was covered with green buds, full blossoms, and ripened almonds, while the other rods were just as they had been the night before. When Mo'ses presented all these rods before Is'ra-el the people were convinced that the Lord had chosen Aa'ron and his family for the priesthood. Then followed a series of instructions concerning the duties of the priesthood, and additional rules regarding certain sacrifices to be made by Is'ra-el.

Thus the thirty-eight years of wandering in the wilderness are covered in several chapters of the book of Num'bers. As this period neared its close, the last of the 600,000 men who had refused to enter Ca'naan when they were at Ka'desh-Barnea the first time had died, and they all had been buried in various part of the A-ra'bi-an desert. The young men who had been under twenty years of age at that time, and others who had been born during the early years of wandering, were now the men of Is'ra-el. They had been brought up under strict religious instruction, and were trained as soldiers.

The time had come when Is'ra-el, a new Is'ra-el, was to pitch camp again on the borders of the Promised Land. Soon the children of Is'ra-el are to enter Ca'naan and begin its occupation.

SUGGESTIONS FOR STUDY

Biblical Index to Helpful References

Punishment for Sabbath Desecration. (Ex. 16:27-31; 31:14; Neh. 13:15.)

The Crime of Conspiracies. (Gen. 37:17-20; Jgs. 9:1-3; 2 Ki. 12:20; Matt. 12:14.)

The Sin of Envy. (Prov. 14:30; 23:17; Gal. 5:26.)

The Sin of Self-Exaltation. (Prov. 17:19; 25:6, 7; Isa. 14:12-17.)

The Blessedness of Meekness. (Zeph. 2:3; Gal. 5:22; 1 Pet. 3:4.)

Sudden Destruction for Perverseness. (Prov. 6:12-15; 24:21, 22; Isa. 30:12, 13.)

Divinely Chosen Instruments of God. (Hag. 2:23; Jno. 15:16.)

Questions

1. What did the Israelites undertake to do after being told of God's judgment for not entering Canaan at once?

2. What reproof did Moses give them?

3. How long did they wander in the wilderness?

4. Tell of the man who violated the law of the Sabbath and what happened?

5. Tell of the rebellion of Korah and others.

6. Why did Korah lead in this conspiracy against Moses and Aaron?

7. What happened to two of these rebels who defied the orders of Moses?

8. What happened to the two hundred and fifty conspirators?

9. What happened to the staff of Aaron as a proof of his priesthood?

10. What event overtook all the male Israelites above twenty at the time of their refusal to enter Canaan during the thirty-eight years in the wilderness?

STORY 54

ISRAEL AT KADESH-BARNEA A SECOND TIME; THE DEATH·OF MIRIAM; THE SIN OF MOSES IN STRIKING THE ROCK

NUMBERS 20:1-14

After thirty-eight years of wandering in the wilderness, the children of Is'ra-el came once more to Ka'desh-Barnea, and once again sorrow befell them. In the first month of the fortieth year after the departure from E'gypt, death came to Mir'i-am, the sister of Mo'ses and Aa'ron. She was then about one hundred and thirty years old; her life had been long and full of interesting events. In her early years she had carefully watched over the life of her infant brother. During the years which followed, while Mo'ses was growing up in the palace of the E-gyp'tian king, she cherished in her heart the hope that some day her people would be delivered from bondage in E'gypt. When Mo'ses fled into Mid'i-an, and while he was lost to his people for forty years, she reflected upon the strange providences of God.

When Mo'ses and her older brother Aa'ron were chosen to lead in the deliverance of her oppressed people, Mir'i-am aided them in every possible way. She was honored as a prophetess, and known as a sweet singer in Is'ra-el.

At one time she became jealous of Mo'ses, envying him for all the honors conferred upon him by the Lord. She persuaded Aa'ron to join her in making false charges against Mo'ses, but was punished for this evil deed by a stroke of leprosy. Mo'ses quickly forgave her, and his prayers caused the leprosy to be removed, but her name does not appear again in the history of Is'ra-el until the account of her death.

Even in obscurity, however, Mir'i-am continued to serve her God and her people, and when she died the whole congregation of Is'ra-el assembled in her honor. For thirty days there was great mourning among the Is'ra-el-ites, then Mir'iam was buried just outside the Promised Land for which she had longed all the days of her life.

When the season of mourning was over, the Is'ra-el-ites began to com-

MOSES SMITES THE ROCK

plain of their unhappy lot, for there was not enough water to meet their needs. It was under these trying circumstances that Mo'ses and Aa'ron committed the sin for which they were not permitted to live to lead Is'ra-el into the Promised Land.

The Lord directed Mo'ses to take Aa'ron, and to call the Is'ra-el-ites together by a great cliff in that vicinity. He told him to speak to the rock, promising that in answer to his voice sufficient water would burst forth to meet all the needs of the Is'ra-el-ites and their herds and flocks.

Once before, during the early days of Is'ra-el's sojourn in the wilderness, he had smitten a rock in the vicinity of Si'nai; a stream of water burst forth, and continued to flow as long as the Is'ra-el-ites were encamped at Si'nai. Now, after forty years in the wilderness, he was told again to speak to a rock for a similar blessing.

When all the people of Is'ra-el had gathered before him, Mo'ses reproached them bitterly, showing a spirit of impatience and anger. His patience had been worn out by the constant murmuring of the people.

Instead of speaking quietly to the rock, as the Lord had commanded, Mo'ses walked up to it and struck two violent blows with a rod. At once a great stream of water began to flow from the rock.

The Lord was greatly displeased by the conduct of Mo'ses and Aa'ron. Mo'ses had fallen short of God's command by his silence before the rock, and had gone beyond his orders by striking it. As a fitting punishment for such disobedience the Lord declared that neither Mo'ses nor Aa'ron should be permitted to lead Is'ra-el into Ca'naan.

What a striking example of human weakness! Mo'ses, who was one of the holiest men who ever lived, gave way to anger in the presence of the Lord. At a time when all his thoughts should have been directed to the solemn duty to which the Lord had called him, Mo'ses could not forget the unjust complaints of the people. For this reason he sinned against God by failing to do what the Lord had ordered, and in performing an evil deed which brought shame to him in the presence of all Is'ra-el.

As an everlasting warning to all future generations the name of the place where Mo'ses and Aa'ron sinned was changed from Ka'desh-Barnea to Mer'i-bah-Ka'desh, which means "place of strife," or "place of bitterness." This name would also serve as a living memorial to the sin of Is'ra-el in rejecting the command which God had given thirty-eight years before, and as a constant warning against similar sins.

This incident also illustrates the need for guarding the strong points of character; for at the very point where one feels secure and considers vigilance unnecessary, the evil one sometimes makes his most subtle attacks. Mo'ses, noted for meekness, becomes petulant; A'bra-ham, celebrated for his faith in God, twice grievously sinned because of doubts; E-li'jah, famed for fearlessness, fled in panic before the vengeance of Jez'e-bel.

SUGGESTIONS FOR STUDY

Biblical Index to Helpful References

Miriam the Sister of Moses and Aaron. (Ex. 15:20; Num. 12:1, 10, 15.)

Times of Great Despair. (Ex. 6:9; Job 7:6; Lam. 3:18.)

The Sin of Ingratitude to God. (Deut. 32:6; Neh. 9:26; Luke 17:17, 18.)

Warnings Against Murmuring Against God. (Lam. 3:29; Phil. 2:14.)

Warnings Against the Sin of Presumption. (Num. 15:30; Isa. 45:9; 1 Cor. 10:9.)

The Duty of Honoring God. (Ps. 107:32; 145:5; Isa. 25:1.)

Questions

1. Tell of the life of Miriam.
2. How old was she when she died?
3. Where did she die?
4. What did the people murmur about at Kadesh-Barnea?
5. What did the Lord tell Moses to do?

6. What did Moses do?
7. Of what sin was he guilty?
8. What punishment did God announce for him?
9. What name was given to Kadesh-Barnea and why?

STORY 55

ISRAEL'S MARCH FROM KADESH
TO THE PLAINS OF MOAB

NUMBERS 20:14-29; 21

When the children of Is'ra-el came for the second time to Ka'desh, which was on the southeastern border of Ca'naan, they planned to enter at once into the land which God had promised them. Just across the border, however, were two strong heathen nations known as the Ca'naan-ites and the Am'o-rites. Mo'ses did not think it wise to make war against these strong tribes at this time, so he decided to take the southern route across the land which was then held by the E'dom-ites. This route would bring them to Ca'naan from the east of the river Jor'dan.

The E'dom-ites were descendants of E'sau, the twin brother of Ja'cob, from whom the blessing of the firstborn had been craftily taken. They were closely akin to the Is'ra-el-ites, so Mo'ses hoped that they would show a brotherly feeling for his people. Mo'ses knew that the Is'ra-el-ites needed help in their plans to occupy the land which the Lord had promised them in the days of their fathers. But the memory of the feud between E'sau and Ja'cob had been kept alive among the E'dom-ites, and they were now envious of the growing power of the Is'ra-el-ites.

Mo'ses sent a messenger to the king of the E'dom-ites with this request: "You know all the misfortunes which have befallen your brethren, the Is'ra-el-ites—how for more than two hundred years we were enslaved in E'gypt—and you know how the Lord delivered us from E-gyp'tian bondage and directed us to occupy the land which He promised to the descendants of Ab'ra-ham, I'saac, and Ja'cob. You also know of the trials we have suffered for forty years in the wilderness of the A-ra'bi-an Peninsula. Now we ask permission to cross your country, that we may enter Ca'naan from the east side. We promise to march only on the highway, and to do no harm to your fields, or vineyards, or other properties; if our people or cattle drink from your wells, we will pay you for the water used."

This request of Mo'ses was coldly refused by the king of E'dom. The old breach between Is'ra-el and E'dom was widened, and the hatred which had been handed down from one generation to another could not

THE DEATH OF AARON

be reconciled. Mo'ses had been told by the Lord that he must not make war upon the descendants of E'sau, so there was nothing else for him to do but seek for another route.

The only other course open to them was a roundabout way near the southern border of E'dom, so they journeyed back toward the Red Sea down a little stream known as Ar'a-bah until they came to the place called Ak'a-bah, or E'zi-on-Ge'ber. Here they turned in a northeasterly direction and travelled through the mountain of Seir to the land of Mo'ab, east of the Dead Sea.

This was a very dreary and desolate country, a frightful desert where the ground was covered with loose gravel and rough stones, so that even a camel found it difficult to pick its way. Round hills of naked stone and gravel rose high into the heavens, there was very little vegetation of any kind, and it was hot and dry. Here the Is'ra-el-ites found very rough going.

During the early days of the march Mo'ses was directed by the Lord to take Aa'ron and his son E-le-a'zar up into the top of a very high mountain called Hor, which was on the east side of the valley of the Ar'a-bah, and not far from the Med'i-ter-ra'ne-an coast line of eastern E'dom. It is the highest and most conspicuous peak of the entire mountain range of that region, raising its twin peaks 4800 feet above sea level, 4000 feet above the Ar'a-bah valley, and 6000 feet above the level of the Dead Sea.

It was here on the top of this mountain that Aa'ron died, not by accident, but according to the will of God. The Lord said, "Aa'ron shall be gathered unto his fathers: for he shall not enter into the land which I have given unto the children of Is'ra-el, because he rebelled against my word at the water of Mer'i-bah."

Just before Aa'ron died on the top of Mount Hor, Mo'ses removed the priestly garments which he wore, and placed them upon E-le-a'zar. Thus by Divine appointment a son of Aa'ron took his place as High Priest of Is'ra-el. In his dying moments Aa'ron had the satisfaction of knowing that his office would 'not die with him, and that his work would be carried on by his own son. When the congregation of Is'ra-el learned of the death of Aa'ron, a thirty day season of mourning was proclaimed. E-le-a'zar was named to take his place, and this appointment was confirmed by the people.

Taking advantage of this period of mourning, one of the kings of southern Ca'naan, whose name was A'rad, attacked the Is'ra-el-ites in the valley of A'ra-bah, and captured some of them. The Is'ra-el-ites then made a solemn vow unto the Lord that when they had taken possession of the Promised Land they would completely destroy Arad's people. This vow was later accomplished, and the place was called Hor'mah, meaning "utter destruction."

While crossing this steep and barren land on their roundabout journey to a place where they might safely enter Ca'naan, the Is'ra-el-ites became very much discouraged, and began to make new complaints against Mo'ses. As a punishment for these murmurings, the Lord caused the poisonous snakes of that region to infest their camp in great numbers. They were called "fiery serpents" from the burning, deadly pain caused by their bites. Is'ra-el had complained for want of water, and the Lord sent a plague upon them which caused a thirst no water could quench; they had shown a preference for death in the wilderness, and the Lord sent death to many of them near the Promised Land.

Then the Is'ra-el-ites repented for their sins, pleaded with Mo'ses to speak to the Lord on their behalf, and asked that the poisonous snakes be driven away from the camp. The Lord not only drove the snakes away, but provided a cure for the people who had been bitten by them.

He directed Mo'ses to make a serpent of brass, similar in every way to the poisonous serpents of the desert, and to place the brazen image on a high pole in the midst of the camps of Is'ra-el. Then those who had been bitten by the "fiery snakes" were told to look upon the "brazen serpent," and all who obeyed this command were healed at once. There was no way by which man could stop the deadly ravages of these serpents, nor was there any earthly remedy for their bites. But the means of cure provided by the Lord was free to all who obeyed His command to look upon the brazen serpent.

The Lord Jesus referred to this image as a token of the Divine cure for sin, and to the faith of those who looked upon it as an example of the simple trust required of all who would be saved from the deadly effects of sin through the "uplifted Savior."

Just as the Is'ra-el-ites who were bitten by those fiery serpents suffered from a communicated, painful, and deadly poison; so humanity under the curse of sin has a fatal spiritual malady. Just as the uplifted Brazen Serpent was provided as a cure by the sovereign grace of God; so God freely gave his own Son in the likeness of the flesh of sin, and for sin, as the only cure for the malady of the soul. Just as Is'ra-el was healed by looking; so men today are healed by believing.

In their superstitious awe the Is'ra-el-ites preserved the brazen serpent, and, in times when they forgot the Lord, some of them would set it up in a high place and bow before it in idol-worship. Four hundred and fifty years later the good king Hez-

THE BRAZEN SERPENT

e-ki'ah, about whom we shall learn in future stories, completely destroyed the image. Thus we are taught that the material things through which God's blessings are brought to us should never be worshiped; the Lord is the source of all blessings, and He alone should be worshiped.

After the snakes had been removed from their camp, the Is'ra-el-ites continued their journey in a northeasterly direction. The names of several encampments are given, but the exact location is not certain until the people reached the plains of Mo'ab directly east of the Dead Sea. The Mo'ab-ites were descendants of Lot, and the Lord had directed Mo'ses not to make war upon them, or to take their land.

The Is'ra-el-ites encamped for some time at a place called Ar, which was on the plains of Mo'ab. Here they dug a well, and praised the Lord in special hymns for the gracious way in which He was leading them on their perilous journeys.

Continuing the journey, and making brief stops at several stations, they arrived at Ja'haz, on the border between the Mo'ab-ites and Am'or-ites. Here Mo'ses sent messengers to Si'hon, king of the Am'or-ites, with a similar request to the one presented to the king of the E'dom-ites. Si'hon's answer to this request was a prompt refusal, and immediate war against Is'ra-el. The Is'ra-el-ites, however, overwhelmingly defeated Si'hon, and occupied his territory. Among the important towns captured was Hesh'-bon, which was Si'hon's capital.

The Am'or-ites were descendants of E'mer, the fourth son of Ca'naan, and were both strong and numerous in the land. Two strong kings ruled over large areas east of the river Jor'dan, and five over territory west of the Jor'dan. Og, who was another king east of the Jordan, was later conquered by the Is'ra-el-ites under Mo'ses, and the territory of Si'hon and Og was given to the tribes of Reu'ben, Ma-nas'seh, and Gad. The five kings west of the Jor'dan were later conquered by Josh'u-a.

After conquering all the territory under the rule of Si'hon, the Is'ra-el-ites carried the war against the Am'or-ites into the northern district of Ba'shan, which was ruled by Og. He and his people were very powerful, and Og himself was so large that he had a bedstead of iron twelve feet long and six feet wide. The giant king and his warriors made the mistake of leaving their fortified cities, and making war against Is'ra-el on the plains. Is'ra-el won a great victory over Og, taking possession of all his territory.

Is'ra-el's warfare against the Am'or-ites east of the Jor'dan was one of extermination. God had commanded them to wipe out these heathen people because of their idolatry and wickedness. And so the lands of the Am'or-ites became the property of God's chosen people, and Is'ra-el was enriched by herds and flocks, and the spoils of many cities.

A triumphant war-song celebrating the victory over these powerful peoples, and giving all honor for it to God, was sung by all Is'ra-el. The people then moved to the plains of Mo'ab, which ran along the eastern border of the Dead Sea and of the river Jor'dan. The city of Jer'i-cho was on the west side of the river, near its mouth, and just opposite the place where Is'ra-el was encamped. Many preparations, however, had to be made before Is'ra-el could cross the river and take possession of the land then known as Ca'naan. The more important of these preparations will be reviewed in our next chapter.

SUGGESTIONS FOR STUDY

Biblical Index to Helpful References

Edomites Descendants of Esau. (Gen. 36:9; Deut. 2:4; 23:7; Jgs. 11:17.)

Inhospitable Treatment of Others Denounced. (Deut. 23:3, 4; 1 Sam. 25:10-13.)

Death of the Righteous Precious to God. (Ps. 116:15; Rev. 14:13.)

Divine Vengeance Against Evil Doers. (Deut. 32:35; Ezek. 25:17; Rom. 12:19.)

Intercessions in Behalf of Sinners. (Isa. 53:12; Heb. 7:25.)

Other Examples of Intercession. (Ex. 32: 32; 1 Sam. 7:5; 2 Chr. 30:18.)

Brazen Serpent Destroyed by Hezekiah. (2 Ki. 18:4.)

Brazen Serpent Type of Christ's Death. (Jno. 3:14.)

Armorites Descendants of Canaan. (Gen. 10:16; 14:17; 15:16; Josh. 24:12.)

Songs of Victory. (Jgs. 5:1; Rev. 14:3.)

Questions

1. Why did not the Israelites enter Canaan from Kadesh-Barnea?

2. From what people did Moses ask permission to pass through their land?

3. Tell who these people were and why they refused?

4. What route did Moses then take?

5. Where did he plan entrance into Canaan?

6. What happened on Mount Hor?

7. Describe the territory through which Israel had to travel.

8. What special punishment was sent upon them for complaining?

9. When Moses prayed for them what remedy did he prepare?

10. What did the people have to do to be healed?

11. What was done with the brazen serpent? Who destroyed it? How long afterwards?

12. Explain the use that Jesus made of this brazen serpent.

13. What territories were conquered by Moses east of the Jordan?

14. To what tribes did he give this territory?

STORY 56

HOW A DUMB ANIMAL TALKED
WITH A PROPHET

NUMBERS 22

The Is'ra-el-ites were now encamped on the plains of Mo'ab on the east side of the river Jor'dan, their camp reaching back five or six miles toward the high plateau of this area. They looked eagerly across the river to the land promised to their fathers, no doubt expecting the Lord to tell them to cross the river at any moment.

But the time had not yet come for Is'ra-el to occupy the land of Ca'naan. There were other territories east of the Jor'dan to be conquered, and the Lord had some important lessons to teach them before they would be ready to conquer the land west of the river.

In much of their recent travels the Is'ra-el-ites had occupied certain parts of the territory of the Mo'ab-ites, and had crossed their borders without opposition. Instead, the most friendly relations had been enjoyed by both nations, and the Mo'ab-ites had sold food and water to the children of Is'ra-el.

But the defeat of the two strong kings of the Am'o-rites, and the conquest of all their territory by the Is'ra-el-ites, had brought suspicion and fear to the heart of Ba'lak, king of the Mo'ab-ites. The army of Is'ra-el numbered 601,730 warriors who had shown great courage and skill in fighting the Am'o-rites. Ba'lak feared that they might attack his own people, and dared not meet them in open battle.

In a small territory near Mo'ab there lived a people called the Mid'-ian-ites. They were a different branch from those of the same name who had given shelter to Mo'ses during the forty years of his exile from E'gypt. This branch had settled on the grassy plains between the lands of the Mo'ab-ites and Am'o-rites before the days of I'saac and Ja'cob. They were stock-raisers, and traded with the caravans which passed through their land. No conflict between them and the Is'ra-el-ites had occurred up to this time. The Mid'ian-ites were neither very strong nor warlike. In their early history they had been defeated by the E'dom-ites, and later were subdued by Si'hon, who made them subjects of the Am'o-rites.

Ba'lak's alarm was without cause, for the Is'ra-el-ites had shown no unfriendliness whatever toward his people. The Lord had instructed them not to harm the Mo'ab-ites, and they had carefully obeyed the order.

Knowing that he could not defeat the Is'ra-el-ites in battle, Ba'lak took a course which he hoped would deprive them of the protection and aid of God which had been so manifest in their battles against the Am'o-rites. There was a magician among the Mid'ian-ites whose name was Ba'laam, and who also possessed the gift of prophecy. He claimed to speak with God, and to have the power of reading the future. Ba'lak decided to have this magician utter a curse against Is'ra-el, and in this way to offset the special favor which they enjoyed from the Lord.

In those days some men were given the power to bless or to curse others, and Ba'laam probably had such power. The most gifted man of God, however, could not bring a curse upon others without reason. No man can curse those whom God is blessing.

Ba'lak sent messengers to Ba'laam to hire him to curse Is'ra-el. In return for this favor to the heathen king, Ba'laam was to be promoted in rank. Valuable gifts were brought to him by the messengers, and he was promised a large sum in gold for uttering the curse.

Ba'laam received the messengers with true Oriental courtesy, inviting them to spend the night in his home. He assured them that he would place Ba'lak's request before the Lord, and would do whatever the Lord commanded.

During the night the Lord appeared to Ba'laam, probably in a vision, and told him neither to return to Ba'lak with these men, nor to pronounce a curse upon the people of Is'ra-el. The next morning he told the messengers of Ba'lak that the Lord had forbidden him to go to the king of Mo'ab at any time. But he did not tell them the most important part of the message from God. An honest report of what had taken place during the night would have ended the matter then and there, but he led the men to think that it was still possible for him to curse Is'ra-el.

Ba'laam is a strange character to many people, but the Bible story gives us a clear picture of him. He was a prophet to whom God revealed certain Divine purposes, and to whom He sometimes gave information concerning worldly matters. Ba'laam was very intelligent, often grasping truths which were too deep for other men to understand. His people were not included in the Is'ra-el-ites' Cov'e-nant, but he professed to believe in the God of the He'brews. He was also well informed concerning the history of Is'ra-el, knowing about their miraculous deliverance from

E-gyp'tian bondage, God's care for them during the forty years in the wilderness, and the hopes which they now held for the future.

At heart, however, Ba'laam was greedy. He simply could not break away from the "wages of divination" which he had received as a magician of the Mid'ian-ites. He tried to serve both God and Mam'mon at the same time.

The messengers returned to Ba'lak with the news that Ba'laam would not come to him at this time. Their words were even more deceptive than those of Ba'laam, for they did not tell their master that the Lord had forbidden Ba'laam to come. This led the Mo'ab-it-ish king to believe that he would come later, and that he would curse Is'ra-el as requested. He suspected that Ba'laam was merely waiting until more money was offered him.

Then Ba'lak sent another group of messengers to Ba'laam. This delegation was larger, and its members were of higher rank than the first

BALAAM AND THE ASS

messengers. They came to Ba'-laam and said, "Ba'lak urges that you come to him at once, and that you let nothing hinder you. He promises that he will give whatever you ask, if you will only curse the Is'ra-el-ites."

Ba'laam already knew that he must neither visit the king, nor curse Is'ra-el, but he let the messengers think that he would finally do both. He said to them, "If Ba'lak would give me his house full of silver and gold, I cannot go beyond the word of the Lord my God, to do less or more."

He should have sent the messengers away at once, but he invited them to tarry with him, speaking as though he thought that the Lord would give him permission to curse Is'ra-el.

The Lord knew that Ba'laam's heart had been turned by his love of money, so He gave him permission to go with these messengers in order to teach him a much needed lesson.

As Ba'laam was riding an ass on the way to the place where Ba'lak lived, a miracle suddenly took place. The animal on which he was riding turned aside into the fields, and Ba'laam angrily forced it back into the road. Again the animal turned suddenly to one side, crushing Ba'laam's foot against a stone wall. Then it fell down, and was beaten severely by its rider. All of these strange actions were caused by an angel of the Lord, who was visible to the animal, but unseen by Ba'laam.

The animal then spoke in human language, saying, "What have I done unto thee that thou hast smitten me these three times?" Apparently not alarmed by the strange fact of having a dumb animal speak to him, Ba'laam answered, "Because thou hast mocked me, if I had a sword I would kill you." After the animal reminded him of its faithful years of service the Lord gave Ba'laam power to see the angel standing in the highway with a sword in his hand. The angel rebuked Ba'laam for his cruelty to the animal, and told him that if it had not turned aside, death would have come to the prophet. The angel also declared that God was trying to save him from the evil which lay in his heart. Ba'laam was permitted to continue his journey, but warned not to curse Is'ra-el.

SUGGESTIONS FOR STUDY

Biblical Index to Helpful References

Moabites Descendants of One of Lot's Sons. (Gen. 19:37; Ezra 9:1; Neh. 13:23.)

Balak's Failure Against Israel. (Josh. 24:9; Jgs. 11:25.)

Balaam's Besetting Sin, Avarice. (Micah. 6:5; 2 Pet. 2:15.)

The Sin of Avarice. (Prov. 15:27; 1 Tim. 6:10; Matt. 26:15, 16.)

Midianites Descendants of Abraham's Son by Keturah. (Gen. 37:28-36; Jgs. 6:7.)

The Evil of Deceit and Fraud. (Ps. 10:7; Prov. 12:5; Jer. 9:5.)

The Practice of Divination. (Jer. 27:9; Zech. 10:2; Acts 16:16.)

Bribery Condemned (Prov. 17:23, Amos 5:12.)

Protection for the People of God. (Ps. 33:12; 78:52; 100:3.)

Angels Executing the Wrath of God. (1 Chr. 21:15; Isa. 37:36; Acts 12:23.)

Questions

1. What two nations formed an alliance against Israel in the plains of Moab?

2. Who were the Moabites?

3. Who were the Midianites?

4. In what way did Balak seek to weaken the Israelites?

5. Who was Balaam? What gifts did he have?

6. Why did he encourage Balak's continued expectation of help from him?

7. What was his besetting sin?

8. What happened as he was riding an ass to visit Balak?

9. Has there ever been any other occasion when a dumb animal talked?

STORY 57

EVENTS DURING THE LAST
DAYS OF MOSES

NUMBERS 25-36   During the months of Is'ra-el's encampment
on the plains of Mo'ab, at a place called A'bel-Shit'tim, many of the people
attended a festival in which the false god called Ba'al-pe'or was worshiped
in rites of an immoral nature. The Is'ra-el-ites had come to the festival
at the invitation of the women of Mo'ab and Mid'i-an, but they should
not have remained in a place where idol-worship was practiced. They
were guilty of forsaking the true God, and of joining the heathen in
acts which they knew were wrong.

The Lord punished Israel by sending a plague which resulted in the
immediate death of twenty-four thousand men. An Is'ra-el-ite named
Zim'ri and a Mid'i-an-ite woman named Coz'bi defamed the name of
God by their evil deeds before the tabernacle, and were put to death by
Phin'e-has, who was a son of E-le-a'zar and grandson of Aa'ron. For
this act of justice in upholding the laws of Is'ra-el he was praised by
Mo'ses, and later was highly honored.

The plague in the camps of Is'ra-el was then removed, but the Lord
directed Mo'ses to make war upon the Mo'ab-ites and Mid'i-an-ites for
the bold, disgraceful manner in which they had turned many of the
Is'ra-el-ites from the worship of God into idolatry.

Because the women of Mid'i-an had been the chief offenders in leading
the Is'ra-el-ites into idolatry and wickedness, the leaders of the army had
been ordered to slay them. But when the war was over, Mo'ses found
that many of his captains had not obeyed these orders, but had made
prisoners of the Mid'i-an-it-ish women. He rebuked them severely, and
ordered that all of these women who had taken part in leading Is'ra-el
into idolatry should be slain at once.

The territory east of the Jor'dan which had been conquered by the
Is'ra-el-ites, from the brook Ar'non on the south to Mount Her'mon on
the north, and extending eastward for many miles to the desert plateaus,
consisted of wide, grassy plains and low hills and plateaus which were
well watered by many streams. It was well adapted for stock-raising, and

was noted for its fine pastures.

Two of the tribes of Is'ra-el, those descending from Reu'ben and from Gad, had very large flocks of sheep and herds of cattle, and were noted for their skill as shepherds. They came to Mo'ses and E-le-a'zar requesting that these lands be given them, and that they be excused from crossing the Jor'dan for the conquest of Ca'naan west of this river.

Mo'ses rebuked the tribes of Reu'ben and Gad for making this request, for it was both selfish and unpatriotic. Their wish to settle on the land east of Jor'dan gave no regard whatever to the welfare of their brethren in the other tribes. It appeared to Mo'ses that they were trying to avoid military service against the strong heathen tribes which held the country west of the Jor'dan, and he felt that such a course would be a reproach upon the unity of Is'ra-el, and a violation of the covenant which they had made with God.

The Reu'ben-ites and Ga'di-tes then changed their proposal. They offered to leave their women and children, and their flocks and herds, on the east side of the Jor'dan while the men crossed over to help the ten other tribes in the conquest of Ca'naan. They would then return and take up their allotment on these lands.

In their new proposal these two tribes agreed to share in the hardships and dangers involved in conquering the entire land of Ca'naan, and they gave up all claim upon any lands west of the Jor'dan. Mo'ses accepted this offer, praised them for acting righteously, and warned them against any unfaithfulness in carrying out the agreement.

Lying to the north of the territory requested by the tribes of Reu'ben and Gad was a rugged, mountainous district known as Gil'e-ad. It was not adapted to stock-raising, so would be of no use to people who had large flocks and herds. Mo'ses directed that this region be given to half of the tribe of Ma-nas'-seh, descendants of one of the sons of Jo'seph. The leaders of this tribe were noted for bravery

IN THE TABERNACLE

and success in war. They had defeated the strong heathen tribe known as the Am'o-rites, and had overcome scores of heavily fortified towns. Gil'e-ad was a frontier district, and would be the natural course of attack upon Is'ra-el by countries of the northeast in later years. For these reasons it was important that this region be held by a strong, courageous tribe.

As mentioned in a previous story, the third census of Is'ra-el during the forty years between their departure from E'gypt and their final occupation of Ca'naan was taken during the encampment at A'bel-Shit'tim. Thousands of Is'ra-el-ites had died since the census which had been taken just before they left Si'nai. Some had been slain in wars, some had perished from plagues sent upon them for acts of disobedience, some from the bite of the fiery serpents, and many from natural causes. Within the entire camp there were only three men above sixty years of age. Of all the men who were twenty years or more of age when they left E'gypt, the only ones now living were Mo'ses, Josh'u-a, and Ca'leb. All the others had perished because of their refusal to enter at once into the Promised Land, as commanded by the Lord, when they were at Ka'desh-Barnea thirty-nine years prior to this last census.

In the last enumeration of Is'ra-el before entering Ca'naan it was found that some of the tribes had grown in numbers during the thirty-eight years of wandering in the wilderness, while others had decreased. The total number of men above twenty years and able to bear arms was 601,730, slightly less than at the last census. This number did not include the men of the tribe of Le'vi, as they were consecrated to special services in the tabernacle.

The numerical strength of each tribe as revealed in this census was made the basis for allotting the land of Ca'naan. Mo'ses, knowing that he would not be permitted to cross the Jor'dan and take part in the conquest of Ca'naan, gave full instructions concerning these allotments, and they were later carried out by his successor, Josh'u-a.

There were many other matters of importance to which Mo'ses gave his attention before he ascended Mount Ne'bo for his departure to heaven. Rules were given for the several feasts which were to be observed by Is'ra-el in their national life. Further instructions concerning the duties of the priests and Le'vites were given, and new provisions were made for their support. The system of tithing was confirmed and carefully outlined. The laws of sacrificial offerings were repeated and made more complete. Mo'ses prepared for future generations a complete account of the journeys of Is'ra-el from E'gypt to Ca'naan, and of the various places where they had encamped. Directions were given for the assignment of certain cities to the Le'vites, and others were set aside as Cities of Refuge.

Mo'ses made a series of speeches in which he recounted all the laws which God had given him, calling special attention to the moral and religious codes. These addresses make up the greater part of the Book of Deu-ter-on'o-my.

In these long speeches Mo'ses reviewed the goodness and mercies of God toward His chosen people, and reminded Is'ra-el of her Divinely chosen place among the nations of the world as the recipient of God's special revelations. He not only urged the necessity of perfect obedience to the laws of God, but also stressed the solemn duty of faithfully teaching them to their children.

In many respects the book in which these addresses are recorded is superior to all the other writings of Mo'ses, for it is a summary of the entire law of God as given to Is'ra-el by Divine inspiration. The four addresses of Mo'ses are the words of a dying father to his children, inspired of God, earnest, and impressive.

SUGGESTIONS FOR STUDY

Biblical Index to Helpful References

The Sin of Forsaking God. (Ezek. 6:9; Isa. 43:22; 1 Jno. 2:19.)

Evil ᐟAssociations Forbidden. (Ex. 32:2; 34:12; Prov. 4:14.)

Results of Evil Associations. (1 Ki. 11:12; 1 Cor. 15:33.)

Divine Wrath Against Forsaking God. (2 Ki. 22:13; Rom. 1:18.)

Phinehas. (Ex. 6:25; Josh. 22:13.)

The Duty of Patriotism. (2 Sam. 10:12; 1 Ki. 11:21.)

Zeal for the Cause of Righteousness. (Ps. 119:139; Isa. 62:1; Jno. 2:17.)

Cities of Refuge. (Deut. 4:42; Josh. 20:2, 9.)

Questions

1. Who seduced many Israelites to attend a heathen festival?

2. What curse was brought upon those who attended?

3. As a result of this evil what war followed?

4. What was done to the women who were responsible for leading these men astray?

5. What tribes requested the territory conquered cast of the Jordan? Why?

6. Why did not Moses give it to them at first?

7. What did they then propose?

8. Did Moses then give them the territory requested?

9. To whom did he give the territory to the north? Why?

10. Why did Moses have a census taken at this time? How many men were there?

11. What else did Moses do while Israel was encamped here?

STORY 58

JOSHUA APPOINTED TO SUCCEED MOSES; THE DEATH OF MOSES

NUMBERS 27:12-23;
DEUTERONOMY 34
    While Is'ra-el was encamped at A'bel-Shit'tim, and just before the death of Mo'ses, the Lord directed Mo'ses and Josh'u-a to enter the tabernacle for a special message. In the sanctuary of the Lord arrangements were made for the departure of Mo'ses, and for the appointment of Josh'u-a as his successor. Mo'ses already knew that he would not be permitted to enter Ca'naan, and he received with perfect calmness the Lord's announcement of his approaching death. He was now one hundred and twenty years of age, but robust in health, full of vigor, and his eyesight undimmed. But the appointed hour for his death was at hand, and he accepted it with the same faith which had marked his entire career. His work was finished, and he was ready to go. There was nothing for him to fear so far as the future peace and happiness of his soul was concerned. His only thought was for the future security and prosperity of Is'ra-el.

Mo'ses did not seek the appointment of a successor from his own family; he asked the Lord to make the choice. When the Lord appointed Josh'u-a as his successor, Mo'ses gladly gave his approval, and prayed that Josh'u-a would be anointed with Divine courage and strength for the very trying work to which he was called.

Josh'u-a was well qualified for the responsible position to which he was divinely appointed. He had been closely associated with Mo'ses throughout the period since Is'ra-el was delivered from E'gypt, and had loyally served as his minister. At Si'nai he had been chosen to accompany Mo'ses to the holy mountain, and had faithfully waited for him during the forty days in which he was alone with God. It was his heroic leadership which had brought victory to Is'ra-el in the war with the Am'a-lek-ites, and he was one of the two spies who reported that Is'ra-el was able to possess the land of Ca'naan when they first stood on the border at Ka'desh-Barnea. It was also under his leadership that the heathen tribes east of the Jor'dan had been conquered.

Josh'u-a was officially placed in office by the priestly services of anoint-

ing and the laying on of hands.
The people accepted his divine
appointment, and publicly declared him to be the successor
of Mo'ses. He was solemnly
charged with the duties of his
office, and given strength by the
assurance of God's presence
with him. Success in the conquest of Ca'naan and in the settlement of Is'ra-el in that land
was promised by the Lord.

Not far from the place where
Is'ra-el was encamped on the
plains of Mo'ab there rose high
into the heavens a series of
mountain ranges. One of the
highest points among these
ranges was called Mount Ne'bo.
From this high peak one may
look out over much of the entire land of Ca'naan.

The Lord directed Mo'ses to
ascend this mountain alone.

JOSHUA IN THE SANCTUARY

With stately step, fearing not, confident of the rest which awaited him,
and fully surrendered to the will of God, Mo'ses walked out from the
camp of Is'ra-el and climbed to the top of Mount Ne'bo. The Is'ra-el-ites
watched him with sorrow, for he had told them that he was going into
the mount never to return.

When Mo'ses reached the top of the mountain he looked down upon
the lands east of the Jor'dan which had been conquered and then allotted
to the tribes of Reu'ben and Gad. Lifting his eyes far to the north, he
gazed with joy upon the land of Gil'e-ad, which was now held by Ma-
nas'seh. Turning to the west, he saw the deep torrents of the Jor'dan
as its waters rushed into the Dead Sea just south of his gaze. Far out
over the western horizon he beheld the hills, mountains, and valleys of the
Promised Land soon to be conquered by Is'ra-el under the leadership of
Josh'u-a. Stretching his sight to the blue waters of the Med'i-ter-ra'ne-an

still further toward the sunlight, the fertile plains of the western shore brought a glow of joy to his heart.

What a glorious spot for a man of Mo'ses' character and career to make his journey into the glories of the world beyond! Surely, no such glorious scenes have ever passed before the dying eyes of another man. The entire landscape of the Promised Land swept before his eyes as he went up into the presence of God. He had once ascended Si'nai to commune with Je-ho'vah, to receive from him comfort and strength and a renewed commission of service; now he ascends Ho'reb to die. Not an untimely death, for he knew how to die as he had known how to live.

There was yet another glorious scene passing before the dying vision of this saintly man which must have greatly cheered his heart. On the plains of Mo'ab his eyes turned to his people Is'ra-el; three million souls compacted into a powerful community, united in spirit and in purpose, ready to cross the Jor'dan at the word of the Lord, and armed for the conquest of the Promised Land. Thus Mo'ses realized that his work would go on.

It is said that Mo'ses was buried by the Lord, and that no man has ever known the last resting place of his body. May it not be that if it was left there on top of Mount Ne'bo at all, it was only for a short time? Is it too much to believe that, like E-li'jah in later history, and like E'noch in times before, Mo'ses was carried bodily into heaven? Did he not appear in transfigured glory when two heavenly visitors talked with Jesus as He was transfigured before three apostles on another mountain?

SUGGESTIONS FOR STUDY

Biblical Index to Helpful References

The Promised Land of Israel. (Gen. 12:7; 17:2; Deut. 8:8; Jer. 2:7.)

The Lord's Provision for His Sheep. (Ps. 79:13; Matt. 10:16.)

Promotion in the Lord's Work. (2 Sam. 7:8; Ps. 75:7.)

Consecration to Divine Service. (2 Ki. 23:3.)

Set Apart by Laying-on-of-Hands. (Deut. 34:9; Acts 6:6.)

Solemn Charges to God's Servants. (1 Ki. 2:1; Acts 20:28.)

Mourning for the Dead. (Acts 9:39.)

Divine Fellowship and Friendship. (Ex. 19:3; 33:11; Jas. 2:23.)

Questions

1. Why was Moses not permitted to enter Canaan?

2. In asking for a successor what did Moses consider of most importance?

3. Who was chosen as Moses' successor?

4. Tell of Joshua's qualifications?

5. Where did the Lord take Moses for his death? Why?

6. Describe the view of the Promised Land from this site?

7. Does any one know where the grave of Moses is?

8. May it not be possible that he was taken to heaven in bodily form?

STORY 59

JOSHUA'S PREPARATIONS FOR THE CONQUEST OF CANAAN

JOSHUA 1, 2

We have already learned many times over in these stories that God sometimes uses man to carry out His plans, but is never dependent upon any one man. When Mo'ses died, Josh'u-a was already prepared to take his place, and to carry forward the conquest of Ca'naan by the Is'ra-el-ites.

And so, after the death of Mo'ses, while the Is'ra-el-ites were still encamped on the east side of the Jor'dan, the Lord appeared to Josh'u-a with a stirring message. He was commanded to lead the children of Is'ra-el across the Jor'dan at once, and to conquer the land which had been promised to their fathers.

The Lord then outlined to Josh'u-a the extent of the land which had been set aside for Is'ra-el. From north to south, it was to begin in the regions of the great river Eu-phra'tes, reaching down to the borders of the land of E'dom and Mo'ab, looking toward E'gypt. From east to west, it was to extend from the great Syr'i-an desert to the shores of the Med'i-ter-ra'ne-an Sea. All this territory, with its many types of soil and vegetation, its beautiful mountains and fertile plains and valleys, its rivers and lakes, its wide forests and unlimited natural resources, was to be conquered as the permanent home for a great nation.

This entire area, except that part east of the Jor'dan which had already been taken from the Am'o-rites, Am'mon-ites, and Mid'i-an-ites, was then held by various heathen tribes. It was not held by one united people, nor ruled by one king; there were many small nations occupying different sections of the country, each of them ruled by its own king. In most cases, the capital of these small tribes would be in a fortified town or city, with the surrounding territory used for farming or stock-raising. These tribal nations were often engaged in wars among themselves. The task of conquering the land was therefore much easier, since there was no probability of united opposition from the various tribes which hated one another.

The Lord not only commanded Josh'u-a to conquer the entire land of Ca'naan, but assured him of His presence. He urged him to be strong

THE SPIES ESCAPE

and of good courage, and to have confidence of victory and success. The laws given by Mo'ses were to be read constantly, and to be carefully obeyed by Josh'u-a and the people. The duties of religion must never be neglected. The Lord cautioned Josh'u-a that he and all Is'ra-el must remain loyal to God and to His teachings, and that true religion must always hold a central place in the national life of the country.

The war which Josh'u-a was commanded to wage against the heathen tribes of Ca'naan was to be one of extermination. These people who had defied God, worshiped false gods and idols, who were given over to the lowest forms of wickedness, and for whom there was no hope of civilization or moral reform, were to be completely destroyed. Such was the will of God, and such were the orders given to Josh'u-a and to all Is'ra-el. Any failure to carry out these instructions would result in punishment from God and great trouble for Is'ra-el.

After receiving full directions from the Lord for the immediate conquest of Ca'naan, Josh'u-a sent officers through the camps of Is'ra-el to prepare the people for this new venture. "Within three days," said Josh'u-a, "we shall begin our march against the Ca'naan-ites. Prepare yourselves to cross the Jor'dan, and to take possession of the land which God has given us." He reminded the members of the tribes of Reu'ben and Gad that the agreement which they had made with Mo'ses must be faithfully kept, and they responded heartily to his order for all the men to join in this march.

It took great courage to cross the river Jor'dan, which separated the Is'ra-el-ites from Ca'naan, for it was a swift stream without bridges or fords. The low lands on either side were narrow, only three to five miles at the widest points. Back of these low lands, on the west side, the hills and mountains rose almost perpendicularly to great heights. At the season when Josh'u-a gave the order for crossing, the narrow banks of the river were flooded by waters from the snow-capped mountains in the north and by rain from the mountains on both sides. The Is'ra-el-ites had no boats to use in crossing this wide, dangerous river, but they had faith that God would help them to carry out the orders of Josh'u-a.

Looking across the Jor'dan from the camp of Is'ra-el, they could see Jer-i'cho, a strongly walled and fortified city of one of the tribes of Ca'naan.

Josh'u-a thought it wise to send two brave, reliable men across the river to spy upon Jer-i'cho. They were to study the city carefully, noting its fortifications and points of weakness, and looking for safe ways of approaching the city. They were also expected to mingle with the people, and to find out whether they were terrified by the possibility of an attack by the Is'ra-el-ites, or whether they were confident that they could defend themselves.

Two men chosen by Josh'u-a swam across the Jor'dan, and thoroughly inspected the surroundings and walls of Jer-i'cho. Then they entered the city to examine its defences, but were discovered and pursued by officers. They sought refuge in the home of a woman named Ra'hab, and she hid them on top of her flat-roofed house, covering them with stalks of flax. When the officers searched the house of Ra'hab they were unable to find the two Is'ra-el-ites, and reported to the king that they had escaped from the city.

Ra'hab evidently knew something about the miraculous dealings of God with the enemies of Is'ra-el, and how He had delivered the Is'ra-el-ites from bondage in E'gypt. She is said to have hidden these spies because of her faith, even though she may have been superstitious and afraid. After the officers had given up their search of her home, she said to the Is'ra-el-ites,

"The people of this city know that your God is mighty, and that He has given you this land. They have heard of His mighty works for you, and are in a state of terror at the thought of your coming into the land. I believe in your God, and would like to serve Him. I beg you to spare my life, and that of my father and mother and brothers and sisters, when you take Jer-i'cho."

The spies knew that she had saved their lives, and they recognized her faith in God, so they promised that no harm would come to her or any member of her family when the city was captured by Is'ra-el. Then they took a cord of deep scarlet color and said, "When our men come to take the city, hang this cord from the window of your house. We pledge our lives that no one will be harmed in the building from which there hangs this scarlet cord."

Ra'hab's house was built on top of the wall of Jer-i'cho, and was a part of the fortifications. It was built of huge basalt rocks, with walls three or four feet thick. She hung a rope from one of the windows outside of the wall, and the two men climbed down the rope and made their way back to the river. Then they swam across the Jor'dan again and arrived safely at the camp of Is'ra-el. They told Josh'u-a how frightened the people were in Jer-i'cho, and said, "Surely the Lord has given us this land, and the people dare not oppose us."

Later, when the Is'ra-el-ites captured the city of Jer-i'cho and destroyed all its people, Ra'hab and her family were spared. She turned fully to the He'brew religion, married one of the princes of the tribe of Ju'dah, thereby becoming an ancestor of the Savior. She is mentioned with honor in the New Testament.

SUGGESTIONS FOR STUDY

Biblical Index to Helpful References

Israel's Promised Inheritance. (Lev. 20:24; Josh. 14:2; 24:28.)

· Invincibility of God's Children. (Deut. 28:7; Josh. 21:44; Songs of Sol. 6:10.)

Divine Constancy. (Isa. 54:10; Heb. 13:5.)

"Be Strong" in the Lord. (1 Ki. 2:2; 2 Chr. 15:7; Isa. 35:4; 2 Tim. 2:1.)

The Duty of Courageousness. (2 Chr. 32:7; Phil. 1:28.)

The Call to Fearlessness. (Ps. 27:3; 118:6; Isa. 12:2.)

The Duty of Straightforwardness. (Prov. 4:27; Phil. 3:13.)

Duty of Steadfastness. (1 Cor. 15:58; 2 Pet. 3:17.)

Wise Meditations. (Ps. 4:4; 19:14; 1 Tim. 4:15.)

Cooperation with God. (1 Sam. 14:45; Ps. 71:12.)

Kindness Rewarded. (Luke 10:34; Acts 16:33; 28:2.)

Questions

1. In what respects was Joshua well prepared for his new duties?

2. Explain the difference in Moses and Joshua and in their work?

3. What command was given to Joshau?

4. What assurances were given him?

5. What was his first step in planning an attack on Jericho?

6. Who protected the Israelitish spies in Jericho? How? How was she rewarded?

7. To whom was Rahab afterwards married?

STORY 60

THE DIVIDING OF THE WATERS OF JORDAN, AND THE COLLAPSE OF THE WALLS OF JERICHO

JOSHUA 3-6

After hearing the report of the two men who had spied upon Jer'i-cho, Josh'u-a directed the children of Is'ra-el to prepare for an immediate removal to the banks of the Jor'dan. The people took down their tents and rolled them up, then gathered their flocks and herds for the march. The priest took down the tabernacle, and prepared it for removal. The furnishings and holy vessels of the tabernacle were also packed in such a way that it would be easy to carry them. The Ark of the Cov'e-nant was covered over with curtains, and two staves were run through the golden rings on each side so that it could be carried by the priests.

Josh'u-a gave orders that those who carried the Ark were to march in front of Is'ra-el, being careful to remain about half a mile ahead. The people were warned not to come any nearer the Ark than that.

Josh'u-a then told the people to dedicate themselves anew to the Lord, saying, "Tomorrow the Lord will do w o n d e r s among you." On the next morning he directed the priests to take the Ark of the Cov'e-nant upon their shoulders and to march down into the waters of the Jor'dan. The people were to follow, carefully observing the rules already given.

THE TAKING OF JERICHO

As the feet of the priests who were carrying the Ark touched the waters of the Jor'dan, a very miraculous thing took place. The fast running currents of the river were suddenly stopped and piled up like a wall clear across the river, while the waters in front ran swiftly on toward the Dead Sea. In a little while there stretched across the entire Jor'dan river-bed a vast, dry highway, the waters to the north forming a great wall held back by an invisible dam.

The priests who were bearing the Ark moved out into the center of the river-bed, then waited there until the entire host of Is'ra-el had crossed to the other side. Only the women and children of the tribes of Reu'ben, Gad, and Ma-nas'seh, with about seventy thousand men who had been left to protect them and to help in caring for the cattle and sheep, remained on the east side of the Jor'dan.

What a startling sight the He'brews must have presented to the Ca'naan-ites on the west side of the river! Nearly five hundred and fifty thousand soldiers armed for battle, about two million women and children, and countless thousands of sheep and cattle moved in one continuous caravan across the Divinely prepared highway for more than eight hours.

After they all had reached the west side of the river, Josh'u-a ordered twelve men, one from each tribe of Is'ra-el, to gather twelve large stones from the river-bed where the priests had stood with the Ark. With these stones he set up a monument which was to remind Is'ra-el at all times of the power of God in providing a way for them to cross the Jor'dan. A second memorial for the same purpose was built in the river where the priests had stood with the Ark. Then the waters of the river began to flow rapidly toward the Dead Sea, just as they had before the miracle took place.

What sacred memories cling to that section of the river Jor'dan! Five hundred and fifty years after the parting of the waters for the passage of Is'ra-el they were again divided. The waters parted for E-li'jah and E-li'sha just before E-li'jah was carried to heaven in a fiery chariot, and again for E-li'sha as he journeyed back to his work on the west side of the river. Then, many hundreds of years later, the Sav'ior was baptized somewhere within this vicinity.

After the two stone memorials had been erected, the Is'ra-el-ites moved to a place called Gil'gal, about six miles west of the river, and within a mile of the city of Jer'i-cho. Here the tabernacle was erected, and the tents of Is'ra-el were set up in the usual order. Gil'gal was to be the camping place of Is'ra-el for many months.

On the fourteenth day of the month, just four days after the crossing of the Jor'dan, the Pass'o-ver was celebrated in all the camps of Is'ra-el. This was the third time that Is'ra-el engaged in the Pass'o-ver feast, the first time being in E'gypt, and the second at Si'nai. It had been neglected for thirty-nine years in the wilderness while Is'ra-el was living in disobedience to the covenant which they violated by not entering Ca'naan when at Ka'deah-Barnea the first time.

The harvest season was at hand when Is'ra-el began the conquest of Ca'naan. The people went into the fields, and vineyards, and orchards to gather food, and this marked the end of the manna. For thirty-nine years this food had fallen from heaven, but now it was no longer needed.

In the course of his preparations for an attack upon Jer'i-cho, Josh'u-a walked around the walls of the city on a tour of inspection. He was met by a heavenly messenger who appeared to be an angel, but who in reality was the Son of God, who many centuries later came into the world as a Sav'ior for all mankind. The same Divine Personage had appeared to Ja'cob hundreds of years before at the ford of Jab'bok, and to Mo'ses in the burning bush in the wilderness. He came to strengthen the faith of Josh'u-a, and to give him courage for the battles which lay just ahead.

In his appearance to Josh'u-a he called himself "Captain of the host of the Lord," suggesting that his presence made holy the ground on which they stood, and advising him that Jer'i-cho would be conquered through the power of the Lord. Josh'u-a bowed before him with great reverence, and humbly accepted the solemn charge placed upon him.

All the Ca'naan-ites and Am'o-rites living west of the Jor'dan had been smitten with terror by the sight of the great host of the Is'ra-el-ites. They had heard of the conquest east of the Jor'dan, and their hearts melted with fear and cowardice as they thought of the power which God gave to His chosen people. The gates of Jer'i-cho had been closed, and no one was permitted to go out. There seemed to be no thought of attacking the Is'ra-el-ites, who were encamped just one mile away.

Is'ra-el's plan of attack against this walled and strongly fortified city was very strange, yet its results were truly miraculous. More than five hundred thousand soldiers marched silently around the outer walls of the city once a day for six days in succession. The Ark of the Cov'e-nant was carried by the priests in the front section of this great army. In the vanguard were picked soldiers, probably the forty thousand men of the tribes of Reu'ben, Gad, and Ma-nas'seh. They marched ahead of the priests who bore the Ark, while the rest of the army marched behind it. Seven priests marched before the Ark, each of them carrying a trumpet, and they all blew upon the trumpets as a signal for the march.

After marching around the city once each day for six days, they made the circuit in a similar manner seven times on the seventh day. At the conclusion of the final march around the city, the entire army stood at attention while the trumpeters blew a long blast. Then all the people lifted their voices in one great shout. At once the foundations beneath the wall sank deep into the ground, and the walls crumpled into a flat mass of stone over which the Is'ra-el-ites could easily pass into the city.

The strange plan of attack was completely successful; the army of Is'ra-el marched over the fallen walls into the city, the entire population was slain, and enormous spoils of war were taken. The city of Jer'i-cho was burned to the ground, and Josh'u-a pronounced a special curse upon any person who should ever undertake to rebuild it on the same site. Many years later another city in that vicinity was called Jer'i-cho, but it

BEARING THE ARK ACROSS THE JORDAN

was on a different site than the one which was utterly destroyed by Josh'u-a.

Before the walls of Jer'i-cho were overthrown, Josh'u-a sent men to rescue Ra'hab and her family from the house in which she had sheltered his two spies. They were put in a safe place outside the camp of Is'ra-el until they had received the ceremonies of purification and adoption by which people who were not Is'ra-el-ites were admitted to the chosen race.

Josh'u-a directed that all the gold and silver and other valuables captured in Jer'i-cho be dedicated to the Lord, and solemnly warned every man against taking anything for himself. One man disobeyed this order, and we shall learn of his punishment in our next story.

In the strange manner in which the city of Jer'i-cho was overthrown the Lord required the trustful, obedient, and laborious service of His people, thereby showing that it is the power of God which brings victory in all the works of His kingdom. The Lord not only conquered the Ca'naan-ites, but won the hearts of Is'ra-el unto Him in faith and love. The destruction of the people of Jer'i-cho, apparently cruel and vindictive, is an example of God's judgments against idolatry and wickedness.

SUGGESTIONS FOR STUDY
Biblical Index to Helpful References

The Original Making of the Ark of the Covenant. (Ex. 25:10-16; 37:1-5.)

Rules for the Removal of the Ark. (Num. 4:5-10.)

The Ark in Israel's Warfare. (Num. 10: 35, 36.)

Preparations Before Great Blessings from God. (Hos. 10:12.)

The Lord Opens a Way for His People. (Isa. 43:16; 49:11, 12.)

The Jordan Divided for Elijah and Elisha. (2 Ki. 2:8, 14.)

Memorial Stones. (Josh. 24:27.)

Institution of the Rite of Circumcision. (Gen. 17:10, 14.)

Institution of the Feast of the Passover. (Ex. 12:11; Num. 33:3; Deut. 16:1.)

Rahab's Kindness and Reward. (Josh. 2: 1; 6:17; Heb. 11:31; Jas. 2:25.)

Questions

1. In the march to the Jordan what position did the bearers of Ark occupy?

2. How far behind the Ark did the Israelites march?

3. Before proceeding to the river's edge what took place?

4. How many people were in this great company? How many cattle and sheep?

5. What happened as the feet of the priests bearing the Ark touched the waters of the Jordan?

6. Where did the priests stand with the Ark as Israel crossed the Jordan?

7. What monuments to this miracle were erected?

8. At what town did the Israelites set up camp?

9. What Jewish rite was performed here? Why had this rite been neglected?

10. What religious festival was celebrated? Why had it been neglected?

11. Who appeared to Joshua at Gilgal? What name did he assume? What message did he give Joshua?

12. Tell of the plan of attack on Jericho? Was it successful?

13. In what manner did Joshua save the lives of Rahab and her family?

14. What directions did Joshua give concerning the spoils of war at Jericho?

STORY 61

ACHAN'S THEFT FROM GOD; THE DEFEAT OF ISRAEL AT AI

JOSHUA 7; 8:1-29

The next place which Josh'u-a planned to capture was a town of the Am'o-rites called Ai. It was situated about twenty miles northeast of Jer'i-cho on the main road leading to the mountainous regions of the interior of Ca'naan. Ai was not fortified like Jer'i-cho, but it was the home of about twelve thousand people, and it must be taken before an attack could be made upon other towns in the district.

Spies were sent to inspect the defenses of Ai, and to find the best way of attacking the town. They soon informed Josh'u-a that there would be no need of sending a large force against it. For this reason only three thousand men were sent to take the town. The men of Ai met this small force of Is'ra-el-ites in battle, and inflicted a crushing defeat upon them. Many of the Is'ra-el-ites were slain, others were captured, and the rest were driven back to their camp.

When the news of this defeat spread through the camps of Is'ra-el the people were struck with terror. Josh'u-a was disappointed and sore at heart. He said, "Is'ra-el has been humiliated before the Ca'naan-ites and A'o-rites, and they will scorn our efforts to take this land." He and the elders of Is'ra-el gathered in the sanctuary of the Lord for prayer. They rent their clothing and threw dust upon their heads, for in those days these were the signs of great mourning. Josh'u-a cried to the Lord, "What shall we do when the children of Is'ra-el turn their backs before their enemies?"

The Lord appeared to Josh'u-a and told him that Is'ra-el's defeat was not because of the strength of their enemies, but because of weakness which had been caused by sin. "Someone among the Is'ra-el-ites," said the Lord, "has taken of the spoils of the conquest of Jer'i-cho which should have been consecrated to the Lord, and has used it for himself." Then he added, "No victory for Is'ra-el is possible until the thief has been found and punished."

The Lord knew who the guilty man was, but He wished Josh'u-a to point him out before the Is'ra-el-ites in such a way that everyone in the camp would be convinced of his guilt. There must be no doubt in the mind of anyone as to the cause of Is'ra-el's defeat at Ai. The criminal himself must be made to realize the terrible wrong which he had committed, and to confess that his punishment was just.

It is not clear exactly how the guilty man was found, but we know that the discovery was made by casting lots. It was learned that the criminal was a member of the tribe of Ju'dah, that he was a descendant of Za'rah, who was one of the five sons of Ju'dah; that he was a member of the household of Zab'di (also called Zim'ri), and that he was a son of Car'mi.

THE PUNISHMENT OF ACHAN

At last the lot fell upon A'chan. Thus the finding of the criminal was marked with terrible certainty, for the Lord had directed the entire process.

When the finger of God pointed him out as the guilty one, A'chan frankly confessed his sin at once. He said, "I have sinned against the Lord, and my guilt has been discovered before all Is'ra-el. I stole a royal garment woven entirely of gold, an ingot of gold shaped like a wedge, and several pieces of silver. All these are hidden in my tent."

Josh'u-a sent men to search the tent, and there they found all the articles mentioned by A'chan. The value of the silver and gold was between seven and eight hundred dollars, and the royal garment was probably worth even more. A'chan had really stolen from the Lord, for it had been commanded that everything taken in Jer'i-cho should be consecrated to His service.

All the members of A'chan's family had known of his theft, and had probably aided him in hiding the stolen goods. For this reason they all received the same punishment as A'chan: they were stoned to death, and their bodies were burned. The place where they were put to death was called A'chor, which means "trouble," and it was marked with a pillar of stones as a warning to all future generations.

All Is'ra-el now knew that the disgraceful defeat at Ai had not been caused by the superior strength of the enemy, but by the sin of A'chan. A golden wedge sinfully hidden in the camp of Is'ra-el was more to blame for their defeat than the many swords of the warriors of a heathen city.

Greatly encouraged by a special message from the Lord, Josh'u-a now. planned a new attack upon the city of Ai. Soldiers were placed in strongholds at different points around the city, and the men of Ai were tempted to come out for battle. While these men were pursuing one group of He'brew soldiers, another group entered the city and set fire to it. The armies of Is'ra-el then turned against the men of Ai in a great battle, and slew every one of them. The king was captured, and was later hanged upon a tree.

Under special permission granted by the Lord, all the cattle, sheep, and other property captured in the city of Ai were given to the soldiers who had taken part in the attack.

After the destruction of Ai, the children of Is'ra-el continued their march across the mountains of central Ca'naan until they came to a place near the ancient city of She'chem. Here Josh'u-a built an altar of stones, and offered burnt sacrifices to God. All the children of Is'ra-el took part in the prolonged service of consecration which was then held.

At the high place where the Is'ra-el-ites gathered for this service two high mountains faced one another, with a narrow depression between them. The mountain to the north was called Mount E'bal, and the one to the south was called Mount Ger'i-zim. Josh'u-a divided the tribes of Is'ra-el into two groups, placing six tribes on Mount E'bal, and the other six on Mount Ger'i-zim. He then read to the assembled Is'ra-el-ites the laws which had been given to Mo'ses. When he read the warnings of God against disobedience, and related the judgments to be imposed upon those who failed to keep God's law, the children of Is'ra-el who stood on the slopes of Mount E'bal shouted, "Amen!" Then he read the promises and words of blessing for those who obeyed the laws of God, and the Is'ra-el-ites upon Mount Ger'i-zim also joined in saying "Amen."

There is great meaning in the fact that the mountains where this ceremony took place were exactly in the center of the land of Pal'es-tine. From Si'don, on the northern boundary, to Ka'deah-Barnea on the south;

and from the Med'i-ter-ra'ne-an Sea on the west to the top of the mountain range of Gil'e-ad on the eastern boundary, the mountains of E'bal and Ger'i-zim are exactly at the half-way point. The renewal of the covenant of Is'ra-el with God at this central point, and at the beginning of the conquest of Ca'naan, was a sign that the children of Is'ra-el would finally take possession of the entire land. It was also a sign of complete obedience to the laws of God in every part of the land which He had given them.

For many centuries after this wonderful ceremony the vicinity of these two holy mountains was the chief place of worship for the children of Is'ra-el. It was at Shi'loh that the Ark of the Cov'e-nant rested for a long period. The prophets of later times often spoke of the sacrifices offered in this neighborhood. Even in the closing years of the He'brew monarchy the history, tales, and legends associated with Mount Ger'i-zim competed in glory with those of Je-ru'sa-lem. In the days of our Sav'ior upon earth, the woman of Sa-ma'ri-a said, "Our fathers worshiped in this mountain."

After the close of the ceremonies on Mount E'bal and Mount Ger'i-zim, which probably lasted for several days, the Is'ra-el-ites returned to their encampment at Gil'gal. Josh'u-a continued his preparations for further combat with the heathen tribes which then occupied various parts of Ca'naan, and for the conquest of the entire land in the name of the Lord.

SUGGESTIONS FOR STUDY

Biblical Index to Helpful References

Achan the Troubler of Israel. (Josh. 22: 20; 1 Chr. 2:7.)

A Similar Crime and Similar Punishment in the New Testament. (Acts 5:1-11.)

Allurements of Sin. (Prov. 9:17; Jas. 1: 14.)

Defeat Because of the Displeasure of God.

(Ps. 44:10, 11.)

Success by Cooperation with God. (1 Sam. 14:45; Mark 16:20.)

Confounding of the Wicked. (Gen. 11:8; Job. 5:12; Isa. 37:27.)

Reading the Book of the Law Solemnly Enjoined. (Deut. 31:26-29.)

Questions

1. What town was next in the plans of attack by Joshua? Locate it. Give size.

2. How many soldiers were sent against it? Why no larger army?

3. What was the result of the attack by the Israelites?

4. What was the cause of the defeat?

5. In what way was the guilty party discovered?

6. What had Achan taken? Give the probable value. Why was his act wrong?

7. After the defeat of Ai where did Joshua lead the Israelites?

8. Describe the consecration services held in the mountains of Ephraim.

9. How are these mountains located in reference to Palestine?

10. Near these mountains was what city? Why important?

STORY 62

JOSHUA CONQUERS SOUTHERN CANAAN; THE SUN AND MOON STAND STILL; THOUSANDS KILLED BY HAILSTONES

JOSHUA 9, 10

The news of Is'ra-el's great meeting on Mount E'bal and Mount Ger'i-zim was soon spread among the various heathen nations of Ca'naan, and they began to seek some way of acting together to keep the chosen people of God out of their land. All the heathen tribes agreed that the victories of Is'ra-el over the Am'o-rites east of the Jor'dan, and the conquest of the lands of Mid'i-an and Am'mon had been won through the favor of God upon the He'brews. They also felt that the destruction of Jer'i-cho and Ai would have been impossible without the Lord's help. They knew that the covenant meeting in the mountains was held for the purpose of dedicating all Is'ra-el to God, and that He had promised to give them the entire land. Their determination to fight Is'ra-el was also a rebellion against God, for in opposing His chosen people they defied His power and rule.

Among the heathen peoples there was one tribe which was impressed by the righteous cause of Is'ra-el, and which was so greatly moved by the fear of God that it deserted the other nations and sought an alliance with Is'ra-el. These people, who were known as the Gib'eon-ites, or Hi'vites, were known to be strong and courageous, but they realized that power and bravery can avail nothing in a fight against God.

For some reason the Gib'eon-ites did not wish to make themselves known in their offer of alliance with Is'ra-el, so they adopted a clever disguise. A group of their wisest and most able men pretented to be common laborers who had come from a distant land. Wearing old, ragged clothing, and carrying torn wine-skins and mouldy bread, they came to Josh'u-a begging for mercy.

They professed to have faith in the true God, showed great respect for the miraculous power which had blessed and protected Is'ra-el, and expressed a strong desire to join the people who had been shown such favor by the Lord. They even suggested that they become servants of the Is'ra-el-ites, promising to do whatever tasks that might be given them.

Josh'u-a was deceived by the request of the Gib'eon-ites. Without knowing who they were, he and the elders of Is'ra-el formed a league with them and agreed to spare the lives of their people. A treaty of peace was then made without seeking the advice of the Lord, and the princes of Is'ra-el gave their word to abide by it.

Three days later the Is'ra-el-ites found out that the Gib'eon-ites were close neighbors, and that they occupied four large and important towns directly east of Is'ra-el's encampment at Gil'gal. Then the Is'ra-el-ites declared that they were no longer bound by a treaty which had been gained by trickery, and that the lives of the Gib'eon-ites should not be spared. But Josh'u-a and the princes of Is'ra-el replied, "We have sworn unto them by the Lord, the God of Is'ra-el; now therefore we may not touch them." The leaders of Is'ra-el felt that a solemn agreement should be kept, even though one of the parties to it has not acted in good faith.

It appears that this treaty had the approval of the Lord, for Saul, who was king of Is'ra-el several hundred years later, was severely rebuked for slaying a group of Gib'eon-ites. Although God condemned them to slavery for their lying and deception, He honored their faith. The league which Josh'u-a and the princes of Is'ra-el had made with them was confirmed and made permanent by the Lord.

It also appears that the occupation of these four cities without warfare was a great advantage to the Is'ra-el-ites. The cities were midway between strong heathen nations to the north and to the south; by occupying them, Josh'u-a was able to thrust his army like a wedge into the center of the unfriendly nations of the country. Thus the alliance of the Ca'-naan-ites was broken up almost before it had gotten under way.

Among the stronger cities of southern Ca'naan there were five which were held by different tribes of Am'o-rites. These were as follows: Je-ru'sa-lem, about twenty miles southeast of Gil'gal; He'bron, one of the most ancient and important cities of the country, located about twenty-five miles south of Je-ru'sa-lem; Jar'muth, about fifteen miles southwest of Je-ru'sa-lem; La'chish, about thirty-five miles southwest of Je-rusa-lem; and Eg'lon, which was just north of La'chish. The people who lived in all these cities, and in the smaller towns which formed a part of each tribal territory, were noted for bravery and military skill.

The king of Je-ru'sa-lem feared that he would be the next to be attacked by Josh'u-a, for his city and territory was nearest to the encampment of Is'ra-el at Gil'gal, and to the royal city of the Gib'eon-ites who had formed

THE SUN AND MOON STAND STILL

a league of peace with the Is'ra-el-ites. He sent an urgent request to the kings of all these other cities to join him in battle against the Gib'eon-ites, thinking that by conquering and occupying the cities of Gib'eon he and his allies would be in a better position to defend Je-ru'sa-lem. In asking for this alliance the king of Je-ru'sa-lem was moved by fear, and by a spirit of revenge. He felt that he was unable to defeat the Is'ra-el-ites, that the Gib'eon-ites who had allied with Is'ra-el should be punished as traitors to the cause of the heathen nations of the land, and that the best way to withstand the Is'ra-el-ites was to conquer their allies.

The kings of these four cities agreed to the request, and there marched against the city of Gib'eon an army of five nations combined. This army was so much greater in numbers and strength that the forces of the Gib'-eon-ites were in grave danger of complete destruction. Terrified by the superior forces of the five nations which gathered before their city, the Gib'eon-ites sent an urgent appeal to Josh'u-a for help.

Josh'u-a's response was prompt and wholehearted. He immediately led the host of Is'ra-el against the armies of the five united kings, marching all night in order to make an attack early the next morning. The distance from Gil'gal to Gib'eon was about eighteen miles, but by daybreak there was an Is'ra-el-ite army numbering at least four hundred thousand ready to go into battle at once. In the meantime the Lord appeared to Josh'u-a in a vision and promised him success, saying to him, "I have delivered them into thy hand." Thus victory was assured before a single blow had been struck.

In the battle which followed, the Is'ra-el-ites fell upon the armies of the Am'o-rite kings like a mighty avalanche rolling down a mountain. The Am'o-rites were slaughtered by the thousands as they fled before the attack, and they were too greatly terrified and confused to make a firm stand. Soon they rushed in mad retreat down the western pass from Gib'eon, pursued by the Is'ra-el-ites, and constantly growing weaker. Then they fled up the steep mountain slopes leading to Beth-Ho'ron, a few miles to the northwest.

The Am'o-rites thought that they had found a place of security in this little city, but the hand of God soon struck them a heavior blow than that which they had just received from Is'ra-el. The Lord caused a great hail storm to fall upon them, some of the stones weighing as much as a pound, and it is said, "more were slain by the hailstones of the Lord than by the swords of Is'ra-el." Just as the fire and brimstone had fallen from heaven upon their ancestors in Sod'om and Go'mor'rah, so deadly weapons of ice now poured down upon the idolatrous Am'o-rites.

While the sun hung in the heavens near the western horizon, and while the Am'o-rites who still lived were fleeing to a smaller town nearby, Josh'u-a made an earnest prayer to the Lord. He asked that the sun and moon in the heavens be made to stand still, and the waning day prolonged, until the last of the enemies of Is'ra-el had been put to death. A poet has described the prayer and its answer in these words:

"Sun, stand thou still upon Gib'eon;
And thou, Moon, in the valley of Ai'ja-lon.
And the sun stood still, and the moon stayed,
Until the nation had avenged themselves of their enemies."

It is said that the day was prolonged to twice its usual length, until the

Is'ra-el-ites had slain every soldier of the five united kings. The kings themselves were captured in a cave where they had sought to hide, and were brought before Josh'u-a. They were forced to submit to a custom of the times which may seem cruel to us. Certain princes of Is'ra-el pressed their feet upon the necks of the kings, thereby showing that humiliating defeat was sure to be inflicted upon all who opposed the conquest of Ca'naan by the Is'ra-el-ites. Then the unhappy kings were hanged on a tree, and after the sun had gone down they were buried in the cave where they had hidden.

Then followed a new series of battles and victories in which five other important cities were destroyed by the Is'ra-el-ites. Before this triumphant campaign ended, the entire southern territory of Ca'naan was conquered by Josh'u-a. Then Josh'u-a and his army returned to Gil'gal, leaving the banners of conquest floating over the entire land from Ka'desh-Barnea on the south to Ga'za on the north, and from the low-lands of the Med'i-terra'ne-an on the west to the city of Gib'eon on the east.

SUGGESTIONS FOR STUDY

Biblical Index to Helpful References

Origin of Heathen Nations in Canaan. (Gen. 10:16-20.)

God's Curse Against the Amorites. (Gen. 15:16; 48:22.)

God's Promise to Give to Israel the Land of Canaanite Heathens. (Ex. 23:23.)

The Alliances of Evil Men Against God. (Ps. 2:2; 56:6.)

God's Help for His People Against Evil Alliances. (Ps. 83:5-18; Mic. 4:11-13.)

The Wicked Put to Shame. (Ps. 25:3; Isa. 25:11.)

The Sin of Deception. (Matt. 2:8, 12.)

The Duty of Guarding Against Deception. (1 Jno. 4:1.)

Questions

1. How did the heathen nations of Canaan feel about the victories of Israel?

2. What five strong nations formed an alliance to war against Israel?

3. From whom had they descended? Did they know of God's favor toward the Israelites?

4. What nation in Canaan refused to fight against Israel and made a league peace with Joshua?

5. Tell of the clever manner in which they sought this alliance?

6. When the Israelites found out their local identity what happened?

7. What service were they required to do in Israel? How did this result?

8. What five cities in southern Canaan formed an alliance against Israel?

9. What people did they attack? Did Joshua go to the aid of Gibeonites?

10. Tell of the route of Israel's enemies?

11. In what way did the Lord aid the Israelites at Beth-Horon?

12. Tell of the sun's halt in the skies while Joshua completely defeated the fleeing enemies?

13. Outline the territories conquered in this campaign of Joshua?

THE CONQUEST OF NORTHERN CANAAN; CALEB WINS HONOR

JOSHUA 11-14

Following the victory of Is'ra-el over the united kings of southern Ca'naan, and the conquest of all their cities and towns, Josh'u-a turned his attention to the vast mountain regions of northern Ca'naan and the plains of the Med'i-ter-ra'ne-an. Only one year was needed in the conquest of southern Ca'naan, beginning with the over-throw of Jer'i-cho, but it took about five years to subdue the northern part of the Promised Land. We come now to the close of this period.

On the way the Lord appeared to Josh'u-a in a vision, saying, "Tomorrow about this time I will deliver this great army into thy hands." It was the largest and best equipped army which Is'ra-el had been forced to meet, and for the first time they were to encounter cavalrymen and war chariots. It was only natural for the Is'ra-el-ites to be alarmed by these new dangers, so the Lord said to Josh'u-a, "Thou shalt smite their horses and burn their chariots with fire."

In the battle on the plains of the waters of Me'rom, Josh'u-a and his army made the attack. Aided by the Lord they descended upon the mighty army of northern Ca'naan with such force that the allied heathen soldiers were completely defeated. Thousands were killed, their horses were slain, and the war chariots were either captured or destroyed. The army of Ca'naan was driven from the field, and forced to retreat eastward toward the coastal city of Zi'don, and into the valley of

THE CRAFTINESS OF THE GIBEONITES

Miz'peh. Is'ra-el pursued the Ca'naan-ites, burning their cities and slaying their kings. The entire country was conquered, and the heathen people were destroyed.

On his return from these victories Josh'u-a paused long enough to destroy the city of Ha'zor and to slay its king. Even the giant-like people of the city of He'bron and the mountains of Ju'dah, who had been so terrifying to ten of the twelve spies who were sent out forty years before, were conquered and slain. Except for a few scattered towns, the entire land was brought under conquest.

When seven years of continuous warfare had finally brought these victories to Is'ra-el, the Lord said to Josh'u-a, "Thou art old and stricken in strength, and their remaineth yet many isolated sections of the country to be conquered. These shall be given to Is'ra-el under my providence and by my power. But before you reach the end of your way, it is to be your privilege and duty to divide the land of Ca'naan among the twelve tribes." So Josh'u-a allotted certain territory to each tribe, and set the boundary lines. Towns and areas yet unconquered within any of the allotted territories were to be taken by the tribes to which they had been assigned.

In making the allotments of land to the twelve tribes of Is'ra-el, one man of the tribe of Ju'dah had shown great ability. It was Ca'leb, who was the only man among the Is'ra-el-ites, except Josh'u-a, who was past sixty years of age when they crossed the Jor'dan into the land of Ca'naan. He was honored in a special manner because of his faithfulness as one of the spies sent out by Mo'ses. The giants which had caused a spirit of fear and cowardice among the Is'ra-el-ites lived in the vicinity of He'bron. In making their report to Mo'ses, Ca'leb and Josh'u-a had said, "We are well able to subdue these mighty people." For forty-five years Ca'leb had waited to make good that statement, and to occupy the city of He'bron which had vividly remained in his memory.

When the time arrived for the land of Ca'naan to be divided among the families of Is'ra-el, Ca'leb came to Josh'u-a and said, "I was forty years old when Mo'ses sent me to spy out this land, and though I am now eighty-five, I am as strong as I was in the day that Mo'ses commanded us to inspect the land of Ca'naan. I am fully capable for the most strenuous demands of warfare with the strongest peoples of these mountainous regions. The Lord promised me that I should have this part of the land, and now I ask that He'bron and the mountains occupied by roving giants be given to me."

This bold request proved the heroic spirit of Ca'leb. In his bravery, however, he counted upon the favor of God for future victories over these strong enemies, and he confessed, "If the Lord shall be with me, then shall I be able to drive out these giants." The request of Ca'leb was granted by Josh'u-a, and a special blessing was pronounced upon him.

A few miles southwest of He'bron there was a place known as De'bir, or Kir'jath-Seph'er, which was strongly fortified by one of the bravest of the tribes of giants. Ca'leb asked for a volunteer to lead in attacking and capturing this stronghold.

Among the bravest men of his army was a captain named Oth'ni-el, who was in love with Ca'leb's daughter Ach'sah. Ca'leb hoped that his daughter would choose for her husband a man who was noted for honor, bravery, and zeal in the conquest of the land, so he proposed to give his daughter in marriage to the man who led in taking De'bir.

Oth'ni-el offered to undertake this task, not only because he was willing to risk his life for the woman he loved, but because he was a man of superior courage and character. His bold attack upon the strongly defended place was successful, Ach'sah was given to him in marriage, and at her request Ca'leb bestowed a dowry more than was customary.

After the death of Josh'u-a, Oth'ni-el was chosen as the first Judge of all Is'ra-el, and he served his nation for many years with honor and distinction.

SUGGESTIONS FOR STUDY

Biblical Index to Helpful References

(See Index to Helpful References in preceding chapter.)

The Promised Inheritance of Israel. (Lev. 20:24.)

The Whole Hearted Consecration of Caleb. (Num. 13:6, 30; 14:24; 26:65.)

Hebron Noted from Days of Abraham. (Gen. 13:18; 23:2; Num. 13:22.)

The Courage of the Righteous. (Ps. 27:3; Isa. 12:2.)

The Duty of Manliness. (Isa. 46:8; Ezek. 22:30.)

Questions

1. How many independent nations were there in northern Canaan?

2. How many allied soldiers were mobilized by Jabin to fight the Israelites?

3. Where did these armies gather for battle?

4. Why were the Israelites hesitant about entering this battle?

5. What encouragement was given Joshua by the Lord?

6. Tell of Israel's great victory.

7. How long had the war for conquest of Canaan continued?

8. What had been the results of the war of conquest?

9. What territory did Caleb ask for? Why?

10. In conquering this territory who did he select to fight against Kerjath-Sepher? Why?

11. What was result of the battle? How was Othniel rewarded?

STORY 64

THE DIVISION OF CANAAN AMONG THE TWELVE TRIBES OF ISRAEL

JOSHUA 15-19

For nearly seven years after the Is'ra-el-ites entered the land of Ca'naan under the leadership of Josh'u-a they were engaged in unceasing war. Several invasions were made in various parts of the land, and the whole country was subdued. The Is'ra-el-ites had succeeded in breaking the power of all the idolatrous nations which formerly occupied the land of Ca'naan.

Before the death of Mo'ses the Mo'ab-ites, Am'mon-ites, and Am'o-rites had been routed from their lands east of the Jor'dan, and this territory had been given to the tribes of Reu'ben and Gad, and to half of the tribe of Ma'nas-seh.

In the southern section of Ca'naan west of the Jor'dan the Am'a-lek-ites, Ke'nites, and E'dom-ites had been overcome by Josh'u-a, and their lands were allotted to the tribes of Ju'dah and Sim'e-on.

In the mountainous central regions west of the Jor'dan the combined forces of Is'ra-el had completely defeated the Hi'vites, Ca'naan-ites, Hit'-tites, Per'iz-zites, and Je'bu-sites, and their lands were assigned to the tribes of Ben'ja-min and E'phra-im, and to the other half of the tribe of Ma'nas-seh.

The northern section of the land west of the Jor'dan was taken from the Am'or-ites, Ca'naan-ites, and Gir'ga-shites, and their lands were given to the tribes of Is'sa-char, Zeb'u-lun, and Naph'ta-li.

The Med'i-ter-ra'ne-an coastal region had been occupied by the Phi-lis'-tines, Ca'naan-ites, and Zi'don-ians, but these strong nations had been subdued by Josh'u-a. The lands in this district were assigned to the tribe of Ash'er on the northwest, to Dan in the west central part of the land, and parts of these grants were added to the territory of E'phra-im and Ma'nas-seh.

Within the territories taken from all these heathen nations there remained many towns and settlements which were not conquered in the general war led by Josh'u-a. Although Josh'u-a was nearly one hundred years old, and his strength was failing, he felt it his duty to go on with the conflict until every city was won and no land was left unpossessed by Is'ra-el.

But the Lord directed him to bring to a close the general war, and to divide the land west of the Jor'dan among the nine tribes of Is'ra-el which had not yet received their allotments, and to provide for the other half of the tribe of Ma'nas-seh. The conquest of the cities and lands which were still unsubdued was to be placed in the hands of the various tribes in whose territory they were situated.

Throughout his faithful ministry Josh'u-a had repeatedly been promised by the Lord that he should cause the Is'ra-el-ites to inherit the Promised Land. One of his greatest desires was to see each of the tribes settled in the territory which was to be allotted, to have the whole land divided among them according to the directions of God. And so the Lord directed him to cease from war, and to divide the land. After this, he was to retire, leaving the conquest of all unpossessed lands and cities entirely in the hands of the various tribes.

God also directed him to remove the tabernacle from Gil'gal, where it had stood for nearly seven years, to a place called Shi'loh in the mountainous region which was to be allotted to the tribe of E'phra-im. This city was situated in the geographical center of the land of the Is'ra-el-ites, and remained the central place of worship for the whole nation for more than three hundred years. The Ark of the Cov'e-nant was thus placed at a point which was convenient for all the people, and the He'brews from every part of the land, including the tribes east of the Jor'dan, were required to go up to Shi'loh for special sacrifices and religious festivals.

Before moving the tabernacle from Gil'gal to Shi'loh, Josh'u-a made allotments for the tribes of Ju'dah and Sim'e-on. After setting up the tabernacle at Shi'loh he called the entire house of Is'ra-el into an assembly for allotting the remaining territory of Ca'naan to the other seven tribes, and to the half tribe of Ma'nas-seh which had so far received no land. A commission of thirty-six men, three from each of the tribes of Is'ra-el, was appointed to make a complete survey of the land not yet allotted, and to set the boundaries for the allotments which were about to be made. After devoting about six months to a survey of these lands, the commission reported its findings to Josh'u-a, and the allotments were made.

In making these allotments great care was taken to follow the prophecies which Ja'cob had made concerning each tribe two hundred and fifty years before, and which had been confirmed by Mo'ses in his farewell

JOSHUA SLAYS THE GIANTS

address. Each tribe was given the territory best adapted to its own habits and occupations, and to the place which it would hold in the future history of the entire nation.

The tribe of Ju'dah was the largest in numbers, there being 76,500 men above the age of twenty who were able to bear arms. It had been honored with the position of leadership, and from it would be born the future kings of the nation and the promised Mes-si'ah. This tribe was therefore given a large mountainous area west of the Dead Sea and extending to the Med'i-ter-ra'ne-an. This tract was filled with fertile valleys and hills, and abounded in fruitful vineyards and green pastures.

The tribe of Sim'e-on was the smallest in numbers, having only 22,200 warriors. It had been predicted that this tribe would be closely associated with the tribe of Ju'dah, and dependent upon them in many respects. Sim'e-on was therefore given a territory south of the allotment of Ju'dah, bordering on the deserts of E'dom. The soil was poor in quality, the climate very dry for most of the year, and the country was unable to sustain even this small tribe. For this reason a number of cities within the borders of Ju'dah were assigned to Sim'e-on.

It had been predicted that Ben'ja-min would be a tribe given to conquest, and in the wars of Ca'naan its members had been noted for courage and bravery. In occupation and habits, the people of this tribe were very much like those of Ju'dah. Since it was comparatively small in numbers, having only 45,600 able bodied men over twenty, there was no need for a large area. Ben'ja-min therefore received a small mountainous territory north of the eastern half of Ju'dah, and not far from the future ruling powers of the nation.

The tribe of Dan was destined for a position of leadership in culture, political power, and the development of crafts. Numbering 64,400 warriors, it was allotted a comparatively small area just north of Ju'dah, and east of the territory given to Ben'ja-min and E'phra-im. This small tract however, was capable of supporting a large and growing population, for it embraced the wide and fertile plans of the Med'i-ter-ra'ne-an.

Special favors had been promised to the tribe of E'phra-im because its members were descendants of one of the sons of Jo'seph. They had shown great courage during the wars of Is'ra-el, and had become prosperous in flocks and herds. Although the tribe at this time numbered only 32,500 men above the age of twenty, it had been promised a multitude of descendants; E'phra-im therefore received a very large area in central Ca'-naan. This territory extended from the Jor'dan on the east to the Med'i-ter-ra'e-an on the west, and was north of Ben'ja-min and Dan. Most of this area was very mountainous, but the soil was rich and fertile, and fresh streams of water flowed in abundance. It was, in many respects, the best part of Ca'naan. Within its borders were the mountains of E'bal and Ger'iz-im, where the covenant had been renewed by Is'ra-el soon after entering Ca'naan; the sacred city of She'chem, and other places memorable in the lives of A'bra-ham, I'saac, and Ja'cob.

The tribe of Ma'nas-seh, descendants of the other son of Jo'seph, had grown in numbers much more rapidly than the tribe of E'phra-im, and its male population over the age of twenty totalled 52,700. Its members had also prospered in flocks and herds, and were noted for skill and bravery in war. To half of this tribe Mo'ses had allotted the territory east of Jor'dan known as Gil'e-ad. To the other half Josh'u-a gave a section of the best territory of Ca'naan lying north of E'phra-im, extending from the Jor'dan to the Med'i-ter-ra'ne-an Sea. Even with these two large areas, the tribe of Ma'nas-seh complained that they needed more land. Josh'u-a told them to help the other tribes in taking some of the cities yet unconquered, and that cities which they took outside of their allotment would belong to them.

The tribe of Is'sa-char was one of the larger of the twelve, having an adult male population of 64,300. It had been predicted that they would be an agricultural people, content with the fruits of peace and industry, and having no desire for the adventures of war. Material prosperity was their chief object in life, yet they did not have enterprise enough to avoid paying tribute to other nations which were stronger. They were given a rather small area just north of Ma'nas-seh, with the Jor'dan forming the eastern boundary, extending north for about thirty miles, and west for

about the same distance. The land was mountainous, but within its borders there were many fertile plains, rich valleys, and several important
towns. The main road leading from the Med'i-ter-ra'ne-an to the interior
of Ca'naan passed through the southern part of their territory.

It had been predicted that the descendants of Zeb'u-lun would become
a great maritime people. This tribe had increased greatly in numbers,
having a male population over the age of twenty of 60,500. The people
were chiefly interested in commerce and industrial growth. They received
a comparatively small district immediately northwest of Is'sa-char, and
bordering on the Med'i-ter-ra'ne-an Sea for a distance of about fifteen
miles. The land was less mountainous than much of Ca'naan, and there
were many fertile plains and valleys. On the west was a part of the plains
of Me-gid'do, famed as a battlefield in both ancient and medieval times,
and over which passed the road from the Med'i-ter-ra'ne-an to the interior
of the country.

According to the prophecies of both Ja'cob and Mo'ses, the descendants
of Naph'ta-li were to be noted for vivacity, timidity, and mildness in manner. From them were to come men and women gifted with eloquence in
both prose and poetry. Ba'rak was descended from this tribe, and most
of the apostles of our Sav'ior who preached the Gospel with such power
came from this region. To this tribe, with its 53,400 men over twenty,
Josh'u-a allotted a large inland area north of Is'sa-char, with Zeb'u-lun
and Ash'er on the west, and bordering on the river Jor'dan to the east.
The southern projections and foot-hills of the famed Leb'anon mountains
extended into this area, giving it richness and fertility. Ha'zor, the capital
city of Ja'bin, who led in the unsuccessful league against Is'ra-el, was
located in this territory. On its southeastern border was the sea of Chin'-
ne-roth, later known as the sea of Gal'i-lee, around which the Sav'ior spent
much of his public ministry.

Ja'cob and Mo'ses had predicted that the tribe of Ash'er would enjoy
great worldly prosperity. Their land was to be one of plenty, providing not
only necessities, but dainties of the richest kind. At the time the allotments were made, Ash'er numbered 53,400 men over the age of twenty.
To them was assigned a strip of territory along the coast of the Med'i-ter-
ra'ne-an extending from Mt. Car'mel on the south to the city of Tyre on
the north, and extending eastward for fifteen to twenty-five miles. This
area was made up of low mountains and rich plains, well adapted to growing the finest grains. The mountains were rich in valuable minerals and

oils. The whole country was covered with olive orchards, gardens of trop-
ical fruits, and broad fields of wheat. It was from this rich district that
Sol'o-mon, several centuries later, supplied food for his friendly neighbors
in Tyre and Si'don. Ac'cho, the best seaport on the Med'i-ter-ra'ne-an
coast, was situated at the southern end of Ash'er, and was the center of
sailing and commerce by men from the tribes of Ash'er and Zeb'u-lun.

The prophetic statements of Ja'cob and Mo'ses concerning the descendants of Gad indicated that these people were to be patient and persevering,
capable of strong resistance in war. They were also skilled in the occupation of stock-raising. To them Mo'ses had assigned a large territory
east of the Jor'dan, extending from the borders of Reu'ben on the south
near the northern end of the Dead Sea to the southern borders of Ma'nas-
seh on the north near the southern end of the sea of Chin'ne-roth. This
tract was about thirty miles wide. It was well watered and adapted to
stock-raising, and was so situated that the Gad'ites could join the people
of Ma'nas-seh in resisting invasions of the wandering tribes of the Syr'i-an
desert east of the borders of Is'ra-el.

Reu'ben, as the eldest son of Ja'cob, was entitled to the first rank among
the tribes, and to a double share in the inheritance of Ca'naan. But he had
lost these privileges by committing a great sin, and by leading a life which
did not do him credit. Ja'cob therefore predicted that Reu'ben's descendants would hold a place of little importance in the inheritance of the
twelve tribes.

The territory allotted to Reu'ben by Mo'ses was on the east side of the
Jor'dan and the Dead Sea, extending from the borders of Gad on the
north to the land of Mo'ab on the south, and was about thirty miles wide.
It was mountainous and well watered. Although the section lying along
the Dead Sea was useless for human habitation or for pasturage, the
remainder of this territory was well adapted to stock-raising, and was
given to the tribe of Reu'ben because of these advantages.

Two hundred and fifty years before the occupation of Ca'naan by the
Is'ra-el-ites, Ja'cob had predicted that the tribe of Le'vi would be scattered
throughout all the other tribes of the nation. Then, forty years before
Is'ra-el entered the Promised Land, Mo'ses had directed that the male
members of this tribe should be set apart for religious services as assistants
to the priests, and that no inheritance or allotment be given to them. So,
in the division of Ca'naan by Josh'u-a, no allotments were made to this
tribe.

Provision was made for them, however, in the appointment of forty-eight cities throughout the various tribes for their residence. While these cities were not owned by the Le'vites, nor occupied by them alone, enough houses were set aside to meet their needs. Provision was made for their support by requiring the people of all the tribes to present tithes from their products of the land and from the increase of their sheep and cattle. Thus these religious workers were distributed throughout the land of Is'ra-el, and their needs were provided for so that all the people could be served by them.

Having completed the allotments of territory for all the tribes of Is'ra-el settled west of the Jor'dan, and having confirmed the allotments made by Mo'ses east of the river, Josh'u-a solemnly warned the people that the Ca'naan-ites must be completely driven out of the territory allotted to each tribe. He then sent all the tribes to the territories to which they had been assigned, and took up residence in the special allotment which had been provided for him. He had faithfully served the interest of the Nation under Mo'ses for forty years; and for seven years he had led Is'ra-el in a continuous war in conquering much of the land of a Ca'naan. He retired to a well earned and much deserved period of rest.

SUGGESTIONS FOR STUDY

Biblical Index to Helpful References

Jacob's Prophecies Concerning Future of Each of the Tribes of Israel. (Gen. 49:1-28.)

Moses' Prophecies Concerning Future of Each Tribe. (Deut. 33.)

Original Consecration of the Tabernacle. (Lev. 8:10.)

Original Directions for Levites. (Num. 1:50; Deut. 12:19; 18:1, 2.)

Questions

1. Name the countries conquered by Moses east of the Jordan.

2. To what tribes was this territory allotted?

3. Name the heathen nations conquered in southern Canaan.

4. To what tribes was this territory allotted? Give the number in each tribe and reasons for the allotment.

5. Name the heathen nations conquered in mountainous central region of Canaan.

6. To what tribes was this territory allotted? Give the number in each tribe and reasons for the allotment.

7. Name the heathen nations of the north conquered by Joshua.

8. To what tribes was this territory allotted? Give the number in each tribe and reasons for the allotment.

9. What heathen nations occupied the Mediterranean coast plains?

10. To what tribes was this territory allotted? Give the number in each tribe and reasons for the allotment.

11. In allotting the territory to the tribes what directions did Joshua give respecting cities not yet conquered?

12. To what place was the tabernacle removed?

13. What provision was made for the tribe of Levi?

STORY 65

JOSHUA'S CLOSING YEARS; HIS FAREWELL MESSAGES TO ISRAEL

JOSHUA 23-24

After all the tribes of Is'ra-el had been allotted their territories, and the borders of each had been clearly defined, a special inheritance was given to Josh'u-a. He had been foremost in the service of his country, but was last to receive a reward. Not until he had brought the whole nation into rich possessions would he accept a home for himself. The same meek spirit which had dominated his entire service in the wars of Is'ra-el prevailed in the division of the land which had been conquered.

He asked of the High Priest E-le-a'zar and of the people that he be given the city of Tim'nath, an obscure place in the heart of the mountains of E'phra-im. Its chief fame in history is that it was founded and built by Josh'u-a, and that his body was buried in its vicinity.

With the smile of God upon him, with the satisfaction of having done his work well, and with the gratitude of Is'ra-el for his faithful services, Josh'u-a retired to this quiet mountain home to spend his declining years. He was then about ninety-three years old, and for forty-seven years all his energy had been devoted to the welfare of Is'ra-el. Grown old at last, and weakened by the toils and hardships of the war in Ca'naan, he was entitled to rest. He had built a nation for Is'ra-el, and now under the kindly providences of God he was permitted to build a humble city for himself. His strength was renewed, and so much of his former vigor restored that he lived to the ripe old age of one hundred and ten.

Then his strength began to fail so rapidly that he knew the hour of his departure was near. In these moments of physical weakness his faith in God grew stronger, and his interest in the future welfare of Is'ra-el became more intense. He sent out an invitation for the elders, the princes and judges, and the leaders of various ranks in all the tribes to come to his home for a special message. A prompt response was given to this invitation, and a group which represented all Is'ra-el gathered to hear his message. He spoke not of the perpetuation of his own honor, but only of the preservation of Is'ra-el's integrity and faithfulness to God.

In recounting his past services for Is'ra-el he boasted of nothing which
he had done, but called attention to the miraculous manner in which God
had fought for Is'ra-el. Nowhere in his message was there a word of self-
esteem or self-praise. He spoke of himself only as a servant of God, and
gave all honor to God as the Captain of the host of Is'ra-el. Every victory
he had won was credited to the guidance and power of God. He had done
nothing, but God had done everything.

Looking to the future of Is'ra-el, he urged these leaders to be very
courageous in doing all that God had commanded them, and assured
them that the same God who had enabled them to conquer so much of
the land would give them strength to drive out the heathens yet remaining within their borders. He earnestly warned them against joining in
the idol-worship practiced by the heathens in their midst and in the neighboring countries. Just as their victories of the past had been won by holding fast to God, so their future triumphs would depend upon their obedience to Him and to his commandments.

Josh'u-a spoke very plainly in his warnings against any social or domestic alliances with the heathen families not yet driven out of Ca'naan. The
Is'ra-el-ites must avoid the "snares and traps" of associating with such
people, for, once they were ensnared by them, "scourges" would pierce
their sides, and "thorns" would pluck out their eyes.

Setting forth the love of God for them, he warned the people that
love sinned against may be turned into fierce anger. Mercy rejected has
its counterpart in cold, stern justice. Transgression of the holy laws of
God demands righteous indignation against the transgressor. Josh'u-a
solemnly warned Is'ra-el that those who disobeyed God's law would perish quickly.

After delivering this message to the leaders of Is'ra-el, Josh'u-a lived
quietly in his home for a few months before death finally came to him.
He lived long enough to deliver a second and final message to all Is'ra-el.
In the first message he had spoken in a personal and private manner, but
in the second he spoke under direct inspiration from God. This address
was delivered before the whole house of Is'ra-el as they assembled at She'-
chem, which was the exact center of the Holy Land.

It was fitting for the last assembly of Is'ra-el to hear the voice of Josh'u-a
to be held at She'chem. It was here that the covenant was first given to
A'bra-ham four hundred and fifty years before. It was in this vicinity
that God appeared to Ja'cob in a vision by night and renewed the cove-

nant, and it was under an oak tree near this city that Ja'cob cast out the strange gods from his family. Twenty-three years before this assembly Josh'u-a had gathered all Is'ra-el on this sacred spot for the renewal of the covenant which God had made with A'bra-ham and I'saac and Ja'cob, and for the public reading of all the laws of Mo'ses. Here God had promised to this generation the inheritance of the whole land of Ca'naan, and here the people had solemnly pledged their obedience to all his laws. How fitting, then, for Is'ra-el to be in a place of so many holy memories to hear Josh'u-a's farewell address!

Josh'u-a began his address by reminding the Is'ra-el-ites of their humble origin. Their ancestors before the Flood had been idol-worshipers. A'bra-ham's father was an idolater, but he had been chosen of God and called out of a land of idolatry. Under the grace and protection of God he had sojourned in the land of Ca'naan, and God had promised this land as a national home for his descendants. The patriarchs I'saac and Ja'cob had dwelt in the land of Ca'naan, and with each of them God had renewed the covenant which he had made with A'bra-ham. Josh'u-a presented these facts as the basis of an appeal for humility, gratitude, and loyalty .

He then spoke briefly of the two hundred fifteen years in E'gypt, and of the slavery into which the Is'ra-el-ites had fallen toward the end of that period. He reminded them of the love of God in giving them Mo'ses to lead them out of bondage in E'gypt, and to impart to them the laws of God; of God's favor in giving them Aa'ron to direct their worship; and of the miraculous way in which God had cared for them and guided them during their forty years in the wilderness. It had been through God's help that they were delivered from the armies of E'gypt,

THE VILLAGE OF GRAPES

from the superior forces of the Am'a-lek-ites, from the scheming of Ba'lak and the greed of Ba'laam, and from the powerful tribes of the Am'o-rites.

The marvelous manner in which God had enabled them to conquer the warlike nations of Ca'naan was quickly reviewed. Strong enemies which might easily have defeated them had they been left to their own strength were overthrown by the Lord. Thirty-one strong heathen nations east of the Jor'dan had been subdued, and their lands and cities given to the Is'ra-el-ites for an inheritance. Under the gracious providence of God they were now living in houses which they had not built, gathering fruits from orchards which they had not planted, enjoying the finest of grapes from vineyards on which they had bestowed no labor, and living in security under His continued blessings.

With these proofs that God had chosen them as His people, with the record of four hundred and fifty years of miraculous favors from God in the past, and with the blessings which they now enjoyed as the basis of his appeal, Josh'u-a urged Is'ra-el to serve God with perfect sincerity. They were called upon to avoid every form of idolatry, and to serve and worship only the true God. Declaring his own allegiance to God, Josh'u-a challenged the faith of the others in these words, "Choose ye this day whom ye will serve."

To this challenge the people of Is'ra-el responded with pledges of absolute loyalty to God, declaring that they would never forsake Him, or serve other gods. Thinking of all the mighty works He had performed for them, they said, "There is no god like our God." With hearts full of gratitude for all that He had done for them, the people declared that they did not belong to themselves, to do as they pleased, but that they belonged to the God who had redeemed them as His very own.

Josh'u-a then warned them that they could not serve God and at the same time worship idols. He declared, "Our God is holy and jealous, and will not give or divide his glory with any other. You cannot serve Him in a half-hearted manner, nor can you serve Him in your own strength."

Although these words of Josh'u-a appeared to suggest that complete loyalty to God was beyond the strength of man, the Is'ra-el-ites replied, "Yes, but we will serve the Lord." They clung to their determination to be true to God and to refrain from every vestige of idolatry even more strongly and persistently than at first.

This declaration of faith and loyalty to Him was accepted by the Lord on condition that the Is'ra-el-ites immediately put out of their hearts every tendency to serve other gods. Josh'u-a reminded them once more that God is jealous, and will accept no divided services of any kind. Truly, God is jealous of his own glory, of the righteousness of his children, of the supremacy of his kingdom in the hearts and lives of his people, and of the influences which his people have over others. This jealousy is wholly unselfish, and is all-important in the happiness and welfare of God's children.

After receiving these solemn pledges of constant allegiance and loyalty to God, Josh'u-a made a covenant with the people. He also erected by the side of the tabernacle in She'chem a stone memorial to the promises which had been given him. This monument was to serve as an everlasting reminder of the pledges given to God on this memorable occasion, and as a witness against Is'ra-el if they departed from the Lord.

The people of Is'ra-el were sent back to their tribal homes, and soon afterwards Josh'u-a died and his body was buried in the borders of Tim'-nath. E-le-a'zar, the High Priest, died a short time later, and one by one the elders of Is'ra-el who had been associated with Josh'u-a also passed away. But Josh'u-a, though dead, continued to speak. His unselfish and holy life became an abiding power to hold those he had faithfully served steadfast in the faith. Through the gloom and heaviness caused by his death the radiant brightness of his noble character continued to shine.

SUGGESTIONS FOR STUDY

Biblical Index to Helpful References

Israel's Promised Inheritance of Canaan. (Lev. 20:24; Deut. 1:38.)

Heathens of Canaan to be Cast Out. (Ex. 34:24; Lev. 18:24.)

Sinful Imitation Denounced. (Ex. 23:2; Lev. 20:23.)

The Sorrows Accompanying Idolatry. (Ps. 16:4.)

The Sin of Backsliding. (Prov. 14:14; Jer. 2:19.)

God's Judgment Against Covenant-Breakers. (Lev. 26:15, 26; Ps. 55; 19, 20.)

The Call to Decision. (Deut. 30:15; Ruth 1:15.)

No Neutral Position Between Serving God and Satan. (Mark 9:40.)

Questions

1. What town was given to Joshua as a permanent home?

2. How old was he at that time? How long had he served Israel? How long did he live after settling in his home?

3. When his strength began to fail what did he ask Israel to do?

4. What warnings did he utter in this address?

5. Where did he later gather Israel for his last message? Why at that place?

6. In what manner did Joshua begin this last address?

7. Relate the events of Israel's past which should have encouraged them.

8. What challenge did Joshua make? What response was given by Israel?

9. Where was the body of Joshua buried?

STORY 66

OTHNIEL AND EHUD, TWO HEROES OF ISRAEL

JUDGES 3:8-31

It hardly seems possible that a people who had been so greatly honored by the Lord, and who had made such strong pledges of loyalty to him, would soon fall into disgraceful idolatry and heathen wickedness. And yet this is exactly what happened within twenty or thirty years after the death of Josh'u-a. A people, chosen of God, highly privileged and well trained, became treacherous in heart and wicked in life. A nation which had been founded by special acts of Divine Providence and blessed with the noblest leaders of any age suddenly forgot the favors of God, fell into a state of idolatry, and disobeyed the known will of God.

Instead of driving the idolaters out of the land, the Is'ra-el-ites mingled with them even to the point of worshiping their false gods. The covenant which they had solemnly made with God was rejected, the fear of God was cast off, His laws were scorned or forgotten, and the worship which belonged to Him was given to lifeless images.

Is'ra-el had avoided the danger of war with the heathens among them by forming sinful alliances, by accepting them as good neighbors, by entering into marriages which the Lord had forbidden, and by lowering their standards of religion. Because of these sins the Lord brought upon them a strong enemy from outside the land of the Is'ra-el-ites.

Chu'shan-Rish-a-tha'im, who was King of Syr'i-a on the Eu-phra'tes, and who was a terror throughout the East, invaded the land of Is'ra-el with a great army. His name stood for lawlessness, violence, and cruelty, and he was called "the crime-committing Chu'shan." He ruled the rich country of Mes-o-po-ta'mia, which lay between the Ti'gris and Eu-phra'tes rivers, and dominated neighboring countries for hundreds of miles around.

Traversing a distance of four hundred miles, this cruel king invaded the land of Is'ra-el from the east, and there followed one of the most tragic stories of the weakness caused by sin. The powerful host of God's people, before whom the armies of the Am'o-rites and Am'mon-ites had melted away like snow under a burning sun, trembled in fear of the invader from the far Northeast. The mighty army which had routed more than thirty kings in Ca'naan quailed in dismay, and the soldiers turned their backs in fright at the appearance of a single chieftain and his army from far away Syr'i-a.

For eight years the Is'ra-el-ites were forced to live under the oppression of Chu'shan. They were treated as though they were slaves, were beaten and tortured, and forced to pay heavy tribute to their masters. It was a period of terrible sufferings, of broken hearts and bruised limbs, and of unspeakable anguish as the people bowed under the iron rule of the dark prince of the house of Ham, notorious for his "double-wickedness." For their abandonment of God's covenant they were abandoned by God, and were left to reap the natural result of their idolatry and wickedness.

These long years of punishment worked out the purposes and mercy of God toward Is'ra-el. They were severely afflicted, not merely for the sake of punishment, but in order to correct and reform them. God was seeking to turn them back to himself. He was seeking to cure them of the dreadful disease which had done so much harm among them. When these purposes were fully accomplished, He raised up from among them a leader who delivered them from the rule of Chu'shan and restored peace and prosperity to the land. When Is'ra-el repented of their sins and cried in righteous sorrow to the Lord, He came to their help as quickly as He had so many times in the past.

THE ANGEL'S REBUKE

In choosing the man of the hour, who must be capable of organizing the Is'ra-el-ites for war against their foreign masters, and of leading them in breaking the yoke of a cruel king who had terrified the people for eight years, the Lord laid his hand on a veteran

EGLON SLAIN BY EHUD

named Oth'ni-el. He was a member of the family of Ke'-naz, was closely related to Ca'-leb, and had won honor in the early wars of Is'ra-el in Ca'naan. In the notable victory at De'bir his name had risen as a star of the first magnitude in the military skies of Is'ra-el.

Oth'ni-el was a man of ripe experience, being fully eighty-five years of age when he was called to judge Is'ra-el. He had learned long before that Is'ra-el's hope of victory in war depended upon faith in God, and that their defeats were always the result of unbelief and departure from the laws of God. He was a deeply religious man, and to him the honor of God's name was more precious than anything else in the world. He attacked the armies of Chu'-shan in the name of the all-powerful God, and at the same time used all his own skill as a leader. All the resources at his command were faithfully employed, and, with practical endurance and perfect trust in God, he accomplished what appeared to be impossible. The Syr'i-ans were driven from the land, and Is'ra-el was given forty years of rest from all enemies.

After the deliverance of Is'ra-el from the oppression of the Syr'i-ans, the worship of God was resumed throughout the nation, and idolatry was overthrown. Civil justice was restored, and the laws and ordinances of God were now fully resumed.

Upon the death of Oth'ni-el, however, the children of Is'ra-el once again fell into idolatrous practices and evils of various kinds. Again the Lord visited them with severe punishments for their sins. He afflicted them to show that He cannot violate his own holiness by allowing his people to worship false gods, that sin is always a deep offense to Him, and that He will not let his own people engage in things which undermine their character and destroy their happiness.

This time He used the Mo'ab-ites to scourge Is'ra-el. For nearly a century these neighboring heathens had looked with envy upon the growth of a people for whom they had a deep hatred. Struck with awe by the power of God which so often aided Is'ra-el, and long having been too weak to attack them, they had patiently awaited an opportunity of gaining vengeance. Finally, when Is'ra-el began to show weakness through neglect of God's law, the time seemed opportune. Eg'lon, the king of Mo'ab, invited the Am'mon-ites and Am'a-lek-ites to join him in an invasion of the land. In some strange way Divine Providence caused the schemes of Eg'lon to succeed, while failure and disaster attended every effort of the Is'ra-el-ites to defend themselves.

The invaders brought the entire land under their control, plundered the country of its products, and oppressed the people with heavy tribute. For eighteen years Is'ra-el was under the iron heel of the combined heathen nations. The city of Jer'i-cho, which had been delivered into their hands by a miracle, was made a Mo'ab-ite stronghold to guard the passes across the Jor'dan, and to force Is'ra-el into subjection. The children of Is'ra-el refused to serve God with the corn and wine and oil which He gave them in abundance, but were forced to include these things in their tributes to the oppressors.

Once again the Is'ra-el-ites were brought to their knees through suffering, and fled to their only refuge in penitence and prayer. The Lord heard their cry, and raised up another deliverer. His name was E'hud, a valiant man of the tribe of Ju'dah who was more skilled in the use of his left hand than he was with his right.

The first duty imposed upon E'hud by the Lord was the removal of Eg'lon, the Mo'ab-ite king who had a palace in Jer'i-cho. Eg'lon was a glutton, very fat, and indolent. He had directed his people in seizing the property of the Is'ra-el-ites, and in many oppressive acts which filled the homes of the land with misery and wailing. For such cruelty he was doomed by the Lord to a shameful death, and E'hud was chosen to bring it to pass.

The man of God called upon Eg'lon to pay the tribute which the Mo'ab-ites demanded of Is'ra-el. Then he returned to the palace, telling the guards that he had a private message for the king. He was admitted to the king's room, where he was left alone with the man he was to destroy in the Lord's name. The guards had not noticed his sword, for he carried it where a right-handed man could not reach it. He then approached the king with the announcement of God's judgment upon him, and suddenly thrust his sword through Eg'lon's body. Locking the parlor door from the inside, E'hud escaped through an unguarded porch and fled to the mountains of E'phra-im. The guards of the palace finally unlocked the door, but were too late to revive the king.

Terror spread quickly through all the encampments of the Mo'ab-ites, for God had provided a way to confuse and alarm all the people of this heathen nation. E'hud sounded a trumpet to summon Is'ra-el to battle, and the army descended upon the Mo'ab-ites at the fords of the Jor'dan. Nearly ten thousand men were slain, and not one Mo'ab-ite escaped death. The land of Is'ra-el was completely freed of the heathen invaders, and there followed a period of peace and prosperity which lasted for eighty years.

SUGGESTIONS FOR STUDY

Biblical Index to Helpful References

God's Warnings Against Forming Alliances with Canaanites. (Ex. 34:12.)

Application of This Law to Christians. (1 Cor. 5:11; 2 Thess. 3:14.)

Warnings Against Forgetting the Laws of God. (Deut. 4:9; 6:12; Ps. 50:22.)

God's Promises to Hear His People When They Cry Unto Him. (Isa. 58:9.)

Deliverers Raised Up by God. (Neh. 9:27; Hag. 2:23.)

Othniel's Past Reputation for Heroism. (Josh. 15:17.)

God's Use of Instruments for Judgment. (Jer. 5:15-19.)

God's Use of Weak Instruments in His Services. (1 Cor. 1:27-29.)

Questions

1. Why does it appear so strange that Israel should fall into idolatry?

2. What sins led to Israel's undoing at this time?

3. What king and nation was used of God to inflict judgment on Israel?

4. How long did the oppression by the Syrians continue?

5. Why did God raise up a deliverer? Whom did he raise up?

6. How long was the period of peace brought in by Othniel's rule?

7. What brought on the next oppression of Israel?

8. What heathen nations united for the oppression of Israel?

9. How long did this oppression last? Name and describe the oppressive king.

10. What was the name of the deliverer raised up to save Israel this time?

11. Tell of his slaying of Elgon. What followed?

12. How long did the period of peace last after Ehud's rule began?

THE TRIUMPH OF DEBORAH THE PROPHETESS AND BARAK THE WARRIOR

JUDGES 4, 5

We are not told how long E'hud lived to rule over Is'ra-el, but his death probably took place toward the close of the period of eighty years of peace which followed his notable defeat of the Mo'ab-ites. We do know, however, that after his death there began another lapse into idolatry which increased in its evil influence upon the life of Is'ra-el until another great affliction was brought upon them by the invasion of a mighty force of Ca'naan-ites from the north.

Prior to the invasion of the Ca'naan-ites from the north, there was a local uprising of the Phi-lis'tines in the coastal cities of western Ca'naan. A hero named Sham'gar organized a group of farmers and crushed this revolt, thereby preventing a war which might have spread throughout the land. Armed only with an ox goad, Sham'gar and his followers slew six hundred Phi-lis'tines in one heroic feat, and thus broke up the disturbance. The ox goads used in those days were eight feet long and about six inches in circumference, and had a sharp prong at one end for driving cattle.

Before long the tribes occupying the northern section of the land were conquered by the Ca'naan-ites, who had reoccupied the city of Ha'zor. This city had been captured by Josh'u-a more than one hundred and fifty years before. Another king of the same name as the one conquered and slain by Josh'u-a had extended his rule over a large area in the northern part of the country, holding several strong coastal towns. For twenty years Ja'bin severely oppressed the people of Naph'ta-li and Zeb'u-lun, forcing the men to cut and hew timbers in the forests for transport to the port of Zi'don. His chief ambition was to win back all the territories which had been taken from his ancestors by Josh'u-a. He stationed a large army in the plains of Jez're-el—also called Es-dra-e'lon and Me-gid'do—in which there were nine hundred war chariots of iron and thousands of well trained soldiers.

Sympathizing with the people of the two tribes who were oppressed by Ja'bin, and realizing that the entire country was in danger from the invasion, all Is'ra-el resorted to prayer. Twice before, under the same circumstances, the nation had turned to God in repentance and prayer— first, in the time of the Syr'i-an oppression, and later when crushed under the iron heel of the Mo'ab-ite king—and both times God had raised up a deliverer.

This time the Lord had ready for the emergency a noble woman called Deb'o-rah, who already held a place of honor in the nation. She was famed as a prophetess, a sweet singer, and a capable judge, and was a

SISERA SLAIN BY JAEL

heroine fully prepared for the dangers of war. So noted was she for giving good advice that all Is'ra-el looked to her for counsel. She was a woman of unfaltering faith in God, believed in His covenant with the chosen people, and relied upon His promises for help.

Having been stirred to the heart by the impulse to overthrow Sis'e-ra and his mighty host, Deb'o-rah called upon Ba'rak, a military leader of renown, to raise an army of ten thousand men from the tribes of Naph'ta-li and Zeb'u-lun for an attack upon the armies of the Ca'naan-ites on the plains of Es-dra-e'lon. Ba'rak felt unworthy of such an appointment, and accepted it only on condition that Deb'o-rah would go with him into the battle. Deb'o-rah granted this request, but told Ba'rak that because of his lack of faith and courage the honor of the victory over Sis'e-ra would be given to a woman.

Ten thousand men, most of whom were from the tribes of Naph'ta-li and Zeb'u-lun, were called to arms by Ba'rak. Many of these soldiers came from the ranks of Ja'bin's slave-workers in the war chariot factories at Ha'zor and in the timber regions of that territory. Armed with axes, hatchets, iron-working tools, and such other weapons as they could gather, the ten thousand men gathered on Mount Ta'bor. From this elevation they could look down upon the great host of Sis'e-ra encamped on the plains of Es-dra-e'lon. With Ba'rak at the head of the Is'ra-el-itish army, and with Deb'o-rah as the guiding spirit of the war, these men prepared to rush down upon the huge army of Sis'e-ra.

Determined to crush the hopes of Is'ra-el for independence, and to press his conquest deeper into their land, Sis'e-ra had gathered a vast army from northwestern Ca'naan. His forces were vastly superior in numbers and equipment to the army of Is'ra-el, but there was one very important factor which Sis'e-ra neglected. "The captain of the Lord's host" was at the head of Is'ra-el's selected army; the Lord God was fighting for His chosen people.

When all was in readiness for the battle to begin, Deb'o-rah was led by the Holy Spirit to tell Ba'rak when the moment had arrived for decisive action against the enemy. Speaking in the name of the Lord, she declared that the God who had performed so many miracles for Is'ra-el in the past would now lead them to victory. With fiery enthusiasm, with courage and faith flashing from her eyes, Deb'o-rah stood before the army of Is'ra-el like an angel sent by the Lord.

Ba'rak and his men were so greatly inspired by Deb'o-rah that all doubts and fears were cast from their hearts, and they swept down upon Sis'e-ra's army like a thundering avalanche from the skies. The Lord confused the forces of Sis'e-ra, bewilderment swept through their camps. Before the iron war chariots could be put into action, or the soldiers properly arrayed for battle, Ba'rak and his ten thousand men swooped down upon them like a whirlwind from the top of Mount Ta'bor. In addition to this fierce attack, the Lord sent a dreadful thunderstorm upon the enemies of Is'ra-el, and heavy hailstones beat upon their faces. The river Ki'shon, which runs across the plain of Es-dra-e'lon, overflowed its banks and checked the movement of soldiers and equipment. Sis'e-ra and his great army were overwhelmingly defeated, the few who escaped slaughter fled in despair, and the cry rang out:

"Let us flee from the face of Is'ra-el, for the Lord fighteth for them against the Ca'naan-ites."

Sis'e-ra himself fled before the armies of Ba'rak in his war chariot. When hard pressed by his pursuers, however, he was forced to alight from the chariot and to seek refuge on foot. Coming to a tent in which a Ke'nite family lived, he was invited to come in by a woman named Ja'el. She seems to have been on friendly terms with the Ca'naan-ites, but at heart was a true Is'ra-el-ite who hoped to aid Ba'rak in his final defeat of their foes. She gave milk and butter to Sis'e-ra, told him to lie down and sleep, and offered to hide him from his pursuers. When he was sound asleep she took an iron tent-peg and drove it through his temples with a hammer. Then she saw Ba'rak searching for the heathen general, so she called him to see how Sis'e-ra had been slain. Thus was fulfilled the prophecy of Deb'o-rah that the honor of the victory should be given to a woman.

SUGGESTIONS FOR STUDY

Biblical Index to Helpful References

God's Use of Harsh Measures for the Punishment of His Sinful Children. (Isa. 5:26-30.)

Notable Women Among God's Instruments. (Ex. 15:20; 2 Ki. 22:14; Luke 2:36.)

Qualities Which Contribute to Woman's Greatness. (Prov. 14:1; 31-30.)

Barak Listed Among the Heroes of Faith. (Heb. 11:32.)

Deliverance Provided by God. (Job 5:19; Ps. 91:3.)

The Multiplied Power of God's Faithful Servants. (Isa. 30:17.)

Faith in God Gives Advance Confidence of Victory. (Num. 14:8; Ps. 3:6.)

God's Power Superior to War Chariots. (Ps. 20:7; Isa. 31:1.)

Questions

1. What people in Northern Canaan began to harass Israel after the death of Ehud? Name the leader and his city.

2. Tell of Shamgar's subduing of a Philistine uprising.

3. Tell how Jabin enslaved and afflicted the tribes of the north.

4. Tell of the woman judge named Deborah.

5. When she planned an attack on the armies of Jabin whom did she select as captain of her armies?

6. How many warriors were raised by Ba-

rak? Why did Deborah go with him for war against Sisera? Where was Sisera's armies encamped?

7. How did Sisera's armies compare with Barak's in number and equipment?

8. What part did Deborah have in the battle?

9. Describe how the Israelites rushed down on their enemies and the result.

10. In what way did the Lord aid the Israelites?

11. What happened to Sisera, the leader of Jabin's army?

THE STORY OF GIDEON AND HIS THREE HUNDRED MEN

JUDGES 6, 7

After the deliverance of their land from the tyranny of Ja'bin, the Is'ra-el-ites lived in peace and prosperity for a long time. Forty years passed before the beginning of the next oppression. The influence of Deb'o-rah and of the thousands who had not yielded to idolatry during the latest religious decline spread throughout the land, raising the people to a higher level of religious and national patriotism. The triumph of Ba'rak over Sis'e-ra and his powerful army brought great fear to the idol-worshippers within the borders of Is'ra-el, and to the heathen nations in surrounding lands.

The death of Deb'o-rah, however, was followed by the same old story of backsliding and idolatry. Once again the children of Is'ra-el fell away from God and followed the false religions of the land. They turned away from the superior light and privileges which heaven had granted, disregarded the truths constantly taught by Divine revelation, forgot the experiences of God's past dealings with them, and ignored the sacred obligations of the covenant which they had made with God.

The story of another decline in the spiritual life of the nation is followed by stories of Divine punishments, of repentance, and of the raising up of another deliverer. This time the nation was afflicted for seven years by the roving bands of warlike Mid'ian-ites from the east. They were descendants of one of the sons of A'bra-ham and Ke-tu'rah, a wandering people who lived principally in the desert lands east of Ca'naan, and in A-ra'bi-a to the south. They had no settled national home, but roamed from place to place, and made their living by plundering and robbing the more civilized people of surrounding lands.

These thieving prowlers brought their own herds of cattle and camels into Ca'naan to eat up the pastures of the Is'ra-el-ites. They took the best of the rich crops of grain, drove the sheep and cattle of the land into their own herds, demanded heavy tribute in money, and plundered the people of all their valuable possessions.

For two hundred and sixty years the Mid'ian-ites had carried in their hearts an old grudge against Is'ra-el. This was caused by the crushing blow which Mo'ses had inflicted upon them at the Lord's command after they had lured thousands of Is'ra-el-ites into sin. The falling away of Is'ra-el from true religion, and the temporary withdrawal of God's protection for this reason, seemed to provide an excellent opportunity for revenge.

In their plundering of the land they were joined by hordes of Ish'ma-el-ites and Am'a-lek-ites, whose habits were much the same. They had no intention of conquering the country, or of making subjects of the inhabitants. Their sole object was robbery, and acts of violence took place only when their banditry was resisted. They would strip the entire country during the harvest season, drive off the cattle and sheep, and sell the stolen goods to caravans of traders on their return to the desert. The Is'ra-el-ites were forced to plant new crops, grow more fruit, and raise more stock; then the invaders would return the next year for similar plundering. The land was so terrorized by them that many of the people were compelled to hide their produce in caves and dens, and no one dared to make war upon the bandits.

When Is'ra-el finally realized that these raids were permitted by the Lord as punishments for their sins, they turned to Him in pentinence and prayer. Again we have the glorious story of God's tenderness and grace. As soon as the people gave proof that their repentance was genuine, He released them from their oppressors.

This time, however, the Lord first sent a prophet to reprove Is'ra-el for her backslidings, and to deepen the conviction of sin among the people. They had shown signs of repentance, but must have a more thorough work of grace in their hearts before a deliverer could be given.

When the Lord searched the land of Is'ra-el for a hero capable of delivering the people from the Mid'ian-ites, his choice fell on a man named Gid'e-on. His father, whose name was Jo'ash, lived at Oph'rah, a secluded town in the rugged hill country of southwestern Ma'nas-seh near She'chem. He was the chief of a clan called the A-bi-ez'rites, and had shown his idolatry by building an altar to Ba'al and a grove to A-she'rah, who was the moon-goddess.

Gid'e-on secretly worshiped the true God, and his heart was burdened by the idolatry and wickedness of his people, and by the calamities which had been brought upon them by the raids of the Mid'ian-ites. His father's household had been plundered by them, and two of his brothers had been captured and slain in the valley of Jez're-el by Mid'ian-ite princes. The fear of being discovered by roving bands of Mid'ian-ites led him to thresh wheat in wine-presses deep in a rocky cave, instead of doing this work on a threshing-floor out in an open field.

While Gid'e-on was engaged in this work he was visited by the "Angel-Je-ho'vah," sometimes called the "Angel of the Cov'e-nant," and better understood as the Mes-si'ah before He came into this world as a man. The visitor, disguised as a man, was not recognized at first as an angel.

In his approach to Gid'e-on, the angel spoke as follows: "The Lord is with thee, thou mighty man of valor." To this true Is'ra-el-ite the voice of even a stranger raised in honor of the true God struck a responsive chord. He had often longed for some congenial friend with whom he could speak freely about the low moral state of his people, and about the hope of a great spiritual revival throughout the land of Is'ra-el.

Gid'e-on therefore answered the angel with words which came from his heart. He said: "Oh, sir, how can you say that the Lord is with us when we are cast away, when desolation reigns over the land, when we are in the grasp of marauding bandits, when our people are brought to such terror that they hide in caves and dens like animals?" Gid'e-on fully believed that the Lord was able to solve any problem, that He could overcome the strongest and fiercest enemy, and that, if He was truly with them, his people would be saved by miracles like those which had been performed in the past.

The Lord then gave Gid'e-on a solemn commission to go forth in his might for the deliverance of Is'ra-el from the grasp of the Mid'ian-ites. In his reply Gid'e-on addressed the angel as the Lord, and acknowledged his faith in the ability of the speaker to deliver Is'ra-el. But he hesitated to accept so great a work, not from any lack of faith, but in modesty and distrust of his own ability. He said, "My tribe is one of the weakest, my family is poor, and I am the least of my father's household. I am wholly unprepared for such a tremendous undertaking."

After the Lord assured him of His presence, and of victory over the Mid'ian-ites, Gid'e-on asked for a sign by which he might know that the speaker was indeed the Lord. And so, when he had brought food for the stranger, the Angel Je-ho'vah touched it with the end of the staff which he carried in his hand, and it was immediately consumed by fire from heaven. The angel then quietly departed, and Gid'e-on built an altar and sacrificed unto the Lord.

Acting under special directions from the Lord, Gid'e-on took ten men and destroyed the altar to Ba'al and the grove to A-she'rah which his father had built as a centre of idolatrous worship by the entire clan. He then built an altar to the Lord on the same spot, and offered burnt sacrifices.

When this act of Gid'e-on was discovered by the men of his father's clan, their anger and threats against the life of his youngest son caused Jo'ash to realize the folly of idol-worship, and he turned to the Lord, supporting Gid'e-on in his new position as the deliverer of Is'ra-el.

While these things were taking place, and possibly aroused by news of Gid'e-on's stand for the Lord, the Mid'ian-ites and Am'a-lek-ites gathered in large numbers on the plains of Jez'reel. For seven years they had plundered this garden spot of Is'ra-el, which was capable of supporting one hundred thousand people. It was here that Sis'e-ra's hosts had been destroyed forty-seven years before, and it was fitting that Gid'e-on should rout the Mid'ian-ites on this famous battlefield.

Gid'e-on was moved by the spirit of God to sound a clarion call for soldiers. His father's household and the entire clan of the A-bi-ez'rites rallied to his support at once. Messengers were sent throughout the tribes, and the men of Ma'nas-seh, Zeb'u-lun, Asher and Naph'ta-li responded

GIDEON CHOOSES THE THREE HUNDRED

heartily. Thirty-two thousand soldiers answered the call, and Gid'e-on began to plan an attack upon the hosts of Mid'ian and Am'a-lek on the plains of Es-dra-e'lon.

The army marched down into the valley of Ki'shon, which was south of the plains where at least one hundred and thirty-five thousand of the Mid'ian-ites and Am'a-lek-ites could be seen. At the sight of so great an army many of the Is'ra-el-ites began to feel faint-hearted, for they were outnumbered four to one.

Then the Lord said to Gid'e-on, "The people with thee are too many." The battle which they faced was in the Lord's keeping, and He could give victory to the many or to the few. He wished to have it clearly shown that the vast armies of the heathens were to be defeated by His power alone, so He directed Gid'e-on to permit all who were craven-hearted to leave the army. Twenty-two thousand of the Is'ra-el-ites immediately took advantage of this offer.

The Lord spoke again to Gid'e-on, saying, "Even though the ten thousand men that you have left are courageous and unafraid, there are yet too many." He then commanded a strange test for determining which of the men were worthy to take part in the defeat of the Mid'ian-ites. Fully equipped for battle they were to march across a stream of water on their way toward the camps of the enemy, and were to pause for a drink of water. Nine thousand seven hundred of them laid aside their weapons, kneeled down at the edge of the brook, and took up water in both hands to quench their thirst. Only three hundred kept their weapons in one hand, watched carefully for signs of the enemy, and dipped water from the brook with one hand, lapping it as a dog drinks.

All the men who had been careless were placed in one group, and the three hundred who had proved themselves to be alert were placed in another. The nine thousand and seven hundred were sent away, and Gid'e-on was ordered to attack the vast armies of Mid'ian with the three hundred warriors who remained. Outnumbered nearly five hundred to one, any victory which they might gain would surely be given by the Lord.

Then the Lord ordered a strategy even more strange than the method which had been used to reduce Gid'e-on's army from thirty-two thousand to a mere three hundred. Gid'e-on was told to divide his men into three separate columns, and to approach the enemy from three different directions, thus giving the impression of an attack by three armies. The time set for the attack was in the middle watch of the night. Ancient Is'ra-el divided the night into three watches: from sunset to ten, from ten to two in the morning, and from two until sunrise. It was probably about midnight when Is'ra-el surrounded the camps of the Mid'ian-ites.

Each of Gid'e-on's three hundred men was given a trumpet, an earthen pitcher, and a lamp which was to be hidden in each pitcher. The small band of Is'ra-el-ites then marched upon the camp of their sleeping enemies from three different directions. At a signal from Gid'e-on the pitchers were broken, the lamps were held aloft in blazing flames, and the trumpets were sounded in loud, shrill blasts. Each man carried out these actions in perfect unison, and then the entire three hundred cried out together, "The sword of the Lord and of Gid'e-on!"

In the deep silence of the midnight hour these three hundred trumpets pierced the air with their shrill blasts, resounding throughout the camp of the enemy like the battle-calls of vast armies. In the dense darkness which shrouded the plain the three hundred lamps flashed like lightning darts from heaven. The thousands of Mid'ian-ites, Ish'ma-el-ites, and Am'a-lek-ites thought that they were being attacked by huge armies. Fear and confusion seized the multitudes of heathen warriors, and terror swept the plain on which they were gathered like a mighty whirlwind from the surrounding mountains. In the mad scramble for safety they became suspicious of one another, and slew thousands of their own men.

Was there ever a battle like this, or such a notable victory? Between one hundred and thirty-five thousand and one hundred and fifty thousand of the cruel invaders were routed by three hundred unarmed Is'ra-el-ites. The battle-field was strewn with thousands of the enemy who were slain in confusion by their own men. Wives and children, cattle and camels, tents and baggage—in fact, everything which the invaders possessed—was left behind to become spoils of war for the victors! Not a single man was lost of Gid'e-on's three hundred. There was really no battle, for the men of Is'ra-el simply stood still and watched the salvation sent by the Lord. It was a miraculous route of the enemy, complete and overwhelming.

As the morning light broke upon the fleeing hordes of Bed'ou-ins, the princes of Mid'ian tried to lead the retreat along the valley eastward to Beth'shan, and then down the Jor'dan valley toward Jer'i-cho, where they might cross the river. In the meantime, however, the nine thousand seven hundred men of Gid'e-on who had not been privileged to take part in the midnight attack massed along the route of escape and slew thousands.

Gid'e-on sent messengers to the E'phra-im-ites, ordering them to gather at the ford of the Jor'dan in order to slay all who might try to cross the river. Three hundred selected, courageous, and loyal men had created and brought a mad dispersion to an army of one hundred and thirty-five thousand Mid'ian-ites; but to conserve the results and to make the victory complete all Is'ra-el must now co-operate. In the final outcome every one had part in crushing these enemies.

Two Mid'ian-ite princes sought refuge, one in the cavern of a rock, and the other in the vat of a wine-press, but both were captured and slain. Two other princes managed to cross the river, but were later pursued and slain by Gid'e-on.

Thus the plunderings and oppressions by the Mid'ian-ites were brought to an end, and for the next forty years there was a period of peace in the land of Is'ra-el. Gid'e-on ruled the land wisely, overthrew idolatry, promoted the worship of the true God, and led the people in ways of righteousness and justice.

SUGGESTIONS FOR STUDY

Biblical Index to Helpful References

The Alliance of Heathen Nations Against the People of God. (Ps. 56:6; Mi. 4:11.)

Israel Humbled Because of Sin. (2 Ki. 17:20; Ezr. 9:7.)

Men's Hearts Filled with Fear Because of Sin. (Isa. 66:4; Heb. 10:27.)

Adversities Brought on by Disobedience of God. (Deut. 32:24; Ps. 16:4.)

God's Mercy in Sending Messengers of Warning. (Jer. 25:4; Matt. 22:3.)

Angelic Ministries in Calling Men for Service. (Ps. 91:11; Acts 27:23.)

Men of Real Worth Made Great Under Providence of God. (Prov. 28:6.)

Needless Fear in the Presence of God's Glory. (Matt. 17:6, 7 Mark 16:5, 6.)

Victories for the Lord Not by Worldly might. (Zach. 4:6.)

Questions

1. Tell of the uplifting influence of Deborah on Israel.

2. Tell of the effect of Barak's victory over Jabin on other heathen people.

3. How long did Israel continue in loyalty to God before another decline?

4. What heathen nation was sent to oppress them this time?

5. Why did the Midianites hate Israel with such vengeance?

6. Describe the plunderings and robberies of the desert nomads.

7. Who was chosen by the Lord as a deliverer at this time?

8. Relate the circumstances of Gideon's call.

9. Where did Gideon begin in his work of reform?

10. Were the Midianites and Amalekites encamped at this time? How many?

11. How many men responded to Gideon's call for warriors?

12. Why were twenty-two thousand allowed to return home?

13. Explain the reduction of the remaining ten thousand to three hundred.

14. Relate the strategy used by Gideon in defeating this great arm.

15. Tell of the spoils of war left behind. Of the slaying of Midianites in their efforts to flee.

STORY 69

JEPHTHAH'S VOW AND THE SACRIFICE OF HIS DAUGHTER

JUDGES 10:6-18; 11

Toward the end of the rule of Ja'ir, Is'ra-el appears to have fallen into a state of idolatry much worse than at any previous time. The worship of false gods became widespread and varied. They forsook the worship of Je-ho'vah, and adopted the gods of Syr'i-a, Si'don, and Mo'ab, and of the Am'mon-ites and Phi-lis'tines.

The gods of Syr'i-a, or A'ram, are not named, but the chief idol among them was called Rim'mon, a symbol of the sun-god. The gods of the Zi'don-ians or Phoe-ni'cians, were Ba'al and Ash'ta-roth; the first being known as the sun-god, while the second was called the moon-goddess. The chief god of the Mo'ab-ites was Che'mosh, which represented the planet Sat'urn. The national god of Am'mon was Mo'loch, or Mil'com, which seems to have been another name for Che'mosh, and to have represented the planet Sat'urn. The chief god of the Phi-lis'tines was Da'gon, the fish-god, or god of increase.

There were striking similarities in the rites and ceremonies practiced in all of these false religions, and all were demoralizing to the moral and social life of the Is'ra-el-ites, leading to a complete breakdown in their worship of the true God.

As a result of the moral and spiritual shortcomings of Is'ra-el, the Lord permitted them to be oppressed by the Am'mon-ites and Phi-lis'tines for a period of eighteen years. The Am'mon-ites afflicted the tribes on the east side of the Jor'dan, while the Phi-lis'tines oppressed the tribes of Ju'dah, Sim'e-on, and Ben'ja-min. In the course of the eighteen years the Am'mon-ites having plundered the land east of the Jor'dan, crossed the river to afflict the tribe of Ju'dah, attacking them from the east while the Phi-lis'tines oppressed them from the west.

Is'ra-el was brought low again; the people confessed their sins and cried to the Lord for deliverance from their oppressors. They concealed nothing, but frankly admitted that they had deserted the true God to worship images of Ba'al and other false gods. The Lord appeared to be unmoved by their cries, and chided them for their ingratitude in leaving

Him after the many blessings which their nation had received in the past. Is'ra-el then humbly accepted the punishment as just, overthrew idolatry throughout the land, and renewed the pledge of loyalty to God. Once again the Lord extended His mercy, and deliverers were raised up under Divine Providence.

When Is'ra-el began to turn away from the false gods of the various heathen peoples in Ca'-naan and the surrounding countries, the Am'mon-ites prepared for war against the tribes east of the Jor'dan. Members of these tribes were led by their captains to a place called Miz'pah, and it was proposed that any hero who was willing to lead them against the Am'mon-ites should be made the permanent ruler of the land.

JEPHTHAH'S DAUGHTER

There had formerly lived in Gil'e-ad a man of great physical strength, boldness, and courage named Jeph'thah. He was the bastard son of a man named Gil'e-ad, and because of the circumstances of his birth was not entitled to dwell in the land of his father's inheritance, but was cast out by his half-brothers. It also appears that Jeph'thah may have been disliked by other members of his clan because he held strictly to the religion of the true God. They may also have been jealous of him because of his bold, enterprising spirit.

Jeph'thah went into a land called Tob, which was in Syr'i-a on the borders of Gil'e-ad to the north or northeast. Because of his adventurous spirit and ability as a leader of men, there soon gathered about him a band of warriors who made frequent raids upon the heathen settlers, including the Am'mon-ites who had plundered the Is'ra-el-ites.

Having learned of Jeph'thah's success and great skill as a warrior, the elders of Is'ra-el invited him to lead his nation in war against the Am'mon-ites, offering to make him the permanent ruler if he succeeded in driving the invaders out of the land. After a series of conferences in which it was admitted that Jeph'thah had been unjustly treated by his brothers, he accepted the commission.

The first act of Jeph'thah was to send a deputation to the Am'mon-ites with a proposal to settle their differences without war. This proposal was scornfully rejected, and Jeph'thah sought again for a friendly settlement of the strife between the Am'mon-ites and his people. The Am'mon-ites sought to justify their hostile attitude toward Is'ra-el on the grounds that their lands had been taken by this nation, and that they had the right to win them back even by the force of arms.

In reply to this argument Jeph'thah reviewed the history of Is'ra-el's dealings with the E'dom-ites, Mo'ab-ites, and Am'mon-ites. He reminded them that Si'hon, king of the Am'o-rites, had been the one who had taken their lands, and that God had enabled the Is'ra-el-ites to defeat him, and to take possession of all his territory. The Am'mon-ites refused to yield to the argument of Jeph'thah, and forced an immediate war upon Is'ra-el.

Lifted far above his natural courage, strength, and wisdom by the anointing of the spirit of God, Jeph'thah raised a large army from the tribes of Ma-nas'seh, Gad, and Reu'ben, and marched against the Am'-mon-ites. His army was assembled at Miz'pah, sacred in the history of Is'ra-el as the place where Ja'cob and La'ban had made a covenant of lasting peace, as one of the forty-eight Le-vit'i-cal cities, as a City of Refuge, and as the capital of Gil'e-ad. Here Jeph'thah made a solemn vow to God that if He would give him victory over the Am'mon-ites, he would offer to Him as a sacrifice whatever came forth to meet him on his return from the field of victory.

In the battle which followed, the Lord enabled Jeph'thah to win a crushing victory over the Am'mon-ites. Many of the invaders were slain, and those who escaped death fled from the land. Twenty cities formerly held by the Am'mon-ites were captured by Jeph'thah's army. The land of Is'ra-el was completely delivered from oppression, and Jeph'thah was made Judge over the tribes east of the Jor'dan.

Jeph'thah had in his home an only child, a lovely young daughter. He loved her very dearly, and she was tenderly devoted to her brave and heroic father. On his return from the great victory over the Am'mon-ites she ran out to meet him, singing for joy, and dancing in praise of her father's triumph over the enemies of Is'ra-el. Jeph'thah was smitten with anguish when he saw her, for he remembered the vow which he had made to God. His heart was filled with grief at the thought of laying his only child, his beloved and cherished daughter, on the altar of sacrifice to the Lord. Calling upon all the heroism of his noble character, he told his daughter of the vow which he had made to God. He solemnly declared, "I have made this pledge to the Lord, and I cannot take it back."

Without pausing for a moment to reflect upon what her words might mean to her and her father, Jeph'thah's daughter said, "Do to me according to that which thou hast vowed." She then asked permission to spend two months in the mountains surrounding Miz'peh that she might "mourn her virginity." To give up the privilege of being a wife and a mother was the supreme sacrifice for an Is'ra-el-it-ish woman. Every Jewish woman hoped, in becoming a mother, that she might give to the world the promised Mes-si'ah of Is'ra-el.

When the two months had passed, Jeph'thah's daughter returned to her home, and the Bible narrative says, "He did with her according to

JEPHTHAH AND HIS DAUGHTER

his vow." Some earnest readers of the Bible believe that Jeph'thah did not put his daughter to death on an altar of sacrifice, for the Scriptures do not say that he actually offered her as a burnt offering to the Lord.

It may be that the sacrifice which Jeph'thah's daughter made was that of giving her life entirely to the service of God, giving up all thought of marriage, and thereby causing the house of her father to pass away without leaving some descendant to bear his name. Such a sacrifice would require both father and daughter to give of their best to the Lord, and would carry out the spirit in which Jeph'thah made his vow unto the Lord.

The word which Jeph'thah used in making his vow was frequently employed in ancient Is'ra-el in the dedication of lands, tithes, or other valuable possessions to the Lord. The object offered in such a ceremony was thought to be so entirely devoted to the Lord that it could belong to no one else. Such an offering did not necessarily require the slaying and burning of the object offered, and certainly would not require the murder of a human being in defiance of one of the Ten Commandments. For these reasons it may well be that Jeph'thah's vow was fulfilled without staining his hands with the blood of his own precious child.

Soon after Jeph'thah's victory over the Am'mon-ites, certain men of the tribe of E'phra-im showed a very ugly spirit. They were jealous of the honor to which Jeph'thah had risen, of the superior courage displayed by the Gil'e-ad-ites, and of their triumph over such powerful foes. Twice before this tribe had shown a haughty, envious spirit toward other tribes of Is'ra-el; first, when the land was allotted by Josh'u-a, and then when Gid'e-on won a great victory over the Ca'naan-ites of the north.

Because of the superior blessing conferred upon their ancestor E'phra-im by his grandfather Ja'cob, the E'phra-im-ites were ambitious to rule over the tribe of Ma-nas'seh, and regarded them as their inferiors. The Gil'-e-ad-ites were descendants of a powerful family of Ma-nas'seh, and therefore were especially envied by the men of E'phra-im.

The E'phra-im-ites took advantage of Jeph'thah's victory to show their hatred for the clan which was rising so rapidly among the tribe of Ma-nas'seh. They pretended that their rank had been ignored because they were not asked to take part in the war against the Am'mon-ites, and threatened to destroy Jeph'thah by burning his house. A large company crossed the Jor'dan and prepared for civil war at Za'phon, which was a small town in the territory of the tribe of Gad. Jeph'thah disproved their charges by reminding them that they had refused to join him in battle, that there was no just cause for their complaint, and that they should be grateful because the land was free from all oppressors.

The men of Gil'e-ad resented the proud attitude of the E'phra-im-ites, and engaged them in a fierce battle. Thousands of them were slain, and the others were forced to flee in confusion. Those who escaped from the battle sought to flee across the Jor'dan to their own territory, but were trapped by a clever plan of the Gil'e-ad-ites.

Jeph'thah placed guards at the fords of the Jor'dan to intercept all the E'phra-im-ites who tried to escape into their own land. In order to tell the tribal membership of those who wished to cross the river, they were required to pronounce the Hebrew word "Shib'bo-leth," which means "an ear of corn." The E'phra-im-ites could not pronounce this word as the tribes east of the Jordan did, but could only say "Sib'bo-leth," and in this way it was known that they were enemies.

The entire length of Jeph'thah's rule as Judge was six years. Peace and prosperity prevailed among the tribes east of the Jor'dan after the defeat of the Am'mon-ites and the civil war with the E'phra-im-ites.

SUGGESTIONS FOR STUDY

Biblical Index to Helpful References

All False Gods Are Alike Idols. (1 Chr. 16:26; Isa. 2:8.)

The Debasing Influence of Idolatry. (Ps. 115:4; Rom. 1:22, 23.)

God's Anger Against Wickedness of Every Kind. (Ps. 7:11; Hos. 12:14.)

The Misery Caused by Forsaking God. (Deut. 28:65-67; Isa. 48:2.)

The Sin of Stubbornness Before God. (Lev. 26:27, 28; Ps. 32:9.)

Seeking Deliverance by the Help of God. (Ps. 43:1; 59:2; 71:4, 5.)

Putting Away Idols. (Gen. 35:2; Josh. 24:14; 1 Sam. 7:3.)

The Re-instatement of the Outcast. (Isa. 11:12; Jer. 30:17.)

Sacred Vows to Be Honestly Kept. (Num. 30:2; Eccl. 5:4.)

The Slaying of Children in Sacrifice Forbidden. (Deut. 12:29-31; Jer. 7:29-31.)

Questions

1. Name the various false gods worshiped by Israel at this time.

2. Why was it so difficult for Israel to refrain from idolatry?

3. What nations now oppressed Israel?

4. In looking for a deliverer who was chosen by the elders of Israel?

5. Why had Jephthah been cast out from his own family?

6. What reputation did he make for himself in the land of Nob?

7. Where was a battle fought against the Ammonites? Why famous?

8. In preparing for this battle what vow did Jephthah make?

9. On his return from the victory, who met him first?

10. Did he keep his vow?

11. Explain how he could do this without violating the law against murder?

STORY 70

EXPLOITS OF SAMSON AGAINST THE PHILISTINES

JUDGES 14, 15

From his mountain home Sam'son could look down upon the plains of the seacoast occupied by the Phi-lis'tines, and upon many communities once held by his own tribe but now in their possession. As he grew in superior physical strength, and as the Spirit of God moved upon him, he must have felt an impulse to begin his work against these oppressors of his nation.

When Sam'son was about eighteen years of age, he visited the town of Tim'nath, which was just a few miles from his home. Many Phi-lis'tine families lived here, so he may have intended to begin his Divinely appointed work of terrorizing the aliens who now held dominion over Is'ra-el. Instead of doing this, however, he fell in love with the daughter of a Phi-lis'tine family.

In keeping with the customs of the age, he asked his parents to arrange for the young woman to be his wife. They were astonished at this request, and rebuked him for seeking a wife from a heathen race, pointing out that it was contrary to the law of God, and would work against his mission of breaking the tryanny of the Phi-lis'tines over the Is'ra-el-ites.

Although they preferred their son to take a wife from his own people, Samson's father and mother finally yielded to his wishes, and visited the parents of the girl to secure their permission for the proposed marriage. While passing near the vineyards in the valley of So'rek, Sam'son grappled with a lion, and killed it with his bare hands. Upon reaching the home of the young woman, and talking with her, he became more deeply attracted than ever.

After waiting for the usual period of six months between the engagement and marriage, Sam'son and his parents went to the home of the Phi-lis'tine girl for the wedding. A festival lasting for seven days was planned, and friends of both families were invited. Among those invited by the bride's family were thirty young men of their own nationality. They were present, not only as friends of the bride, but as spies upon Sam'son, should any trouble arise.

As Sam'son and his parents made the journey to Tim'nath, they passed near the place where Sam'son had slain the lion six months before. Bees had made a hive in the skeleton of the lion, and it was filled with honey. Samson gathered and ate some of the honey, and gave some to his father and mother.

During the festivities of the first day of the wedding feast Sam'son told the thirty young men that he would ask them a riddle. If they were unable to solve it within seven days, they were to give him thirty shirts and thirty changes of clothing; and should they give the answer within this time, he would give them the same things. They agreed to the proposal, and Sam'son stated his riddle in these words:

"Out of the eater came forth meat, and out of the strong came forth sweetness."

For five or six days the young men tried as hard as possible to guess the answer, but without success. Then they urged Sam'son's wife to find out the answer, threatening to set fire to her house if she failed. They also

SAMSON'S RIDDLE

accused her of marrying a foreigner in order to rob her own people. Under the pressure of these threats, she begged and cried to her husband until he told her the answer to the riddle. Then she told the young men, and they waited until the close of the seventh day before they said to Sam'son, "We have the answer. What is sweeter than honey? And what is stronger than a lion?"

Sam'son was not slow in detecting the treachery of the young Phi-lis'-tines, so he charged them at once with underhanded plottings with his wife. Their scheme had been so unfair that he would have been justified in refusing to pay the things which had been promised. Rather than be charged with failure to keep his word, however, Sam'son took advantage of the occasion to begin his mission of smiting the Phi-lis'tines. He went to the Phi-lis'tine stronghold of Ash'ke-lon, slew thirty prominent men, and brought the shirt and fine outer garment of each one back to the men of Tim'nath in payment of his wager. Thus the schemers received their ill-gotten gains through the death of their own countrymen.

Moved to anger by the deceit of his bride, and by the apparent plot of her family and friends to bring contempt upon the Is'ra-el-ites, Sam'son returned to his home without his wife. Her father then gave her in marriage to the leader of the spies who had sought to outwit Sam'son by treachery, and thus a strange Providence put an end to a marriage which was forbidden by the Lord.

Although the Lord had been merciful in breaking Sam'son's marriage with an idolatrous woman, the mighty man of Is'ra-el tried to win her back. With a special gift in hand, he went to her father's house in the hope of meeting her once again. His father-in-law then showed the lack of respect for marriage which prevailed among the Phi-lis'tines by admitting that he had given Sam'son's wife to another man, and by suggesting that he console himself with a younger daughter who was more attractive.

Knowing that the Phi-lis'tine people of the community agreed with his father-in-law, and feeling a new impulse to carry out his mission against the oppressors of Is'ra-el, Sam'son performed a daring feat of destruction upon the crops and vineyards of the entire neighborhood.

He went into the forest and caught three hundred foxes, tied their tails together in pairs, placed burning firebrands upon them, and turned the foxes loose in the fields of ripened grain. Frightened by the fiery torches, maddened by the painful burns, these animals swept like streaks of lightning through fields and vineyards, setting fire to the grain, and completely ruining the vineyards.

When the owners of these fields and vineyards were told that Sam'son was responsible for the destruction of their crops and fruits, and that he had done this because his father-in-law had given his wife to another man, they took vengeance upon their neighbor by burning his house down upon him and his daughter.

SAMSON'S STRENGTH

Sam'son then turned upon the murderers of his faithless bride, and single-handed slew vast numbers of the Phi-lis'tines in Tim'nath and its surroundings.

Aroused by the depredations of the giant Is'ra-el-ite, yet fearing to attack him, the Phi-lis'tines raised a huge army to force the people of Ju'dah to surrender Sam'son to them. Three thousand of the men of Ju'dah went out to meet the army of the Phi-lis'tines, not to engage in battle with them, but to make a disgraceful surrender. With unspeakable cowardice they yielded to the demands of their oppressors, failing to rally around the champion of their liberties in a battle which might have freed them forever from tyranny.

The pages of history contain no act more cowardly than that which is here recorded of the Ju'de-ans. Three thousand of them approached the lone Sam'son in his mountain retreat, and denounced him for arousing the Phi-lis'tines to acts of violence against Is'ra-el. They were willing to give up their Divinely appointed deliverer in exchange for peace with their cruelest enemies.

When these traitors promised not to harm him, Sam'son agreed to be bound with strong ropes and delivered to the enemy. When the Phi-lis'tines saw Sam'son being led to them with strong ropes around his hands, they set up a terrific howl of scorn and triumph. This awakened the power which slumbered in the arms of the giant, and the cords which held him fast were instantly parted like flax touched by a flame of fire. "The Spirit of the Lord came mightily upon him," and Sam'son made use of the jaw-bone of an ass to slay a thousand Phi-lis'tines. The whole army was paralyzed with terror, unable to fight against the sudden ava-

lanche of power which appeared among them. Those who were not slain fled in confusion, and Sam'son voiced his triumph in these words:
"With the jawbone of an ass, heaps upon heaps,
With the jawbone of an ass have I smitten a thousand men."
Suffering from thirst in a place where no water could be had, Sam'son cried unto the Lord, "Thou hast given this great deliverance by the hand of thy servant; and now shall I die for thirst, and fall into the hands of the heathens." The Lord miraculously opened a spring of water where Sam'son threw the jawbone, and the name of the place was changed to En-hak'ko-re, which means "the spring of him that called."

Thus in the zenith of his supernatural power Sam'son left to all future generations a memorial to the fact that his exploits and triumphs were dependent on faith and prayer. The Phi-lis'tines, like an over-running flood, had swept over the land of Is'ra-el. In a manner unthought of and unheard of up to this time, God had raised up one lone man to serve as a breakwater against these destructive torrents. By super-human strength he manifested sufficient power to defeat a whole nation. But it was only when Sam'son fully relied upon Divine help, looked to God in faith and with humble supplications, that he triumphed against his enemies.

SUGGESTIONS FOR STUDY

Biblical Index to Helpful References

God's Law Against Mixed Marriages. (Deut. 7:3.)

Wedding Festivals of Ancient Times. (Gen. 29:21, 22; Est. 2:17, 18; Jno. 2:1-11.)

Israel's Enslavement to Alien Nations Because of Sin. (Deut. 28:48.)

The Use of Riddles in Ancient Times. (1 Ki. 10:1; Ezek. 17:2.)

The Treachery of Faithless Wives. (2 Sam. 6:16; Mark 6:17.)

The Sin of Deceitful Practices. (Ps. 5:6; Prov. 20:17.)

The Crime of Betrayal. (1 Chr. 12:17; Matt. 24:10, 26:16.)

The Declaration of God's Vengeance. (Deut. 32:35; 2 Pet. 2:3.)

Questions

1. What was the probable object of Samson's visit to the Philistine town of Timnath? What actually happened?

2. When he told his parents of his wish to marry a Philistine maiden what did they say?

3. What occurred as Samson and his parents journeyed to Timnath?

4. Tell of Samson's proposed riddle to the young men of the Philistines.

5. Were they able to answer it? How did they find out the answer?

6. What course did Samson then take to secure the garments with which to pay the wager won by the cheating Philistines?

7. Did Samson take his bride home with him? What did her father then do?

8. When Samson sought to reclaim his wife, what act of vengeance did he perform against the Philistines?

9. What did the enraged Philistines do to Samson's wife and family?

10. Tell of Samson's slaying a thousand Philistines.

STORY 71

SAMSON'S WEAKNESS ATONED BY HIS DYING FEAT

JUDGES 16

Following the account of Sam'son's remarkable exploit in the valley of So'rek, it is stated that he judged Is'ra-el for twenty years. Although it does not appear that the dominion of the Phi-lis'tines was broken during this period, it seems that for a long number of years there was no open warfare between the two peoples. The Is'ra-el-ites yielded meekly to their cruel masters, and continued to mingle with them in ways of idolatry and wickedness. Nowhere is there the slightest evidence that they repented of their idolatry or improved their moral conduct.

Among the few privileges granted to Is'ra-el was that of having a Judge, and this office was held by Sam'son. The nation was unready and unwilling to accept freedom from the alien people into whose idolatrous ways and wicked habits they were now completely entangled, and Sam'son's efforts to gain independence for Is'ra-el had been cowardly rejected. For these reasons the career of Sam'son was free of further exploits against the Phi-lis'tines until his reign of twenty years was nearly over.

It is probable that the intervening years were spent quietly by Sam'son at his home in Zo'rah, and that no stirring events worthy of record took place. He no doubt advised the Is'ra-el-ites in their domestic and civil problems, acted as a judge in settling their differences, and had authority in other matters where there was no conflict with the Phi-lis'tine rule.

For some unknown reason Sam'son decided to visit Ga'za, which was the Phi-lis'tine capital, and one of their strongest cities. It is probable that he went there seeking an opportunity of performing some mighty feat which would amaze and distress the Phi-lis'tines.

While it is evident that Sam'son did not go down to Ga'za with any intention of doing wrong, he was guilty of entering the path of the wicked unguarded from temptation. Led on by his hasty, impulsive nature, he entered a house where he had no business.

Ga'za was a walled city, and the gates were closed and locked at night. When the Phi-lis'tines saw Sam'son enter the home of a woman innkeeper

SAMSON CARRIES AWAY THE GATE OF GAZA

for the night, they surrounded the place and posted guards at the city gates, expecting to capture and slay him on the next morning. Sam'son was in the stronghold of his bitterest enemies, shut in by strong walls and locked iron gates, surrounded by plotters who were eager to seize him, and exposed to probable death at the hands of an angry mob.

In some way Sam'son discovered the plot against his life. He was filled with fury by the thought that he might be trapped in a prison of death. What were high walls and iron gates before his miraculous strength! Determined to spoil the plans of his enemies, he left the building at midnight, and made his way secretly to the gates of the city. Taking a firm hold upon the folding iron gates, he tore the heavy posts from the ground; placing the gates and posts on his back, he boldly marched away.

Ten miles or more from Ga'za was the city of He'bron, noted as the religious and political center of the tribe of Ju'dah, and situated on a high mountain. As a sign of contempt for the Phi-lis'tines, Sam'son carried the gate of their capital and strongest city far up the mountain road leading to the rallying point of his own people, and cast it to the ground.

As usual, Sam'son appears to have gone on his way without the slightest regret or penitence for the sins which had very nearly cost him his life. More than once God had saved him from evils caused by his own hasty, self-confident deeds, but never do we read of a prayer for forgiveness. His fondness for idolatrous women, if persisted in, would surely lead to his downfall.

In spite of his many worthy traits of character, Sam'son seems to have lost his sense of moral uprightness, and to have forgotten the Lord's command against marriages between the children of Is'ra-el and heathens. Soon after the episode in Ga'za, he fell in love with a Phi-lis'tine woman named De-li'lah. With the treachery so common among the Phi-lis'tines, she used her charm over him for his own downfall. Blinded and enslaved by his unholy affection for her, he permitted himself to be led step by step into a violation of his Naz'a-rite vow, and thus to his ruin.

The leaders of the Phi-lis'tines were constantly spying upon Sam'son, seeking to find some way by which they might trap him, discover the source of his tremendous strength, and finally subdue him. They knew that he must have some higher, secret power than that of his body, and felt that they could overcome him as soon as they discovered the secret of his strength. They knew of Sam'son's affection for De-li'lah, so they offered her a great sum of money if she would find out and reveal to them the secret of her lover's strength.

De-li'lah accepted the bribe of the Phi-lis'tine officers, and began at once to lure Sam'son into telling her the secret of his superhuman power. At first he made light of the matter, telling her in a jocular manner that if he were bound with seven green fibers of wood he would be as other men. When he was bound according to these directions, a number of Phi-lis'tines rushed in upon him from an adjoining room, but the strong twisted fibers parted like tow when it is touched by fire.

Determined to learn the secret at any cost, De-li'lah continued to plead with Sam'son, accusing him of trifling with her, and using increasing charm upon his lessening resistance. Again Sam'son suggested a test of his strength, but the new ropes with which he was bound broke like small threads when the Phi-lis'tine spies rushed in upon him.

For the third time De-li'lah sought to have Sam'son tell her his secret, and for the third time he was able to deceive her. This time, however, he came dangerously near the point of revealing the truth. He told her that if the seven locks of his long hair were woven into a web, he would

SAMSON AND DELILAH

be no stronger than other men. Using a loom which was in her home, De-li'lah wove Sam'son's hair into a perfect web, and then fastened the web to the floor with a strong tent pin. But when she told him that the Phi-lis'tines were upon him, he quickly arose, released the pin, and shook his hair free from the web.

Day after day the pleadings continued, with De-li'lah using every charm and allurement at her command. She reproached Sam'son incessantly with the tormenting accusation that, if he really loved her, he would keep no secrets from her. She argued that between two such lovers there should be no deception whatever, and that she was entitled to know everything about him. There were doubtless well disguised promises that she would make no improper use of the information given, if he would only reveal to her the secret which he had safely guarded for forty years.

Sam'son finally yielded to De-li'lah's persistent urging and allurements, and told her that the secret of his strength lay in keeping the Naz'ar-ite vow which required him not to cut his hair. He admitted that if his head were shaven he would be no stronger than other men.

Casting aside all the promises that she had made, and all pretense of love for the man to whom she had feigned wholehearted devotion, and without shame or apology, the hard-hearted traitress proceeded at once to carry out her purpose. She sent for the Phi-lis'tine leaders to bring her the money which they had promised, assuring them that she had stolen from Sam'son the secret of his power, and that she would deliver him helpless into their hands.

She then lured Sam'son to sleep on her knees, and called in a barber to remove the seven locks of her betrayed lover. Arousing him from his fatal slumbers, she taunted him and turned him over to the spies who lay in waiting. Sam'son tried to show his former power, not realizing that the Spirit of God had left him helpless in the hands of his enemies. The Phi-lis'tines seized him roughly and gouged out his eyes, a cruel punishment which was often inflicted upon prisoners in ancient times.

In his blinded and weakened condition Sam'son was carried to Ga'za, where he became the slave of his captors. He was given the humiliating work of grinding corn with mill stones which were turned by hand. As an object of ridicule and scorn in the city where he had performed one of his mightiest feats, and jeered by people who once had been terrified by him, Sam'son spent his closing days in unspeakable disgrace and shame. Yet now when Samson had lost his eyesight he saw more clearly the most valuable spiritual things of life: the folly of fraternizing with the forces of evil whom God had sent him to destroy; the gross sin of trifling with the sacred vows of consecration to God; the realization that spiritual power can be retained and exercised only while living in harmony with the will of God; that restoration is secured by repentance.

The Phi-lis'tines regarded their final subjection of Sam'son as a triumph of their fish-god Da'gon over the God of Is'ra-el, and all the nobles of the land gathered in the fine temple at Ga'za to engage in a great festive celebration of Sam'son's humiliation. The whole temple was filled with throngs of people, and more than three thousand made merry on the roof-garden. Sam'son was brought to the festival that he might be jeered and buffeted, and to be ridiculed in every possible way.

But the Lord had shown mercy toward Sam'son, whose hair was beginning to grow again. He felt his former strength returning, and sought an opportunity of using it once more in vengeance upon his enemies. He had learned of the manner in which the temple was built, and had probably seen it before his eyes were put out.

Standing in the center of the great hall of the temple were two huge pillars which supported the beams for the galleries and for the central part of the roof-garden. Sam'son was placed in the middle of the crowd so that they could make sport of him as he blindly danced before them. He asked the boy who was guiding him to let him lean against the pillars to rest. Standing between the two huge pillars, Sam'son prayed:

"O Lord God, remember me, I pray thee, and strengthen me, I pray thee, only this once, O God, that I may be at once avenged of the Phi-lis'tines for my two eyes."

Then he took hold of the two pillars and surged at them with all his might, saying as he did so:

"Let me die with the Phi-lis'tines."

The pillars began to sway, they tottered, they were broken; and the whole building collapsed into one terrible mass of ruins, bringing death to the vast throngs of Phi-lis'tines who were engaged in drunken revelry and jeers against the true God of Is'ra-el. The clamors of revelry and idolatry were suddenly changed into shrieks of agony and dying groans as thousands perished.

Among the thousands of slain Phi-lis'tines there lay the body of the hero of Is'ra-el who, for twenty years, had held the oppressors of his nation in a state of constant fear by his superhuman exploits. He had now given his life in one final mighty deed against the enemies of God.

His kinsmen and friends from the tribe of Dan were permitted to remove the body from the ruins of the temple of Da'gon, and it was buried with honor in the cemetery of his father near the mountain home where he had resided throughout his remarkable career. The stories of his exploits became highly prized in the later development of Is'ra-el as a nation, and Sam'son's name has been immortalized by poet and musician.

SUGGESTIONS FOR STUDY

Biblical Index to Helpful References

Presumptuous Attitude Toward Evil Denounced. (Prov. 12:15; Luke 18:11.)
The Hatefulness of Presumptuous Sins. (Ps. 19:13; Jas. 4:17.)

Warnings Against Trifling with Temptation. (Matt. 26:41; Eph. 6:10.)
The Danger of Self-Deception. (Ps. 81:11, 12; Jas. 1:22, 26.)

Questions

1. How long did Samson rule as judge in Israel?

2. In what manner did he probably spend the time after his exploit at Sorek?

3. What mistake did he make in visiting Gaza? How as he trapped?

4. In what manner did he escape this trap of the Philistines?

5. Tell of Samson's continued disregard for God's law in the marriage laws.

6. Relate the story of Delilah's persistent seductions in stealing the secret of Samson's strength.

7. Tell of her final success and of Samson's humiliating capture by the Philistines.

8. What atrocity did the Philistines perform against Samson?

9. Tell of the great feasts in Gaza by the Philistines.

10. What did they require of Samson during this feast?

11. Tell of Samson's overthrow of the Philistine banquet hall.

12. What great significance is attached to this final triumph of Samson?

THE BEAUTIFUL STORY OF NAOMI, RUTH, AND BOAZ

RUTH 1, 2

The story of Ruth and Na-o'mi and Bo'az which follows the book. of Judges in our Bible is one of the gems of sacred literature,—so beautiful that it is unequalled in any writings of fiction or fact. The incidents related are among the most fascinating of the entire Bible. They took place sometime during the period of Judges, and are in striking contrast to the irreverence, idolatry, tumults, and cruelties so common during that era.

With poetic beauty and simplicity, and moving to its happy ending with delightful directness and continuity, the story presents an entrancing picture of rural life in ancient Is'ra-el. It tells of the reverses and sorrows of a devout family, of the trials and hardships of poverty, of noble deeds by two heroic and beautiful women; and relates in a most charming manner stories of romance, marriage, and domestic happiness.

The first scene of this lovely story opens in the peaceful little town of Beth'le-hem in Ju'dah, later made famous as the home of David and the birthplace of Je'sus. Living in the hill country near this town was a farmer whose name was E-lim'e-lech, with a wife named Na-o'mi, and two sons who were called Mah'lon and Chil'i-on. The town had been visited by a severe drought, the crops had failed, and there was a great famine in that part of the country. Pressed by poverty, E-lim'e-lech decided to take his family to the fertile plateaus of Mo'ab, across the Jor'dan and southeast of the lands of Reuben.

The scene changes, and we find the devout little family of four living among idolatrous people, surrounded by heathen altars, and with no neighbors who loved and served their God. Settled on a farm in their newly chosen home their material circumstances were greatly improved, but their religious loyalty and devotion were placed under a great strain. These four noble Is'ra-el-ites, however, lived true to the faith of their fathers, withstood all temptations of idolatry, and, instead of being influenced by their neighbors to take part in the evils of Mo'ab, they led them to respect the true God and the religion of the Is'ra-el-ites. There soon grew up between this He'brew family and the Mo'ab-ites a spirit of tolerance in religion, and of friendly regard in the common interests of life.

The happiness of the little family was soon disturbed by the coming of the angel of death. E-lim'e-lech, the faithful husband and loving father, was called to his eternal home. Na-o'mi's heart was filled with unutterable grief, and the two boys were lonely and distressed. Because of the poverty to which they had been reduced by the famine in Ju'dah and the long journey which they had made, it was impossible for them to carry their dead back to the native land. Thus they were obliged to bury E-lim'e-lech's body in a strange land and among a strange people.

In the course of a few years Mah'lon and Chil'i-on married young women of Mo'ab; one was called Or'pah, and the other's name was Ruth. Soon the family was visited with a double sorrow. Both of the young men died, and, instead of one lone widow cheered by two loyal sons and two devoted daughters-in-law, there were three heart-broken widows. What a tragic picture of grief and trial! A lonely widow, well advanced in years, far away from home, in a strange land and among strange people; two lonely widows, young and strong, their lives made more desolate because they had married outside their own race; and the loneliness of all three deepened because there were no children to comfort them.

Na-o'mi became strongly attached to her two daughters-in-law, and they both loved her very dearly. The three bereaved women lived together in perfect understanding and sympathy. No ill-feeling arose because of racial or religious differences. Na-o'mi's pious nature and upright conduct gradually turned both Ruth and Or'pah toward the Jewish religion.

News came to Na-o'mi that the famine was ended in the land of Ju'dah, and she began to feel a strong impulse to return to her native land and kindred. For ten years she had lived in a foreign land without complaint, but now she longed to go home. Tenderly she told Ruth and Or'pah of her decision, and advised them to return to their parents. They were young, so Na-o'mi expressed the hope that they would find good husbands among their own people, and that the blessings of God would rest upon them.

Ruth and Or'pah loved Na-o'mi so deeply, and their relations with her had been so friendly, that they could not bear the thought of being separated from her. They begged Na-o'mi either to stay with them in Mo'ab, or else to let them go back with her to the land of Ju'dah. When she insisted in returning to her native land, they both journeyed with her to the border between Mo'ab and Is'ra-el. It was truly a touching scene when they reached the place and time for final partings. Or'pah yielded to the advice of her mother-in-law, bade her a fond farewell, and went back to live among her own people. But Ruth clung to Na-o'mi, refused to leave her, and poured the depth of her love into these beautiful words:

"Entreat me not to leave thee,
Or to return from following after thee:
For whither thou goest, I will go;
And where thou lodgest, I will lodge;
Thy people shall be my people,
And thy God my God:
Where thou diest, will I die,
And there will I be buried:
The Lord do so to me, and more also,
If ought but death part thee and me."

Na-o'mi graciously accepted this wonderful appeal, and the two women journeyed together on the road down to the Dead Sea, walked along the

RUTH AND NAOMI

borders of this Sea to the north, crossed the Jor'dan, and made their way up the rugged mountain road to the little town of Beth'le-hem.

The scene changes again to this lovely Jewish town and the surrounding country side. Ruth, in her wholehearted love for Na-o'mi and for Na-o'mi's God, had given up her nationality, the gods of her fathers, and the hope of marriage among her own people; by these sacrifices she proved her desire to become an Is'ra-el-ite in spirit and in practice. With noble unselfishness she began a life of toil and self-denial in her new home, thinking only of the welfare and security of her mother-in-law.

With many fond hopes Na-o'mi took Ruth into the full enjoyment of her rights as an Is'ra-el-ite, and planned for her marriage to some member of the family of E-lim'e-lech in order to provide an heir to the rights and honors of Ruth's deceased husband.

Na-o'mi was given a hearty and gracious welcome by her relatives and friends. She was glad to be back among them, but in her heart-broken state over the loss of her husband and two sons, she cried, "Do not call me Na-o'mi, but call me Ma'ra: for the Almighty hath dealt very bitterly with me." The name Na-o'mi means "pleasantness", while Ma'ra means "bitterness". Adding to these sorrows was the impoverished condition of the two widows. Since there was no one else to provide a livelihood for them, Ruth was obliged to look for some kind of work.

The hand of Providence directed Ruth to glean in one of the fields owned by Bo'az. She received permission from the steward in charge of the reapers to gather scattered barley behind the harvesters. In the hot, broiling sun she worked hard all day, not even taking time to return to her home for a brief rest. Toward evening Bo'az went out into the field to see what progress had been made by his reapers, and greetings were exchanged with all his workers. Attracted by the patient toil of a stranger among the women who were gleaning in the field, he asked of his steward, "Whose damsel is this, and what is her nationality?" He was told that she was the woman of Mo'ab who had returned with Na-o'mi. He had heard many favorable comments concerning her, but up to this time had not been given an opportunity of meeting her.

Bo'az walked over to where Ruth was gleaning, but she was so busy that she did not hear him when he first spoke to her. Then he spoke again, saying, "Hearest thou not, my daughter?" He told her to continue to glean in his field, and to avoid the fields of others. He then tenderly assured her that he had arranged for her protection, and kindly asked her to take refreshment from the water brought into the fields for the harvest hands. Ruth courteously expressed her thanks for this favor, bowing her head to the ground in the custom which prevailed in those days.

Then followed in the harvest field a romantic conversation which is unrivalled in all other stories. The words of Bo'az were thoughtful, respectful, and deeply religious.

With great tenderness Bo'az asked Ruth to share his hospitality in the meal which he had brought to the field. He also tactfully ordered his reapers to see that enough grain was purposely left behind them to give Ruth an abundance of food when she returned in the evening to the home of her mother-in-law.

Ruth continued to glean in the fields of Bo'az throughout the harvest season. The admiration of Bo'az for the charm and virtue of this woman of Mo'ab soon developed into deep affection. Ruth, moreover, soon fell deeply in love with Bo'az, not merely because he had been kind to her, but because she had found him worthy of her heart.

SUGGESTIONS FOR STUDY

Biblical Index to Helpful References

Famines Threatened as Punishments for Sin. (Lev. 26:19, 20; Deut. 28:23, 24; Ps. 107:33, 34.)

Famines Recognized as Divine Instruments for Chastisements. (2 Sam. 24:13, 14; Ezek. 5:16; Amos. 4:6, 7.)

Christian Duties in Time of Famine. (1 Ki. 8:35-37.)

Moabites Descendants of Lot. (Gen. 19:36, 37.)

Moab an Asylum for Troubled Israelites. (1 Sam. 22:3, 4; Isa. 16:4; Jer. 40:11.)

The Lord's Provision for His Needy Children. (1 Ki. 17:4-10; Ps. 37:3, 7, 19; Ps. 145:17.)

Prayer in the Parting of Loved Ones. (Gen. 28:1-3; Acts 20:36-38.)

The Law of Gleanings. (Lev. 19:9, 10; Deut. 24-19.)

True Character Manifest in Words of Kindness. (Prov. 31:26; Col. 4:6.)

Questions

1. What were the general conditions in Israel when the incidents of this story took place?

2. Relate some of the reasons for the value of this story.

3. Why did Elimelech and his family leave Bethlehem? Name the other members.

4. Where did they go, and why?

5. What sorrow soon came to this home?

6. What events of interest took place with the two sons?

7. What second great trial soon followed?

8. Describe the happy relations between Naomi and her two daughters-in-law?

9. What happened when Naomi prepared to return to Bethlehem?

10. What kind of work did Ruth do in Bethlehem? In whose field?

11. How was she treated by Boaz?

12. How did Ruth feel toward Boaz?

THE MARRIAGE OF RUTH AND BOAZ

RUTH 3, 4   Na-o'mi was very happy when Ruth told her
in whose field she had gleaned, and of the courtesy shown her by the
owner. Bo'az had also been kind to E-lim'e-lech before the family had
gone to Mo'ab, and Na-o'mi called this to mind with deep gratitude
for God's continued goodness.

The law of Lev'i-rate Marriage was a custom of the Is'ra-el-ites which
required the closest unmarried male relative of a man who died without
children to purchase the family inheritance and to marry the widow.
Na-o'mi knew of this law, but seems to have thought at first that it would
not apply to Ruth, who belonged to a foreign nation. After Ruth was
converted to the Jewish religion, however, and because the friendship
with Bo'az seemed to be ordered by Divine Providence, Na-o'mi felt that
the law should be carried out for the benefit of her son's widow. She
therefore encouraged Ruth in her friendship with the noble and highly
respected kinsman of her deceased husband, and the courtship which followed had her blessing.

It is evident that neither Na-o'mi nor Ruth resorted to any question-
able designs on the heart of Bo'az. Na-o'mi did not direct Ruth in the
choice of the field in which she gleaned, nor did Ruth know to whom the
field belonged when she entered it. Her application was made to the
steward in charge of the harvest. Bo'az himself took the first steps in
their acquaintance and in the close friendship which grew up among
them. Ruth did not know of his relation to her deceased husband, nor
did she know of the law of Lev'i-rate Marriage. The growth of their
friendship was the natural result of the love and respect which they felt
for one another.

In taking such an active part in guiding Ruth in her relations with
Bo'az, Na-o'mi performed a solemn duty of both religion and friendship.
Under the religious laws of her people her dead son Mah'lon had certain
claims upon Bo'az, and she hastened to press these claims. In her deep
love for Ruth she felt it her duty to make sure that adequate provision
was taken for her future security and happiness.

Under the laws of Lev'i-rate Marriage it was customary for the woman to take the lead in presenting her claims. Although Bo'az had shown warm affection for Ruth, she must make the first move in offering to become his wife. She was modest and timid, so the customary procedure in this matter had to be arranged by her mother-in-law Na-o'mi. The method adopted by Na-o'mi was wholly proper under Oriental customs; though it might be frowned upon to-day, the purity and honor of the entire procedure is proved by its happy result.

Ruth modestly confessed the love and esteem which existed between them, asked for the guardianship and protection to which she was entitled from him, and sincerely renounced the claims of all others. In his reply Bo'az showed complete respect for the will and law of God, praised Ruth for her kindness and virtue, and promised to remove all obstacles to their early marriage.

There was one other serious

RUTH AND BOAZ

impediment in the way of the marriage of Ruth and Bo'az. Another Is'ra-el-ite, who was a nearer kinsman to Mah'lon, was entitled to the heart and hand of Ruth; only after he had given up all claims to this right and responsibility could Bo'az legally proceed with the marriage which he desired so much.

It is Bo'az who takes the leading part in the final act of this fascinating drama. Throughout the story his character has stood out in superb glory, but now it shines forth in the brilliance of the noonday sun. We have seen him as a successful farmer; honoring, and honored by, his workmen; we have looked upon him in his generous regard for the poor, quick to perceive virtue and to honor it; he has lived and walked before us as a deeply religious and wholly righteous man, wise and self-controlled; and we have admired him as a manly and sincere lover, always pure in thought and deed.

Now we are to behold him as a hero dealing fairly with a rival, meeting with honor every requirement of the laws of his people, and acting as a redeemer for the woman he loved. Going at once to the place of civil judgment, he acted in a spirit of candor and fair dealing. In the presence of witnesses he stated the facts, giving the lawful heir to Mah'lon's inheritance, which included the obligation of taking Ruth as a wife, a fair opportunity to claim all that the law allowed him.

When the kinsman of Mah'lon refused to carry out his responsibilities in the Lev'i-rate Marriage, Bo'az paid the required redemption fee, and he and Ruth were married at once.

There was born to them a son whom they called O'bed, who later became the father of Jes'se, and the grandfather of David, the great king of Is'ra-el. Thus Bo'az and Ruth became the ancestors of a long line of kings who ruled over Is'ra-el and Ju'dah, and of the Mes-si'ah who came into the world to save mankind from sin and to head a great spiritual kingdom.

SUGGESTIONS FOR STUDY

Biblical Index to Helpful References

The Duty of Caring for Loved Ones. (Job 39:13-16; 1 Tim. 5:8.)

Moabites Not Included in the Law Against Marrying Aliens. (Deut. 7:1-3.)

The Law of Levirate Marriage. (Deut. 25:5-10.)

The Good Fortune of Having a Worthy Wife. (Prov. 12:4, 31:10-31.)

Ruth an Ancestress of Christ. (Matt. 1:3-6.)

Questions

1. Why was Naomi happy when she was told in whose field Ruth had gleaned?

2. Did Naomi or Ruth act in a wrong spirit in pursuing Boaz in courtship?

3. What is meant by the "Levirate Marriage Law"?

4. Why could not Boaz marry Ruth at once under the "Levirate Marriage Law"?

5. What steps did he take to remove this impediment?

6. What name was given to the son of Boaz and Ruth?

7. Of what great personalities did Ruth thus become an ancestress?

THE HIGH PRIEST ELI AND THE BOY SAMUEL

1 SAMUEL 1-3

About thirty years before Sam'son began to rule in the west and southwestern parts of Is'ra-el, there was raised to the office of High Priest in Shi'loh a man named E'li. He held this position for forty years, the last ten of which coincided with the first ten years of Sam'son's twenty year reign. During his tenure of office as High Priest in the tabernacle he also held a place of much influence in the nation as a magistrate. Strictly speaking, he was not a "Judge," although it is said that he "judged Is'ra-el for forty years." This statement is due to the fact that during his priesthood there was no Judge whose reign extended over the entire land. In his priestly office, therefore, E'li advised the people in respect to civil matters, and decided legal problems.

The time had now come for great changes in the national life of Is'ra-el. For nearly three hundred years there had been no centralized national authority, and the tribes had been very loosely related to one another and to the nation. What is known as the Period of Judges had witnessed many disgraceful sins, frequent lapses into idolatry, constant failures to uphold true religion; and the country had suffered periodic invasions and oppressions from the heathen nations adjoining their land.

But in spite of the bloodshed, lawlessness, and superstition of that troubled period, it is easy to trace the progress of God's plan for uniting the widely separated and disordered tribes of Is'ra-el. Running through the entire story is the thread of God's purpose to purify the nation which was to become the great religious teacher of the world, and in whose land the Sav'ior was to be born. Chief among the factors which had brought the tribes into greater unity were their common faith in the religion of Je-ho'vah, their sense of racial unity, the pressure of common danger from foreign oppressors, and the brave leadership of great heroes raised up by God.

The tribes of the west and southwest were oppressed by occasional raids from the Phi-lis'tines, but there was no general war nor invasions of the land by foreign nations. A general state of irreverence and religious de-

THE CHILD SAMUEL

cline prevailed throughout the land, but notable exceptions to this rule are seen in t h e stories of Na-o'mi, Bo'az and Ruth. The Lord was preparing Is'ra-el for a great religious awakening, and for a closer union of worship and nationality.

The stories drawn from the books of Sam'u-el cover important events in the period which led to the formation of the great Is'ra-el-it-ish monarchy under Saul as the first king.

As we learned in previous chapters, the office of High Priest of Is'ra-el was held exclusively by descendants of Aa'ron, and that this honor was given to the eldest son of each generation, unless there were good reasons why he could not serve. In the case of E'li, he was a descendant of Ith'a-mar, the youngest son of Aa'ron. The rank was probably given to him because at the death of the last High Priest of the family of E-le-a'zer, the eldest son of Aa'ron, his son was too young or inexperienced to assume the office.

E'li was a devout and pious man of God, and served the people with honor for a long period of time. He was lacking, however, in one very important respect: he was careless in the religious training of his sons, failing to restrain them from ways of immorality and blasphemy. For these failures he was severely punished, and his family doomed to lose their priestly heritage.

In his declining years E'li turned over many duties of the priesthood to his two sons, Hoph'ni and Phin'e-has. Even while performing these sacred duties, they acted very wickedly. They were greedy, selfish, and depraved in conduct. They brought religion into disrepute and contempt, and caused the people to "abhor the offering of the Lord." Reports of their doings were brought to E'li, but he merely remonstrated with them in a feeble manner, letting them go on in their evil ways. He was not only High Priest, but a magistrate in Is'ra-el, and should have sternly punished his sons, who were so wicked that the Bible record speaks of them as "sons of Be'li-al who knew not the Lord."

An unnamed messenger of the Lord was sent to E'li with a solemn warning that the wickedness of his sons would end in their death on the same day. But even this stern warning fell upon deaf ears, so weak was E'li in the discipline of his wicked sons.

There was living in the days of E'li, at the little town of Ra'mah in the mountains of E'phra-im, a devout man by the name of El'ka-nah. He was a direct descendant of Ko'hath of the tribe of Le'vi, but for some unknown reason did not serve as a Le'vite. He was fairly prosperous, was faithful in his religious duties, and took his family up to Shi'loh for regular worship and sacrifice unto the Lord. In spite of the notorious unworthiness of those who acted as priests he did not neglect the duty of worship.

El'ka-nah was the husband of two wives, Han'nah and Pe-nin'nah. He had probably married Pe-nin'nah because of Han'nah's childlessness, as this was a common practice in those days. From the time of Creation it has always been wrong for any man to have more than one wife; even though El'ka-nah was justified by the customs of his times, he could not escape the sure punishment which follows the violation of God's law. So the little home in Ra'mah, though prosperous and devout, was not happy.

The plural marriage of El'ka-nah embittered the life of the home, bringing unhappiness to every member of the family. Han'nah was the lawful and favorite wife, so Pe-nin'nah was jealous of her; Han'nah, moreover, was jealous because Pe-nin'nah had children, while she had none. As we have already learned, children were regarded by the He'brews as a sign of His favor, while to have no children was a reproach and a disgrace. Han'nah was continually taunted by Pe-nin'nah, and in her distress of spirit sought help from the Lord in prayer.

One year when El'ka-nah's family had gone up to Shi'loh for worship and sacrifice, Han'nah lingered in the tabernacle in great bitterness of soul, earnestly pleading with God to take away her reproach. So deep was her anguish, and so intense her prayer, that she uttered no sound with her lips, but spake in her heart to the Lord.

When the aged priest E'li saw Han'nah lying prostrate in the tabernacle, her lips silently moving, and tears streaming down her face, he thought that she was the victim of strong drink, and spoke harshly to her. Although she must have been deeply wounded by the false accusation of the one person in the world from whom she might have expected sympathy and understanding, her reply was calm and respectful.

In the deep sorrow of her heart she did not tell the High Priest the reason for her anguish and fervent prayers, but asked only that she be recognized as a "handmaiden of the Lord," and that he pronounce a blessing upon her. E'li's attitude was completely changed, and the stern rebuke spoken in ignorance was turned into a heavenly benediction as he said to her, "Go in peace, and the God of Is'ra-el grant thee the petition that thou hast asked of him." God answered Han'nah's prayer, and in the course of time she became the mother of a son whom she gave the name Sam'u-el, which means "asked of the Lord."

In the birth of this son Han'nah gave to the world one of the greatest characters of Biblical history. Sam'u-el was destined to become the chief interest of God in leading Is'ra-el from a disordered group of twelve rival tribes into a strongly united nation. While silently pleading with the Lord,

ELI DIRECTS SAMUEL

Han'nah had said in her heart, "If thou wilt give unto thine handmaid a man-child, then I will give him unto the Lord all the days of his life." In her deep consecration she had promised that the most cherished gift of her heart would be returned to the Divine Giver; that God's gift to her would be her consecrated gift to God.

For the first three years of Sam'u-el's life Han'nah watched over him tenderly, not even going up to Shi'loh for the annual feast days and sacrifices unto God.

When Sam'u-el was about three years old, his father and mother prepared special offerings to be made unto the Lord, and carried the young child to the tabernacle at Shi'loh. Han'nah told E'li that she was the woman who had come to the temple years before to pray for a son, and acknowledged God's favor in giving her the child. Sam'u-el was then dedicated to the service of the Lord, and was left in the tabernacle to be trained for his mission by ministering unto the Lord before E'li. Han'-nah and her husband returned to their home in Ra'mah, where unceasing prayer was made for their young son. Once a year, when Han'nah went up to Shi'loh for the sacrifices, she brought a little robe for her son.

Through the days of his childhood and youth Sam'u-el was constantly engaged in the services of the Lord's house. In E'li's declining years he became the personal assistant and companion of the aged priest. There grew up between them a deep and abiding affection, and E'li looked upon the boy as if he were a beloved son, for his own sons had long since disgraced themselves by evil deeds.

When Sam'u-el was about twelve years old he was sleeping in a room which adjoined that of the High Priest. Suddenly he heard a voice calling, "Sam'u-el, Sam'u-el." Thinking that E'li needed him for some service, he rushed into the next room and said, "Here I am, did you not call me?" E'li told Sam'u-el that he had not called him, and directed him to return to his own room. The same experience was repeated, and then took place for the third time. E'li then told Sam'u-el that the voice which had come to him must be that of the Lord, and that if he heard it again, he should say, "Speak, Lord, for thy servant heareth." Once more Sam'-u-el heard the voice calling him by name, and this time he did as E'li had directed. The Lord then revealed to his young servant a message of doom which must be delivered at once to E'li.

When Sam'u-el awoke from the dream he hesitated to bring E'li the message from God. But when E'li urged him to relate what the Lord had said, and solemnly charged him to keep back nothing, he told the aged priest of God's judgments against his house because of the wickedness of his sons.

Even the confirmation of the doom previously announced to him by the unnamed messenger of God failed to stir E'li to any serious effort to prevent his sons from going on in their evil ways. Giving up all priestly and parental authority, he said, "It is the Lord, let him do what seemeth him good."

As proved by future events, this incident was more significant in the life of Sam'u-el than in that of E'li. For the first time the Lord had revealed Himself to the lad who was afterwards to be known as "the prophet of the Lord." God opened the spiritual hearing of Sam'u-el, and whispered to him the secret of His own will and purposes. From that very moment the reality and personal contact of God with him became a constant experience; he kept his ears open for every utterance of the Divine voice, and was recognized by the people as a prophet of the Lord. He grew in favor with God and with man, and "the Lord was with him, and did let none of his words fall to the ground."

SUGGESTIONS FOR STUDY
Biblical Index to Helpful References

God's Judgments Begin at His Own House. (John 2:14-17; 1 Pet. 4:17.)

Guilt of Failing to Restrain Sin in Others. (Ezek. 33:8, 9.)

The Tabernacle Set Up at Shiloh by Joshua. (Josh. 18:1; Jgs. 21:19.)

Elkanah's Descent From Kohath. (1 Chr. 6:22-25, 35, 36.)

God's Law of Monogony. (Gen. 2:24; Matt. 19:5; 1 Cor. 7:2.)

God's Promise to Meet His People at His House. (Exo. 29:43; Deut. 16:14.)

Bitterness of Heart in Secret Anguish. (Prov. 14:10.)

Prayer the Source of Help in Trouble. (Ps. 69:13-20; 1 Cor. 4:13.)

Prayer Without Words. (Ps. 19:14; 27:8.)

Secret Bitterness and Prayer Observed by God. (Ps. 139:1, 2; Rom. 8:26, 27.)

Vows to God to Be Fulfilled Without Delay. (Eccl. 5:4.)

Difference Between Levitical and Nazarite Consecration. (Num. 8:24, 25; Num. 6:1-21.)

Samuel the Beginning of Prophet's Office. (2 Chr. 35:18; Acts 3:24.)

Questions

1. What was the office of Eli? Why is he called a "judge"?

2. How long did he serve as high priest and "judge"?

3. What was the general condition of Israel at that time?

4. In what was Eli deficient? What judgment did God announce against him?

5. Why was Hannah in bitterness? To whom did she go for help?

6. What vow did she make and how did she fulfill it?

7. Where was Samuel placed for training and service for the Lord?

8. What message was given to him for Eli?

9. What was the significance of this nightvision to Samuel?

10. What office did Samuel occupy in Israel?

DISASTERS CAUSED BY THE ABUSE OF THE ARK OF GOD

1 SAMUEL 4-7:2   As noted in previous chapters, the Is'ra-el-ites at this time were under the dominion of the Phi-lis'tines who held the rich plains of the Med'i-ter-ra'ne-an in the south and southwest, and who made frequent raids upon the tribes which lived near them. It appears that Sam'u-el directed the people of Is'ra-el to make war upon these Phi-lis'-tines in the latter days of E'li, and that the Is'ra-el-ites were badly defeated in a battle fought near A'phek, which was not far from Miz'pah in the territory of Ben'ja-min.

The moral and spiritual state of Is'ra-el at the time was at a very low ebb. E'li's sons had neither confessed their guilt nor amended their ways, and the people had not turned to God in penitence for idolatry or in prayer for help against their enemies. There was, however, a superstitious and idolatrous regard for the Ark at Shi'loh, and the Is'ra-el-ites were influenced by the customs of their heathen neighbors, who carried images of their gods into battle in the hope of victory, to have their elders bring the Ark of the Cov'e-nant to the battle-field.

A great uproar and clamor was raised by the Is'ra-el-ites whenever the Ark was brought up to the line of battle, and the Phi-lis'tines were filled with terror when they learned the reason for such rejoicing by their enemies. The Phi-lis'tines, however, determined to fight on with greater force and courage than they had shown at any time before.

On the next day the Is'ra-el-ites resumed the battle in a rather light-hearted manner, and with superstitious reliance upon the presence of the Ark to bring them victory. They tried to throw off the yoke of the Phi-lis'tines without submitting to the yoke of God. They failed to offer repentance and obedience to the Lord whose presence among them was falsely represented by the misuse of the Ark, and therefore the Lord's hand was against them. The defeat of the previous day was turned into a rout, with the loss of thirty thousand soldiers. Hoph'ni and Phin'e-has, the two wicked sons of E'li, were slain, and the Ark of the Cov'e-nant was taken by the Phi-lis'tines.

THE IDOL DESTROYED

Is'ra-el had relied upon the presence of a symbol, while ignoring the God represented by that symbol. They had trusted in the power of magic while the emblem of Divine power was abused in profane hands; they had pretended to be loyal to the laws of God while their hearts were separated from Him by great sins.

The aged High Priest E'li waited at the gates of Shi'loh for news of the result of the battle. His heart sank in despair when a Ben'ja-mite messenger told him of the shameful defeat of his people, and of the death of his two sons and of thirty thousand footmen. When he learned that the Ark of God had been captured by the Phi-lis'tines, he suddenly fell over backwards, and his neck was broken by the fall. When the wife of Phin'e-has was told that her husband was dead, and that the Ark had been taken by Is'ra-el's enemies, she gave her new-born child the name of Ich'a-bod, which means "the glory of the Lord has departed." Thus, according to the word of the Lord, the doom pronounced upon the house of E'li was carried out.

The Phi-lis'tines carried the Ark to Ash'dod, which was one of the five noted cities of their nation, located about thirty-two miles north of Ga'za and one mile from the Sea. It was placed in the temple of Da'gon, the fish-god of this heathen nation. Da'gon was represented by an image with a human body and a fish's tail.

Just as the abuse of the Ark had proven a curse to the Is'ra-el-ites, so its presence among the Phi-lis'tines became the source of terrible calamities. When the people came into the temple to worship on the next morning they found the image of Da'gon lying on its face before the Ark. On the next morning a still worse thing happened, for they found that not only had Da'gon fallen again, but his head and hands, the emblems of his strength, were cut off. Neither priests nor people dared to cross the threshold of the temple. In addition to the mysterious disasters which befell their fish-god, the people of the city and surrounding coast-lands were afflicted with a plague of boils, which caused great suffering and death.

Overwhelmed by their sufferings and by the clear supremacy of the God of Is'ra-el over their chief god, the people of Ash'dod hastily sent the Ark off to Gath, another chief city of the nation ten miles to the east. When the same affliction came upon the people of that city, they rushed the Ark off to Ek'ron, where the same punishments were repeated.

The cry of the people against these disasters was so intense that the lords of the Phi-lis'tines gathered in council. It was then decided to send the Ark back to Is'ra-el with an offering of golden jewels; this was done in the hope of appeasing the anger of God against them. Under the instructions of the magicians of the land they prepared five golden emerods to represent the plague of boils, and five golden mice in token of the hordes of these pests which had infested the land. This was in keeping with the heathen custom of presenting to their gods offerings which expressed the mercy desired.

A new cart drawn by two milch kine was used for the removal of the Ark. It was carried to Beth-she'mesh within the borders of Ben'ja-min, placed on a large stone in the field of a man named Josh'u-a, and there the cows were offered as a burnt sacrifice to the Lord.

The people of Beth-she'mesh did not treat the Ark with proper reverence,—some of them even looking into it—so the Lord punished thousands of them with death. The Ark was then removed to Kir-jath-Je'a-rim, a much larger town in the territory of the tribe of Ju'dah on the road toward Shi'loh. Here it was placed in the home of A-bin'a-dab, and his son E-le-a'zar was appointed to protect it from all irreverence. The Ark remained in the house of A-bin'a-dab for seventy years or more, and was later restored to the tabernacle by David.

The twenty years which followed these events are passed over in silence. It appears that the Phi-lis'tines continued to dominate Is'ra-el, and that the sanctuary at Shi'loh fell into ruins and disuse. Never again, however, do we hear of any attempts among heathen nations to unite the He'brew religion with idolatry.

Sam'u-el vanished from sight during this period of twenty years, but we may be sure that the following statement concerning his life was true: "And the Lord was with him, and did let none of his words fall to the ground; and he was established among the people from Dan to Be'er-she'ba to be the prophet of the Lord." He no doubt spent these years in causing a great spiritual revival throughout the land, for we read toward the close of the period, "And all the house of Is'ra-el lamented toward the Lord."

It was the holy influence of Sam'u-el's character and the unassuming services rendered during that twenty years that led to permanent reforms in Is'ra-el, and finally broke the Phi-lis'tine oppression. Occupying a position of preëminence in the history of the He'brews for purity of life and for devotion to the welfare of his people, and standing above all others as an intercessor before God, he was a perpetual power for good.

SUGGESTIONS FOR STUDY

Biblical Index to Helpful References

God's Victory in the Proper Use of the Ark. (Num. 10:33; Josh. 3:14-16.)

God's Law of Success or Failure in the Battles of Israel. (Deut. 28:1, 7, 15, 25; Ps. 81:8-15.)

Reasons for Honoring the House and Oracles of God. (Ps. 87:2; Ps. 26:8.)

The Worthlessness of Idol-Gods. (1 Cor. 8:4.)

God's Judgments Against Oppressors of Israel. (Isa. 51:22, 23.)

Heathens Forced to Acknowledge the Power of God. (Exo. 9:27.)

Questions

1. Why did the Lord permit the Philistines to defeat the Israelites?

2. What superstitious act did Israel engage in after their first defeat?

3. What happened in the second battle?

4. What calamities were brought upon the Philistines by the abuse of the Ark?

5. Name and locate the three cities in which the Ark was placed.

6. What did the Philistines finally do with the Ark?

7. Why was a plague sent upon the people of Bethshemesh?

8. In what city and in whose home was the Ark then placed?

STORY 76

ISRAEL DEMANDS A KING; SAUL IS CHOSEN

1 SAMUEL 8-10

When Sam'u-el was about sixty years old the weakness of increasing age led him to appoint his two sons to assist him in ruling over Is'ra-el. They were placed at Be'er-she'ba, in the south-western part of the land, while Sam'u-el remained at the head of the nation and continued to serve in the cities of Ra'mah, Beth'el, Gil'gal, and Miz'peh. Sam'u-el had no idea of making the office of Judge a heritage of his own family, but was merely doing what seemed best at the time.

In his earnest desire to have his two sons grow up to be godly men, Sam'u-el had given each of them a name which had a deep religious meaning, One he called Jo'el, which means "Je-ho'vah is God," in protest against the idolatry of the land; the other was called A-bi'ah, which means "Je-ho'vah is father," as a proof of his faith in the close relationship of God with all His children. He had set before them the example of a godly life, and had faithfully taught them the principles and duties of true religion. But sad to say, Sam'u-el's sons did not follow in their father's steps. They turned aside into evil ways, took bribes, and scorned justice.

The feebleness of Sam'u-el and the misconduct of his two sons gave rise to the demand for a king. The elders of Is'ra-el came to him at Ra'mah, declaring that the people desired a king to rule over them as in other nations. This injured the feelings of Sam'u-el, for he thought that the people had rebelled against God's plan for the nation, and had scorned his authority as chief ruler. True to his usual custom, he carried the matter to the Lord in prayer. The Lord told him to yield to the wishes of the people, even though their demand had the appearance of rejecting God.

While this request of Is'ra-el for a king seems to have been hasty, and not entirely free from wrong motives, it must be remembered that God had promised both A-bra'ham and Ja'cob that kings should come from their offspring. Ja'cob had declared in his prophetic blessing upon Ju'dah that the scepter should not depart from his tribe until Shi'loh came, and Ba'laam had prophesied that a scepter should rise out of Is'ra-el. In giving the law to Mo'ses the Lord had made special provision for the kingdom into which Is'ra-el should later be formed.

Is'ra-el did wrong, therefore, in not waiting patiently for God's time, and in failing to ask Sam'u-el to inquire of the Lord whether or not the time had come when they might have a king. They had been chosen by the Lord as a holy nation, unlike the nations around them, and it was wrong for them to wish to imitate the heathen peoples of the world. If their demand had been based upon a desire for better government or a closer national unity for the accomplishment of God's will, then the change could have been made in keeping with the plan of God, and without any unhappy results. But, since the demand was in advance of God's time for setting up a kingdom in Is'ra-el, the early history of the kingdom was marked by unnecessary strife and turmoil.

The Lord granted the request of Is'ra-el with the solemn warning that certain burdens for which they were not prepared would be laid upon them by the appointment of a king at this time, and that their self-imposed yoke would be more irksome than the one placed upon them by their Divine King.

Sam'u-el told the people of the Lord's decision, dismissed the elders, sent the people home, and gave careful thought to the necessary steps in selecting a king. Such was the reverence of the people for God, and so great was their confidence in his prophet, that the task of finding and appointing the right man to be their king was left entirely in the hands of Sam'u-el.

The incidents leading up to Sam'u-el's discovery of the first king for Is'ra-el present a rather curious story, but are in perfect keeping with the customs and superstitions of those days. There was living in the tribe of Ben'ja-min a wealthy man by the name of Kish, who owned large herds of cattle and asses. According to the habit of Oriental shepherds in pastoral regions, Kish let his animals roam at large during the grazing season, and later sent men to search for them. He had a son to whom he assigned the responsible and honorable task of taking charge of his large herds of asses. The son's name was Saul, and he was tall, handsome, and industrious.

When it was time to gather in the roaming herds Saul and one of his servants left Gib'e-ah, a few miles north of Je-ru'sa-lem, and traveled northwest toward the mountains of E'phra-im in search of his father's herd of asses. After searching for several days without success, Saul proposed to his servant that they return. Their supply of food had given out, and Saul did not wish his father to be alarmed by their long absence.

Since they were not far from Ra'mah, which was the home of the prophet Sam'u-el, Saul's servant suggested that before giving up the search they should consult the man of God. In the land of Ca'naan at that time it was a common thing for people to consult "seers" for help in finding things which had been lost or stolen, or for advice in private matters of importance. Sam'u-el had no doubt encouraged this practice in order to prevent his people from going to heathen magicians, and as a means of opening the way for his more important duties as a prophet of God.

Saul hesitated to follow the suggestion of his servant, for he had no

SAMUEL AT RAMAH

money to pay the customary fee for such advice. But when the servant told him of the small piece of money which he had, Saul agreed to go to the prophet's home.

As we learned in a previous chapter, Ra'mah was one of the centers of worship which Sam'u-el had provided after the abandonment of the tabernacle at Shi'loh. Preparations for a religious festival were in progress when Saul and his servant reached the town. Making inquiry of some young women, they were told that the prophet was expected to attend the festival to be held that day.

On the day before, as Sam'u-el was in prayer to God about the choice of a king, he was told that the Lord would bring him a man of the tribe of Ben'ja-min, and that he should make him the prince of Is'ra-el. When Saul and his servant drew near, the prophet had a Divine intuition that this was the man of whom the Lord had spoken. Never having met Sam'-u-el, Saul asked if he could direct him to the seer of God.

Sam'u-el then made himself known, and invited Saul to join him in the offerings and feast on top of the high place where there was an altar to the Lord. "As to the asses," said Sam'u-el, "do not be troubled about them, for they have been found." Then the prophet said something about the desire of Is'ra-el being set on his father's house and upon him, but Saul did not know what was meant by these words. With great modesty, therefore, Saul replied, "Is not my tribe the smallest in Is'ra-el? And is not my family the least of the tribe of Ben'ja-min?"

At the religious festival which followed there were about thirty guests, yet Saul was given the place of honor and was served with the choicest food. When the feast was over, Sam'u-el took Saul and the servant to his own home to be his guests for the night. Out on the flat roof of the building, with no other light than that of the stars, the prophet told the young man that he was to be appointed king of Is'ra-el. The next morning they arose early, and Sam'u-el journeyed with Saul and his servant toward the gates of the town.

When they reached the border of Ra'mah, Sam'u-el directed the servant to leave him alone with Saul. He then took a vial of the oil used in anointing the priests of God, and poured it on the head of young Saul; he also kissed him as a sign of homage to the new king. Sam'u-el then directed the course for Saul's homeward journey, telling him of certain things that would happen as signs of his Divine selection for the office of king.

Seven days after the private anointing of Saul, Sam'u-el ordered all Is'ra-el to gather at Miz-peh to cast lots for the choice of a king. Prayer was made to God that His choice be revealed through this method commonly used in Is'ra-el for deciding such matters. Slips of paper representing each tribe were placed in a vessel, and one was drawn out. The lot fell to the tribe of Ben'ja-min. Then slips of paper on which were written all the families of Ben'ja-min were placed in the vessel; this lot fell to the family of Kish. Then the names of the sons of Kish were placed in the vessel, and one was drawn out. It bore the name of Saul. As a result of this election the people felt that Saul had been chosen for the office by the Lord.

When a cry went up that Saul be presented to the people, there was no response. A search was made for him, and he was found among the baggage of the people who had gathered for the solemn occasion—hiding in shyness. He knew from the words of Sam'u-el seven days before that the choice would probably fall to him, and he modestly fled from assuming such a responsible position.

Saul was then brought before the people, and they were greatly pleased with his tall, impressive appearance. God had read the mirror of their hearts, and had given them a man after their own desires.

SUGGESTIONS FOR STUDY

Biblical Index to Helpful References

The Best of Men Make Mistakes. (Prov. 20:9; Eccl. 7:20; Rom. 3:23.)

Bribery and Injustice Denounced. (Ex. 23:8; Prov. 17:23; Isa. 1:23.)

National Peace to Be Sought. (Rom. 14:19; Heb. 12:14.)

The Perils of National Strife. (Jer. 51:46.)

God's Warnings Against Sinful Imitations. (Ex. 23:2; 2 Ki. 17:5.)

Warnings Against Trusting in Man Instead of God. (Ps. 118:9; 146:3.)

The Danger of Looking on Outward Appearances Only. (Matt. 23:27; Jno. 7:24.)

Rulers to Be Honored. (Gen. 41:43; Acts 26:2.)

Mizpeh Place of Sacred Events. (Gen. 31:48, 49; Josh. 11:8.)

Duties of Rulers. (2 Sam. 23:3; Ps. 2:10.)

Questions

1. Why did Samuel appoint his sons to assist in judging Israel?

2. Name these sons and give the meaning of each name.

3. What was the reason for Israel's demand for a king?

4. Was it in the plan of God that Israel should become a kingdom?

5. What was wrong then with the request for a king at this time?

6. Tell of the prosperity of Kish and the duties of his son Saul.

7. Why did Saul and his servant consult the prophet Samuel?

8. Tell of Samuel's conversation with Saul.

9. Tell of Saul's private anointing by Samuel.

10. Tell of the election of Saul at Mizpeh. How was the ballot taken?

11. Where was Saul when the time came for his public anointing?

12. Tell of Samuel's instructions to the people and their new king.

STORY 77

KING SAUL'S GOOD BEGINNING; SAMUEL'S RESIGNATION ADDRESS

1 SAMUEL 11, 12   Although Saul had been privately anointed king by Sam'u-el at Ra'mah and his appointment had been publicly approved at Miz'peh, it seems that he did not assume the office at once. Instead, he returned to his father's farm, and continued to engage in the work of agriculture and stock-raising. It was not long, however, before the occasion arose through which he was led by the Lord to take his place of leadership over all the tribes of Is'ra-el.

On the east side of the Jor'dan there lived a clan known as Gil'e-ad-ites, who were members of the tribe of Ma-nas'seh. The territory which they occupied had once belonged to the Am'mon-ites, but had been taken by the Am'o-rites and later conquered by the children of Is'ra-el under the leadership of Mo'ses. The Am'mon-ites claimed the right to take back this territory, and frequently pressed their claims by making war upon the Gil'e-ad-ites. It was in subduing one of their attacks that Jeph'thah rose to the rank of Judge in Is'ra-el. A threatened war by them against the Gil'e-ad-ites was one of the circumstances which led the Is'ra-el-ites to demand a king.

After the newly elected king failed to assume the leadership of Is'ra-el and returned to his father's farm, the Am'mon-ites decided that he lacked the courage and ability to resist their demands upon Gil'e-ad. They therefore marched against Ja-besh-Gil'e-ad, the capital of the Gil'e-ad-ites, knowing that the people there were too few and too weak to oppose them. In great fear the people of that city offered to become subjects of the Am'mon-ites, provided that their lives be spared.

Na'hash, king of the Am'mon-ites, agreed to accept their offer of surrender on condition that his soldiers be permitted to put out the right eye of all the men of the city. By this cruel measure the Gil'e-ad-ites would be made unfit for army service, since the left eye was covered by a shield in battle, and the right eye was used in aiming the spear.

The elders of Ja-besh-Gil'e-ad asked for a truce of seven days, during which to seek help from the other tribes of Is'ra-el, and agreed to submit

DAVID PLAYS FOR SAUL

to the cruel demands of Na'hash if help did not come within that time. Messengers came to Gib'e-ah, the home of Saul, with news of the tragedy facing the Gil'e-ad-ites, and the people cried out in fear and sympathy. When Saul came in from the fields where he had been working and saw the entire town bowed in wailings, he asked for an explanation. They told him of the plight of their brethren at Ja'besh, and as he listened a spirit of supernatural power came upon him. He expressed his feelings by cutting two oxen into twelve pieces, and sending the pieces among the tribes of Is'ra-el by special messengers. He then summoned all Is'ra-el to join him and Sam'u-el in a war against the Am'mon-ites, saying, "Whoever fails to come, so shall it be done unto his oxen."

From every tribe of Is'ra-el there came a hearty response to the call, and more than three hundred thousand people gathered at Be'zek, on the plains of Jez're-el within the territory of Is'sa-char, to follow the leadership of their new king in the first crisis of his reign.

Saul then sent messengers to Ja'besh with the good news that on the next day he would attack the Am'mon-ites who were gathered before their gates. The men of Ja'besh then notified the Am'mon-ites that they would come out on the following day and submit to having their right eyes put out. Saul organized his army in the evening and marched all night, moving over the mountains of central Ca'naan to one of the fords of the Jor'dan, crossing the river, and climbing the plateau of Gil'e-ad. Early the next morning, therefore, the Am'mon-ites were trapped between the men of Ja'besh and the armies of Is'ra-el.

In the furious battle which followed, the Am'mon-ites were badly beaten, many of them were slain, and those who escaped death were so confused that not even two of them could be found together.

Now that Saul's military courage and skill had been fully proved, the people of Is'ra-el shouted in honor of their new king. He was given a great public ovation, and his loyal subjects demanded that those who had spoken contemptuously of him should be brought forth and put to death. In reply to the demand for vengeance upon his enemies, Saul showed a fine spirit of self-control and forgiveness. He declared, "There shall not a man be put to death this day, for today the Lord hath set his people free from their enemies." In this victory over self and in his acknowledgment of the Lord's power, Saul showed his fitness to be a king more convincingly than he had in the defeat of the Am'mon-ites. The tragedy of his life, as we shall learn in future chapters, is that he did not live up to the nobility and piety of these early days of his reign.

At the invitation of Sam'u-el, the people gathered for a great religious celebration at Gil'gal in the Jor'dan valley. Burnt offerings were made to the Lord, and all the people joined in giving Saul a vote of confidence. Sam'u-el announced his resignation as civil ruler over the nation, but declared his intention to continue as their spiritual adviser.

In his farewell address as ruler, Sam'u-el recalled his faithfulness during the long years of his service, reminding the people that he had ruled justly, had wronged or defrauded no one, had never accepted a bribe, or oppressed the people in any way. There was a note of sorrow in his remarks, for it was hard to give way to another ruler, but he did not complain. To all his claims the people readily agreed. There was not a single blot on his entire life, and the people did not blame him for the weakness and sins of his two sons.

Sam'u-el also reviewed God's past favors upon the nation, and called attention to the truth that all their past misfortunes and periods of oppression by heathen nations had been sent by the Lord, because of their idolatry and sinful association with heathen people. With great devotion to the nation which he loved, he urged perfect loyalty to God. They were setting up a new form of government, and there would come many temptations to turn away from their unseen Ruler. He stressed the fact that both king and people must continue to recognize God as their chief Ruler, that the laws of God must remain supreme in the land, and that the conduct of both civil affairs and warfare must be carried forward under Divine guidance.

Solemn warnings were given by the prophet against the tendency to lean upon their own understanding and to depend upon their earthly king, instead of relying upon the wisdom and power of God. The people were assured that, even though they had acted in an unworthy and unbelieving manner in demanding a king, the Lord would give them continued security and progress for as long as they remained faithful to His commandments.

The address closed with a glorious climax as Sam'u-el said:

"Moreover, as for me, God forbid that I should sin against the Lord in ceasing to pray for you, but I will teach you the good and right way. Only fear the Lord, and serve Him in truth with all your heart; for consider how great things He hath done for you. But if you shall still do wickedly, you shall be consumed, both you and your king."

SUGGESTIONS FOR STUDY

Biblical Index to Helpful References

Israel's Previous Efforts to Avoid War With the Ammonites. (Deut. 2:19-23.)

Duty of Promptness in Obeying the Call of Duty. (Ps. 119:60; Gal. 1:15, 16.)

The Power of Unity in Fighting Enemies. (Jgs. 20:11; Neh. 4:16, 17.)

The Lord Draws His Enemies Into Snares. (1 Ki. 22:19-23; Mic. 4-12, 13.)

The Duty of Forbearance and Forgiveness. (Col. 3:18.)

Questions

1. Did Saul enter at once upon his duties as king?

2. Who were the Ammonites? The Gileadites?

3. What demands did Nahash of the Ammonites make of the Gileadites?

4. When news of these demands came to Saul, what did he do?

5. What was the result of the battle in which Saul led the Israelites?

6. Tell of the fine spirit showed by Saul after the battle.

7. Relate the main points in Samuel's resignation address.

8. In what work did Samuel continue after resigning as judge of Israel?

A PRINCE MORE NOBLE THAN
HIS FATHER

1 SAMUEL 13-14:1-46

When Sam'u-el first informed Saul that he was to become king of Is'ra-el, he stressed the fact that his first duty would be to rid the nation of the Phi-lis'tines. But instead of following up his brilliant victory over the Am'mon-ites with an immediate war against the ancient foes of Is'ra-el, he settled down quietly in his home at Gib'e-ah and began to surround himself with the royal courts and splendors enjoyed by heathen kings. In his public acceptance of the throne he had pledged his loyalty to the laws announced by Sam'u-el. These promises were soon forgotten, and he became a king in name only.

The Phi-lis'tines were much more advanced in the arts and crafts than the Is'ra-el-ites, and were well supplied with such implements of war as swords, spears, and iron chariots. They forbade the Is'ra-el-ites to have ironworkers, so their only weapons of war were axes and mattocks and similar farming tools. The Is'ra-el-ites were obliged to go to the ironworkers of the Phi-lis'tines to have their tools repaired and sharpened.

The condition of the nation seemed to be hopeless, and Saul was making no effort to break off the yoke of the Phi-lis'tines. The spirit of the Is'ra-el-ites became so broken that many of them entered into friendly relations with their oppressors.

It was in the midst of this sad state in Is'ra-el that the Lord moved the heart of one of Saul's sons to take the lead in war against the Phi-lis'-tines. Jon'a-than, a young man of great courage and piety, was placed at the head of an army of one thousand men stationed at Gib'e-ah. His father Saul headed another army of two thousand men which occupied the town of Mich'mash, about seven miles north of Je-ru'sa-lem. A strong Phi-lis'tine garrison occupied an elevated position between Gib'e-ah and Mich'mash.

While Saul and his two thousand men remained inactive and afraid to move against the Phi-lis'tines, Jon'a-than and his army made a sudden attack upon the garrison, overwhelmingly defeating the heavily armed enemy. This victory aroused the spirit of Saul, and he ordered all Is'ra-el to gather with him at Gil'gal in the Jor'dan valley. The confidence of the nation in Saul's ability as a leader had been so shaken by his years of idleness that only six hundred men responded.

Realizing that the Lord had deserted him because of his shameful inactivity over a number of years, and because of his religious backslidings, Saul asked Sam'u-el to come to Gil'gal that he might sacrifice unto the Lord in his behalf. Growing impatient and worried by the delay in Sam'u-el's arrival, Saul presumptuously made the burnt offering himself, thus incurring greater disfavor from God. When Sam'u-el finally came to Gil'gal he denounced Saul for his irreverent act, declared that because of such unworthiness the Lord would choose another to take his kingdom, and then left the king in a state of confusion.

Finding that hundreds of his men had deserted him, and that he had only six hundred warriors left, Saul joined Jon'a-than in the fortress which he had captured from the Phi-lis'tines. In the meantime the Phi-lis'tine army at Mich'mash had been divided into three bands which raided the valleys to the north, west, and east.

While Saul and his six hundred men were encamped on a high rock near Gib'e-ah, from which place the Phi-lis'tine garrison at Mich'mash might easily be observed, Jon'a-than suggested a daring exploit to his armor-bearer. The two of them went down into the valley between the outposts of the opposing armies, and approached the camps of the Phi-lis'tines at a point where there was a great cliff. Thinking that they were deserters from the army of Is'ra-el, the Phi-lis'tine sentries scornfully invited them to climb the rocks to their camp.

With daring faith in God, Jon'a-than said to his armor-bearer, "This is a sign that the Lord hath delivered them into our hand." Then they scaled the rocks, slew twenty of the sentries, and spread confusion through the entire camp of the enemy. Simultaneous with this bold adventure of Jon'a-than, the Lord sent a terrific earthquake into that vicinity, and all the Phi-lis'tine bands were dispersed in terror.

When the sentries of Saul observed the tumult among the armies of the Phi-lis'tines, they tried to discover who had left their camp. When it was found that Jon'a-than and his armor-bearer were absent, Saul ordered the priest in the camp to bring out the ephod and pray for victory. His army of six hundred men, strengthened by thousands who left their places of hiding and alliances with the Phi-lis'tines, pursued the scattered forces of the enemy. It was a great victory, and the Phi-lis'tines who escaped the slaughter were glad to return to their own land. Thus the power of the Phi-lis'tines over Is'ra-el was temporarily broken.

The two unhappy incidents which accompanied this great victory are to the discredit of Saul. Although he did not enter the field of battle until the enemy had already been routed by Jon'a-than, he assumed full credit for the triumph. There was no word of recognition for the bravery of his son, nor acknowledgment of the Divine power which had given the victory to Is'ra-el. Saul pretended to be very religious, but inwardly his heart was wrong with God. He took advantage of a natural mistake of his soldiers to excuse his own sin.

So eager was Saul to "avenge himself of his enemies" that he ordered his men to pursue the Phi-lis'tines when they were already in a weakened state, at the same time forbidding them under oath to take any food. When the day had passed, his soldiers were so hungry that they slew the animals taken from their enemies and ate them without properly draining the blood according to the law of Mo'ses. For this act Saul charged them with sin, and they were punished by being forced to bring offerings to the Lord from their own sheep and oxen.

Even Jon'a-than, who was responsible for the defeat of the Phi-lis'tines, did not know that Saul had charged his men to eat nothing during the

JONATHAN TASTES THE HONEY

day. In the woods where they pursued the Phi-lis'tines there was an abundance of wild honey, so Jon'a-than had relieved his hunger by eating of it. When told of his father's strict order, Jon'a-than said, "My father hath troubled the land, see how I am refreshed by the honey; and if the people had been permitted to eat freely of the spoils of the enemy, our victory would have been far greater."

In the meantime Saul had sought counsel of the Lord, but the ear of God was deaf to his prayers. Instead of looking into his own heart for the cause of the Lord's refusal to hear him, he sought to lay the blame upon someone else.

When he was told of the act of Jon'a-than, Saul declared that the failure of the Is'ra-el-ites to wipe out the Phi-lis'tines was the result of a violation of his solemn oath. He also declared his intention to have Jon'a-than slain.

The people rose up in violent rebellion against this blindness to the heroism of his son and deafness to the voice of reason. Saul's unjust sentence upon Jon'a-than: "Thou shalt surely die" was met by the united voice of the people, "There shall not one hair of his head fall to the ground." Up to this moment they had been faithful to the command of the king, but when he acted unwisely they felt justified in rescuing from his unholy decree the noble young man who had led them to victory.

The Lord permitted Saul to remain in office for a number of years, sparing him until he could find a successor worthy to occupy the throne of Is'ra-el.

SUGGESTIONS FOR STUDY

Biblical Index to Helpful References

The Law of God Against Oppression and Cruelty. (Ps. 62:10.)

Condemnation for Rulers Living in Ease While Subjects Suffer. (Amos 6:4.)

Despondency and Despair Caused by Afflictions. (Job 10:1; Ps. 31:10.)

The Sin of Presumption and Rashness. (Prov. 19:21; Isa. 45:9; Acts 19:36.)

The Duty of Courage in Life's Battles. (Deut. 31:6; Job 40:7.)

Fearlessness When Contending for the Right. (Ps. 3:6; Isa. 12:2.)

The Curse of Envy and Jealousy. (Ps. 73:3; Prov. 14:30.)

Questions

1. In what respect did Saul fail after the victory over the Ammonites?

2. What oppressors of Israel did he fail to destroy?

3. Describe the despair that prevailed throughout the land.

4. Who took the lead in fighting against the Philistines?

5. Describe the feat of Jonathan in defeating the Philistines at Michmash.

6. Tell of the battle that followed and give reasons for Israel's victory.

7. Was any credit due Saul for this victory? Did he claim the honor?

8. What cruel exactions did Saul make of his warriors?

9. Tell of Jonathan's violation of Saul's orders in eating some honey.

10. How was Saul's intention to kill Jonathan prevented?

SAUL'S DOWNFALL AND REJECTION BY THE LORD

1 SAMUEL 14:47-52;15 As a result of their victory over the Phi-lis'tines
the children of Is'ra-el were freed from the invasions of these enemies
for a number of years, and Saul seems to have taken a renewed interest
in the affairs of the nation. He enjoyed once again the confidence of
Is'ra-el, and the people rallied to his leadership in wars against various
nations on every side of the land.

Saul drove back the Mo'ab-ites who were threatening the security of
Is'ra-el from their lands southeast of the Dead Sea. The Am'mon-ites,
who were a constant menace to the tribes east of Jor'dan, were routed
again, and threatenings from the E'dom-ites south of Ju'dah and Sim'e-on
were also suppressed. To the north, between Da-mas'cus and the
Eu-phra'tes river, Saul was successful in a war with the strong, wealthy
kingdom known as Zo'bah. Several years were probably spent in inter-
mittent wars against these various heathen nations.

The prophet Sam'u-el, who seems to have avoided Saul after rebuking
him for his unworthy conduct in the battle with the Phi-lis'tines, now
appeared with a special message from God which called for an attack
upon the Am'a-lek-ites. They were a fierce, roving people who lived
south and southwest of Ca'naan in the A-ra'bi-an Peninsula, and were
descendants of Am'a-lek, a grandson of E'sau. The Lord's command that
they be destroyed goes back to their hostility toward Mo'ses in the wilderness. They had allied with the Ca'naan-ites at Ka'desh, with the Mo'ab-
ites in the capture of Jer'i-cho in the early days of the Judges, and with
the Mid'i-an-ites in the oppression of Is'ra-el prior to the days of Gid'e-on,
and were now bent upon robbery and murder once again.

God's command to Saul at this time was that he "utterly destroy" this
nation and all their live-stock. Nothing was to be spared or offered for
redemption. Such a course, cruel and barbarous as it may seem to us,
was justified because long years of persistent evil doing had removed all
possibility of salvation for the Am'a-lek-ites.

Saul organized an army of two hundred and ten thousand men, and proceeded at once into the land of the Am'a-lek-ites. Living among these wild people of A-ra'bi-a was a small tribe of the Mid'i-an nation known as Ken'ites. They had shown special kindness to the people of Is'ra-el on more than one occasion, and a covenant of friendship had been made with them. Saul ordered them to leave, so that they would not be included in the destruction of the Am'a-lek-ites.

Saul then attacked the Am'a-lek-ites and won an overwhelming victory. Their entire land was smitten from the southeast to the west and northwest. The people were slain, and the king, whose name was A'gag, was taken prisoner. But in the destruction of the live-stock the command of God was only partially obeyed. The best of the sheep and oxen and fatlings and lambs were spared, and were carried back to Ca'naan as spoils of war. Saul again showed a spirit of self-will and rashness. He placed his own wishes above the direct command of God, feeling, no doubt, that his way was better than that of God.

The Lord was greatly displeased with the conduct of Saul. He appeared again to Sam'u-el, telling him that He regretted the appointment of such a self-willed, disobedient man to the throne of Is'ra-el. Sam'u-el's anger

SAMUEL SLAYS AGAG

was kindled against Saul, and he was greatly disturbed by the Lord's threat to remove him from the throne. He spent the whole night in prayer, asking mercy for the wilful and disobedient king.

Next to Mo'ses, Sam'u-el was the greatest pleader for mercy in Is'ra-el, but his prayers in behalf of Saul could not offset the king's persistent disobedience to God's known commands. The Divine arm was not shortened, nor the Divine ear deaf, but even God could do no further mighty works for the unbelieving Saul. No prayer from the greatest saint could now remove the just punishment upon an unrepentant sinner.

Sam'u-el was therefore obliged to forego his earnest pleadings for Saul, and become the messenger of Divine judgment. The earnest intercessor must now be changed into the stern accuser. And so on the next morning he went to Saul with the decree of God.

When the king saw him drawing near, he said to him, "Blessed be thou of the Lord, I have performed the commandment of the Lord."

To this greeting the faithful prophet replied, "What meaneth then this bleating of the sheep, and the lowing of the oxen which I hear?"

Saul then tried to take refuge in evasions and falsehoods; he sought to blame the people for his own sin, and said that the best of the sheep and oxen had been taken for sacrifices unto the Lord. By every word that fell from his lips he revealed the complete breakdown of his moral character, forfeited his own self-respect, and foretold his own ruin. He had spared the life of A'gag merely for the glory of displaying a distinguished captive, and he even boasted of the capture when faced by Sam'u-el's charge of unfaithfulness to the command of God. Step by step he added a worse lie to the previous one until he wove about himself a web of self-condemnation from which it was impossible to escape.

Sam'u-el cut short the excuses of the king by reminding him of the humble station in life from which he had been raised to the highest place in the nation, and of the marked difference between the modesty and humility which he possessed at the time of his call and the proud, conceited spirit which he now displayed. In his final words of condemnation the prophet uttered this sublime, eternal truth:

"Behold, to obey is better than sacrifice, and to
hearken than the fat of rams."

Then he announced the solemn judgment of God in these words:

"Because thou hast rejected the word of the Lord,
He hath also rejected thee from being king."

Saul then confessed his sin, admitting that he had disobeyed the command of God. He used the words of true repentance, but lacked the spirit of it. He spoke as if in sorrow, but there was no genuine sorrow in his heart. He pleaded with Sam'u-el for forgiveness, but there could be no forgiveness for him.

When Sam'u-el turned to leave him, he became desperate at the thought of being disgraced before the people. He seized the prophet's robe in such frenzy that it was torn, pleading with him to remain for worship, lest he be put to shame at once. Sam'u-el agreed to stand beside him while he worshiped, thus retaining honor before the elders of Is'ra-el for the time being.

Sam'u-el then asked that A'gag, the captive king of the Am'a-lek-ites, be brought to him. With his own hand he executed the judgment of God against the wicked heathen king, stabbing him with a mortal blow. The story then concludes with these tragic words: "Sam'u-el came no more to see Saul."

SUGGESTIONS FOR STUDY

Biblical Index to Helpful References

The Command of God for the Extermination of Heathen Nations. (Num. 31:7.)

God's Judgment Against the Amalekites. (Ex. 17:14; Deut. 25:17-19.)

Victories in Battles Won by the Help of God. (2 Chr. 32:8; Psm. 24:8.)

Obedience to God Must Be Wholehearted. (Deut. 26:16; Josh. 11:15.)

The Curse Resulting From Avarice. (Prov. 15:27; Jer. 17:11; 1 Tim. 6:10.)

God's Curse on Deceit and Lying. (Nah. 3:1; Psm. 101:7.)

Forsaken by God Because of Sin. (Josh. 7:11-12; Isa. 59:2.)

Final Destruction of Those Who Forsake God. (Jer. 11:11; 1 Thess. 5:3.)

Prayers Unanswered Because of Iniquity in the Heart. (Psm. 66:18; Hos. 5:6.)

Questions

1. Following the successful war against the Philistines how did Saul rule?

2. Name the different heathen nations defeated by him during the following five or six years.

3. What particular nation did Samuel direct Saul to destroy?

4. Who were the Amalekites and how completely were they to be destroyed?

5. What was the outcome of Saul's invasion of the land of Moab?

6. What did Saul do in this victory which displeased the Lord?

7. Tell of Samuel's prayer for Saul, and why it could not be answered.

8. When Samuel reproached Saul for his grievous wrong how did he act?

9. Quote the sublime words of eternal truth uttered by Samuel in passing judgment against Saul.

10. Quote the final word of Divine judgment against Saul.

STORY 80

A SHEPHERD BOY CHOSEN KING

1 SAMUEL 16

Although the Lord had twice announced to Sam'u-el that Saul was rejected as king and that another should be chosen to occupy the throne of Is'ra-el, He had not told him how soon this was to take place, or whether Saul should be permitted to remain as head of the government until removed by death. Thus we find that Saul continued in office for a number of years, although the Lord had withdrawn His blessings from him after his rejection at Mich'mash.

In the meantime the Lord directed Sam'u-el in the private selection and anointing of the young man who was to take the place of Saul. He was

DAVID PRESENTED TO SAMUEL

a mere boy at the time, and years of preparation and training were needed before he would be capable of ruling over Is'ra-el. But the Lord wished Sam'u-el to know His choice for two reasons. First, that he might act as a prophet of God in preparing the Divinely chosen king for his work; secondly, that he might act as the religious leader of Is'ra-el in making the nation ready for the enthronement when the time had come.

One day when Sam'u-el was still discouraged because of God's judgments against Saul, and much worried over the future welfare of Is'ra-el, the Lord came to him with a rebuke for his persistent mourning over Saul. He directed the prophet to prepare a horn of holy oil and to go at once to the home of Jes'se in Beth'le-hem to anoint one of his sons, saying, "For I have provided me a king among his sons."

Sam'u-el, who seldom showed any reluctance or fear in doing the bidding of the Lord, was now in grave fear for his personal safety in performing such a duty. Saul was often subject to moody spells and fits of sudden anger, so the worst might be dreaded when he discovered that Sam'u-el had appointed another king. The Lord then told Sam'u-el to provide a calf for an offering in Beth'le-hem, and to tell anyone who might be interested that he was going to this town to make a sacrifice. Such concealment was necessary for the protection of both Sam'u-el and the young king.

You will remember that since Sam'u-el's retirement as the civil ruler of Is'ra-el he had continued his service as a spiritual adviser, and that he made frequent trips through the land to reprove and punish wrong doing, to offer sacrifices, and to stimulate the people in their religious life. A visit to Beth'le-hem, therefore, would not be regarded with suspicion by anyone. He, therefore proceeded at once on his journey, walking over the mountain roads from Ra'mah to Beth'le-hem, a distance of about ten miles.

When the officers of the little hill town saw the prophet coming, they anxiously inquired why he had come. He told them that his purpose was to sacrifice unto the Lord, and issued a call for all the people to make the preparations required by law for such services, making sure that Jes'se and his sons were properly set apart to the Lord.

There were eight sons in the family of Jes'se, and seven of them were present at the gathering. After the sacrifice had been offered, Sam'u-el inspected these seven young men, one after another. As he stood before the eldest, whose name was E-li'ab, and who was tall and handsome, he felt sure that this was the man whom the Lord would choose to be king. But then the Lord spoke these words to the heart of the prophet:

"Look not on his countenance, or on the height of his stature; because I have refused him: For the Lord seeth not as man seeth; for man looketh on the outward appearance, but the Lord looketh on the heart."

The Lord wished Sam'u-el to understand that outward beauty is not a guarantee of inward worth; that a pleasing appearance and imposing height do not make a man a good king. Saul had all of these advantages, but had failed miserably because his heart was not right. The new king must be chosen for his purity of spirit and righteousness of heart.

Jes'se then caused the other six sons who were present to pass before the prophet, and each time the Lord said to Sam'u-el, "He is not the man." Turning to Jes'se, the prophet asked, "Are these all the children you have?"—"There remaineth yet the youngest," said Jes'se, "and he is in the field watching over the sheep." Sam'u-el asked that he be brought before him at once, and the moment he saw him the Lord said, "Arise and anoint him, for he is my choice for the throne of Is'ra-el." He was a boy of about fifteen years, with a fine, rosy complexion, sparkling eyes, and an appearance that was good to behold.

Thus David, the youngest son of Jes'se was solemnly anointed by the aging prophet of God while his father and brothers looked on in wonder. The boy was too young and inexperienced to assume the heavy burdens of ruling Is'ra-el, so perhaps he was not told at this time of the full meaning of the ceremony performed by the man of God. He did, however, enter a new stage in the development of his inner life, which was fully consecrated to God. The gifts with which he was richly endowed by nature began to unfold. As he continued tending his father's flocks the goodness and glory of God was made known to him on every hand. In the mild, starry nights he learned how "The heavens declare the glory of God; and the firmament showeth his handiwork." The holy teachings of the books of Mo'ses, in which he had been instructed from his earliest years, became more clear to him as he read them over and over again.

It was during these formative years that he received the inspiration for many of the beautiful psalms which were afterwards put into permanent form for use in the worship of Is'ra-el. His poetic and musical gifts were cultivated as the days and weeks went by, and his kingly qualities were rapidly developed. Whether he knew that he was destined to become ruler of his nation or not, he lived in constant remembrance that the anointing by Sam'u-el had consecrated him to a life of service to God and his people. The faithful discharge of his duties as a shepherd of sheep prepared him to become the righteous and successful shepherd of Is'ra-el. The sense of duty and responsibility daily displayed in protecting his flock from bears and lions strengthened him for the eminent ruler he afterwards became. The Lord was making him ready for a great career.

Neither Saul nor the people of Is'ra-el were informed of the selection of young David to succeed to the throne of Is'ra-el, nor do his father and brothers seem to have known the secret of the prophet. Apparently several years passed before Saul suspected God's plan for the noble young man, and through these years Divine Providence brought David the training and discipline required for a great career on the throne of Is'ra-el.

While the Spirit of God was guiding David, an entirely different thing was taking place with Saul. The Holy Spirit having left him because of his sins, he was tormented by an evil spirit which led him into fits of melancholy and extreme irritation. Unrestrained by the good Spirit, he was goaded by Sa'tan into ungovernable madness and rage. His servants were so distressed by the change that they sought some way of quieting his temper. Even in those early days music was looked upon as a means of soothing a troubled spirit and subduing anger, so the servants suggested that a musician of great skill be engaged to play the harp for

Saul. The unhappy king consented, and search was made at once for a gifted harpist.

One of the king's servants knew of David's talent as a musician, of his handsome appearance, gentle disposition, and courageous spirit. He therefore suggested that the young man be engaged as musician to the king, and Saul sent a messenger to Jes'se with the request that David be sent to him at once.

By a strange providence the young man who had been chosen of God to be Saul's successor was brought to the court at the king's own request. As he modestly stood before the king with his harp in hand and began to play, the magic touch of his fingers on the strings produced an effect which immediately soothed the troubled spirit of Saul. As the sweet sounds

DAVID TAKES PRESENTS TO SAUL

of music fell upon Saul's ears, and the unspoken prayers of David's heart reached the ears of God, the king's heart went out to this young nobleman with great affection. Thus was the plan of God and the liberty of man combined for the preparation of Da'vid to become Is'ra-el's greatest king: for Da'vid in his devotion to his harp had no thought of thereby rising to royal favor; and the servant who suggested his name knew not that he had been chosen as Saul's successor.

David was engaged as court musician and personal armor-bearer for the king, and for a time they were fast friends. We do not know just how long the friendship lasted, but shall find that within a few years Saul became intensely jealous of David's growing popularity and turned against him with murderous hatred.

David continued to live at his father's home in Beth'le-hem, and much of his time was spent in caring for his father's sheep. Under the anointing power of God's spirit he continued to grow in strength and bravery. In protecting the sheep from the ravenous beasts of that land he relied upon the ancient weapon known as a sling. By constant practice he soon became expert with the sling, and was able to hurl the small stones exactly where he wished them to go. His strength was also developed until he was able to perform some of the mighty deeds of Sam'son, such as killing bears and lions with his own hands. God was preparing him for a miraculous victory over the Phi-lis'tines, and we shall soon learn about it.

SUGGESTIONS FOR STUDY

Biblical Index to Helpful References

Jesse a Descendant of Ruth and Boaz. (Ruth 4:18-22.)

The Course of Wisdom Sometimes Requires Concealment. (Prov. 11:13; 12:23.)

The Lord Secretly Guides His Faithful Servants. (Acts 9:6.)

God Looketh on the Heart. (1 Ki. 8:39; Luke 16:15.)

The Lord Chooses the Way of His Servants. (Acts 22:14, 15.)

The Laws of Spiritual Growth. (Rom. 14:19; 1 Cor. 14:12.)

Music to Be Used in Praising God. (Psm. 33:2; 81:2; 92:3.)

Questions

1. Did Saul continue to act as king for long after his rejection by the Lord?

2. In what state of mind was Samuel during this time?

3. To what family was he directed to choose a king?

4. How many sons did Jesse have?

5. Relate how each of the first six were not chosen and why.

6. Tell of David's choice. Describe his age and appearance.

7. What was David's employment? How did he spend much of his time?

8. Tell of Saul's moody and mean spells.

9. Tell of David's employment as Court Musician.

A SHEPHERD BOY SLAYS THE PHILISTINE GIANT

1 SAMUEL 17

Some time after David was employed by Saul for occasional service at the court as musician and armor-bearer, and several years after the defeat of the Phi-lis'tines at Mich'mash, the warlike heathens decided upon another war against Is'ra-el. Their armies marched into a village of the hill country between the mountains of Ju'dah and the plains of the Med'i-ter-ra'ne-an, about eleven miles southwest of Je-ru'sa-lem and Beth'le-hem. Here they encamped for battle along a range of low hills facing a fertile plain called E'lah. The armies of Is'ra-el went out against them, camping on the range of hills along the opposite side of the valley.

In those days it often happened that when two opposing armies were in position for battle, but neither dared to attack, a champion from each side would meet in single combat. It was agreed that victory would belong to the army whose champion defeated his rival in the single combat.

The champion of the Phi-lis'tines in this battle was a giant warrior named Go-li'ath. He was nearly nine feet tall, wore armor made of metal plates which overlapped like the scales of a fish and weighed three hundred pounds, protected his head with a helmet of brass, and had the lower part of his legs covered with heavy metal guards. He carried a short spear thrown over his shoulders, and a sword five feet long which weighed twenty-five pounds.

Every day he marched out on the plain between the two armies and scornfully challenged the Is'ra-el-ites to send out a champion to fight a duel with him. For forty days he cast ridicule and contempt upon the armies of Is'ra-el as Saul's slaves, and taunted them for their cowardice in failing to send out a man to meet him in battle.

During all this time the king who had once led Is'ra-el in slaying forty thousand Phi-lis'tines in one day sat cowering in weakness while a single Phi-lis'tine braggart held the armies of Is'ra-el in check. Why the difference? Because in the previous victory the noble prince Jon'a-than had been anointed by the Spirit of God, and Saul had taken advantage of the confusion caused by his daring exploit to gain a decisive triumph. At this time, however, Jon'a-than had been rejected by his ungrateful father, and the Lord had withdrawn from Saul. Courage had left the army because the Lord was no longer with their king.

Three of Jes'se's sons were among the soldiers encamped on the edge of the valley of E'lah and Da'vid often journeyed back and forth from the royal palace and his father's home, caring for the sheep when his services were not needed by the king. It is likely that he wished to join his brothers in the army opposing the Phi-lis'tines, and that he often spoke of his desire to aid in ridding the land of the cruel oppressors, but neither the king nor Da'vid's older brothers thought him old enough to be a soldier.

One day Jes'se sent Da'vid to the camp of the soldiers, just a few hours' walk from Beth'le-hem, to carry food to his brothers and to ask about their welfare. It so happened that he reached the camp just as the two armies were facing one another ready for battle. He left the provisions which he had brought with the keeper of the army supplies and rushed to the side of his brothers. While he was talking with them, the Phi-lis'tine champion came out on the field with his usual scornful challenge. The soldiers all fell back in fear, but Da'vid looked on with growing anger. Some of the men told him that this had been going on morning after morning for forty days, and that the king had offered a great reward for any man who would slay the giant.

Da'vid then declared that he was ashamed of the cowardly manner in which the Is'ra-el-ites permitted the heathen giant to

THE DEFIANCE OF GOLIATH

terrify them, and said that the insult to Is'ra-el and the living God of the nation must be wiped out. The remarks of his younger brother were bitterly resented by E-li'ab who said that Da'vid was neglecting his duties in caring for his father's sheep, and that he had no business even to visit the king's armies. It appears that E-li'ab remembered with envy the time when Sam'u-el had rejected him in favor of Da'vid for the sacred anointing. Da'vid showed both forbearance and reason in his reply, "Have I come without an errand? Is there not a need for someone to meet this defiance of our God?" Then he turned to others and made similar remarks.

The soldiers were delighted with Da'vid's bravery in proposing to meet the Phi-lis'tine giant, and hastened to report his courageous offer to Saul, who demanded that the young man be sent to him at once. When Da'vid stood before the king, his first words were, "Let no man's heart fail because of him; thy servant will go and fight with this Phi-lis'tine." The king tried to dissuade him from meeting the giant in single combat by telling him that he was too young and inexperienced to go against one who had been trained in war for so many years. But Da'vid persisted in his demand, telling Saul of the mighty deeds he had already performed with the help of God. The young man closed his appeal with these words: "The Lord that delivered me out of the paw of the lion, and out of the paw of the bear, he will deliver me out of the hand of this Phi-lis'tine."

The confidence of this young hero, joined as it was with his unfaltering faith in the help of God, overcame the hesitancy of Saul. He agreed to Da'vid's request to champion the cause of Is'ra-el before the giant Go-li'ath, but was unwilling to let him enter what seemed to be an unequal combat without the benefit of the best armor and weapons which could be had.

Saul then brought out his own armor and sword, and asked Da'vid to use them in the battle soon to come. Da'vid felt however, that he would do better with weapons with which he was more familiar. After putting on the king's armor and taking his sword in hand, he decided that the sling which he had learned to use with such telling force would serve him better. The man-made armor of an unbelieving and rejected king was only an encumbrance to a youth whose faith was approved of God. By using the sling he would not have to come into close grips with a man who was much larger and more powerful than he. As an expert with the sling, he could take sure aim and hurl a stone with the strength

DAVID WITH SAUL'S ARMOR

of God lending force to his arm.

On his way to the field of battle, Da'vid picked up five smooth stones from the brook which ran through the valley between the two armies. Placing these stones in the shepherd's bag which he carried, and with his staff and sling in hand, Da'vid marched out between the armies of Phi-lis'ti-a and Is'ra-el to meet the giant warrior. The Is'ra-el-ites looked on with mingled feelings of amazement, hope, and prayer, while the hosts of the Phi-lis'tines gazed at the young man with scorn and ridicule.

Go-li'ath felt insulted when he and his armor-bearer stood before the young shepherd of Is'ra-el. Here was a mere boy, armed only with a staff and sling, going out to meet the greatest warrior of the Phi-lis'tine nation as though he were about to kill a dog with a club. Go-li'ath then announced that he would feed the flesh of his opponent to the birds of the air and to the beasts of the field.

The taunts of Go-li'ath were quietly answered by Da'vid with confidence in God's help, and with an assurance of victory which could have been given to him only by the Lord. He boldly met the defiance and scorn of the giant with these inspired words:

"Thou comest to me with a sword, and with a spear, and with a shield; but I come to thee in the name of the Lord of hosts, the God of the armies of Is'ra-el, whom thou hast defied. This day will the Lord deliver thee into mine hand; and I will smite thee, and take thine head from thee; and I will give the carcasses of the hosts of the Phi-lis'tines this day unto the fowls of the air, and to the wild beasts of the earth; that all the earth may know that there is a God in Is'ra-el. And all this assembly shall know that the Lord saveth not with the sword and spear, for the battle is the Lord's, and he will give you into our hands."

Da'vid then took one of the smooth stones from his shepherd's bag, placed it in his sling, and hurled it with deadly aim at the forehead of the giant. The stone pierced the skull of the giant, and Go-li'ath fell to the ground. Da'vid then rushed up to the fallen giant, drew Go-li'ath's sword, cut off the head of his enemy, and carried it back to the camps of Is'ra-el as a trophy of his victory.

This super-human feat of Da'vid was accomplished by his grasp upon the unseen forces of God. He fully believed that God who had delivered him out of the paw of the lion, and out of the paw of the bear, would also deliver him out of the hand of the giant Phi-lis'tine. His previous life had been a life of faith unseen, and hence he was ready for any emergency. It was to the living God that he turned for his pivotal victory.

The death of their champion struck terror into the heart of the Phi-lis'tine armies, and they fled toward their own land, different groups taking three separate routes in their efforts to escape death at the hands of the pursuing Is'ra-el-ites. The armies of Is'ra-el slew thousands of the fleeing Phi-lis'tines, pursuing the remnants of the defeated army even to the gates of their cities of Ek'ron and Gath. Da'vid meanwhile took the head of Go-li'ath to Je-ru'sa-lem, and later delivered it to Saul in person.

SUGGESTIONS FOR STUDY

Biblical Index to Helpful References

Unbelief Produces Cowardice. (Num. 13:31; Josh. 14:8.)

Scorn and Contempt for the Righteous. (Neh. 2:19; Ps. 80:6; Matt. 13:55, 56.)

David's Errand Similar to That of Joseph. (Gen. 37:12-14.)

Deadly Aim of Expert with the Sling. (Jgs. 20:16; 1 Chr. 12:2.)

Strength in the God of Hosts. (Ps. 124:8; 125:1.)

Reason for David's Reliance on God. (Ps. 18:16-21; 63:7.)

Foes Within One's Own House (Ps. 41:9; 55:12-14; John 12:25.)

Inadequacy of Earthly Weapons Alone. (Ps. 44:6; Hos. 1:7; Ps. 33:13.)

God's Use of Humble Instrumentalities. (1 Cor. 1:27-29.)

Questions

1. Where did the Philistines again attack Israel?

2. What method was proposed by the Philistines for determining the victor?

3. Describe the champion of the Philistine armies.

4. What effect did his presence have on Saul's army?

5. How was David employed at this time?

6. On what errand was he sent to Israel's armies?

7. What did he propose to do in regard to the Philistine champion?

8. How did Saul receive David's proposal?

9. What weapons did David use?

10. Describe the weapons of the Philistine giant.

11. What did David's brother Eliab say about David's proposal?

12. Tell what happened in the duel between David and Goliath.

13. What did David do with Goliath's head?

SAUL'S INCREASING JEALOUSY; JONATHAN'S LOVE FOR DAVID

1 SAM. 18-19

After the heroic feat of Da'vid in slaying Go-li'ath in single combat, Saul showed the same ungrateful, selfish spirit which had possessed him after the victory of his eldest son Jon'a-than at Mich'mash. He pretended not to know who Da'vid was, and tried to deprive him of the honor in which he was held by the people. The love which Saul had once felt toward his young musician was now turned into envy, for the king could not bear to hear anyone praised but himself.

Da'vid came back from his great victory carrying the head of Go-li'ath, which he presented to the king. Under the circumstances, Saul was forced to acknowledge Da'vid's bravery by suitable honors and rewards, so he received him into his own house and made him an officer in the army.

A few days passed before the armies returned from pursuing the Phi-lis'tines, and the usual celebrations of victory took place. When the soldiers returned, Da'vid took his place among them in the triumphal march, for his victory over Go-li'ath had done more than anything else to end the war.

Even though Saul had already publicly honored the heroism of Da'vid and had appointed him as an officer in his army, he could not overcome his envy; to hear the people sing the praises of one who had put his own glory to shame deeply aroused the king's anger. Da'vid's loyalty to the army won him the good-will of the other officers and soldiers, while his courage in warfare made him more popular than ever with the Is'ra-el-ites. Much as he hated to do it, Saul was obliged to show Da'vid the same courtesy and favor which the other officers enjoyed, and to send him out in battle whenever the peace of Is'ra-el was threatened by further uprisings of the Phi-lis'tines.

These circumstances brought great unhappiness to Saul, and he fell once again into fits of melancholy and fierce unrest. He was constantly haunted by Sam'u-el's report that the Lord had chosen another to take his place upon the throne. The black moods which had been the occa-

sion for bringing the shepherd
boy to him some years before
now became worse than ever.
So Da'vid was invited once
more to play the harp for him
with the hope that these trying
spells might be driven away.
This time, however, the sweet
music of Da'vid no longer
soothed the troubled spirit of
the king. Saul's heart was
filled with murderous jealousy, for he began to suspect
that the young hero was the
Lord's choice for the throne of

DAVID AT PRAYER

Is'ra-el. Twice he tried to kill Da'vid by throwing a javelin at him, but
each time the young man was able to dodge the deadly weapon.

Convinced that the Lord was with Da'vid, and that he himself was rejected of God, Saul decided to place him in command of a thousand men
in some outpost where he would not see him. But even this plan
did not overcome his determination to do away with Da'vid. He began
to seek some means of having him killed by some of the officers, or by
the Phi-lis'tines in battle.

Saul pretended to have great admiration for Da'vid because of his
bravery and prudent behavior, and offered to give him his eldest daughter
in marriage. Of course, he did not really wish to have Da'vid become his
son-in-law, but the offer was made in the hope of encouraging him to
attempt such dangerous exploits in war that he would eventually be killed.
Saul had no intention of keeping his promise, and when the time came
for Da'vid to marry Me'rab, the princess who had been promised him
in marriage, it was found that she had been given to another officer in
the army.

In the meantime Saul's younger daughter Mi'chal had fallen in love
with the noble young officer, and the king proposed once more to make
Da'vid his son-in-law. He was no more sincere this time than before,
and his failure to keep the promise concerning Me'rab seems to have
led Da'vid to pay little attention to the second proposal.

Saul was so determined to entrap Da'vid in some scheme which would cost him his life that he sent his courtiers to the brave officer with a new proposal. They told Da'vid that he would be given the hand of Mi'chal in marriage when he had slain one hundred Phi'lis'tines. He accepted this challenge to his bravery, went out against the Phi-lis'tines, and slew twice the number required by the crafty king.

The king then had no other choice than to permit the marriage of Da'vid and Mi'chal, which took place at once. The Phi-lis'tines thought that Da'vid would follow the He'brew custom which exempted newly married men from military service for one year, so they planned a series of attacks upon Is'ra-el in revenge for the losses which they had suffered at the hands of this great warrior.

Instead of taking advantage of this privilege, Da'vid remained on active service in the army and proved himself more valiant than ever; so successful was he in these new combats that Saul's jealousy and determination to have him killed became more fierce with every passing day. As Da'vid continued to grow in favor with the people, Saul's hatred for him broke out in desperate attacks upon his life.

The one earthly source of cheer and hope for Da'vid during these trials was his friendship with Jon'a-than, Saul's eldest son. They were drawn together by kindred qualities of nobility, heroism, and love to the Lord. Just as the shepherd lad had proved his courageous faith by meeting the giant in single combat, so the young prince of Is'ra-el had shown the same boldness when he scaled the rock and entered the garrison of the Phi-lis'tines. They were both possessed with great concern for the welfare of Is'ra-el and by the spirit of humility which always accompanies true greatness.

It is not strange, therefore, that when the young shepherd stood before Saul and proved his holy motives both by humble conduct and noble words, Jon'a-than's heart went out to him with an affection stronger than life or death. "He loved him as he loved his own soul," and there began on that day a friendship which has long been famed in history. The hearts of the two young men were bound together in a spiritual union which has seldom been equalled.

Jon'a-than then displayed the highest mark of honor which a prince can bestow upon a subject. He gave to Da'vid his own royal robes and official weapons for war, and announced his willingness to give up his own advantages as the son of the king for the good of his friend. A perpetual covenant of friendship between the two young men was made

Moses Striking the Rock *by Adam van Noort*
MUSEUM OF DUESSELDORF : GERMANY

Boaz and Ruth *by Gerbrand van den Eeckhout*
BOYMANS MUSEUM : ROTTERDAM

Samuel Anointing David
by *Jan Victors*
BRUNSWICK MUSEUM : GERMANY

David's Triumph
by *Matteo Rosselli*
PITTI PALACE : FLORENCE

Daniel in the Lion's Den
by Alfred Rethel
STAEDTISCHES KUNST INSTITUT : FRANKFURT

Elijah Goes to Heaven by *Eduard Jakob von Steinle*
ARCHBISHOP'S GALLERY : ZAGREB

that day, and it withstood the strains of the civil war and revolution in which Da'vid became an outlaw and a fugitive.

Not many days passed before Jon'a-than had an opportunity to prove his friendship. Saul announced to his officers that he intended to kill Da'vid at once, and Jon'a-than came forward to plead for the condemned officer. He then secretly warned Da'vid of his great danger, advising him to go into hiding until he could intercede with his father.

Jon'a-than then boldly, but with proper respect for his father defended his young friend. In gentle tones he reminded Saul of Da'vid's willingness to give his life for the welfare of the nation when he slew Go-li'ath, or when he attacked the Phi-lis'tines, and of his unquestioned loyalty to the king in all his services. The king's anger was quieted for the time, and he gave his word that Da'vid should not be slain. The young captain was welcomed once more at the king's house, and was encouraged to resume his service in the army. This he did, and slew large numbers of the Phi-lis'tines in battle.

Before long, however, Saul was troubled again by fits of depression and unrest, so Da'vid tried to soothe him by playing the harp. Once again the king's sudden anger led him to hurl a javelin at the one who sought to help him, but again Da'vid was unharmed. Men were sent to guard the home of Da'vid so that he could not escape, and Saul declared that he should be slain the next morning.

Mi'chal's quick thinking saved the life of her husband on this occasion. After helping him escape through a window, she placed an idol in Da'vid's bed and told the messengers of Saul that he was too ill to be disturbed. Her trick succeeded, but the next day Saul ordered that Da'vid be brought to him in his bed, so that he might slay him at once. Saul then rebuked his daughter severely for deceiving him, and she defended herself by saying that Da'vid had threatened to kill her if she did not help him. This was not true, but it made many people believe that she was secretly in league with her father in the effort to take the life of Da'vid.

After making his escape, Da'vid went directly to the home of the prophet Sam'u-el in Ra'mah and told him of Saul's repeated efforts to kill him. It must have brought great relief and peace of mind to Da'vid to enjoy once again the friendly help and advice of the religious leader of the nation. They talked together for a long time, and then went to a place called Na'ioth, where a group of young prophets were engaged in worship. How long Da'vid remained here we are not told, but it was probably for a considerable time. It is thought by some that it was during this restful period in company with the prophets that he wrote the part of the 119th Psalm which so beautifully describes the security of those who trust in the law of the Lord. Here are some of the gems from that Psalm which may well describe Da'vid's feelings at the time:

> "Princes did also sit and speak against me;
> But thy servant did meditate in thy statues.
> The proud have had me in derision,
> Yet have I not declined from thy law.
> Trouble and anguish have taken hold on me;
> Yet thy commandments are my delights.
> Oh how I love thy law!
> It is my meditation all the day.
> The law of thy mouth is better unto me
> Than thousands of gold and silver.
> I know, O Lord, that thy judgments are right,
> And thou in faithfulness hast afflicted me.
> It is good for me that I have been afflicted;
> That I might learn thy statutes."

SUGGESTIONS FOR STUDY

Biblical Index to Helpful References

Examples of Dissimulation and Its Sin. (2 Sam. 14:2; Luke 20:20; Acts 23:15.)

Celebrating Victory in Song, Music, Dancing. (Ex. 15:1-21; Jgs. 5:1.)

The Sin of Jealousy and Envy. (Gen. 37:4; Jgs. 8:1; Luke 15:28.)

Examples of Treachery. (Jgs. 16:19-21; 1 Ki. 21:8; Matt. 26:49.)

Cowardice Resulting from an Evil Conscience. (Isa. 66:4.)

Examples of True Friendship. (2 Ki. 2:2; John 13:1; Rom. 16:4.)

The Constancy of True Friendship. (Ruth. 1:16; Prov. 17:17.)

Friends Not to Be Forsaken. (Prov. 27: 10.)

Questions

1. How did Saul show his littleness after David's victory over Goliath?

2. How did he act toward Saul's insult?

3. What did the women say in the victory march?

4. What effect did this have on Saul?

5. In what way did Saul try to kill David himself?

6. What proposal did Saul make with the hope of having David slain?

7. What offer did Saul make to David in the proposed marriage of his younger daughter to him?

8. How many Philistines did David kill to meet this offer?

9. Why were Saul's son Jonathan and David drawn together so closely?

10. Describe the friendship between them.

11. How did David escape Saul's plan to have his officers kill him?

12. Where did he then go?

STORY 83

JONATHAN'S ARROW WARNS DAVID OF SAUL'S ANGER •

1 SAMUEL 20

While Da'vid was at Na'ioth, Saul made two unsuccessful attempts to have him captured. He sent messengers to arrest him and bring him back to the king's court, but on each occasion the messengers were so carried away by the religious zeal of the prophets that they took part in the worship, and finally returned without Da'vid. Saul then decided to go after Da'vid himself, but as he came near Sam'u-el's house he was suddenly filled with a strange religious excitement; all day and all night he was in the power of the Spirit of God, calling upon His name as if he were a prophet. While the king was in this exalted state Da'vid went to his friend Jon'a-than for advice. Saul's anger seems to have been subdued by his strange experience at Na'ioth, for he went quietly home after yielding to Sam'u-el's urgings that he give up his unjustified hatred for Da'vid.

It appears that by this time there was an understanding between Jon'-a-than and Da'vid that no member of Saul's family should be permitted to succeed him as king, and that Da'vid was destined to become the ruler of Is'ra-el. In the heart of Jon'a-than, however, there was no resentment to the will of God nor ill-feeling toward Da'vid.

In the meeting between Jon'a-than and Da'vid at this time their covenant of perpetual friendship was renewed, and Da'vid promised that in the event of Jon'a-than's death he would always show kindness to the family and descendants of his friend.

On the day after this meeting there began at the king's house a festival in honor of the new moon. This festival lasted for two days, and it was customary for all members of the king's family to attend. Da'vid and Jon'a-than knew that it would be dangerous for the young captain to appear at Saul's table for the festival, but they also felt that his absence might be taken as an insult to Saul. It was important that Da'vid find out Saul's intentions toward him before renewing his visits to his home.

The plan adopted by the two bosom friends at this time was most unusual. Since there was a religious festival going on at Beth'le-hem at the same time, it was decided that Da'vid should stay away from the gathering at Saul's house, and that Jon'a-than should explain the absence by saying that he wished to be with his family during the services at Beth'le-hem. It was felt by both of these young men that the manner in which Saul accepted the absence of Da'vid from the feast in his home would indicate his future intentions.

Jon'a-than and Da'vid arranged a clever plan by which the latter could be secretly informed of Saul's feelings toward him. On the day following the close of the festival Da'vid was to hide behind some cliffs in the shallow valley between Gib'e-ah and Nob, while Jon'a-than was to take his bow and shoot three arrows in the direction of Da'vid's hiding place. If the arrows were shot beyond the hiding place, it would be a sign of danger; if they fell short, it meant that Saul intended no harm toward Da'vid. A boy was to be brought along to pick up the arrows, and Da'vid was to learn the message from his friend through the directions given to the boy.

On the first day of the feast Da'vid's place was vacant, but Saul made no inquiry. On the second day the king noticed the absence of Da'vid

DAVID IN THE WILDERNESS OF ZIPH

and asked Jon'a-than why he had not been there on either day of the festival. Jon'a-than mentioned Da'vid's wish to attend the service at Beth'le-hem, and told his father that he had given him permission to go. Saul was so vexed with his son for taking the part of Da'vid that he hurled a spear at him. He accused the young prince of forming the strongest ties of friendship with a rival to the throne, and tried to turn him against Da'vid by appealing to his own ambition and self-advantage. Saul then declared with vehement anger, "As for Da'vid, he shall surely die"; and ordered his men to see to it that the young officer was brought to him at once.

On the following day Jon'a-than went to the place agreed upon with Da'vid and shot the arrows beyond the place of hiding, shouting to the boy he had brought with him, "The arrow is beyond thee!" Then he sent the boy away and went into the field to meet Da'vid. The two devoted friends embraced and kissed each other over and over again, weeping bitterly as they faced a separation which might be long. Da'vid, who seems to have been the more deeply affected of the two, clung to Jon'a-than a long time before he could bear to let him go; then he said, "Go in peace, the Lord shall be between me and thee, and between my children and they children forever."

From this time to the end of Saul's reign, Da'vid led the life of a roaming exile and hunted outlaw. He wandered over the country, spending most of his time in the wilderness south of Je-ru'sa-lem, constantly pursued by the soldiers of the angry king.

SUGGESTIONS FOR STUDY

Biblical Index to Helpful References

Feast of New Moon. (Num. 10:10; 28: 11.)

Covenants Between Friends. (Gen. 21:27; 2 Sam. 5:3; 1 Ki. 5:12; Jer. 34:8.)

Bow and Arrows in Symbolic Use. (2 Ki. 13:15-19.)

(See Biblical Index on preceding chapter.)

Questions

1. Why were Saul's officers unable to take David at Naioth?

2. What happened to Saul when he went for him himself?

3. Describe the bond of friendship between David and Jonathan.

4. Why did David decline attendance at the monthly feast in Saul's house?

5. How did his absence effect Saul?

6. Explain the plan agreed upon between Jonathan and David by which David was advised about Saul's anger.

7. Describe the parting of Jonathan and David.

8. What did David now become?

STORY 84

DAVID PURSUED BY SAUL

1 SAMUEL 21-23   When Da'vid said farewell to Jon'a-than and
went away in exile, never to return to the house of the king, he must have
known that Saul had been rejected by the Lord, and that he was destined
to occupy the throne of Is'ra-el. Instead of leading a revolution, however,
he merely sought to protect his own life. He went away, not as a rebel,
but as a loyal subject of the king whose unjust hatred and murderous
envy had forced him to flee.

During the trying times which followed he may have done some
things which seem far beneath the nobility of character and uprightness
of conduct which had marked his career up to this time, but never was
he guilty of the slightest act of treason or disloyalty to the king. Even
while he was being sought by Saul under the false charge of outlawry,
he led his followers in war against Is'ra-el's enemies, and on more than
one occasion saved his nation from attacks by invading heathens. Twice
he spared the life of Saul when the king was completely in his power.

Soon after leaving Jon'a-than, Da'vid visited a place called Nob, which
was not far from Je-ru'sa-lem on the road to the north. A priest named
A-him'e-lech was in charge of the place of worship in this little town,
and his son A-bi'a-thar acted as an assistant. Da'vid was very hungry,
but did not think it safe to ask the townspeople for food; knowing that
the priest would not betray him to Saul, he asked for bread. The priest
replied that the only food he had was the shewbread which was being
removed from the sacred table, the time having come when it must be
replaced with fresh bread. It was unlawful for anyone except the priests
to eat this bread. However, A-bi'a-thar was so touched by Da'vid's urgent
need that he gave him the shewbread, and the conduct of both Da'vid
and the priest was approved hundreds of years later by the Sav'ior.

Da'vid thought it best not to tell A-him'e-lech that he was fleeing from
Saul because the king sought his life, but did say that he had left the
king's house in such haste that he had failed to provide himself with
a sword. He probably knew that the weapon which he had taken from
Go-li'ath after their memorable combat had been placed in the shrine
at Nob for safekeeping, and for this reason asked the priest for a sword.

The priest told him that this was the only sword at hand, and gladly gave it to him.

The visit of Da'vid to Nob was followed by a sad event in which Saul was guilty of a terrible crime. An E'dom-ite named Do'eg, a chief herdsman of Saul, happened to be present when Da'vid was given the shewbread to eat. He reported the incident to Saul, and the angry king summoned A-him'e-lech and all the priests of his family to come to Gib'e-ah at once. After accusing them of befriending an enemy of the king, Saul commanded his guards to slay them, but the soldiers shrank in holy fear from laying violent hands upon the priests of God.

Even though A-him'e-lech explained that he had befriended Da'vid without knowing that he was an outlaw, and denied that he or any of the priests were disloyal to the king, and even though the soldiers refused to slay the priests, Saul was not to be baffled in his hatred toward anyone who showed the slightest kindness to Da'vid. Do'eg was ordered to slay the priests, and that day saw the murder of eighty-five religious leaders of Is'ra-el. Only A-bi'a-thar escaped, and he joined Da'vid at the first opportunity.

It must have pained the heart of Da'vid to learn of the terrible outcome of his visit with the priest at Nob, and perhaps he felt somewhat to blame. He received A-bi'a-thar with great kindness, and assured him that his life would be safeguarded. Not satisfied with the slaughter of the priests, Saul had sent his men to Nob and utterly destroyed the town.

Feeling that it was no longer safe for him to remain anywhere in the land of Is'ra-el, Da'vid then fled into Phi-lis'ti-a and sought refuge in the city of Gath. He probably thought that he would no longer be recognized there as the one who had slain the Phi-lis'tine giant, and that these people would be glad to welcome anyone who was fleeing from Saul. He was recognized, however, and saved his life only by pretending that he had lost his mind.

Da'vid then fled back across the border of Is'ra-el into the hill country and took refuge in the limestone cliffs and caverns in a place called A-dul'-lam, which was in the region southeast of Beth'le-hem. His brothers and kinsmen learned where he was hiding and hastened to join him. Many people in the land who had suffered from Saul's failure to protect them, or who had been oppressed by him, rallied to the cause of Da'vid. Before long he had a company of four hundred men, many of whom were noted for their bravery and devotion to the right.

It was while Da'vid was hiding in the cliffs of A-dul'lam that he was joined by some of the men who were later known as his "mighty men" or heroes. Among them were his nephew Ab'i-shai, who became a famous general; Be-na'iah, whose great strength was shown in slaying a lion single-handed, and in killing two lion-like men of Mo'ab; E-le-a'zar, who once smote the Phi-lis'tines until his hand was so weary that it clave to his sword; and Je-hoi'a-da, who slew an E-gyp'tian with his own sword after tearing it from the hands of his enemy.

Among the brave followers who joined Da'vid at this time was a band of Ga'dites, who swam the Jor'dan when its banks were overflowed and scattered all enemies who tried to halt their march. When the time arrived for Da'vid to leave his hiding place in A-dul'lam, his band of loyal friends had grown to six hundred men, all noted for their courage and patriotism.

DAVID AND AHIMELECH

Meanwhile Da'vid performed an act of kindness for his father and mother which clearly proves the nobility of his character. He secretly crossed the river Jor'dan just north of its entrance to the Dead Sea, went up into a mountain fasteness in the land of Mo'ab to the southeast, and arranged for his parents to have a home where they would be secure from the anger of Saul during these troubled times. He may have appealed to the Mo'ab-ites for this favor in the name of his great-grandmother Ruth, who had been a member of their nation, and it is possible that his parents were lodged in the home of some of the descendants of Ruth's family.

About this time the Phi-lis'tines were making new invasions into the territory of Ju'dah, and the Lord planned to have Da'vid put an end to these raids. He, therefore, sent to Da'vid a prophet named Gad to tell him to go at once into Ju'dah, for Saul was too greatly disturbed in mind to be of service in checking these attacks from the ancient foes of Is'ra-el.

The town of Kei'lah in Ju'dah, not far from He'bron, had been captured by the Phi-lis'tines, who had robbed the people of their grains and fruits. Da'vid inquired of the Lord, saying, "Shall I go and smite these Phi-lis'tines?" God answered his prayer by telling him to go and save the town. Da'vid's men hesitated to make this effort, for they were in danger of attack from both the Phi-lis'tines and the armies of Saul. When Da'vid inquired again of the Lord, and was given the same command, his men rallied to his leadership and won a great victory over the Phi-lis'tines. Large quantities of war-spoils were taken, and Kei'lah and its inhabitants were saved.

No sooner had Saul been informed of Da'vid's capture of Kei'lah than he formed a plot by which he hoped to entrap Da'vid and his men within the walls of this own of Ju'dah. Again Da'vid turned to the Lord for guidance, asking whether the men of Kei'lah would protect him or yield to the demand of Saul that he and his men be given to him as prisoners. When told that they would give in to the will of Saul, Da'vid led his men out into the wilderness of Ziph, moving from place to place among the rocks and isolated spots of that wild territory.

When Saul was told that Da'vid had fled from Kei'lah, he gave up his plans to attack that town, but continued his pursuit of Da'vid and his men. Every time that news came to him of possible hiding places for them in the mountains he would send an army to search for his enemy, but the Providence of God kept Da'vid out of the way of the pursuing armies. Even the treachery of the Ziph'ites, who proposed to find Da'vid's hiding place and aid the army of Saul in capturing him, was brought to failure by the hand of God.

At last, when it appeared that Saul's armies had caught Da'vid and his men in a trap, a messenger told the cruel king that the Phi-lis'tines were attacking his home country, and that he must send the army back at once to meet the invasion. Thus victory over his hated rival was denied Saul, and he was forced to turn his armies from the pursuit of Da'vid to the defense of their own land.

It was during these perilous days in the wilderness of Ziph, just after the shameful conduct of the men of Kei'lah, and just before the treachery of the Ziph'ites, that Da'vid was given strength by a friendly visit from Jon'a-than. Moved by his great love for Da'vid, this noble young prince ran the risk of death at the hands of his father by making a secret visit to his friend in exile. He urged Da'vid not to be afraid, for the Lord would not permit him to be captured by Saul, and assured him that he was soon to become the king of Is'ra-el. With deep religious feeling on the part of both, the covenant of friendship between these two great souls was renewed, and Da'vid's hopes for the future were made much stronger.

SUGGESTIONS FOR STUDY

Biblical Index to Helpful References

The Duty to Honor Civil Rulers. (Ex. 22: 28; Rom. 13:1; 1 Pet. 2:17.)

The Shewbread Prepared for Priest Alone. (Ex. 25:30; Lev. 24:5; Num. 4:7.)

Jesus Commended Giving Shewbread to David. (Mark 2:26:)

The Violence of an Angry Ruler. (Prov. 16:14; 28:15; Ezek. 39:9.)

Care for Aging Parents Commanded. (Ex. 20:12; Prov. 23:22; Deut. 27:16.)

David's Great Grandmother a Moabite. (Ruth 4:17.)

Divine Guidance to be Sought in Emergencies. (Ps. 5:8; 25:5.)

Questions

1. When David fled from Saul was he a rebel or traitor?

2. Did he ever engage in war against Saul's armies?

3. While in exile did he have war with any of Israel's enemies?

4. Where did he go for food?

5. What kind of bread did the priest give him?

6. For whom was this bread prepared exclusively?

7. What attitude did Jesus take toward this act of David?

8. In what cave did David and his men hide? Where is it?

9. What provision did he make for his parents?

10. Tell of the Philistine capture of Keilah and of David's recapture of it.

11. Why did David flee Keilah and where did he go?

12. What happened which turned Saul's attack on David to other wars?

13. Who visited Davil while in the wilderness of Ziph?

STORY 85

DAVID SPARES THE LIFE OF SAUL

1 SAMUEL 24

Da'vid took advantage of the rest provided by Saul's engagement with the invading Phi-lis'tines to escape into the wilderness of En-ge'di, a region filled with steep mountains, deep ravines, and hundreds of caverns, on the western shores of the Dead Sea about thirteen miles northwest of Ma'on. As soon as Saul's armies had succeeded in driving off the Phi-lis'tine raid, the angry king sent three thousand picked soldiers in pursuit of Da'vid. It was during this pursuit that there occurred one of the two incidents in which Da'vid showed his nobility of character by sparing the life of the king when it was placed within his power by a strange providence.

Da'vid and his men were hiding among the rocks and caverns of that region, which was so steep and dangerous that only wild goats lived there. It so happened that Saul lay down to sleep at the entrance of one of the great caverns in which Da'vid and a few of his bravest men were taking refuge. While the king slept, unaware of his danger, Da'vid's men urged that he be put to death. They declared that the Lord had given them this opportunity of vengeance upon the wicked king who had sought to kill them without just cause.

How many strong, but conflicting desires must have throbbed in the heart of Da'vid! Apparently God had placed his cruel enemy in his power, and the urge to take revenge must have been hard to resist. Had not the time now come to bring peace to the land by ending the reign of a king who had been rejected by the Lord? Would he not bring a blessing to the entire nation by carrying out the sentence which had long since been pronounced upon the man who had been unfaithful to the Lord? Should he not take advantage of a remarkable opportunity which seemed to make it possible for him to become king at once?

Against these natural feelings of Da'vid and the urgent persuasions of his men, who insisted that he rid himself at once of his chief enemy, there remained the fact that Saul was still the king of Is'ra-el, and that Da'vid had never lifted up his hand against "the anointed of the Lord." Da'vid, therefore, gave up all thought of revenge, and forbade his men to harm the king. The fear of God held first place in his heart, so every

DAVID SPARES SAUL'S LIFE

idea of harming Saul was overcome by the teachings of true religion. Da'vid merely cut off a small part of the king's robe, intending to show it to Saul at some later time as proof that he had spared his life when he might easily have taken it.

Later, when Saul awoke from sleep and renewed his search for the young exile, Da'vid ran after him, waving the piece which he had cut from the king's robe, and calling to him to stop. Da'vid then made a wonderful speech in his own defense, declaring anew his loyalty to the king, and denying that he had ever rebelled against him.

Never has there been a man with better reasons for deserting his leader than Da'vid. He deserved Saul's deepest gratitude, but was shown nothing but ingratitude and cruelty. He was a loyal subject of the king, and his flight had been one of self-defense rather than defiance. While he could not honor Saul as a man, he respected his position and authority as king of the nation. In his moving defense of his own conduct, Da'vid appealed to Saul's reason and to God's justice. Addressing him as "My lord the king," he said:

"Why do you give heed to the people who tell you that Da'vid seeks your harm? See how the Lord has this day delivered you into my hand, and my men urged me to kill you; but I have spared your life and will not put forth my hand against my lord, for you are the Lord's anointed."

He then went on to say, "The skirt of your robe which I hold in my hand is proof that I bear no ill-will against you, although you wickedly seek my life." Referring to his own feeling of unworthiness to meet the armies of Is'ra-el in battle, he added, "I am as harmless as a flea, and as insignificant as a dead dog, and should be regarded as beneath the dignity of your pursuit." Appealing to God's justice, Da'vid ended his sublime words of defense by saying, "May the Lord judge between me and you, observe the injustice of your pursuit upon my life, and deliver me out of your hand."

Saul was overcome by these words of Da'vid and by the mercy shown by one whose life he had sought. His cruel, hardened heart was melted by the forgiving spirit of the noble exile, and for a moment his sense of justice was awakened. When he realized that his life had been spared by Da'vid's mercy to a bitter foe, he said, "You are a better man than I, for you have returned me good when I had done you evil. When the Lord placed me within your power, you did not kill me; and may God give you a good recompense for your kindness. I know that you are to be king of Is'ra-el, and I beg that you give me an oath that you will not cut off my sons after me, and that you will not destroy my name in the annals of Is'ra-el's history."

Saul then gave up the war against Da'vid and he and his men went home. Sad to say, however, his confessions of guilt and shame were not sincere, for he soon renewed his determination to kill Da'vid and all who befriended him.

SUGGESTIONS FOR STUDY

Biblical Index to Helpful References

Returning Good for Evil. (Gen. 45:15; Num. 12:13.)

Honoring Rulers Even When Attacked by Them. (Eccl. 10:20; Acts 23:5.)

Retaliation Forbidden. (Prov. 20:22; 24: 29; Matt. 5:39.)

Vengeance Belongeth to God. (Deut. 32: 35; Ps. 94:1, 2; Ezek. 25:17.)

Questions

1. Where did David go while Saul was engaged in war with the Philistines?

2. What did Saul do as soon as the war with the Philistines was over?

3. How did he fall into the hands of Saul?

4. What were the arguments in favor of David having Saul killed then?

5. For what reasons did David not kill Saul?

6. What did he do that he might have proof that he might have killed him?

7. What did David do when Saul awoke?

8. Tell of the speech which David made to Saul.

9. How did David's forbearance affect Saul?

STORY 86

ABIGAIL CONQUERS DAVID'S ANGER

1 SAMUEL 25

Da'vid seems to have realized that Saul's more friendly attitude would be short-lived, and that it was not safe for him to dismiss his followers and return to normal life again. He therefore removed to the wilderness of Pa'ran, which was an extended tract of country along the southern border of Ca'naan adjoining the Si'na-it'ic desert. There were two reasons which probably led him to choose this outlying district. One was the recent death of Sam'u-el, whose influence in Is'ra-el had done much to support the cause of Da'vid; the other, because it was becoming difficult to provide for his six hundred followers in the wilderness of Ju'dah.

Living not far from the place where Da'vid had taken his new refuge was a wealthy man by the name of Na'bal. He owned large herds of sheep and goats, and employed many shepherds. Da'vid and his men had given aid to these shepherds in protecting their flocks from the roving tribes of the desert, and for this reason felt justified in calling upon Na'bal when they were greatly in need of food.

Da'vid sent ten of his most courteous men to Car'mel, which was the home of Na'bal, with instructions to greet him in the name of the Lord, tell him of their friendly aid to his shepherds, and to explain the dire need of Da'vid's men for food. They were to ask Na'bal to send any food which he might spare from the feast which had been prepared for his shepherds and sheep-shearers, or from that which had been provided for the festivities of the seasons. All the circumstances justified Da'vid in making this request, and he had every reason to expect a generous response.

Da'vid was soon to be disappointed, however, for Na'bal had the heart of a miser, taking no thought for those who were less fortunate than himself. He had been blessed by the Lord with an abundance of earthly goods, but instead of thinking of what he owed to the Lord and all around him who were in need, he used his wealth only for his own enjoyment. He spoke of his possessions as "my bread, my meat, my water, and my shearers." He was also most ungrateful, for had Da'vid's men not protected his flocks both day and night, he would have had fewer sheep to shear and less wealth of which to boast.

Na'bal heard the request of Da'vid's men without the slightest feeling of obligation or generosity. He denied the request, speaking of Da'vid as a run-away slave who was in need because of misconduct.

When Da'vid's men reported Na'bal's unfriendliness and insults, their leader became very angry. He ordered four hundred of his men to gird on their swords and follow him, planning to swoop down upon Na'bal's farm with vengeance and deadly destruction. He was wrong in allowing his temper to rule for the moment, but Divine Providence kept him from carrying out his intentions against Na'bal and his household.

Na'bal's wife, whose name was Ab'i-gail, was an intelligent, kindly and deeply religious woman. She knew of Da'vid's excellent character and of his exile under the persecutions of Saul, and had been informed of the kindness of Da'vid's men to Na'bal's shepherds when they were in peril from bandits while out in the desert. When she learned of her husband's boorish treatment of Da'vid's young men in refusing their request, she felt that Da'vid would be justified in causing trouble for Na'bal.

ABIGAIL KNEELS BEFORE DAVID

She decided to take steps at once to save her husband and household from possible slaughter, and to prevent Da'vid from any rash deeds.

One of the shepherds urged her to act before it was too late, and spoke of Na'bal as "such a son of the Devil that no one could advise him." Ab'i-gail hastened to provide gifts which might appease Da'vid. Gathering two hundred loaves of bread, two bottles of wine, five dressed sheep, five clusters of parched corn, one hundred clusters of raisins, and two hundred cakes of figs, she had them loaded on beasts of burden and rushed off to meet Da'vid.

Her arrival was just in time, for she and the servants who went with her had not traveled far before they met Da'vid at the head of his four hundred men. He was in an angry mood, and was muttering in his heart, "I guarded all that this prosperous man had in the wilderness, so that nothing was lost; and for this goodness he has requited me evil. I shall surely be avenged by slaying him and every man in his company."

Ab'i-gail quickly dismounted, fell on her face before Da'vid, and cried, "Upon me, upon me, my lord, let this iniquity rest; and permit me, I beg you, to have audience with you." She then freely admitted that he had been badly treated by her husband, but pointed out the fact that Na'bal's very name means "fool" in the He'brew language. She also explained that she knew nothing of the request of the young men until they had gone, and that they would have received generous aid, had they applied to her. She then appealed to the deepest emotions of Da'vid's heart, expressing herself in words to this effect: "I am happy to deal with a man who, though sometimes at fault in word or deed, is a true servant of the Lord, and who will not deliberately break His law." She went on to assure Da'vid of her sympathy in the persecutions suffered from Saul's hatred, saying that she was confident that he would be raised to the throne of Is'ra-el, and adding this beautiful prophecy: "Your soul shall be found in the bundle of life with God, and the souls of your enemies shall be flung out in the cup of the sling."

Ab'i-gail then made a very touching appeal in which she reminded Da'vid that it would bring him great unhappiness, after he was king, if he had to look back upon any act in which he had shed blood without a cause. She then begged him to accept the provisions which she had brought to make up for the discourtesy shown by Na'bal, and earnestly sought forgiveness.

Da'vid was completely overcome by the appeal of this noble woman, and was deeply impressed with her personal charm and worth. In reply to Ab'i-gail he said, "May the Lord God of Is'ra-el be blessed, who sent you to me! Blessed be your counsel, and blessed may you be, because you have kept me this day from shedding blood and from avenging a personal grievance with my own hand. Had you not hurried and come to me, then certainly by tomorrow morning there would not have been left a single one of Na'bal's men." He then accepted the gifts which she had brought and sent her home in peace.

When Ab'i-gail returned to her husband she found him drunkenly enjoying the festivities of the sheep-shearing season, wholly unmindful of the peril from which his noble wife had saved him. She waited until the next morning, when he had sufficiently recovered from his drunkenness to understand what she said, to tell him how she had appeased the anger of Da'vid, and of the certain death from which she had saved her unworthy husband. Na'bal was so shocked by the news that he fell into a state of paralysis, and ten days later he died.

When news was brought to Da'vid of Na'bal's death, he sang once again a song of praise to God for the deliverance from evil which had been brought to him through the wise counsel and prudent acts of Ab'i-gail. His admiration for her noble character and deep piety soon grew into a strong affection, and Ab'i-gail became a faithful and devoted wife of the young hero.

SUGGESTIONS FOR STUDY

Biblical Index to Helpful References

Duty of the More Fortunate to the Less Fortunate. (Deut. 15:7; Ps. 4:1.)

Dangers of Prosperity. (Deut. 6:10-12; 32:15; Jer. 5:28.)

The Baseness of Selfishness. (Prov. 11:26; Matt. 25:43; Luke 10:31, 32.)

The Baseness of Inhospitality. (Num. 20: 18; 21:21-23.)

The Baseness of Ingratitude. (Eccl. 9:15; Prov. 17:13; Jer. 18:20.)

The Glory of a Wise Woman. (Prov. 11: 16; 14:1; 31:10, 30.)

The Blessing of Wise Counsel. (Prov. 12: 15; 13:10.)

Questions

1. Where did David now take his followers? Why?

2. What destitution faced David and his men?

3. Why did he call on Nabal for food?

4. What were Nabal's material circumstances in life?

5. Why would he have extra food on hand at this time?

6. How did Nabal treat David's request for aid?

7. What did David propose to do to Nabal?

8. Who prevented his harsh measures as planned?

9. What happened to Nabal when Abigail told him what she had done?

10. What did David later do in reference to Abigail?

STORY 87

SAUL VISITS THE WITCH OF ENDOR; HIS TRAGIC DEATH

1 SAMUEL 28, 31;
1 CHRONICLES 10

The stage was now set for a tragic ending to the career of Saul. Violent warfare was raging betwen the Phi-lis'tines and the Is'ra-el-ites, and preparations were made for a decisive battle on the plains of Jez're-el at the foot of Mount Gil-bo'a. Saul appears to have had strange warnings of the disaster soon to come. His efforts to secure Divine aid through prayer and by an appeal to the priests of the land had met with an appalling silence from God. No help came to him through revealing dreams, the advice of a priest, or the words of a prophet. He should have known at once that the Lord had left him to his own evil ways, but it was a long time before this knowledge filled him with terror.

With the armies of Is'ra-el assembled in the foothills of Mount Gil-bo'a, and with the forces of the Phi-lis'tines massed on the plains of Jez're-el, Saul was overcome by fright. He remembered the timely messages of the prophet Sam'u-el during the earlier days of his reign, and now, even though the man of God was dead and buried, Saul felt that he must find some way of communicating with him. There were people in those days, just as there are now, who pretended to be able to speak with people long dead. Women who practiced this art were known as "witches," and God had told Is'ra-el through the Mo'saic Laws that all such deceivers were dominated by evil spirits and should be slain. This law against witches had been strictly enforced by Saul, but one woman who lived in a secluded spot in the Little Her'mon mountain had escaped the executioners of the king. In his troubled spirit Saul decided to ask her aid in communicating with the spirit of Sam'u-el.

Saul disguised himself in the clothing worn by common people, took two servants with him, and sought a secret meeting with the witch of En'dor. The place where she was in hiding was located beyond the camps of the Phi-lis'tines, so it was necessary for Saul to pass around his bitter foes in his secret mission. It was a dark and perilous night for the despairing king as he kept to the east of the plains of Jez're-el, crossed the valley to the adjoining Little Her'mon, and climbed the rugged path to En'dor.

The witch at En'dor did not recognize Saul at first, and thought that her visitor, whoever he might be, had come merely to entrap her. She reminded the unknown visitor that Saul had driven from his land all people who claimed to speak with the dead, and accused him of laying a snare for her. Saul then took oath that no harm should befall her for anything which she might do to help him, so the woman said, "Whom among the dead shall I summon for you?" Saul replied, "Bring me up Sam'u-el." This request convinced the woman that her visitor was none other than the king of Is'ra-el, and she cried out in anger, "Why have you deceived me? You are Saul." The king then admitted his identity, but told her once again that she need fear no harm if she granted his request.

The woman evidently knew of Sam'u-el's frequent warnings to Saul during his life, of Saul's rejection by the Lord, and of his constant fear of losing the throne to Da'vid. She was acquainted with all that had taken place in the life of the king, and knew that his mind was now filled with many fears. She remembered the appearance of Sam'u-el during his earthly life, and was able to duplicate it well enough to make Saul think that the prophet himself was called up from death to speak with him.

SAUL FALLS UPON HIS SWORD

The entire interview was a fraud, based upon the superstitious, false belief that departed spirits may be called back to speak with the living. It is plainly taught in God's revealed truth that a return of the spirits of the dead to this world is impossible. All through the Bible the practice of witchcraft or sorcery is closely connected with spirits of evil, and is severely denounced by the Lord. There are a number of incidents recorded in which miraculous deeds of a certain kind are attributed to the servants of Sa'tan. It is clearly said in the Scriptures that "Sa'tan fashioneth himself into an angel of light," and certain forms of his works are said to be "with all power and signs and lying wonders." The story of Saul's visit to the witch of En'dor and of his conversation with the dead prophet must be understood in the light of the Lord's plain teaching on this subject.

It is directly stated in connection with this story that "God answered Saul no more," and it was for this reason that he turned to a sorceress for help. It is therefore obviously true that nothing which was said during the visit with the witch of En'dor came from God. It was Sa'tan himself, or one of the evil spirits at his command, who led the witch to say what she did to Saul. All that was said was true, and all that was predicted came to pass, but Sa'tan was merely taunting the man whose evil deeds had brought him wholly within his power. Sa'tan ruins men, and then laughs at them in their misery.

For more than twenty-four hours Saul had been in such anguish of mind and spirit that he had not taken any food; in this weakened condition he was overcome by the shock of apparently receiving a message from the spirit of Sam'u-el, and suddenly fell to the ground. The witch was terrified by the thought that the king might be found dead or injured in her home, which would mean certain death for her. She therefore begged him to take some food in order to revive his weakened body. Saul refused at first, but was finally persuaded by the witch and his own servants to eat a full meal. Presently he rose up and went back to the camps of his soldiers while it was still night.

On the next day the Phi-lis'tines attacked the Is'ra-el-ites with great force. The battle was waged fiercely by both sides, but its tide was against Is'ra-el. Three of Saul's sons—Jon'a-than, A-bin'a-dab and Mal-chi-shu'a —were slain, and Saul himself was severely wounded by the archers. In his pain and despair he said to his armor-bearer, "Draw your sword and thrust it through my body, lest the heathen Phi-lis'tines slay me." When the armor-bearer refused to do it, Saul placed the point of his sword against his body and threw himself upon it with all his weight. He died instantly, and was soon followed in death by the devoted armor-bearer, who took his life in the same way.

When news of the shameful manner in which the bodies of Saul and his three sons had been left hanging on the walls of Beth-she'an reached the ears of the people of Ja'besh-Gil'e-ad, which was far across the Jor'dan to the northeast, some of their valiant men resolved to put an end to such treatment. Travelling all night in order to reach Beth-she'an as soon as possible, they took down the bodies of their dead king and his sons, and had them cremated. Then they carried the ashes to Ja'besh for burial, and declared seven days of fast and mourning.

These Gil'e-ad-ites showed a fine spirit of gratitude and courage in their noble deed. In the early days of his reign, many years before his tragic death, Saul had gone to the defense of the city of Ja'besh-Gil'e-ad when it was attacked by the Am'mon-ites. The great victory which he had won for them in the name of God had not been forgotten.

SUGGESTIONS FOR STUDY

Biblical Index to Helpful References

Powerlessness Because of Sin. (Lev. 26: 37-39; Jgs. 16:6-8.)

Powerlessness Because of Unbelief. (Mark. 9:18; John 15:5.)

Unanswered Prayer Because of Sin. (Deut. 1:45; Ps. 66:18; Prov. 1:24-38; 28:9.)

Forsaken by God Because of Wickedness. (2 Chr. 30:7; Ps. 81:11, 12; Matt. 23:38, 39.)

God's Law Against Witchcraft. (Ex. 22: 18; Lev. 19:31; 2 Ki. 23:24; Micah 5:12.)

God's Law Against Patrons of Witchcraft. (Lev. 20:6; Isa. 8:20.)

Witchcraft a Work of the Flesh. (Gal. 5: 19, 20.)

Saul's Punishment for Turning to a Sorceress. (1 Chr. 10:13.)

Sorcerers Given Power of a Certain Kind by Satin. (Ex. 7:11-22; Acts 16:16.)

Satan Transforms Himself Into an Angel of Light. (2 Cor. 11:14.)

Satan's Wiles and Strange Powers. (Matt. 4:6; 2 Thess. 2:9, 10.)

Sorrowful Death of the Wicked. (Ps. 37: 35-36; Prov. 5:23; Isa. 50:11.)

Saul's Deliverance of Jabesh-Gilead. (1 Sam. 11:1-11.)

Questions

1. When the Philistines encamped against Israel how did Saul feel?

2. Why could he receive no answer to his prayers?

3. To whom did he turn for advice and counsel?

4. What had God said about witches and witchcraft?

5. To whom did Saul wish to have the witch conjure from death?

6. Did Samuel actually come back and talk to Saul?

7. Does the Bible anywhere teach that the dead may talk to the living?

8. What influence gave this delusion to the witch and to Saul?

9. What message did the witch purport to receive from Samuel?

10. Was this message what Saul expected to hear?

11. Tell of Saul's death? Of the disgrace of his body by the Philistines?

12. Who provided burial for Saul and his sons? Why?

STORY 88

DAVID'S LAMENT OVER SAUL AND JONATHAN

2 SAMUEL 1

The news of the defeat of the Is'ra-el-ites by the Phi-lis'tines and of the death of Saul and his sons was brought to Da'vid three days after he and his men had returned to the ruins of Zik'lag. There rushed into the camp a man in tattered clothes and with the appearance of having gone through a terrific struggle. Thinking that Da'vid would be pleased to hear the unhappy end of the one who had persecuted him for so many years, the stranger told Da'vid of the tragic death of Saul. No doubt seeking a reward from Da'vid, he pretended that he had taken an important part in the tragedy, saying:

"I happened by chance to come upon Saul as he leaned upon his spear, hard pressed by the chariots and horsemen of the enemy; and at his own request, because he did not wish to undergo the shame of being slain by the Phi-lis'tines, I slew him with my own hands. I have brought you the metal cap which he wore to protect his temples and as an emblem of power; and his armlet, the mark of his royal dignity."

This man, who said that he was an Am'a-lek-ite, misjudged the nobility of Da'vid. The story which he told was only partially true, and the claims which he made for himself were wholly false. Instead of bringing praise and reward, his scheme brought down upon his head the anger of the man he sought to please and the punishment of death.

Da'vid's heart was filled with sorrow at the news of the death of Saul and of his bosom friend Jon'a-than. His feelings broke forth in overwhelming grief and in violent anger toward the man who claimed to have slain the king. He proclaimed a season of deep mourning among his men for Saul and Jon'a-than and for all the Is'ra-el-ites who had fallen by the sword of the Phi-lis'tines.

He then called for the man who had brought the news of the death of Saul and his sons, and asked him who he was. The man replied that he was an Am'a-lek-ite who had moved into the land of Is'ra-el. Then the one who had never been disloyal to his king, and who had twice spared his life, said to the stranger, "Thou art condemned by the words of thine own mouth, for the penalty of death must be inflicted upon any man

HEBRON

who slays the Lord's anointed." He then directed one of his valiant men to execute the self-confessed criminal, and the sentence was immediately carried out.

Da'vid then uttered a lament over the death of Saul and Jon'a-than which holds an honored place among ancient writings of this kind. It is arranged in three strophes, gradually diminishing in power and scope:

"Thy glory, O Is'ra-el is slain upon the high places!
    How are the mighty fallen!
Tell it not in Gath,
    Publish it not in the streets of As'ke-lon;
Lest the daughters of the Phi-lis'tines rejoice.
    Ye mountains of Gil-bo'a,
Let there be no dew nor rain upon you, neither fields of offerings:
    For there the shield of the mighty was vilely cast away,
The shield of Saul, not anointed with oil.
    From the blood of the slain, from the fat of the mighty,
The bow of Jon'a-than turned not back,
    And the sword of Saul returned not empty.
Saul and Jon'a-than were lovely and pleasant in their lives,

And in their death they were not divided:
They were swifter than eagles,
   They were stronger than lions.
Ye daughters of Is'ra-el, weep over Saul,
   Who clothed you in scarlet delicately,
Who put ornaments of gold upon your apparel.

How are the mighty fallen in the midst of battle!
   Jon'a-than is slain upon thy high places.
I am distressed for thee, my brother Jon'a-than:
   Very pleasant hast thou been unto me:
Thy love to me was wonderful,
   Passing the love of women.

How are the mighty fallen,
   And the weapons of war perished!

What a remarkable insight into the heart of Da'vid is provided in the words of this beautiful ode! He sang high praises in memory of the man who had made his youth and early manhood a time of constant danger and worry. Is'ra-el had lost a king who, with all his faults, had certain qualities of greatness; and in his tribute to the dead, Da'vid forgot and forgave his faults, while magnifying his virtues. Instead of being gratified by the end of an enemy and rejoicing that his persecutions were over, Da'vid bowed in genuine grief. To his heart, Is'ra-el's shame and the insult to God in the triumph of the Phi-lis'tines were more important than the prospects of a safe return to his native land and the probability of immediate advancement to the throne of Is'ra-el. Such nobility is rare in the history of mankind; and is possible only because one makes God, and not himself, the center of the universe. This nobility was Da'vid's safeguard against the baneful influences of both adversity and prosperity.

SUGGESTIONS FOR STUDY

Biblical Index to Helpful References

Freedom from a Retaliatory Spirit. (Prov. 20:22; 24:29; 1 Pet. 3:9.)

Treachery Detected and Punished. (Neh. 6:2, 15, 16; Esther 3:8; 7:10.)

The Wicked Snared by Their Own Acts. (Job 18:8; Ps. 9:15; Prov. 22:5; 28:10.)

Grief for the Dead. (Job 1:19-21; Jer. 31:15; Acts 9:39.)

Questions

1. What false representations were made to David about the death of Saul?

2. How did David feel about the death of Saul and Jonathan?

3. What punishment did he inflict upon the man who claimed to have killed Saul?

4. Describe the character of the ode penned by David on the death of Saul and Jonathan.

STORY 89

DAVID'S SEVEN YEARS OF REIGN OVER JUDAH

2 SAMUEL 2-5:1-5

Although Da'vid had known for many years that he was eventually to become king of Is'ra-el, and though it appeared that the death of Saul had opened the way for his immediate rise to the throne, he made no move until directed by the Lord. Eight years before the death of Saul he had been anointed by Sam'u-el as the future king of the nation; for several years after that momentous occasion he had faithfully served as harpist in the royal court and as a captain in the army; for the past two years or more he had been persecuted as an outlaw and an exile; and, now that the king was dead, one would expect Da'vid to press his demand for a prompt enthronement. Both Saul and Jon'a-than had admitted that the house of Saul had been rejected by the Lord, and had told Da'vid more than once that he would be the next king. True to his usual course at critical times, however, Da'vid sought the Lord's guidance for his next step.

The Lord not only told him to return to his native land at once, but directed him to go to the city of He'bron in the mountains of Ju'dah, which was twenty miles south of Je-ru'sa-lem and about the same distance north of Be'er-She'ba. Taking along all his men and their families, that those who had shared his hardships might also enjoy his prosperity, Da'vid went directly to the city appointed by the Lord. Here, in that most ancient city of the world, made sacred in the days of Ab'ra-ham, famous as the burying place of the great patriarch, given to Ca'leb for his bravery, and situated in the heart of Ju'dah, which was the royal and Mes-si'an-ic tribe, Da'vid was made king by the people of his own tribe.

The first official act of Da'vid was to send messengers to Ja-besh-Gil'e-ad to thank the princes and nobility for their kindness in providing an honorable burial for the ashes of Saul and Jon'a-than.

It would seem to us that all Is'ra-el would have rallied to the banner of Da'vid, and that he should have been recognized at once as the rightful king of the entire land. The people must have known of God's will in this matter, and the crushing defeat suffered at Gil'bo-a should have con-

ABNER SLAYS ASAHEL

vinced them that the time had come for the Divinely appointed ruler to take his place at the head of the nation.

Some of the tribes to the north and on the east side of the Jor'dan, however, were opposed to the rule of Da'vid. Under the leadership of Ab'ner, who had commanded Saul's armies for a number of years, they refused to accept David's coronation at He'bron, choosing as their king Ish-bo'sheth, a surviving son of Saul. Thus still greater trials were brought to Da'vid, for civil war prevailed in Is'ra-el over a period of seven years. For three or four years Da'vid had refused to lead a revolt against Saul, but now that he was king he had to face the rebellion of an ambitious army captain.

Ab'ner had known Da'vid for a number of years, and seems to have felt kindly toward him at the time of his triumph over Go'li-ath. During the days of Da'vid's service as captain in Saul's armies he must have had many occasions to observe the bravery of the young hero. Even while Da'vid was in exile, and was being constantly hunted down by Saul's armies, Ab'ner had been forced to recognize the loyalty which twice led him to spare the life of the king. He well knew the nobility of Da'vid's character, and he was familiar with the Divine command that the kingdom be transferred from the house of Saul to that of Da'vid; yet he was responsible for the raising up of Ish-bo'sheth as a rival to Da'vid and for the civil war which followed.

The first open clash between the rebels led by Ab'ner and Da'vid's men took place at Gib'e-on, in the western part of Ben'ja-min about six miles north of Je-ru'sa-lem. Ab'ner brought over from Ish-bo'sheth's capital on the east side of the Jor'dan a great force of men, and was apparently bent on subduing Ju'dah to the rule of Ish-bo'sheth. Three of Da'vid's nephews, Ab'i-shai, As'a-hel, and Jo'ab, were brave officers in Da'vid's army; Jo'ab being the commander. They led a small company of men to meet Ab'ner at Gib'e-on, and it was agreed that twelve men from each side should engage in single combat. After all these men had been mortally wounded, there came a battle in which twenty of Da'vid's men and three hundred and sixty of Ab'ner's followers were slain. As'a-hel pursued Ab'ner from the field of battle, but was killed by the crafty general.

Darkness fell before Da'vid's men could complete their victory, and Ab'ner led his scattered forces to the top of a high hill, with Jo'ab and his army in close pursuit. The next morning a truce was proposed by Ab'ner, and both armies returned to their homes. A state of war continued, however, and there were frequent conflicts between the followers of Da'vid and those who were loyal to the house of Saul. As time went on, the cause of Da'vid steadily gained in power, while the followers of Ish-bo'sheth grew weaker.

Ab'ner was an ambitious politician who made use of Ish-bo'sheth in setting up a rival kingdom to that of Da'vid, but who had no real love for the son of the lamented Saul. When he saw that he was taking part in a losing cause he began to seek some excuse for deserting Ish-bo'sheth, hoping to ally himself with Da'vid. A violent quarrel with his master finally gave Ab'ner his opportunity, and it was then that he admitted his knowledge of God's decree that Da'vid should be king over Is'ra-el, and that he declared his intention of turning the hearts of the people to their rightful king.

When Da'vid learned of Ab'ner's wish to join him, he demanded as one of the conditions the immediate return of his wife Mi'chal, who had been taken from him by Saul and given to another man. Although this request no doubt was prompted by a spirit of love for Mi'chal, Da'vid may also have considered the political advantages of his remarriage to the daughter of Saul. Ish-bo'sheth yielded to this demand, and permitted Ab'ner to return Mi'chal to David, even though the man to whom she had been unlawfully married made a bitter protest.

Ab'ner then set out to win the princes of the tribes of Is'ra-el to the support of Da'vid, reminding them of their former wish to have him as their king, and of God's decree in the matter. He also pointed out their need of Da'vid's help in resisting the continual raids of the Phi-lis'tines. Their consent was readily obtained, for it was only through Ab'ner's persistent efforts that Ish-bo'sheth's authority over them had been secured and maintained. The results of this appeal to the leaders of the rebellious tribes were carried to Da'vid in his court at He'bron, and plans were made for an immediate public treaty uniting the two factions. After a covenant feast at which Ab'ner and twenty of his friends were guests of honor, Da'vid sent Ab'ner home to complete the arrangements for the treaty.

While all this was taking place, Jo'ab was away on official duty; when he returned and heard of Ab'ner's proposal, he protested vigorously against a league of peace with the former leader of a rebellion against Da'vid. He gave as reason for his views a complete lack of faith in Ab'ner, but seems to have been prompted chiefly by the fear that this older, more renowned general might be given his place at the head of Da'vid's armies.

After bitterly denouncing Da'vid for being deceived by a cunning plotter, Jo'ab sent messengers to Ab'ner with the request that he return for a conference. This invitation may have been sent in the name of the king, for it aroused no suspicion in the mind of Ab'ner. He promptly came back to the capital, where Jo'ab took him aside under the pretense of a private conversation, and thereupon assassinated him. Jo'ab tried to justify this cruel deed as an act of revenge for the death of his brother As'a-hel, and by the claim that Ab'ner was a traitor to Da'vid and an enemy of God, but few believed that this was his real motive.

Da'vid's sense of justice was outraged by the treachery of Jo'ab, and he felt that the proposed alliance of the rebellious tribes with his kingdom would be greatly hampered by this cruel deed. He disclaimed all responsibility for the act of his general, pronouncing a curse upon Jo'ab and his family. As a token of honor for the slain Ab'ner he proclaimed a season of mourning, and himself took part in the lamentations. In his funeral dirge he declared:

"Ab'ner died, not as a worthless man, nor as one guilty of any crime worthy of death; he was overpowered without suspecting evil, and was murdered as a defenseless hero. A prince and a great man has fallen this day in Is'ra-el."

Da'vid's lament at the grave of Ab'ner and his fair-minded praise won him the increased support of all Is'ra-el, and the union of all the tribes was quickened rather than delayed by the tragedy.

When the news of Ab'ner's death reached Ish-bo'sheth, this weak king lost all courage to keep on as a rival of Da'vid, and his followers lost hope of maintaining their separate government. The military group which had been the chief support of the puppet king became disorganized, and treason broke out among the officers.

Two of the rebellious officers treacherously murdered Ish-bo'sheth while he was quietly resting on his bed. With the hope of gaining a reward they cut off the head of their master and brought it to Da'vid. Like the Am'a-lek-ite who claimed to have slain Saul at his own request, these men failed to grasp the nobility of Da'vid, and were denounced for their wicked deed. Da'vid ordered their immediate execution, and gave instructions for an honorable burial of the head of Ish-bo'sheth.

Even though these men had paid for their treachery with their lives, the death of the puppet king removed the last barrier to a united nation. The princes of all the tribes of Is'ra-el which had previously rejected the rule of Da'vid, and had allied with Ab'ner in his effort to establish the weak Ish-bo'sheth firmly on the throne of Is'ra-el, now came to He'bron to offer Da'vid the homage of all the nation. After seven years of civil war, during which he had been acknowledged as king only by the tribe of Ju'dah, Da'vid was now the ruler of all the twelve tribes, and Is'ra-el entered upon a period of great prosperity.

SUGGESTIONS FOR STUDY

Biblical Index to Helpful References

Hebron Made Sacred by Abraham. (Gen. 13:18; 23:2.)

Hebron Visited by the Spies. (Num. 13:22.)

Hebron Given to Caleb. (Josh. 10:36-37; 14:14.)

Abner, the Captain of Saul's Armies. (1 Sam. 14:51; 17:55; 26:7.)

David's Reign of Seven Years in Hebron.

(1 Chr. 3:4; 29:27.)

David's Life in God's Hands. (Ps. 25:20-22; 31:15.)

Examples of Treachery. (Jgs. 16:19; 1 Sam. 18:17; 2 Sam. 20:10.)

Mourning for the Dead. (Gen. 50:3, 10; Num. 20:29; Deut. 34:8.)

Michal, Saul's daughter. (1 Sam. 14:49; 18:20, 27; 19:12.)

Questions

1. Did David hasten to seek the kingship of Israel after Saul's death?

2. Where did the Lord direct him to go? What importance attached to Hebron?

3. What tribe of Israel crowned David king?

4. Who was made king over the other tribes? By whom?

5. How long did David reign over Judah before becoming king of all Israel?

6. What conditions existed during this time between Judah and Abner's following?

7. Why did Abner desert Ishbosheth and seek alliance with David?

8. What condition did David impose on Abner?

9. Who among David's officers resented the actions of Abner?

10. What did he do?

11. How did David feel about the slaying of Abner?

· STORY 90

DAVID IS CROWNED KING OF ALL ISRAEL

2 SAMUEL 5:1-5
1 CHRONICLES 11:1-3   After the shrewd generalship and crafty efforts of Ab'ner had failed to make Ish-bo'sheth king over all Is'ra-el, but had brought death to both general and king, there was left only one member of the house of Saul to contest Da'vid's claims to the throne. The one heir was the lame Me-phib'o-sheth, who was only twelve years old. The leaders of the eleven revolting tribes therefore went to He'bron and asked that Da'vid be made king of the entire nation.

Among the reasons given for this request were the following: the suspicions aroused by Da'vid's enforced alliance with the king of Gath had been fully removed by his active interest in the welfare of all Is'ra-el; his splendid record as a soldier fitted him to lead Is'ra-el against their enemies;

THE PLATFORM OF THE DOME OF THE ROCK

and the Lord had clearly indicated his choice of Da'vid for the office of king.

In the coronation ceremonies at He'bron the qualifications and duties of the king were placed on a much higher plane than before. For the first time he was placed over Is'ra-el as a pastor; the duty of love and humility and proper respect for the liberty, property, and life of the people was stressed, and the king was charged with the responsibility of watching over his people as a shepherd watches his flocks.

The whole procedure was carried out in a deeply religious spirit. The religious unity of the nation, which had been established by Sam'u-el and then weakened by Saul, was fully restored. Da'vid "made a league with Is'ra-el before the Lord," and the representatives of all the tribes of Is'ra-el pledged their loyalty and obedience to him as "the anointed of the Lord." It was the beginning of a new era for Is'ra-el and for her Divinely chosen king.

Da'vid was now thirty years old, and the hopes which he had humbly cherished in his heart for fifteen years were now at last fully accomplished. The sufferings and discipline and training of these long years had often tested his faith in God and man, but he had come out of the fires of trial and temptation fully prepared to be a great ruler.

His confidence in God had been strengthened by the Divine grace which had been granted him in manifold trials, and he was well qualified for the great honor to which he had been consecrated by the prophet Sam'u-el fifteen years before.

SUGGESTIONS FOR STUDY

Biblical Index to Helpful References

God's Everlasting Covenant with David. (2 Sam. 23:5; Isa. 55:3.)

Coronation of Kings. (1 Ki. 12:1, 20; 2 Ki. 11:12.)

Anointings as a Sign of Consecration. (Lev. 8:30; 1 Ki. 1:39; 19:16.)

Justice and the Fear of God Required of Rulers. (Deut. 17:6; 2 Chr. 19:6; Prov. 16: 12; 29:4.)

The Shepherding Duty of Kings. (Prov. 29:14; Ezek. 34:23.)

Questions

1. What immediate events opened the way for David's enthronement over all Israel?

2. Who came to Hebron and asked that he be made king over all Israel?

3. What reasons did they give for this request?

4. In what respects were the qualifications and duties of the king elevated?

5. In whose name did David make a league with the elders of Israel?

6. What distinction was given to David in making him king?

STORY 91

DAVID CAPTURES JERUSALEM AND MAKES IT HIS CAPITAL

2 SAMUEL 5:6-25
1 CHRONICLES 11:4-25;
14:8-17   The first task of Da'vid after becoming the ruler of all Is'ra-el was to decide which city should be his capital. For seven years the seat of his government had been at He'bron, sacred to all the people of the nation for many reasons, but he did not wish it to appear that the eleven tribes were being annexed to the little government of Ju'dah. He felt that to keep his capital at He'bron would cause undue pride among the people of Ju'dah, and make the other tribes jealous. He also wished to avoid the mistake of Saul, who made his home town of Gib'e-ah capital in spite of the fact that it was a place of little national importance, and was scorned by the people as the scene of one of the worst outrages in the history of the nation.

For personal reasons, Da'vid preferred his native city of Beth'le-hem for the capital, but its situation would not permit the building of proper defenses. His problem was to choose a capital which was not then held by any of the twelve tribes; otherwise, there would be jealousy among the tribes; and to find a city which might be taken by the combined efforts of all the tribes, thereby giving them a sense of unity as a nation.

For all these reasons, therefore, Da'vid set his heart on taking Je-ru'sa-lem, a strongly for-

BENAIAH SLAYS A LION

tified city, situated between the land of Ju'dah and Ben'ja-min, and thus belonging to neither. It was then held by the Jeb'u-sites, a strong Ca'naan-it-ish tribe which had occupied the mountainous section of Ju'dah when the Is'ra-el-ites first entered the land. Neither Josh'u-a, who conquered them after a great struggle, nor the children of Ju'dah, who seized the lower part of the city, nor the Ben'ja-mites, to whom the city had been assigned, were able to take the strong citadel of Je'bus on Mt. Zi'on.

The Jeb'u-sites were so strongly fortified on the eastern hill of the city that they looked with scorn upon any who dared to attack them, and cried from the walls of their citadel that even the blind and the lame could defend it. It was shut in by deep valleys on three sides, and was not easily approached from the other. Through the centuries it had defied all attempts to scale its heights and break down its fortifications; to capture the fort of Je'bus was regarded as an impossible feat.

Da'vid, however, had relied upon the strength of the Lord to do what had seemed impossible in days gone by, so he believed that he could take this powerful fortress. He led his armies in the attack, and was successful; not by strength of arms or skill in warfare, but by the unseen forces of the God of Is'ra-el. The city was given to Da'vid as a servant of the Lord God of hosts, and as a blessing to all the world, for the stronghold of Je'bus was thereby made the fortress of Zi'on, and Je-ru'sa-lem became a city unequalled in importance by any other in the history of the world.

Greater wisdom was never displayed in the selection of the capital of any nation. Je-ru'sa-lem was, indeed, a "mountain throne" for the kings of Is'ra-el, and a "mountain sanctuary" for the people of God. High above Jer'i-cho in the Jor'dan valley, the Phi-lis'tine strongholds on the plains of the Med'i-ter-ra'ne-an, the Phoe-ni'ci-an cities of Tyre and Si'don, and Da-mas'cus of Syr'i-a, it stood in defiance of all enemies for hundreds of years. Situated in a mountain fastness on the edge of one of the highest table-lands of Ca'naan, in the most prominent part of the mountain range which extended from the desert country on the south to the plains of Es-dra-e'lon on the north, the holy city of Je-ru'sa-lem was the pride and glory of God's chosen people throughout their history. Not until the Mes-si'ah set up His worldwide dominion did it lose its importance, and long after the Advent it held a position of honor.

The coronation of Da'vid as king over all the tribes of Is'ra-el and the capture of the fort of Je'bus served as the occasion for new invasions by the Phi-lis'tines. During Ish-bo'sheth's seven yeàrs of rule over the eleven tribes the Phi-lis'tines had set up garrisons in various cities of the land, and, when it appeared that Da'vid would lead a united nation against them, they immediately took the offensive. Not knowing whether it would be the wiser course for him to allow the Phi-lis'tines to attack the newly won fortress at Je-ru'sa-lem, or to go out and meet them in battle in some other part of the land, David turned to the Lord for guidance. He obeyed the Lord's command to meet them in open battle, and won two great victories. The Phi-lis'tines were driven from the land all the way from Gib'e-ah in Ben'ja-min to Ge'zer, which was at the extreme north of the Phi-lis'tine country.

DAVID'S VALIANT MEN

It was probably during the first engagement with the Phi-lis'tines that three of Da'vid's valiant men crept through the enemy lines in order to bring their king water from the famous well of his home town. Grown weary with the strain of this new campaign, and filled with longing for the happy days when he was a shepherd lad among the hills of Beth'le-hem, Da'vid thought of the old well by the gate where he had often rested, listening to the stories of warriors and shepherds. In the stress and strain of the moment he sighed:

"Oh that one would give me drink of the water of the well
   of Beth'le-hem!"

Three of his men cautiously made their way through the territory filled with the strong and cunning Phi-lis'tines and brought Da'vid the water for which he had longed. Touched more by the courage of his men than by having the water he had requested, Da'vid performed a symbolic act of worship by pouring the water on the ground and dedicating it to the Lord.

Looking upon the bottle of water for which he had so deeply yearned, Da'vid said, "Is not this the blood of men who went in jeopardy of their lives?" Stimulated by the loyalty and courage of his men, and regretting any selfishness he might have shown during his moments of homesickness, Da'vid took new courage for the battles against his enemies. The Phi-lis'tines were so completely routed that they left on the battlefield the images of their gods which they carried as a superstitious means of protection.

There followed a season of peace, with Da'vid growing in favor with the people as he established his rule in Je-ru'sa-lem. Other children were born in his family, and a royal palace was built for his home. Friendly relations were established with Hi'ram, King of Tyre, who sent valuable materials and skilled workmen to help in erecting government buildings in the capital.

SUGGESTIONS FOR STUDY

Biblical Index to Helpful References

Jebusites Conquered by Joshua. (Josh. 11:3.)

Judah Unable to Drive the Jebusites from Jerusalem. (Josh. 15:63.)

The Benjamites Unable to Conquer Jerusalem. (Jgs. 1:21.)

Israelites Intermingle with Jebusites. (Jgs. 3:5; 19:11.)

Contempt for the Righteous. (Neh. 2:19; Ps. 80:6; 119:22.)

David's Praises to God for His Help. (Ps. 40:1-5; 52:7-9.)

The Lord's Choice of Mt. Zion. (Ps. 132:13; Joel 3:17; Zech. 1:17.)

Hiram the Friend of David and Solomon. (2 Chr. 2:2; 1 Ki. 5:15; 9:10.)

Questions

1. Why did David desire a new capital for the united kingdom?

2. What place did he wish for his new capital?

3. Describe the location and advantages of this desired place?

4. In whose possession was Jerusalem at that time?

5. Why had it not been taken by the Israelites before now?

6. Tell of David's capture of Jerusalem.

7. What position did Jerusalem hold after that in history?

8. Why did the Philistines renew their attacks upon Israel at this time?

9. What were the results of David's wars against them?

10. Tell of the brave men who secured water from Bethlehem for David.

11. With whom did David then make friendly alliance?

STORY 92

JERUSALEM MADE THE CENTER OF WORSHIP

2 SAMUEL 6; 1 CHRON-
ICLES 13:15-16
 In setting up the new kingdom of Is'ra-el under Da'vid, strong efforts were made by both king and people to model the government after the pattern which God had revealed to Mo'ses, and the position of the king as head of the religious life of the nation was fully recognized. The relationship of the king to the people was given a new development by the thought that his chief duties were those of a shepherd to his flock. Henceforth the king was not to make use of his office and his people for the accomplishment of selfish purposes, but his life was to be consecrated to the civil, moral, and spiritual welfare of his subjects.

It was God's will to make Is'ra-el a great nation without letting the people forget that He was still their chief ruler. For this reason the head of the civil government was also to be the representative of God in the religious life of the people. The chief reason for Saul's miserable failure had been his rejection of God's will and the ideal which should prevail in all true worship.

Da'vid had been faithful to this ideal in his limited authority by setting up a center of worship at He'bron, and in maintaining the High Priest A-bi'a-thar as an officer in his government. When the twelve tribes were united in a central government with headquarters at Je-ru'sa-lem, he planned at once to make this city the center of He'brew worship. One of the first steps taken in carrying out this purpose was the removal of the Ark of the Cov'e-nant to Je-ru'sa-lem. This was a strong testimony of Da'vid's faith in God, and a call to Is'ra-el to restore the God of their fathers to His rightful place in their national life, thus providing a secure foundation upon which to build their future national unity.

In planning to make Je-ru'sa-lem the religious center of the nation, Da'vid did not stubbornly insist on having his own way. He called together representatives of all the tribes of Is'ra-el, consulted with them, and acted only after their enthusiastic agreement. Before establishing a central place of worship he asked "if it seemed good to them," and did not

DAVID DANCES BEFORE THE ARK

carry out this plan until assured that "it was of the Lord."

The people did more than merely agree to Da'vid's suggestions; they joined wholeheartedly in the movement, determined to restore the religious life which had been neglected during the reign of Saul, and resolved to establish one great center of worship as formerly commanded by the Lord. Da'vid arranged the priests and Le'vites in regular order for the services of the Lord's house, reorganized the worship of the nation, and gave an important place to music in Divine services,

It was then decided that the Ark of the Cov'e-nant, which had been Divinely appointed as the symbol of God's presence among his people, should be set up in the house of the Lord in the royal city. The sacred chest had been completely ignored by Saul, and was probably almost forgotten by thousands of the Is'ra-el-ites. It had rested in the house of A-bin'a-dab in the town of Kir-jath-Je'a-rim, on the border between Ju'dah and Ben'ja-min eight miles west of Je-ru'sa-lem, for about seventy years.

As we learned in previous chapters, the Ark had been captured by the Phi-lis'tines in the days of Sam'u-el, then returned to the Is'ra-el-ites because of the terrible calamities which it brought to its heathen captors. Since the tabernacle at Shiloh had fallen into disuse, the Ark was placed for safe keeping in the home of A-bin'a-dab. There it had remained during the twenty years which elapsed before Saul became king, for the forty years of his reign, and from the time of Saul's death until Da'vid made this change.

A procession made up of a military force of thirty thousand men and representatives of all the tribes, led by Da'vid himself, marched off to attend the removal of the Ark to Je-ru'sa-lem. Da'vid had a new cart made to carry the Ark; this was against the Lord's command, but was probably done in a thoughtless, impulsive moment. The entire procedure was moved by love to the Lord, a sincere desire to restore the appointed worship of God, and reverence for the symbol of God's presence among His people, but we shall find that the performance of a worthy deed in a manner contrary to the expressed will of God resulted in a great calamity.

Upon reaching the home of A-bin'a-dab, Da'vid had the Ark placed on the new cart, and the procession started on the journey back to Je-ru'sa-lem with the priests in charge of the Ark leading the way. As the procession moved along the highway there was great rejoicing, with music from various instruments, joyful singing, and religious dancing. The entire company was filled with unrestrained happiness. Suddenly the joy of the festival was turned into great sorrow and superstitious fear.

The Lord was not pleased with the substitution of cattle for the priestly hands which should have carried the Ark; there were no sacrificial offerings, and the worship which did take place was more selfish than spiritual. The breaking of one law led to another violation which was more serious; as the cart passed over the rough road the Ark was so tossed about that it seemed likely to fall, and one of the company tried to steady it. This man, whose name was Uz'zah, suddenly dropped dead, and panic spread through the entire procession.

Da'vid was greatly alarmed by the death of Uz'zah, and dreaded the further displeasure of God if the march was continued. He may have remembered that the Ark was to be carried only by appointed Le'vites, that no unconsecrated hands were to touch it, and that all acts in service of the Lord must be performed according to His own directions.

As a result of this tragic judgment upon the sin of Da'vid and his servant, the Ark was placed in the home of a priestly family by the name of O-bed-e'dom, where it was left for three months. Then Da'vid assembled another company, but this time he had the Ark carried by the priests who were specially appointed for this duty. The procession played upon musical instruments, sang hymns of joy, and danced as they had done at the beginning of the previous march. Da'vid himself laid aside his royal robes and took an active part in the celebration. The Ark was joyfully carried into the city of Je-ru'sa-lem and placed in a tent which Da'vid had made ready as a place of worship. Sacrifices were offered to the Lord at certain intervals on the march to Je-ru'sa-lem, and prolonged ceremonies were observed after the Ark had been placed in its new stronghold.

The final triumphant removal of the Ark to Je-ru'sa-lem was not, however, without an unhappy incident. Da'vid's wife Mi'chal, who should have led the women in their part in the celebration, looked out from a window of the palace with unfriendly eyes. To her, the joy of Da'vid was like the excitement of a madman, and his demonstrations of deep feeling were foolish and degrading. She reproved him sharply for taking off his royal robes and wearing the white garments of those who were celebrating, and for his dancing in the streets of the capital. Da'vid answered these reproaches by the statement that he was dancing to the Lord, and that he would continue to return thanks for the distinction and blessings given through God's favor.

The inaugural service held in the tent prepared for the Ark was one of the grandest of its kind in the history of Is'ra-el. Burnt offerings were made for the sins of the people, peace offerings were given in thanks

A STREET IN MODERN JERUSALEM

for God's favors, and the Le-vit'i-cal service of song was introduced. Da'vid pronounced a special benediction upon the people, and generous amounts of bread, meat, and wine were given to them. A song of thanksgiving composed by Da'vid especially for this occasion was sung by all the people.

This Psalm represented a form of service to be rendered in the restoration of tabernacle worship, celebrated the redemption which had been unfolded in the history of Is'ra-el, called for wholehearted praises to the Lord, and presented the love of God as the foundation for all true worship. This code of worship was embodied, with slight variations, in several of the Psalms which were later composed for use in the worship of God. The Lord's majesty and power over all the nations of the earth was gloriously set forth, and the ultimate conquest of the world by the Sav'ior was beautifully foretold.

> "The truth that Da'vid learned to sing,
> Its deep fulfillment here attains,
> 'Tell all the earth the Lord is king!
> Lo, from the cross a King he reigns!' "

SUGGESTIONS FOR STUDY

Biblical Index to Helpful References

The Advantages of Recognizing Leaders. (1 Chron. 15:25; 26:26; 28:1.)

David's Sleepless Concern for a Resting Place for the Ark. (Ps. 132:4, 5.)

Commendable Zeal for the House of God. (Isa. 62:1; Jer. 20:9; John 2:17.)

Celebrations in Music and Dancing. (Ex. 15:20; Jgs. 11:34.)

Rules for Carrying the Ark. (Ex. 25:14, 15; Num. 4:15.)

Required Consecration in Removal of Ark. (Lev. 10:3; 1 Chr. 15:12.)

The Abomination of Religious Services Performed in the Wrong Manner. (Prov. 21:4; Hos. 7:14; 1 Cor. 11:20.)

Psalms Probably Used in This Festival. (14; 15; 24; 29; 30; 68; 132; 141.)

Obed a Door-keeper in the Lord's House. (1 Chr. 15:18; 16:5.)

Questions

1. What was given first place by David in setting up his government?

2. What was in the mind of God in changing Israel to a monarchy?

3. With whom did David confer in his plans for religious interests?

4. Where had the Ark of the covenant been for seventy years?

5. How had this sacred vessel of the Lord been regarded by Saul?

6. Tell of the procession organized by David for the removal of the Ark.

7. What Divine order did he violate?

8. What happened as a result of this irreverence?

9. Where was the Ark left after Uzza dropped dead from touching it?

10. Tell of the second effort to remove the Ark.

11. Tell of the gorgeous celebrations by David and the people.

12. What criticism did Michal make of David's conduct? Why?

STORY 93

THE LORD REFUSES TO LET DAVID BUILD A TEMPLE OF WORSHIP

2 SAMUEL 7;
1 CHRONICLES 17

As Da'vid enjoyed a brief respite from war amid the peaceful delights of the magnificent palace which he had built in Je-ru'sa-lem, there came into his heart a burning desire to build for the Lord a more spacious and elegant structure.

Da'vid made known his desire to build a house for the Lord to Na'than, a young prophet whose name first appears in the Scriptures at this time, and who later became closely associated with the king and his family. Na'than heartily praised the king for his noble impulse, encouraged him in the desire to bring his own people and the surrounding nations into closer relation with the God of Is'ra-el, and advised him to do whatever was in his heart. The prophet gave this advice, however, without consulting the Lord, and that night he was told in a vision that God did not wish a new temple to be built at that time.

The Lord's refusal to let Da'vid build the house later erected by Sol'o-mon was not based upon any unfitness of Da'vid, nor did He reject the holy impulse of the king. The Lord said, "It is good that this desire is in Da'vid's heart," but the time was not ripe for the construction of such a building. Neither the political nor religious condition of Is'ra-el was ready for such a development.

In refusing Da'vid's proposal, the Lord gave him much more than he had asked. He assured him that his kingdom would endure, promised him a son who would erect the temple which he desired to build, and foretold the elevation of a descendant of his line to the throne of an everlasting and universal dominion. Through the reign of this descendant, who would be called the Son of God, it was promised that all the families of the earth should be included in the Mes-si'an-ic blessings.

The Lord gave to Na'than in a prophetic vision a dim outline of a kingdom far more glorious than that of Da'vid. He revealed to him that Da'vid's descendant, who was also Da'vid's Lord, would establish his house forever; that the honor which Da'vid had earned because of the great national blessings brought about through his splendid rule would be far exceeded by his Mes-si'an-ic heir, and that the reign of the Mes-si'ah over a great spiritual kingdom would bring salvation to all the world. The glorious truth of this vision was later revealed more clearly to Da'vid, and he made it the theme of some of his most beautiful Psalms:

"Je-ho'vah saith unto my Lord, Sit thou at my right hand,
Until I make thine enemies thy footstool.
Je-ho'vah will send forth the rod of thy strength out of Zi'on;
Rule thou in the midst of thine enemies.
Thy people offer themselves willingly
In the day of thy power, in holy array.
Je-ho'vah hath sworn, and will not repent:
Thou art a priest forever
After the order of Mel-chiz'e-dek."

To Da'vid's son Sol'o-mon was given Divine inspiration for the utterance of similar truths in some of the Psalms which he wrote; among the most striking lines are these:

"Yea, all kings shall fall down before him;
All nations shall serve him;

DAVID'S GATE ON MT. ZION

For he will deliver the needy when he crieth,
And the poor that hath no helper."

"He will have pity on the poor and needy,
And the souls of the needy he will save.
He will redeem their soul from oppression and violence;
And precious will their blood be in his sight:
And they shall live; and to him shall be given of the gold of Sheba:
And men shall pray for him continually;
They shall bless him all the day long."

"His name shall endure forever;
His name shall be continued as long as the sun:
And men shall be blessed in him;
All nations shall call him happy."

Eager as Da'vid was to build a house for the Lord, his disappointment at the Lord's refusal was completely overcome by his joy in the promise of greater blessings. He received the vision of Na'than with wonder and deep gratitude. The promise of God's favor in years to come was accepted in a spirit of humility and adoration for the greatness and goodness of God.

SUGGESTIONS FOR STUDY

Biblical Index to Helpful References

God's Ancient Prophecy of a Central House of Worship. (Deut. 12:10, 11.)

The Lord's Reason for Refusing David's Request. (1 Chr. 22:8; 28:3; 1 Ki. 5:3.)

David's Spirit of Humility. (Ps. 8:4, 5; 144:3)

God's Covenant with David for Perpetuity of His Kingdom. (2 Sam. 23:5; Ps. 89: 28, 29.)

Nathan's Services for David. (2 Sam. 12:1, 7; 1 Ki. 1:10, 32.)

Nathan Author of Lost Book. (1 Chr. 29:29.)

Messianic Prophecies. (Gen. 49:10; Num. 24:17, 19; 1 Chr. 28:1.)

A Messianic Psalm of David. (Ps. 110.)

A Messianic Psalm of Solomon. (Ps. 72.)

The Fulfillment of These Prophecies. (Luke 2:33.)

Questions

1. What prompted David in his desire to build a house for God?

2. To whom did he make known this desire? What did he reply at first?

3. Why did he afterwards change his advice?

4. Why was David not permitted to build a house for God?

5. What revelation did the Lord make to Nathan concerning a future kingdom?

6. Did David utter any prophecies concerning the Messianic kingdom?

7. How did David accept God's refusal to allow him to build the temple?

DAVID SHOWS KINDNESS TO JOHNATHAN'S CRIPPLED SON

2 SAMUEL 9

Da'vid was often troubled in mind by the tragedies which befell the house of Saul, even though they brought him to the throne of Is'ra-el. The death of Saul brought deep sorrow to his heart, and he mourned the loss of his friend Jon'a-than in the battle with the Phi-lis'tines. No vengeance was ever shown by Da'vid toward Ish-bo'sheth and Ab'ner for the revolt which they had led against his enthronement at He'bron. Their tragic deaths were a source of pain to him. The embarrassing situation in which he was placed during the seven years of his reign at He'bron, however, prevented any investigation concerning possible surviving members of Saul's family, and after he was made king of the entire nation his energies were so occupied with foreign wars that no thought could be given to such matters. When he was firmly established in Je-ru'sa-lem as the new capital, however, he resolved to find out who was left of Saul's family, and to show them kindness in the name of the Lord.

It was discovered that a son of Jon'a-than called Me-phib'o-sheth was living in seclusion at Lo-de'bar, far away on the east side of the Jor'dan. At the time of Jon'a-than's death he was a lad of five, and had been crippled for life by being dropped by his nurse. He had grown to full manhood and was married, but had remained in obscurity. This was no doubt a result of his unwillingness to appear as a rival of Da'vid for the throne of Is'ra-el, or because of the infirmity which had made him lame in both legs.

Me-phib'o-sheth was living in the home of Ma'chir, a man of position and wealth. Da'vid had him brought to the palace at once, and the lame man fell on his face before the king in fear. He was awed by the splendor of the king's palace and embarrassed by the great kindness shown to him. David said to him:

> "Fear not; for I will surely show thee kindness for Jon'a-than thy Father's sake, and I will restore thee all the land of Saul thy grandfather; and thou shall eat bread at my table continually."

Due to his deformity and long years of residence in an obscure country, Me-phib'o-sheth had become exceedingly bashful, and felt unworthy of the high honor of a place in the king's home. He was grateful for the kind offer of Da'vid, but his answer was full of humility. Da'vid proceeded at once, however, to arrange for his removal to his own home, and directed that the entire landed estate of Saul be turned over to Jon'a-than's son who was the only surviving heir.

The lands formerly owned by Saul had passed to the crown, and were then in charge of Zi'ba, one of Saul's former servants. Da'vid appointed him as an overseer under the command of Me-phib'o-sheth; directing him to cultivate the soil and to care for the herds and flocks, with instructions that all profits be used for the support of Me-phib'o-sheth's family. Zi'ba had fifteen sons and twenty servants, and· all these were employed in caring for Me-phib'o-sheth's property and in attending to his wants.

It was indeed a very noble act of Da'vid to remember the covenant made with Jon'a-than when they were close friends, and to show respect for his dead friend by kindness to his crippled son. His friend's death was not used as an excuse for neglecting the repayment of his debt of gratitude. Jon'a-than could not be next to him in the rule of Is'ra-el, but his son, who was unable to perform any active service in the king's court, could enjoy the hospitality of his table.

SUGGESTIONS FOR STUDY

Biblical Index to Helpful References

Covenant Between David and Jonathan. (1 Sam. 20:14-17.)

Mephibosheth's Injury at the Age of Five. (2 Sam. 4:4.)

Kindness to the Living in Memory of the Dead. (Ruth 2:11-17.)

The Character of True Friendship. (Prov. 17:17; 2 Tim. 1:16.)

Advantages of Having the King's Favor. (Prov. 16:15; 19:12.)

Characters of Real Worth Humble in Estimation of self. (Prov. 30:2; 1 Cor. 15:9.)

Questions

1. Describe David's feelings toward the house of Saul.

2. Tell of the discovery of Mephibosheth and of his unfortunate condition.

3. Whose son was Mephibosheth? Why was David under special obligation to care for him?

4. What did David do for Mephibosheth?

5. Describe the spirit of Mephibosheth in accepting these favors.

6. What do you think of the spirit of David in this act?

STORY 95

DAVID'S GRAVEST ERROR, HIS PENITENCE AND FORGIVENESS

2 SAMUEL 11, 12:1-23;
Psalms 51   The incidents reported in this chapter took place in the private life of Da'vid while Jo'ab was leading a part of the armies of Is'ra-el in an attack upon the Am'mon-ites' royal city of Rab'-bah. Contrary to his usual practice, Da'vid had remained in the capital when his armies were engaged in a crucial war with foreign enemies. After taking his noon-day rest one day, he strolled out on the roof of the palace. This was a custom of the people in that country, and such time was usually spent in religious meditation. Da'vid seems however, to have been in a restless mood, and, instead of praying, let his thoughts wander into paths of evil. Had he followed the counsel of one of his own Psalms, in which he asked the Lord to "Turn away mine eyes from beholding vanity," a great temptation and a great sin would have been avoided.

It appears that Da'vid was attacked by Satan in an unguarded moment. His mind was filled with thoughts of recent victories and the increasing prosperity of his kingdom, his standards of conduct were lowered by a state of ease and idleness, and his heart was led astray by selfish pride and sinful desire. Glancing about into the court-yards of neighboring homes, he saw a very beautiful woman, and fell in love with her without giving a thought to the fact that she might already be the wife of another man.

In those days it was not considered wrong for a man to have more than one wife. Da'vid had already married several times, and was the father of a number of children. In this defiance of God's law which provided that a man should have only one wife, Da'vid had so weakened the voice of conscience that he now felt free to claim the woman who had attracted him. He soon learned that her name was Bath-she'ba, and that she was the wife of a man named U-ri'ah, who was one of the valiant men in Jo'ab's army.

Had Da'vid possessed the self-control and sense of God's presence which had previously guided him, he would have instantly dismissed the thought of taking Bath-she'ba as his wife. Unfortunately, however, he yielded to the impulse of the moment, took unfair advantage of his power as king, and sent messengers to bring the beautiful woman to his palace. Had Bath-she'ba been faithful to her marriage vows, she would have refused such a summons, even from the king.

When the wrong committed by Da'vid had advanced to a stage beyond repair, his error gave rise to still greater sins. His first move was to order U-ri'ah to return home from the army on a furlough. U-ri'ah felt that it was not right for him to enjoy the comforts and security of home while the armies of Is'ra-el were engaged in an important battle at Rab'bah, so he insisted that he be returned to his duties at once. Da'vid then sent a message to Jo'ab, commanding him to place U-ri'ah in a dangerous position when the army made an attack upon the walls of the Am'mon-ite city. Jo'ab carried out this order, and U-ri'ah died in battle. The news of his death was brought to Da'vid by special messengers, and no word of reproach was spoken by the king for the death of other brave soldiers who had been sacrificed by Jo'ab in bringing the end of Da'vid's rival.

Bath-she'ba spent the customary time in mourning after learning of the death of her husband, then Da'vid hastened to make her his wife. Two grievous wrongs had been committed, however, and dire suffering was in store for the king who had become a weakling when faced by a temptation which might easily have been avoided. In the course of time a son was born to Da'vid and Bath-she'ba, and the child was greatly loved by its father. Up to this time Da'vid seems to have kept his wrong as a secret in his own heart and that of the wife whom he had cowardly taken from a loyal soldier, but there had been long hours of heartaches and pangs of conscience. For months Da'vid suffered constant unrest in his heart as he tried to conceal his wrong-doing. He later described this unbearable anguish of soul in these pathetic words:

"When I kept silence, my bones wasted away
Through my groaning all the day long.
For day and night thy hand was heavy upon me:
My moisture was changed as with the drought of summer."

During these trying days he probably hid the great evil which he had done from most of the people, but it was an open sore upon his conscience, and could not be concealed from the all-seeing eye of God. The Lord was greatly displeased by such unworthy conduct, and took a course which soon forced Da'vid to admit his great sin and seek forgiveness.

A few days after the birth of Bath-she'ba's child, the prophet Na'than, who was a close friend of the king and a man of unquestioned honesty, came to the king for a private interview. Na'than pretended to be seeking the king's judgment upon a certain evil-doer among his subjects, but in reality he had been sent by the Lorld to open Da'vid's conscience to a still deeper sense of the terrible wrongs which he had committed; and to lead him into a genuine state of repentance. This was no easy task. It is one thing to rebuke a man plainly for his errors, and another to arouse his conscience so gently and lovingly that he will repent. Na'than, however, was given Divine wisdom for the unpleasant duty assigned to him. He began by telling an imaginary story with such feeling that the king thought it had actually taken place. Na'than said:

"There were two men in one city; the one rich, and the other poor. The rich man had a large number of flocks and herds; but the poor man had nothing, save one little ewe lamb, which he had bought and nourished. It grew up together with him and his children; and he fed it morsels from his own food, and gave it drink from his own cup. He carried it in his bosom as though it was his precious daughter. One

DAVID SEES BATH-SHEBA BATHING

day there came a traveller to the rich man, and instead of taking from his own flocks and herds to provide food for the wayfarer, he took the poor man's lamb, killed it, and dressed it for his visitor."

Na'than then paused, waiting for the response of Da'vid. The king was enraged by the injustice and cruelty of the rich man in Na'than's story, and sternly declared:

"In the name of the living God, the man who has done this wicked thing shall surely die; and he shall restore the lamb fourfold."

Given courage by the Spirit of God, Na'than looked Da'vid squarely in the eyes and said, "Thou art the man." The king had unwittingly passed judgment upon his own cruel act, the sword of just anger had been thrust into his own heart, and he stood convicted at the judgment bar of his own conscience and before God.

Na'than then went on to give a complete account of the wrongs which Da'vid had committed, wrongs which he thought no one knew but himself. With heart-searching directness he pointed out to Da'vid how the rich man's plenty was a striking picture of his own abundance, while the poor man's one ewe lamb was an equally striking picture of U-ri'ah's poverty. Then the prophet said, "Even though you have many wives, like the rich man who took the one lamb of the poor man, you have taken the one wife of U-ri'ah. You have added to the injustice of this deed by having a noble soldier murdered at the post of duty in an effort to cover up your sin."

The favors and mercies which God had given so freely to Da'vid were reviewed by the prophet, the unpardonable nature of his sin was clearly set forth, and the stern judgments of God were solemnly pronounced upon the king. Da'vid bowed his head in deep sorrow, confessing that he had not only wronged U-ri'ah, but had sinned against the Lord by bringing shame upon His cause before the world. He poured out his heart in tears of penitence, confessions of guilt, and earnest prayers for pardon and restoration to God's favor.

These confessions of guilt and prayers of the broken hearted king were accepted by the Lord, and the prophet said to him: "The Lord hath put away thy sin; thou shalt not die. Howbeit, because by this deed thou hast given great occasion to the enemies of the Lord to blaspheme, the child that Bath-she'ba hath born unto these shall surely die."

On returning to his home, Da'vid found his new born child dangerously ill. For a week it lay between life and death while Da'vid earnestly prayed to the Lord for mercy; wracked with the pangs of genuine love for his little son, and with a deep sense of guilt, he would neither take food nor talk with any one for seven days. On the seventh day the child passed away, and the servants of the king feared to tell him, lest his grief be too much to bear. Noting the whisperings among those who had cared for the child, Da'vid asked, "Is the child dead?" Then they told him the sad news.

To the amazement of his friends, Da'vid arose from his prostration, asking that food be prepared for him. He explained his strange actions by telling those about him that while the child lived, there was hope and the need for prayer and fasting; now that there was no hope, he must submit to the will of God and accept the sorrow as a Divine punishment. With heroic faith in the will of God he uttered these memorable words: "I shall go to him, but he shall not return to me."

SUGGESTIONS FOR STUDY

Biblical Index to Helpful References

The Hittites in the Land of Canaan. (Gen. 15:20; 23:7.)

The Mosaic Law Against Unchastity. (Ex. 20:14.)

God's Warnings Against Lustful Passions. (Prov. 6:25; Matt. 5:28.)

The Duty of Restraining Evil Passions. (Rom. 13:14; 1 Cor. 9:27.)

The Duty of Self-Control. (Rom. 6:12; 1 Cor. 6:12.)

Secret Sins Known by God. (Job 24:15, 16; Ps. 19:12; 90.8; Isa. 29:15.)

Courage in Rebuking Evil Doers. (1 Ki. 21:20; 22:14.)

God's Punishment of His Own Children for Wrong Doing. (Ps. 2:5; 60:1; Amos 3:3.)

Promise of Forgiveness to Penitent Confessors. (1 Jno. 1:9; Ps. 130:4.)

Questions

1. Tell of the circumstances under which David fell in love with Bathsheba?

2. What prayer did he fail to offer which he afterwards prayed?

3. On the discovery that Bathsheba was married what should David have done?

4. Instead of doing this, what did he do?

5. How did David feel while refusing to confess his wrong?

6. Who went to David to rebuke him for his wrong?

7. In what way did he force David to pass judgment on his own sin?

8. Relate this parable.

9. Tell of David's repentance.

10. Tell of the illness of David's baby and of his prayer and fasting.

11. Describe David's conduct after the death of the baby.

STORY 96

TROUBLES IN THE KING'S HOUSEHOLD, THE REBELLION OF ABSALOM

2 SAMUEL 13-15:1-18

In pronouncing judgment upon Da'vid for his sins, Na'than predicted many other sorrows in addition to the loss of Bath-she'ba's son. Although the Lord had forgiven him, and his sin had been put away, it was predicted that certain natural evils would follow, bringing severe trials and much sorrow to the heart of the king. Repentance for sin and Divine forgiveness often fail to remove the shameful stains on the character of an evil doer, or to prevent the natural train of evils which follow in the wake of criminal conduct. This is exactly what happened in the life of Da'vid.

In close succession came one unhappy incident after another in a chain of events which ended in the rebellion and death of Da'vid's favorite son Ab'sa-lom. The trouble began with his eldest son Am'non, whose mother was not of noble Is'ra-el-it-ish blood. He fell in love with his half-sister Ta'mar, who was a full sister of Ab'sa-lom. Following a scheme suggested by his cousin Jon'a-dab, Am'non pretended to be ill and asked his father to send Ta'mar to prepare food for him. Knowing nothing of the evil intentions of Am'non, Da'vid granted the request. When Am'non tried to press his unwelcome attentions upon Ta'mar, she did everything possible to prevent his act of folly. Her efforts were unsuccessful, however, and Am'non's conduct toward her became base and brutal. He then turned against her with hatred, forcing her to leave in shame and under grave reproach.

Ta'mar went to the home of her brother Ab'sa-lom with the sad report concerning Am'non, and he resolved to avenge the wrong committed against his sister. It was a custom in those days for brothers to safeguard the honor of their sisters, and to avenge all acts which injured their reputation.

When the unworthy conduct of Am'non was reported to Da'vid, the king was greatly angered, but did nothing whatever about it. In his love for his children he was often too lenient toward their wrong-doing, and in this matter he may have been haunted by the memory of his own recent unlawful behavior in taking Bath-she'ba as a wife. The entire matter seems to have been dropped without any punishment being inflicted upon Am'non for his wicked deed.

Ab'sa-lom did not forget the wrong which had been done his sister. Though he said nothing about it, he was deeply wounded by the weak manner in which his father passed over the sin of Am'non. For two full years he awaited an opportunity to carry out the vengeance which he cherished in his heart. Then he planned a feast for the time of sheepshearing, and invited his father and all his brothers to attend, making sure that Am'non would be present. When the festivities had reached their highest point, he commanded his servants to slay Am'non. Panic broke out among those who were present, and Ab'sa-lom's surviving brothers leaped to their horses and rode away as fast as they could. News of the incident spread rapidly, and someone told Da'vid that Ab'sa-lom had slain all of his brothers. Later Da'vid learned that only Am'non was dead, for it was against him alone that Ab'sa-lom had cherished the thought of revenge for two years.

Ab'sa-lom then became an exile in the land of Ge'shur, where he remained for three years before being permitted to return to his native land.

ABSALOM CAUSES AMNON TO BE SLAIN

In the meantime Da'vid missed him more than he did Am'non, and gradually was moved to forgive the violent manner in which Ab'sa-lom had sought to avenge the wrong which had been done to his sister.

These tragedies brought increasing sadness into the life of Da'vid, and his heart was greatly depressed. His deepest feelings were torn in two directions; swayed one day by grief over the death of Am'non, and at other times by a feeling of vengeance toward Ab'sa-lom for slaying his own brother. Most of all, however, Da'vid was moved by love for his exiled son. Hoping to relieve the distress of his king, and at the same time to retain the good will of Ab'sa-lom, who was heir to the throne, Jo'ab devised a clever scheme to have the king grant permission for the return of his wayward son. He selected a shrewd woman of Te-ko'ah to visit the king, clothed in mourning and pretending great sorrow. The plan which Jo'ab taught her to employ with Da'vid may be described as follows:

> "I am indeed a widow, for my husband is dead. I had two sons who quarreled one day in the field, and one of them killed the other in the heat of his anger. All my kindred have risen against me, and are seeking to have the avengers of blood, according to an ancient law in Is'ra-el, slay my son who is now in hiding. Should he be slain, the only heir to my husband will be taken away, and there will be none to carry on the family. I plead with these, O king, do not allow the avengers of blood to slay my only son."

Just as Jo'ab had hoped, the heart of Da'vid was deeply touched by the story of this woman, and he promised to protect her son. "In the name of the living God," said Da'vid, "not one hair of his head shall be permitted to fall to the ground."

Then the woman proceeded at once to deliver the speech which Jo'ab had prepared for her: "You, O king, are doing the very thing which the avengers of blood are threatening to do to my son. The mercy which you have proposed for a stranger should be extended to your own son, who is in exile, and who lives in daily fear of your revenge." Then she went on to remind Da'vid of the shortness and uncertainty of human life, and of the folly of holding in his heart a grudge against the present heir to the throne. Becoming more eloquent and personal in her appeal, she said, "We must needs die, and are as water spilt upon the ground which cannot be gathered up again. God will not fail to show mercy to one who deviseth means that his banished be not exiled from him."

The justice and righteousness of this speech moved the heart of Da'vid to sympathy. He understood the purpose of the woman's visit, and suspected that it was part of Jo'ab's plan to soften his attitude toward Ab'sa-lom, yet he was so deeply affected by the tale that he gave orders for Jo'ab to bring Ab'sa-lom back to Je-ru'sa-lem at once.

When Jo'ab obeyed his master's orders and brought the exile back to the capital, Da'vid refused to let his own son come into his presence, and directed that he should be sent to live in a place outside the palace. For two years Ab'sa-lom lived in his own house in Je-ru'sa-lem, and was denied all the privileges of the king's court. However, he was winning his way into the hearts of the people, for he was a handsome, attractive man with many winning ways, and was always able to make friends.

Before long the continued refusal of Da'vid to admit him to his presence became unbearable to the spirit of the young prince, and he resolved to have Jo'ab take him before the king. He sent for Jo'ab on two different occasions, but each time there was no response. Then he had his servants set fire to a field of ripening barley near his home which belonged to Jo'ab. When Jo'ab came to ask why he had done this, he told the general of his wish to appear before the king at once, declaring that he should have preferred to remain in exile in a foreign country rather than to be ignored by his own father.

Jo'ab then made another plea to the king in behalf of Ab'sa-lom, and this time succeeded in bringing about what appeared to be a complete renewal of friendly relations between father and son. When Da'vid looked upon the face of the son who had once been his favorite, but had been exiled for five years under the curse of his wrath, he kissed him tenderly as a sign of forgiveness. Ab'sa-lom was given a place in the royal court, and Da'vid's feeling toward him became as kindly and indulgent as his former attitude had been severe and unforgiving.

Ab'sa-lom became the proud owner of many horses and chariots, lived in royal style, and set himself up as a great man. He also stooped to crafty ways of making himself popular at the expense of his father. Standing in the gates of the royal court, he whispered against the king, saying that not enough judges had been provided to hear the grievances of the people, and declaring that if he were in authority their interests would be given better care. He pretended to have deep affection for all the people with whom he talked, taking them into his arms and kissing

them. By this shrewd, deceitful practice he "stole the hearts
of the men of Is'ra-el."

This went on for four years
without the slightest suspicion
on the part of Da'vid that his
son was scheming to seize the
throne of Is'ra-el. Little did the
king think that for nearly ten
years the heart of his son had
been filled with a burning desire to take the place of his
father. When the time seemed
ripe for carrying out his plan,
Ab'sa-lom asked his father for
permission to go up to He'bron
to fulfill a vow which he said
he had made to the Lord while
in Ge'shur. The baseness of his
revolt was made even worse by
this pretense of religious duty.
Once he had decided to strike
openly for the throne, no means
was too low to be used in gaining his purpose.

Da'vid was easily deceived by
the pretended religious purpose

ABSALOM

of Ab'sa-lom, and was delighted by the thought that he wished to perform
special worship in the sacred city of his fathers. But no sooner had Ab'sa-
lom been granted the favor which he sought, than he organized a group of
his friends into a revolution against David. Spies were sent throughout
all Is'ra-el to inform those who had been won to Ab'sa-lom's scheme to be
ready for the sudden announcement of civil war. A-hith'o-phel, who had
been one of Da'vid's most trusted advisers, joined Ab'sa-lom at He'bron
to help in planning the revolution. Many people who were admirers of
the young prince, but ignorant of his intended revolt against Da'vid, were
swept into Ab'sa-lom's marching armies by the excitement. Before long
it looked as though the entire country had risen in revolt against Da'vid,

and it was proclaimed throughout the land that Ab'sa-lom had been made king at He'bron.

Thousands of Is'ra-el-ites renounced their allegiance to Da'vid to follow one who was in all respects his inferior, and who had no worthy claims on their support. How severely this must have pained the heart of the aging king whose rule had been productive of great good to the nation. But by far the greatest aggravation of Da'vid's trials must have been in the consciousness that he had brought them upon himself by failing to order his household in accordance with the will of God.

When Da'vid learned that Ab'sa-lom was leading a revolution, and that he was followed by A-hith'o-phel and other trusted servants of the king, he was panic-stricken. For several years he had lived in seclusion in his palace, and was not well informed on what had been happening. He had fully trusted Ab'sa-lom after restoring him to the privileges of the royal court, and had never dreamed that he would treacherously turn against his father. Within a few hours Da'vid gathered his valiant men, left ten servants in charge of the palace, and fled toward the wilderness of Ju'dah with all the other members of the royal household. There followed a bitter civil war in which Ab'sa-lom was slain by Jo'ab.

SUGGESTIONS FOR STUDY

Biblical Index to Helpful References

Absalom the Son of an Alien Woman. (2 Sam. 3:3.)

The peril of Following Evil Counsel. (Num. 31:16; Job 2:9.)

The Evil of Deception. (1 Ki. 13:18; 2 Ki. 6:19.)

Warnings Against Evil Passions. (Gal. 5:24; 1 Thess. 4:5.)

Examples of Fratricide. (Gen. 4:8; 2 Chr. 21:4.)

God's Law Concerning the Treatment of Fugitives. (Deut. 23:15.)

Other Examples of Fugitives. (1 Ki. 11:40; Matt. 2:13.)

Examples of Revenge. (1 Ki. 19:2; Matt. 14:8.)

The Danger of Unholy Ambition. (Luke 22:24.).

Questions

1. With whom did Amnon fall in love? Was it wrong for him to marry her?

2. What scheme did he adopt to have Tamar visit him?

3. Name Tamar's full brother who was also guardian of her honor?

4. When Tamar told him of Amnon's unbecoming conduct what did he resolve to do?

5. Tell how Absalom schemed the slaying of Amnon?

6. Where did Absalom then go? Would his father allow him to return home?

7. What scheme did Joab use to secure David's permission for Absalom's return home?

8. Did David restore Absalom to his rights as a prince?

9. What scheme did Absalom then take to secure further help from Joab?

10. How did Absalom conduct himself after being restored to the king's favor?

11. Tell of Absalom's revolt and conspiracy against his father.

STORY 97

SHEBA'S REVOLT—ATONEMENT TO GIBEONITES

2 SAMUEL 20, 21

Da'vid's trials were by no means ended on the death of Ab'sa-lom. Jealousy broke out at once between the northern and southern tribes because of the greater honor given to Ju'dah in restoring Da'vid. She'ba, loyal to the memory of Saul and ambitious for personal advancement, made use of this rivalry to plot another revolution. He led a large company into the mountain cities of E'phra-im with the hope of setting up a new kingdom. Da'vid ordered his new commander Am'a-sa to summon volunteers from Ju'dah to meet this revolt, but the response was so slow that he commanded Ab'i-shai to lead the army stationed at Je-ru'sa-lem in an immediate attack on She'ba.

Jo'ab, who had been displaced as commander of Da'vid's armies, proved his loyalty to the king by going with Ab'i-shai. Upon reaching Gib'e-on they were joined by the soldiers which Am'a-sa had rallied. Jo'ab went to meet Am'a-sa with a sword hidden in his left hand, and put his rival to death. Taking charge of the combined armies, he then pursued She'ba to the town of A'bel.

The people of A'bel were probably ignorant of the revolt of She'ba, but were unwilling to protect him and his followers from Da'vid's armies; they did not wish their town to be destroyed by an invading army. A woman who was noted for her wisdom demanded an interview with Jo'ab before he began the siege. After learning of the character of She'ba and his revolt against Da'vid, she agreed to have him beheaded; and, in proof of the execution, delivered his head to Jo'ab. Jo'ab was then returned to the command of Is'ra-el's armies; though Da'vid did not approve of the manner in which Am'a-sa had been slain, it was necessary to have a fearless warrior at the head of his troops.

Some time after the defeat of She'ba, the land of Is'ra-el was visited by a terrible famine. After two years of want, Da'vid became greatly alarmed; there was a feeling that God had sent the drought in punishment of some sin for which proper atonement had not been made. The Lord then told Da'vid that the famine had been sent because of the crime which Saul had committed against the Gib'e-on-ites. When the cruel king had sought to destroy them, he had broken the covenant of friendship between Gib'e-on and Is'ra-el.

Da'vid then summoned the leaders of the Gib'e-on-ites asking what they would require in atonement for the crime of Saul. They replied that they sought no money, nor did they wish the Is'ra-el-ites to suffer for the sin of their former king. The request was made that seven descendants of the blood-guilty king be turned over to them for public execution in Saul's home town of Gib'e-ah. Accordingly Da'vid delivered to the Gib'e-on-ites two sons of Riz'pah, and five sons of Me'rab, who was one of Saul's daughters. These men were all hanged in the streets of Gib'e-ah. Me-phib-o-sheth, the son of Jon'a-than, was spared because of the covenant which Da'vid had made with his father.

The bodies of the executed men were left unburied until rain fell, in proof that full atonement had been made for Saul's crime. Riz'pah, the mother of two of these men, sat upon a rock near the bodies until the rains came, to see that they were not molested by carrion birds or wild beasts. When news of her devotion was brought to Da'vid, he graciously provided for the burial of all the victims. Their bodies, with those of Saul and Jon'a-than—which had been buried by the men of Ja-besh-Gil'e-ad in their own town—were given an honorable burial in the sepulcher of Saul's father Kish.

SUGGESTIONS FOR STUDY

Biblical Index to Helpful References

Famines Threatened Because of Sin. (Lev. 26:36; Jer. 14:16.)

Covenant Between the Gibeonites and Is-raelites. (Josh. 9:3-14.)

The Law of Blood-Avenge. (Deut. 19:11, 12.)

Expiation by Payment of Money Forbidden. (Num. 35:31.)

The Law of Retribution. (Ps. 34:14, 15; Heb. 10:30.)

Rizpah, Concubine of Saul. (2 Sam. 3:7.)

Merab, Wife of Adriel. (1 Sam. 18:19.)

Questions

1. What caused suffering and alarm to David after Sheba's death?

2. What did he think was the cause of the famine?

3. When he sought information from God what was he told?

4. Tell of the covenant between the Gibeonites and Israelites.

5 How had Saul violated this covenant?

6. What expiation did the Gibeonites ask of David?

7. Whose sons were given to meet this demand?

8. How did Rizpah show her grief and devotion to her sons?

9. What did David do when he learned of her noble vigil?

STORY 98

DAVID INSISTS UPON NUMBERING ISRAEL

2 SAMUEL 24;
1 CHRONICLES 21
An era of peace and prosperity had now come to the kingdom of Is'ra-el and Da'vid allowed his heart to be puffed up with pride. In a spirit of self-confidence he decided to make a boastful show of the glory of the nation. Partly to satisfy his own vanity, and partly to set forth Is'ra-el's claim to a place of superior rank among the nations, he ordered a complete census of all the people of the land. There was no good reason for taking a census at this time, as there had been on previous occasions when Mo'ses numbered the people, and Da'vid's motives were displeasing to God. He later confessed: "In my prosperity I said, I shall never be moved; thou didst hide thy face, and I was troubled."

Jo'ab protested that the census would endanger the nation and result in the judgment of God upon the king, but Da'vid would neither accept the advice of a friend nor seek the counsel of God. Nine months were required to complete the census. It was found that the population exceeded six millions, but this record was never included in the annals of the nation. The omission was probably due to the confusion which was caused by God's disapproval, and by the calamities which followed the taking of the census.

DAVID'S WELL

The results of the census were confusing to the nation and disappointing to Da'vid. To add to this unhappy outcome, the Lord announced through the prophet Gad a severe judgment upon Da'vid. The king was given his choice of three punishments: seven years of famine, three months of war, or three days of pestilence. Da'vid proved his love for the people by choosing the form of punishment which might be expected to strike him more severely than it would the nation. A great pestilence swept over the land, causing the death of seventy thousand persons in one day.

Breaking out at opposite ends of the country, the pestilence spread rapidly toward Je-ru'sa-lem. The Lord then mercifully commanded a pause before the city was smitten, and Da'vid saw an angel hovering over Je-ru'sa-lem with a drawn sword. Da'vid and the elders of Is'ra-el put on garments of sackcloth as a token of mourning, and bowed to the ground in earnest prayer to the Lord. Then Da'vid asked that the people be spared, and that the plague be caused to strike him and his family alone. In answer to this prayer the plague was halted.

The Lord then directed the prophet Gad to tell Da'vid to provide an altar on the highest point of the city, which place was a threshing floor then owned by a Jeb'u-site named Or'nan. An angel appeared at this site, which Or'nan offered to give for the building of an altar, and to provide both wood and an animal to be offered, as a burnt sacrifice. Da'vid insisted, however, on paying the full market price for the land.

An altar was built, and Da'vid made burnt offerings and peace offerings to the Lord. These offerings were accepted with the sign which the Lord had given when the Great Altar was set up at Si'nai in the days of Mo'ses: fire was sent from heaven to consume the offerings. The plague was then removed, and the city of Je-ru'sa-lem was spared. The place where the offerings had been made was set apart by the Lord as a center for true worship, and as the spot on which the temple was later built.

SUGGESTIONS FOR STUDY

Biblical Index to Helpful References

Previous Numberings of Israel. (Num. 1: 1-4; 26:2.)

The Curse of False Pride. (Prov. 11:2); 16:18.)

Examples of Kingly Pride. (2 Chr. 26:16; 32:25; Dan. 5:23.)

The Sin of Rejecting the Counsel of God. (2 Chr. 36:16; Psm. 50:17.)

Pestilence Sent by God Because of Sin. (Psm. 78:50; Amos 4:10.)

Angels of Wrath. (Gen. 19:1; 2 Chr. 32: 21.)

Judgments Removed Because of Penitence. (2 Ki. 22:19; Jonah 3:6-9.)

Sacrificial Offerings to the Lord. (Luke 21:4; 2 Cor. 8:3, 4.)

Questions

1. What prompted David to have Israel numbered?

2. Was there any reason why a census needed to be taken?

3. Who protested against this census?

4. How long was required for taking this census?

5. Were the results ever accurately tabulated? Why not?

6. What curse was sent upon the land for David's sin in this census?

7. How many people perished?

8. In what way did David cause the Lord to stay the pestilence?

9. Where did he build the altar for making sacrifices unto God?

10. What building was later erected on this spot?

DAVID PREPARES TO BUILD THE TEMPLE

1 CHRONICLES 22-29 The closing years of Da'vid's reign were
blessed with freedom from foreign wars. After the suppression of the
revolt of the northern tribes under She'ba, there were no serious problems
to be solved within the land. The king was free to give all his time and
energy to the domestic welfare of the nation.

Early in his reign Da'vid had expressed a strong desire to build a temple
in Je-ru'sa-lem, but had been told by a prophet of the Lord that the time
was not ripe. He was given the promise, however, that the Lord would
give him a son to succeed him on the throne, and to whom the privilege
and responsibility of building the temple would be given. This promise
was fulfilled in the birth of Sol'o-mon.

Sol'o-mon was carefully instructed in the word of God by both father
and mother, and early in youth was placed under the prophet Na'than
for further religious training. His father was deeply concerned over the
development of the national life of Is'ra-el under the rule of Sol'o-mon,
and was eager to have everything in readiness for the immediate building
of the temple.

For twenty-five or thirty years Da'vid gathered treasures and funds for
the construction of the temple. Both in times of war or domestic troubles,
and during periods of peace and prosperity, he laid aside great stores of
gold and silver to be used for the building which held first place in his
heart. The enormous treasures which he had taken as spoils of war were
consecrated to the Lord for this purpose.

The threshing floor of A-rau'nah the Jeb'u-site was chosen by the Lord
as the site for the temple to be built by Sol'o-mon. Da'vid received the
pattern and directions for the temple from the Lord, just as Mo'ses had
received the plans for the tabernacle in the wilderness. The finest, most
costly materials were to be used, and the highest quality of workmanship
must be employed, for the temple was to be perfect in every detail.

For the task of preparing the materials of iron and brass, timber and
stone, and gold and silver, Da'vid summoned the finest workmen of
Is'ra-el, and sent to his friend Hi'ram, King of Tyre, for skilled craftsmen.
The finest cedars of Leb'a-non were purchased from Hi'ram, and the best

HIRAM, THE FOUNDER OF THE
TWO PILLARS

building stone in the country was quarried and brought to Je-ru'sa-lem. The gold which Da'vid had accumulated in his zeal for the temple would be worth about two billion dollars today, while the silver set aside for this purpose would exceed one billion dollars in value.

Enormous as these sums appear, Da'vid knew that there would be need of more before the temple could be completed and furnished. There must be a great number of costly furnishings, and many of the vessels for use in certain acts of worship were to be of finest gold. For this reason he invited the people to bring in free-will offerings, and commanded his officers to lead a great campaign to raise money. No one was to be taxed, but all were to be given an opportunity to make donations.

Da'vid led the way in this free-will offering, giving generously of his most valuable possessions. The people promptly responded to the king's example, bringing in gifts which made up a huge sum. Many of those who had no money to give sent ornaments or materials which could be used for the temple.

A glorious thanksgiving service followed the free-will offering, and Da'vid uttered a prayer which applies to the spirit in which all gifts should be made.

This prayer was followed by burnt offerings, in which a thousand bullocks, a thousand rams, and a thousand lambs were sacrificed unto the

Lord. For the second time the people approved the appointment of Sol'o-mon as king, and there was a season of great rejoicing in Is'ra-el.

The plan of God and of Da'vid to have Sol'o-mon occupy the throne and build the temple immediately after his father's death seems to have been generally known throughout Is·ra-el. So Da'vid, some months before his death, called Sol'o-mon into his court and imposed a very solemn charge upon him. He explained why the Lord had not permitted him to build the temple himself, gave Sol'o-mon the pattern which he had received from the Lord, and said to him, "I have prepared, you are to use the materials; I have gathered, you are to expend the funds; I have been hindered by wars and domestic trials; you are to have peace and quietness. Carry this work to completion promptly, and may the Lord be with you and prosper you."

In addition to the elaborate preparations made for the building of the temple, Da'vid carefully organized the religious and political affairs of the nation before resigning the throne to Sol'o-mon. The orders of the priesthood and of the Le'vites, and of a large group of musicians and singers, were set up, and the order of their services was arranged. Da'vid passed on to Sol'o-mon a thoroughly trained standing army of three hundred thousand warriors. Besides this great force there was a special king's guard of thirty thousand men. In all of these ways the tribes of Is'ra-el were strongly united before Da'vid entered his heavenly reward.

SUGGESTIONS FOR STUDY

Biblical Index to Helpful References

The Building of a House for the Lord. (Deut. 12:5; 2 Chr. 3:1.)

David's Holy Desire to Build a House for God. (2 Sam. 7:2; 1 Ki. 8:17, 18; 1 Chr. 17:1.)

God's Promise to David That His Son Should Build the Temple. (2 Sam. 7:13; 1 Ki. 5:5.)

The Wisdom of Advanced Preparations. (Prov. 6:8; 24:27; Luke 12:33.)

Freewill Offerings for Religious Work. (Num. 15:3; 29:39; Ezra 1:4; 3-5.)

Questions

1. How long had David anticipated the building of the temple by Solomon?

2. What preparations had he made during that entire time?

3. From what source did David receive plans and specifications for the temple?

4. What preparations did he make for the erection of the temple during the closing years of his life?

5. How much were the monies and treasures accumulated by David worth in present day monies?

6. In what way did he collect additional funds?

7. Who led the way in these freewill offerings?

8. Tell of the charge David gave to Solomon respecting the building of the temple.

STORY 100

THE CONSPIRACY OF ADONIJAH

1 KINGS 1

It seems to have been generally understood throughout Is'ra-el that Sol'o-mon had been chosen as king by the Lord. On at least two occasions Da'vid had shown that he approved the choice of Sol'o-mon, but still certain leaders tried to place Ad-o-ni'jah on the throne. It appears that he was the fourth son of Da'vid, the eldest who was living at the time—and that he had been greatly indulged by his father. He seems to have been a handsome man with an attractive personality, and was able to gain strong support for his unjust claims to the throne of his father.

Without waiting for the death of his father, and taking advantage of his increasing weakness, Ad-o-ni'jah plotted to have himself made king. He knew that Da'vid preferred Sol'o-mon for this office, and that the Lord had decreed the succession of Da'vid's favorite son, but he was resolved to seize the throne at any cost. He was supported in this plan by Jo'ab, who promised the aid of the armies which he commanded, and by the High Priest A-bi'a-thar, who gave his blessing to the crafty attack upon the throne of Is'ra-el.

Ad-o-ni'jah gave a great feast at En-ro'gel, and invited those who were in favor of his conspiracy, including Jo'ab, A-bi'a-thar, and many of the royal family. Za'dok, the High Priest next in rank to A-bi'a-thar; Be-na'iah, the bodyguard of Da'vid; Na'than, the prophet who advised Da'vid and Sol'o-mon, and Bath-she'ba and her son Sol'o-mon, were all omitted from the list of people invited to this feast. The plan was to have Ad-o-ni'jah anointed by the High Priest, and then proclaimed king in a great demonstration.

The prophet Na'than learned of the plot, and hastened to call upon Bath-she'ba in secret. He told her of the conspiracy of Ad-o-ni'jah, and urged her to inform Da'vid at once. It was arranged that while she was relating the facts to Da'vid the prophet would suddenly appear with full proof of Ad-o-ni'jah's plot.

On being received by Da'vid, Bath-she'ba bowed humbly before him and said:

"My Lord, you have sworn in the name of the Lord God unto your handmaid, saying, Assuredly Sol'o-mon thy son shall reign after me, and he shall sit upon my throne. And now behold, Ad-o-ni'jah reigneth; and now, my lord the king, thou knowest it not: and he hath prepared a great feast, and hath called all the sons of the king, and A-bi'a-thar the priest, and Jo'ab the captain of the host; but Sol'o-mon thy servant hath he not called. And thou, my lord the king, the eyes of all Is'ra-el are upon thee, that thou shouldst tell them who shall sit on the throne of my lord the king after him. Otherwise, it will come to pass, when my lord the king shall sleep with his

DAVID'S TOMB

fathers, that I and my son Sol'o-mon shall be counted offenders."

While Bath-she'ba was speaking, in rushed the prophet Na'than. He repeated the news which had just been given by Bath-she'ba, making it more definite. He told Da'vid that the people were already shouting, "God save Ad-o-ni'jah the king," and explained that he and Za'dok and Be-na'iah had taken no part in the conspiracy. Then Da'vid repeated his former oath to Bath-she'ba, and promised to carry it out at once.

Da'vid's three loyal friends, Na'than, Za'dok, and Be-na'iah, were told to raise Sol'o-mon to the throne without delay. They were to place Sol'o-mon upon the royal mule and let him ride through the streets of the city —an honor granted only to a king, or to one about to be crowned. The friends of Da'vid were to lead the procession to Gi'hon for the public anointing of the young prince. There Za'dok and Na'than anointed Sol'-o-mon with the holy oil which had been taken from the tabernacle of the Lord.

The anointing was followed by great celebrations; the people danced for joy, crying out with a loud voice, "God save Solomon the king." Back toward the city marched the procession, with Sol'o-mon riding upon the royal mule in the front rank. The rejoicing of the people showed that their deepest feelings had been against the conspiracy of Ad-o-ni'jah, and that Da'vid's resignation in favor of Sol'o-mon was heartily approved.

In the meantime the festivities Ad-o-ni'jah's friends were over, and the plotters were alarmed by a thunderous noise in the streets of the capital. Jo'ab asked in amazement, "What is the meaning of this great uproar?" As if in answer to his question, there rushed into the crowd a son of A-bi'a-thar named Jon'a-than. He brought the news that Da'vid had given up the throne, and that Sol'o-mon was now the ruler of all Is'ra-el. In fear and trembling the guests of Ad-o-ni'jah quietly stole through the streets to their homes. They hid themselves, lest they be arrested as rebels.

Conscience stricken for his wicked plot, and fearing that he might be put to death at once, Ad-o-ni'jah sent a plea to the young king for mercy. Sol'o-mon was touched by the news of his brother's penitence, and wisely showed mercy to him. He pardoned the crime of Ad-o-ni'jah, and restored all his privileges as a member of the royal family on condition that he prove himself a man of valor and worth.

SUGGESTIONS FOR STUDY

Biblical Index to Helpful References

Adonijah, Fourth Son of David. (2 Sam. 3:4; 1 Chr. 3:2.)

The Sin of Exalting One's Self. (Prov. 30:32; 17:19.)

The Wicked Snared. (Job 18:8; Ps. 69:22, 23.)

The Triumph of the Wicked Short. (Job. 20:5; Ps. 55:23; Prov. 10:27.)

The Downfall of Those Who Trust in Worldly Pomp. (Ps. 20:7, 8; 101:7, 8.)

Benaiah David's Body Guard. (2 Sam. 8: 18; 20:23.)

David Six Hundred Valiant Men. (2 Sam. 23:8-39; 1 Sam. 25:13.)

The Divine Promise Concerning Solomon. (1 Chr. 22:8, 9; 2 Sam. 11:11-13.)

Watchfulness and Fidelity of Servants Commended. (Isa. 62:6; Ezek. 33:7.)

The Benefits of Good Counsel. (Prov. 11:14; 15:22; 24:6.)

Solomon the Son of Bathsheba. 2 Sam. 12: 24, 25.)

Questions

1. Was it generally known that Solomon had been Divinely chosen to be king?

2. Who sought to exalt himself to be king?

3. What two members of David's official supported him in his efforts?

4. In what way did Adonijah plan to conclude his conspiracy?

5. Who took steps to advise David of the scheme of Adonijah?

6. Why did he request Bathsheba to carry the news to David?

7. Repeat what Bathsheba said to David.

8. Who came in while she was speaking and confirmed what she said?

9. Describe what David directed to be done at once.

10. How did the people respond to the anointing of Solomon?

11. What happened among the conspirators associated with Adonijah?

12. What did Adonijah do?

13. Tell of Solomon's leniency toward Adonijah.

DAVID'S PARTING WORDS TO SOLOMON

1 KINGS 2:1-12

Da'vid was now in his seventieth year, and his once robust health had broken under constant hardship and suffering. For forty years he had borne the problems of a most trying period in the history of Is'ra-el. Seven years of his reign had been spent at He'bron, where he was constantly troubled by his rival Ish-bo'sheth. For thirty-three years he had guided the nation through many foreign wars, and in the midst of much internal strife and opposition. He had brought Is'ra-el to her golden era, and the nation now held an envied position among other kingdoms of the world.

His eventful career had not been free from grievous wrongs, nor had his private life always been above reproach, but he had never failed to show true repentance when found at fault. He had finished his course, had fought a good fight, had kept the faith; henceforth there was laid up for him a crown of righteousness. He was now ready to lay down the armor of earth, and to be clad with the garments of heaven.

The death-bed scenes of great men are always solemn and impressive, and the last words of a dying hero are cherished by those who are left to carry on his unfinished work. With awed silence we look upon the enfeebled form of a man who had slain lions, bears, and even the giant Go-li'ath, but who was

SOLOMON IS MADE KING

now about to fall before the arm of a mightier power. No greater charge ever fell from the lips of dying mortal than that which Da'vid gave to Sol'o-mon:

"I go the way of all the earth: be thou strong therefore, and show thyself a man; and keep the charge of the Lord thy God, to walk in his ways, to keep his statutes, and his commandments, and his judgments, and his testimonies, as it is written in the law of Mo'ses, that thou mayest prosper in all that thou doest, and withersoever thou turnest thyself: that the Lord may continue his word which he spake concerning me, saying, If thy children take heed to their way, to walk before me in truth with all their heart and with all their soul, there shall not fail thee a man on the throne of Is'ra-el."

How timely were these words to a youth of twenty years! How Helpful to one of a quiet, yielding disposition who was suddenly thrust into a position which called for great wisdom, patience, and perseverance. It was supremely important for him to observe the Law in all its forms, and to devote himself to his royal duties with intelligence, unwearying toil, and constant vigilance.

Da'vid's warning that the promises of God would be granted according to Solomon's obedience to His law was very important; had Sol'o-mon kept this advice always before him, he would have avoided many of the misfortunes later suffered. In all his career, he suffered only when he departed from the law of God.

SUGGESTIONS FOR STUDY

Biblical Index to Helpful References

The Feebleness of Old Age. (Ps. 71:9; Eccl. 12:3, 5.)

Honorableness in Old Age for the Righteous. (Prov. 16:31; 20:29.)

God's Special Presence with the Righteous in Old Age. (Isa. 46:4.)

The Call for Manliness. (Job 38:3; Ezek. 22:30.)

Walking Before the Lord. (Ps. 56:13; 116:9.)

Walking in Truth. (Ps. 26:3; 86:11; 2 Jno. 4.)

Fulfillment of Divine Promises Conditional. (Ps. 132:12; Jno. 7:17; 14:23.)

God's Promise to Establish David's Throne. (2 Sam. 7:16; Jer. 33:17.)

Duty of Showing Kindness to Friends of Ancestors. (Prov. 27:10.)

Questions

1. What was the general physical condition of David when Solomon's choice to be king was made?

2. How old was he when he died?

3. Why were the scenes of David's deathbed solemn? His last words cherished?

4. Repeat the charge made by David to Solomon.

5. Why were they so timely to Solomon?

6. What directions did he give concerning Joab? Were these words vindictive?

7. What charge did he give concerning Barzillai? Why?

SOLOMON MAKES HIS RULE SUPREME

1 KINGS 2:13-46; 3:1  Sol'o-mon's rule was seriously threatened immediately after the death of his father, and he was forced to deal sharply with hostile acts on the part of Ad-o-ni'jah, A-bi'a-thar, Jo'ab and Shim'e-i.

Although Ad-o-ni'jah's effort to seize the throne had met with defeat, and though he had pretended to be loyal to Sol'o-mon henceforth, he soon formed another conspiracy. Ab'i-shag, a beautiful Shu'nam-mite maiden, had served as Da'vid's nurse during his last illness, and was generally regarded as one of the king's widows. With the object of basing his claims to the throne upon the fact that he was the eldest son of Da'vid and the husband of Ab'i-shag, Ad-o-ni'jah sought permission to make her his wife. Instead of going directly to the king with this request, he tried to gain the support of Sol'o-mon's mother.

Bath-she'ba failed to detect the motive in Ad-o-ni'jah's request, and immediately went to Sol'o-mon with it. He saw through the crafty plan of his brother, showed his mother how she had been deceived by the flattery of Ad-o-ni'jah, and ordered the immediate execution of the traitor. He had once been pardoned on the condition that he reform, and the second offense deserved nothing less than the penalty of death.

Sol'o-mon also discovered that the High Priest A-bi'a-thar, who had taken part in Ad-o-ni'jah's previous conspiracy, was still supporting the pretender to the throne. Summoning the disloyal priest to the court, Sol'-o-mon said to him, "Thou art worthy of death." This stern judgment was fully justified in view of A-bi'a-thar's sin of ingratitude toward Da'vid, with whom he had been on the most friendly terms for forty or fifty years. Then Sol'o-mon added these words of mercy to his verdict, "But I will not at this time put thee to death, because thou bearest the ark of the Lord, and

LOWER POOL OF SILOAM

because thou hast been afflicted with my father."

Jo'ab was executed by Be-na'iah while he held on to the horns of the altar in the house of God because of his support of Ad-o-ni'jah in his second conspiracy. Shim'e-i was slain for his persistent disloyalty to the house of Da'vid manifested in the violation of a covenant made with Sol'o-mon.

The youthful king was now past twenty years of age, and still unmarried. In taking a wife he formed an alliance with the king of E'gypt, marrying a daughter of the Pha'raoh who was then on the throne. Since this marriage is nowhere condemned in the Scriptures, it may be concluded that Pha'raoh's daughter became a convert to the Jewish religion.

Sol'o-mon's marriage to the daughter of Pha'raoh, and the alliance with E'gypt which went with it, brought Is'ra-el into friendly relations with the most ancient and splendid of the eastern monarchies, and opened the way for his fame among the nations of that age. It was the first political connection of Is'ra-el with E'gypt since their exodus four or five hundred years before. The time had now come when a king of the land in which Sol'o-mon's ancestors had been oppressed as slaves should give his daughter in marriage to a young Jewish prince. As a result of this alliance, E'gypt was destined to contribute in large measure to the strengthening of a nation formed from the descendants of those people who had once been persecuted and "fed with the bread of affliction" by a Pha'raoh of long ago.

SUGGESTIONS FOR STUDY

Biblical Index to Helpful References

Adonijah's Proposal Contrary to Mosaic Law. (Lev. 18:8.)

Words and Counsels of Deceit Devise Iniquity. (Psm. 36:3, 4; 37: 12,13.)

The Prophetic Judgment Against the House of Eli. (1 Sam. 2:31-36.)

The House of Ithamar Rejected. (1 Chr. 24:5, 6.)

Marriage Commended. (Prov. 18:22; Heb. 13:4.)

Regulations in the Choice of Wife. (Gen. 24:3; 28:1; Deut. 7:3; Josh. 23:12.)

Questions

1. What threatened the stability of Solomon's throne after David's death?

2. What intriguing scheme was adopted this time by Adonijah?

3. What was the real purpose of his request for Abishag as a wife?

4. Did Bathsheba see through the duplicity of his request? Did Solomon?

5. What punishment did Solomon inflict upon Adonijah?

6. When Joab learned of Adonijah's execution, what did he do? Why?

7. What orders did Solomon give respecting Joab? Where was he slain?

8. Why did Solomon depose Abiathar from being high priest?

9. Why did he not have him killed also?

10. Why did he have Shimei executed?

11. Whom did Solomon marry? Did she become a proselyte to the Jewish faith?

12. What benefits came to the nation through this marriage?

SOLOMON'S PRAYER FOR WISDOM

1 KINGS 3:3-15; 4:29-34;
2 CHRONICLES 1   The piety of Sol'o-mon during the early years
of his reign was strikingly demonstrated in a great religious service held
at Gib'e-on. To this place he summoned all the people of the nation to
offer sacrifices unto God. Sol'o-mon himself presented on the brazen
altar one thousand burnt offerings in token of his deep and abiding love
to the Lord.

During the night which followed the grand religious meeting at Gib'-
e-on, the Lord appeared to Sol'o-mon in a dream and said to him, "Ask
what I shall give thee." In reply to this invitation, Sol'o-mon uttered one
of the most noble prayers recorded in all the Bible. It was Divinely ordained, for the one who made it had been given notice in advance. He
stood in the presence of the great King of Kings under the sceptre of
peace, for a state of perfect love to the Lord ruled in his heart.

The prayer of Sol'o-mon began with words of gratitude for the mercies
and blessings already received. Trembling with a sense of the greatness
of the work to which he was called, Sol'o-mon admitted that his own
strength was not enough to sustain him in the trying hours which lay
ahead. He then humbly and sincerely uttered the prayer which shall
stand long after all his worldly fame is forgotten:

"Give therefore thy servant an understanding heart to judge thy people,
that I may discern between good and bad: for who is able to judge this
thy so great a people?"

The Lord was greatly pleased by this request of the young king, and
said in reply:

"Because thou has asked this thing, and hast not asked for thyself long
life; neither hast asked riches for thyself, nor hast asked the life of thine
enemies; but hast asked for thyself understanding to discern judgment;
behold, I have done according to thy words. And I have also given thee
that which thou hast not asked, both riches and honor: so that there shall
not be any among the kings like unto thee all thy days."

The prayer which Sol'o-mon thus made early in his career was fully answered, as promised by the Lord; his life, however, was cut short because
of his failure to abide by the ways and statutes and commandments of the

Lord. The knowledge of Sol'o-mon surpassed anything known before or since. Endowed with the gift of poetry and song, he wrote some of the finest Psalms contained in the Sacred Scriptures, and was also the author of three thousand proverbs, hundreds of which are preserved in the word of God.

Soon after his rise to the throne of Is'ra-el, Sol'o-mon's court became a center where the great and learned of all nations gathered to improve their knowledge. A new day dawned for Is'ra-el when the wonders of ancient E'gypt, the commerce of the Zi'don-ians, and the romance of A-ra'bi-a swept across the barriers which had long separated her from the rest of the world. Tremendous advantages were thrust upon the chosen people of God, but with them dire perils. Had the nation been content to carry out the revealed will of God as a separate people, instead of trying to rival the great pagan empires, the story of the next three centuries would have been vastly different.

Sol'o-mon's wisdom was, to a very large extent, the gift of God and a sign of Divine favor, and the early years of his reign were marked with trust in God and sincere efforts to direct the nation in perfect harmony with His will. These years were blessed with heaven's choicest favors, and with great material prosperity.

SUGGESTIONS FOR STUDY

Biblical Index to Helpful References

Marks of True Piety. (Deut. 10:12; Eccl. 12:13; Mic. 6:8.)

Requirements in True Worship. (Deut. 26:10; 1 Chr. 16:29; Psm. 5:7.)

God's Revelations to his Saints in Dreams. (Num. 12:6; Jer. 23:28.)

Notable Visions in Dreams. (Gen. 28:12; Jgs. 7:13; Matt. 1:20.)

True Wisdom Secured from God in Answer to Prayer. (Jas. 1:5; Psm. 90:12; Eph. 1:17.)

The Supreme Value of True Wisdom. (Prov. 4:7; 9:1; Jas. 3:17.)

True Wisdom an Excellent Gift of God. (Job 28:12-28.)

Questions

1. In what manner did Solomon show his love for God?

2. How many burnt offerings did he make in the feast at Gibeon?

3. In what way did the Lord appear to Solomon at Gibeon?

4. Tell of the notable prayer made by Solomon and the answer.

5. Repeat the prayer. Repeat what the Lord said in reply.

6. How did Solomon's knowledge and wisdom compare with other kings?

7. How many proverbs is he said to have written? Where do we find many of them?

8. What other writings of Solomon have been preserved?

9. Tell of kings and princes visiting Solomon's court.

10. Tell of the advantages thrust upon Israel through Solomon's wisdom.

STORY 104

SOLOMON BUILDS THE TEMPLE ON MOUNT MORIAH

1 KINGS 5-8;
2 CHRONICLES 2-7   You will recall that for twenty years or more Da'vid gathered treasures to be used in building a temple, and that he turned over to Sol'o-mon money and materials which would be valued at nearly five billion dollars today. He also gave his young son full instructions for building the temple.

Now that Sol'o-mon had firmly established his rule, he devoted all his energy to the chief undertaking of his great career. The plans for the temple prepared by Da'vid under the direction of God did not call for a large building, but its style and design, and the quality of the materials to be used, demanded enormous sums of money and much labor. Nothing but the highest quality of stone and marble, the finest copper and brass, and the best timbers of cedar and cypress could be used. Many of these materials had to be secured from foreign countries, and their preparation and transportation required the employment of thousands of common laborers and skilled workmen.

The friendship which had existed between Da'vid and Hi'ram, King of Tyre, was continued and deepened by Sol'o-mon. A trade agreement was made, with Hi'ram to provide the finest timbers of cedar and fir, and Sol'o-mon to send the Phoe-ni'ci-ans vast quantities of grain, oil, and wine. Skilled workmen of Phoe-ni'ci-a were engaged to cut and prepare the timbers, and others were hired to transport them to Je-ru'sa-lem. Hi'ram also supplied men to work in the quarries in preparing stones and marble for the temple.

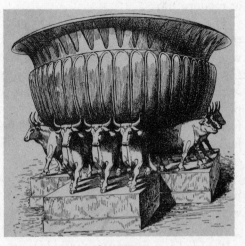

A LAVER

Sol'o-mon showed remarkable ability in organizing and directing the workmen in the preparation of materials for the temple. Thirty thousand men of Is'ra-el were assigned to help in cutting and preparing timbers and stones. These men were arranged in three groups, so that one third of the men worked for one month out of every three, and were thus given two months for labors at home. One hundred and fifty thousand men from the native Ca'naan-ites and from the prisoners of war which had been taken by Da'vid were employed, of which eighty thousand were hewers of timber and stones, and seventy thousand served as common laborers in the forests and quarries.

The site selected for the building of the temple was Mount Mo-ri'ah, made sacred several hundred years before as the scene of A'bra-ham's offering of I'saac unto the Lord, purchased from A-rau'nah the Jeb'u-site by Da'vid for the building of an altar for burnt sacrifices, and then pointed out by the Lord as the place where the temple should be erected. The date when Sol'o-mon began actual construction of the temple was the second month of the fourth year of his reign, and the time required for the completion of the building and its furnishings was more than seven years.

In magnificence the temple was superior to anything ever built before or since, and its cost exceeded that of any similar structure known to man. Its completion marked the greatest epoch in the history of Is'ra-el, and was the occasion of a religious celebration unequalled in either ancient or modern times.

The interior proportions of the temple were: ninety feet in length, thirty feet in width, and forty-five feet from the floor to the ceiling. It was divided into two rooms: the Holy Place, which was sixty by thirty feet; and the Holy of Holies, thirty by thirty feet. The walls and ceiling of these two rooms were made of expensive carved woods, and were completely overlaid with gold. On the front of the temple was a porch thirty feet in length and fifteen feet in width—which was also completely overlaid with gold—and two monumental pillars made of solid brass and artistically decorated.

The furnishings of the temple were similar to those of the tabernacle, but were larger, more richly decorated, and much more costly. Some were made of brass, others of solid gold, and some were overlaid with gold.

The dedication services took place several months after the completion of the temple, and were very elaborate and solemn. The Ark of the Cov'e-nant was removed to the Holy of Holies with impressive ceremonies, in which parts were taken by the elders of the tribes, chiefs of the fathers, judges, Levites, and priests. There was an orderly procession in which the king, with his royal guard, took the lead. The Le'vites bearing the Ark came next in order, followed by a great choir of Le-vit'i-cal singers and a large number of priests. Sacrifices of burnt offerings and peace offerings were made on the great altar in front of the temple.

As the procession marched about the temple, chanting songs, and giving praise to God for the completion of a central house of worship for the entire nation, the house was filled with a brilliant cloud from heaven— a token of God's acceptance of the temple and His blessings upon it. Sol'-o-mon delivered a matchless address to the people, and offered a long prayer of dedication which contains some of the finest passages in the Old Testament. His words of exaltation of God for His greatness, faithfulness, and goodness are unsurpassed in human language; the tenderness, patriotism, and sympathy with which he prayed for his people are unexcelled in sacred literature; while his prayers took account of every circumstance and condition of Is'ra-el at that time and for all future generations.

SUGGESTIONS FOR STUDY

Biblical Index to Helpful References

David's Desire to Build a House for the Lord. (2 Sam. 7:13; 1 Chr. 17:12.)

Why David Was Not Permitted to Build the Temple. (1 Chr. 22:8; 28:3.)

David's Charge to Solomon Respecting the Building of the Temple. (1 Chr. 22:6-16.)

David's Alliance with Hiram, King of Tyre. (2 Sam. 5:11, 12; 1 Chr. 14:1, 2.)

God's Promise to Dwell in His Sanctuary. (Ex. 25:8; Lev. 26:11, 12.)

The Lord Confines Himself to No Earthly Building. (Isa. 66:1, 2; Acts 7:47-50.)

Mount Moriah in Sacred History. (Gen. 22:2.)

Questions

1. How long was David engaged in gathering funds for building a temple?

2. Tell of David's charge to Solomon respecting the building of a temple.

3. With whom did Solomon form an alliance for temple materials?

5. How many skilled workmen were employed in preparing materials? How many common laborers?

6. What famed sculptor and engraver was brought to work on the temple?

7. Tell of his parentage. Of his fame.

8. What site was selected for the temple? Why?

9. Define the size and expensiveness of the temple.

10. Tell of the dedication of the temple.

11. Explain the important position of the temple in Jewish history.

ACTS OF SOLOMON LEADING TO HIS DECLINE

1 KINGS 9-11;
2 CHRONICLES 8-9   After the dedication of the temple at Je-ru'-sa-lem, Sol'o-mon faced the temptations which accompany periods of material prosperity and national growth. Successful in his commercial enterprises, and at the highest point of imperial grandeur, he was in danger of falling into the traps of worldly glory and selfish indulgence. The Lord, therefore, appeared to him in a second special vision, seeking to encourage him in the path of righteousness, and warning him of the dangers which resulted from disobedience to the Divine law.

It was not long, however, before Sol'-o-mon began to boast and take pride in his worldly successes, and the sacred ritual of the temple became a mockery. The worship of various pagan gods was set up in Je-ru'sa-lem in rivalry to the services of the temple, and worldliness and idolatry became widespread.

Instead of sending the thousands of conscripted laborers back to their homes after the temple was built, Sol'o-mon decided to employ them in a vast building program. A royal palace was built—second only to the temple in splendor and cost—and furnished lavishly, with decorations of gold, silver, and precious stones. The plates and drinking vessels for the banquet halls were of solid gold, and all the other equipment was of similar extravagance. Other public buildings of great cost were erected in Je-ru'sa-lem, and the city was inclosed in massive walls and mighty fortifications, strengthened with a huge tower. Garrison cities were built in various parts of the country, and many elaborate public buildings were erected throughout the land. Luxurious pleasure resorts were provided at great cost, and the entire nation was swept into a whirlpool of materialism and worldliness.

The royal court of Sol'o-mon was maintained on a scale of magnificence and luxury similar to those of the richest heathen empires, boasting an enormous train of servants and courtiers. A constant succession of guests came from all over the world. The king and his attendants moved about in gorgeous array, and a blaze of glory filled the palace at all times. No expense was spared in the display of material wealth and worldly glory.

As an example of the extravagant manner in which foreign rulers were entertained at the king's court, we have the story of the visit of the Queen of She'ba. She came from a distance of more than a thousand miles with a long train of camels, richly clad attendants, and valuable presents for the king.

The Queen of She'ba seems to have possessed everything necessary for worldly happiness—wealth, rank, and power. And yet, having heard of Sol'o-mon's fame for wisdom and glory, she spared neither time nor expense in making a visit to his court. She brought presents of gold, precious stones, and fragrant spices; appearing before Sol'o-mon in all the glory of a rich and powerful A-ra'bi-an princess. She asked him hard questions, and was rewarded with a wonderful display of superior wisdom and knowledge. Sol'o-mon received her with a magnificence which surpassed that of her own court, showing her the splendors of the temple and the royal palace. She was overwhelmed by so dazzling a spectacle. The luxury and splendor of the banquet hall, the rare, expensive foods, the orderly arrangement of hundreds of servants, the gorgeously dressed courtiers—all these evidences of wealth and glory were enchanting and bewildering. In her amazement she declared:

"It was a true report that I heard in mine own land of thine acts and of thy wisdom. Howbeit, I believed not their words, until I came, and mine eyes had seen it; and, behold, the half of the greatness of thy wisdom was not told me."

Another field in which Sol'o-mon's prosperity was rapidly enlarged was the foreign commerce of the nation. As a result of his alliance with Hi'ram, King of Phoe-ni'ci-a, a fleet of ships was built, and trade relations were extended to the ancient countries of the East, and to the nations to the north and west. The kingdom of Is'ra-el began to copy many of the customs of the great pagan nations of that age, and the moral character of the people was weakened by the season of worldly success and splendor. The territory of Is'ra-el was extended to take in many alien peoples, but instead of winning them to the Jewish faith, the Is'ra-el-ites adopted many of the false ideas and wicked practices of false religions.

The love which Sol'o-mon had once felt for God, and the perfect faith which he had formerly shown, were destroyed by his burning desire for worldly wisdom. He became the victim of his own proud self-sufficiency, a suicide to the regal splendor which had become so dear to him.

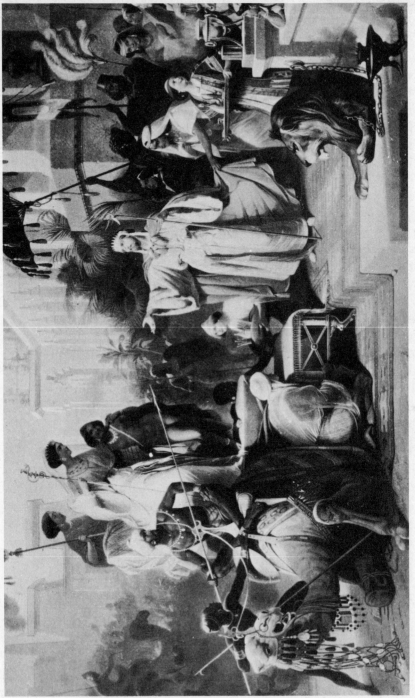

THE QUEEN OF SHEBA AT SOLOMON'S COURT

Although Sol'o-mon had attained all the elements regarded as important in the office of a monarch—riches, splendor, and fame—his greatness
in these respects led to his downfall. The high state of prosperity to which
he had brought the nation was soon reduced to a sad condition of want
and dissatisfaction. The vast companies of men which had been employed
in erecting public buildings and fortifying many cities throughout the
land, the increase in the standing army, the huge sums required by thousands of royal officers, and the enormous outlay in the purchase of luxuries
from foreign lands—all these governmental expenditures resulted in heavy
taxes upon the people.

Added to these causes of Sol'o-mon's decline was his unwise practice
of taking many wives. A large number of the wives of Sol'o-mon were
from foreign countries—daughters of pagan kings, and worshipers of various false gods. He broke the laws of his own religion by building temples
to the pagan gods of his wives not far from the house of God, by visiting
these heathen shrines, and by taking part in ceremonies which were forbidden by the principles of true religion. By so doing, Sol'o-mon tried
to mingle the worship of God with pagan rites, an arrangement which
had long been attractive and dangerous to the Jewish mind, and which had
often led the nation into gross evils. Thus the glory of Sol'o-mon's reign
was brought to a shameful end, and the kingdom was broken asunder
soon after his death.

SUGGESTIONS FOR STUDY

Biblical Index to Helpful References

The Peril of Great Riches. (Matt. 16:26;
1 Tim. 6:9, 10.)

The Folly of Trusting in Worldly Achieve-
ments. (Psm. 20:7; 52:7; Prov. 11:28.)

Safety of Nations Not in Material Success.
(Psm. 33:16, 17; Prov. 21:31; Isa. 31:1.)

God's Judgment Against Arrogant Rulers.
(Isa. 10:13-16.)

Luxury at the Expense of the Poor Condemned. (Amos 6:4, 5; Luke 16:19.)

The Law Against Cruel Marriages. (Deut.
17:17.)

The Queen of Sheba Commended for Her
Search of Wisdom. (Matt. 12:42.)

Wisdom the True Source of Power for
Rulers. (Prov. 8:15, 16.)

Questions

1. What new charge did God give Solomon after the dedication of the temple?

2. What great temptation faced the king at
that time?

3. Tell of Solomon's extensive building
enterprises.

4. Tell of the visit of the Queen of Sheba
and of her royal entertainment.

5. With what nation did he form an alliance for sea commerce?

6. How did Solomon allow his material
prosperity to effect his religious life?

7. To what condition was the nation reduced by high taxes?

8. What other great wrong did Solomon
commit which led to his downfall?

SOLOMON REJECTED BY THE LORD

1 KINGS 11   One of the most pathetic pages in the Scripture record is the story of Sol'o-mon's spiritual decline and his rejection
by the Lord. Tragic, indeed, are these sentences:

"And Sol'o-mon did evil in the sight of the Lord, and went not fully
after the Lord."

"Wherefore the Lord said unto Sol'o-mon, Forasmuch as this is done
of thee, and thou hast not kept my covenant and my statutes, which
I have commanded thee, I will surely rend the kingdom from thee, and
will give it to thy servant."

To look upon a man who has enjoyed greatness in its full degree falling
into ruin; to see a man who once was noted for his loyalty to God drifting
into the lowest forms of idolatry—surely no other scene could bring deeper
grief to human hearts! That is the picture which passes before our eyes
in the downfall of Is'ra-el's greatest king. Sol'o-mon's riches were almost
beyond belief; his power was unquestioned; his glory unsurpassed.

Sol'o-mon's decline was the result of his unholy association with idol-
worshipers, his fondness for worldly pleasures, and his complete devotion
to material things. Nowhere in his great mind was there a place for God. In his marriages with women of the Mo'ab-ites, Am'mon-ites, E'dom-ites, Hit'-tites, and Si'don-ians he scorned the principle upon which God had based the development of the Jewish nation, and thereby brought into Is'ra-el all manner of idolatrous worship. In his efforts to bring heathen nations under the rule of Is'ra-el, and to join his people with pagan world, he broke one of the most solemn commands of God. His

WIVES OF SOLOMON

plans to make Is'ra-el a world power were contrary to God's purposes in planting the nation in the isolated land of Ca'naan. For all these unholy alliances and schemes he was denounced and rejected by God.

In punishing Sol'o-mon for his disloyalty, the Lord permitted certain foreign enemies to harass him during his last years, and a conspiracy against his rule was led by his own servant Jer-o-bo'am. Ha'dad, a royal child of E'dom who had escaped into E'gypt when war raged between Is'ra-el and his own people, returned to E'dom after the death of Da'vid and Jo'ab in the hope of restoring the kingdom of his fathers. Jer-o-bo'am, a trusted officer of Sol'o-mon, spread a feeling of discontent among his friends, and stirred up opposition to the king's heavy taxes among the people. Thus Sol'o-mon's last days were troubled by the threat of a revolution. Through the mercy of God, however, the splitting up of the kingdom was delayed until after Sol'o-mon's death.

The Book of Ec-cle'si-as-tes appears to have been written by Sol'o-mon after his rejection by the Lord. Throughout this book are many evidences of penitence and forgiveness for the very sins which led to Sol'o-mon's downfall. The entire book is the confession of a heart which, disappointed in the pursuit of worldly fame and selfish indulgence, turns at last to the Lord as the source of all true forgiveness and happiness. Many expressions in this book reveal the spirit of doubt and confusion which is natural to a heart which has been disappointed by all that the world can give, but it ends with a triumph of faith in these glorious words: "Let us hear the conclusion of the whole matter: fear God, and keep his commandments; for this is the whole duty of man."

SUGGESTIONS FOR STUDY

Biblical Index to Helpful References

Deflection from God the Result of Sinful Affinities. (1 Cor. 15:33.)

God's Anger Against Disobedient Children. (Isa. 13:13; Jno. 3:36.)

God's Punishment for Disobedience Without Violating His Covenant. (Rom: 3:3; 2 Tim. 2:13.)

God Honored by the Wrath of His Enemies. (Psm, 76:10.)

Solomon the Beloved of the Lord. (Neh. 13:26.)

Questions

1. Why was the spiritual decline of Solomon such a tragedy?

2. Quote the condemning words of God concerning his apostasy.

3. What were the chief contributing causes of Solomon's downfall?

4. In what manner did the Lord punish Solomon?

5. What evidences have we that Solomon was restored to God before his death?

STORY 107

THE DIVISION OF THE JEWISH EMPIRE

1 KINGS 12:1-24; 2
CHRONICLES 10; 11:1-4   The death of Sol'o-mon made his eldest son
Re-ho-bo'am the natural heir to the throne of Is'ra-el. Moved by the
spirit of unrest and discontent which existed among the tribes outside of
Ju'dah, the people summoned Re-ho-bo'am to an assembly at She'chem,
the ancient capital of E'phra-im, for the ceremony of coronation. In the
meantime Jer-o-bo'am, who had fled to E'gypt after Sol'o-mon's threats
against him for treachery, had returned to the land of Is'ra-el as the
spokesman for the rebellious people of the nation.

The discontent which had spread throughout the nation may be traced
to three main causes: oppressive taxation, corruption of the worship of
God by the introduction of idolatry in Je-ru'sa-lem and many other centers of the land, and the jealousy of the tribe of E'phra-im. Speaking for
the people, Jer-o-bo'am said to the heir to the throne:
"Thy father made our yoke grievous: now therefore make thou the
grievous service of thy father, and his heavy yoke which he put upon us,
lighter, and we will serve thee."

Instead of giving this request the prompt answer which it deserved,
Re-ho-bo'am asked for a delay. He wisely sought the advice of his
father's aged and experienced counselors who advised appeasement of
the people in their reasonable demands. This good counsel was rejected
and following the wishes of his young, conceited, and reckless friends,
he answered the people roughly, saying, "My father chastised you with
whips, but I will chastise you with scorpions." Thus insulted, the people revolted.

The rebellion spread rapidly, and the way was opened for setting up a
rival kingdom under the rule of Jer-o-bo'am, as previously announced by
the Lord in His judgment upon Sol'o-mon for extravagance and idolatry.
The work of one hundred and twenty years, in which Saul, Da'vid, and
Sol'o-mon had built up the Jewish kingdom, was undone in a single day.

Re-ho-bo'am unwisely sent Ad-o-ra'im, an officer who had been in
charge of the levy of forced labor, and whose presence would naturally
enrage the people, to subdue the rebellion. The people stoned him to
death, and Re-ho-bo'am was forced to flee in his chariot. The enraged

multitude was in a violent mood, and only the hand of Providence checked what would have been a bloody revolution. The revolting tribes, which included all of Is'ra-el except Ju'dah, then made Jer-o-bo'am their king.

Returning to his capital city, Re-ho-bo'am determined to crush the revolt, and to win back to the crown of Ju'dah the tribes which had set up a rival kingdom. He raised an army of one hundred and eighty thousand brave warriors from the tribe of Ju'dah and the neighboring territory of Ben'ja-min, and ordered an immediate attack upon Jer-o-bo'am and his followers. But the Lord sent the prophet She-ma'iah to Re-ho-bo'am with this message:

"Thus saith the Lord, Ye shall not go up, nor fight against your brethren the children of Is'ra-el: for this thing is of me."

Thus was fulfilled the prophecy which A-hi'jah the Shi-lo-nite had spoken to Sol'o-mon some years before. The folly of Re-ho-bo'am and his gay young advisers, their utter failure to regard the discontent of the people, and their own sins of pride and weakness—these were the human agencies for the accomplishment of God's judgments. Beneath these unhappy developments was the kindly purpose of God to preserve the tribal life of Ju'dah and the royalty of the house of Da'vid for the coming of the Mes-si'ah hundreds of years later. This will be seen more clearly in the course of our review of the history of the two kingdoms.

SUGGESTIONS FOR STUDY

Biblical Index to Helpful References

Usual Procedure in Anointing Kings. (1 Sam. 10:24; 1 Ki. 1:29.)

Shechem's Important Position in Israel's History. (Gen. 33:18-20; Josh. 24:1.)

Shechem Scene of Bimelech's Usurpation of Regal Power. (Jgs. 9.)

Rehoboam's Mother an Ammonite. (2 Chr. 12:13.)

Regal Tyrannies Foretold by Samuel. (1 Sam. 8:11-18.)

A Soft Answer vs. Harsh Words. (Job 22:5; Prov. 15:18; 30:33.)

Warnings Against Strife. (Prov. 16:28.)

Adoram (also called Adoniram) Overseer of Levy Labor. (1 Ki. 4:6; 5:14; 2 Sam. 20:24.)

Questions

1. Who was the natural heir to the throne after the death of Solomon?

2. Where did the people assemble for his coronation? Why?

3. What demand did the people make of Rehoboam?

4. With whom did he counsel before replying? Quote his reply.

5. What resulted from his harsh and inconsiderate reply?

6. Who was chosen as the spokesman for the discontents?

7. How many tribes revolted? Who was chosen as their king?

8. Why did Rehoboam give up his efforts to suppress the revolt?

STORY 108

JEROBOAM LEADS ISRAEL INTO SIN

1 KINGS 12-14;
2 CHRONICLES 13:4-20 The breaking up of the empire ruled by Sol'o-
mon reduced the territory of Re-ho-bo'am to the mountainous regions
of Ju'dah and Ben'ja-min. This area extended from the Jor'dan on the
east to the plains of the Med'i-ter-ra'ne-an on the west, and included the
arid lands to the south formerly occupied by Sim'e-on, for members of
this tribe had either united with Ju'dah or joined the A-ra'bi-ans. The
cities on the plains of the Med'i-ter-ra'ne-an sea coast remained in the
hands of the Phi-lis'tines.

The territory ruled by Jer-o-bo'am included all the lands of Is'ra-el
north of Ju'dah and Ben'ja-min, and east of the Jor'dan. In area and in
population it was almost three times as large as the southern kingdom,
and for this reason became known as Is'ra-el—though sometimes called
the Northern Kingdom or E'phra-im. Re-ho-bo'am's kingdom was
known either as Ju'dah, or the Southern Kingdom.

Jer-o-bo'am made She'chem his capital, and reigned there for twenty-
two years. A sad commentary on his entire reign is found in this text:
"He did that which was evil, because he set not his heart to seek the
Lord." He is often referred to in the Scriptures as, "Jer-o-bo'am, the son
of Ne'bat, who made Is'ra-el to sin."

The events which followed his coronation were sad and depressing.
Fearing that the attendance of the Is'ra-el-ites at the temple in Je-ru'sa-lem
would turn their hearts back to the house of Da'vid, Jer-o-bo'am cleverly
provided two central places of worship within his own territory: one at
Dan, in the extreme northern part of the land; and the other at Beth'el,
near the southern border. Temples were erected, and in each he placed
a golden calf, saying to the people: "It is too much for you to go up to
Je-ru'sa-lem; behold thy gods, O Is'ra-el, which brought thee up out of
the land of E'gypt."

One of the most popular festivals of the Jewish religion was the annual
Feast of Tab'er-na-cles, a national thanksgiving following the harvest season. The date established by the Law of Mo'ses for this festival was the
fifteenth day of the seventh month. Jer-o-bo'am ordered that this feast
be held at Beth'el, and set the date a month later

One day when the people were gathered at Beth'el for worship, Jer-o-bo'am committed the sacrilege of burning incense before the altar. While he was still engaged in this reckless violation of one of the strictest laws of God, there suddenly appeared a mysterious prophet who had come up from Ju'dah. Like a meteor out of the heavens, he bravely faced the king who set himself up as a priest; against the unworthy king and the desecrated altar he uttered this solemn prediction:

"O altar, altar, thus saith the Lord, Behold a child shall be born unto the house of Da'vid, Jo-si'ah by name; and upon thee shall he offer the priests of the high places that burn incense upon thee, and men's bones shall be burnt upon thee."

More than a hundred years later the words of the prophet were carried out to the least detail by Jo-si'ah, king of Ju'dah.

When Jer-o-bo'am heard the rebukes of this strange man of Ju'dah, he raised his hand in an angry gesture and ordered that the prophet be seized. Suddenly the arm of the king was paralyzed. The altar was rent asunder so that ashes poured out of it, and the wicked king was so terrified that he begged the man of God to pray for the healing of his arm. The prophet agreed, and the arm was made well at once. With a show of gratitude and acknowledgment of the power of God, Jer-o-bo'am then offered a reward to the prophet, but it was promptly declined.

It appears that the Lord had sent the unnamed prophet on a mission to Jer-o-bo'am with strict orders not to enter into any fellowship what-

THE UPLANDS OF EPHRAIM

ever with the people of the Northern Kingdom. At first he withstood all temptations to break the instructions of the Lord, but finally yielded to the urgent request of an aged prophet of Beth'el to enter his house and dine with him. Although the man of Beth'el made the false claim that God had directed him to give the invitation, the Ju'de-an prophet was wrong in accepting the word of any man without direct permission from God to change his original instructions.

While they were eating and drinking together, the old man of Beth'el turned against the prophet, rebuking him severely for disobeying the command of God. The old man declared that for this sin he would die in some violent manner before reaching his home, and that his body would never be buried among his own people. Soon after the Ju'de-an prophet resumed his journey he was slain by a lion. Hearing of this misfortune, the man of Beth'el placed the body in his own sepulcher, saying as he did so, "Alas, my brother, alas!" He then declared that the predictions of the unnamed prophet against the unholy altars of Is'ra-el should come to pass.

Jer-o-bo'am's young son A-bi'jah, upon whom he doted as the heir to his kingdom became seriously ill. Turning from the idolatrous shrines and hireling priests in whose help he had no confidence, he sent his wife to the prophet A-hi'jah at Shi'loh for aid. This was the man of God who had predicted his rise to the throne of the ten tribes, and who had solemnly warned him against disobeying the laws of God. Having ignored this warning, and fearing the reproach of his own priests for calling upon A-hi'jah, Jer-o-bo'am ordered his wife to disguise herself. The Lord, however, had forewarned the prophet of the coming of Jer-o-bo'am's wife, so when she arrived at the door of his house he said,

"Come in, thou wife of Jer-o-bo'am; why feignest thou thyself to be another? For I am sent to thee with heavy tidings."

Then A-hi'jah told her to carry back to her husband the news of God's judgment upon his wickedness. In this message the prophet reminded Jer-o-bo'am that he had been raised up by the Lord, and given honor and power even to the shame of the chosen tribe of Ju'dah; and that he had been most ungrateful for the blessings of God. He went on to predict the cutting off of his descendants by the most horrible punishments, and foretold the final ruin of the nation which he had been permitted to set up. Instead of giving Jer-o-bo'am's wife any hope for the recovery of the sick child, the prophet of God faithfully told her that the child would die the moment she reached home. Just as the prophet of God predicted, God's judgment against this idolatrous king resulted in the immediate death of his innocent and pious son.

Jer-o-bo'am's insincerity in sending to the prophet for aid was fully manifested in his continued course of evil. He foolishly tried to take advantage of A-bi'jah's youth and inexperience to invade the territory of Ju'dah. The purpose of this invasion was to subdue the house of Da'vid, and to make Jer-o-bo'am the ruler of all Is'ra-el. With complete disregard for the splendid address by which A-bi'jah sought to dissuade him from the daring attempt to subdue the kingdom of Ju'dah, the self-willed Jer-o-bo'am forced a great battle. Human odds were strongly in favor of the proud, conceited king, for his army far outnumbered that of A-bi'jah, and Jer-o-bo'am was a shrewd general. But God was on the side of Ju'dah, and the hordes of the Northern Kingdom suffered a shameful, crushing defeat. Thousands of soldiers were slain, a number of important cities were taken by the victors, and the unholy ambitions of Jer-o-bo'am were utterly crushed.

SUGGESTIONS FOR STUDY

Biblical Index to Helpful References

The Making of Images a Violation of God's Commandment. (Ex. 20:4, 5.)

The Priests and Levites Remained Loyal to Rehoboam. (2 Chr. 11:13, 14.)

The Sin of Appointing Idolatrous Priests. (Jgs. 17:5.)

The Legal Date for the Feast of Tabernacles. (Lev. 23:34, 39, 41.)

Divinely Promised Sons Named by Angels.

(Gen. 17:19; 1 Chr. 22:9.)

The Boldness of the Righteous in Condemning Wrong. (Prov. 28:1; Acts 4:3.)

Custom of Rewarding Prophets. (1 Sam. 9:7, 8; 2 Ki. 8:7-9.)

The Fulfillment of the Predictions of the Unnamed Prophet. (2 Ki. 23: 15-20.)

The Natural Downward Course of Sin. (Jno. 8:34; 2 Tim. 3:13.)

Questions

1. Define the territory over which Rehoboam ruled.

2. Define the territory over which Jeroboam ruled.

3. How long did the kingdom of Israel continue? How many kings ruled? How many dynasties represented?

4. Tell of Jeroboam's forgetfulness of God's warnings.

5. Where did he set up places of worship? Why? What idols were made?

6. What change did he make in respect to the Feast of Tabernacles? Why?

7. Tell of Jeroboam's sacrilege in burning incense.

8. Tell of the visit of the prophet and what happened.

9. What happened to the unnamed prophet later? Why?

10. Why did Jeroboam send his wife to the prophet Ahijah?

11. What message did Ahijah send back to Jeroboam?

12. Tell of the war between the king of Israel and the king of Judah.

13. How long did Jeroboam reign? Who succeeded him?

STORIES OF POLITICAL SCHEMES AND IDOLATRY IN THE NORTHERN KINGDOM

1 KINGS 15:25-34;
16:1-28; 2 CHRONI-
CLES 16:1-5　　　　Re-ho-bo'am died four years before Jer-o-bo'am, and his son A-bi'jah reigned over Ju'dah for three years. After his death his son A'sa ruled for forty-one years, or to the sixty-first year after the division of the kingdom. Including the year that Jer-o-bo'am reigned after A'sa became king, the kingdom of Is'ra-el was in six different hands during the reign of A'sa over Ju'dah. The record of that period is stained with conspiracies, increasing wickedness, and bloodshed.

Na'dab, Jer-o-bo'am's son, reigned only two years, and followed in the steps of his wicked father. He was weak in character, unable to hold the respect of his own subjects. When he was treacherously slain by Ba'a-sha, one of his officers, during a battle with the Phi-lis'tines at Gib'be-thon, not one Is'ra-el-ite came forward to avenge the murder. This was the first time in the tumultuous history of the Northern Kingdom that a king had been murdered.

Ba'a-sha, an obscure military adventurer, and a bold, merciless plotter, assumed the throne of Is'ra-el. He was a member of the undistinguished tribe of Is'sa-char, and seems to have been of low reputation among his own people. Having seized the crown through the treacherous murder of Na'dab, he slew all the descendants and relatives of the house of Jer-o-bo'am; thus came to an early end the dynasty of the first king of the northern tribes, as foretold by the prophet of God some years before.

The reign of Ba'a-sha covered a period of twenty-four years, during which there were frequent outbreaks of war with A'sa. We have the record of a fierce battle which took place in the thirty-sixth year of the kingdom, and in the twelfth year of Ba'a-sha's reign. Ba'a-sha tried to recapture the city of Ra'mah, which had been taken from the Northern Kingdom in the victory of A-bi'jah over Jer-o-bo'am. A'sa secured the help of Syr'i-an warriors, who smote the towns of I'jon, Dan and A'bel-Ma'im, and all the store cities of Naph'ta-li, thereby forcing Ba'a-sha to abandon his plans for taking Ra'mah.

As Ba'a-sha plunged deeper into idolatry and evil, leading Is'ra-el into more grievous sins than ever, the Lord sent a prophet named Je'hu to announce judgment upon him. Je'hu told him that because he had followed in the sins of Jer-o-bo'am the same punishment would come to his dynasty; just as he had destroyed all heirs of the former king, so his own line would be completely wiped out.

Ba'a-sha died in the twenty-fourth year of his reign, and his son E'lah then held the throne for two years. He inherited the low, intemperate habits of his father, but none of his energy and ability. While his armies were fighting the Phi-lis'tines, he spent his time carousing and drinking, pouring out strong wine for his own pleasure while his men were pouring out their life-blood in barbarous war. In the midst of drunken revelry at the home of one of his friends in Tir'zah he was murdered by Zim'ri, the commander of half of his chariots. Zim'ri, slew the entire household of the king, but reigned for only seven days.

When news of Zim'ri's murder of E'lah and his seizure of the throne reached the army at Gib'be-thon, the soldiers elected their captain Om'ri as king. Under his leadership the army returned to Tir'zah and besieged the city. Zim'ri was afraid to meet the avengers of the murdered king, so he took refuge in the palace, set fire to it, and perished in its flames.

Fierce anarchy and disorder then broke out; rival claimants to the throne carried on a murderous combat for many months. A large number of Is'ra-el-ites rebelled against Om'ri, and elected Tib'ni as their king. In the civil war which followed, Om'ri won out after the death of Tib'ni.

Om'ri's reign began with his coronation at Gib'be-thon, but it was several months before he became the unquestioned ruler. He reigned for twelve years, but the chief comment upon these years is found in the brief statement, "He did worse than all that were before him." He led the people into gross idolatry, going further than any king before him in this respect. There was no longer any pretense of the worship of Je'hovah at the shrines set up by Jer-o-bo'am, for pagan rites were encouraged by the law of the land. Jer-o-bo'am had made it possible for Is'ra-el to worship idols, but Om'ri made this sin compulsory.

The only good deed to Om'ri's credit was the purchase of the hill of She'mer, where the city of Sa-ma'ri-a was later built. This hill became the place of residence of the kings of Is'ra-el, and Sa-ma'ri-a was the capital of the Northern Kingdom until Is'ra-el was taken captive by the Assyr-i'ans, and the nation passed into oblivion.

Sa-ma'ri-a was ideally located, situated in a vast circle of mountains, about six miles from She'chem, and near the center of the country. She'-mer's hill was a beautiful round mountain, rising five or six hundred feet above the surrounding valleys. Its wide, level top gave a splendid view of the fruitful lands and lovely valleys of the region. The city has held an important place in the history of Pal'es-tine, and is often mentioned in the New Testament.

Om'ri reigned at Tir'zah for six years, and at Sa-ma'ri-a for the same length of time. Records found among other nations of that period indicate that he was a shrewd politician, and that he did a great deal to enlarge and strengthen his country. In spite of his sins against the Lord, he brought the nation into closer unity, and laid the foundation for a new epoch in the history of the northern tribes. He died a natural death, and the crown was kept in his family by the choice of his son A'hab as the next king.

SUGGESTIONS FOR STUDY

Biblical Index to Helpful References

Sin of Rulers Ruinous to Nations. (Prov. 14:34; 16:12.)

Lowliness of the Tribe of Issachar. (Gen. 49:14, 15.)

The Curse of Sinful Imitation. (Ex. 23:2; Deut. 12:30; 1 Sam. 8:19, 20.)

Omri's Statutes of Idolatry. (Mic. 6:16.)

Tirzah Conquered by Joshua. (Josh. 12:24.)

God's Decrees That the Wicked Shall Be Cut Off. (Job 22:15, 16; Psm. 37:22, 38.)

The Peril of Provoking God. (Num. 14:11, 12; 16:30; Deut. 31:20, 21; Ezra 5:12.)

Warnings Against Drunkenness and Profligacy. (Prov. 23:20; Isa. 5:11; Eph. 5:18.)

Hardness of Heart and Certain Doom Caused by Rejecting God's Warnings. (Psm. 81:11, 12; Ezek. 33:4.)

The Wicked Soon Forgotten After Death. (Psm. 37:35, 36; Eccl. 8:10; Jer. 16:4.)

Questions

1. Rehoboam and Jeroboam were contemporaneous kings for how long?

2. Who succeeded Rehoboam? Who was the third king of Judah? For how long?

3. How many kings ruled over Israel during Asa's reign in Judah?

4. Who succeeded Jeroboam? How long did he reign? What kind of king was he?

5. How did Baasha usurp the throne of Israel? What kind of man was he?

6. How long did Baasha reign? Tell of his efforts to retake Ramah?

7. Who succeeded Baasha? What kind of man was he? How long did he reign?

8. Tell of the assassination of Elah. By whom? How long did Zimri reign?

9. Who was chosen king by the army of Israel? What became of Zimri?

10. Tell of the civil war which broke out in Israel and why.

11. How long did Omri reign? What sins did he cause Israel to do?

12. In what respects was Omri worse than all previous kings?

13. Where did he build a new capital? Tell of the advantages of this place.

STORY 110

JEZEBEL'S POWER OVER AHAB;
A GREAT PROPHET OF GOD APPEARS

1 KINGS 16:29-34;
17:1-6   The rise of A'hab to the throne of Is'ra-el
marked the beginning of a great era for the Northern Kingdom. For
the next thirty-five years the nation stood out as the chief power of the
land. A'hab remained on friendly terms with Je-hosh'a-phat, the king of
Ju'dah, and there was a long period of peace between the rival kingdoms.
In addition to his own ivory house in Sa-ma'ri-a, A'hab built many strong
cities throughout the land, and carried on successful wars against the
Syr'i-ans. Although he worshiped idols himself, he had the good judgment to choose as his chief minister a godly man who was faithful to the
law of Mo'ses. O-ba-di'ah, the most prominent member of the court,
was a righteous man who feared only the Lord.

The wisdom and statesmanship of A'hab was made of little account,
however, by his marriage to an ambitious heathen woman of Phoe-ni'ci-a.
Under her influence he was led to make Ba'al-worship the national religion of Is'ra-el. Though strong in many noble qualities, he became
a weak and yielding character in the hands of this wicked woman. The
Bible sums up his career in a few brief, striking words; typical comments
are the following:

"And A'hab, the son of Om'ri, did evil in the sight of the Lord above
all that were before him."

"He took to wife Jez'e-bel, the daughter of Eth'ba-al, king of the
Zi'don-ians, and went and served Ba'al, and worshiped him."

"But there was none like unto A'hab, which did sell himself to work
wickedness in the sight of the Lord, whom Jez'e-bel his wife stirred up.
And he did abominably in following idols."

The marriage of A'hab to Jez'e-bel was the first serious mistake of his
career. It was undertaken chiefly for political reasons, and with complete disregard for the laws of God. Although Jez'e-bel was a princess
of a powerful nation, she was alien in race and religion. She had all the
reckless, daring traits of the Ca'naan-ites, combined with the shrewdness
of an Oriental queen. Her father had slain his own brother, and had

given himself up completely to idol-worship. Jez'e-bel also worshiped Ba'al, and took advantage of her position as queen to establish altars to this heathen god all over Is'ra-el. By clever management she became the power behind the throne; never openly advising the king, but seeing to it in tactful ways that her wishes soon became the law of the land.

Through the marriage of Jez'e-bel to A'hab there was transplanted into the royal family an alien poison which finally resulted in the destruction of the line of Om'ri. Her evil influence over the throne became so strong that it could not be checked even by the sons of A'hab who reigned after his death.

It was through Jez'e-bel's influence that Phoe-ni'ci-an idolatry was introduced into Is'ra-el, encouraged by royal authority, and finally made the state religion.

A'hab's reign of twenty-two years, and the reigns of his sons after him, were notorious for idolatry, treachery and murder, and every form of ungodliness. All this was the work of a woman called the wife of A'hab, and the mother of his sons, but in reality the satanic master of their lives.

AHAB AND JEZEBEL

As an example of the impiety of A'hab's times, we have the record of an attempt to rebuild the city of Jer'i-cho. The curse of God had been pronounced by Josh'u-a upon anyone who should rebuild the city, and for hundreds of years God's will had been respected. Then a native of Beth'el called Hi'el, no doubt encouraged by A'hab, undertook to rebuild the ancient stronghold of Ca'naan. In return for his boldness, he lost his first son when he began to lay the foundation of the walls, and his youngest as he completed the task of setting up the gates. All this took place exactly in keeping with the curse of Josh'u-a.

Although the nation had turned aside from the righteous ways of God, and was now moved to despair by the cruelty of a shrewd, heartless queen, there were thousands of Is'ra-el-ites in the land who had not "bowed the knee to Ba'al." Prophets moved quietly among the people, teaching them the word of God, and encouraging them to refrain from every form of idolatry. In many homes the laws of Mo'ses were still read and obeyed, altars of prayer were kept aflame with praise and supplications, and hearts were warm with the hope of better days to come.

Suddenly, like a thunderbolt from the heavens, one of these prophets appeared unannounced in the courts of the wicked, idolatrous king. His name was E-li'jah, which mean "My God is Je-ho'vah," and his abrupt appearance was a stern rebuke to the idol-worshiping king. He was called "the Tish'bite," having come from the little town of Tish'bi in the mountainous regions of Gil'e-ad east of the Jor'dan.

E-li'jah was uncouth in appearance, with his hair and beard long and unkempt, and his dress a rough mantle of skin, but he was a man of sterling character and complete devotion to the Lord. He was a prophet of few words, but one always ready to act. His mission was to proclaim the all-powerful and ever-living God of Is'ra-el in opposition to A'hab's dead and powerless idols. A grander, more romantic character the world has never known. He was raised up by the Lord to denounce the proud spirit of idolatry, and to demonstrate the power of the only true religion in the world at that time. He was filled with the Spirit of God, and given power to perform mighty deeds and wonders for the confusion of all the enemies of God. To meet the needs of so dark an age, God gave Is'ra-el the brightest light which shone in the world prior to the coming of the Sav'i-or.

With no other introduction to the king than that which he made for himself, without the support of friends, and standing as the lone servant of God in so great an assembly, E-li'jah solemnly said to A'hab:

"As the Lord God of Is'ra-el liveth, before whom I stand, there shall not be dew nor rain these years, but according to my word."

Then the prophet departed as suddenly and mysteriously as he had come. Like a man fading away into thin air he was gone, leaving the king with mingled feelings of fright and curiosity. At the command of God, E-li'jah went into a secluded spot somewhere in the mountainous regions toward the Jor'dan called the brook Che'rith. He was to remain in hiding until his words had been proved true by the long drought, and until the people had been given time to learn their need of him and of his God. He was to be protected from all violence at the hands of the king, and from the rage of the wicked Jez'e-bel.

The first act of the mysterious prophet had been performed with great speed and severity. He had struck a blow at the very roots of Ba'al-worship. The priests of Ba'al and other false gods had told the people that the images they worshiped were able to control the forces of nature, so all Is'ra-el must be shown that the Lord alone is ruler of everything in nature. It must be made perfectly clear that the dew and the rain were not of Ba'al's giving, but were wholly in the hands of God. For more than three years the drought continued, finally breaking down the obstinacy of A'hab, and E-li'jah remained in seclusion until the Lord was ready to prove the sincerity of his prophet by sending rain at his word.

SUGGESTIONS FOR STUDY

Biblical Index to Helpful References

Self-Seeking Presumption Leads to Ruin. (Isa. 65:11-15.)

Marriage with Heathens Prohibited by God's Law. (Gen. 24:3; Deut. 7:3; Ezra 9:12.)

The Baneful Influence of an Evil Wife. (Jgs. 16:4, 15-19; Est. 5:14.)

Joshua's Curse Against Rebuilding Jericho. (Josh. 6:26.)

Drought Sent as Punishment for Sin. (Lev. 26:19; Deut. 11:15, 16.)

Elijah, a prototype of John the Baptist. (Matt. 3:4.)

Questions

1. Tell of the new era ushered in by Ahab.
2. What was the chief cause of his turning away from God?
3. Define the national origin and character of Jezebel.
4. Tell how she shrewdly managed her husband.
5. Through Jezebel's baneful influence what religion was imported into Israel?
6. Why was it wrong to undertake the rebuilding of Jericho?
7. Had all the Israelites turned away from God to worship Baal?
8. What prophet abruptly appeared before Ahab?
9. What national calamity did he foretell?
10. What became of him immediately after announcing this judgment?

ELIJAH MIRACULOUSLY PROVIDES FOOD FOR A WIDOW; RAISES HER SON FROM THE DEAD

1 KINGS 17:7-24

Our last story introduced us to one of the most majestic figures of the Old Testament. No heroic character of the Bible holds the mind of the student with more rapt attention than that of E-li'jah. His dramatic appearance at the very center of idolatry in the land—with no information regarding his parentage, training, or former activities—startles us today even as it did the royal household of A'hab and the people of Is'ra-el. There are mysteries in the stories connected with his life which attract and charm even a hasty reader. During his lifetime he was respected by friends and enemies alike, and today the tales of his fearless attacks upon idolatry command the admiration of both unbelievers and Christians.

It is clear to the sympathetic reader that God had prepared him in the wild, rocky mountains of Gil'e-ad to become a sweeping tornado against the evils of idolatry in Is'ra-el, but to some of little faith the lack of definite information in these matters casts doubt upon his strange career. All Is'ra-el trembled in fear and helplessness before the strong minded and evil hearted Jez'e-bel. A'hab was like putty in her hands; no one in the royal court dared to oppose her wishes. Only by the mighty deeds of a Divinely appointed hero could the proud spirit of the heathens be broken. Thus the Lord suddenly plunged upon benighted Is'ra-el the bright rays of a truly noble character. Let us now trace the chief events in the career of one who was sent by the Lord.

Although E-li'jah remained in such deep seclusion that neither A'hab nor the people knew his hiding place during the prolonged drought, the Bible record gives us some knowledge of his life in exile. For a long time he lived in the caves and deserts near Che'rith, drank from the sparkling waters of the brook, and was fed by ravens.

It was truly miraculous for such wild, unreasoning creatures to bring food to the man of God, but with God nothing is impossible. Should

RAISING OF THE WIDOW'S SON

it be His will, any creature under the heavens could serve as the means through which help might be brought to a deserving subject. Such a miracle took place for the benefit of one who accepted the word of God without question, and who did not permit even the prospect of starvation to interfere with his mission.

As a result of the continued lack of dew and rain, the waters of the brook upon which E-li'jah depended for his daily needs gradually diminished, and were finally dried up. Then the Lord appeared to His servant, and said:

"Arise, go to Zar'e-phath, in the region of Zi'don, and dwell there: behold, I have chosen a widow woman there to sustain thee."

This command was most unexpected, for the town of Zar'e-phath (better known as Sa-rep'ta) was situated between Zi'don and Tyre in Phoe'-ni-ci-a, which was the native land of Jez'e-bel. The Phoe'ni-ci-ans were idolators of the most fanatical type, and it was from their land that the worship of Ba'al had been introduced into Is'ra-el. It was the last place in the world where a worshiper of the true God might be expected to live, or where someone could be found who would befriend the man sent of God to oppose the cruel daughter of the Zi-do'ni-an king in her efforts to impose the worship of Ba'al upon Is'ra-el.

The brave E-li'jah, however, set out at once on his long and dangerous journey, travelling through the mountains to the north, and making his way through secret passes in order to escape the searching parties of an angry king. Upon reaching the outskirts of the little town of Zar'e-phath he saw a widow gathering wood to prepare the meal which she thought would be the last for her son and herself. The tired and bedraggled E-li'jah, looking more like a hermit than a prophet of God, called to the Gentile woman in these words:

"Fetch me, I pray thee, a little water in a vessel, that I may drink."

As the woman moved to grant this request, the prophet said,

"Bring me, I pray thee, a morsel of bread in thine hand."

To this request the woman of Sa-rep'ta replied:

"As the Lord thy God liveth, I have not a cake, but a handful of meal in a barrel, and a little oil in a cruse: and, behold, I am gathering two sticks, that I may go in and cook it for me and my son, that we may eat it, and die."

It was clear to E-li'jah that the Lord had brought him to this house, and the woman was also Divinely guided to recognize the stranger as a prophet of God. She confessed her faith in God in responding to the request of the hungry man at her gate. The prophet's next words opened the way for a deep, spiritual friendship which resulted in many blessings for both. Said he to the woman of Sa-rep'ta:

"Fear not; go and do as thou hast said: but make me thereof a little cake first, and bring it unto me, and after make for thee and thy son. For thus saith the Lord God of Is'ra-el, the barrel of meal shall not waste, neither shall the cruse of oil fail, until the day that the Lord sendeth rain upon the earth."

With a faith unrivalled by any to be found in Is'ra-el, this Gentile woman prepared her last bit of food for the prophet. Like the widow praised by the Sav'i-or nine hundred years later, she gave "all her living" to the Lord's service, and thus made possible the sending of daily provisions by the Lord. Had she not given, she would have famished; by giving, she was freely supplied with all that she needed.

We do not know how much longer the drought continued, but the barrel of meal and the cruse of oil did not run out. The same power which multiplied the two loaves of bread and five fishes for the hungry throng on the shores of Gal'i-lee now replenished the meal and oil for the widow of Sa-rep'ta.

Soon her faith was put to a severe trial. Her son was stricken with a mysterious disease, and suddenly died. Bowed down with the grief which only a mother can know, her first impulse was to drift back into the pagan religion of her own people, and to blame the prophet of God for the calamity.

ELIJAH FED BY AN ANGEL

E-li'jah was a man of spirit, quick to resent any disrespect to the God of Is'ra-el, but his one feeling at this moment was sympathy for the bereaved mother. He therefore asked the Lord for a favor which had never been granted before—the power to restore life to a dead body. Three times he placed his warm, living body upon the cold form of the widow's son, earnestly praying to God as he did so. Then the prayer was answered, and he took the boy to his mother alive and well. In great joy the woman said, "Now by this I know that thou art a man of God, and that the word of the Lord in thy mouth is truth."

SUGGESTIONS FOR STUDY

Biblical Index to Helpful References

Elijah Sent from His Own Land Because of Rejection by His Own People. (Luke 4: 24-26.)

The Necessity for Seclusion from the World. (Mark 6:30, 31; 7:34; Luke 9:10.)

Faith That Staggers Not at Improbabilities. (Psm. 27:3; Rom. 4:20, 21.)

The Woman's Consecration Like That of Another Widow. (Mark 12:42; Luke 21: 12.)

The Power of the Prayers of the Righteous. (Deut. 9:25, 26; Jas. 5:16.)

Other Resurrections of Old Testament Days. (2 Ki. 4:35; 13:21.)

Questions

1. Mention some of the things about Elijah which hold our attention.

2. How long did he live in seclusion before the drought was broken?

3. Where did he spend the earlier part of this seclusion? How was he fed?

4. Why did he leave Cherith? Where did he go? Why? Explain the danger incurred.

5. Tell of Elijah's meeting with the woman of Sarepta.

6. Describe fully the miracle that provided food for the widow and her son.

7. Tell of the death of her son and how Elijah restored him to life.

8. Was this the first instance of raising the dead to life? Can you name any others that took place afterwards?

STORY 112

ELIJAH CALLS DOWN FIRE FROM HEAVEN

1 KINGS 18

The drought which E-li'jah had predicted in his message to A'hab continued for three and a half years, covering the entire land of Is'ra-el and the countries to the north with desolation and barrenness. The sheep and cattle went hungry, and soon even the people were facing starvation. At last the wicked king was obliged to travel far and wide in search of food for his own horses. His God-fearing servant O-ba-di'ah was sent in one direction, while the king himself went in another. In the meantime the Lord had appeared to the prophet E-li'-jah, saying: "Go, show thyself unto A'hab; and I will send rain upon the earth."

In the course of his journey E-li'jah met A'hab's servant O-ba-di'ah— not by accident, but under the providence of God. O-ba-di'ah recognized the prophet at once, and fell on his face before him. E-li'jah told O-ba-di'ah to arrange an immediate interview with the king, but A'hab's servant protested that such an errand would endanger his own life. He re-

ELIJAH CALLS DOWN FIRE FROM HEAVEN

minded E-li'jah of his faithfulness to God, relating how he had hidden one hundred prophets from the wrath of Jez'e-bel, and how he had fed them from his own meager store of food. E-li'jah, however, assured O-ba-di'ah that he would show himself to the king that very day, and A'hab's servant was forced to report the coming visit of the prophet.

Soon the wicked king stood face to face with the prophet of God. A'hab spoke first, saying, "Do I at last meet thee; thou bringer of trouble upon Is'ra-el?" In reply to this accusation, E-li'jah boldly said to A'hab, "I have not troubled Is'ra-el; but thou, and thy father's house, in that ye have forsaken the commandments of the Lord God, and hast followed after Ba'al-im." The prophet then went on to direct the king to summon all Is'ra-el to Mount Car'mel for a decisive combat between the power of God and that which was claimed for Ba'al. The worshippers of Ba'al acknowledged him as the god of fire; E-li'jah challenged this claim in the test proposed. Such a test was fair to the Ba'al-ites.

Four hundred and fifty prophets of Ba'al, as well as four hundred other heathen priests who were fed by Jez'e-bel, were sent to Mount Car'mel to meet the lone prophet of God in a test of faith. Gathered to witness the contest were thousands of Is'ra-el-ites from all parts of the country, for all the people were eager to know who was the true God of Is'ra-el.

When the people had assembled, and all the priests of Ba'al were there, E-li'jah spoke as follows:

"How long halt ye between two opinions? If the Lord be God, follow him: but if Ba'al, then follow him. Now prepare two bullocks for sacrifice; let the priests of Ba'al offer one on an altar, and I will offer the other on an altar which I shall build. No fire is to be placed under either offering; the priests of Ba'al shall call upon their god, and I will call upon the God of Is'ra-el. The god that answereth by fire, let him be God."

The people were so strongly in favor of the proposed test that the priests of Ba'al dared not refuse to take part in it. Since the challenge came from E-li'jah, the servants of Ba'al had to go first in taking the test. They built an altar, prepared a bullock for sacrifice, and tried to call down fire from heaven. According to an ancient tradition, one of the heathen priests hid beneath the altar in an effort to set fire to the offering, but was suffocated before he could do so. Whether this is true or not, we know that for three long hours they cried in vain for Ba'al to send fire upon their offering. Then they danced wildly around the altar, shouting "O Ba'al, hear us!" Louder and louder became their cries, but to no avail; in despera-

tion they began to cut themselves with knives and lan-
cets, hoping to gain the
favor of their god by pouring out their blood as a
sacrifice.

The prophet of God
seized this opportunity of
mocking the worshipers of
Ba'al, saying to them taunt-
ingly, "Cry louder, for Ba'al
is a god: either he is talking, or has gone on a journey, or perhaps he is asleep,
and must be awaked!" The
taunts of the prophet drove
the servants of Ba'al to
even greater frenzy. They
danced more wildly than
ever, shouted at the top of
their voices, and cut themselves more deeply until

KING AHAB

they fell in utter exhaustion. But still Ba'al was silent, and no fire came
from heaven.

Then E-li'jah built his altar, taking care to follow the ancient law of
Is'ra-el—and to give all honor to God. He took twelve stones, one for
each tribe of Is'ra-el, and prepared the bullock for sacrifice as commanded
in the Le'vit-i-cal law. To prove that there could be no trickery, he had
twelve barrels of water poured over the offering, so that the altar was
completely drenched. When the hour arrived for the usual evening sacrifice, he called the people near the altar and prayed:

"Lord God of A'bra-ham, I'saac, and Is'ra-el, let it be known this day
that thou art God in Is'ra-el, and that I am thy servant, and that I have
done all these things at thy word. Hear me, O Lord, hear me, that this
people may know that thou art the Lord God, and that thou hast turned
their heart back again."

At once fire came down from heaven! From the clear evening sky there
swept down a beam of fire from God which consumed the offering,

burned the altar itself to ashes, and licked up every drop of water in the trenches around the altar. Thus two brief sentences, uttered in prayer by a lone man of God, had accomplished what the frantic cries of four hundred heathen priests for a whole day had failed to do. The name of Jeho'vah was brought back to the lips of the people; the neglected God of Is'ra-el had triumphed, and the people's faith in him was renewed.

The conquering prophet of God then directed the people to seize and put to death all the priests of Ba'al, and promised the king that rain would now surely fall upon the scorched land. Leaving A'hab to partake of food, E-li'jah went up into one of the high peaks of Car'mel to pray for rain. He sent a servant to a point from which he could look out upon the Med'i-ter-ra'ne-an Sea for a sign of the rain which he knew in his heart the Lord would send. But there was no sign of rain. Seven times the man of God prayed, and six times the servant returned with news of failure. After the seventh prayer, however, the servant reported that he had seen a cloud about the size of a man's hand in the western horizon. "That is enough," said the old prophet, "there is a sound of abundance of rain." The faith of E-li'jah was wonderfully rewarded, for in a short time the rains came in refreshing downpours over the entire land.

SUGGESTIONS FOR STUDY

Biblical Index to Helpful References

The Duty of Power of Self-Denial. (1 Thess. 3:3; 1 Cor. 9:12-27.)

Providential Meetings. (Gen. 24:15; 29:9.)

The Duty of Courage in Reproving Evil Doers. (Lev. 19:17, 18; Prov. 27: 5; Gal. 2:14.)

The Sin of Indecision. (Matt. 6:24.)

The Sin of Double-Mindedness. (2 Ki. 17:41; Psm. 12:2; Jas. 1:8.)

Directions for Building Altars for the Lord. (Deut. 27:5, 6; Ex. 20:25.)

The Fire of God Sent Upon His Altar. (Lev. 9:24; 1 Chr. 21:26; 2 Chr. 7:1.)

The Penalty of Death for Idolatry. (Deut. 17:2-5.)

Elijah's Power in Prayer. (Jas. 5:17, 18.)

The Availing Power of the Prayer of the Righteous. (Psm. 34:15; 1 Jno. 3:22.)

Questions

1. Describe the desolation caused by the long drought in Israel.

2. Did Ahab show any signs of repentance?

3. What did the Lord tell Elijah to do?

4. Whom did he meet and what message did he send to Ahab?

5. Why was Obadiah afraid to tell Ahab of Elijah's coming?

6. What did Elijah request Ahab to do?

7. Explain his proposed test between the power of God and of Baal.

8. How many priests of Baal were present at this test?

9. Tell of tho long prayers and fanaticism of the priests of Baal.

10. Describe how Elijah prepared his altar and sacrifice.

11. What happened when he uttered a brief prayer?

12. What was done to the priests of Baal?

13. Tell of Elijah's prayer for rain.

STORY 113

A BRAVE PROPHET IN THE
DEPTHS OF DESPAIR

1 KINGS 19

Following his great triumph over the prophets of Ba'al and the answer to his prayer for rain, E-li'jah hastened to the city of Jez're-el; expecting, no doubt, to find the queen overwhelmed with shame. Jez'e-bel, however, was neither terrified by the miracle which had taken place at Car'mel nor humbled by the Power which had given rain to the parched land of Is'ra-el. All the cruelty of her evil nature was aroused by the news of the execution of her idolatrous priests, and she swore vengeance with a threat to have E-li'jah slain within two days.

E-li'jah's usual courage forsook him when he learned that the queen had ordered his death, so he fled across the mountains of Ju'dah to the vicinity of Be'er-she'ba. After a hard day's travel he took shelter under a juniper tree, faint, hungry, and completely overcome with despair. In his utter lack of hope he prayed:

"Now, O Lord, take away my Life; for I am not better than my fathers."

Some people have looked upon the flight of E-li'jah as an inexcusable act of cowardice, but the Lord had not a word of reproach for him. Instead of granting his request for death, God refreshed the prophet with peaceful sleep. Food was prepared by angel hands while he slumbered, and twice he was awakened and told to partake of food to strengthen him for the long journey which lay ahead. E-li'jah then tasted no other food during his journey of forty days and nights to Mount Ho'reb, which was about two hundred miles from Be'er-she'ba. He could have travelled this distance in a direct course within five or six days, but he wandered about in the wilderness of Si'nai forty days—which reminds us of the forty years spent by the children of Is'ra-el in this same desert country.

The scenes about Ho'reb must have awakened many holy memories in the mind of E-li'jah. It was in the vicinity of these famous mountains that Mo'ses was hailed by the voice from a burning bush, and received the call to deliver Is'ra-el from E'gypt. It was from the top of Mount Si'nai that God had given the Ten Commandments, and it was here that Is'ra-el had encamped for the year during which the tabernacle was built and a new form of worship established. Made humble in spirit by the memory of these sacred events, E-li'jah lodged in a cave on the side of Mount Ho'reb; here the Lord said to him, "What doest thou here, E-li'jah?"

In answer to the Lord's question E-li'jah said:

"I have been devoted to the Lord God of hosts, but the children of Is'ra-el have forsaken thy covenant, thrown down thine altars, and slain thy prophets with the sword. I alone am left, and now they seek to take my life."

The Lord then healed the broken spirit of his prophet in a most wonderful way. While E-li'jah stood on the summit of Mount Ho'reb, the Lord showed His power in storm, earthquake, and fire. First a mighty wind swept through the mountains, rending great boulders from the cliffs of Ho'reb, and shattering them into small fragments. This sign of God's power was quickly followed by a terrific earthquake, and the prophet felt that he would soon receive a Divine Message. Like the disciples of the Sav'ior hundreds of years later, he no doubt wished to turn the force of the earthquake upon the enemies of God, but there was no message in the earthquake for E-li'jah. Storm and earthquake were followed by a third wonder. Shining above the brightness of the sun, a great fire swept through the mountains, roaring and devouring as it played from cliff to cliff. As the stern enemy of idolatry watched the tongues of flame melt the rocks about him he must have remembered the judgment of God upon idolatrous Sod'om, and longed for the same sort of Divine punishment upon Sa-ma'ri-a. God had spoken to Mo'ses from the top of the mountain, but still His

ELIJAH DWELLS IN A CAVE

voice was withheld from E-li'jah.

While the prophet stood in awed silence, marveling at the power of God, a fourth symbol was given. This time it came as a still, small voice; God spoke to his mind and heart through the Holy Spirit. Thus it was made clear to the despairing man of God that the victory of truth over error must be won through spiritual powers, and that idolatry and sin must be overthrown, "not by power nor by might, but by my Spirit, saith the Lord." In deep humility, and fully committed to the will of God, E-li'jah wrapped his face in his mantle and returned to the cave. Again the Lord appeared to him, and said, "What doest thou here, E-li'jah?"

Then the Lord directed the prophet to return to the land of Is'ra-el for other urgent duties; thus relieving his despair by enlarged work. His loneliness was cured by the Divine assurance that there were "seven thousand in Is'ra-el who had not bowed the knee to Ba'al." Comforted, refreshed, and reassured, E-li'jah resumed his important work in Is'ra-el.

The Lord's command for the anointing of E-li'sha as a companion and successor to the aged prophet was obeyed at once. Finding the young man ploughing one of the rich fields owned by his father Sha'phat, a prosperous farmer, the prophet cast his sheepskin mantle on the shoulders of E-li'sha: the ceremony used in those days in the adoption of a son or the appointment of a successor to a sacred office.

SUGGESTIONS FOR STUDY
Biblical Index to Helpful References

Hatred and Persecution of the Righteous. (Matt. 10:22; 2 Cor. 4:11.)

Human Frailty and Weakness. (Psm. 103: 14; 1 Cor. 3:2.)

The Depressing Influence of Loneliness. (Psm. 38:11.)

Despondency Under Persecution. (Psm. 71:4, 10.)

Death Sought in Despair. (Num. 11:14, 15; Job 7:15.)

Unwise Prayers. (Jonah 4:3; Matt. 20: 21.)

God's Care for His Children. (Psm. 115: 12; Matt. 6:32.)

Ministrations of Angels. (Psm. 91:11, 12; Isa. 63:9.)

Zeal for the Cause of God. (Phil. 4:12, 13; 2 Cor. 6:4-10.)

Questions

1. Explain the new side to Elijah's character now presented.

2. Why did Elijah flee into hiding?

3. Explain his despondency under the juniper tree.

4. How did God relieve his despair?

5. Where did Elijah then go? How long was the journey?

6. Tell of the Lord's appearance to Elijah in the cave at Horeb.

7. Describe the three symbols of God's power given to Elijah on Horeb.

8. Did God speak to him in any of these? How did God speak to him?

9. What was the significance of these manifestations and the still voice?

10. What commission was given Elijah after this experience?

11. Who was selected and anointed as Elijah's successor?

STORY 114

AHAB DEFEATS THE SYRIANS; JEZEBEL'S CRIME AGAINST NABOTH

1 KINGS 20, 21

The history of Is'ra-el now turns to brief accounts of two wars in which the Is'ra-el-ites were attacked by the Syr'-i-ans. Ben-Ha'dad, a son of the Syr'i-an king by the same name who had aided king A'sa of Ju'dah in a war against A-bi'jah, and had captured several cities of Is'ra-el, led a powerful army against the city of Sa-ma'ri-a. The cowardly A'hab then agreed to surrender his wives, children, and treasure to Ben-Ha'dad. But when the cruel Syr'i-an king made further demands upon him, A'hab consulted the elders of Is'ra-el and decided to go to war.

Undeserving as A'hab was of the Lord's mercy, the people who he had led into idolatry were saved from the invaders by a miracle. An unnamed prophet assured the people of deliverance, and organized an army of seven thousand men and two hundred and thirty officers for an attack upon the Syr'i-ans. Although greatly outnumbered in men, the Is'ra-el-ites were given courage for the battle by their faith in God.

The proud, self-confident king of the Syr'i-ans celebrated the expected conquest of Sa-ma'ri-a in drunken revelry with his thirty-two courtiers, thus making it easier for the Is'ra-el-ites to succeed in their attack. Given but little support and encouragement by their drunken leaders, the Syr'-i-an troops were slain in thousands, and Ben-Ha'dad and his chieftains barely escaped with their lives. Is'ra-el had been given a great victory by the God whom the people had forsaken. The prophet of God warned A'hab, however, that the Syr'i-ans would attack again, and urged him to be ready for another war within a few months.

The Syr'i-ans felt that they had failed to conquer Is'ra-el because of the power of Je-ho'vah, whom they regarded as a god of the hills. In planning their next attack, therefore, they resolved to avoid the hills, and to fight on level plains where their chariots would be most effective. In defiance of the God of Is'ra-el they marched into the most beautiful and fertile valleys of the land. The Is'ra-el-ites cautiously kept to the hills, and for six days constantly harassed the heathen invaders as they marched along the plains. In comparative numbers and strength, Is'ra-el was like a lamb in the midst of wolves, but the arm of Je-ho'vah led her to victory. On the seventh day the Is'ra-el-ites swept down upon the great hosts of the Syr'i-ans, routed them in confusion, and slew thousands of them as they fled toward the town of A'phek. Suddenly the walls fell down upon the terrified Syr'i-ans who huddled beneath them, and twenty-seven thousand warriors were crushed to death. Thus the Lord God of Is'ra-el proved that victory does not depend upon mere strength or numbers.

Once again A'hab showed a spirit of ingratitude by failing to carry the victory to a complete triumph over Ben-Ha'dad. The heathen king of Syr'i-a had been placed in the hands of Is'ra-el for utter destruction, and the power of his nation was to be broken forever. But A'hab accepted a plea of mercy from Ben-Ha'dad, who agreed to return to Is'ra-el the cities which his father had taken.

A prophet of God then told A'hab a parable which concerned a trusted servant who had proved himself disloyal. In passing judgment upon such conduct, A'hab unwittingly denounced himself, just as Da'vid had done before the prophet Na'than. The prophet then revealed himself as a messenger of God, and plainly declared to A'hab that his dynasty would be overthrown as a penalty for his failure to destroy Ben-Ha'dad.

After A'hab had been miraculously delivered from the Syr'i-ans by the power of God, he gave himself up completely to a life of ease and comfort, spending much time in enlarging the gardens of his summer residence near Jez're-el. Not content with his already vast possessions in the beau-

NABOTH IN HIS VINEYARD

tiful plains of the Jez're-el valley, he coveted a neighboring vineyard which belonged to Na'both. Since the laws of Is'ra-el required that the vineyard be kept for his children, Na'both declined to sell the property. Then A'hab showed his weakness of character, sulking like a spoiled child, and giving way to fits of temper and irritation.

When Jez'e-bel learned the cause of the king's unhappiness, she took the matter into her own hands with typical deceit and cruelty. By means of forged letters Na'both was accused of treason, removed from his position of rank, and stoned to death; and his property seized by A'hab. These crimes, however, did not escape the notice of God; and as A'hab took possession of Na'both's vineyard his way was suddenly blocked by the stern prophet E-li'jah. Smitten in conscience, A'hab cried, "Hast thou found me, O mine enemy?" E-li'jah solemnly replied:

"I have found thee: because thou hast sold thyself to work evil in the sight of the Lord. God hath declared that he will cut off your descendants for the provocation of his anger, and for causing Is'ra-el to sin. As for thy wife Jez'e-bel, the Lord hath decreed that the dogs shall eat her flesh by the wall of Jez're-el; and there shall not one be left of thine or of her offspring." Ahab was spared, but these predictions were later fulfilled.

SUGGESTIONS FOR STUDY

Biblical Index to Helpful References

The Insatiable Demands of Avarice. (Prov. 16:8.)

The Insolence of a Corrupt Heart. (Jer. 17:9.)

The Duty of Vigilance Against Enemies. (Eph. 6:10; 1 Pet. 5:8.)

Jehovah the God of All Nations. (Ex. 19:5; Psm. 24:1.)

Boldness in Denouncing Sin Required of God's Ministers. (2 Tim. 4:2.)

Self-Pronouncement of Doom. (2 Sam. 12:5, 6.)

Possessions of Executed Criminals Become the Property of the Crown. (Deut. 13:16.)

Questions

1. Tell of the Invasion of Israel by Ben-Hadad.

2. Did Ahab seek help of Baal? Why not? Did he ask aid of God? Why not?

3. Did the Lord intervene? Why?

4. What element of weakness was displayed by Ben-Hadad and his chieftains?

6. Describe the outcome of the war.

7. Tell of the excuses offered by the Syrians for their defeat.

8. Where did they plan for the next war to take place?

9. How long did the invasion continue before the main battle?

10. Describe the victory of the Israelites. What happened at Aphek?

11. Describe Ahab's failure to perform his full duty.

12. What judgment did he pronounce upon himself? How was this brought about?

13. Tell of Ahab's wish to have Naboth's vineyard and of his peevish fit.

14. Relate the plot by which Jezebel had Naboth slain and took the vineyards.

15. Tell of Elijah's visit to Ahab in Naboth's vineyard.

Story 115

ELIJAH CARRIED TO HEAVEN IN A FIERY CHARIOT

2 KINGS 2:1-18 For six or eight years after E-li'jah called
E-li'sha to the Lord's service, and began to train him as his successor, the
two prophets avoided the rulers of Is'ra-el.

The moral and religious condition of Is'ra-el was somewhat improved
under the reign of Je-ho'ram. He was not a good king, but was less wicked
than A'hab and A-ha-zi'ah. He destroyed the image of Ba'al which his
father had set up in Sa-ma'ri-a, and was more tolerant of those who worshipped the true God. He followed the course of Jer-o-bo'am in supporting calf-worship, which was a mixture of idolatry and worship of Je-ho'-
vah. These changed conditions
called for a different type of
work by the prophets of God.

The time had come for the
work of the stern, fiery E-li'jah
to be handed over to his mild
mannered successor. E-li'jah's
ministry of harsh reproof and
stern vengeance had been completed, and it was time for him
to enjoy his eternal reward. It
was Divinely revealed to E-li'-
jah that he should be carried to
heaven without suffering death,
and E-li'sha and the young
prophets were somehow given
to know when the hour of
E-li'jah's departure was at hand.

E-li'jah and E-li'sha were at
Gil'gal in E'phra-im when the
Lord told the aged prophet that
his time of departure was near.

THE CHARIOT OF FIRE

Wishing to lay down his office as quietly as he had entered upon it, E-li'jah suggested to his young companion that he remain at Gil'gal while he journeyed down to Beth'el. But E-li'sha declared his loyalty in these memorable words, "As the Lord liveth, and as thy soul liveth, I will not leave thee."

Upon reaching the waters of the Jor'dan, E-li'jah smote them with his mantle, dividing the waters so that he and E-li'sha passed over on dry ground. E-li'jah realized that he was soon to exchange the trials and hardships of earthly life for the joys of heaven. In these last moments, however, the aged prophet said to his friend and successor: "Ask what I shall do for thee, before I be taken away from thee."

E-li'sha then requested that he be given a double portion of the spirit of his master; to which E-li'jah replied, "Thou hast asked a hard thing, nevertheless, if you see me taken to heaven, it shall be done."

There soon followed a scene which can never be fully described in human language. Suddenly a flaming chariot descended from heaven, drawn by horses of fire. The aged prophet bowed his head, realizing that his hour of departure had come; then he was drawn into the chariot and carried up by a whirlwind into heaven. It was a fitting end to the earthly journey of one whose career had been like a flame of fire from heaven, bursting out from time to time with consuming wrath against idolatry and wickedness in high places.

The Lord opened the eyes of E-li'sha to the full meaning of the spectacle, and permitted E-li'jah's mantle to fall at the feet of his successor. Convinced by these signs that he was Divinely chosen to carry on the work of his master, E-li'sha picked up the mantle and walked to the edge of the Jor'dan. Remembering that just an hour before the waters had divided at the touch of the prophet's mantle, he smote the waters as his master had done. Once again the waters divided, and he walked to the other side of the Jor'dan on dry ground. Here he was met by the fifty young prophets who had looked with wonder upon the fiery chariot as it bore E-li'jah to heaven. Thus ended in a blaze of glory the earthly career of a great prophet, and thus began the mission of one who was worthy to follow in his steps.

SUGGESTIONS FOR STUDY

Biblical Index to Helpful References

The Virtue of Constancy. (Ruth 1:16; Matt. 27:55.)

The Whirlwind a Symbol of Destruction for the Wicked. (Prov. 1:27; Isa. 17:13.)

ELISHA BEGINS HIS WORK AS SUCCESSOR TO ELIJAH

2 KINGS 2:19-25; 3

The contrast between E-li'jah and his successor was striking, both in traits of character and in the nature of their ministries. E-li'jah was stern and vehement; E-li'sha was gentle and calm by nature. E-li'jah appeared in the king's court abruptly, without having been mentioned before; E-li'sha began his work after six or eight years of training. E-li'jah loved the solitude of caves and dens in the wilderness; E-li'sha spent much of his time in Jer-i'cho and Shu'nem, had his own home in Sa-ma'ri-a, and frequently visited the schools of the prophets. E-li'jah appeared before kings only to rebuke them; E-li'sha was often their counsellor.

E-li'sha was accepted as the successor to E-li'jah by the young prophets at Jer'i-cho, and began his ministry healing the bitter waters of a spring near the city. He then decided to visit the young prophets at Beth'el, but on the way was scoffed at by a band of children. They mocked and jeered him, saying, "Go up, thou bald head!" These children may have been pupils of the school of calf-worship at Beth'el and probably knew of E-li'-sha's appointment as a prophet. Their insults were really directed against the Lord, and for such blasphemy E-li'sha pronounced a curse upon them. Two bears came from the nearly wood, tearing to pieces forty-two of the blasphemers.

> "Hear the just doom, the judgment of the skies:
> He that hates truth shall be the dupe of lies;
> And he who will be cheated to the last,
> Delusions, strong as hell, shall bind him fast."

The next appearance of E-li'sha was on behalf of the kings of Is'ra-el, Ju'dah, and E'dom in a war against the Mo'ab-ites. After the death of A'hab the Mo'ab-ites revolted against Is'ra-el, refusing to pay the heavy annual tribute they had been accustomed to render. While marching across the desert lands near the border of E'dom, the allied armies found themselves in a place where no water could be had. Je-ho'ram, the king of Is'ra-el, knew that it was useless to call upon the idols of his people for help, and was so completely overcome by the emergency that he wrung his hands in utter helplessness. But Je-hosh'a-phat, the king of Ju'dah, was a devout believer in the true God; he called for a prophet, and eagerly sought the help and counsel of E-li'sha.

At first E-li'sha scornfully suggested that Je-ho'ram turn to the false prophets of his father and mother, adding these words: "Were it not that I regard the presence of Je-hosh'a-phat, the king of Ju'dah, I would not even look toward thee." As a means of soothing and elevating his mind, E-li'sha called for religious music; then he assured the three kings of an abundance of water, and a complete victory over the Mo'ab-ites.

The soldiers were ordered to dig great trenches to hold the water which E-li'sha declared would come, not from rain in the valley, but in some miraculous way known only to God. That night sudden rains fell upon the mountains of E'dom, and the next morning the overflow of water filled the trenches which had been dug at the prophet's command. Just as E-li'jah had brought down fire at the time of the evening sacrifice, so E-li'sha brought down an abundance of water at the time of the morning sacrifice.

CHILDREN SLAIN BY BEARS

Then a strange optical illusion was caused by the Lord to deceive the Mo'ab-ites. Looking upon the trenches filled with water under the blazing sun, they mistook them for streams of blood, and concluded that war had broken out between the men of Is'ra-el and of Ju'dah. The leader of the Mo'-ab-ites ordered his men to march upon the camps of the invading armies, thinking to capture the spoils left by those who had fallen in a civil war among his enemies.

Too late to change his course of action, he discovered the delusion under which he had labored, and was forced to meet the refreshed, well armed Is'ra-el-ites in open battle. His armies were utterly routed, his fruitful country laid bare and desolate. In heathen frenzy the king of the Mo'ab-ites offered his own son as a human sacrifice on the walls of his beleaguered capital.

Although this great service of E-li'sha did not lead Je-ho'ram away from the worship of calf-idols, it evidently raised the prophet to a place of influence in the land. He and his friends in the schools of the prophets were shown many courtesies by the rulers of the nation, and permitted to carry on their reforming work among the people. E-li'sha himself was permitted to make his home in the royal city, to travel at will throughout the country on his errands of mercy and salvation, and to offer his advice when the king faced unusual difficulties. His struggles with idolatry were often unavailing, but his labors healed many afflictions in the land of Is'ra-el.

SUGGESTIONS FOR STUDY

Biblical Index to Helpful References

Healing Poisonous Waters. (Ex. 15:21.)

Mocking of Good Men. (2 Chr. 30:10; Neh. 4:1; Acts 2:13.)

Scoffers Condemned. (Psm. 73:11; Jer. 17:5; 2 Pet. 3:3.)

Warnings Concerning Scorners. (Prov. 1: 22; 14:6.)

The Righteous Must Suffer Derision. (Psm. 42:10; 69:12; Luke 16:14.)

The Peril of Evil Alliances. (Isa. 30:2; Jer. 2:25.)

The Sin of Half-Heartedness. (Jer. 3:10; Hos. 10:2.)

False Illusions. (Jas. 4:13, 14.)

Questions

1. Describe the differences in Elijah and Elisha.

2. What was the first miracle performed by Elisha? The second?

3. Tell of the scoffing of the young people of Bethel.

4. What was the occasion of war between Israel and Moab?

5. Who became allied with Israel in this war?

6. Describe the distress in which the armies found themselves.

7. What was the feeling of Jehoram? Of Jehoshaphat?

8. Tell of the miracle by which Elisha relieved the peril of Israel.

9. Tell of the illusions of the Moabites and the result.

10. Did the miraculous deliverance effect any real change in Israel?

STORY 117

ELISHA'S MIRACLES FOR THE RELIEF OF INDIVIDUALS AND GROUPS

2 KINGS 4; 6:1-7; 8:1-6

The transitions in the life of E-li'sha were abrupt and startling. One day he miraculously supplied three great armies with water; soon afterward he performed a miracle which saved a poor and helpless widow from starvation and her sons from slavery.

The widow was hopelessly in debt, and had no money. The laws of the land provided that under such circumstances her two sons could be sold into bondage in order to pay her obligations. After one of her creditors had taken steps to have this done, the poor woman appealed to E-li'sha for help. The prophet was filled with pity, but took a wise, considerate course in relieving her distress. Instead of giving her direct aid, he found a way in which she could do something to help herself.

E-li'sha said to the unfortunate woman, "What hast thou in the house?" She replied, "I have nothing in the house, save a pot of oil." The prophet then directed her to borrow a large supply of empty vessels from her neighbors, to shut herself and her two sons in the privacy of her own home, and to pour oil from the one pot that she had into the others until they all were filled.

Without pausing to doubt the prophet's word, or to explain why he was asking her to do something that was impossible, she hastened to do what she was told. She poured a quantity of oil into the first empty pot from her own scant supply, and immediately the empty vessel was filled; the same miracle took place as she passed from vessel to vessel—each filling to the brim as soon as she had poured in a few drops from her own store —until presently all the borrowed vessels were full.

Filled with amazement and joy, the woman told the prophet what had happened and asked for further directions. She was told to sell enough of the oil to pay her debts, and to use the remainder for herself and her sons.

In the course of his missionary journeys E-li'sha often visited the little town of Shu'nem, located on the plain of Es-dra-e'lon at the foot of Mount Her'mon. A noble woman of considerable wealth often invited him to dine with her family as he passed through the community, and suggested to her husband that they prepare a guest room for the prophet, so that he would have a convenient place to rest when stopping in the village for any length of time.

One day when E-li'sha and his servant Ge-ha'zi were visiting at this home, the prophet expressed a desire to return her kindness by granting some favor. He offered to secure any favor of the king's court that she might desire, but the woman was content in her own home and among her own people, and had no desire for social honors or other marks of distinction. E-li'sha was perplexed, and said to Ge-ha'zi, "There must be some way in which we may command the blessings of God upon this noble woman for her generosity to us."

Ge-ha'zi then reminded his master that the good woman was too modest to speak about the one great trial in her life. There was no child in her home, and nothing would bring her greater joy than to be blessed with a son. E-li'sha quietly informed the woman that in return for her kindness to the servants of Je-ho'vah she would be rewarded with the gift of a son. In due time the son was born as promised by the man of God.

Within a few years the woman's joy was turned to anguish. The son who had brought supreme happiness to her home was now the means of bringing over it the deepest shadows. One day the child was struck down by the fierce rays of the harvest sun, and was brought home unconscious. By noon he was dead, and the parents were bowed down in grief.

As soon as the shock of this terrible blow had subsided, the faith of the noble woman came to her rescue. By a miracle God had given her this son, and she believed that he could be restored through a similar miracle. She tenderly carried the lifeless body up to the guest room set apart for the prophet E-li'sha, and hopefully made plans to lay her sorrow upon the heart of the miracle-working man of God. Without telling her husband of the death of the child, she asked that one of the servants go with her to Car'mel, where she might confer with E-li'sha. Upon reaching Car'mel she begged the prophet for help, refusing to leave him until he agreed to return with her to the room where the dead child lay upon the prophet's own bed.

E-li'sha quietly entered the room, closed the door, and began to pray. Alone with God and the dead child, he pleaded before the throne of grace; while the anxious mother waited patiently for news. Only once before had the dead been made alive in this world, and that had taken place through the prayers and miracle-working power of E-li'sha's departed master. E-li'sha had been promised the anointing power of God like that of E-li'jah, and now the promise must be put to its severest test. Like his master before him, E-li'sha first prayed, then placed his own warm body upon the cold flesh of the child. Suddenly the child awoke from the slumber of death, and was returned to his mother's arms, alive and well.

The prophet then warned the mother that a drought would soon torment this community for seven years, and advised her to seek a home in some neighboring land. She and her family journeyed to the land of the Phi-lis'tines, where they made their home until the famine was ended. During their absence the family estate was taken over by another, and on her return the woman went directly to the king with a plea for justice.

At the time of her plea before the king, the prophet's servant Ge-ha'zi had just told him of E-li'sha's miracle in restoring to life the son of the Shu'nam-mite woman. She then confirmed the account which Ge-ha'zi had given, and asked that the king give orders for the restoration of her property. The influence of E-li'sha's reputation and the just plea of the woman prompted the king to grant her request; her lands were restored at once, with the payment of rent for the time that they had been used by others.

Sometime after these events E-li'sha visited the school of the prophets at Gil'gal at a time when food was scarce. Some of the young prophets had gathered wild herbs, and were cooking them in a pot. As they began to eat of this

DWELLING OF THE SHUNAMMITE

pottage one of the men cried out, "O man of God, there is death in the pot!" It was suddenly discovered that the wild gourds which they had gathered were poisonous. E-li'sha called for a handful of meal, and cast it into the deadly food with these words, "Pour out for the people, that they may eat." By this simple act the prophet performed a miracle which overcame the power of deadly poison.

Two other notable miracles were performed in connection with the school of the prophets at Jer'i-cho. A friend of the institution brought from the first fruits of his harvest twenty small barley cakes and a small sack of fresh ears of corn. There were a hundred students, and of course this small amount of food was not sufficient to feed so many. The prophet, however, told his servant to set it before them, saying, "they shall eat and have some left." The meager meal was multiplied so that they all had an abundance. In the other miracle the prophet caused "iron to swim." The school had outgrown its quarters and a group of students was sent to cut timbers on the banks of the Jor'dan for its enlargement. One young man, too poor to own any tools, borrowed an axe; and as he felled the trees the iron head dropped into the deep waters of the river. E-li'jah cast a small stick into the waters and the axe gently rose to the surface; was recovered, and the young prophet was enabled to continue his work.

SUGGESTIONS FOR STUDY

Biblical Index to Helpful References

Laws Governing Slavery for Debt. (Ex. 21:2-6; Lev. 25:39-40; Deut. 15:12.)

God's Attentive Ear to the Cry of the Poor. (Psm. 34:6.)

The Lord's Help in Hours of Distress. (Isa. 66:13; Jno. 11:25.)

The Lord Our Provider of Food. (Psm. 145: 15, 16.)

Benevolent Deeds for God's Servants Rewarded. (Matt. 10:42; 25:40.)

Women Noted for Benevolent Services. (Prov. 31:10-31.)

Miracle-Born Children. (Gen. 18:10-15; 1 Sam. 1:19-20.)

The Dead Child Raised by Elijah. (1 Ki. 17:17-33.)

Questions

1. Tell of the variety in Elisha's miracles.

2. Explain the troubles of the woman unable to pay her debts. Who was she?

3. Tell of the method adopted by Elisha for her relief.

4. What kindness was shown Elisha by the woman of Shunem?

5. What miracle was performed as a reward for her?

6. How did the blessing of this child become the source of sorrow?

7. Tell of the Shunammite's appeal to Elisha for help.

8. What did Elisha do?

9. What other favor did Elisha bestow upon the Shunammite woman?

10. Tell of Elisha's two miracles at Gilgal.

11. Explain the miracle of causing iron to swim.

STORY 118

THE HEALING OF NAAMAN, THE SYRIAN LEPER

2 KINGS 5

North of Is'ra-el was a country known as Syr'i-a, which often made war upon the Is'ra-el-ites, taking away grain and cattle and prisoners. The commander of the Syr'i-an army was Na'a-man, a great warrior who was a favorite of the king. He enjoyed great honors and wealth, but was far from happy; across his life there fell the dread shadow of leprosy, a foul and incurable disease.

Among the servants in Na'a-man's household was a Jewish maiden who had been carried away by the Syr'i-ans in one of their raids upon Is'ra-el. Instead of holding thoughts of hatred and revenge against her master, she looked upon his suffering with pity and compassion. In her concern for the welfare of Na'a-man she said to his wife, "Would God that my master were with the prophet who is in Sa-ma'ri-a! He would heal him of his leprosy."

When these words were repeated to Na'a-man a ray of hope entered his breast, and he immediately sought the advice of the king. Laden with valuable presents he then went directly to the king of Is'ra-el, to whom he presented the following message from the king of Syr'i-a:

"Now when this letter is come unto thee, behold, I have therewith sent Na'a-man, my servant, that thou mayest recover him of his leprosy."

Je-ho'ram, the king of Is'ra-el, entirely misunderstood this message, and accused the king of Syr'i-a of seeking a quarrel. When E-li'sha was told what had happened, he sent this message to the king:

"Why hast thou rent thy clothes in anger? Send the man to me, and he shall know that there is a prophet in Is'ra-el."

Na'a-man and his large band of attendants then went to the home of E-li'sha, expecting the prophet to come out to meet them. Instead, E-li'sha sent his servant to the gate to tell the proud general:

"Go and wash in Jor'dan seven times, and thy flesh shall come again to thee, and thou shalt be clean."

This was a severe blow to Na'a-man's pride, and he turned away in a rage, saying contemptuously, "Are not Ab'a-nan and Phar'par better than all the waters of Is'ra-el?" He was insulted at the thought of bathing in the turbid waters of the Jor'dan instead of the clear, limpid streams of Da-mas'cus. E-li'sha had given him a very simple thing to do, but he was disappointed at not being instructed to do something more in keeping with his honorable rank; it also irked him to receive instruction from a mere servant, instead of from the prophet himself.

Under the wise counsel of his servants, however, he obeyed the prophet's directions. He went down to the Jor'dan, dipped himself seven times in its waters, and was amazed to find his body completely healed of leprosy. As he realized more fully the miracle which had been performed through the power of Is'ra-el's God, Na'a-man rushed back to E-li'sha to give him a suitable reward. He had brought with him ten talents of silver—worth fully fifteen thousand dollars today—a considerable amount of gold, and a number of costly Oriental garments. All of these treasures were offered to the prophet of God in return for the miraculous cure which he had received.

E-li'sha declined any reward, saying: "As the Lord liveth, before whom I stand, I will receive nothing." He wished the healed man of Syr'i-a to understand that the blessings of Is'ra-el's God were "without money and

RIVERS OF DAMASCUS

without price," and that no true prophet of Je-ho'vah would use a Divinely given power for his own gain. Na'a-man was fully convinced of the superiority of Je-ho'vah over the gods of Syr'i-a, and went home with a firm resolve henceforth to worship the true God.

In refusing to accept remuneration from Na'a-man for the great blessing that he had brought to him, E-li'sha displayed the spirit of self-denial and superlative honesty required of those who minister in spiritual things. He had given up a comfortable home, separated himself from family and friends, and endured many hardships in his arduous and dangerous travels; but he would accept no luxuries, no prospects for worldly wealth, for the miracle-working power which enabled him to help suffering humanity. Scorning earthly wealth, he possessed spiritual riches; avoiding even the appearance of a low mercenary spirit, he won heavenly glory through self-sacrifice.

True ministerial powers can not be bribed; and legitimate gifts are refused when the cause of religion would suffer by accepting them;

"Then learn to scorn the praise of men,
And learn to lose with God;
For Jesus won the world through shame,
And beckons thee His road."

SUGGESTIONS FOR STUDY

Biblical Index to Helpful References

Youthful Piety and Its Influence. (1 Sam. 2:18, 26; 2 Chr. 24:1, 2; 2 Tim. 1:5.)

The Lord's Use of Humble Instruments. (1 Cor. 1:27-29.)

The Loathesomeness of Leprosy. (Lev. 13:2; Deut. 24:8.)

The Sin of Suspicious Uncharitableness. (Math. 7:1-4.)

Divine Blessings Prevented by Pride. (Prov. 11:2; 13:10.)

The Curse of Avarice. (1 Tim. 6:10.)

The Sin of Using Religion for Pecuniary gain. (Acts 5:8.)

Wealth Gained by Lying and Dishonesty a Curse. (Prov. 21:16; Jer. 17:11.)

Naaman's Faith Commended by Jesus. (Luke 4:27.)

Lepers Healed by Jesus. (Matt. 8:2; Luke 17:12.)

Questions

1. What are some of the truths suggested by the story of Naaman?

2. Define Naaman's position in Syria. His affliction.

3. Tell of the kindness of the Jewish maid-slave.

4. To whom did Naaman first appeal for aid? With what effect?

5. Why did he go to Elisha? How was he received by Elisha?

6. What did Elisha direct him to do and what was his immediate action?

7. In what manner was Naaman healed? How did he seek to show his gratitude?

8. Why did Elisha refuse his gifts?

9. Tell of Gahazi's treacherous conduct.

10. What happened to Gahazi afterwards?

STORY 119

ELISHA SAVES HIS NATION FROM SYRIAN CRUELTY

2 KINGS 6:8-33; 7   Ben-Ha'dad, the king of Syr'i-a, made secret plans for invading Is'ra-el in a series of raids and plunderings. E-li'sha was enabled by the Lord to know the secret councils of the Syr'i-an king, and to inform Je-ho'ram of the time and place of attacks planned against Is'ra-el. When these crafty attacks were so often repulsed by the Is'ra-el-ites, Ben-Ha'dad suspected that traitors among his own warriors were giving away his plans to the king of Is'ra-el. He was told, however, that the prophet E-li'sha had full knowledge of the most secret plans of the Syr'i-an court, and that he informed Je-ho'ram of these plans. Ben-Ha'dad then ordered a band of soldiers to find and arrest E-li'sha, with the intention of having him slain.

E-li'sha and his young servant were then at Do'than, a village twelve miles north of Sa-ma'ri-a. Ben-Ha'dad sent a large army of horsemen and chariots to surround the little village and to capture the prophet. These soldiers encircled the town during the night, and E-li'sha's servant was greatly alarmed when he saw the early morning sun shining upon glistening spears and chariots. E-li'sha, however, was unafraid; he said to his frightened servant, "Fear not; for they that be with us are more than they that be with them." Then he prayed to the Lord to open the spiritual eyes of the servant, and the faint-hearted young man saw a host of fiery horses and chariots filling the mountains which surrounded the village.

The house where E-li'sha dwelt was soon surrounded by a group of Syr'i-an warriors, but they were suddenly smitten with blindness. E-li'-sha then said to those who had come to capture him, "Follow me, and I will take you to the man whom ye seek." He led them over the twelve mile road to Sa-ma'ri-a, and prayed that their sight be restored. In bewilderment and defeat these Syr'i-an warriors faced the humiliating experience of being captured by the one lone man whom they had sought to take prisoner.

When the king of Is'ra-el saw how these Syr'i-an warriors had been miraculously delivered into his hands, he wished to put them to death at once. But the prophet came to the rescue of the prisoners; at his suggestion they were released unharmed, with instructions to return to their home land.

Thus through the wisdom of E-li'sha the land of Is'ra-el was spared further invasions of the Syr'i-ans, and the nation was made secure for the time being. Before long, however, the cruel designs of Ben-Ha'dad took a more determined plan of attack upon Is'ra-el. The mercy which had been shown to his captured soldiers was forgotten, and Ben-Ha'dad made war upon Sa-ma'ri-a with a vast army. The city was besieged with such overwhelming numbers that it was soon brought into a state of starvation, and the pangs of hunger became so strong that mothers slew their own children for food.

Je-ho'ram blamed the prophet of God for the calamities which had fallen upon his capital city, and ordered that E-li'sha be arrested and slain. After due thought, however, he saw that his people were suffering for his own sins; he therefore restrained his officers from carrying out his former command for the murder of E-li'sha. The king then uttered a prayer which may be summarized in these words: "I admit that this calamity is a punishment for my own sins; I am chastened sorely by the Lord; and it will be better for my people to surrender to our foes."

BEN-HADAD AND THE KINGS

But the prophet of God sensed an entirely different outcome. He knew that God would deliver the people from their sufferings, and that the invading Syr'i-ans would be routed by a miracle. He then came forward with a prediction which very few of the people understood:

"Thus saith Je-ho'vah, Tomorrow about this time shall a measure of fine flour be sold for a shekel, and two measures of barley for a shekel, in the gate of Sa-ma'ri-a."

So impossible did the fulfillment of such a prediction appear that a prominent member of Je-ho'ram's court scoffed at the prophet's words in this language: "If Je-ho'vah should make windows in heaven, this thing could not be." With the mockery of unbelief he laughed at the idea of the Lord pouring down meal and grain like rain. So offensive to God was this speech that the prophet declared, "Thou shalt see it with thine eyes, but shalt not eat thereof."

That very night the word of E-li'sha was fulfilled in a most unexpected manner. The Lord caused the Syr'i-ans to think that they heard the tumult of vast armies coming to attack them, and they fled in dismay, leaving great stores of food, arms, and horses. Thus Sa-ma'ri-a was miraculously delivered from its enemies, and at the same time supplied with quantities of much needed food in fulfillment of E-li'sha's prophecy.

SUGGESTIONS FOR STUDY

Biblical Index to Helpful References

God's Knowledge of Evil Plottings. (Job 34:12; Prov. 15:11; Matt. 12:25; 22:18.)

The Duty of Making Known Malicious Plots. (Acts 23:16.)

The Confounding of the Wicked. (Isa. 37:27; 41:11, 12.)

The Lord's Defense of Those Who Trust Him. (Psm. 5:11.)

The Fearlessness of the Righteous. (Psm. 3:6; 27:3; 91:5.)

The Power of Habitual Prayerfulness. (Psm. 5:3; 55:17; Acts 10:2.)

The Woes Resulting from Famines. (Deut. 28:23.)

Doubting Scoffers Denounced. (Psm. 78:19; Isa. 53:1.)

The Lord's Use of Delusions. (2 Sam. 5:24.)

Questions

1. What secret plots did Ben-Hadad make against the Israelites?

2. Who made known these plots to Jehoram? How did he know about them?

3. What efforts did Ben-Hadad make for the arrest of Elisha? With what results?

4. When Elisha's servant became afraid, what happened?

5. What miracle was performed against the soldiers seeking Elisha?

6. How were they later treated by Elisha?

7. In what way did Ben-Hadad later undertake his raid against Israel?

8. What was the distressed condition of the people of Samaria?

9. Tell of the manner in which the Lord confused the Syrian armies.

10. Tell of Elisha's prophecy and of its fulfillment.

STORY 120

THE FALL OF THE HOUSE OF AHAB; BAAL WORSHIP DESTROYED

2 KINGS 8:7-15; 9-10

God now led E-li'sha into Da-mas'cus, the capital of Syr'i-a, and a center of idolatry and bitter hatred toward the people of Is'ra-el. E-li'sha's reputation as a man of God had great influence among the rulers of this heathen land, and his counsel was often sought in times of misfortune. Ben-Ha'dad did not believe in Is'ra-el's God, but he was unable to forget the miraculous healing of Na'a-man's leprosy. When the news of E-li'sha's presence in Da-mas'cus reached his sick bed, the king immediately sent his servant Haz'a-el to ask the prophet whether or not his illness should be fatal.

Haz'a-el, who had been a trusted servant of Ben-Ha'dad for many years, called upon E-li'sha with a train of forty camels laden with rich presents, and asked whether his master would recover. E-li'sha saw treachery and deceit in the eyes of the servant, read the true character of his murdrous plans, and had the courage to rebuke him in these words: "Go, say unto Ben-Ha'dad, Thou shalt surely recover; howbeit, Je-ho'-vah hath showed me that he shall surely die."

This puzzling message meant that the king would not die from disease, but at the hands of Haz'a-el.

Under the sorrow caused by a vision of Haz'a-el's future cruelties to Is'ra-el, the faithful prophet of God began to weep; when asked the reason for his tears, he related in detail the evils which the man standing before him would inflict upon Is'ra-el. Haz'a-el reigned for more than forty years, oppressing the Is'ra-el-ites just as the prophet had foretold.

Returning to his master, Haz'a-el reported that E-li'sha had said that he would recover from his illness, but kept to himself the prediction concerning the king's death. Within twenty-four hours he smothered Ben-Ha'-dad, choosing this form of assassination because it would leave no signs of violence on the body. He then succeeded Ben-Ha'dad as king of Syr'i-a, and soon after ascending the throne began war against Is'ra-el.

The scene of activity for E-li'sha now changes back to his native land. War was raging between Syr'i-a and Is'ra-el, and A-ha-zi'ah, king of Ju'-

dah, joined Je-ho'ram as an ally. He was the son of Ath-a-li'ah, the daughter of A'hab and Jez'e-bel who had been married to one of Je-hosh'a-phat's sons. In a fierce battle at Ra-moth-Gil'e-ad Je-ho'ram was wounded, and soon afterward returned to Jez're-el for treatment, leaving Je'hu in command of the army.

E-li'sha directed one of his disciples—thought by many to have been Jo'nah—to go secretly to Ra-moth-Gil'e-ad and anoint Je'hu as king of Israel. Twenty years before this incident the old prophet E-li'jah had foretold the agencies through which the house of A'hab should be destroyed, and Je'hu, the grandson of Nim'shi, was named among them. It had been fifteen years since Je'hu and one of his servants had been associated with A'hab in the taking of Na'both's vineyard, and had heard E-li'jah utter the words of doom upon A'hab's dynasty. Although he had probably never realized that he was to be one of the chosen instruments for carrying out this doom, the circumstances of his life had fully prepared him for such work.

JEHORAM PIERCED BY AN ARROW

The time had now arrived for the utter destruction of the dynasty of Om'ri, the most disastrous in the history of Is'ra-el and stained with the darkest crimes. Such a succession of weak and wicked rulers could not continue, and the crime of introducing into the royalty of the chosen race Phoe-ni'cian blood of the vilest type must be avenged. The doom of A'hab's household has been sealed; the hour is at hand.

Jehu's long years of war-like training had developed in him the traits required in the grim task of destroying every trace of the dynasty of Om'ri, and of the descendants of Jez'e-bel in the royal house of Ju'dah. The familiar text, "It is the driving of Je'hu, for he driveth furiously," fittingly describes his reckless, violent spirit. He did not plot or conspire to become king, but accepted his Divine appointment with boldness and zeal.

Having first assured himself of the loyal support of his army officers, Je'hu resolved to be the first to confront the deposed king. He rode furiously toward Jez-re'el, seized the messengers of Je-ho'ram who came out to meet him, and awaited the arrival of the rejected king and his ally A-ha-zi'ah. The meeting took place, fittingly enough, on the site of Na'-both's vineyard; Je'hu fatally wounded Je-ho'ram with an arrow, and the fleeing A-ha-zi'ah was slain by one of Je'hu's men.

Having learned of Je'hu's sudden rise to power, Jez'e-bel put on her finest royal garments and jewels, hoping to overawe the new king by her majesty and beauty. When she appeared at a window in the palace, Je'hu called to the servants to know who were on his side, and ordered that she be thrown into the street. Thus she was put to death, and her body was trampled in the streets of Jez-re'el by horses. E-li'jah had prophesied that "the dogs shall eat Jez'e-bel by the walls of Jez-re'el" and the Divine judgment was fulfilled with such precision that her body was not recognizable.

There were seventy male descendants of A'hab connected with the royal family in Sa-ma'ri-a. Je'hu challenged those who were loyal to the slain Je-ho'ram to choose a king from this number, intimating that such a course would be followed by civil war. The rulers in Sa-ma'ri-a yielded to Je'hu, and declared their allegiance to him as king of Is'rael. Then Je'hu ordered the immediate assassination of the seventy sons of the house of A'hab, thus carrying out the Divine decree against the idolatrous family. Then, on his triumphal march to the capital, Je'hu met forty-two princes of Ju'dah who were members of the house of Ath-a-li'ah, and under his orders they were put to death.

The next move of Je'hu was to order the death of all the priests and followers of Ba'al. Is'ra-el was in danger of being completely lost in idolatry, and the laws of Mo'ses had declared that worshippers of false gods should be punished with death. The warnings of two of God's greatest prophets had not been heeded, but now Je'hu was raised up by the Lord to blot out this evil.

The Lord praised Je'hu for his zeal in uprooting idolatry in Is'ra-el, but disapproved of his shrewd military tactics. Later he fell under the judgment of God because his reforms were incomplete. Instead of restoring true forms of worship in the nation, he turned to the evils of Jer-o-bo'am in calf-worship. A sad comment on his reign of twenty-eight years is found in the text: "Je'hu took no heed to walk in the law of the Lord God of Is'ra-el with all his heart." His reforms were carried out with an iron hand, were employed too much for selfish ends, and failed to check the downward trend of the nation. He reigned longer than any of his predecessors, and the throne of Is'ra-el remained under the rule of his dynasty for seventy-six years after his death, but idolatry and evils of every kind persisted in the nation.

SUGGESTIONS FOR STUDY

Biblical Index to Helpful References

Elisha Carries Out Elijah's Commission for Anointing Hazael. (1 Ki. 19:15.)

Hazael's Later Oppressions of Israel. (2 2 Ki. 12:17, 18; 13:3-7.)

"Am I a Dog" Term for a Despicable Man. (1 Sam. 17:43.)

Weeping Over the Sufferings of a Doomed People. (Luke 19:41; Rom. 9:1-3.)

Elisha Fulfills Elijah's Commission to Anoint Jehu. (1 Ki. 19:17.)

Baalism Introduced Into Israel by Jezebel. (1 Ki. 18:19.)

Destruction of House of Ahab and of Jezebel Foretold. (1 Ki. 21:21-24.)

Divine Vengeance Certain and Terrible. (Ezek. 25:17; Mi. 5:15; Rom. 12:19.)

Death, the Penalty for Idolatry in Israel. (Deut. 13:1-15; 17:2-4.)

The Wicked to Be Cut Off. (Job 22:15, 16; Psm. 37:22, 38; 73:17.)

The Curse of Evil Women. (Prov. 22: 14; Ezek. 13:18; Mark 6:22.)

Questions

1. Why did Elisha visit Damascus? How was he regarded in Syria?

2. What inquiry was made of him by Hazael?

3. Explain the answer given by Elisha. How was this answer fulfilled?

4. What prediction did he make concerning Hazael's treatment of Israel?

5. Tell of the anointing of Jehu to be king of Israel.

6. Tell of his extermination of Ahab's descendants.

7. In what manner did Jezebel meet death? What other descendant of Ahab was also slain?

8. Tell of Jehu's further sanguinary work.

9. Why did Jehu fall under the condemnation of the Lord?

STORY 121

A DEAD MAN REVIVED BY THE TOUCH OF ELISHA'S CORPSE

2 KINGS 13

Je'hu was succeeded on the throne of Is'ra-el by his son Je-ho'a-haz, who reigned for seventeen years, and who "did that which was evil in the sight of Je-ho'vah, and followed the sins of Jer-o-bo'am wherewith he made Is'ra-el to sin." The Lord allowed the Syr'i-ans to continue as His scourge upon Is'ra-el for persistent idolatry. The wealth of the nation was exhausted, and the people were ground down like dust.

Je-ho'a-haz was succeeded by his son Je-ho'ash, who reigned for sixteen years, and who also led Is'ra-el into sin. The peace of the nation was still threatened by Syr'i-a, for the Lord was ever alert to punish idolatry. Sometime after Je-ho'ash became king it was reported to him that the prophet E-li'sha had been stricken with a fatal illness. He was then more than ninety years old, worn out from long years of service for Is'ra-el, and rapidly coming to the end of his notable career. Although unfaithful to God himself, Je-ho'ash felt that the counsels and prayers of the aged prophet were Is'ra-el's only guarantees of security.

He therefore hastened to the bedside of the dying prophet to receive

VALLEY OF AJALON, FROM THE WEST

his last message. It was revealed to him that the passing away of the Lord's servant would have no effect upon the Divine protection of Is'ra-el as long as the king and people relied upon His presence among them. Then the king was directed to take a bow and arrow; E-li'sha, as God's representative, placed his hand on that of the king; the window was opened, and the arrow shot eastward. As it flew in the direction of the Syr'i-an conquest east of the Jor'dan, the prophet said, "The arrow is the arrow of the Lord's deliverance of his people out of the hand of the Syr'i-ans." Then E-li'sha directed the king to take up a number of arrows, and to shoot them into the ground; signifying victories to be won over the Syr'i-ans. Je-ho'ash betrayed the weakness of his faith and his unwillingness to press the combats against this powerful nation by shooting only three arrows into the ground. The meaning of this sign was that after winning three victories, Is'ra-el would be defeated by the Syr'i-ans. Had the king been more confident, more victories could have been won.

After this interview with Je-ho'ash, "E-li'sha died, and they buried him," but they did not bury his wholesome influence in the world. Sometime after the death of E-li'sha, the Mo'ab-ites invaded Is'ra-el on a plundering expedition, and a fierce battle took place. One of the Is'ra-el-ites was killed in action, and his comrades were so hard pressed by the enemy that they hurriedly thrust his body into the tomb of E-li'sha. As the body of the dead warrior touched the remains of E-li'sha, it suddenly sprang back to life. It was not the dead body of the prophet, but the living God of E-li'sha that gave life again to the dead, and the miracle showed that the powerful influence of the prophet of God had not ceased.

SUGGESTIONS FOR STUDY
Biblical Index to Helpful References

Sinful Imitations Denounced. (Ex. 23:2; Rom. 12:2.)

Mercy Promised to Those Who Return to God. (Psm. 34:4; Jer. 2:13.)

Godly Teachers a Nation's Greatest Security. (Matt. 5:13.).

God's Use of Signs. (Jgs. 6:38; Isa. 7:14; Luke 2:12.)

Power Limited by Unbelief. (Matt. 13:58; 17:19-20.)

Posthumous Influence of a Good Man. (Matt. 26:3; Heb. 11:4.)

Questions

1. What scourge of Israel continued under reign of Jehoahaz?

2. Who was reigning in Israel when Elisha became fatally ill?

3. Why did he visit the sick prophet?

4. What assuring message did Elisha give Jehoash?

5. Explain the sign used.

6. What further sign was directed illustrating victories over Syrians?

7. Why did Elisha become angered at Jehoash?

8. Tell how a dead man was made alive by touching Elisha's corpse.

STORY 122

THE WICKED REIGN OF JEROBOAM II

2 KINGS 14:23-29
PROPHECY OF AMOS   This chapter covers a period of splendor and prosperity for the Northern Kingdom of Is'ra-el. Adversity having failed to turn the hearts of the people back to God, it appears that the Lord gave them one last chance for repentance in a season of vast material blessings.

Je-ho'ash was succeeded by a son who is known as Jer-o-bo'am II, a man who was able as a statesman and skilled in warfare. Although he worshiped idols himself, he was used by the Lord to deliver Is'ra-el from foreign enemies, and to raise the nation to a height of success and glory unequalled in its past history. He reigned for forty-one years, longer than any other king of Is'ra-el, and brought the country into a flourishing state.

Wars against Syr'i-a were carried on with greater vigor, the lands recovered by his father were made more secure against further attacks, and the city of Da-mas'cus was subdued. The territory of Is'rael was extended to Ra'math in the northern Leb'a-non on the O-ron'tes, and the southern boundaries of the country reached the lower extremity of the Dead Sea. The wheels of commerce were again set in motion, and material prosperity covered the entire land.

These blessings, however, brought no religious improvement to Is'ra-el. Moral and spiritual reforms were neglected, and no attention was paid to the warnings of prophets of God. It is said of the king: "And Jer-o-bo'am did that which was evil in the sight of the Lord, and departed not from the sins of calf-worship."

The prophet Jo'nah—probably a servant of E-li'sha—appeared during the reign of Je-ho'ash, and predicted a reprieve in the judgments of God upon the nation, during which time there would be great prosperity. He encouraged Jer-o-bo'am II to extend the narrow borders of Is'ra-el until the country almost reached the grandeur of Da'vid's empire. Other notable prophets were sent with earnest calls to repentance, and with solemn warnings of destruction if the nation persisted in idolatry and wickedness.

It was during the reign of Jer-o-bo'am II that the prophet A'mos—the first of the He'brew seers to commit his message to writing—began his work. From the book which bears his name we have a clear picture of the luxury, idleness, and self-indulgence of Is'ra-el at that time. The ruling classes of the nation lived in wealth and idleness, utterly heedless of the sufferings of the poor. Thousands of peasants were crushed under the burdens of debt, and the provisions of mercy for such classes given in the Mosaic Law were ignored. The judges were so corrupt that A'mos denounces them as "sellers of the righteous for silver, and the needy for a pair of shoes." Weights and measures were untrue, hard earned wages were withheld, excessive interest charges were made for loans, and the poor were shamefully abused.

Worst of all, the practices of greed and oppression were carried on hand in hand with flourishing rites of idolatry. The altars at Beth'el and Gil'-gal, at Dan and Be-er-she'ba, burned with sacrifices of mixed worship to the calves of gold and to Je-ho'vah. The duties of true religion and the laws of the Sab'bath irked the people, and so were wickedly cast aside.

The prophet A'mos, though a native of Ju'dah, devoted his ministry to the Northern Kingdom—probably because of its greater wickedness at the time, and because its doom was more nearly at hand.

In vision after vision, with burning attacks upon self-satisfaction and indifference, with calls to repentance and reformation, and with predictions of dire calamities, this eloquent prophet appealed to Is'ra-el without avail. The nation sank deeper into sin year by year. When Je-ro-bo'am II died, after forty-one years on the throne, he left the kingdom at the highest pinnacle of material prosperity, but in the depths of moral and spiritual ruin.

SUGGESTIONS FOR STUDY

Biblical Index to Helpful References

The Perils of Material Prosperity. (Deut. 8:13, 14; Psm. 62:2.)

Earthly Wealth Fleeting and Uncertain. (Prov. 23:5; Jer. 17:11.)

Israel's Misfortunes Brought on by Idolatry and Sin. (Jer. 2:19; Hos. 9:7-13.)

Beneficent Laws for the Care of the Poor. (Ex. 23:11.)

Justice for the Poor Required. (Psm: 82:3; Prov. 19:17.)

Extortion and Injustice Condemned. (Isa. 10:2; Ezek. 22:12.)

Oppression and Pitilessness Denounced. (Psm. 35:15; 69:21; Prov. 22:16; 28:3.)

Questions

1. What was the material state of Israel under Jeroboam II?

2. With what country did Jeroboam carry on successful wars?

3. Did these improved material conditions benefit the nation religiously?

4. What prophet was sent to warn Israel against the sins of this age?

6. Describe the conditions why he bitterly denounced.

7. Quote some striking parts of his announcements of judgment.

Story 123

JONAH COMMISSIONED TO PREACH IN NINEVEH

THE BOOK OF JONAH

Among the prophets of the Northern Kingdom during the reign of Jer-o-bo'am II was a man named Jo'nah. In his youth he was probably an assistant of E-li'sha, and in later life was a contemporary of A'mos and Ho-se'a. He labored among the people of the Ten Tribes during the Syr'i-an oppression, and sent a special message to the king which has not been preserved.

In the midst of his work among the Ten Tribes of Is'ra-el, Jo'nah suddenly was called by the Lord to a dangerous mission. He was to go to Nin'e-veh, the capital of the great As-syr'i-an Empire, and announce that it would be destroyed within forty days unless the people turned away from their wickedness. This was a startling proposal, for As-syr'i-a had long been hated by Is'ra-el. For centuries Nin'e-veh had been filled with spoils of war taken by the As-syr'i-an kings from other nations, and had now attained a place of supremacy among the cities of the world. Her glory was stained with blood and robbery, idolatry and witchcraft, and she was notorious for her pride and defiance of God.

Jo'nah was deeply opposed to giving Nin'e-veh an opportunity of escaping its doom, and sought to relieve himself of the duty imposed by God by quitting his own land and fleeing to the city of Tar'shish at the end of the Med'i-ter-ra'ne-an Sea. Instead of going east as directed, he went west; instead of entering the field of action appointed by the Lord, he sought a safe retreat; instead of going to Nin'e-veh, he went down to Jop'pa and paid the fare for passage on a ship to Tar'shish.

The boat on which Jo'nah fled was soon overtaken by a great storm, and the heathen sailors felt that they were being punished by a god who resented the presence of an unbeliever. Jo'nah had been found sleeping at the bottom of the ship, and was awakened by the command. "What meanest thou, O sleeper? arise, call upon thy God, if so be that God will think upon us, that we perish not." All eyes were turned upon him witth suspicion as the sailors cast lots to determine who had offended their god. The lot fell upon Jo'nah, and the sailors began to question him closely.

Realizing that he had been overtaken by the Lord, Jo'nah declared that he was a He'brew who worshiped Je-ho'vah, the one true God of heaven and earth. After admitting his sins and blaming himself for the terrible storm, Jo'nah invited the sailors to put themselves under the protection of Je-ho'vah. To the question of what should be done with him he replied, "Throw me overboard into the sea, and the raging tempest will cease."

The sailors did not know what to do: if Jo'nah remained on board, they feared that they would be lost in the storm; if they cast him into the sea, they believed that Jo'nah's God would take their lives in vengeance. Hoping to save both Jo'nah and themselves, they took oars and rowed desperately to bring the ship to shore. Failing in these efforts, they finally cast Jo'nah into the sea, pleading with God not to let the guilt of murder rest upon them. At once the sea was calmed, and the grateful sailors worshiped Je-ho'vah with vows and sacrifices.

The sailors expected Jo'nah to be drowned, but the Lord had prepared a living sepulcher from which he would arise unharmed after three days. Jo'nah was carried through the depths of the sea in the belly of a great fish; for three days he lived entombed beneath the waters of the Med'i-ter-

JONAH'S TOMB AT NINEVEH

ra'ne-an, miraculously preserved by the power of God. While imprisoned in the depths he uttered one of the most notable prayers recorded in the Bible, admitting his sin in words of true penitence, and pledging himself to obey whatever commands God might give him if he was rescued. Then the Lord caused the great fish to cast Jo'nah up on the shores of his home-land, and the prophet sang a song of praise to God for his deliverance.

After Jo'nah's miraculous rescue, he received a second call to preach in Nin'e-veh which he promptly obeyed. The entire city heeded his warnings, repented, and turned to God; and the judgment of utter de-struction was lifted. God's mercy toward Nin'e-veh angered Jo'nah, who was unwilling for any people outside his own race to enjoy the favor of Je-ho'vah. The Lord dealt with his sullen behavior with mixed reproach and tender pity in which he condemned the spirit of religious intolerance.

The story of Jo'nah seems to have been included in the sacred writings of ancient Is'ra-el as an example of God's displeasure with the pride and exclusiveness of His chosen people. It shows God's love for all nations, and His will that the blessings of forgiving grace be extended to all the peoples of the world, and its chief lesson is: "God is no respecter of per-sons, but whosoever feareth him is accepted."

SUGGESTIONS FOR STUDY

Biblical Index to Helpful References

God's Call for Service Demands. Speedy Obedience. (Psm. 119:60; Eccl. 9:10.)

Natural Forces Used as Messengers of God's Judgment. (Job 37:1-7; Psm. 147:15-18.)

Impossible to Flee from God. (Jer. 16:16-18; Amos 9:2-4.)

Omni-Presence of God. (Psm. 139:7, 12.)

The Lord's Power Over the Raging Sea. (Psm. 89:9 93:3; 107:29.)

Driven to Prayer by Trouble. (Isa. 26:16-18; Acts 16:25-30.)

Prayer the Source of Help in Emergencies. (Prov. 3:6; 1 Pet. 5:7.)

Deliverance from Horrible Sufferings. (Psm. 34:4; Isa. 38:17.)

Questions

1. In whose reign did Jonah prophecy in Israel?

2. What unusual commission was given him by God?

3. Describe the size and moral state of Nineveh.

4. Why was Jonah unwilling to go to Nineveh?

5. How did he seek to flee from God?

6. Through what providence did God apprehend him?

7. When faced with his sin by the sailors what did Jonah do?

8. What happened to him when thrown into the sea?

9. What did he do while in the whale's belly?

10. What response did he give to the second call from God?

11. What is the lesson of the story of Jonah?

STORY 124

THE DESTRUCTION OF THE NORTHERN KINGDOM OF ISRAEL

2 KINGS 15:8-31; 17

When Zach-a-ri′ah, the son of Jer-o-bo′am II, ascended the throne of Is′ra-el the land was at peace, and its borders were almost as wide as those of the united kingdom in the days of Sol′o-mon. Yet trouble was soon to come from the far northeast; As-syr′i-a was developing into a military power much greater than any with which Is′ra-el had previously contended. The prophet A′mos had declared, even in the flourishing days of Jer-o-bo′am, that this powerful empire would crush Is′ra-el, and the prophet Ho-se′a had clearly outlined the scourge that As-syr′i-a would wield over all A′si-a.

Worse than any threatening foe from the outside was the civil strife which broke out in Is′ra-el as the result of wickedness and idolatry. Zach-a-ri′ah was assassinated by Shal′lum after a reign of only six months, and of the five kings who ruled the nation during the next forty years, only one died a natural death. Shal′lum reigned six months, and then was slain by Men′a-hem, who ruled for ten years. In order to prevent an attack by the king of As-syr′i-a, Men′a-hem paid the heavy tribute of a thousand talents of silver—which sum was raised by taxing every wealthy citizen fifty shekels of silver.

Men′a-hem died a natural death, and was succeeded as king by his son Pek-a-hi′ah. After two years of troubled rule the new king was slain by his officer Pe′kah, who then held the throne for twenty years. It was during his reign that Tig-lath-Pil-e′ser, king of As-syr′i-a, invaded the lands east of the Jor′dan and carried away the tribes of that region into captivity. The nation had now become so feeble that Pe′kah does not seem to have made the least effort to resist the As-syr′i-ans, and Is′ra-el was soon reduced to a small province surrounding Sa-ma-ri′a.

Ho-she′a then seized the throne by assassinating Pe′kah, and reigned for nine years. He seems to have slain Pe′kah at the command of Tig-lath-Pil-e′ser, and so began his reign as a vassal of the As-syr′i-an king. Before long, however, he made a bold stand for national freedom. When Shal-ma-ne′ser V became king of As-syr′i-a and demanded the tribute which

Is'ra-el had been accustomed to pay for a number of years, Ho-she'a revolted. With the aid of So, the king of Egypt, he warded off the demands
of As-syr'i-a for a few years; at length, however, the E'gypt-ian allies were
forced to defend their own country from the As-syr'i-ans. Shal-ma-ne'ser
then sent his general Sar'gon with a strong army against Is'ra-el, imprisoned Ho-she'a for life, and laid siege to Sa-ma-ri'a.

Sa-ma-ri'a held out for three years, but was finally overcome after indescribable horrors and sufferings, all of which had been foretold by the
prophets Ho-se'a, A'mos, and I-sa'iah. The records of Sar'gon state that
he took 27,200 of the people of Sa-ma-ri'a into captivity, seized fifty chariots, and imposed heavy tribute upon those who were left in the land.

Although it is said of Ho-she'a that "he was not as bad as the kings of
Is'ra-el that were before him," it is also stated that "he did that which was
evil in the sight of the Lord." He did not practice idolatry nor force it
upon the nation with the determined opposition to Je-ho'vah which earlier
kings had shown, but Is'ra-el seems to have been lost beyond hope of
recovery.

The kingdom came to an end, and the ten tribes disappeared forever
from history. Many of the people who were carried away as captives
mingled with the heathens to such an extent that they lost all trace of
their He'brew identity. The country which God had given to His chosen
people, except for the territory then occupied by Ju'dah, was given over to

CHALDEANS DESTROY THE BRAZEN SEA

aliens settled there by As-syr'i-a, and many of the Jews who remained were allowed to intermarry with them, forming the mixed race later known as Sa-mar'i-tans.

There sprang up in the wake of Is'ra-el's downfall an abominable mingling of true and false religion. Efforts were made to blend the teachings of Judaism with the pagan religions brought in by the As-syr'i-an col onists, so that the strange statement is made: "They feared the Lord, and served their own gods." Priests were chosen from the lowest types of the mixed population, and the resulting worship was deeply tinged with idolatry and wickedness.

It was from this mixture of heathen cults with Ju'da-ism and from the inter-marriage of Jews left in Pal'es-tine with the colonized captives sent there by the As-syr'i-ans that the Sa-mar'i-tan community was born, which was so loathed by the Jews in the time of Christ.

While the tribal existence of the ten tribes cannot be discovered in the annals of history after the As-syr'i-an captivity, it appears certain that many families were settled in cities which were occupied one hundred years later by the captives of the Ju-de'an kingdom. These people were represented by the returned exiles after the Bab-y-lo'ni-an captivity who were unable to trace their tribal ancestry, and among the millions of dispersed Jews of later history. It also appears that many of those who were left in their native land renewed their loyalty to Ju'dah, joining the He'brews of the Southern Kingdom.

SUGGESTIONS FOR STUDY

Biblical Index to Helpful References

The Certainty of the Lord's Word. (Ezek. 12:25.)

Israel Made as Dust Under God's Judgment. (Psm. 18:42.)

Judgments for Sin Effect Future Genera-tions. (Ex. 20:5; 24:7; Deut. 5:9.)

The Sin of Deserting God and Relying on Man. (Hos. 5:13; 7:11; 8:9.)

Horrors of the Siege of Samaria. (Isa. 28: 1-4; Hos. 10:11-14; 13:16; Amos 6:9-14.)

Questions

1. What were the apparent conditions when Zachariah became king?

2. In reality what great war power was threatening the nation?

3. What worse plague than outside foes existed?

4. Tell of the regicides of a brief forty year period.

5. When did Tiglath-Pileser conquer the territory east of the Jordan?

6. Tell of Hoshea's tumultuous reign.

7. How long was Samaria able to hold out against the siege of the Assyrians?

8. Tell of Samaria's fall and the end of the empire.

9. What religious conditions prevailed in the land after Israel's defeat?

10. What became of the ten tribes conquered by Assyria?

STORY 125

JUDAH PUNISHED FOR IDOLATRY

1 KINGS 12:21-24;
14:21-31; 15:1-8;
2 CHRONICLES 11-13   As a result of the division of Sol'o-mon's king-dom the territory governed by his son Re-ho-bo'am was confined to the tribes of Ju'dah and Ben'ja-min equal in area to about one-third of that governed by Jer-o-bo'am. After the Lord had checked his warlike plans for subduing the revolt of the ten tribes, Re-ho-bo'am showed signs of in-creasing wisdom. He established his capital at Je-ru'sa-lem, the city of Da'vid, and avoided the mistakes of the kings of Is'ra-el who shifted their capital from place to place for personal convenience.

Immediately after the rebellion of the ten tribes the Le'vites who had been stationed within this territory returned to Ju'dah, offering their serv-ices to the house of Da'vid. For three years or more Re-ho-bo'am encour-aged true worship and humbled himself before God. He made a serious mistake, however, in failing to oppose every form of idolatry in the land. The pagan temples built by his father in Je-ru'sa-lem were not destroyed, and the people were allowed to build high places and groves to Ba'al and other heathen gods.

Re-ho-bo'am became proud and conceited, and forsook the law of God. He became more interested in building for worldly grandeur than in maintaining the honor of God. The services of the temple and of the priesthood were abused, and the ideals of true worship were forsaken. He tolerated the most horrible sins among the people, and indulged him-self in many luxuries and vices contrary to the laws of God. He violated the Mosaic Law by taking many wives, and set aside the rights of his first born son in favor of A-bi'jah, because of his fondness for his mother.

The personal sins of Re-ho-bo'am soon led to national degeneracy and weakness. There was a rapid spread of immorality, the worst forms of vice prevailed under the sanction of idolatrous religions, and the apostasy of the nation became grievous and universal.

"Thus men go wrong with an ingenious skill,
Bend the straight rule to their own crooked will."
But God reserves His own appointed agencies for the punishment of national sins; and in due time allowed Re-ho-bo'am to be forced into war.

There was ruling in E'gypt at this time a mighty warrior king known as Shi'shak. With a large number of foreign allies, twelve thousand chariots, sixty thousand horsemen, and a huge army on foot, Shi'shak invaded the land of Ju'dah. After capturing many strong cities he marched against Je-ru'sa-lem, and the king and his officers trembled in fear of the E'gypt-ians.

Re-ho-bo'am gathered all the princes of the nation in Je-ru'sa-lem for counsel, and the Lord sent the prophet She-ma'iah to tell him that the invasion was in punishment of the sins of His chosen people. Re-ho-bo'am and the princes of Is'ra-el admitted their sins, and humbled themselves before the Lord. God then pardoned them, and ordered the prophet to announce that Je-ru'sa-lem would not be destroyed nor the nation overthrown at that time. The king was forced, however, to yield to Shi'shak, and the nation became tributary to E'gypt. The temple and palaces were robbed of their treasures, and the golden spears borne by the king's bodyguard were taken as a sign of Ju'dah's humiliation.

After ruling for seventeen years, Re-ho-bo'am died, and was succeeded by his son A-bi'jah. Jer-o-bo'am, king of Is'ra-el, took advantage of his youth and inexperience in an effort to gain control of Ju'dah, raising an

THE MOUNT OF OLIVES, FROM MOUNT ZION

army of eight hundred thousand men for this purpose. A-bi'jah was able to gather only four hundred thousand warriors, but went out to meet Jer-o-bo'am in battle. Standing on a point which overlooked the armies of Jer-o-bo'am, he urged them not "to fight against Je-ho'vah, the God of their fathers," warning them that they would not prosper in such a war. He upbraided Jer-o-bo'am and his followers as rebels, and denounced the Northern Kingdom for its calf-worship and other forms of idolatry. Ju'-dah was praised for its loyalty to the Mosaic laws and forms of worship, and A-bi'jah called upon the Lord to strengthen the armies of the house of Da'vid.

While A-bi'jah was making his speech, Jer-o-bo'am ordered his armies to encircle the forces of Ju'dah and make an immediate attack. The men of Ju'dah cried unto the Lord for Divine aid, and the priests blew trumpets as a signal for united combat with the armies of Jer-o-bo'am. Although outnumbered two to one, the men of Ju'dah were given such strength and courage by the Lord that they won a great victory. They slew five hundred thousand of Jer-o-bo'am's men, captured a number of important cities, and utterly defeated the attempt to seize control of their country.

In spite of the honors and success which the Lord granted him, we are told that A-bi'jah's heart "was not perfect, and he walked in the sins of his father." His religion seems to have been reserved for great emergencies, and entirely forgotten in the ordinary pursuits of life. He was an eloquent speaker and an able leader, but in his heart was divided in loyalty, trying to serve both the true God and the graven images of Ba'al.

SUGGESTIONS FOR STUDY

Biblical Index to Helpful References

The Permanency of the Tribe of Judah. (Deut. 3:7; Jgs. 1:2.)

God's Unbreakable Covenant with David. (Psm. 89:34-37.)

Promises and Conditions for Prosperity of Offspring. (Psm. 132:12.)

Acknowledgment of God's Justice in Retri-butions. (Ezra 9:15; Neh. 9:33.)

God's Use of Heathen Attacks in War for Judgment. (Isa. 5:26-30; Jer. 6:22-25.)

The National Disgrace of a Defenseless Capital. (Prov. 25:28.)

The Law Violated in Choice of Abijah. (Deut. 21:15, 16.)

Questions

1. Define the territory ruled by Rehoboam.

2. What act of the Levites strengthened Judah's religious state?

3. How long did Rehoboam remain loyal to God?

4. Describe his later religious apostacy.

5. What nation made war on Rehoboam?

6. What was the outcome of this war?

7. How long did Rehoboam reign? Who succeeded him?

8. Tell of the war between Jeroboam and Abijah.

STORY 126

ASA, THE REFORMER KING OF JUDAH

2 CHRONICLES 14-16;
1 KINGS 15:9-24

A'sa was a deeply religious man, careful at all times to honor Je-ho'vah. No sooner had he risen to the throne than he began to undo the evils inflicted upon the land by his father and grandfather. He struck at the very root of the nation's woes by pulling down the altars and high places used in heathen worship, breaking to pieces the images of Ba'al, and utterly destroying all the relics of pagan gods in Je-ru'sa-lem and other cities.

The first ten years of his reign were quiet and prosperous. Taking advantage of the current weakness of E'gypt, which had dominated the land of Ju'dah since the invasion by Shi'shak, A'sa fortified many of his cities and raised a large militia to resist any future attacks from E'gypt or other foes from the south. The people were taken into his confidence, and their wishes were considered in levying taxes, raising the army, and deciding other problems of the government.

Soon after Ze'rah became king of E'gypt, that country regained much of its former military strength. Ze'rah decided to invade Ju'dah in order to bring the land under E-gyp'tian control once more, and led an expedition of one million soldiers to the town of Mar-re'shah, near the southern border. A'sa then called out all his warriors and met the invaders in a valley near Ma-re'shah. Before entering the battle, A'sa turned to the Lord in prayer. He knew that "there is no restraint to the Lord to save by many or by few," and relied upon Divine power for help.

As A'sa and his victorious armies returned from the pursuit of the E-gyp'tians, they were met by the prophet As-a-ri'ah. He reminded them that God had given them the victory, and warned them that His continued favor would depend upon obedience to His laws. A'sa heeded the warnings of the prophet, and his reforms were carried on with even greater zeal. The destruction of idols was extended to Ben'ja-min and the cities which had been taken from the Phi-lis'tines. He would not even allow his mother to keep the idol which she served, but had it burned and the ashes cast into the brook Ki'shon. The altars of the Lord which had been desecrated by Re-ho-bo'am and A-bi'jah were repaired, and neglected sacrifices to God were resumed.

No religious revival in Is'ra-el was complete without a renewal of the covenant with God. To such a gathering A'sa invited all members of the tribes of Ju'dah and Ben'ja-min, as well as representatives of the northern tribes who had remained loyal to Je-ho'vah. The people joined in solemn pledges to keep the laws of God and to punish all who worshiped idols, and offered seven hundred oxen and seven thousand sheep in sacrifice to the Lord. There followed a number of years of peace and prosperity for the nation.

During the last years of this good king a state of rivalry between Ju'dah and the Northern Kingdom led him to make a great mistake. Ba-a'sha had slain the descendants of Jer-o-bo'am, seized the throne of Is'ra-el, and now threatened the Southern Kingdom. He strengthened himself in his warlike designs by allying with the king of Syr'i-a, who also had made a treaty of peace with Ju'dah. The town of Ra'mah was situated on the border between Ju'dah and Is'ra-el, and Ba-a'sha decided to make it the site of a strong fortress which would interfere with the commerce of the people of the Northern Kingdom and Je-ru'sa-lem. This action greatly alarmed A'sa, who felt that the freedom of his country demanded defeat of Ba-a'sha in his stronghold at Ra'mah.

HAIFA, AT THE FOOT OF MOUNT CARMEL

Instead of turning to God for counsel, A'sa relied upon his own shrewdness. He bribed the king of Syr'i-a to break his agreement with Ba-a'sha, and to lend military aid in a threatened war against Is'ra-el; thus the Northern king was forced to give up the fortifications at Ra'mah. A'sa had won a temporary victory, but at a price unworthy of his previous career. He was guilty of using the very treasures which he had dedicated to the Lord's service in payment of his bribe to the king of Syr'i-a.

The Lord sent the prophet Ha-na'ni to reprove A'sa for his folly and sin. The prophet rebuked him in these words: "Because thou hast relied on the king of Syr'i-a, and not on the Lord thy God: therefore is the host of the king of Syr'i-a escaped out of thy hands; and from henceforth thou shalt have war." The strife between the two He'brew kingdoms continued unabated, and the bribed Syr'i-ans proved unreliable in their support of Ju'dah.

The rebuke of the prophet embittered A'sa, who had him thrown into prison; but God's means of reproof and punishment were not exhausted. The king was soon humbled by a serious ailment which brought him unspeakable sufferings for two years prior to his death. He added sin to sin by turning to physicians who depended upon charms and magic for healing diseases, and was again filled with disappointment. Though his faith had grown less in his declining years, he was highly honored in his burial. He was succeeded by his son Je-hosh'a-phat.

SUGGESTIONS FOR STUDY

Biblical Index to Helpful References

God the Dispenser of Quietness Among Nations. (Psm. 46:9.)

God's Sovereignty Over All Nations. (Job 12:19; Prov. 21:1.)

God's Ancient Covenant with Israel. (Ex. 22:20; Heb. 10:28.)

God's Curse on the Land That Deserts Him. (Isa. 9:9.)

Covenant Meetings in Israel's History. (Ex. 24:3-8; 2 Ki. 23:3; Neh. 10:28, 29.)

The Peril of Turning from God for Reliance on Man. (Psm. 146:3.)

God's Promises Certain of Fulfillment. (Isa. 65:16; Jer. 10:10.)

Questions

1. Tell of Asa's reforms on assuming the throne of Judah.

2. What was the state of the nation for the first ten years of his reign?

3. Tell of Asa's national defense policies.

4. What king of Egypt made war on Asa? Why?

5. Tell of the victory of Judah's armies over Zerah.

6. What warnings were given Asa by the prophet Azariah?

7. How did Asa respond to these warnings?

8. Tell of Asa's mistake in connection with the Northern Kingdom.

9. What prophet reproved Asa for this error? How did he receive this reproof?

STORY 127

THE REIGN OF THE GOOD
KING JEHOSHAPHAT

2 CHRONICLES 17-20;
1 KINGS 22:1-50
Je-hosh'a-phat stands out as a man of honor, even though his life was not entirely free from mistakes. He was strongly opposed to the calf-worship and other idolatries of the Northern Kingdom, and continued the work begun by his noble father in destroying heathen images in all the land which he governed. Upright in character, and wholehearted in his loyalty to Je-ho'vah, he sought to restore the true forms of worship, to instruct the people in the laws of God, and to establish justice throughout the land.

During the declining years of his father, the Northern Kingdom had grown in power under the reign of A'hab, and was now showing decided hostility toward Ju'dah. Je-hosh'a-phat, therefore, began his reign by fortifying the cities of Ju'dah and training an army of more than one million men. Thus the threat of war was checked, and the nation commanded the highest respect of neighboring countries.

One of the wise moves of Je-hosh'a-phat was the appointment of a commission of sixteen to tour the nation on an educational campaign. Five of the members were princes, whose duty it was to inform the people concerning the government; there were also nine Le'vites, to teach the Mosaic ritual and laws of worship; and two priests, to explain the laws of sacrifice.

The one great mistake in the career of this noble king was his permission of the marriage of his son Je-ho'ram to Ath-a-li'ah, the daughter of A'hab and Jez'e-bel. This marriage was evidently sought by Jez'e-bel out of envy for the riches and honor of Je-hosh'a-phat, and from her idolatrous designs on the Southern Kingdom. Je-hosh'a-phat gave his consent in the hope of establishing peace between the two kindred nations, and without suspecting the probable evil results. This marriage, as we shall later see, brought the kingdom of Ju'dah and the royal house of Da'vid to the brink of ruin. It involved Je-hosh'a-phat in an unholy alliance which very nearly resulted in his death on the battlefield with A'hab. When warned by the prophet Mi-ca'iah of the disastrous outcome of the war into which A'hab had drawn him, he had gone too far to withdraw.

For his unholy alliance with A'hab, Je-hosh'a-phat was severely rebuked by the prophet Je'hu, who said: "Thou hast helped the ungodly, and loved them that hate the Lord." He assured the king, however, that the Lord would continue his blessings because of the many good qualities which he possessed.

After the death of A'hab there was war between the Northern Kingdom and the Mo'ab-ites, and Je-hosh'a-phat responded to Je-ho'ram's urgent appeal for help. The E'dom-ites, who were subjects to Ju'-

AHAB PIERCED BY AN ARROW

dah at that time, also joined in the war against the Mo'ab-ites. When the combined armies of the three nations faced certain defeat because of the lack of water in the territory in which they were encamped, Je-hosh'a-phat suggested that the prophet E-li'sha be called to their aid. As a result of the miraculous supply of water which came in answer to E-li'sha's prayer, and of the confusion produced among the Mo'ab-ites by the miracle, the united armies won a great victory. In revenge for the part which Je-hosh'-a-phat had played in their humiliating defeat, the Mo'ab-ites later secured the aid of the Am'mon-ites in an unexpected invasion of the land of Ju'dah. The combined armies were a dangerous threat to Ju'dah, and the heart of the good king was filled with grave doubts.

Although alarmed, Je-hosh'a-phat was equal to the occasion. He issued a call for a national fast in Je-ru'sa-lem, and gathered the people in the temple for prayer. He then bowed before the Lord, acknowledging the utter helplessness of his people, expressing his complete dependence upon the Lord in delivering the nation from the invaders. There was a note of confidence in his supplications as he declared: "Thou art our God, who didst drive out the inhabitants of this land before thy people Is'ra-el; our eyes are upon thee."

While the king and people stood humbly before Je-ho'vah, the Spirit of

God came upon a prophet named Ja-ha'zi-el, who said to the king: "Thus saith the Lord unto you, Be not afraid or dismayed by reason of this great multitude; for the battle is not yours, but God's. Tomorrow go down against them: ye shall not need to fight in this battle: set yourselves, stand ye still, and see the salvation of the Lord with you."

Encouraged by these assurances from the prophet of God, the people of Ju'dah went out to meet the hordes of the Mo'ab-ites and Am'mon-ites. The strangest battle in history followed. Singers were appointed to lead the procession in joyful praise to God, and the whole company joined in reverent worship. Songs of victory were sung without a single stroke in battle. Panic fell upon the mixed armies of the enemy, and they turned their weapons upon one another in great confusion and fear. It was truly "not a battle of the He'brews, but of the Lord" as He seized the officers of the enemy with madness and turned the soldiers into a blind frenzy. The work of destruction was ended even before the men of Ju'dah could reach the field, which was strewn with dead bodies. The armies of Je-hosh'a-phat spent four days gathering treasures and spoils of war, and then returned to Je-ru'sa-lem with the same religious celebrations which had preceded the Divinely given triumph.

After a brilliant reign of twenty-five years Je-hosh'a-phat's health became enfeebled, and his son Je-ho'ram was allowed to rule the nation during the last four years of the king.

SUGGESTIONS FOR STUDY
Biblical Index to Helpful References

The Institution of a Central Court for Israel. (Ex. 18:19-26; Deut. 7:8-13.)

Warnings Against Alliances with the Wicked. (Prov. 4:14; 23:6-8.)

Satan Working Through Professed Followers of God. (Zech. 1:10.)

God's Chosen Servants Sometimes Placed in Wicked Hands. (Job 16:10; Lam. 3:30.)

Consulting Prophets Before Beginning War. (1 Sam. 28:16.)

Conscience Makes Cowards of Sinners. (Prov. 28:1.)

Evil Men Ensnared in Their Own Traps. (Prov. 12:13; 24:15, 16.)

Iniquity Its Own Punisher. (Prov. 5:22; 11:3.)

Questions

1. How does Jehoshaphat's reputation appear?

2. What precautions did Jehoshaphat take against trouble from Northern kingdom?

3. Tell of Jehoshaphat's educational program.

4. What was the one big mistake of Jehoshaphat's life?

5. By whom was he rebuked for this wrong?

6. What was the occasion of Jehoshaphat's alliance with Northern Kingdom?

7. What was the outcome of the first war with Moabites?

8. In what way did Jehoshaphat win against the attacks of Moab?

9. What was the reason for Jehoram's taking the throne before his father's death?

THE NATION SUFFERS FROM AN UNHOLY MARRIAGE

2 CHRONICLES 21-22;
2 KINGS 8:16-29;
9:27-29; 11:1-3 This chapter covers the darkest period in the history of Ju'dah, and shows the terrible calamities which result from unholy marriages. Je-hosh'a-phat was one of the noblest kings of Ju'dah, but his son Je-ho'ram and grandson A-ha-zi'ah were two of the most ignoble. The history of these two wicked kings shows how the evil influence of one woman corrupted the house of Da'vid and disgraced the kingdom of Ju'dah, besides destroying the royal line of Om'ri in the Northern Kingdom. Ju'dah became infected with the same idolatry which had enfeebled Is'ra-el, and the morality of Je-ru'sa-lem sank almost as low as that of Sa-ma'ri-a.

Je-hosh'a-phat showed wisdom in appointing all his other sons to responsible positions over cities and provinces, and by endowing them with rich gifts of silver and gold. Je-ho'ram, being the eldest son and natural heir to the throne, had no reason to be jealous of his heritage; when he became king, however, he had his six brothers murdered. He was no doubt driven to this inexcusable deed by the evil influence of his wife and her mother.

Although Je-ho'ram had the benefit of his father's wise counsel and holy life during the first four years of his reign, he chose to follow in the wicked steps of A'hab. He became vile in his manner of life, and compelled Ju'dah to adopt the worship of Ba'al. King and people alike forsook Je-ho'vah and the services of His house, taking up the abominations of heathen worship. Je-ho'ram thus made himself notorious as the first king to lead Ju'dah into the worship of foreign gods.

E'dom, which had been subject to Ju'dah since the days of Da'vid, revolted and set up its own king. Je-ho'ram tried to subdue this rebellion, but his soldiers became so demoralized that they gave up the battle and returned to their own homes. E'dom was lost to the nation, and this misfortune was soon followed by the rebellion of the A-ra'bi-ans who had been conquered by A'sa, and by the loss of the important city of Lib'nah.

Taking advantage of the weakened condition of Ju'dah, the Phi-lis'-

tines joined the A-ra'bi-ans in an invasion of the land, plundered Je-ru'sa-lem and the royal palace, and took into captivity all of the royal family except Je-ho'a-haz, the youngest son. The prophet E-li'sha of the Northern Kingdom was directed by the Lord to·write a letter of warning to Je-ho'ram, announcing that he would be smitten with an incurable disease and die in shame. At the early age of forty Je-ho'ram became the victim of a loathsome plague; he died in disgrace, unloved and unmourned by the people whom he had led away from God, and denied burial in the royal sepulcher.

Je-ho'ram was succeeded by his son A-ha-zi'ah, who persisted in the worst features of his father's unholy example, and who was guided by his idol-worshiping mother. After reigning for only one year, A-ha-zi'ah fell under the Divine judgment upon the dynasty of

THE DEATH OF JEZEBEL

Om'ri in Is'ra-el and the destruction of all the descendants of A'hab and Jez'e-bel. His uncle Je-ho'ram, king of Is'ra-el, had been wounded in a battle with the Syr'i-ans and had returned to his palace at Jez're-el for treatment. Je'hu, the commander of Is'ra-el's armies, had been anointed king under the direction of the prophet E-li'sha, and Je-ho'ram and all the house of A'hab, including Jez'e-bel, were slain in the revolt which followed. Under the providence of God A-ha-zi'ah went to visit his wounded uncle, and was thus included in the wholesale slaughter by Je'hu and his men.

When Ath-a-li'ah received the news of the murder of her son, and of the complete destruction of her father's descendants in Is'ra-el, the fierce temper of her Phoe-ni'ci-an blood took possession of her. When the body of A-ha-zi'ah was brought to Je-ru'sa-lem, and full information given her concerning the slaughter of forty-two princes of her own house by Je'hu, her bloodthirsty ambition knew no bounds. In her desperation she launched a work of murderous revenge seldom equalled in history. She caused the foul murder of her own grandchildren and all the descendants of the brothers of her dead son, then pushed aside the widowed queen, and seized the throne of Ju'dah. For six years she carried on her evil work among the chosen people of God.

The Lord had promised, however, that the house of Da'vid should be continued on the throne of Is'ra-el, and no wicked queen could prevent the promise from coming true. God raised up a good woman to defeat the plan of murdering all of Da'vid's descendants. Jo'ash, the infant son of A-ha-zi'ah, was hidden in the temple by Je-ho-she'ba, wife of the High Priest Je-hoi'a-da. She was a daughter of Je-ho'ram, but not of Ath-a-li'ah, for her mother had been another wife of the former king. By this courageous act a good woman preserved the only surviving heir of Da'vid, and Jo'ash, the great religious reformer, was spared to carry on an extremely important link in the Divinely ordained ancestry of the Sav'ior.

SUGGESTIONS FOR STUDY

Biblical Index to Helpful References

The Unhappy Outcome of Bad Marriages. (Gen. 24:3; Josh. 23:12; Neh. 13:25.)

No Permanent Profit in Wickedness. (Prov. 10:2.)

Policies Based on Evil Certain to Fail. (Prov. 12:3.)

Edomites Subject to Israel Since Days of David. (1 Ki. 22:47; 2 Ki. 3:9.)

The Companion of Fools Certain of Destruction. (Prov. 13:20.)

Counsels of the Wicked Lead to Ruin. (Prov. 12:5; Mi. 6:16.)

David's House Established Forever. (2 Sam. 7:16; 1 Ki. 2:45.)

Restoration Promised to the Repentant. (Jer. 30:17.)

Questions

1. Describe the baseness of Jehoram and Ahijah?

2. Through what woman were they largely influenced?

3. How long did this period of evil continue? How long did each ruler reign?

4. What two heathen people invaded Judah during Jehoram's reign?

5. How did Jehoram die?

6. How did Ahaziah meet death?

7. Tell of the atrocious crimes of Athaliah in assuming the throne.

8. Who was saved from her wholesale murder of the royal family? How?

STORY 129

JOASH MADE KING AT THE AGE OF SEVEN

2 CHRONICLES 23, 24;
2 KINGS 11, 12   During the six years of Ath-a-li'ah's unlawful
reign over Ju'dah, Je-ho-she'ba and her husband carefully trained the
young child Jo'ash in the fear and worship of God. The High Priest
whose wife had saved the child was required by his sacred office to watch
over the religious life of the people, and to protect the throne from all
abuses. United with the royal family by marriage, he was placed by the
Lord in an excellent position to restore the throne to the house of Da'vid.

Directed by the Spirit of God, he boldly struck when the time was ripe.
Taking advantage of a great religious festival which filled the streets
of Je-ru'sa-lem with multitudes from all parts of the country, and which
required the presence of many civil officers, priests, and Le'vites in the
temple, Je-hoi'a-da made arrangements for the coronation of the young
Jo'ash. At a given signal the boy was brought into the temple and proclaimed king by certain wisely chosen officers. The people clapped their
hands in joy, shouting, "Long live the king!", and the trumpets of the
priests announced that a new king was beginning his reign.

Ath-a-li'ah naturally took no part in the religious festivals of Is'ra-el,
and was enjoying quiet repose in her palace. When she heard the great
tumult of the people at the coronation of Jo'ash, she rushed boldly into
the temple, shouting, "Conspiracy, conspiracy!" She counted upon her
authority as queen to command the support of the people in crushing the
revolt, but instead she was seized by officers wisely appoined by Je-hoi'-
a-da, carried from the house of God, and justly put to death.

The coronation of Jo'ash and the slaying of Ath-a-li'ah were followed
by a religious assembly in which Je-hoi'a-da made a solemn renewal of
the ancient covenant between God and Is'ra-el. The young king pledged
himself to rule according to the laws of God, and the people swore to
obey him as a servant of the Lord. This meeting was immediately followed by a popular uprising against idolatry and the complete overthrow
of Ba'al-worship in Je-ru'sa-lem. Ath-a-li'ah had built a temple to Ba'al
in the holy city, had plundered the temple of Je-ho'vah to enrich the

shrine of her favorite heathen god, and had made Ba'al-worship the national religion. This unholy temple was destroyed, Ba'al's altars and images shattered to pieces, and the leaders of idolatry put to death.

The worship of Je-ho'vah was fully restored, priests appointed to their regular courses, and sacrifices offered according to the ancient laws of Is'ra-el. Porters and singers were assigned to their usual duties, the service of praise and thanksgiving filled the Lord's house, and Divine worship completely revived. Je-hoi'a-da was given an important place in the life of the nation, and the office of High Priest given new honor and dignity.

Since Jo'ash was only seven years old, the High Priest was naturally the ruling power behind the throne. As long as Je-hoi'a-da lived, the young king remained under his holy influence and counsel. He faithfully observed the covenant made between Je-ho'vah and the people, and "did that which was right in the sight of the Lord." When Jo'ash reached the years of manhood, he turned his attention to the repair of the temple. For fifteen years the house of God had been allowed to deteriorate and decay, had been robbed of its treasures, and some of the stones actually removed for the building the temple to Ba'al. When the priests were slow and careless in raising funds for restoring the temple, Jo'ash ordered that such contributions be kept separate from the regular funds for the support of the priests, and that they be honestly used in the purpose for which they were given. Now that confidence was restored, liberal offerings were made, and the work was carried forward to a glorious success.

Je-hoi'a-da lived for seven years after the repair of the temple, reaching the ripe old age of one hundred and thirty years. In the thirtieth year of his reign, however, Jo'ash suffered a great loss in the passing away of the noble High Priest. Accepting the advice of some of the young princes of Ju'dah who had become jealous of the growing influence of the priest-

ATHALIAH AND JOASH

hood, the king drifted away into a state of religious neglect and idolatry. The people turned away from God and set up the worship of idols in groves and high places, so prophets of the Lord were sent to warn them of national calamities that were sure to come in punishment of their sins. The most notable of these prophets was Zech-a-ri'ah, a son of Je-hoi'a-da, but the ungrateful king ordered him to be stoned to death. In his dying moments the prophet of God declared to Jo'ash that the Lord would punish this failure to remember the kindness of his father.

Before long the Syr'i-ans subdued the Phi-lis'tine stronghold at Gath, and then Haz'a-el sent an invading army against Je-ru'sa-lem. Jo'ash robbed the temple of its treasures and gave them to the Syr'i-ans as tribute, but the invaders slew many of the princes of Ju'dah, and took large amounts of plunder to Da-mas'cus.

Jo'ash was then smitten with an incurable disease, and a group of his own officers took advantage of his helplessness to conspire against him; finally he was slain by his own servants. He had reigned forty years, thirty years as a good king richly blessed of God, and ten years as one stained with disgrace and unworthy of his office. His body was buried in Je-ru'sa-lem, but not in the royal sepulcher. Am-a-zi'ah, his son, reigned in his stead, and for many years did that which was pleasing to God.

SUGGESTIONS FOR STUDY

Biblical Index to Helpful References

The Distinction of an Understanding Heart. (1 Chr. 12:32; 22:12.)

The Lord's Intimate Knowledge of the Heart. (Jer. 12:3.)

David's Throne Established Forever. (Psm. 89:37.)

Counsels of Wisdom Spoken in Seclusion. (Eccl. 9:17.)

The Command to Utterly Demolish Idols. (Isa. 2:8.)

Seducers to Idolatry Under Penalty of Death. (Deut. 13:5, 6; 17:2-7.)

Capital Punishment the Law of God. (Lev. 10:2; Num. 15:36.)

The Reproach of Neglecting the House of God. (Hag. 1:4.)

God's Ancient Covenant with Israel. (Deut. 4:6; 27:9.)

Questions

1. How was the life of Joash preserved for six years?

2. Tell of his coronation by Jehoiada.

3. What happened to Athaliah when she tried to interfere?

4. What reformations were inaugurated after to coronation of Joash?

5. Who was really the ruler during Joash's early reign?

6. What work was inaugurated by Joash when he reached manhood?

7. How long did Jehoiada live?

8. What happened in the life of Joash after Jehoiada's death?

9. How did Joash die?

DISASTERS IN JUDAH UNDER THE RULE OF AMAZIAH

2 CHRONICLES 25;
2 KINGS 14:1-20

Am-a-zi'ah began his reign with every outward appearance of righteousness, but he was lacking in deep, spiritual loyalty to God. He was double-minded and half-hearted; outwardly obedient to Je-ho'vah, but secretly in favor of idol-worship. There was a striking similarity between his career and that of his father Jo'ash. Both began by professing zeal for the worship of Je-ho'vah, and afterwards lapsed into idolatry; both refused to hear the warnings of God's prophets, and both were slain by assassins after rejecting the Lord.

Among the first acts of Am-a-zi'ah's reign was the just punishment of those who had slain his father. Contrary to the usual custom of the East, he spared the children of the murderess. From the beginning of his reign, Am-a-zi'ah showed great military ambitions, and he organized the nation after the ancient order of Is'ra-el, in companies of fifty, one hundred, and one thousand, according to family and tribal lineage.

In preparing for war against the E'dom-ites, Am-a-zi'ah hired 160,000 soldiers from the Northern Kingdom. Then, being warned by a prophet that an expedition of mercenaries would fail, he sent these men back to Sa-ma'ri-a. Angered by this course, the soldiers of Is'ra-el ravaged the land of Ju'dah, slew three thousand people, and carried away much plunder. The war against E'dom succeeded, however; ten thousand being slain and ten thousand prisoners being captured. In a moment of madness the king

TAANACH

ordered these prisoners slain, and his success was turned into a curse.

As a result of the victory over E'dom, Am-a-zi'ah, became proud, conceited, and ambitious for further conquest. Hoping to avenge the brutal deeds of the dismissed soldiers from the Northern Kingdom, and to extend his rule over the Ten Tribes, he challenged Je-ho'ash, king of Is'ra-el. In reply to this challenge Je-ho'ash sent a parable which likened Am-a-zi'ah to a low thistle and himself to a mighty cedar, while the armies of the Northern Kingdom were represented as wild beasts crushing under foot the frail thistle. The warnings of Je-ho'ash merely increased Am-a-zi'ah's determination to fight, and the two armies met at Beth-she'mesh. The Southern Kingdom was utterly defeated, Am-a-zi'ah was taken prisoner, and the war was carried against Je-ru'sa-lem. The walls of the city were broken down, the temple robbed of its treasures, and prisoners carried to Sa-ma'ri-a as hostages to prevent further attacks upon Is'ra-el.

Am-a-zi'ah had now lost the respect and loyalty of his people, and a plot was made to assassinate him. He fled to La-chish, where he was overtaken and slain by the plotters; then his body was carried back to Je-ru'sa-lem in the royal chariot and buried in the sepulcher of the kings of Ju'dah. After a reign of twenty-nine years, disgraced by the barbarous execution of helpless prisoners, dishonored by the worship of heathen images, and finally ruined in a war of his own making, Am-a-zi'ah went down to his grave disowned by his people and rejected by the Lord. He was succeeded by his son Uz-zi'ah also called Az-a-ri'ah, who reigned fifty-two years in Je-ru'sa-lem.

SUGGESTIONS FOR STUDY

Biblical Index to Helpful References

Double-Mindedness and Half-Heartedness Denounced. (Zeph. 1:4, 5; Luke 16:13.)

Children Not to Be Punished for Sins of Fathers. (Deut. 24:16; Ezek. 18:4, 20.)

Vindictiveness Condemned. (Luke 9:54, 56; Jno. 18:10, 11.)

The Downfall of the Proud and Presumptuous. (Prov. 16:18; 18:12.)

Retributions for Forsaking the Lord. (Isa. 65:6; Jer. 23:2.)

Contrivances of the Wicked Cruel. (Prov. 12:5, 10.)

God's Endless Sovereignty. (Psm. 9:7; 11:4; Isa. 6:1.)

Questions

1. Compare the characters of Joash and Amaziah.

2. How did Amaziah begin his reign?

3. Tell of Amaziah's war against Edom and its results.

4. What sort of spirit did Amaziah display after victory over Edom?

5. What was the outcome of his war against the Northern Kingdom?

6. Tell of Amaziah's end.

STORY 131

SIXTY-EIGHT YEARS OF PROSPERITY IN JUDAH

2 CHRONICLES 26-27;
2 KINGS 15:1-7; 35-38

Uz-si'ah was crowned king of Ju'dah when he was only sixteen years old, and ruled for fifty-two years. During his early life he obeyed the counsel of the prophet Zech-a-ri'ah, just as the young Jo'ash had depended upon the High Priest Je-hoi'a-da.

Uz-zi'ah's reign was marked by great vigor and prosperity, corresponding to the meaning of his double name: Az-a-ri'ah, which means "the strength of Je-ho'vah; and Uz-zi'ah, "the help of Je-ho'vah." He rebuilt the city of E'loth, an important seaport captured by his father from the Phi-lis'tines; waged successful wars against the people of the Med'i-terra'ne-an plains; and founded Jewish colonies in large areas of the Phi-lis'-tine country. He also conquered the A-ra'bi-ans and other wandering tribes in the country south of Ju'dah, and forced the Am'mon-ites east of the Jor'dan to pay tribute.

As the country became prosperous under his reign, there arose many

THE PLAINS OF 'AKKA FROM THE SLOPES OF CARMEL

abuses which were severely condemned by the prophets I-sa'iah, Ho-se'a, Jo'el and A'mos. The luxury, indolence, and oppression of the poor by the wealthier classes were the sins chiefly responsible for the decline which soon followed. The people thought more of making money than of leading a good life; the use of false weights and treacherous dealings was widespread among the traders of the land; and these conditions became unbearable under the succeeding reign of the good king Jo'tham.

Toward the close of his reign Uz-zi'ah became puffed up with pride, and boldly set himself up as a priest, burning incense in the temple of the Lord. He persisted in this unlawful act even after being warned by the priests, and was suddenly smitten with incurable leprosy. He lived in misery for some years, being isolated from all people because of his disease. He died at the age of sixty-eight, and was succeeded by his son Jo'tham, who had performed the duties of king during Uz-zi'ah's illness.

The prosperity of Ju'dah was continued under the rule of Jo'tham, who reigned for sixteen years. He was faithful to the Lord in most respects, but was lenient with certain forms of idolatry which persisted among the people. The defenses of Je-ru'sa-lem and of many other cities of Ju'dah were strengthened, precautions taken against possible revolt by any of the vassal states, and Jo'tham became noted "because he prepared his way before the Lord." A rebellion by the king of the Am'mon-ites was promptly subdued, and the tribute paid by the Am'mon-ites was greatly increased. Pious toward God, just in his dealings with all men, and ever mindful of the welfare of his people, Jo'tham served the land of Ju'dah without reproach or judgment from God.

SUGGESTIONS FOR STUDY

Biblical Index to Helpful References

Zealousness Commended. (Isa. 62:1; Acts 18:25.)

Acknowledging God in All the Ways of Life. (Psm. 37:5.)

The Value of a Good Name. (Prov. 15:30; 22:1; Eccl. 7:1.)

The Sin of Arrogance and Presumption. (Prov. 27:1; Isa. 45:9.)

Burning Incense an Exclusive Priestly Service. (Num. 18:7.)

Leprosy as a Judgment from God. (Deut. 24:8, 9; 2 Sam. 3:29.)

Questions

1. How old was Uzziah when crowned king? How long did he reign?

2. Upon whom did he lean for instruction?

3. What distinction marked his entire reign?

4. What heathen enemies did he conquer?

5. What were some of his wise domes-

tic policies?

6. What grievous sin did he commit near the close of his reign?

7. In what manner was he punished?

8. How long did Jotham reign?

9. Describe the national affairs of his reign.

STORY 132

JUDAH ENDANGERED BY THE WICKED REIGN OF AHAZ

2 CHRONICLES 28;
2 KINGS 16;
ISAIAH 7:1-12   A'haz was one of the few men in Biblical history of whom nothing good is recorded. Under his weak, evil rule Ju'dah sank to the verge of complete ruin. Instead of following in the steps of his godly father, he adopted the idolatrous ways of the Northern Kingdom. The principles of true religion which had brought success to the nation were wholly rejected in favor of the inhuman rites of Mo'loch, in which he sacrificed his own children to this heathen god. A brazen image of Mo'loch was made red hot, and A'haz forced his own sons to walk into the glowing arms as a burnt sacrifice.

Not satisfied with setting up false gods in every city of the land, A'haz turned the temple of Je-ho'vah into a heathen shrine. The priests of God were forced to take part in the most abominable heathen rites, and true religion was almost forgotten in the land. The nation was so enfeebled

THE PLAINS OF JERICHO, FROM THE WEST

by the disgraceful rule of A'haz that it became a prey to successful invasions by the Syr'i-ans, the Phi-lis'tines, the E'dom-ites, and Is'ra-el.

Pe'kah, the king of Is'ra-el, and Re'zin, the king of Syr'i-a, united in plundering Ju'dah. Thousands of brave warriors were slain, thousands of men, women, and children were captured and removed from the land, and enormous spoils of silver and gold were carried away. The allied kings threatened to appoint a vassal prince, in the hope that Ju'dah would aid them in resisting the attacks of the As-syr'i-ans from the far north east. The E'dom-ites raided the southern borders of the nation, carrying away many captives and rich booty; while the Phi-lis'tines subdued all the cities of the western plains and the hill country. The great wealth accumulated under the good rule of Jo'tham and Uz-zi'ah was swept away, and sixty-eight years of prosperity and good government was wiped out.

With the nation greatly empoverished, and with threats of revolt being muttered among the people, Ahaz pleaded with the As-syr'i-an king for help. In order to secure the desired aid, he paid a heavy tribute, consisting largely of treasures taken from the temple of God. The As-syr'i-ans responded to his appeal, and a large army was sent into Ju'dah; instead of helping A'haz, however, they inflicted great damage upon the country.

In spite of all the calamities brought upon himself and the nation by his desperate wickedness, and in spite of the pleas and warnings of the prophet I-sa'iah, A'haz persisted in his evil ways. His name has been included in the list of those upon whom the curse of God descended. He was cut down when only thirty-six years of age, but the evil influence of his idolatrous reign persisted in the life of Ju'dah until the nation was carried away into captivity.

SUGGESTIONS FOR STUDY

Biblical Index to Helpful References

The Perils or Luxury, Worldliness, Drunkenness. (Isa. 2:7; Hos. 12:8; Amos 3:1.)

The Mosaic Law Against Sacrifice of Human Life. (Lev. 18:21; 20:2; Deut. 18:10.)

Offering Children in Sacrifice to Idols Denounced. (Jer. 7:31; 19:4, 5.)

Success in War the Result of the Wickedness of Enemies. (Deut. 9:5.)

Ensnared in One's Own Iniquities. (Prov. 5:22; 11:6.)

Questions

1. What unenviable reputation has Ahaz?

2. Describe the low moral and spiritual state of Judah under his reign.

3. Besides ordinary idolatrous practices, what sin did he commit respecting his sons?

4. What foreign powers invaded Judah during his reign?

5. Tell of the harassments by Pekah and Rezin.

6. Tell of his tribute to Assyria and the outcome.

NOTABLE REFORMS UNDER THE RULE OF HEZEKIAH

2 CHRONICLES 29-31;
2 KINGS 18:1-8
A'haz, the most wicked king of Ju'dah, was succeeded by his twenty-year-old son Hez-e-ki'ah, the best and holiest of all the monarchs of the nation. Throughout his reign of twenty-nine years he followed the policies laid down in the laws of God, and raised the nation to a place of power and fame among the nations.

The good king began his reforms by undoing the unholy work of his father, who had turned the temple of Je-ho'vah into a heathen shrine. He ordered the priests and Le'vites to purify themselves for the work of cleansing the house of God from every taint of idolatry. The altar which his father had raised to a Syr'i-an god was removed, alterations in the temple and its furnishings were repaired, and the sanctuary of the Lord was restored in every detail. When the work was complete, Hez-e-ki'ah assembled the princes and court officers for a service of reconsecration; presenting sin offerings, burnt offerings, and peace offerings according to the laws of Mo'ses.

The revival of true worship was then extended to the entire nation. Every city, village, and hamlet was invited to send representatives to a great service in the temple. The ancient orders of the priests, Le'vites, and singers were reorganized, and for sixteen days the city of Je-ru'sa-lem was thronged with devout worshipers of God.

As soon as the hearts of the people had been turned back to God in true worship, the work of destroying idolatry was readily accomplished. The entire country had been studded with heathen shrines by A'haz, the brazen serpent which had healed the Is'ra-el-ites four hundred and fifty years before was now made an object of idol-worship. Hez-e-ki'ah, however, told the people that the idol was nothing but a piece of brass, and he broke it into small pieces. The people were thus encouraged to destroy images, altars, shrines, and every vestige of idolatry in the land.

This great spiritual awakening was soon followed by a celebration of the ancient feast of the Pass'o-ver. It was the greatest gathering in Je-ru'-sa-lem since the days of the dedication of the temple by Sol'o-mon. The

FRUIT OFFERED IN TITHES

people came from every part of the country, brought liberal offerings to God, and joined with gladness in the fourteen days of worship.

After the national observance of the Pass'o-ver, the people continued their work of destroying whatever traces of idol-worship which remained in the land. The Mosaic laws which required the offering of the first fruits of the land and the payment of tithes were restored, and the people responded so heartily that extra preparations had to be made to take care of the enormous contributions received at the temple in Je-ru'sa-lem.

SUGGESTIONS FOR STUDY

Biblical Index to Helpful References

The Blessings of Godliness. (Psm. 73:24, 25; 104:1; 2 Pet. 3:11.)

The Blessing of Fearing and Trusting God. (Gen. 39:9; Psm. 48:14.)

The Advantages Secured by Good Counsellors. (Prov. 11:14; 15:22.)

God's Counsels to be Given First Consideration. (Psm. 33:10-16; Prov. 19:21.)

Required Purification of Priests and Levites. (Ex. 19:22; Lev. 11:44.)

Required Sin Offerings Under Mosaic Law. (Lev. 1:4; 4:15, 24.)

Required Burnt Offerings Under Mosaic Law. (Lev. 4:19.)

Offerings of First Fruits and Tithes. (Ex. 23:19; Num. 18:12-18.)

Promises of Prosperity to Liberal Givers. (Prov. 11:25; Mal. 3:10-12.)

Questions

1. How does Hezekiah stand among all the kings of Judah?

2. What were his handicaps and how were they overcome?

3. How did Hezekiah begin his reign?

4. To what extent did he carry forward his reformations?

5. Tell of his great national celebration of the Passover.

STORY 134

AN ANGEL DELIVERS JERUSALEM
FROM THE ASSYRIANS

2 CHRONICLES 32:1-23;
2 KINGS 18:13-37; 19;
ISAIAH 10: 12; 14   Hez-e-ki'ah was permitted to succeed with his reforms before the nation was seriously threatened by foreign wars or invasions. In the fourteenth year of his reign, however, a king of Syr'i-a by the name of Sen-nach'e-rib invaded the land of Ju'dah. After capturing forty walled cities, and posting his armies at La'chish, a stronghold twenty-five miles southeast of Je-ru'sa-lem, the heathen king prepared to attack the capital city of Ju'dah. Hoping to prevent this attack, Hez-e-ki'ah robbed the temple of its treasures in order to send an enormous tribute to Sen-nach'e-rib.

The As-syr'i-an king was determined to capture Je-ru'sa-lem, and sent one of his most noted generals to plan a siege. In the meantime Hez-e-ki'ah had strengthened the defenses of the city, and made a conduit for water in order to prevent the soldiers and people from being weakened by thirst during the attack which was soon to come.

The proud armies of Sen-nach'e-rib demanded the immediate surrender of the holy city, and the crafty general Rab'sha-keh made a speech in which he tried to turn the people from their loyalty to Hez-e-ki'ah. The As-syr'i-an officer scoffed at the religious reforms of the king, charging him with shutting his people up in the capital to die of starvation and thirst, and suggesting that they would greatly improve their condition by surrendering to Sen-nach'e-rib. These threats were spoken in vain, for the silence of the besieged people forced him to admit to the king that his mission had failed.

Sen-nach'e-rib then sent an insulting letter to Hez-e-ki'ah, making light of the possibility of a successful resistance to his great armies. The good king turned to the Lord in prayer, laying before Him the tablets of clay on which the letter was written. He also sent a special request to the prophet I-sa'iah for advice and prayer, and an immediate answer came from the Lord. The prophet sent the rival kings an inspired letter rebuking Sen-nach'e-rib and predicting that he would retreat in disgrace, and declaring that Je-ho'vah Himself would deliver the besieged city.

The next morning found the bodies of one hundred and eighty-five thousand As-syr'i-an soldiers lying dead upon the ground. Just how the Lord caused this wholesale slaughter is not known, but it is clear that the prophecy of I-sa'iah was fulfilled, and that Je-ho'vah himself had delivered his people by a miracle.

> "Like the leaves of the forest when summer is green,
> That host with their banners at sunset were seen;
> Like the leaves of the forest when autumn hath blown,
> That host on the morrow lay withered and strewn.
>
> For the Angel of Death spread his wings on the blast,
> And breathed in the face of the foe as he passed;
> And the eyes of the sleepers waxed deadly and chill,
> And their hearts but once heaved, and forever grew still!
>
> And the widows of As'shur are loud in their wail,
> And the idols are broke in the temple of Ba'al,
> And the might of the Gentile, unsmote by the sword,
> Hath melted like snow in the glance of the Lord!"

The people of Ju'dah knew that it was the Lord who had delivered

THE SLAYING OF THE ASSYRIANS

them, so there was a burst of national thanksgiving which is recalled in
these words of praise:

"In Ju'dah is God known:
His name is great in Is'ra-el.
In Sa'lem also is his tabernacle,
And his dwelling place in Zi'on.
There he brake the arrows of the bow;
The shield, and the sword, and the battle.

Glorious art thou and excellent,
From the mountains of prey,
The stout hearted are made a spoil,
They have slept their sleep;
And none of the men of might have found their hands.
At they rebuke, O God of Ja'cob,
Both chariot and horse are cast into a dead sleep."

Sen-nach'e-rib returned to Ninevah, his capital city, in humiliation and
disgrace. He was no longer able to command the support of his people
in combatting the Bab'y-lon-ians, who were threatening to overthrow As-
syr'i-a. His own sons conspired against him, and treacherously put him
to death. No more did the As-syr'i-ans cross the Jor'dan, and within forty
years the power which had terrified all A'si-a suddenly vanished from
the earth.

SUGGESTIONS FOR STUDY

Biblical Index to Helpful References

The Folly of Depending on Worldly Help.
(Psm. 56:5; Isa. 31:3; Jer. 17:5.)

Victory by the Lord's Help. (Psm. 27:9.)

The Lord's Power to Kill or to Make
Alive. (1 Sam. 2:6-10.)

The Death Angel of Jehovah. (Ex. 12:23.)

The Sin of Reviling and Ridiculing God.
(1 Sam. 17:43; Isa. 37:17, 23, 24; 1 Pet.
3:9.)

The Psalm of Jehovah's Triumph. (Psm.
76.)

Questions

1. What power from the northeast threatened the peace of Hezekiah's reign?

2. How many cities of Judah did Sennacherib conquer?

3. What mistake did Hezekiah make in
trying to pacify Sennacherib?

4. Tell of Rabshakeh's insulting address
to Jerusalem.

5. How was this followed up by Sennacherib?

6. What recourse for help did Hezekiah
take? Who else prayed for him?

7. What answer was given by Isaiah?

8. Tell how the armies of Sennacherib
were defeated.

STORY 135

HEZEKIAH'S LIFE PROLONGED FIFTEEN YEARS IN ANSWER TO PRAYER

2 CHRONICLES 32:24-
32; 2 KINGS 20;
ISAIAH 38   Immediately after the deliverance of the nation from the As-syr'i-ans, Ju'dah was faced with another threatened calamity. The beloved king whose faith in God had saved his people was smitten with a fatal illness. All hope for his recovery was lost, and the prophet I-sa'iah solemnly announced that death was at hand.

Hez-e-ki'ah was still a young man, in the very prime of his usefulness, and many of the good works which he had undertaken remained unfinished. There was no son to take his place on the throne, and to carry on the line of Da'vid, so the prophet's direction that he "put his house in order" was an order for him to select someone to succeed him as king.

In this dark hour the prayer and faith of the good king triumphed again, rolling back even the tides of death. We do not know the words which Hez-e-ki'ah uttered before the throne of grace, but the answer was quickly given. The Lord spoke to I-sa'iah, who was leaving the palace in despair, and said:

"Turn back, and say to Hez-e-ki'ah, the captain of my people, Thus saith Je-ho'vah, the God of Da'vid thy father, I have heard thy prayer, I have seen thy tears: behold, I will heal thee; on the third day thou shalt go up unto the house of Je-ho'vah. And I will add unto thy days fifteen years; and I will deliver thee and this city out of the hand of the As-syr'-i-ans; and I will defend this city for mine own sake, and for my servant Da'vid's sake."

Hez-e-ki'ah asked for some sign that the promise was true. The prophet told him that the shadow of the sundial in his window would turn back ten degrees. The sign was given before his eyes, and within three days the king was restored to full health and vigor.

SUGGESTIONS FOR STUDY

Biblical Index to Helpful References

Sickness Sometimes Brought on by Sin. (Deut. 28:22-24, 58-61.)

God's Protective Power in Times of Sickness. (Psm. 94:12-19; Jno. 9:3; 11:4.)

STORY 136

THE LONG REIGN OF MANASSEH

2 CHRONICLES 33;
2 KINGS 21   During the closing years of Hez-e-ki'ah's reign many heathen people came into Ju'dah from the neighboring countries of Bab'y-lon, Chal-de'a, and Phoe-ni'ci-a, and from remnants of the former Northern Kingdom. There soon arose two rival forces: the national party, made up of those who were loyal to the ideals of Hez-e-ki'ah, and led by the prophets; and the patrician party, made up of people of rank and wealth, which favored foreign alliances and idol-worship. During the strife between these two parties many of the Jews were led away from their ancient worship and customs, and idolatry became widespread.

Ma-nas-seh was only twelve years old when his father died, and for this reason was dominated by the scheming court attendants during the early part of his reign. It is therefore said of him, "He did that which was evil in the sight of Je-ho'vah, after the abominations of the nations whom God cast out before the children of Is'ra-el." He reigned for fifty-five years, longer than any other king of either Jewish nation, and for more than half of that long period inflicted upon Ju'dah her darkest era.

The young prince began his rule with a strong effort to wipe out the reforms of his father; in a short time he destroyed all the good which Hez-e-ki'ah had accomplished in many years. Where his father had refused to worship any but the true God, Ma-nas'seh borrowed pagan deities from Phoe-ni'ci-a and Chal-de'a, and set up countless soothsayers and magicians among the people.

The prophets Ho-se'a, Jo'el, Na'hum, Ha-bak'kuk, and I-sa'iah tried to warn him of the terrible consequences of his sins, but they were met with a furious outbreak of murderous persecution. The streets of Je-ru'sa-lem ran with the blood of courageous patriots, earnest teachers, and devout prophets. A Jewish tradition declares that the venerable prophet I-sa'iah was sawed asunder by agents of the patrician party.

In order to punish the nation, and the wicked king in particular, the Lord permitted an invasion of Ju'dah by hordes of the growing power later known as Bab'y-lon-i-a. Ma-nas'seh was taken prisoner, bound in chains, and carried to Bab'y-lon, where he was cast into a dungeon.

As Ma-nas'seh sat in the dungeon under the twinkling stars which he had vainly worshiped, his heart was filled with penitence. The memory of his wickedness in forcing God's chosen people to worship foreign gods, and the terrible results of his godless rule, drove him to his knees. He humbly pleaded with God for pardon, and asked for an opportunity to prove his change of heart. His prayer was granted by a merciful God, and he was allowed to return to the good ways which he had so long deserted.

Upon returning to his throne in Je-ru'sa-lem the king spent the remainder of his days in a genuine effort to blot out the evil deeds of other days. The temple was cleared of its infamous idols, the shrines of pagan gods throughout the land were overthrown, and the people were commanded to worship Je-ho'vah alone. The king himself bowed before the altar of the Lord and worshipped Him with burnt offerings according to the ancient Law. At the age of sixty-seven he died, and was given an honorable burial in the sepulcher which he had prepared for himself; then his son A'mon was made king.

A'mon's reign was brief and uneventful, except that he followed in the steps of the earlier life of his father. He did evil in the sight of God, making sacrifices to many heathen gods. As so often happens among the forces opposed to God, quarrels broke out among the leaders of the patrician party; after reigning for only two years, A'mon was slain as the result of a plot among his own officers.

SUGGESTIONS FOR STUDY
Biblical Index to Helpful References

The Destructive Power of Evil Associations. (Hos. 7:9; 1 Cor. 15:33.)

The Corrupting Influence of Evil Seductions. (Isa. 8:19; Ezek. 13:10; 1 Jno. 2:26.)

Sorceries and Witchcraft Forbidden. (Deut. 18-10.)

Sacrilege Denounced. (Lev. 19:18; Rom. 2:22.)

Obduracy in Evil Leads to Certain Ruin. (Zech. 7:11; Jer. 44:16; Acts 7:51.)

Stubborn Resistance of Good Counsel Denounced. (Psm. 32:9; 78:8; 2 Pet. 2:10.)

Restoration Promised to the Penitent. (Psm. 51:12; Mi. 7:19.)

Questions

1. What produced great evil influences in Judah during closing years of Hezekiah's reign?

2. How old was Manasseh when he began his reign? Under whose influence was he largely dominated during early years?

3. What characterized the early years of his reign?

4. Name the prophets who sought to turn him from his evil.

5. What were the immediate results of the work of these prophets?

6. What nation invaded Judah as a punishment?

7. Tell of Manasseh's imprisonment and its result.

8. What reforms marked the closing years of his reign?

STORY 137

JOSIAH'S REFORMS; THE FINDING OF THE LOST BOOK OF THE LAW

2 CHRONICLES 34-35;
2 KINGS 22, 23: 1-30

Jo-si'ah, the son of A'mon, was crowned king when only eight years of age, and ruled over Ju'dah for thirty-one years. Under Jewish law he was a minor until he reached the age of thirteen, so the government was no doubt directed by court officials during these years. There is no record of any official acts on his part until he was sixteen, when it is stated, "In the eighth year of his reign, while he was yet young, he began to seek after Je-ho'vah." When he was twenty he began to drive every trace of pagan worship out of the land.

For six years Jo-si'ah fought against idolatry, and his efforts met with success. Many of the heathen altars were torn down, graven images were ground into dust, and idolatrous groves were uprooted. The temple of Je-ru'sa-lem was cleansed of its pagan altars and images, and the ancient order of worship under the priesthood was reorganized. Abundant offerings and tithes were brought to the temple by people from the entire land, and there was a surplus on hand after ample provision had been made for the priests.

In the eighteenth year of his reign Jo-si'ah gave orders for the repair of the temple, which had been allowed to deteriorate for two hundred and fifty years. It was during this praiseworthy task that one of the most notable events in Jo-si'ah's reign took place. The original copy of the five books of the law written by Mo'ses eight hundred and fifty years before was discovered by the workmen, given to the High Priest Hil-ki'ah, and later delivered to the king. The scroll had originally been placed in the Ark of the Cov'e-nant, and Divine orders had been given that it be kept within the sacred chest. During the profanation of the temple by A'haz the ark had been removed, and the ancient scroll was either discarded or cast into the rubbish by accident.

No doubt there were partial copies of the ancient laws in the hands of the priests, but the loss of the original scroll was a great calamity. For at least half a century there had been no public reading of the Law; the people had no knowledge of the written word of God, and were thus

WHERE NECHO DEFEATED JOSIAH

compelled to depend on the traditions of the priests and prophets.

When the stern judgments of God against idolatry and wickedness found in the Book of the Law were read to Jo-si'ah, his heart was alarmed, and he asked that prayer be made to God for the removal of his wrath against the nation. He also called for a prophet, and as Jer-e-mi'ah was absent from Je-ru'sa-lem at the time, the prophetess Hul'dah was brought to him. She boldly announced that the nation would soon come under the extreme penalties announced in the Law; but advised Jo-si'ah that he would be "gathered into his fathers" before the fall of the nation. In an effort to save the nation from its impending doom, Jo-si'ah led the people in a great Covenant Meeting and in nationwide efforts to overthrow all pagan worship.

The downfall of the kingdom was delayed by the good works of Jo-si'ah, but it could not be avoided. The heart of the nation was not really changed by the fervor of the noble young king, nor by the restoration of outward forms of the worship of Je-ho'vah. The political and military affairs of the great world-powers were rapidly taking shape for the overthrow of Ju'dah. The rival monarchies of E'gypt and As-syr'i-a were struggling for supremacy, and the Bab'y-lon-ian empire was about to claim world domination. Pal'es-tine was a coveted frontier territory, and was essential for the world supremacy of any great power. It was destined to become a great battlefield in the rivalry between As-syr'i-a and E'gypt.

Jo-si'ah's notable career came to an end while he was still in the prime of life, and the tragedy was caused by war between the powerful neighbors of Ju'dah. Wishing to establish his rule in As-syr'i-a before the Babylonians forestalled him, King Ne'cho of E'gypt led a huge army through Pal'es-tine on his way to the famous battlefield of Car'che-mish. Feeling honor bound to support the interests of his northern master, Jo-si'ah opposed the passage of the E'gyp-tian army through his territory. He engaged Ne'cho in battle on the plains of Es-dra-e'lon—famed for many great combats in history—and lost his life in the struggle.

All Ju'dah and Je-ru'sa-lem mourned the slain king, and Jer-e-mi'ah composed a funeral elegy which was chanted by the Jewish people for many centuries afterward. Though apparently at the height of his notable career, there was a kind providence in his removal before terrible disasters befell his beloved Ju'dah. God's promise spoken by the prophetess Hul'-dah had been accomplished in a strange manner, and Jo-si'ah departed this life in honor and in peace.

SUGGESTIONS FOR STUDY

Biblical Index to Helpful References

Seeking and Finding the Lord. (Mal. 2:7, 8.)

The Blessing of Early Religious Training. (Psm. 78:6-7; Eph. 6:4.)

The Book of the Law Deposited in the Ark. (Deut. 31:25, 26.)

Sections of the Mosaic Writings Probably Read to Josiah. (Lev. 26; Deut. 28:32.)

Bible Should Be Read and Studied. (Matt. 21:42; Jno. 5:39; Acts 17:11.)

Bible Should be Read with Reverence and

Faith. (Psm. 85:8; 119:66; Jas. 1:21.)

Illumination and Cleansing Secured in Bible Reading. (Psm. 119:130; Jno. 15:3.)

Men Employed for Copying Scriptures. (Prov. 25:1.)

Original Regulations for Observance of Passover. (Ex. 12:7-28.)

Necessity for Purification for Religious Services. (1 Cor. 5:7; Gal. 6:16.)

Prophecy Against Altar at Bethel. (1 Ki. 13:1-3.)

Questions

1. How old was Josiah when he began his reign?

2. Describe his early piety and devotion to God.

3. What changes had taken place in the king's court?

4. In what manner did Josiah carry on reforms for six years? How old was he when this work was begun?

5. What special work did he begin in the eighteenth year of his reign? How long since the temple had been repaired?

6. What book was found during the repair of the temple?

7. Who was the constant adviser of Josiah in his reign?

8. Who was called on to read and explain the book of the law to Josiah?

9. What unusual blessings following the public reading of the law?

10. Why was the political life of Judah threatened at this time?

11. How did Josiah meet his death?

STORY 138

THE DISMAL END OF THE KINGDOM OF JUDAH

2 CHRONICLES 36;
2 KINGS 23:31-37;
24-25; JEREMIAH 22-28   The kingdom of Ju'dah virtually ceased with the death of Jo-si'ah. The four kings who succeeded him were mere servants of E'gypt and Bab'y-lon, and Pal'es-tine became the scene of continuous bloodshed, conquests, and deportations. The prophet Jer-e-mi'ah bravely tried to turn the hearts of the people back to God, and to delay the judgment upon the nation, but his efforts were of no avail. The sins of Ju'dah were too deep to be removed, and the wrath of God could no longer be checked.

Je-ho'a-haz, not the eldest son of Jo-si'ah, but a favorite of the people because of his determination to resist E'gypt, was chosen king. After three months of rule he was taken prisoner by Ne'cho, King of E'gypt, and died in captivity. Ju'dah was made a vassal of E'gypt, being forced to pay in tribute a sum which in present day money would be about fifty thousand dollars.

Ne'cho then placed E-li'a-kim, the second son of Jo-si'ah, on the throne of Ju'dah, and changed his name to Je-hoi'a-kim. Instead of following in the steps of his noble father, Je-hoi'a-kim defied God, persecuted His prophets, and made evil hirelings of the priests and princes of Is'ra-el. After four years Ne'cho was forced to withdraw from the east and north, and Ju'dah passed under the rule of the new Bab'y-lon-i-an Empire. Je-hoi'a-kim refused to pay tribute to the Bab'y-lon-i-ans, who were then too much occupied in warfare to subdue his revolt. They did, however, command their vassal states surrounding Ju'dah to make war upon the Jewish nation, and for nearly three years the Syr'i-ans, Mo'ab-ites and Am'mon-ites harassed Je-hoi'a-kim.

In the meantime the prophet Jer-e-mi'ah warned the Ju-de'an king of the uselessness of fighting against the Bab'y-lon-i-ans, of the folly of trusting in E'gypt for defense, and announced that Neb-u-chad-nez'zar was a Divine agent raised up to punish the nation for its repeated backslidings. Je-hoi'a-kim was slain by his own outraged subjects, and his eighteen-year-old son, Je-hoi'a-chin succeeded him. Within three months he surrendered to Neb-u-chad-nez'zar's armies, was carried to Bab'y-lon with ten thousand nobles, warriors, and craftsmen.   Neb-u-chad-nez'zar then placed on the throne the weak and vacillating son of Jo-si'ah, Mat-ta-ni'-ah; changing his name to Zed-e-ki'ah.   After eight years he joined Am'-mon in revolt against Bab'y-lon.

Once again Neb-u-chad-nez'zar led his armies into Pal'es-tine, and sent a large army to besiege Je-ru'sa-lem.   An E'gyp-tian army was sent to help Zed-e-ki'ah, but military needs at home soon caused this force to be re-called.   Jer-e-mi'ah strongly advised the surrender of Zed-e-ki'ah and the people, declaring that the nation was doomed by the Lord.   For this ad-vice he was denounced by the friends of E'gypt, accused of treason, and thrown into a muddy cistern, from which he was rescued through the friendly intervention of a slave and the aid of the king, who respected the prophet even though he did not hearken to his warnings.

Je-ru'sa-lem held out against the Bab'y-lon-i-ans for eighteen months, in spite of famine and pestilence.   Finally a breach was made in the north wall of Je-ru'sa-lem, and the famed capital of the Jewish kingdom was

BY THE WATERS OF BABEL

utterly destroyed. The city was sacked, its palaces and public buildings demolished, and its walls and fortifications torn down. The temple was pillaged and burned to the ground. Zed-e-ki'ah and his family were seized, his sons were slain before his eyes, and then his eyes were gouged out; after this he was carried to Bab'y-lon, where he spent the rest of his days in prison.

Thousands of the people of Ju'dah were forced to migrate to the land of Bab'y-lon, while a few were allowed to remain as slaves of the Bab'y-lon-i-an Empire. Jer-e-mi'ah preferred to remain in Pal'es-tine, where he continued his work of reformation. Neb-u-chad-nez'zar appointed a Jewish governor named Ged-a-li'ah, but this vassal prince was soon assessinated in an uprising led by Ish'ma-el. Stricken with despair, and fearing the terrible results of the madness which swept the land, many of the surviving Jews took refuge in E'gypt.

Thus Ju'dah was humbled in the height of its glory, and a great number of her citizens were carried away as the slaves of a foreign power; hundreds fled to the land from which their forefathers had been miraculously delivered from slavery centuries before, and hundreds were left scattered over the land which God had given them. All this took place because the nation had forsaken the Lord, and was now reaping the fruits of idolatry and sin.

SUGGESTIONS FOR STUDY

Biblical Index to Helpful References

Israel's Captivity Foretold. (Deut. 28:36; 1 Ki. 14:15; Isa. 39:7, Jer. 13:9.)

Prophecies Fulfilled in Captivity. (2 Ki. 15:29; 17:6; 18:11; 2 Chr. 28:5.)

Warnings Against Stubbornness. (Psm. 32:9; 78:8; Isa. 46:12; 48:4.)

Warnings Against Impenitence. (Jer. 7: 13; Amos 4:6; Hag. 2:7; Matt. 11:20.)

God's Use of Wicked Nations as Instruments of Punishment for His People. (Deut. 28:49-52; Isa. 5:26-30; Jer. 5:15-19; 6:22-23.)

Sin Separates from God's Protection. (Josh. 7:11, 12; Isa. 59:2; 64:7; Hos. 5:6.)

Questions

1. When did the kingdom of Judah practically end?

2. Who was chosen king after Josiah's death?

3. What country made Judah a vassal province? Who was made king?

4. What changes resulted in Judah becoming a vassal to Babylon?

5. What prophet warned Jehoiakim against rebellion against Babylon?

6. What was the outcome of his rebellion?

7. Who succeeded Jehoiakim as king?

How long did he reign? How long a prisoner in Babylon? How honored in late life?

8. Who was appointed king by Nebuchadnezzar? To what was his name changed?

9. How many Jews were carried to Babylon when Jehoiachin was overthrown?

10. What kind of king was Zedekiah?

11. Tell of the siege of Jerusalem by Nebuchadnezzar's armies.

12. What distribution was made of the Jewish people?

STORY 139

DANIEL'S THREE COMPANIONS IN THE FIERY FURNACE

DANIEL 1, 2, 3, 4   The first deportation of He'brews to Bab'y-lon by Neb-u-chad-nez'zar during the reign of King Je-hoi'a-kim consisted of the elite of the nation; and among them were four young princes of noble countenance, superior intelligence, and upright character. In keeping with the practice of victorious rulers of the East these notable captives were chosen for service in the royal court of the king; and were placed in training for a period of three years; in which they were taught the language, customs, and learning of the Chal'de-ans. The names of these four highly favored He'brews were: Dan'iel, Han-a-ni'ah, Mi'shael, and Az-a-ri'ah; who were given the Chal'de-an names of Bel-te-shaz'zar, Sha'drach, Me'shach, and A-bed'ne-go.

Among the privileges conferred upon these young princes during the period of training was that of being supplied with food from the king's own table—meats which had been set apart to idols worshiped by the Bab'y-lon-i-ans, and alcoholic beverages. Dan'iel felt that it would be wrong for him and his companions to eat this food, or to drink intoxicating wines; and asked, therefore, that they be given plain vegetarian food and water. With reluctance the steward granted this request, and at the expiration of a ten days' test was surprised to find that their countenances appeared fairer, and they were fatter in flesh than all the youths who ate of the king's meat.

These four He'brews advanced rapidly in Chal'de-an learning, and were well prepared for the responsible positions awaiting them in the king's court. Their capacity for learning, combined with their diligent application and the blessings of God, made these Jewish exiles ten times more able in answering the king's questions than all the wise men of the Bab'y-lon-i-an Empire. The luxury and idolatry of the heathen court, a course of study filled with superstition and sorcery, and constant association with heathens of low moral standards were unable to turn their hearts from God.

In the course of events, the wisdom of Dan'iel was put to a severe test.

Neb-u-chad-nez'zar had a dream which greatly troubled him; the details of which he was unable to remember. Having called upon all the magicians of his realm for a revelation of the dream, and for the interpretation of its meaning, without any satisfactory solution; he finally accepted the offer of Dan'iel to tell him the dream and to explain its meaning. After recovering the dream and giving its interpretation, Dan'iel was made governor of the realm and his three companions were appointed to responsible positions in the king's court.

Neb-u-chad-nez'zar was a mighty king who extended his dominion over most of the known world of his time. He made Bab'y-lon one of the most beautiful cities the world has ever seen, built splendid palaces, roof-gardens, and public buildings, and set up a great image in the plain of Du'ra near Bab'y-lon. It was a statue ninety feet high and nine feet square; covered with gold from top to bottom, its shining pinnacle was visible for fifteen miles. A decree was issued which required all the people to bow down before this image at the sound of a trumpet. Daniel appears to have been away on some business for the king at the time, but his three companions were employed in high positions in the king's court. They refused to bow before the image, because such an act would have been a violation of their religious beliefs.

IN THE FIERY FURNACE

The princes of Bab'y-lon, already jealous of the young He'-brews because of their superior intelligence, informed the king of their failure to obey his command. Neb-u-chad-nez'zar then ordered the young princes to come before him for examination, declaring that they would be cast into a fiery furnace if they did not bow before the image within three days. In reply to the king's proposal the young noblemen replied: "We do not wish any time; our answer is ready now; we will not disobey the law of our God."

Remaining steadfast in their faith they declared that their God was able to deliver them from the fiery furnace. Neb-u-chad-nez'zar was enraged at their defiance of his law, and ordered that they be cast into the furnace at once.

When the king came later to look into the highly heated furnace into which the three He'brews had been cast, he was amazed to find four men walking among the flames unhurt, and the fourth appeared like the son of God. Smitten with awe by the sight, and convinced of the righteousness of these faithful servants of God, Neb-u-chad-nez'zar asked them to come out of the furnace. He then declared, "There is no other God who can deliver after this sort," and a decree was issued forbidding anyone to speak against the God of the He'brews.

Sha'drach, Me'shach, and A-bed'ne-go were given positions of higher rank in the service of the Bab'y-lon-i-an king, and after a period of about ten years Neb-u-chad-nez'zar issued a noteworthy proclamation. In this message to his entire realm the king set forth Je-ho'vah's greatness, truth, and justice, and acknowledged His sovereignty over all the world. The upright, fearless conduct of Dan'iel and his three companions, combined with their prayers for the heathen king, had now borne fruit in his conversion.

Neb-u-chad-nez'zar had another dream which none of the wise men of Bab'y-lon could interpret; although it foretold dire afflictions for the king, Dan'iel faithfully revealed its meaning. In his dream Neb-u-chad-nez'zar had seen a tree which grew and grew until its height reached into the heavens, and the sight thereof to the end of the earth. The leaves were fair and the fruit abundant, and its branches provided food and shelter for men and beasts throughout the world. Then the king heard, in his dream, one of the holy ones of heaven order the tree to be cut down, leaving the stump and its roots in the earth. Further details of the dream suggested that someone would become insane, and live among the beasts until restored by the power of God.

Dan'iel then explained that the tree represented Neb-u-chad-nez'zar at the height of his prosperity, and warned him that he was later to be deprived of his reason, driven out to live among the beasts of the field, and forced to eat grass. The leaving of the stump and roots of the tree in the earth indicated that after a period of years the king's reason would be restored, and his kingdom preserved. Thinking of the king's welfare, Dan'iel followed his interpretation of the dream with an earnest appeal that he give up sin, live uprightly, and show mercy to the poor.

One day as Neb-u-chad-nez'zar was walking in the splendid roof gardens of Bab'y-lon, glorying in the work of his own hands, he was suddenly smitten with a type of madness which causes the victim to think that he is an animal and to act as such. He was removed from the throne at once, and cast out to live with the wild beasts. Having set himself up as more than a man, God punished him by causing him to become something less; having thought of himself as a rival to his Maker, he was reduced to a place lower than that of his humblest subjects. Neither physicians, sorcerers, or magicians were able to relieve him of the strange madness.

There was a power which could help him, as revealed in the explanation of the dream by Dan'iel. Neb-u-chad-nez'zar's own story of that power was, "I lifted up mine eyes unto heaven, and my understanding returned unto me." His mental powers were restored, and a great spiritual change took place in his heart. Neb-u-chad-nez'zar acknowledged to the whole world that his cure had been wrought by the Most High God of heaven; for the remainder of his life he showed a spirit of true religion, and sought always to honor the God of the He'brews.

SUGGESTIONS FOR STUDY

Biblical Index to Helpful References

The Deadly Evil of Envy and Jealousy. (1 Sam. 18:8; Prov. 6:34; 14:30.)

Refusing Evil Makes One a Prey to Envy. (Isa. 59:15; Jer. 15:15.)

Overcoming the World Through Faith. (1 Jno. 5:4.)

God's Presence in Fiery Trials. (Isa. 43:2.)

Standing Fiery Tests. (1 Pet. 4:12.)

Loyalty to God Winning Over Enemies. (Psm. 146:6.)

Flowering Trees Symbols of Prosperity. (Ezek. 17:22; 31:3.)

Periods of Chastisements Under Symbolic Figure Seven. (Lev. 26:18, 24, 28.)

The Sin of Robbing God of His Glory. (Psm. 9:4, 17.)

God's Power to Heal Incurable Madness. (Matt. 8:28-32.)

Hope for Those Who Forsake Their Evil Ways. (Isa. 55:7, 8.)

Blessings Following Repentance. (Joel 2:14.)

Questions

1. Tell of Nebuchadnezzar's greatness and of Babylon's glory.

2. What did Nebuchadnezzar's pride lead him to do?

3. Why did Daniel's three companions refuse to bow before this image?

4. Why did the princes of Babylon hasten to report them to the king?

5. Tell of the casting of these three noblemen into the fiery furnace.

6. When the king looked into the furnace what did he see?

7. What favors were then conferred upon Shadrach, Meshach, and Abednego?

8. Tell of the king's dream about a great tree and of Daniel's interpretation.

9. How did this dream afterwards come true?

THE HANDWRITING ON THE WALL; THE FALL OF BABYLON

DANIEL 5

After Neb-u-chad-nez'zar's death the throne of Bab'y-lon was occupied by Ne-bon'i-dus, who shared the government with his eldest son Bel-shaz'zar. Daniel and his three companions appear to have been banished from the royal court after the death of Neb-u-chad-nez'zar, but the reputation of the prophet of God was still remembered by many of the leaders of the nation.

Bel-shaz'zar was weak in moral character; he lived in reckless dissipation, and paid no attention to the solemn warnings given to his grandfather Neb-u-chad-nez'zar. Trusting in the strong defenses, lofty walls, and brazen gates of Bab'y-lon, he revelled in sin with a false feeling of security. While the country was being overrun by Cy'rus and his strong Persian armies, and the city of Bab'y-lon was in grave danger, Bel-shaz'zar and his princes engaged in a riotous feast. During the drunken revelry the king sent for the sacred vessels which Neb-u-chad-nez'zar had taken from the temple of God nearly seventy years before, and profanely used them by drinking toasts to heathen gods. As a thousand of his notable men, with their wives and companions, gave themselves up to wild carousals, the festivities were halted by a startling sight. Suddenly the form of a hand appeared, and ghostly fingers traced on the wall certain words which no one in the company could understand.

There was a sudden break in the merriment of the party, the drunken king was stricken with terror, and magicians and soothsayers were hastily summoned to decipher the mysterious lettering. When the wise men were unable to read the message, the aged queen-mother suggested that Dan'iel be sent for. At length the venerable prophet of God was brought before the king; although rich rewards had been promised for reading the strange message, Dan'iel made it clear at once that he would accept nothing for his services. He began by reminding Bel-shaz'zar of God's dealings with Neb-u-chad-nez'zar for his pride, rebuked him for failing to heed the lessons of his grandfather's experience, and denounced him for profaning the vessels of the temple. Then he solemnly read the inscrip-

BELSHAZZAR'S FEAST

tion on the wall, announcing the doom upon Bab'y-lon in these words: "MENE, God hath numbered thy kingdom and brought it to an end." "TEKEL, thou art weighed in the balances and art found wanting." "PERES, thy kingdom is divided and given to the Medes and Per'si-ans."

While Dan'iel was speaking, the Medes and Per'si-ans were entering the city by the brass river-gates, which had been left unlocked as predicted in a judgment spoken by another prophet of God. Hordes of foreign soldiers swept through the streets of Bab'y-lon with bloodstained swords; rushing into the royal banquet hall they slew all who stood in their way, including Bel-shaz'zar. Thus was brought to an end the Bab'-y-lon-i-an Empire, and the next great world-power came into supremacy. An uncle of the Per'si-an conqueror Cy'rus, Da-ri'us by name, was make king of Bab'y-lon. Da-ri'us immediately placed one hundred and twenty governors over the realm, and Dan'iel was made chief of the three presidents who directed them.

The Per'si-an Empire was the third of the great world powers about which we read in the Bible. The first was the As-syr'i-an kingdom which had Nin'e-veh for its capital; and was the nation used of God for the destruction of the Northern Kingdom of Is'ra-el. The second was the Bab'y-lon-i-an, or Chal-de'an, and was God's instrument for the punishment of Ju'dah for her idolatry. Now Per'si-a is to be used in restoring Is'ra-el.

SUGGESTIONS FOR STUDY
Biblical Index to Helpful References

The Vanity of False Religions. (Matt. 15: 9; Col. 2:23.)

The Sin of Sacrilege. (Lev. 10:1; Matt. 21:13.)

The Helplessness of Enchanters. (Isa. 47: 12, 13.)

The Peril of Surfeiting and Drunkenness. (Luke 21:34.)

Mocking Destruction of Strong Drink.

(Prov. 20:1; 23:20.)

Certain Damnation of Hardened Offenders. (Prov. 29:1; 2 Pet. 2:3.)

The Utter Destruction of Revelling Fools. (Eccl. 7:6.)

Smitten with Guilty Fear. (Mic. 7:17; Heb. 10:27.)

Medes and Persians Fulfilling Judgments of God. (Isa. 21:2; 45:1, 2; Jer. 51:28-39.)

Questions

1. Who reigned over Babylon after the death of Nebuchadnezzar?

2. With whom did he share the government?

3. Describe the character of Belshazzar.

4. What had happened to Daniel and his companions?

5. Tell of the riotous feast given by Belshazzar.

6. What startling event took place during the drunken revelries?

7. Who was first called to read and interpret the handwriting on the wall?

8. Why was Daniel sent for? Tell of his explanation of the writing.

9. What occurred while Daniel was giving the meaning of the handwriting?

STORY 141

DANIEL IN THE LIONS' DEN

DANIEL 6

When Da-ri'us became king of Bab'y-lon through the merging of the country with Me'di-a and Per'si-a, he respected the honors which had been conferred upon Dan'iel by Bel-shaz'-zar, and continued him in office as the chief governor of the realm. This act of the king in promoting an alien Jew to the highest rank of authority angered the governors of the provinces and presidents of the court; and they began at once a jealous plot for his downfall. They knew, however, that no fault could be found against his character or official conduct, and therefore made their attack on his religion.

These enemies of Dan'iel formed a conspiracy by which they induced Da-ri'us to issue a decree that no man in the realm be permitted to offer a petition to any God or man, except the king; the penalty for disobedience being death at the mercy of ferocious lions. Certain that this decree would entrap Dan'iel, for his habit of praying three times a day to Je-ho'vah was common knowledge, these vicious plotters gathered near his house to spy on him. Presently they saw him kneel before an open window facing toward Je-ru'sa-lem, and bursting into his private room they seized him and rushed him before Da-ri'us; wickedly accusing him of scorning the authority of the king.

Da-ri'us was greatly upset and troubled; not toward Dan'iel, but with himself for being tricked into issuing a decree which threatened the life of his most trusted officer. He spent a whole day in trying to find some way to avoid casting Dan'iel into the lions' den, but under the rigid law of the Medes and Persians there was no way out. The man of God was therefore flung into the den of hungry, ferocious lions, and a stone was placed over the mouth of the cave.

After a long, sleepless night in which the king was tortured by thoughts of the injustice done to Dan'iel, much of it spent in prayer that the God of heaven would prevent any harm to his loyal servant, Da-ri'us rushed to the lions' den, calling out in a voice mingled with hope and despair, "O Dan'iel, servant of the Most High God, is thy God, whom thou servest continally, able to deliver thee from the lions?" A cheerful voice from the den of lions assured the king that God had "stopped the lions' mouths that they did him no harm." While the king had tossed upon his royal bed, haunted by demons of fear and self-reproach, the prophet had slept peacefully surrounded by fierce animals whose mouths were closed by the God in whom he trusted. Dan'iel was rescued and the men who had plotted his death were cast to the vicious animals.

SUGGESTIONS FOR STUDY

Biblical Index to Helpful References

The Curse of Jealousy and Its Attendant Evils. (Rom. 1:29; Tit. 3:2.)

Plottings of the Wicked Against the Righteous. (Prov. 4:16; Psm. 10:9.)

The Privilege of Prayer Under Trials. (1 Thess. 5:17, 18; Phil. 4:6.)

Jehovah a Prayer-Hearing God. (Psm. 65: 2; 91:15.)

Angels Employed to Protect the Lord's Saints. (Psm. 103:20, 21.)

God's Deliverance from Trouble. (Job 5: 19; Psm. 23:4; 1 Pet. 3:13.)

Questions

1. What plot did the officers effect for the downfall of Daniel?

2. Why did they choose an attack on his religious integrity?

3. What decree did Darius issue under suggestion of Daniel's foes?

4. What did Daniel do concerning the edict of the king? Why?

5. What punishment was inflicted upon Daniel?

6. Compare the state of the king and of Daniel during the night following.

7. What did the king find the next morning when he called to Daniel?

8. Who shut the lions' mouths?

9. What was done with the enemies of Daniel?

DANIEL IN THE LIONS' DEN

STORY 142

THE STORY OF ESTHER, QUEEN OF PERSIA

THE BOOK OF ESTHER 📖 One of the most unusual stories of the Bible is the patriotic romance of Es'ther, who saved the Jewish people of Per'si-a from destruction. Mingled with the history of her noble deeds is an account of the heroic public services of her uncle Mor'de-cai, the faithful aid of her Per'si-an servant Hatach, and the support and prayers of the Jewish population of the empire.

A-has-u-e'rus, king of Per'si-a and Me'di-a, gave a great feast at his palace in Shu'shan for all his princes, nobles, and prominent citizens; and Vash'ti, the queen, provided a similar feast for the women of the court. On the seventh day of the feast, when the king was befuddled with wine, he ordered his seven chamberlains to bring the queen to his feast, that he might display her unusual beauty before the guests. Angered by her refusal to obey his request, the king carried out the suggestion of some of his officers and declared that Vash'ti was no longer queen. Then he ordered his servants to assemble a number of eligible young women of the realm, and planned to choose one of them as queen.

Among the minor officers of A-has-u-e'rus at Shu'shan there was a Ben'ja-mite Jew named Mor'de-cai, who had been carried away from Je-ru'sa-lem by Neb-u-chad-nez'zar. He was kind and noble spirited, and had adopted an orphan niece, whom he faithfully brought up in the Jewish faith. The child's Jewish name was Ha-das'sah, meaning "a lovely flower of promise," but was later given the name of Es'ther, which means "star of hope." Recalling her beauty and charm, and ambitious for her future rank in their adopted land, Mor'de-cai arranged for Es'ther to be among the young women from whom the new queen was to be chosen.

Each of the candidates in turn was required to appear before the king but Es'ther refused to be adorned with jewels or other artificial displays of beauty; when the time came for her presentation, she relied wholly upon her natural charm and the radiant goodness of her personality. A-has-u-e'rus was so enraptured by Es'ther that she was chosen at once, for "he loved Es'ther more than all the other maidens, and set the royal

ESTHER ACCUSING HAMAN

crown upon her head, and made her queen instead of Vash'ti." The king did not know that she was a Jewess, for Mor'de-cai had told her not to reveal her nationality. She was selected solely because of her native beauty and wisdom, and under the guiding hand of an all-wise Providence.

Soon after the marriage feast was celebrated, and Es'ther had received all the honors of state, she was given her first opportunity to render a great service to the king. Two of the royal chamberlains had formed a conspiracy to murder A-has-u-e'rus, and Mor'de-cai, having discovered the plot, advised his niece to report the matter to the king. An investigation was made, and as a result the two plotters were hanged.

Five or six years after Es'ther had become queen there appeared among the officers of A-has-u-e'rus a man who set his heart on destroying the Jews. His name was Ha'man, and through some strange fancy of the king had been made chief of the royal officers. He was vain and self-conceited, and managed to secure an order from the king which compelled everyone to pay him the reverence due only to the gods. Such an act was forbidden by Jewish laws of religion, so Mor'de-cai refused to pay homage to the wicked Ha'man.

Ha'man was so greatly angered by Mor'de-cai's refusal to honor him that he determined to have the He'brew put to death. Having warned that Mor'de-cai was a Jew, he planned the destruction of all the Jews in the Persian Empire with one blow. He, therefore, told the king that the Jews lived apart from the natives of Per'si-a, clinging stubbornly to their own laws and customs; and that their presence was a threat to the safety of the empire. Then he asked the king for a decree calling for the massacre of all people of Jewish blood, agreeing to make a large donation from his own fortune toward the expenses involved, and promising to take full responsibility for the massacre. A-has-u-e'rus gave his consent to this cruel demand apparently without investigating the charges made by Ha'man, and ordered copies of the decree to be sent to all the governors of the one hundred and twenty-seven provinces of the empire.

The date for the proposed massacre was determined by casting lots, and Divine Providence caused a delay of several months—thus giving Mor'-de-cai and Es'ther time to thwart the wicked schemes of Ha'man against their people. Not content with apparent success in his plan to destroy all the Jews in Per'si-a on a given date, Ha'man prepared for the immediate execution of the one man who refused to salute him as if he were a god. At the suggestion of his wife, who seems to have been in favor of the shameful deed, Ha'man built a gallows seventy-five feet high, so that all the people could see the hanging of Mor'de-cai.

When news of the king's edict reached the ears of Mor'de-cai, the godly man was filled with sorrow—not for himself, but for his kindred. He clothed himself in sackcloth, scattered ashes over his head, and stood at the gate of the palace crying out in bitter lamentations. In every Jewish home of the land laughter and joy were silenced, and the people wept in sore distress. Queen Es'ther's servants told her of Mor'de-cai's outcries of sorrow, but she did not know that the destruction of her people had been ordered. She sought to relieve her uncle's sorrow by sending him new raiment to take the place of the sackcloth which he wore, but he would not receive it.

It was then that Es'ther turned to her trusted chamberlain Ha-thach to carry messages to and from Mor'de-cai. He brought the Queen news of the plight of her people, showed her a copy of the king's edict, and presented an urgent request from Mor'de-cai that she plead with A-has-u-e'-rus for the life of her people. Under the rules of the Per'si-an court all persons were forbidden, under pain of death, to appear before the king uninvited; and for the past month she had not been asked to visit him. When she reminded Mor'de-cai of these facts, he sent a still more urgent message, saying, "Who knoweth whether thou art not come to the kingdom for such a time as this?"

This message from Mor'de-cai was a Divine summons to Es'ther to make use of her position for the rescue of her people, and an indication of God's purpose in making her Queen of Per'si-a at a critical moment in the history of the He'brews. In reply to the appeal of her uncle she directed that all the Jews of the realm spend three days in fasting and prayer, while she found some way of inducing the king to spare her people.

Wearing her royal robes Es'ther went into the court, and stood modestly before the throne. The king looked upon her with kindly interest, and raised his golden scepter as a sign that she was welcome; then he said, "What wilt thou, Queen Es'ther?" She replied that she wished the king and Ha'man to come to a banquet which she had prepared. The invita-

MORDECAI HONORED BY THE KING

tion was accepted, and the king sent for Ha'man to join him at Es'ther's feast. When the guests were seated at the banquet, Es'ther invited them to feast with her again on the next day, A-has-u-e'rus had urged Es'ther at the banqueting table to present her petition, assuring her that he would grant it, even to the half of his kingdom. She felt, however, that the time was not ripe to make her request.

Ha'man left the first banquet puffed up with pride by the honors shown him by the Queen, but still moved with a spirit of revenge toward Mor'de-cai. That night A-has-u-e'rus was unable to sleep, and his mind was troubled by the unseen hand of Je-ho'vah. When he took his place upon the throne on the following morning, the same foreboding spirit clung to him. Feeling that this moody spell was brought on by some neglected duty, the king called for the reading of certain documents in which there was recorded an account of Mor'de-cai's service in saving the life of the king from two murderous plotters. He asked whether Mor'de-cai had been duly rewarded, and was told that nothing had been done for him.

At that very moment Ha'man appeared in the court, intending to ask for an order to have Mor'de-cai hanged on the gallows which he had built. Before he could speak, however, the king asked, "What shall be done unto the man whom the king delighteth to honor?" Thinking that the king referred to him, Ha'man replied: "For the man whom the king delighteth to honor, let the royal apparel be brought which the king is accustomed to wear, and the horse that the king rideth upon, and the royal crown which is set upon his head; and let this apparel and horse be delivered to one of the king's most trusted princes, that the man whom the king delighteth to honor may be arrayed in all these; and bring him on horseback through the streets of the city with the proclamation: Thus shall it be done unto the man whom the king delighteth to honor."

A-has-u-e'rus then ordered Ha'man to do all that he had suggested— not for himself, but for Mor'de-cai. Thus he was forced to bestow all the honors of royalty upon the man whom he had planned to hang on that very day. Overcome with chagrin, Ha'man went to his wife and friends for further advice, but was told that his scheme would fail if the man against whom he had plotted was a Jew. Disguising his feelings as well as he could, Ha'man then went to the second royal feast prepared by Es'ther.

At the second festival prepared by Es'ther for the king he remembered that the Queen had visited him for a special purpose, and for the third time urged her to make known her request; assuring her that it would be granted. At last the moment for Es'ther to save her people had come; and she earnestly related to the king the plot for the massacre of herself and her whole nation. When A-has-u-e'rus asked "who durst presume in his heart to do this?" Es'ther denounced Ha'man to the king in his own presence. The king was so enraged that he went into the garden to reflect upon the terrible plight under which he had fallen under the influence of an evil officer.

Caught in his own trap, and awed by the guilt of his conscience, Ha'-man begged for mercy from the Queen. Finding the wicked officer prostrate before Es'ther the king ordered his arrest at once, and being reminded of the gallows already erected for Mor'de-cai, commanded that Ha'man himself be hanged thereon. The property of the plotter was given to Es'ther, and Mor'de-cai was promoted to the office which the enemy of the Jews formerly held. Es'ther then secured an order from A-has-u-e'rus permitting the Jews to protect themselves with arms against those who sought to execute the order of Ha'man; thus saving her race.

SUGGESTIONS FOR STUDY

Biblical Index to Helpful References

The Sin of Glorying in Earthly Splendor. (Acts 25:23.)

Ill-Effects of Drunkenness and Revelry. (Prov. 21:1, 17; Isa. 56:12.)

The Commendation of Modesty. (Gen. 24:65; 1 Tim. 2:9, 10; 1 Pet. 3:1, 2.)

Duties of Wives. (Prov. 31:27; Eph. 5: 22; 1 Tim. 3:11.)

Conjugal Love. (Gen. 24:67; Prov. 5:19; Eph. 5:28.)

The Sin of Envy and Malice. (Psm. 140: 1-3; Prov. 30:14.)

The Sin of Vindictiveness. (2 Ki. 6:21; Psm. 137:9.)

Persecution of Jews. (Psm. 74:8; 83:4, 5; Dan. 3:8.)

Self-Sacrificial Spirit. (Gen. 44:33; Ex. 32:32; Ruth 2:11.)

Vanity of Riches. (Prov. 11:4; Eccl. 6:2; Zeph. 1:18.)

Proud and Wicked Humiliated. (Job 9: 13; Prov. 11:5; 22:14.)

The Worthy Promoted. (Gen. 39:5.)

Questions

1. Relate the interesting historical setting of the story of Esther.

2. Tell of the feast of Ahasuerus and of Vashti's refusal to attend.

3. What punishment was inflicted on Vashti for her insubordination?

4. Who was Esther? Tell of her choice to become queen.

5. Describe the character of Haman.

6. Why did he become angry and envious of Mordecai?

7. What shrewd. trick did he play against the Jews?

8. Tell how Esther won the consideration of the king.

10. What became of Haman? Of Mordecai?

9. What course was taken to save the Jews?

STORY 143

THE RETURN OF THE JEWISH
EXILES FROM BABYLON

THE BOOKS OF EZRA
AND NEHEMIAH   The captivity of Ju'dah in Bab'y-lon was a decisive era in the history of ancient Is'ra-el and in the preparations for the
coming of the Mes-si'ah. For a period of seventy years the government
of God's chosen people had been broken up, and their nationality had
collapsed. They had been carried into captivity because they turned away
from Je-ho'vah and walked in evil ways. The Lord had sent such notable
prophets as I-sa'iah and Jer-e-mi'ah to warn them of the swift destruction
from the North, but the warnings were rejected and the prophets treated
cruelly. Under a just Providence they were forced to live among people
of an alien tongue who knew nothing of Je-ho'vah, scorned the Jew'ish
religion, and hated the captives.

In ancient times the object of wholesale deportations of conquered
nations was to break down the patriotism and common religion which
held the people together. The Bab'y-lo-ni-an conquerors thought that by
removing the He'brews from their native land they would destroy their
spirit of nationalism, draw them away from God, and force them to lose
their racial identity through intermarriage.

The plans of the Bab'y-lo-ni-ans, however, worked out in a way exactly
opposite from what they had intended. Removed from their God-given
land because of their sins, forced to live among heathen mockers without
a religious temple, and deprived of the freedom once enjoyed under the
blessings of Je-ho'vah, the Jews were convinced that their misfortunes had
been visited upon them by a loving God who was working out their
salvation in His own way. In a deeply penitent spirit they turned to the
teachings of the Mosaic Law and other sacred writings for instruction,
and developed a higher standard of personal religion than they had
known before.

A special message from the prophet Jer-e-mi'ah, who had remained
among the Jews left in Pal'es-tine advised them to become loyal to the
Bab'y-lo-ni-an government, and to take every opportunity of advancement
in the land in which they had been settled by the Providence of God.

The prophet E-ze-ki'el had been raised up among them, and he labored faithfully in the interests of pure, devout religion in the homes and private life of the people. In addition to such patriots as Dan'i-el and his companions, and later such leaders as Ze-rub'ba-bel, Ez'ra, and Ne-he-mi'ah, there were no doubt many others who rendered valuable services for the captive nation. It is known that the leaders of the people occupied themselves with collecting and editing the sacred books of the Law, books of history, prophecies, psalms, and sayings of wisdom.

The overthrow of the Bab'y-lo-ni-an Empire by Cy'rus opened the way for great prosperity and progress among the Jewish exiles. They were scattered throughout the hundred and more provinces of the new Me-do-Per'si-an empire, and many of them became financial and industrial leaders. The Jews carried their sacred books wherever they went, and clung to the faith of their fathers. Thus there was kept alive the hope of an eventual return to their native land for the rebuilding of the temple.

Cy'rus was quick to recognize the eagerness of his Jewish subjects to return to Pal'es-tine. Seeing the advantages of having a contented people settled in Ju'dah as a bulwark against possible attacks from the south, he issued a call for volunteers to return to Ju'dah. Those who did not wish to return at this time were asked to contribute to the aid of those who accepted the offer of the king.

Ze-rub'ba-bel, a prince of the house of Da'vid, was chosen to lead the returning band of exiles; and Josh'u-a, a priest descended from Aa'ron, was to help him. They were given the treasures which Neb-u-chad-nez'-zar had taken from the temple, and large donations were received from patriotic Jews in every part of Per'si-a. In the year 538 B. C. a caravan of more than forty thousand persons set out on the march by way of the Eu-phra'tes valley and Syr'i-a, and reached Je-ru'sa-lem after travelling for months over a distance of nearly one thousand miles. The first thing they did upon arrival was to set up the great brazen altar and observe the Feast of Tab'er-nac-les. This was done not only in celebration of the ancient deliverance of Is'ra-el from E-gyp'tian bondage, but also in honor of their return from exile.

The first task to which the returned exiles set their hands was the rebuilding of the temple. This was the chief purpose of their return to their native land, and was clearly set forth in the royal edict of Cy'rus. When the foundations were laid and the materials assembled, some of the older people discouraged the workers by complaining that the proposed temple would be much inferior to the one destroyed by Neb-u-chad-nez'zar.

Serious opposition also sprang up from the Sa-mar'i-tans, whose request to take part in the work had been refused by Ze-rub'ba-bel on the grounds that their degraded form of religion made them unworthy to associate with pure blooded He'brews. Largely as a result of the opposition of the Sa-mar'i-tans, the work was halted for a time. Meanwhile the Lord raised up the prophets Hag'ga-i and Zech-a-ri'ah, who aroused Ze-rub'-ba-bel and Josh'u-a, and encouraged the people to resume work on the temple. When the Per'si-an governor asked by what authority the re-building of the temple was undertaken Da-ri'us searched the archives of the kingdom until the original decree of Cy'rus was found. He then ordered the work to be continued, directing the governor of Syr'i-a to provide funds as needed from the government treasury.

In 516 B. C. the restored temple was dedicated with the offering of countless sacrifices, and with the observance of the national festival of the Pass'o-ver. Generous free will offerings were brought to the temple, and the forms of worship established by Mo'ses and Aa'ron were fully restored. From that day until the temple was rebuilt by Her'od the Great, the house built by Ze-rub'ba-bel remained as the center of the religious life of the Jews.

NEHEMIAH AND THE KING

About sixty years after the dedication of the temple a Jew-ish patriot named Ez'ra, who was a priest of the captive Jews in Per'si-a, led a small band of returning exiles to Je-ru'sa-lem. He had spent much time in compiling the ancient writings of the Jew'ish people, and with the aid of E-ze-ki'el had carefully arranged the system of worship. On his arrival at Je-ru'sa-lem he made improvements in the temple worship, and put into effect many reforms in the civil and religious life of the colony.

Things were going badly for the little band of He'brews in Ju'dah, and alarming reports reached the Per'si-an government concerning the failure of the colonists to solve their problems. There was at that time in the Per'si-an court of Ar-tax-erx'es a young Jewish prince by the name of Ne-he-mi'ah. He was a man of deep piety, a true Jewish patriot, and an influential member of the Per'si-an court. Upon learning of the sad state of affairs in Je-ru'sa-lem—how the city itself remained largely in ruins, and that the ancient walls had never been restored—he fasted and prayed before the Lord. When the king asked the reason for his sadness, Ne-he-mi'ah sought permission to go to Je-ru'sa-lem on a mission of reform. Ar-tax-erx'es appointed him governor of the province, and gave him authority to lead a third band of returning exiles to Ju'dah. Provision was also made for Ne-he-mi'ah to be assisted in his mission by the governors of neighboring provinces.

Upon reaching Je-ru'sa-lem, Ne-he-mi'ah made a complete survey of the desolation secretly by night, determined to plan at once for rebuilding the walls of the city. Then he called together the elders and princes of Je-ru'sa-lem, and the leading Jews of surrounding communities, and laid his plans before them. He was bitterly opposed by the Sa-mar'i-tans and other alien residents of Ju'dah, but through wise planning and united effort was able to carry on the work. The governors of neighboring provinces tried to thwart the work of Ne-he-mi'ah: first by open opposition, then by ridicule, and then by proposing a compromise in which they would be given a part in the undertaking.

San-bal'lat, the leader of the governors who sought to hinder the work, bribed a Jewish priest to tell Ne-he-mi'ah that his life was in danger, and threatened to tell the king of Per'si-a that the Jews were plotting to set up an independent kingdom. All opposition was overcome, however, and the walls of the city were rebuilt within the short space of fifty-three days.

When the walls were completed, Ez'ra suddenly appeared upon the scene, taking part in the great service of dedication. A national fast was proclaimed, and for two days the law of God was read aloud to the people. The ancient covenant was renewed, and the leaders of the colony signed the solemn agreement to keep themselves from the idolatry of the heathens about them, and to be true to all the duties of the Jewish religion.

Ne-he-mi'ah then returned to the Per'si-an capital, but resumed his post as governor of Ju'dah after a lapse of twelve years. On his return he found many evils which had to be removed. The rich were defrauding and oppressing the poor, the lands of the lower classes were heavily mort-gaged, and the laws of Mo'ses were wholly set aside. Among the abuses which had taken place was the marriage of the High Priest to a daughter of To-bi'ah, an Am'mon-ite ruler, and the presence of this heathen woman within the temple. Ne-he-mi'ah at once cast out the High Priest E-li'a-shib, ordering devout priests to purify the temple. He also denounced those who broke the Sab'bath and oppressed the poor, and forbade inter-marriage with the heathens of the land.

Cured of idolatry by the Bab'y-lo-ni-an Captivity, the Jews continued their racial and religious institutions under the dominance of the suc-ceeding world-powers of Greece and Rome. They passed through many severe struggles and trials during the A-poc'ry-phal period of three hun-dred years; but held tenaciously to the laws of Mo'ses, the teachings of the prophets, and the hope of the coming Mes-si'ah. They were scattered to every part of the world, and their holy Scriptures were translated into Greek and other important languages. Thus the Jews in Palestine were prepared for the coming of the Mes-si'ah in the land of ancient Is'ra-el, and the world was made ready for the advent of his kingdom.

SUGGESTIONS FOR STUDY

Biblical Index to Helpful References

Israel's Sad Plight in Babylon. (Psm. 137.)

Divine Promises of Israel's Restoration. (Deut. 30:3; Isa. 11:11; Jer. 16:15; 23:3; Zeph. 3:20; Zech. 10:10.)

Cyrus the Instrument of Jehovah for Is-rael's Restoration. (Isa. 44:28.)

Advantages in Co-operative Labors. (Ex. 17:2; Jgs. 20:11; 2 Ki. 6:2; 1 Chr. 12:38.)

Free-will Offerings for Religious Work. (Num. 15:3; 29:39; Deut. 12:6; 16:10.)

Solicitude for Israel. (Isa. 22:4; 62:1; Jer. 4:19; 8:21; Lu. 13:24; Rom. 9:2.)

Examples of Intercession. (Ex. 32:32; Num. 14:17; 1 Sam. 7:5; Psm. 106:23.)

God's Hand Gives Blessings to His Ser-vants. (2 Chr. 30:12; Psm. 37:24; 104:8.)

Prosperity for the Righteous. (Gen. 39:3; 1 Chr. 22:13; 2 Chr. 31:21.)

False Accusations Against the Righteous. (Job 2:5; 22:6; Jer. 37:13; 1 Pet. 3:16.)

Promise of Deliverance from False Ac-cusers. (Psm. 18:28.)

Questions

1. How long did the Israelites remain in Babylonian captivity?

2. Why were they thus punished?

3. What was the object of Babylon in re-moving them to Babylon?

4. What effect did Babylonian captivity have on the Jews?

5. What advice did Jeremiah give them?

6. Under whose reign were the Israelites permitted to return to Judea?

7. Who led the first caravan of returning exiles? Who greatly aided him?

8. What people opposed these colonists? Who were the Samaritans?

9. What was the first work done by Zerub-babel and Joshua?

10. Who led the second caravan of re-turning exiles?

11. Who led the third? What great work did he do?

BEAUTIFUL BIBLE STORIES

from

THE LIFE AND TEACHING OF JESUS CHRIST

HARMONIZING THE GOSPEL RECORDS
WITH VALUABLE SUGGESTIONS
FOR STUDY

THE GOOD SHEPERD

STORY 144

THE ANGEL GABRIEL VISITS ZACHA-RIAS AND THE VIRGIN MARY

LUKE 1

The holy drama of the New Testament opens with the appearance of two important characters: an angel from heaven, and a devout man on earth. On.one hand was a priest of Is'ra-el who was noted for his righteousness in the sight of God, and for his blameless conduct toward men. On the other hand was the angel Ga'bri-el, sent on an errand of love to a world steeped in sin. The names of only two angels are given in the sacred writings: Ga'bri-el, who announces God's purposes in glad tidings; and Mi'cha-el, who carries out God's commands.

The priest Zach-a-ri'as and his devout wife lived in the hill country of Ju'de-a near the town of He'bron. Though their quiet home life was happy in every other respect, they often lamented the absence of children, and for many years had prayed earnestly to the Lord to remove this misfortune. As time went on it became clear that only a miracle could answer their prayers for a child, and for many centuries there had been no such miracles among the chosen people of God.

For the opening scene in the drama of the New Revelation we are taken to the sanctuary of God's house in Je-ru'sa-lem, to the place of holy meditation where the aroma of burning incense filled the room with an air of praise and worship. The hour was that of public prayer; Zach-a-ri'as was taking his turn in the services of the temple, and the saints of Is'ra-el were gathered in the outer court to ask the blessings of Je-ho'vah. Suddenly there stood by the right side of the altar a heavenly visitor—though startled by the miraculous appearance, Zach-a-ri'as was quickly put at ease by the gentle words of the angel, who said:

"Fear not, Zach-a-ri'as: for thy prayer is heard; and thy wife E-lis'a-beth shall bear thee a son, and thou shalt call his name John. And thou shalt have joy and gladness; and many shall rejoice at his birth. For he shall be great in the sight of the Lord, and shall drink neither wine nor strong drink; and he shall be filled with the Holy Ghost. And many of the children of Is'ra-el shall he turn to the Lord their God. And he shall go before him in the spirit and power of E-li'as, to turn the hearts of the fathers to the children, and the disobedient to the wisdom of the just; to make ready a people prepared for the Lord."

Zach-a-ri′as simply could not believe this message, and asked the angel for a sign. It was given at once, for the angel replied that he would be unable to speak until the promise was fulfilled; when Zach-a-ri′as came out to pronounce a benediction upon the people, he was stricken dumb, and was forced to bless them by means of signs.

The second scene of the holy drama took place about six months later. The angel Ga′bri-el appeared to a maiden in the little town of Naz′a-reth, which was situated far back among the hills of Gal′i-lee, in the heart of a province regarded as little better than heathen. The maiden was called Ma′ry, and she was betrothed to Jo′seph, a member of the house of Da′vid who was a humble carpenter in the little town so much despised by the Jews. Ma′ry was one of the many descendants of Da′vid who had fallen into obscurity and poverty, but she was deeply religious—earnest in her search of the prophetic Scriptures, and firm in her belief that the promised Mes-si′ah would come. As she pondered the messages concerning the coming Sav′ior she was often filled with the hope that Je-ho′vah might "condescend to her low estate" and make her the mother of the "Son of the Highest."

The angel appeared to Ma′ry in a vision as she was quietly meditating in her home. She seems to have shown no signs of fright at his presence, but her heart was filled with wonder when he said:

"Hail, thou that art highly favored, the Lord is with thee: blessed art thou among women."

In these words the angel of the Lord did not declare that Ma′ry was a saint, nor that she was the fountain of grace; he merely announced the grace which God had bestowed upon her. As the maiden stood in silent wonder, overcome by an emotion too deep to be put into words, the angel continued his message to her in these words:

"Fear not, Ma′ry: for thou hast found favor with God. And behold, thou shalt bring forth a son, and shall call his name JE′SUS. He shall be great, and shall be called the Son of the Highest: and the Lord shall give unto him the throne of his father Da′vid: and he shall reign over the house of Ja′cob for ever; and of his kingdom there shall be no end."

Without in the least doubting the word of the angel, Ma′ry asked how so great a miracle could take place. Ga′bri-el then said to her:

"The Holy Ghost shall come upon thee, and the power of the Highest shall overshadow thee: therefore that holy thing which shall be born of thee shall be called the Son of God."

After these words of explanation the angel told Ma'ry of the blessing soon to come to her cousin E-lis'a-beth, proving that neither barrenness nor old age could check the power of God in fulfilling the promise of a son given to her saintly husband. This miracle was to be a sign to Ma'ry that the promise which she had received would also come true.

Ma'ry was overwhelmed with joy at the news of her part in the Divine plan, and meekly replied: "Be it unto me according to thy word." In this humble, trusting way she received the greatest summons ever sent from heaven to a mortal creature. Her privilege it was to bring into the world the One who would undo all the evils which had been brought upon the human race.

From this soul-stirring experience Ma'ry returned to the humble paths of her life in Naz'a-reth, pondering in her heart the wonderful blessing promised by the Lord, but telling no one in Naz'a-reth of her secret. Presently she set out on a journey through the hill country of Ju'de-a to visit her cousin E-lis'a-beth, who told her the wonderful news of the angel's promise to Zach-a-ri'as; while Ma'ry told the glad tidings of Ga'bri-el's visit to her. As they rejoiced together Ma'ry burst into song, and her words have come down through the centuries in the hymn which is known as "The Magnificat":

"My soul doth magnify the Lord,
    And my spirit hath rejoiced in God my Sav'ior.
For He hath regarded the low estate of His handmaiden:
For, behold, from henceforth all generations shall call me blessed.
For He that is mighty hath done to me great things;
    And holy is His name.
And His mercy is on them that fear Him
    From generation to generation.
He hath showed strength with His arm;
He hath scattered the proud in the imagination of their hearts.
He hath put down the mighty from their seats,
    And exalted them of low degree.
He hath filled the hungry with good things;
    And the rich He hath sent empty away.

THE "MAGNIFICAT"

He hath holpen His servant
   Is'ra-el,
In remembrance of His mercy.
As He spake to our fathers,
To A'bra-ham, and to his seed
   for ever."

Ma'ry remained for a time
with E-lis'a-beth, and then returned to Naz'a-reth. In due
time a son was born to E-lis'a-
beth, and on the eighth day was
taken to the temple in Je-ru'sa-
lem for presentation to the Lord
according to the ancient laws of
Is'ra-el. E-lis'a-beth's relatives
and friends wished the child to
be named for his father, but she
insisted that he should be called
John. When Zach-a-ri'as was
asked to choose a name for his
son, the aged priest, who was
still unable to speak, wrote these
words on a tablet: "His name
is John." Suddenly Zach-a-ri'as
recovered his power of speech,
and praised the Lord in a beautiful song which is called the
"Ben'e-dic-tus":

"Blessed be the Lord God of Is'ra-el;
For he hath visited and redeemed his people,
And hath raised up an horn of salvation for us
In the house of his servant Da'vid;
As he spake by the mouth of his holy prophets,
Which have been since the world began:
That we should be saved from our enemies,
And from the hand of all that hate us;
To perform the mercy to our fathers,

And to remember his holy covenant;
The oath which he sware to our father A'bra-ham,
That he would grant unto us,
That we, being delivered out of the hand of our enemies,
Might serve him without fear,
In holiness and righteousness before him,
All the days of our life.

And thou, child, shalt be called the prophet of the Highest:
For thou shalt go before the face of the Lord to prepare his ways;
To give knowledge of salvation unto his people
By the remission of their sins,
Through the tender mercies of our God;
Whereby the dayspring from on high hath visited us,
To give light to them that sit in darkness
    and in the shadow of death,
To guide our feet into the way of peace."

After uttering this beautiful prophetic hymn concerning his God-given son, Zach-a-ri'as and E-lis'a-beth dedicated the remainder of their days on earth to the holy task of preparing him for the great work of priest, prophet, and forerunner of the coming Mes-si'ah.

SUGGESTIONS FOR STUDY

Biblical Index to Helpful References

Ministry of Angels. (2 Ki. 6:17; Psm. 34:7.)

Angel-Appearances in Path of Duty. (Gen. 32:1.)

The Angel Gabriel. (Dan. 8:16; 9:21.)

The Angel Michael. (Dan. 10:13, 21; 12:1; Jude 9; Rev. 12:7.)

Human Incredulity When Prayers Are Answered. (Acts 12:12-16.)

Delighting to Do the Will of God. (Psm. 40:8.)

The Divine Nature of Jesus. (John 5:19, 23; 8:28; 14:10, 11.)

Another Woman Called "Blessed." (Jgs. 5:24.)

The Messiah an Offspring of David. (Psm. 2:7; 89:27; 132:11.)

The Meaning of the Name JESUS. (Matt. 1:21.)

Questions

1. How does the drama of the New Testament open?

2. What two angels are named in the Bible? Mission of each?

3. Describe the character of Zacharias and his wife Elisabeth.

4. What promise did the angel give to Zacharias?

5. What happened to him when he asked for a sign?

6. Tell of the angel's appearance to the Virgin Mary.

7. What promise did he make to her?

8. To whom was she betrothed?

9. Repeat from memory the "Magnificat."

10. Repeat from memory the "Benedictus."

STORY 145

THE BIRTH OF THE CHRIST CHILD

LUKE 2:1-20;
MATTHEW 1:18-25   After her visit with her cousin E-lis'a-beth,
Ma'ry returned to her home in Naz'a-reth. Here the problems of her
strange experience were greatly increased by Jo'seph's distressed state of
mind. He had learned that his betrothed wife was soon to become a
mother, but did not know of the visit of the angel Ga'bri-el to Ma'ry,
or of her overshadowing by the Holy Ghost. While he was planning to
break the engagement an angel of the Lord appeared to him in a vision at
night, saying:

"Jo'seph, thou son of Da'vid, fear not to take unto thee Ma'ry thy betrothed: for that which is conceived of her is of the Holy Ghost. And she
shall bring forth a son, and thou shalt call his name JE'SUS: for he shall
save his people from their sins."

The marriage was quietly solemnized according to the laws of the Jew'-
ish religion, and Jo'seph meekly accepted the task which Divine Providence assigned to him as the protector of Ma'ry, and the foster-father of
her Divine Child. Ma'ry and Jo'seph made their home in their little
native town, but according to the prophecies of ancient Is'ra-el the Mes-
si'ah was not to be born in Naz'a-reth. The next scene in the holy drama,
therefore, was moved under the providence of God to the little city of
Beth'le-hem, the native home of Da'vid, six miles south of Je-ru'sa-lem.

Au-gus'tus Cae'sar, the Roman Emperor who ruled most of the known
world at that time, unwittingly became the servant of God in bringing
about the events which led to the birth of Ma'ry's son in the city of Da'vid
as prophecied hundreds of years before. He issued a decree for the enrollment of all his subjects, and Pal'es-tine was a part of the Roman Empire.

In Ju'de-a the enrollment was carried out in keeping with Jewish customs, which required the people to enroll in the town of their ancestors.
Jo'seph and Ma'ry were both of the house of Da'vid, and therefore, had
to leave their home in Naz'a-reth of Gal'i-lee and journey to Beth'le-hem
of Ju'de-a. It was a long, tiresome journey over the mountainous regions
of Pal'es-tine and along the borders of the Jor'dan—a distance of about
eighty miles—and must have been a severe ordeal for the saintly woman
who was soon to become the mother of the Lord. At the end of their

weary march, Ma'ry and Jo'-seph climbed the little hill that led to Beth'le-hem, seeking lodging in the village inn. They had come too late, however, for the inn was already filled to capacity with others who had come to be enrolled. Nor could they find some friendly home to provide the comfort and shelter so much needed at the moment, but were forced to lodge in a cavern stable.

Thus the scene was prepared for the birth of the Sav'ior in the city ordained by the Lord, and the lowly manger of an ox-stall was the first resting place for the Son of God. To open the way for man's enjoyment of an eternal inheritance, He was

THE FLIGHT INTO EGYPT

born under the most humiliating conditions; his infant body was placed in the manger where lay the food for cattle, and his earthly career was begun without a sign of the glory to come.

Hidden from the eyes of a thoughtless and wicked world, possessed of a dual inheritance of royalty, and destined to receive a name that has no equal in heaven or earth, the Son of God made his silent entrance into the world. The unfathomable depths of Divine wisdom were becoming more clear, the fountains of God's immeasurable love were pouring out blessings upon all mankind, and the founder of a spiritual kingdom which is to have no end had now come into the world—yet not even the chosen people of God knew of the momentous event which was taking place in the lowly stable in Beth'le-hem.

In the hill country near Beth'le-hem a group of shepherds were watching the sheep needed for the daily sacrifices in the temple at Je-ru'sa-lem. They were humble and devout Is'ra-el-ites, strengthened in their duties and trials by the promise of a Divine Deliverer of the nation, and always quick to perceive the revelations of God. In the darkness of night an angel of Je-ho'vah appeared among them, and they were smitten with fear. Then the heavenly messenger spoke to them in these words:

"Fear not: for, behold, I bring you good tidings of great joy, which shall be to all people. For unto you is born this day in the city of Da'vid a Sav'ior, which is Christ the Lord."

The shepherds were then told that in proof of this message they would find a babe wrapped in swaddling clothes lying in a manger. Suddenly the heavens were opened with a halo of Divine light, and there appeared a multitude of the heavenly host singing:

"Peace on earth; goodwill among men; glory to God in the highest."

Hastening to the city of Beth'le-hem, the shepherds found the streets empty, with no sign of the good news which they had received from the angel. They searched until the humble place of the Sav'ior's birth was found, and there they saw the new-born King lying in a manger. Kneeling at His feet, they paid the homage which shall some day be rendered by all the redeemed family of God. They told Ma'ry and Jo'seph of the message, of the angel and the heavenly chorus, and returned to their flocks praising God for all the things which they had seen and heard.

> "So would I love Thee, Blessed Lord,
> And in Thy praise will sing,
> Because Thou art my loving God,
> And my redeeming King."

SUGGESTIONS FOR STUDY

Biblical Index to Helpful References

Birthplace of the Messiah Foretold. (Mic. 5:2.)

Divinely Appointed Time for the Coming of the Messiah. (Dan. 9:24, 25.)

God's Revelations in Dreams. (Jgs. 7:13; 1 Ki. 3:5; Dan. 2:1; 4:5.)

The Son of God Incarnated in Human Flesh. (Jno. 1:14; Rom. 8:3; Phil. 2:7.)

Prophecies of the Divine Incarnation (Isa. 7:14; 9:6.)

The Great Host of Heavenly Angels. (Dan. 7:10.)

Angels Praising the Savior. (Psm. 148:2.)

Evidences of Jesus' Humanity: Hunger (Lu. 4:2.), Sleep (Lu. 8:23), Sorrow (Matt. 26:37), Weariness (Jno. 4:6.)

Questions

1. Tell of the message of God to Joseph.

2. Why was it necessary for Mary and Joseph to visit Bethlehem?

3. Had the Lord revealed the place of the Savior's birth?

4. How far was Bethlehem from Nazareth? Tell of journey of Mary and Joseph.

5. Tell of the reasons for Mary and Joseph having to stop in a stable.

6. Tell of the great meaning of the birth of her baby.

7. To whom did angels announce the birth of Jesus?

8. Tell of their visit to see the Child Jesus.

STORY 146

THE PRESENTATION OF THE CHILD JESUS IN THE TEMPLE

LUKE 2:21-38

After the crowded condition in Beth'le-hem was relieved, Ma'ry and Jo'seph moved into a humble dwelling place where they made their home for two months or more. At the end of the forty days required for the "purification of motherhood" under the Mosaic Law, Ma'ry and Jo'seph went up to the temple to make the customary offerings and to present the infant Je'sus to the Lord. A lamb and a pigeon were the usual offerings, but because of their poverty Ma'ry and Jo'seph were allowed to offer two pigeons instead.

There was then living in Je-ru'sa-lem an aged Is'ra-el-ite who was noted for piety and virtue, and who had been assured by the Holy Spirit that

he would not die until his eyes had looked upon the promised Mes-si'ah. As Ma'ry and Jo'seph were presenting the infant before the altar of God, the venerable man was moved by a Divine intuition to recognize him as the Mes-si'ah. Taking the child into his arms, and speaking with deep emotion, the faithful old man said:

"Lord, now lettest thy servant
    depart in peace, according to
    thy word:
For mine eyes have seen thy
    salvation,
Which thou hast prepared before the face of all people;
A light to lighten the Gentiles,
And the glory of thy people
    Is'ra-el."

JESUS PRESENTED AT THE TEMPLE

The beautiful words of Sim'e-on told Ma'ry and Jo'seph nothing which had not already been made known to them by the angel Ga'bri-el, but they were amazed that a total stranger should possess so deep an insight into the destinies of the Holy Child. Sim'e-on then pronounced a benediction upon Ma'ry and Jo'seph, and added these words to Ma'ry alone:

"Behold, this child is set for the fall and rising again of many in Is'ra-el; and for a sign which shall be spoken against; yea, a sword shall pierce through thine own soul also."

How tragic were these predictions! And how truly did Ma'ry become "The Mother of Sorrows" as she suffered the grief of seeing her Divine Son despised and rejected, wearied with the labors of love for the good of others, yet treated with ingratitude and contempt until He was finally murdered on the shameful cross.

To the inspired testimony of Sim'e-on there was added the hallowed witness of a devout woman. There lived in the temple an aged prophetess named An'na, a widow whose time was wholly employed in the service of God with fastings and prayers night and day. In her was represented the ten tribes of the Northern Kingdom lost in As-syr'i-an captivity, for she was a member of the tribe of Ash'er. Coming into the temple about the time that Sim'e-on uttered his last word to Ma'ry, she told all the people who were gathered there of the work of redemption which the infant Mes-si'ah would accomplish in Je-ru'sa-lem.

SUGGESTIONS FOR STUDY

Biblical Index to Helpful References

The Law of Purification. (Num. 31:20.)
The Duty of Keeping the Law. (Josh. 23:6.)
Recognizing God's Claims Upon Our Children. (Num. 3:13.)
Waiting Upon the Lord. (Psm. 33:20; 40:1; Isa. 25:9; 33:2.)

Messianic Hopes. (Mark 15:43; Jno. 4:25.)
Blessings for Those Who Wait in God's Sanctuary. (Psm. 84:4; Mic. 4:2.)
Christ to Be the Light of the World. (Isa. 9:2; 42:6; Eph. 5:14.)
Another Prophetess in the Temple. (2 Chr. 34:22.)

Questions

1. Where did Mary and Joseph live during the infancy of Jesus?
2. Why did they go, up to Jerusalem at the expiration of forty days?
3. What aged saint was present in the temple?

4. What did he say when he saw Jesus?
5. What prediction did he make concerning Mary?
6. Who else in the temple prophesied concerning the Child Jesus?

WISE MEN OF THE EAST PAY HOMAGE TO THE INFANT PRINCE

MATTHEW 2

After the presentation of the Child Je'sus in the temple at Je-ru'sa-lem, Ma'ry and Jo'seph returned to Beth'le-hem, intending to make their home in the little city of Da'vid. It was sometime later that the wise men from the East made their visit to the new born Prince of Is'ra-el.

In the ancient Eastern countries of Me'di-a, Chal-de'a, and A-ra'bi-a, the people made a close study of the stars, and many of them believed that they could read the future in this way. Three of the wise men, who probably lived in Me'di-a, had seen an unusual star which they thought was the sign of the birth of a new king in the land of Is'ra-el. It was not a star like others, of course, but could be seen only by those whose eyes were opened to spiritual truths by the Lord.

It is probable that the wise men were familiar with the ancient prophecies of the He'brews concerning the Mes-si'ah, for translations of the Jewish Scriptures had been widely distributed and read by scholars of other religions. No doubt there were also devout Is'ra-el-ites living in Media who told others of their hopes for the coming of the promised Deliverer of their nation. In some such a way, therefore, the wise men knew when the time had come for them to start on the long journey to the land of Ju-de'a in search of the new born king. As was the custom, they took with them gold and other precious things to be presented when they paid homage to the king.

Upon reaching the land of Ju-de'a, they went directly to the capital city for information, asking: "Where is he that is born King of the Jews?" The wise men then explained their search by saying, "For we have seen his star in the east, and are come to worship him."

When the words of the wise men were carried to Her'od, who was not a "born king," but ruled over Ju-de'a through the friendship of Mark An-to'ny of the Roman government, he was greatly disturbed. He was an able ruler, and had done many fine things for the Jews; but was deservedly unpopular because of his lack of principle. In his determination to remove every obstacle to his claim to the throne of the Jewish province he had utterly destroyed the house of the Mac'ca-bees, and, shortly before this incident, his peace of mind had been disturbed by the refusal of six thousand Phar'i-sees to take the oath of allegiance to him. He had wrecked the hopes of the Jews of Pal'es-tine for an independent kingdom, but in so doing had reawakened in the hearts of thousands of devout Jews the hope of the restoration of the house of Da'vid on the throne of Is'ra-el in the coming of the Mes-si'ah.

For all these reasons Her'od was greatly troubled by the announcement that there had been born somewhere in the land a "king of the Jews" and called upon the chief priests and elders to tell him where the Mes-si'ah should be born. On being told that the city of Beth'le-hem had been named in the prophecies as the birthplace of the promised king, he directed the wise men to this little city six miles away.

Before sending them away, however, the crafty king demanded that, when they had found the young Child, they should return to the capital and tell him the place, so that he might also worship the new king. Hidden beneath this request was an evil design to have the infant slain, thus removing a possible rival to his throne.

The star which had guided the wise men to Je-ru'sa-lem, and which had disappeared during their interview with Her'od, now guided them to the house in Beth'le-hem where they found the Infant Prince in the arms of his mother. Kneeling before the Child they rendered the homage usually paid to kings on the throne. Opening their treasures they laid before him gold, frankincense, and myrrh—the traditional gifts to a ruling Prince. Then, being warned in a dream that they should not return to Her'od, the wise men took another course on their journey back to their native land; thus leaving the evil ruler in still greater worry.

Soon after the departure of the wise men, an angel of the Lord appeared to Jo'seph, saying: "Arise, and take the young Child and his mother, and flee into E'gypt, and be thou there until I bring thee word: for Her'od will seek the young child to destroy him." Coming so soon after the wise men had paid homage to the Child, the news that the ruler of the land was seeking his life must have filled the hearts of Ma'ry and Jo'seph with despair. They would have to travel more than eighty miles before crossing the borders of E'gypt; since much of the way was over rugged hills and through desert country, the trip would require several days. The sojourn in E'gypt would involve considerable expense, but the Lord had made ample provision for this in the rich gifts of gold which the wise men had laid at the feet of the Child.

Preparations were quickly made for the journey, and the shades of night found the holy family on the way toward E'gypt. It is well that they hastened, for Her'od sent his soldiers into the little town of Beth'le-hem to slay all the male children under two years of age, expecting in this way to destroy the young child whom the wise men had declared to be the King of the Jews.

Ma'ry and Jo'seph readily found friends in E'gypt, for thousands of dispersed Is'ra-el-ites were living there at that time. During the two or three years of their stay in E'gypt, Jo'seph no doubt worked at his trade of carpentry. By this time Her'od had died, and the Lord sent His angel to Jo'seph with the message: "Arise, and take the young child and his mother, and go into the land of Is'ra-el: for they are dead which sought the young child's life."

When the holy family reached the province of Ju-de'a it was learned Ar-che-la'us reigned in his father's stead, and for this reason they did not think it safe to return to Beth'le-hem. They, therefore, went back to their old home in Naz'a-reth, for the province of Gal'i-lee was outside the territory ruled by Ar-che-la'us.

SUGGESTIONS FOR STUDY

Biblical Index to Helpful References

Deliverer for Israel Promised. (Num. 24: 7; Psm. 72:8-11.)

Christ as King. (Isa. 9:7; Dan. 7:14; 1 Cor. 15:25.)

Gifts for the King. (Isa. 60:3; 6; Psm. 72:10; Eccl. 2:9.)

Christ Worshiped. (Heb. 1:6; Rev. 5:8.)

God's Direction Given in Dreams. (Gen. 15:1; 46:2.)

Flight Into Egypt Foretold. (Hos. 11:1.)

Lamentation in Bethlehem Foretold. (Jer. 31:15.)

Questions

1. Where did Mary and Joseph live after presenting Jesus in the temple?

2. What directed the wise men in searching for Jesus?

3. Why did these men expect to find a new-born king in Judea?

4. Who was king in Judea at that time? What kind of man was he?

5. Where did the priests say Jesus should be born?

6. When the wise men found the Child Jesus, what did they do?

7. What request had Herod made of them? Why did they not comply with it?

8. What message was given Joseph in a dream?

9. Where did Mary and Joseph carry Jesus for safety?

10. Would they find friends in Egypt? Where did they get money for the trip?

11. How long did they remain in Egypt?

STORY 148

JESUS VISITS THE TEMPLE AT THE AGE OF TWELVE

LUKE 2:41-52

When Ma'ry and Jo'seph returned from their sojourn in E'gypt, Je'sus was a child of not more than three years. Believing that it was unsafe to return to Beth'le-hem, the holy family remained in Naz'a-reth until Je'sus was thirty years of age. Although the Gospel record makes only one reference to these "silent years," it is possible to form many interesting conclusions. From other information given in the New Testament we know that Ma'ry and Jo'seph became the parents of several children, including at least four boys and probably two girls. Since Je'sus is spoken of as both a carpenter and a carpenter's son, it appears that he assisted Jo'seph in the work of his chosen trade. Referring to the nine or ten years which Je'sus spent at Naz'a-reth before going up to the temple in Je'ru-sa-lem at the age of twelve, the Bible record says:

"The child grew, and waxed strong in spirit, filled with wisdom: and the grace of God was upon him."

These were years of physical health and development, of intellectual and moral growth, and of faithful, loving service to his heavenly Father. He lived a plain, blameless life; unaware of the high calling which soon awaited him. He grew up as did other Jewish boys of that age, taking part in the youthful sports of his day, mingling with neighbors of the community, and joining in the social and religious activities of his people.

Je'sus was the eldest of a family of seven children: four brothers, James, Joses, Ju'das, and Si'mon; and two sisters. He was therefore, given the advantages of being raised in a large, happy family, and was forced to adapt himself to the joys and trials brought into the home by so many brothers and sisters. His superior traits of goodness were no doubt envied by his younger half-brothers, for they rejected his claim to the Mes-si-an'ic office until after his death and resurrection. Since no mention is made of Jo'seph after he began his public ministry, it is believed that his foster-father must have died sometime after the visit to the temple when Je'sus was twelve years old.

Jo'seph and Ma'ry belonged to the poorer element in the land of Ju-de'a, so Je'sus was brought up in humble circumstances. The house in which he lived was plain and simple; its walls were of whitewashed stones, and its floors were of bare earth. The furniture consisted of a small table or two, a wooden chest for clothing, woven baskets for food, earthen jars for water, and a stand on which a stone lamp gave out a flickering light. The beds were woven rugs, which were kept on a platform at one end of the room during the day and spread on the earthen floor at night. Luxuries were unknown in the home of the growing Child Je'sus, and the necessities of meagre comfort were often scarcely sufficient.

JESUS IN THE TEMPLE

In a tiny case fastened upon the door post of the humble home there was a writing from the ancient law of Mo'ses; Ma'ry faithfully taught the children the principal teachings of the Law, and the entire family joined heartily in singing the beautiful Psalms of the Old Testament Scriptures. At the age of five Je'sus was no doubt sent to school in the village synagogue, where he was taught to read. He was also instructed in the word of God from scrolls containing the books of the Old Testament, and required to memorize long passages from the Law, the Prophets, and the Psalms. Twice each week, and always on the Sab'bath, he attended worship in the synagogue, listened to the Rabbi's explanation of the Scriptures, and joined in singing the Psalms. Often some member of the congregation would be called upon to explain the Scriptures, and no doubt Je'sus sometimes gave his interpretation of certain verses.

It was the custom for Jews in all parts of Pal'es-tine to go up to Je-ru'-sa-lem to observe certain feasts, especially the Feast of the Pass'o-ver, which was held every spring. Children, however, were never taken to the festivals until they had reached the age of twelve, at which time a

Jewish child legally became of age and was held responsible for keeping the precepts of the law.

When Je'sus was a boy of twelve, therefore, he was allowed to accompany Ma'ry and Jo'seph to Je-ru'sa-lem for the annual feast of the Pass'-o-ver. This was the feast which recalled the sparing of the Is'ra-el-ites many centuries before, when the angel of death stalked the land of E'gypt, taking the eldest child in every home which was not protected by the blood of a lamb sprinkled on the door. It is significant that the first visit of Je'sus to the capital was for the celebration of that momentous event in the history of the nation. Just twenty-one years later he fulfilled the meaning of the Pass'o-ver lamb in his own death upon the cross for the salvation of all mankind.

As Je'sus walked among the courts of the temple, looked upon the great altar with its burning sacrifices, watched the priests in their white robes as they ministered about the altar, and heard the Rabbis explain the laws of Is'ra-el, he was strongly tempted to begin his holy mission at once. His mind was so filled with these thoughts that he did not realize that his relatives and friends had started on the journey back to Naz'a-reth.

There was a large caravan of pilgrims travelling the road which Ma'ry and Jo'seph took on their way home, and they went for a whole day before the absence of their young son was discovered. They returned to Je-ru'sa-lem at once to search for him, inquiring first among their kinsfolk and friends; then on the third day they went up to the temple, where they found him conversing with the learned teachers and astonishing them with his wisdom. They gently reprimanded him for staying behind, and he replied, "Wist ye not that I must be about my Father's business?"

But the time had not come for Je'sus to begin his public ministry. He was to be trained by his parents and instructed in the laws of Is'ra-el until he was fully prepared for the great work which lay ahead. Thus he returned to Naz'a-reth with Ma'ry and Jo'seph, and "was subject unto them." Not until he was thirty years of age—the usual age for priests and religious teachers to begin their work—did he appear again in the public ministries of his appointed office. The Gospel record describes the eighteen years between his visit to Je-ru'sa-lem and the beginning of his ministry in these words:

"And Je'sus increased in wisdom and stature, and in favor with God and man." Of those days of childhood and youth He could truly sing:

"Thy mercy heard my infant prayer,
Thy love, with all a mother's care,
Sustained my childish days:
Thy goodness watched my ripening youth,
And formed my heart to love Thy truth,
And filled my lips with praise."

These must have been momentous years in the life of the young Naz'a-rene. Shut in from the outside world, he spent much time in silent communion with his heavenly Father. Looking across the hills and mountains from his humble home, he could behold the great plains of Es-dra-e'lon and recall the stories of Is'ra-el's victories on that noted battlefield. From the high hills of Naz'a-reth he could look down upon the road leading from the north country and watch the pilgrims on their way to Je-ru'-sa-lem, and could also see the trade route over which great caravans of Mid'i-an-ites wended their way toward the commercial centers of E'gypt. Looking in another direction, he could view the great Roman highway leading from De-cap'o-lis on the Sea of Gal'i-lee to the port of Acre on the Med'i-ter-ra'ne-an, and perhaps he sometimes talked with the legions of Roman soldiers who marched over this road. Thus for eighteen years the Sav'ior was prepared for his great work of human redemption, and for setting up an everlasting kingdom here upon earth.

SUGGESTIONS FOR STUDY

Biblical Index to Helpful References

Requirements for Attendance at Feasts. (Deut. 16:16.)

Feast of the Passover. (Lev. 26:6; Num. 9:5.)

Christ's Wisdom. (Isa. 11:2; Matt. 13:54; 1 Cor. 1:24.)

Christ's Words of Power. (Mark 13:31; Jno. 6:63, 68; 7:46.)

Parental Solicitude. (Gen. 37:14; Est. 2:11.)

Devout Mothers of Israel. (Gen. 21:6; 1 Sam. 1:22; 2 Tim. 1:5.)

Jewish Requirements for Education of Children. (Deut. 6:7; 31:13; Prov. 22:6.)

Questions

1. Where did Mary and Joseph settle after their return from Egypt?

2. How did Jesus spend his years as a boy?

3. How old did a Jewish boy have to be before attending the feasts?

4. What feast at Jerusalem did Jesus attend at this age?

5. Tell of the thoughts of Jesus as he walked about the temple.

6. What happened when his parents started on their return home?

7. Where did they find Jesus on the third day afterwards?

8. What was he doing?

9. What happened in the life of Jesus during the next eighteen years?

STORY 149

THE MINISTRY OF JOHN THE BAPTIST; THE BAPTISM OF JESUS

MATTHEW 3; MARK
1:1-11; LUKE 3:1-22   During the years in which Je'sus was being
quietly prepared for his mission, the Lord was making ready another
great character in the work of redemption. John the Bap'tist, as he was
later called, was the son of Zach-a-ri'as and E-lis'a-beth. The prophets
had foretold his birth as "the forerunner of the Mes-si'ah," and his mission was to prepare the way for the Lord's work of salvation. He had
been consecrated to the Lord in the Naz'a-rite vow, and was being trained
for his ministry in the seclusion of the wilderness areas of Ju-de'a. Spending much of his time in the hills near He'bron and in the deserts of southern Ju-de'a, he enjoyed close fellowship with God. Filled with the Holy
Spirit from his birth, he was truly upright and heroic soul—the greatest
saint of his times.

Having received his official call at the age of thirty, he began his ministry in a startling manner in the wilderness of Ju-de'a. The unusual nature
of his labors was clearly foretold by the ancient prophets:

"The voice of one crying in the wilderness;
Prepare ye the way of the Lord.

Every valley shall be filled,
And every mountain and hill shall be brought low;
And the crooked shall be made straight,
And the rough ways shall be made smooth:
And all flesh shall see the salvation of God."

Instead of seeking a hearing in the synagogues of the towns and cities
of Pal'es-tine, or of trying to reach the people in the centers of population,
John the Bap'tist preached in the thinly populated districts along the
banks of the river Jor'dan. Beginning at a point near the entrance of the
Jor'dan into the Dead Sea, the field of his labors extended north into the
regions of the Jor'dan valley, taking in parts of Pe-re'a, Sa-ma'ri-a, and
Gal'i-lee. He made his headquarters in the wilderness area of the land,

providing himself with locusts and wild honey for food, and wearing a rough garment made of woven camel's hair.

The theme of John's preaching was "the kingdom of heaven is at hand," and his work was that of a pioneer who opens the way for the coming of the King. Through his ministry proud, lofty spirits were brought low, the crooked ways of crafty men were made straight, fraud and dishonesty were rebuked, obstacles of every kind that stood in the way of spiritual reform were removed, and the humble and contrite in heart were made receptive to the teachings of the Mes-si'ah. These moral and spiritual preparations for the coming of Christ could be accomplished only through the repentance which was so urgently demanded in all of John's stirring sermons.

The political and religious conditions of Ju-de'a and the surrounding world were ripe for the coming of the Mes-si'ah. The Jewish nation had completely lost its independence; Pal'es-tine was divided into three Roman provinces ruled by idle, luxury-loving politicians; even the mighty Roman Empire was weakened by the dissolute rule of Ti-be'ri-us Cae'sar.

The state of religion in Ju-de'a had fallen so low that the sacred office of the High Priest was claimed by An'nas, who had been deposed by the Romans, and his son-in-law Ca'ia-phas, who was equally undeserving of respect. The religious leadership of the nation was in the hands of the rival sects of the Phar'i-sees and Sad'du-cees, the one so proud, self-conceited, and debased in character that its members were rightly described as "a generation of vipers" and "whited sepulchres"; the other made up of infidels who denied the fundamental principles of

THE RIVER JORDAN WHERE JESUS WAS BAPTISED.

true religion. The people who tried to cling to the faith of their fathers were burdened with meaningless rites and man-made traditions, and Is'ra-el as a whole was sorely oppressed with political tyranny and religious corruption.

For more than three hundred years Is'ra-el had been without the voice of a prophet; then, like a thunderbolt from a clear sky, the rugged Naz'a-rite began to preach to the great masses of the common folk, raising to the highest pitch their hopes for the coming of a great Deliverer. Many of the people thought that John was himself the promised Mes-si'ah, but he declared:

"One mightier than I cometh, the latchet of whose shoes I am not worthy to unloose." . . . .

During his ministry in the wilderness of Ju-de'a, John introduced the religious rite called baptism. All who responded to his call to repentance, who gave proof of a sincere desire to enter the kingdom of God soon to be set up by the Mes-si'ah, and who openly confessed their sins in declaring their loyalty to God, were baptized in the Jor'dan. By word and by deed John solemnly proclaimed the message of the ancient prophets:

"Wash you, make you clean; put away the evil of your doings from before mine eyes."

"In that day there shall be a fountain opened in the house of Da'vid, for the inhabitants of Je-ru'sa-lem, for sin and for uncleanness."

While these things were taking place in the valley of the Jor'dan, the thoughts of Je'sus back in the hills of Naz'a-reth were going out to a world steeped in sin, and the Divine purpose for his coming into the world began to assert itself in his heart. Looking out over the land of memorable battles where ancient Is'ra-el had won many triumphs in the name of Je-ho'vah, he yearned to take his appointed place in showing the world the spiritual meaning of those victories. Conscious of powers which no other man possessed, of the immortal destiny for which he was born, and of the infinite resources of God at his command, he realized that the work of his forerunner was a sign for him to enter his public ministry.

Bidding his mother a fond farewell, Je'sus left his home in Naz'a-reth and made the sixty mile journey down the Jor'dan valley to the place where John was preaching and baptizing. John's announcement that "The kingdom of God is at hand" must be proclaimed by the Sav'ior, but first he must be inducted into his public office by his forerunner.

One evening after all the people, who had come for baptism on that day had received the blessed rite, Je'sus asked that he, too, should be baptized. Knowing that there could be no need of repentance on the part of Je'sus, and conscious of his own inferiority, John protested:

"I have need to be baptized of Thee, and comest Thou to me?"

To this argument Je'sus meekly replied:

"Suffer it to be so now: for thus it becometh us to fulfill all righteousness."

Although John did not fully understand all that was involved in the request of Je'sus, he knew that it was important for the baptism to be performed. As the solemn rite was being administered, the heavens were suddenly opened with a Divine halo, the Spirit of God descended upon Je'sus in the form of a radiant dove, and the voice of God was heard to say:

"This is my beloved Son, in whom I am well pleased."

These words made it perfectly clear to John that he had baptized the long promised Mes-si'ah. The title, "Son of God"; the endearing expression, "Beloved"; and the Divine commendation, "Well pleased," could truly be applied only to the Mes-si'ah. The "opened heaven" indicated that Je'sus would enjoy the light of heaven; while the descent of the Holy Spirit upon him showed that he was truly Im-man'u-el, or "God with us." From that day onward the message of John stressed the fact that Je'sus was "The Lamb of God that beareth away the sins of the world."

SUGGESTIONS FOR STUDY

Biblical Index to Helpful References

John's Mission as Fore-Runner of the Messiah. (Isa. 40:1-3; Mal. 3:1.)

The Ministry of Preaching. (Acts 9:20; 10:36; 1 Cor. 1:23; 2 Cor. 4:5.)

Repentance and Remission of Sins. (Luke 24:47; Acts 2:38.)

John's Humility. (Jno. 1:19-23.)

John's Courage. (Matt. 14:4.)

John's Holiness and Burning Zeal. (Mark 6:20; Jno. 5:35.)

John Performed No Miracles. (Jno. 10: 41.)

The estimate of John by Jesus. Matt. 11: 11; Luke 7:24-27.)

Questions

1. In what way did John the Baptist spend his first thirty years?

2. Describe the peculiar character of his ministry.

3. What announcement did he make?

4. What was the theme of his preaching?

5. What were the religious and political conditions in Judea at the time?

6. Tell of the wide-spread interest in John's preaching.

7. Tell of the coming of Jesus to John for baptism.

8. What three-fold sign of Jesus' Messianic office were given at his baptism?

STORY 150

JESUS TEMPTED IN THE WILDERNESS

MATTHEW 4:1-11;
MARK 1:12-13;
LUKE 4:1-13   Immediately after his baptism by John, Je'sus spent forty days in the region near Jer'i-cho where he was severely tempted by Sa'tan. Having gone without food for this entire period the Sav'iour was intensely hungry. In the first temptation Sa'tan suggested to Je'sus that he use his power to turn stones into bread and thus satisfy his hunger. The Sav'iour refused, saying "Man lives not by bread alone."

Sa'tan knew that Je'sus was deeply concerned with the problem of commanding the respect and attention of the masses which he had come to save, so he spoke after this fashion: "If you wish to convince the people at once that you are the Mes-si'ah, do something startling—make a public exhibition of your power as the Son of God. Cast yourself down from the highest pinnacle of the temple in Je-ru'sa-lem; when you arise unhurt, the people will surely hail you as the Mighty One." Sa'tan tried to justify his temptation by quoting from the sacred Scriptures, so he added: "For it is written, He shall give his angels charge concerning thee; and in their hands they shall bear thee up, lest at any time thou dash thy foot against a stone."

Je'sus cast off the temptation, refused to turn his authority to selfish purposes, and silenced his tempter with a quotation from the Scriptures, saying: "It is written, Thou shalt not tempt the Lord thy God."

It was then that Sa'tan made his master stroke, suggesting a wicked scheme for the immediate accomplishment of world domination for Je'sus. He knew that God had promised the

TEMPTATION OF CHRIST

Mes-si'ah an everlasting kingdom, and that under his reign the kingdoms of this world would be united in service to the Lord. He also knew that the road which Je'sus would follow toward his ultimate conquest would be one of suffering, shame, and death.

And so the devil said to Je'sus: "Son of God, I know that you are destined to become the ruler of the world, but I also know that the way over which you must travel will involve great self-denial, many sorrows, and the shedding of your life-blood. Come with me to the highest mountain, let us observe all the wealth and glory of the world. You may have complete mastery of all the world if you will only bow down and worship me." In this offer Sa'tan claimed to have control of all worldly kingdoms, and proposed to give Je'sus a place of dominance. The mission of the Son of God, however, was to set up an entirely different kingdom—a spiritual kingdom in which the principles of righteousness should prevail.

Had Je'sus accepted the offer of Sa'tan, the entire plan of the Messianic kingdom would have been destroyed, and the Divine provision for man's redemption would have been set at naught. Je'sus therefore said to the devil: "Get thee hence, Sa'tan: for it is written, Thou shalt worship the Lord thy God, and him only shalt thou serve." This was a death-blow to the hopes of Sa'tan, who left him for a season. We may be sure, however, that the temptations made by the devil at that time represented the persistent urgings of the evil one which forever dogged the steps of Je'sus.

"Touched with a sympathy within, He knows our feeble frame;
He knows what sore temptations mean, for He has felt the same."

SUGGESTIONS FOR STUDY
Biblical Index to Helpful References

Jesus Tempted in All Points Like Unto Us. (Heb. 2:18; 4:15.)

The Malignant Work of Satan. (Job. 1: 9-11; Zech. 3:1; Lu. 9:42; Jno. 8:44.)

The Defeat of Satan by Jesus. (Jno. 12: 30, 31; Heb. 2:14; 1 Jno. 3:8.)

Deity of Christ Challenged. (Mark 15:31, 32; Lu. 5:21; 20:1, 2; Jno. 5:8; 8:53.)

Spiritual Weapons for Combatting Satan. (Eph. 6:11; 1 Thess. 5:8; Rev. 12:11.)

Resisting Temptation. (Gen. 14:23; 2 Ki. 5:6; Job 2:9, 10; Acts 8:20.)

Duty of Resisting Temptation. (Prov. 1: 10; 4:14; Rom. 6:13.)

The Devil to Be Resisted. (Jas. 4:7; 1 Pet. 5:8, 9.)

Questions

1. When did this long period of temptation take place?

2. Why was it necessary for Jesus to be tempted?

3. What was the first temptation? Why wrong for Jesus to comply to Satan's suggestion to provide food?

4. What was the second temptation? What wrong involved in complying?

5. What was the third temptation? Why wrong to have complied?

6. What happened after these tests by Satan?

THE EARLY MINISTRY OF JESUS IN JUDEA

JOHN 1:19-4:42

Immediately after his triumph over Sa'tan in the wilderness, Je'sus returned to the scene of John's ministry in Beth'a-ny beyond the Jor'dan. The fore-runner of Je'sus had already declared that he was not the Mes-si'ah, and that his role was only to prepare the way for One whose shoes he was not worthy to unloose.

When Je'sus appeared for the second time in the crowds that followed John, the man of God pointed to the coming sacrifice of the Sav'ior in the sublime words: "Behold the Lamb of God which beareth away the sin of the world." To make sure that the people would understand that he was not expressing a mere personal opinion, he announced the Divine message which had been given at the time of Je'sus baptism.

The next day John repeated his testimony concerning Je'sus, this time in private conversation with two of his followers. It was the last time that he would see the Mes-si'ah, so he was eager to be of service in gathering followers for him. The two men to whom he gave this private testimony immediately expressed a desire to follow the Lord. Je'sus received them cordially, and invited them to come to his place of abode. After many hours of intimate conversation they yielded their hearts to him as the promised Mes-si'ah, and became his helpers in setting up his kingdom among men.

One of the two converts was An'drew, who hastened to bring his brother Si'mon to the Lord. When Je'sus looked upon Si'mon he said, "Thy name shall be changed to Ce'phas, or Pe'ter, which means a rock." Si'mon immediately accepted membership in the group of followers being assembled by the Sav'ior, and afterwards became a strong, outspoken leader of the group.

The name of An'drew's companion is not given, but there is evidence that it was John, who was later known as "The Beloved Apostle," and who is the author of four books in the New Testament. He doubtless brought with him his brother James, who also became prominent among the leaders of the Sav'ior's kingdom upon earth.

THE CALL OF JAMES AND JOHN

The four men who became the first disciples of Je'sus resided in the province of Gal'i-lee, and were engaged in the fishing enterprise conducted by Zeb'e-dee, who was the father of James and John. They had been drawn to the scene of John the Bap'tist's ministry by the announcement that the coming of the Mes-si'ah was near at hand. Among other Gal'i-le-ans who were present was Phil'ip, an acquaintance of James and John, and a devout student of the sacred Scriptures. As Je'sus and his small band of followers were starting on a trip to Gal'i-lee, Phil'ip was invited to join them. His hearty response to the call of Je'sus is shown in his urgent invitation to Na-than'a-el, to whom he said, "We have found him of whom Mo'ses in the law, and the prophets, did write, Je'sus of Naz'a-reth, the son of Jo'seph."

Having read nothing in the Scriptures about the Mes-si'ah coming from Naz'a-reth, and knowing of the ill repute of that little town, Na-than'a-el was incredulous until Phil'ip said, "Come and see." As soon as he beheld Je'sus power, he announced his loyalty in that splendid confession, "Most excellent Teacher, Thou art the Son of God; Thou art the King of Is'ra-el." Na-than'a-el was later called Bar-thol'o-mew, and is so listed among the twelve apostles of Je'sus.

Je'sus knows your need, as He did Na-than'a-el's; you may truly say:
"He sees my wants, allays my fears,
And counts and treasures up my tears."

SUGGESTIONS FOR STUDY

Biblical Index to Helpful References

The Righteous Practice Self-Abasement. (Gen. 18:27; Ex. 3:11; Prov. 3:2.)

John's Testimony Concerning Christ. (Jno. 3:28-36; 5:33; 10:41.)

Christ the Lamb of God. (Isa. 53:7; 1 Pet. 1:19; Rev. 15:3.)

Christ the World's Sin-Bearer. (Isa. 53:12; 1 Pet. 2:24.)

The Anointing of Christ by the Holy Spirit. (Isa. 11:2; 42:1; Acts 10:38.)

The Blessing of Knowing Jesus. (Hos. 6:3; Jno. 8:12; 12:26.)

The Gracious Benefits of Bringing Men to Jesus. (Prov. 11:30; Dan. 12:3; Jan. 5:20.)

Questions

1. Where did Jesus go after his temptation?

2. How did John point him out as the Messiah?

3. Who were the first two disciples of John that followed Jesus?

4. What did they immediately do?

5. Who did Jesus then invite to follow him?

6. What did Nathaneal say when invited to come to Jesus?

7. Was he easily convinced that Jesus was the Messiah when he came?

JESUS AT CANA; THE FIRST MIRACLE

JOHN 2:1-11   Three days after the call of Na-than'a-el, Je'sus and five or six disciples attended a marriage festival at Ca'na, a little village of Gal'i-lee within a few miles of his former home at Naz'a-reth. Here Je'sus performed his first miracle, turning plain water into the finest wine.

The family at whose home the wedding was taking place were either relatives or close friends of Ma'ry and Jo'seph, so Je'sus and his followers were invited to attend. Ma'ry seems to have had charge of the festivities, which had probably been going on for several days before the arrival of Je'sus, for wedding feasts in Pal'es-tine lasted for seven days or more. For some reason the supply of wine gave out, and Ma'ry quickly reported the news to her son. Up to this time Je'sus had never attempted to use the wonderful powers which had been given him over nature, but Ma'ry seems to have had an intuition that the time had come for him to prove his Divinity by performing a miracle.

In reply to his mother's appeal Je'sus said, "Woman, what have I to do with thee? Mine hour is not yet come." These words of the Master are perplexing until we remember that Ma'ry's son had already begun his work as the world's Sav'ior, and that in his eternal kingdom Ma'ry held no higher rank than any other woman who believed in him. From the time that Je'sus entered upon his work of redemption, and until he made his ascent into heaven, he never recognized Ma'ry as higher than any other saintly woman. Even from the cross, he addressed her with the same respectful title, "Woman"; for she who had been his mother was now no more than his sister in God.

Je'sus took pity on the family which was so greatly distressed by the lack of wine for their guests, and quickly provided a new supply. He ordered the servants to fill six large waterpots to the brim with water, and then to take them to the director of the feast. The jars were then opened, and the servants who had filled them with water were amazed to see good wine poured out. Those who attended the feast probably did not know of the miracle which had taken place, for Je'sus had been careful to spare his host any embarrassment. All who were present, however, marveled at

THE MARRIAGE FEAST AT CANA

the quality of the wine, declaring that it was better than any they had been given before. Apparently it was the custom at such festivals to serve good wine at first, but to replace it with an inferior quality as soon as the guests had dulled their sense of taste.

In the miracle which Je'sus performed at Ca'na we have a striking example of his friendly spirit toward all humanity. He was at ease in all ranks of society, accepted all worthy invitations, and mixed with men and women in every walk of life in order to spread his teachings as widely as possible. We read later of his dining with Phar'i-sees and publicans, of his ministrations to the outcasts of society, and of his blessed announcement that "He came not to call the righteous, but sinners to repentance."

SUGGESTIONS FOR STUDY

Biblical Index to Helpful References

Christian Workers to Practice Social Fellowship. (Luke 10:7; 14:8, 12; Jno. 12:2; 1 Cor. 10:27.)

Christ Entertained as a Guest. (Matt. 9: 10; Mark 14:3; Lu. 7:36; 10:38; 14:1; 19:7.)

Telling Jesus Our Needs. (Matt. 8:25; Mark 6:35, 36; 10:51; Lu. 5:5.)

Cooperative Effort with Christ. (Mark 3:5; Lu. 5:4; Lu. 17:14.)

Christ's Power Over Natural Law. (Matt. 14:25; Mark 4:39.)

Questions

1. Where did Jesus attend a wedding?
2. Who had charge of the festivities?
3. What embarrassing situation arose?

4. What did Mary do in this emergency?
5. What was the answer of Jesus? Mary's reply?
6. Describe the miracle that followed?

JESUS CLEANSES THE TEMPLE; TALKS WITH NICODEMUS

JOHN 2:13-25; 3:1-21

Following the wedding feast at Ca'na, Je'sus and his small band of disciples made a brief visit in Naz'a-reth. Then, accompanied by his mother and brothers, they went down to Ca-per'-na-um on the shores of the Sea of Gal'i-lee, where they remained for a few days. He appears to have engaged in no public ministries at either place on these short visits.

Je'sus then went to Je-ru'sa-lem to attend the Feast of the Pass'o-ver, leaving his mother and brothers and some of the disciples in Ca-per'na-um. Thousands of Is'ra-el-ites thronged the streets of the holy city and crowded the courts of the temple. For more than a thousand years the temple had been the center of the religious life of the Jewish people. It had been erected as a house of prayer and holy sacrifices, yet Je'sus found it abused and profaned. It had been turned from sacred to secular uses, and its holiness had been violated by the greed of the religious rulers, who had converted the entire system of worship into a money-making scheme.

Within the sacred portals of the temple, where one should come only for worship and prayer, Je'sus found a throng of money-changers and merchants. They had not come to worship, but to ply their trade in the hope of profit. Indignant at this abuse of the holy ordinances of religion, Je'sus seized a "whip of cords," and drove out those who had profaned the temple.

When challenged to give a sign of his authority for thus cleansing the temple, he replied, "Destroy this temple, and in three days I will raise it up." The people thought that he spoke of the magnificent building, which had required forty-six years for its completion; but he spoke of his own body, which was raised up on the third day after the crucifixion. With the death of his earthly body the temple lost its place as the center of the religious life of the Jews, and it was literally destroyed a few years later.

Among those who were deeply impressed by the teachings and miracles of Je'sus in Je-ru'sa-lem was Nic-o-de'mus, who was a member of the

San'he-drin. He came to Je'sus secretly by night, not as a representative of that official body which later condemned the Mes-si'ah, but in his own interests. The calmness and earnestness of the Sav'ior's conduct, the authoritative manner in which he had cleansed the temple, and the Divine power which he had shown in performing miracles, commanded the respect of this Jewish leader. Reverently addressing Je'sus he said:

"Most excellent Master, we know that thou art a teacher come from God: for no man can do these miracles that thou doest, except God be with him."

This gave Je'sus an opportunity to deliver one of the most important discourses ever recorded. In pointing out the fact that one must be born again in order to be saved, Je'sus completely reversed the ideas of the Jewish leaders concerning the Mes-si'ah and his kingdom. He emphasized the truth that membership in his kingdom is secured by spiritual rebirth, and not by natural heritage, external law, religious rite, or official decree. He laid down God's love in giving His son for the sins of the world as the basis for human redemption, and explained the simple process through which the blessings of the gospel are made available to all who have faith.

CHRIST DRIVING OUT THE MONEY CHANGERS

Sermon on the Mount [Detail] *by Carl Heinrich Bloch*
FREDERIKSBORG, CASTLE : COPENHAGEN

The Wedding of Cana
by Julius Schnorr von Carolsfeld
KUNSTHALLE : HAMBURG

CAMERA CLIX

Flight into Egypt by Giovanni Bellini
NATIONAL GALLERY OF ART : WASHINGTON, D. C.

THREE LIONS

Adoration of the Shepherds *by Bartolomé Esteban Murillo*
THE PRADO : MADRID

THREE LIONS

The Annunciation *by Fra Filippo Lippi*
PINAKOTHEK : MUNICH

Nic-o-de'mus listened reverently to the wonderful message of the Sav'-ior, and then went back to his official duties in the San'he-drin. It is evident that he became a secret believer, for no mention is made of his having taken part in the proceedings through which the Jewish court found Je'sus guilty of blasphemy. After the crucifixion it was Nic-o-de'mus who paid honor to the Lord's body.

The discourse with Nic-o-de'mus was intended for all the world, and has been preserved by Divine Providence for the enlightenment of humanity in every age. Je'sus spoke of heavenly things with full knowledge and authority, revealing the spiritual nature of the kingdom which he had come to establish among men. The Jews were expecting the coming of their Mes-si'ah to be solely for the punishment of their enemies, and firmly believed that he would set up an earthly kingdom. Yet Je'sus now declared that God had sent him to redeem all mankind, and that the only condemnation which rests upon any race or nationality is that which they bring upon themselves by failing to believe in him.

The message reached its climax in the statement that God had sent His son not to condemn mankind, but to bring salvation and eternal life. He summed up the entire teaching of the gospels in one sentence which has given hope, peace, and consolation to untold generations:

"For God so loved the world, that he gave his only begotten Son, that whosoever believeth in him should not perish, but have everlasting life."

SUGGESTIONS FOR STUDY

Biblical Index to Helpful References

Pollution of God's House. (2 Chron. 33: 7; 36:14; Jer. 7:30; Zeph. 3:4.)

Divine Indignation. (Psm. 69:24; 78:49; Isa. 10:5; Jer. 10:10.)

Reverence for the House of God Demanded. (Lev. 19:30; Eccl. 5:1.)

Previous Cleansings of the Temple. (2 Chron. 29:15; Neh. 13:9.)

The Zeal of Christ. (Isa. 59:17; Jno. 9:4; Acts 10:38.)

Skeptical Demands for Signs. (Matt. 12: 38; Lu. 11:16; 1 Cor. 1:22.)

Believers in Christ Delaying Open Confession. (Jno. 7:13; 12:42; 19:38.)

The Heavenly Doctrine of the New-Birth. (Ezek. 36:26; Jno. 1:13; 2 Cor. 5:17; 1 Jno. 5:1.)

Questions

1. Where did Jesus go after leaving Cana? Where then? Where next?

2. What was the occasion of his visit to Jerusalem?

3. What did he do when he found the house of God filled with traders?

4. When challenged to give his authority, what did he say? What did this mean?

5. Who sought out Jesus at night for an interview?

6. What strange doctrine did Jesus preach to him?

7. What other truths did he expound?

8. What kind of disciple did Nicodemus become?

STORY 154

JESUS TALKS WITH A SAMARITAN WOMAN

JOHN 4:1-44

After the conversation with Nic-o-de'mus, Je'sus and the disciples who were with him went into the rural districts of Ju-de'a near the river Jor'dan. For some weeks he remained near the Jor'dan, preaching the gospel and calling the people to repentance. Those who responded to his call were baptized by the disciples, under his authority and direction.

The news of the increasing popularity of Je'sus led some of John the Bap'tist's followers to make a complaint to their master. Instead of showing an envious spirit toward the man who appeared to some to be his rival, John bore witness to the superior character and work of Je'sus. He told his followers that his own work was only in preparation for that of the Mes-si'ah, and that the greater success of Je'sus was due to the fact that he came directly from God. Contrasting Je'sus with himself, he said that the Sav'ior belonged to heaven, while he was of the earth; and that the Mes-si'ah had power to grant salvation, while he could only call men to repentance.

In the meantime there was growing opposition to the new doctrines preached by John, and to his bitter denunciation of sin. Her'od An'ti-pas, the ruler of the province of Gal'i-lee, finally had the noble preacher cast into prison for uttering just words of condemnation which applied to him. Having learned of the imprisonment of John, and of the growing hatred of the Phar'i-sees for all who preached the new doctrines, Je'sus decided to leave Ju-de'a. He therefore departed for his long ministry in Gal'i-lee, journeying across Sa-ma-ri'a on his way to Ca-per'na-um.

The province of Sa-ma-ri'a was inhabited by a half-pagan people who were scorned by all devout Jews. There was such bitter hatred between the Sa-mar'i-tans and the He'brews that they had no dealings with one another. Many of the social customs and religious practices of the Sa-mar'i-tans, however, resembled those of the Jews, and they revered certain parts of the Old Testament Scriptures.

Early one afternoon the Lord reached the historic Ja'cob's well, and paused for rest. He sent his disciples away to buy some food, and was sitting quietly by the well when suddenly a Sa-mar'i-tan woman came to draw water. Je'sus said to her, "Give me a drink," but she expressed great surprise that one who was a Jew should ask a favor of a Sa-mar'i-tan. Then the Sav'ior told her of "the water of life" which he would gladly give her, explaining that once she drank of this water "it would become a well of water within her heart, springing up into everlasting life."

The woman did not understand the spiritual meaning of the Sav'ior's words, but promptly asked him to give her the water of which he spoke. Then Je'sus lifted the veil from her past life in such an amazing way that she was convinced that he must be a prophet. When she asked where one ought to worship, Je'sus uttered one of the great truths of the gospel: "The hour cometh, and now is, when true worshipers shall worship the Father in spirit and in truth."

Thus in a tactful manner Je'sus brought the woman to realize her own sinfulness, and to understand something of his Divine personality. Like

AT JACOB'S WELL

all the Sa-mar'i-tans, she was looking for the coming of a Mes-si'ah, "a prophet like unto Mo'ses," who would reveal all things. The insight which he had shown into her past life, and the words he had spoken concerning true worship made her think that he might be the long awaited Mes-si'ah. When her words indicated her thoughts in this respect, Je'sus declared, "I that speak unto thee am he."

Although the Sa-mar'i-tan woman made no reply to this announcement, her soul was filled with new hope, and she took an entirely different outlook upon life. Her deeds fully proved her acceptance of the Sav'ior, for she immediately became a missionary to her countrymen. She said to her neighbors, "Come see a man, which told me all things that ever I did: is not this the Christ?" Through her influence many came to hear Je'sus, and some were converted.

When the disciples returned with food for Je'sus they were amazed at his interest in the Sa-mar'i-tans, and were perplexed by his refusal to eat. In reply to their question about his refusal to eat the food which they had brought, he spoke another great truth concerning the work of his kingdom:

"My meat is to do the will of him that sent me, and finish his work."

SUGGESTIONS FOR STUDY

Biblical Index to Helpful References

Successful Work in Samaria by Philip. (Acts 8:5-8.)

Rules of Exclusiveness. (Gen. 43:32; Acts 10:28.)

The Error of Discourtesy. (1 Sam. 25:3; Prov. 18:23.)

The Harmfulness of Racial Prejudices. (Acts 11:3; 19:34; Gal. 2:12.)

The Water of Life Given by Christ. (Isa. 12:3; Jno. 7:38, 39; Rev. 7:17.)

The Secrets of the Heart Known. (Jer. 17:10; 23:24; Rom. 8:27.)

Tender Reproaches of Christ. (Psm. 141: 5; Eccl. 7:5; Heb. 12:5.)

Exposure of Sin Under Searching Eye of God. (Job 20:27; Prov. 26:26; Jer. 16:17.)

The Joy of Open Confession of Christ. (Rom. 10:9; 1 Jno. 4:15.)

Witnessing for Christ. (Psm. 66:16; Jer. 20:9; Mal. 3:16.)

Questions

1. Where did Jesus go after leaving Jerusalem?

2. Why did he find it advisable to leave Judea?

3. Where did he pause for rest?

4. With whom did he talk at the well of Samaria?

5. When she declined to give him water, what did he say to her?

6. Describe the remainder of the conversation?

7. What proof have we that the woman was converted?

8. What did Jesus say about the food brought by his disciples?

STORY 155

JESUS BEGINS HIS WORK OF PREACHING AND HEALING IN GALILEE

Visit to Cana—Healing of Nobleman's son. (Jno. 4:43-54.)
Visit to Nazareth—First Rejection. (Luke 4:14-30.)
Preaches at Capernaum. (Matt. 4:17-22; Mark 1:14-20.)
The Calling of Four Fishermen. (Luke 5:1-11.)

After spending two days in the neighborhood of Sy'char in Sa-ma'ri-a, Je'sus passed into the interior of Gal'i-lee, returning first to the village of Ca'na. The news of his miraculous turning

HEALING OF SIMON'S WIFE'S MOTHER

of water into wine had spread throughout the country, and the fame of the great Teacher had already penetrated the entire province of Gal'i-lee.

Living in Ca-per'na-um, fifty miles distant from Ca'na, there was a nobleman whose son was seriously ill. On learning of Je'sus' return to Ca'na, he hastened to make the long journey, and urgently requested him to come to his house and heal the boy. Je'sus said to him, "Except ye see signs and wonders, ye will not believe." Instead of being turned away by this apparent rebuff, the nobleman pleaded more earnestly; and Je'sus then said to him, "Go thy way; thy son liveth."

The next day, when the nobleman was about half way home, he was met by some of his servants, who told him that the dying boy had suddenly been healed. Upon inquiry it was found that he was made well at the very hour when Je'sus said, "Thy son liveth." The nobleman and his entire household then believed in Je'sus as the Mes-si'ah, and were numbered among his earliest disciples in Ca-per'na-um.

Je'sus then made a brief visit in Naz'a-reth, where he openly announced his Divine mission. On the Sab'bath he attended worship in the synagogue, and was asked to read a selection from the writings of the prophets. The selection which he read is from the prophecy of I-sa'iah.

"The Spirit of the Lord is upon me, because he hath anointed me to preach good tidings to the poor; he hath sent me to heal the broken hearted, to preach deliverance to the captives, and recovery of sight to the blind, to set at liberty them that are bruised, to preach the acceptable year of the Lord."

Je'sus then explained the Scriptures which he had read, saying, "This day is this Scripture fulfilled in your hearing." In the sermon which followed Je'sus set forth the principles of his eternal kingdom. It has a message of healing for hearts crushed by sin, and a balm for those who were wounded by disappointment, bereavement, or misfortune. It broke the chains of intemperance, profanity, and impurity, and made men spiritually free.

The announcement of the blessings which his gospel would bring to the world was given to neighbors and friends who had known Je'sus intimately for nearly thirty years. They had been impressed by his blameless conduct among them, but nothing in his career had been supernatural. News of his miraculous works in Je-ru'sa-lem and elsewhere had reached their ears, but most of the people remained skeptical. Presently some of them began to say, "Is not this the carpenter's son, and are not his brothers

CHRIST PREACHING FROM A BOAT

and sisters living here among us?" Perceiving their opposition to him because of his humble relations in the community, Je'sus severely rebuked their unbelief. Angered by his rebukes, certain members of the congregation rose up to thrust him out of the city, but the invisible hosts of heaven enabled him to escape unharmed. Je'sus then went down to Ca-per'na-um, where he was a guest in the home of Si'mon Pe'ter. It was later said, "He could do no mighty works in Naz'a-reth, because of their unbelief."

Soon after Je'sus began his work in Ca-per'na-um he invited a number of his most devoted followers to give all their time and energy to the work of the new kingdom which he was setting up. In the great missionary campaign which the Lord conducted in the province of Gal'i-lee for a period of about two years there was need of devoted helpers. Thousands of afflicted people were to be restored to health and happiness, countless hours must be spent in meeting and talking with those who were attracted by the Mes-si'ah's fame, and endless instruction given concerning the laws of His kingdom. It was impossible for one person, however richly endowed with Divine gifts, to attend to all these matters, so Je'sus chose as helpers those who had proved their faith.

Among the most loyal of his followers were the four fishermen: Si'mon, and his brother An'drew; John, and his brother James. Although they had been present on many important occasions in the ministry of the Sav'ior, they had not given up the fishing business in which they were partners. One day as Je'sus was teaching on the shores of the Sea of Gal'i-lee, the throngs pressed so closely upon him that he found it necessary to continue his preaching from a boat. Borrowing the boat from Si'mon and An'drew, and thrusting out a little from the shore, he preached to the multitude.

While he was speaking, James and John were washing their nets not far away. After the people had been sent away, Je'sus said to Si'mon, "Launch out into the deep, and let down your nets for a draught." Si'mon replied that they had fished all night without success, but added, "Nevertheless, at thy word I will let down the net." When he and An'-drew cast their nets into the water at the point selected by Je'sus, they took so great a number of fish that the nets began to break. Then they beckoned to their partners in the other ship to help them bring the great catch to shore.

The humble fishermen were overwhelmed by the miraculous catch,

CHRIST AMONG THE FISHERMEN

and Si'mon Pe'ter bowed before Je'sus, saying, "Depart from me; for I am a sinful man, O Lord." Then the Sav'ior assured him that there was no reason to be afraid, and gave the invitation, "Follow me, and I will make you fishers of men." Thus the fishermen received the Divine commission to forsake their worldly labors for full time service in the cause of Christ.

On the Sab'bath following the call of the first four Apostles, Je'sus astonished the congregation at Ca-per'na-um with his messages of authority and spiritual power. He spoke with such conviction that his words went straight home to the hearts of his hearers. Even the demons which dwelt within one of the listeners trembled with fear, and cried out, "Let us alone, Thou holy One of God." After silencing the unclean spirit which had spoken through the voice of its victim, Je'sus commanded the demons to leave the unfortunate man.

Upon reaching the home of his disciple Si'mon Pe'ter, Je'sus found that Simon's mother-in-law was seriously ill with a deadly fever. The Sav'ior rebuked the fever, took the sick woman by the hand, and she was immediately restored to health. The recovery was so complete that she arose at once to minister to the needs and comfort of her healer.

So great was the excitement caused in Ca-per'na-um on that memorable Sab'bath, that at sunset, when the Sab'bath restrictions were no longer in effect, "all the city gathered at the door" of the house in which Je'sus was a guest, bring many persons to be healed of disease and possession by demons.

SUGGESTIONS FOR STUDY

Biblical Index to Helpful References

Notable Parental Prayers. (Gen. 17:18; 2 Sam. 12:16; 1 Chr. 29:19; Job 1:5.)

Faith Testings. (Josh. 6:3; Jgs. 7:7; 1 Ki. 17:9, 13.)

Blessing Promised to Attendants at the House of God. (Psm. 84:4; Mic. 4:2.)

Promises of Divine Anointing for Jesus. (Isa. 42:1; 61:1.)

The Call to Become "Fishers of Men." (Matt. 18:15; 1 Cor. 9:19, 20.)

Self-Renunciation to Follow Jesus. (Phil. 3:8; 2 Cor. 4:11.)

What Is Involved in Following Christ. (1 Pet. 2:21; Rev. 14:4.)

Questions

1. Tell of the fame of Jesus.

2. Who came to Cana to ask for the healing of his son?

3. Did Jesus go to this man's house for the healing of his son?

4. Tell of the attendance of Jesus at church in Nazareth. What occurred?

5. In this message, what did Jesus say as to his mission in the world?

6. Did the people of Nazareth believe in Jesus? Why not?

7. Describe the territory of Galilee where Jesus spent much of his life.

8. What was the burden of Jesus' preaching in Galilee?

9. Tell of the call of some fishermen to give up their work and follow Jesus.

10. Tell of the healing of the mother of Peter's wife. What followed?

STORY 156

JESUS BEGINS HIS FIRST TOUR
OF GALILEE

Healing of a Leper. (Matt. 8:2-4; Mark 1:40-45; Luke 5:12-16.)
Healing of a Paralytic. (Matt. 9:2-8; Mark 2:1-12; Luke 5:17-26.)
Calling of Matthew; His Feast. (Matt. 9:9-13; Mark 2:13-17; Luke 5:27-32.)
Defends His Disciples. (Matt. 9:14-17; Mark 2:18-22; Luke 5:33-39.)
Heals an Incurable Disease. (Matt. 9:20-22; Mark 5:25-34; Luke 8:43-48.)

Having begun his work in Ca-per'na-um with such clear proof of the favor and power of God, Je'sus entered upon a missionary tour of Gal'i-lee. The spirit in which he began this ministry is indicated in the record that he arose early in the morning, a great while before day, and went into a secluded place for prayer. When sought out by Si'mon Pe'ter and other disciples, and told that he was being sought by all men, he said to them: "Let us go into the next towns, that I may preach there also: for therefore came I forth."

Gal'i-lee was a densely populated district of more than two hundred villages and towns, each containing several thousand inhabitants. In these towns the Jewish synagogues were the centers of worship. The difficulties of going up to the temple at Je-ru'sa-lem had led many of the people to abandon these long, inconvenient journeys, and the services held in the community centers had gradually become more important in their religious life than the festivals held in the capital. It was our Lord's custom to attend Divine worship in whatever town he might be, and to take the opportunity of preaching the gospel. He did not limit his efforts to this work alone, for many of his mightiest works and greatest discourses took place in the open air, or in the humble homes of the people.

The first tour of Gal'i-lee covered a period of at least one year. The record of this ministry is not complete, but we are told of eight miracles of healing which took place, of two instances in which the dead were called back to life, of the commission of the twelve Apostles, and of the anointing of his feet by a grateful woman who was saved from a life of shame by his grace. Partial records of five or six of his most notable discourses have been preserved, among them the Sermon on the Mount. It was during this period that Je'sus defended his disciples when they were criticized for not fasting, that he refuted the Phar'i-sees on three occasions, and uttered his great testimony concerning John the Bap'tist. He also rebuked the cities of Gal'i-lee for their failure to grasp the heavenly opportunities offered in his ministry, and called into his service Mat'-thew, otherwise known as Le'vi, who later became the author of the first gospel.

The first notable event of this tour was the healing of a leper. Leprosy, which was one of the most loathsome diseases of the Orient, caused the skin to become hard and cracked, breaking out into great, ugly sores, and resulting in the gradual loss of external parts of the body until death released the sufferer. Lepers were regarded as "unclean," and so were forced to live apart from other people, and to cry out in warning when others came near. This dread disease was thought to be a plague sent by the Lord in judgment, and was regarded as incurable. Only two instances of its cure are mentioned in the Old Testament: the first being in the case of Mir'i-am, who was healed in answer to the prayer of Mo'ses; and the other, the miraculous healing of Na'a-man by the prophet E-li'sha.

The leper of Gal'i-lee fell on his knees before Je'sus, saying: "Lord, if thou wilt, thou canst make me clean." Tenderly Je'sus put forth his hand, touching the poor man who was shunned by everyone else. At once the deadly disease was cured, and the weak, disfigured body restored.

When it was learned in Ca-per'na-um that Je'sus had returned for a brief visit in the home of Si'mon Pe'ter, great multitudes flocked to the house, bringing their sick and helpless friends. The Lord performed hundreds of miracles on that occasion, but the details of only one are given in the gospel record. A paralytic was brought to Je'sus by four of his friends, but they could not get into the house because of the great throngs. Thereupon they went to the roof of the building, removed some of the tiling, and let the palsied man down before the Sav'ior. Je'sus suddenly paused in his sermon, and seeing their faith, he said to the sick man, "Thy sins be forgiven thee."

These words were instantly seized upon by certain of the Scribes who were present, for they had come solely in the hope of finding some flaw in the work of Je'sus. They did not accept him as the Son of God, and knew that "none but God can forgive sins." For this reason Je'sus decided to convince the unbelievers of his divine power. Turning again to the sick man, he said, "Arise, take up thy bed, and go unto thine house." The man was made well at once; taking up his bed, he startled the multitude by carrying it through the streets to his home.

During his stay in Ca-per'-na-um, Je'sus went out on the shores of the lake to preach to the people. As he passed the office of the tax-collector Mat'-thew, he said to him, "Follow me." Mat'thew had evidently met Je'sus, or at least heard his wonderful message, for he left everything and followed the Master. Although his occupation had naturally brought the hatred of the Jews upon him, he was a devout student of the ancient Scriptures, and was quick to accept Je'sus as the Mes-si'ah.

THE CALL OF MATTHEW

In proof of his complete acceptance of the Sav'ior, Mat'thew prepared a great feast in His honor, inviting a number of his friends in the hope that they, too, might follow Him. When Je'sus mingled with the friends of his new disciple, the scribes and Phar'i-sees complained that he, "received sinners, and ate with them." This criticism led Je'sus to utter one of the most profound truths concerning the purpose of his mission, "I came not to call the righteous, but sinners to repentance."

The Phar'i-sees also raised the question of fasting, a common religious practice of the age, but one which Je'sus and his followers ignored. The priestly class at Je-ru'sa-lem had established many days of fasting, and the religion of many Jews consisted almost entirely of the observation of these fasts and other rites. Je'sus then explained that such acts of self-denial should be practiced only when some emergency demand deep penitence and prayer, and then in the spirit of true sacrifice. He also declared that some of the traditions of the Jews were like "old wine bottles made of skin," and that the "New wines of the Mes-si-an'ic kingdom" could not be preserved in them. Such traditions must be cast aside as worthless, and the gospel must be presented in new spiritual rites and ordinances.

About this time a certain ruler named Ja-i'rus asked that Je'sus come to his home at once, for his little daughter was sick unto death. As the Sav'ior journeyed toward the home of Ja-i'rus, he was pressed from every side by the multitudes which followed him. Among those who sought his help was a woman whom the best physicians had labored in vain to heal for twelve long years. So strong was her faith in the healing powers of Je'sus that she said in her heart, "If I can only touch the hem of his garment, I shall be made well."

Although hastening to a chamber of death, the Sav'ior paused long enough to allow his Divine power to heal a disease which had baffled all human skill; although eagerly besought by multitudes of ailing people, he singled out this woman as most worthy of his aid. Her faith, though expressed with a certain degree of superstitious fear, was honored by a complete cure.

The story of the healing of this woman not only illustrates the spontaneous compassion of Je'sus for suffering humanity manifest in all His works of beneficence; but strikingly sets forth His compassionate and respectful regard for womanhood.

Je'sus consistently and perpetually dignified womanhood, improved every opportunity for her relief and elevation, and gave to her a place of pre-eminence in the work of His kingdom. The religion founded by Je'sus recognizes the intellectual and spiritual insight of woman, and exalts her to positions of responsibility and power.

SUGGESTIONS FOR STUDY
Biblical Index to Helpful References

Secret Prayers of Jesus. (Mark 6:46, 47; Lu. 5:16; 6:12; 9:18; 22:41, 42.)

Leprosy a Foul and Incurable Disease. (Lev. 13:10; 14:2, 34; Deut. 24:8.)

Ceremonial Rites for Healed Lepers. (Lev: 14:1-32.)

The Synagogue the Center of Religious Life. (Acts 13:5, 14; 14:1; 18:19.)·

God's Knowledge of Man's Heart. (1 Sam. 2:3; Ps. 69:5; 139:2.)

Universal Mission of Christ. (Acts 8:14; 11:19; Gal. 2:9; 3:28.)

The Folly of Self-Righteousness. (Prov. 12:15; 30:12; 2 Cor. 10:12.)

Fasting When Distressed by Sin or Afflictions. (Joel 1:14; 2:12; 1 Sam. 7:6.)

Questions

1. By what spirit of devotion was the life of Christ characterized?

2. Describe the population of Galilee.

3. Describe the position of the Jewish synagogue in the life of the people.

4. How long did the first circuit of Galilee continue?

5. How many miracles of healing recorded during this circuit? Resurrections?

6. Describe the character of leprosy.

7. Tell of the healing of the paralytic in Capernaum.

8. How did Matthew show his gratitude for his call? Who were guests?

9. How did Jesus answer the charge against his disciples about fasting?

10. Tell of the healing of the woman with an incurable disease.

STORY 157

THE DAUGHTER OF JAIRUS
RAISED FROM DEATH

(Matt. 9:18-26; Mark 5:22-24; 35-43; Luke 8:41-42; 49-56.)

The delay in reaching the home of Ja-i'rus brought Je'sus face to face with a new situation. When he and the distressed father reached the home they were met by friends who said, "Thy daughter is dead: why troublest thou the Master further?" Overwhelmed with grief and despair, they felt that nothing more could be done. Yet

THE RAISING OF JAIRUS' DAUGHTER

this apparently hopeless case was an opportunity for Je'sus to exert his greatest power. Asking the mourners to leave the building, he said to the broken-hearted father, "Be not afraid, only believe."

Selecting for his companions the three disciples who were always nearest to him in hours of trial, Je'sus entered the room where the little girl lay motionless in the sleep of death. Tenderly grasping the lifeless hands of the child, he said: "Damsel, I say unto thee, Arise."

The restoration was immediate and complete, for the little girl rose up at once, and began to walk about in the room. As a means of proving that she had been brought back to normal health, Je'sus ordered that she be given food; then astonishment and gratitude filled the hearts of all who were present as the damsel took the food that was offered.

The next two recorded miracles of the Lord took place in the home of Si'mon Pe'ter. Two men who were suffering from blindness came to him for healing, calling upon him as "Thou Son of Da'vid." More and more the true identity of Je'sus as the promised Mes-si'ah was gripping the hearts of the people, and more and more he gave proof of his divinity. To these blind men he said, "Believe ye that I am able to do this?" Touching their eyes, he then added, "According to your faith be it unto you."

As the two men whose sight had been restored went out, there was brought to Je'sus a man who was dumb and possessed of a demon. Je'sus immediately cast out the evil spirit, and the man began to talk. This miracle caused great astonishment, for persons in such a condition were thought to be beyond all earthly help.

SUGGESTIONS FOR STUDY

Biblical Index to Helpful References

Examples of Love of Fathers for Children. (Gen. 31:28; 37:35; 2 Sam. 12:16.)

Scoffers Denounced. (Psm. 73.11; Isa. 5:19; Jer. 17:15.)

Seclusion for Raising the Dead. (1 Ki. 17:19; 2 Ki. 4:33; Acts 9:40.)

Two Other Occasions for the Inner Circle of Jesus' Disciples. (Matt. 26:77; Mark 9:2.)

Faith Assures Success in Prayer. (2 Chr. 20:20; Jas. 1:5, 6.)

Questions

1. Why did the delay of Jesus in reaching the home of Jairus cause hopelessness in that home?

2. In what way did Jesus encourage Jairus?

3. Name the disciples selected as his companions in entering the chamber of death.

4. Did Jesus bring this dead maiden back to life?

5. How many miracles of raising the dead did he perform? Explain the progressive elements in each.

6. Tell of the healing of the two blind men.

STORY 158

JESUS VISITS JERUSALEM;
HEALS A LAME MAN

Healing of Lame Man. (Jno. 5:1-16.)
Discourse on His Relation to God. (Jno. 5:17-47.)
Controversies with Pharisees. (Matt. 12:1-14; Mark 2:23-3:6; Luke 6:1-11.)

Je'sus interrupted his Gal'i-le-an ministry by making a brief visit to Je-ru'sa-lem during one of the great religious festivals. It was either the Feast of the Pass'o-ver, or that of Pu'rim, which takes place a month earlier. Soon after his arrival in the Holy City, Je'sus visited a place called Be-thes'da, where there was a mineral spring with an irregular flow of waters. These waters were thought to heal certain kinds of disease, so a house with five porches had been built for the convenience of those who had come to enter the pool. At the time of Je'sus'

JESUS GOES UP TO JERUSALEM

visit the porches were filled with a multitude of ailing people; some were blind, others lame, or paralyzed. and all were eagerly awaiting the next moving of the waters. It was generally believed that the first person to reach the waters when they flowed was sure to be healed.

Among the great company of ailing men and women was a man who had been crippled for thirty-eight years; he was utterly helpless, and had no friends to carry him to the waters, nor money to hire some one to aid him. The heart of the great Physician went out in pity for the friendless sufferer, and He asked the man, "Wilt thou be made whole?"

The lame man then explained that he had no one to help him go down to the waters at the proper time, but Je'sus said, "Arise, take up thy bed, and walk." Instantly he was healed, and walked the streets of the city with great joy. The Jewish leaders, however, accused him of breaking the Mo-sa'ic laws which forbade such activity on the Sab'bath. In reply to their charges the healed man said, "He that made me whole said to me, 'Take up thy bed, and walk.' " He had been healed without learning the name of the miracle worker, and in his joy had rushed away. Soon afterward he went to the temple to give praise to God for his wonderful cure; here he met Je'sus, who said to him, "Go, and sin no more; lest a worse thing come upon thee." Out of gratitude to his new found Sav'ior, and hoping to bring the Jewish leaders to recognize Je'sus as the Son of God, the man hastened to make public the source of his cure.

The Jewish leaders then accused Je'sus of violating the Sab'bath, and threatened to have him slain. In defending his act of mercy Je'sus said, "My Father worketh till now, and I work." Then the persecution became more bitter, and Je'sus was accused of blasphemy in making himself equal with God. This charge opened the way for a wonderful discourse on the unity of Je'sus and His Father, in which he proved God's identity with him in the Mes-si-an'ic labors, and proclaimed eternal salvation for all who sincerely believed on Him.

"Verily, verily, I say unto you, He that heareth my word, and believeth on him that hath sent me, hath everlasting life, and shall not come into judgment; but is passed from death unto life."

The next two incidents in the ministry of Je'sus further illustrate the growing hostility of the Phar'i-sees; one relating to their complaint that his disciples had broken the Sab'bath, the other concerning their fault finding with Je'sus himself for healing on the Sab'bath.

The ruling classes were becoming more and more envious of Je'sus

BESIDE THE POOL AT BETHESDA

and were constantly on the watch for some act which would expose him
to prosecution in the Jewish courts. To the original laws of Mo'ses respecting Sab'bath observance they had added many regulations of their
own, until a devout Jew could hardly lift his finger without breaking
some law. There were laws forbidding the sick to send for a physician
on the Sab'bath; against a tailor carrying his needle with him on Friday
night, lest he break the Sab'bath by carrying it about with him on the
next day; against writing down as many as two letters of the alphabet;
and scores of other regulations which were contrary to the original purpose of the Sab'bath. Knowing that Je'sus paid little attention to such
trivial things, his enemies constantly sought to trap him on the Sab'bath
day.

The disciples of Je'sus, several of them formerly men of good circumstances in life, had given up all for His cause, and were often in dire need
of food. While crossing through a field one Sab'bath day, they took
advantage of a merciful provision of the Mo-sa'ic law in plucking a few
ears of corn and rubbing out some grains in order to relieve their hunger.

The Phar'i-sees then declared that in so doing they were guilty of reaping and winnowing, and had therefore broken the Sab'bath.

Je'sus defended his disciples on the ground of their personal need, and called to mind an incident in the life of Da'vid when ceremonial rules were set aside by the higher law of human distress.

The other incident took place on another Sab'bath day when Je'sus was attending worship at the synagogue. Among those present was a man whose right hand was lame, so the Phar'i-sees were watching closely to see what the Sav'ior would do. Reading their thoughts, Je'sus commanded the infirm man to stand forth. This time he met their hostility before they had made a complaint, and appealed to the principle that petty rules of conduct on the Sab'bath must be set aside for acts of mercy toward the unfortunate. Then he said to the man, "Stretch forth thy hand." The Phar'i-sees were enraged by the miracle of healing which then took place, and began to plan among themselves for the destruction of the Sav'ior.

In neither of these incidents did Je'sus question or violate the holiness of the Sab'bath. He recognized its Divine appointment as a day for rest and worship, and identified himself with its Founder in these words, "For the Son of man is Lord even of the Sab'bath day."

SUGGESTIONS FOR STUDY

Biblical Index to Helpful References

Hebrew Festivals. (Ex. 23:14; Lev. 23:2; Num. 15:3.)

Sicknesses Sometimes Caused by Sin. (Lev. 26:15, 16; Mic. 6:13.)

Other Cures of Chronic Ailments. (Mark 5:25; Jno. 9:1.)

The Misfortune of Friendlessness. (Psm. 31:11; 142:4.)

The Lord Helps in Extremities. (Psm. 116:6; Acts 12:6; 27:20, 24.)

The Sin of Sanctimonious Pretensions. (Isa. 29:13; 65:5.)

Seven-Fold Testimony to Deity of Jesus. (Jno. 1:34; 5:36, 37, 39; 8:14; 15:26, 27.)

The Sin of Uncharitableness. (Isa. 29: 20; Acts 28:4.)

Questions

1. What place did Jesus visit in Jerusalem? Why?

2. Tell the condition of the poor lame man at the pool of Bethesda.

3. Tell of his cure by Jesus.

4. Did the man know who Jesus was at the time of the cure?

5. Where did Jesus later find him? What did he tell him to do?

6. How did Jesus answer the hostility of the Pharisees?

7. How did he explain his miraculous works of healing?

8. What three great truths did he then proclaim?

9. What proofs did he offer concerning his oneness with the Father?

10. Name some of the extraneous rules of the Pharisees regarding the Sabbath.

11. How did Jesus defend his disciples for plucking corn on the Sabbath?

12. Tell of the healing of the man's lame hand.

STORY 159

THE CALLING OF THE TWELVE;
THE SERMON ON THE MOUNT

Selection of the Twelve Apostles. (Matt. 10:1-21; Mark 3:7-12.)
Sermon on the Mount. (Matt. 5:1-7:27; Luke 6:20-49.)

After the controversies with the Phar'i-sees, Je'sus withdrew to the open areas on the Sea of Gal'i-lee, where he was followed by great multitudes from all parts of Gal'i-lee and from Ju-de'a, from Id-u-me'a, from beyond the Jor'dan, and from the Phoe-ni'ci-an cities of Tyre and Si'don. He spoke to them from a boat which was thrust back a little from the land because of the great throngs of people which pressed forward to hear him, and hundreds were healed of all kinds of physical and mental ailments.

Following this strenuous day of teaching and healing, Je'sus went out into Mt. Hat'ten, about five miles west of the Sea of Gal'i-lee, and spent the entire night in solitary prayer. On the next day a vast throng of his followers gathered in this mountain under his call, and twelve of them were named as Apostles. A threefold purpose was given in the choice of the twelve and in their ordination: First, they were to abide with Christ, share in his temptations and trials, witness his glory and majesty, and enjoy his full confidence and trust. Secondly, they were to go forth preaching his gospel, proclaiming to all Is'ra-el that the long promised Mes-si'ah had now come with gracious words of healing and salvation. Finally, they were to prove the truth of their testimony by healing the sick and casting out demons.

All of these men, with the possible exception of Ju'das Is-car'i-ot, had been disciples of Je'sus for a year or more; they had listened attentively to his sublime teachings, witnessed his miracles of every kind, and come to know him intimately. They may be divided into three groups: the first, composed of Pe'ter and An'drew, James and John, were men of deep spiritual insight who became leaders in the progress of Christ's kingdom in the world; the second, made up of Phil'ip, Bar-thol'o-mew, Thom'as, and Mat-thew, were notable for insistence upon clear proofs of the Mes-si-an'ic claims of Je'sus; while the last group, numbering James, the son of Al-phae'us, Jude, Si'mon the Zeal'ot, and Ju'das Is-car'i-ot, may be described as practical and common-place. Ju'das Is-car'i-ot, of course, was not a true disciple.

The disciples were chosen from the common walks of life, and no Rabbis or prominent religious leaders of the Jews were included. That they were men of unusual intellectual ability is proved by the writings of some members of the group, and by their wonderful deeds in promoting the kingdom of Christ after his ascension. They have been called ignorant, unlettered men, but such statements apply only to their lack of rabbinical training. Four of them—Mat'thew, John, Pe'ter, and Jude—are among the foremost writers of the New Testament.

The superior force of Pe'ter's character is revealed in the vigor of his writings and deeds. John's writings, as well as the recorded events of his life, show that he was a profound, imaginative thinker. Mat'thew's history of the teachings and deeds of the Sav'ior displays the grasp of a real scholar in his knowledge of Old Testament prophecies. James must have been outstanding in his ability to present the gospel of Christ, for

THE TWELVE APOSTLES ORDAINED

he was the first of the noble company to suffer martyrdom.

By virtue of his powers of leadership and vigorous character, Pe'ter became the spokesman of the disciples, but there is no evidence that he was given a superior rank among them. During the history of the Apostolic Church his leadership was supplanted by that of Paul, the great missionary to foreign fields.

Ju'das Is-car'i-ot was the "wolf in sheep's clothing." He showed his selfish, greedy nature on several occasions, and finally betrayed his Master into the hands of his enemies for the price of thirty pieces of silver—about seventeen dollars in present currency. His ignoble career was soon brought to a close by suicide.

Little is known of the other disciples beyond the fact that they remained loyal to the Lord Je'sus, were constant in witnessing for him during his sojourn upon earth, and spread the gospel throughout the world after his ascension. They were witnesses to the fact that he rose from the dead, were present when he breathed the Holy Spirit upon them after the resurrection, and were among those who were blessed at Pen'te-cost.

After selecting and ordaining the twelve Apostles, Je'sus proclaimed the laws of his kingdom in the Sermon on the Mount. In this discourse he gave to the human race the highest moral and spiritual rules ever known; the standards of the Mosaic laws were raised to new levels of spirituality. The Jews had thought that the Mes-si-an'ic kingdom was to be a golden age of wealth and worldly power, an Is'ra-el-it-ish Empire in which they would enjoy world wide dominion. In this Divinely inspired address, however, Je'sus' defined the Mes-si-an'ic reign as a spiritual kingdom, one that would flourish in a world of opposition and persecution.

The Divine Law Giver then described the spiritual qualities of the members of his kingdom in the verses which are known as the Beatitudes. True followers of the Lord were to be "Poor in spirit"; not proud, or self-satisfied. "Mournful in heart"; not inclined to excuse or tolerate sin, but ever ready to bow in godly sorrow. "Meek in temperament"; not self-willed, easily angered, or rebellious, but gentle, forebearing, and forgiving. "Hungering after righteousness"; not carried away by earthly pleasures, but yearning for perfect obedience to God's law. "Merciful in spirit"; not cruel or indifferent toward the unfortunate, but sympathetic, helpful, and generous. "Pure in heart"; not unclean in thought or will, but upright in mind and heart. Finally, the members of Christ's kingdom were to be "Peacemakers" in a world torn by strife and hatred.

THE SERMON ON THE MOUNT

Je'sus concluded the Beatitudes with an assurance that those who were persecuted for righteousness' sake, or reviled for His sake, were blessed in the sight of God. They had only to stand firm when attacked by the worldly-minded to share in the heavenly reward now enjoyed by the prophets who had gone before them. To those who trusted fully in God, persecution would be only a means of making them more nearly perfect.

In setting forth the relation of the citizens of his kingdom, Je'sus emphasized the purifying force of his followers upon a benighted society. He made it clear that he was not seeking to destroy the Mo-sa'ic law or the testimony of the prophets, but to broaden and deepen the authority of both in the life of his followers. Those who believed on Him were urged to obey the spirit as well as the letter of the law, and were reminded that they were not worthy of His kingdom until their righteousness exceeded that of the Phar'i-sees.

Je'sus then gave five illustrations of the principle that mere outward obedience to God's law is not enough. He applied the principle first to murder, showing that anger and violent thoughts are of the same evil nature. He also explained that the commandment against adultery forbids unclean thoughts, that the practice of oath-taking must not be abused by profanity, that evil treatment should not be returned in kind, and that one should love even his enemies, praying for those who are guilty of spiteful conduct.

Turning his attention to matters of worship, Je'sus gave instruction concerning almsgiving, which held an important place in the religion of the Jews. The Master told his followers that they should make no display of their generosity in giving alms to the poor, but should perform such deeds secretly. Similar counsel was given in regard to prayer and fasting. The model prayer which was then given is known as "The Lord's Prayer," but since it is for our use a better name is "The Disciples Prayer."

Thus the Lord laid down broad, comprehensive rules for every phase of the moral and spiritual conduct of his followers, stressed their mission as a holy society in a world of error and sin, and uttered stern warnings against the evils of the external world. Self-seeking and worldly ambitions among the leaders of his kingdom were bitterly denounced, and the chief basis for rank among his followers was placed on the high spiritual plane of self-denying service.

With a keen insight into human character Je'sus warned his followers against worry of mind and fretfulness of soul. Both of these errors were foolish and sinful, because they interfere with one's full use in life and deny the ability of God to care for all his children. He gave full assurance of the security and happiness of all who sincerely obey the laws of his kingdom, declaring that all who build their hopes upon him and his word are safe from all the perils of time and the future judgment of God.

SUGGESTIONS FOR STUDY

Biblical Index to Helpful References

Distinctiveness of the Office of the Apostles. (Acts 1:13, 26; 1 Cor. 4:9; 9:1; Eph. 2:20; 4:11.)

"Poor in Spirit"—Sensible of Spiritual Poverty. (Isa. 57:15; Prov. 29:23.)

"Mournful in Heart"—Penitent for Sin. (2 Chr. 7:14; Ezr. 10:1.)

"Meek in Temperament"—Tranquil, Affable. (Gal. 5:22, 23; Jas. 1:21.)

"Hungering After Righteousness"—Yearning for Goodness. (Psm. 38:9; Isa. 26:9; 1 Pet. 2:2.)

"Merciful in Spirit"—Sympathetic, Generous. (Prov. 3:3; 11:17; Mic. 6:8.)

"Purity of Heart"—Rectitude, Sincerity, Holiness. (Psm. 24:3, 4; 1 Tim. 1:5.)

"Peace-Makers" — Composing Disturbances, Peaceableness.—(Prov. 12:20; Rom. 14:9; Heb. 12:14.)

Spiritual Mindedness. (Rom. 8:6; Phil. 2:5; 4:8.)

Evil Thoughts and Imaginations Denounced. (Jer. 4:14; Rom. 1:21.)

Retaliation Forbidden. (Prov. 20:22; 24: 29; Rom. 12:17; 1 Pet. 3:9.)

Heavenly Citizenship. (Luke 10:20; Phil. 3:20; 1 Pet. 1:4.)

Spiritual Investments. (Phil. 3:8; 1 Tim. 6:19; Rev. 3:18.)

Double - Mindedness in Religion Denounced. (2 Ki. 17:33; 1 Cor. 10:21.)

Questions

1. Tell of the throngs which came to hear Jesus in Galilee.

2. Following a busy day, how did he spend the whole night?

3. How many were chosen to be apostles? Give the three purposes for calling them.

4. How long had they been disciples of Jesus? What had they learned?

5. Define in a general way the characteristics of these men.

6. How did Christ's kingdom differ from Jewish expectations?

7. Name and explain the seven Beatitudes. The supplementary Beatitude.

8. Explain other striking features of the Sermon on the Mount.

STORY 160

THE RAISING OF THE WIDOW'S SON; OTHER MIRACLES IN GALILEE

Healing of the Centurion's Servant. (Matt. 8:1-13; Luke 7:1-10.)
Raising of the Widow's Son. (Luke 7:11-17.)
Response to Messengers from John. (Matt. 11:2-19; Luke 7:18-35.)
Cities of Galilee Upbraided. (Matt. 11:20-31.)
Jesus Feet Anointed by a Sinful Woman. (Luke 7:36-50.)
A Dumb and Blind Man Healed. (Matt. 12:32-45; Mark 3:19-30.)
Jesus Sought by Mother and Brothers. (Matt. 12:46-50; Mark 3:31-35; Luke 8:19-21.)
Parables of the Kingdom. (Matt. 13-1-50; Mark 4:1-32; Luke 8:4-18.)
Stilling of a Storm at Sea. (Matt. 8:18-27; Mark 4:35-41; Luke 8:22-25.)
Healing of a Demoniac. (Matt. 8:28-34; Mark 5:1-20; Luke 8:26-39.)
Second Rejection at Nazareth. (Matt. 9:1, 13:54-58; Mark 5:21, 6:1-6; Luke 8:40.)

Returning to Ca-per'na-um, Je'sus resumed his work of preaching and healing among the masses of Gal'i-lee. The healing of a centurion's servant was notable for several reasons; the Roman officer was a Gentile, yet he confessed his unworthiness to have Je'sus enter his house, and believed that the Sav'ior could heal the servant merely by speaking a word. To the centurion he said, "Go home, your servant is healed."

Je'sus and his followers then journeyed toward the little town of Na'in, where they met a funeral procession bearing the body of a widow's son to the cemetery outside the walls of the village. Moved with compassion for the bereaved mother, Je'sus bade her cease from weeping; moving nearer to the body, he commanded the youth to arise. "He that was dead sat up, and began to speak," and the people declared, "A great prophet has arisen among us; God has visited his people."

News of the increasing activities of Je'sus came to the ears of John the Bap'tist, who had long been imprisoned through the wrath of Her'od. Wondering how the Sav'ior could be so indifferent to his sufferings, John sent messengers to Je'sus with the inquiry, "Art thou he that should come, or do we look for another?" In his reply Je'sus reminded John of the blessings which had attended his ministry—the restoration of sight to the blind, recovery of the lame, cleansing of lepers, and the preaching of good news to the poor. He then turned to those who stood by, and said:

RAISING OF THE WIDOW'S SON AT NAIN

"Among them that are born of women there is none greater than John: but he that is least in the kingdom of heaven is greater than he."

After this Je'sus accepted an invitation to dine in the home of a Phar'i-see. While enjoying this hospitality, he was suddenly approached by a woman of ill repute, who wept at his feet; taking a box of costly spikenard, she then anointed the feet of the Sav'ior. The silence of Je'sus filled the mind of his host with wonder; sensing this, the Master spoke a parable concerning two debtors. One of them had been forgiven much, and therefore, should be the more grateful. The point of the story was quickly understood, for the depth of the woman's affection had been shown in an act of beautiful devotion which the Phar'isee had neglected.

There soon followed a miracle in which Je'sus healed a demon-possessed man who was both blind and dumb. This mighty work so greatly impressed the onlookers that they said, "Is this not the son of Da'vid?" Such popular acclaim served only to increase the opposition of the scribes and Phar'i-sees, who charged for the second time that Je'sus was casting out demons by the power of the chief of devils. The Sav'ior proceeded to show the folly of such a charge, pointing out that no kingdom or house divided against itself could possibly stand, and uttering a solemn warning against blasphemy. When the Phar'i-sees demanded that he give them a sign of his Divinity, he declared that no sign would overcome their prejudice and hatred, but that in due time the sign of Jo'nah should be fulfilled in him.

Standing upon the shores of the Sea of Gal'i-lee among vast throngs of people, Je'sus delivered eight parables which relate to His kingdom. The Parable of the Sower describes the various ways in which those who hear the gospel respond to its Divine invitation. The Parable of the Wheat and Tares illustrates the mingling of the children of the kingdom with the children of the wicked one in the common interests of life, while the Parable of the Mustard Seed points to the sure, steady growth of His kingdom.

As an illustration of the silent power of his kingdom within human hearts and society, Je'sus uttered the Parable of Leaven in the Meal. Two parables were devoted to the superior worth of faith in the kingdom in the hearts of man: the Treasure Hidden in the Field, for which a man would sell all that he had; and the Pearl of Great Price, for which a merchant would surrender all his treasures. Then, in token of the process by which members of his kingdom are to be gathered from a world of sin, Je'sus spoke the Parable of the Net.

Exhausted by his labors among the great throngs on the shores of the Sea of Gal'i-lee, Je'sus and some of his followers took refuge in a boat. While Je'sus was quietly resting in sleep, a fierce storm suddenly swept down upon Gen-nes'a-ret. The disciples awakened him with the cry, "Lord, save us: we perish." Je'sus then reproached the disciples for their lack of faith, and calmed the raging winds and billows by the command, "Be still."

Upon reaching the shores of the country known as Gad-a-ra', Je'sus was faced by two maniacs who made their home among the tombs, and who were a constant source of terror to all who passed that way. Moved by the evil spirits which dwelt within them, these men cried out, "What have we to do with thee, Je'sus, thou Son of God?" Sensing that their doom was near at hand, the evil spirits asked permission to take refuge in a herd of swine feeding nearby.

SWINE DRIVEN INTO THE SEA

The request of the evil spirits was granted, and immediately the herd of swine rushed wildly down the slope into the sea, where they were drowned. The keepers of the swine fled into the city to report the incident to their master, and all the people of that district begged Je'sus to leave their neighborhood.

The next appearance of Je'sus was in his home town of Naz'a-reth, where he attended worship in the synagogue. For the second time, however, he was rejected by his old friends and neighbors, even though they had received full reports of his mighty works in other parts of Gal'i-lee and Ju-de'a.

This rejection of Je'sus for the second time by the people of His own home-town, because they knew Him as the carpenter's son, and the members of His family were familiar to them, led the Sav'ior to remark with tinged disappointment: "A prophet is not without honor, save in his own country." A yet more distressing comment was given by one of the Gospel writers in which it is stated: "And He could do no mighty works in Naz'a-reth because of their unbelief."

SUGGESTIONS FOR STUDY

Biblical Index to Helpful References

Praying for Another's Relief from Trouble. (Job 42:10; Psm. 106:23.)

Confessions of Unworthiness. (Matt. 25: 37-39; 1 Cor. 15:9.)

Other Examples of Great Faith. (Matt. 9: 18, 28; 14:36; 15:28; Mark 5:28.)

Other Gentile Believers. Luke 23:47; Acts 8:12; 10:2; 18:7.)

Special Consideration for Widows in Sorrow. (1 Ki. 17:9; Acts 6:1; 9:39.)

Promises to the Afflicted. (Psm. 30:5; 34: 19, 20; Rev. 21:4.)

Christ, Conqueror of Death. (Isa. 25:8; 1 Cor. 15:25, 26; Rev. 1:18.)

Divine Sympathy for Momentary Doubtings. (Gen. 15:8; Jgs. 6:17; Acts 12:14, 15.)

Convincing Argument of Good Works. (Jas. 2:18; 1 Pet. 2:12.)

Judgment According to Privilege. (Lu. 12:48; Rom. 2:12.)

Jesus the Friend of Sinners. (Lu. 19:7; Rom. 5:8; 1 Tim. 1:15.)

Questions

1. What is notable about the Centurion's plea?

2. What doubts were suffered by John? Why?

3. Why did Jesus upbraid certain cities of Galilee?

4. What occurred as Jesus sat at dinner in a Pharisees' home?

5. What indictment was brought against Jesus by the Pharisees?

6. Explain the answer of Jesus to his mother and brothers.

7. Name and explain the "parables of the kingdom."

8. Tell of the casting of the demons which entered a herd of swine.

STORY 161

CLOSING MONTHS OF THE GALILEAN MINISTRY

The Twelve empowered for Special Mission. (Matt. 9:35; 11:1; Mark 6:7-13; Luke 9:1-6.)

Death of John The Baptist and Terror of Herod. (Matt. 14:1-12; Mark 6:14-29; Luke 9:7-9.)

Retirement to Bethsaida; Five Thousand Fed. (Matt. 14:13-22; Mark 6:30-46; Luke 9:10-17; Jno. 6:5-14.)

Jesus Walking on The Sea. (Matt. 14:24-33; Mark 6:47-52; Jno. 6:16-21.)

Mighty Works of Healing in Gennesaret. (Matt. 14:34-36; Mark 6:53-56.)

Sermon on Bread of Life. (Jno. 6:22-71.)

Defense of Twelve on Ceremonial question. (Matt. 15:1-20; Mark 7:1-23; Jno. 7:1.)

Withdrawal to Tyre and Sidon; Daughter of Greek Woman Healed. (Matt. 15:21-28; Mark 7:24-30.)

Withdrawal toward Decapolis; Deaf and Dumb Man Healed. (Mark 7:31-37.)

Feeding of four Thousand. (Matt. 15:29-38; Mark 8:1-9.)

Pharisees refuted in Magdala. (Matt. 15:39; 16:1-4; Mark 8:10-12.)

Retirement to Bethsaida; Rebuke of disciples. (Matt. 16:5-12; Mark 8:13-21.)

Blind man healed. (Mark 8:22-26.)

Opinions of Christ; Peter's confession. (Matt. 16:13-20; Mark 8:27-30; Luke 9:18-21.)

Predictions of Death and Resurrection. (Matt. 16:21-28; Mark 8:31-9:1; Luke 9:22-27.)

The Transfiguration. (Matt. 17:1-8; Mark 9:2-8; Luke 9:28-36.)

Instructions to Peter, James and John. (Matt. 17:9-13; Mark 9:9-13.)

Healing of Demoniac Child. (Matt. 17:14-21; Mark 9:14-29; Luke 9:37-42.)

Return to Galilee, Second Prediction of Death and Resurrection. (Matt. 17:22-23; Mark 9:30-32; Luke 9:43-45.)

Miracle of Tax Money taken from Fish. (Matt. 17:24-27.)

Selfish Ambitions and Contentions among Apostles. (Matt. 18:1-5; Mark 9:33-37; Luke 9:46-48.)

John's mistaken Zeal. (Matt. 18:6-14; Mark 9:38-50; Luke 9:49-50.)

Offenses and Forgiveness; Parable of Wicked Servant. (Matt. 18:13-35.)

Overcoming Hindrances to following Jesus. (Matt. 8:19-22; Luke 9:57-62.)

Declines Advice of brothers to go to Jerusalem. (Jno. 7:2-9.)

Journeys through Samaria to Jerusalem. (Luke 9:51-56; Jno. 7:10.)

After the Gal'i-le-an ministry of Je'sus had continued for nearly two years, marked with success in nearly all of the towns which he visited, the Master began to entrust his followers with greater responsibilities in spreading the gospel. He called the twelve Apostles into a solemn meeting, gave them the power to heal the sick

CHRIST'S CALL TO THE SICK AND WEARY

and to cast out demons, and sent them out in pairs to preach in the cities throughout the land. Later he sent seventy others on a similar mission. All of these servants were directed to travel in the simplest and humblest manner, and were told to rely upon the hospitality of friends for all their needs. In communities where they paused for missionary labors they were to select a family which seemed worthy, and to remain in that home as long as their work continued.

Meanwhile the opposition to Je'sus was becoming more determined among the religious leaders of the Jews, and the Phar'i-sees, Sad'du-cees, and Her'od-i-ans were combining in their schemes to entrap him. John the Bap'tist had been beheaded under orders of Her'od An'ti-pas, whose wife he had rebuked for her illegal marriage to the king. News of the increasing power of Je'sus reached Her'od's court, and dark forebodings filled the heart of the

CHRIST WALKING ON THE SEA

guilty king. When it was suggested to him that John the Bap'tist had risen from the dead, he expressed a desire to interview Je'sus in person.

Much of the remaining ministry of Je'sus in Gal'i-lee was, therefore, spent in seclusion, and there is the record of four different withdrawals for the sake of continuing the saving work. During one of these periods of retirement Je'sus miraculously provided food for five thousand men and the women and children who accompanied them from five small cakes of barley and two little fishes. When the feast was over, twelve baskets of food were gathered from what remained. So great was the excitement caused by this miracle that the people clamored to make Je'sus a king. This plan, however, was checked by the Sav'ior when he sent his disciples across the sea, while he took refuge in a secluded spot in the mountains for prayer.

The boat in which the Apostles were crossing the sea was soon beset by a terrible storm, but suddenly the Sav'ior appeared, walking serenely over the very waves which had filled their hearts with fear. With the boldness for which he was noted, Pe'ter asked to be given the power to do the same thing. For a time he was able to walk upon the waves, but soon his faith was disturbed by the sight of the angry waters, and he began to sink. Then the hand of Je'sus lifted him to safety with the gentle rebuke, "O thou of little faith, wherefore didst thou doubt?"

Referring to the multitudes of people who followed him because of the loaves and fishes, which he had provided in his miraculous feeding of the five thousand, Je'sus delivered a matchless address in the synagogue at Ca-per'na-um. Speaking on the subject, "The Bread of Life," he referred to himself as "the living bread which came down from heaven."

The second period of withdrawal carried Je'sus and his disciples into the regions about Tyre and Si'don in the land of the Phoe-ni'ci-ans. Here he was asked by a Greek woman to heal her daughter, who was grievously tormented by a demon. At first Je'sus appeared to be wholly indifferent to the cries of this Gen'tile woman, and the disciples did not wish her to trouble the Master. When she persisted in her request, Je'sus said to her, "Do you think it right that I take the children's meat and give it to dogs?" These words were not as harsh as they seem; in so speaking, Je'sus merely reminded the woman that the blessings of the Mes-si'ah must first be offered to the children of Is'ra-el, and then be extended to the Gen'tiles. The Gre'cian woman understood that such must be the case, but replied, "But even the dogs may eat of the crumbs which fall from the table of the children." The meaning of these remarks is more clear when we remember that the Jews often referred to all Gen'tiles as "dogs."

Returning to the land of Gal'i-lee for his third withdrawal, Je'sus went into the hill country of De-cap'o-lis. Here he healed a deaf and dumb man, and doubtless performed other acts of mercy. The second miracle of providing food for an enormous number of hungry people was performed when he fed four thousand people from seven barley cakes and a few little fishes.

Miracle of the Loaves

During the fourth withdrawal Je′sus led his Apostles into the regions of Beth-sa′i-da and Caes-a-re′a Phi-lip′pi, where he warned his followers against the evils of the Phar′i-sees, and rebuked them for their forebodings and lack of faith because of failure to bring food with them. While at Beth-sa′i-da he healed a blind man through a gradual return of his sight, and then requested him not to tell others of the miracle.

While in the regions of Caes-a-re′a Phi-lip′pi he questioned the Apostles concerning their belief in him, asking also what others thought about him. They reported that popular opinion varied; some saying that he was John the Bap′tist risen from the dead, others that he was E-li′jah, or Jer-e-mi′ah, or some other of the great prophets. When pressed to give their own belief, Si′mon Pe′ter acted as spokesman for the disciples in the noble confession, "Thou art the Christ, the Son of the living God." Je′sus then declared that this faith had been wrought in their hearts by the Spirit of God, and that upon this fact he would build his church, against which the gates of hell should never prevail.

In further proof of his Divinity, Je′sus took his three most intimate Apostles, Pe′ter, James, and John—far away into the top of Mount Her′-mon, and there they were permitted to·look upon the Sav′ior at the moment of Trans-fig′u-ra′tion. While he was engaged in prayer his countenance was illumined with a brilliance like that of lightning, his garments shone like the sun, and he was so completely enveloped in the glory of heaven that no earthly witness could describe the full glory of the spectacle. While in this transfigured glory Je′sus was visited by two heavenly saints: Mo′ses, representing the law, and E-li′jah, representing the prophets. They conversed with the Master about his approaching death for the sins of the world, while the disciples fell into a trance.

When the three disciples had recovered sufficiently to understand who the heavenly visitors were, Pe′ter suggested that three tabernacles be built; one for Mo′ses, one for E-li′jah, and one for the Sav′ior. His proposal was met by the voice of God out of the heavens, saying, "This is my Beloved Son, hear ye him." Suddenly Mo′ses and E-li′jah vanished into the heavens above, and Je′sus told the disciples to tell no man of what had happened until after he had ascended into heaven.

Upon returning to the foot of the mountain, Je′sus found the other nine Apostles greatly distressed by their failure to cure a demon-possessed child which had been brought to them by the father. One word of rebuke from Je′sus drove out the demon, and the Sav′ior explained to the disciples that some desperate cases could be healed only by prayer and fasting.

Je'sus then returned to Gal'-i-lee, where he made the second prediction of his approaching death and resurrection. At Ca-per'na-um he was asked to pay a temple tax, and performed a striking miracle in providing a coin of the exact amount of the tax. He sent Pe'ter on a fish-ing errand, telling him that he would find the needed piece of money in the mouth of a fish. Needless to say, this is exactly what happened.

While still in Ca-per'na-um, Je'sus found it necessary to re-buke the disciples for a conten-tion among them over the rank which they would hold in the kingdom of God. Placing a young child among them, Je'sus

THE TRANSFIGURATION

said: "Except ye be converted and become as little children, ye shall not enter into the kingdom of heaven." He added that it would be better for a man to be cast into the sea than to offend one of these little ones, and concluded with these gracious words: "Take heed that ye despise not one of these little ones; for I say unto you, that in heaven their angels do always behold the face of my Father."

In answer to Pe'ter's question concerning the forgiveness of offenses, Je'sus declared that a brother should be forgiven until seventy times the seven acts of mercy which Pe'ter had thought to be sufficient. To illus-trate the principle of forgiveness he then uttered the Parable of the Un-merciful Debtor. In this parable a wicked servant who had been forgiven an enormous debt—perhaps eight million dollars in present money—was so little moved to mercy that he imprisoned a man who owed him the trivial sum of fifteen dollars.

CHRIST BLESSING LITTLE CHILDREN

Preparing for the close of his ministry in Gal'i-lee, and for the journey through Sa-ma'ri-a to Je-ru'sa-lem, Je'sus pointed out some of the difficulties and hardships which must be borne by those who followed him. His brothers, who had not yet accepted him as the Mes-si'ah, came to him with the challenge that, if he were indeed the Sav'-ior, he should present himself in Ju-de'a. The suggestion that he go at once to Je-ru'sa-lem for the Feast of Tab'er-na-cles was rejected with the explanation that "his hour was not yet at hand." A few days later, however, he left Gal'i-lee on his way to Je-ru'sa-lem.

SUGGESTIONS FOR STUDY

Biblical Index to Helpful References

The Power and Wisdom of the Apostles. (Acts 4:33; 6:10; 9:40.)

The Gift of Healing. (1 Cor. 12:9.)

Biblical Requirements for Support of the Ministry. (1 Cor. 9:14; 1 Tim. 5:18.)

The Need for Solitude and Rest. (Gen. 32:24; Psm. 55:7; Jer. 9:2.)

Provisions of Spiritual Food. (Ezek. 34: 14; 1 Cor. 10:3, 4; Rev. 2:7, 8.)

Worthlessness of Mere Ceremonialisms. (Acts 15:10; Gal. 4:9; Heb. 9:10.)

Invincibility of Faithful Believers. (Deut. 11:25; 28:7; Songs 6:10.)

The Glory of Christ in Transfiguration. (2 Pet. 1:17, 18.)

Mountain Top Revelations. (Gen. 22:2; Ex. 19:11, 20; 1 Ki. 18:19, 20.)

The Sin of Worldly Ambition. (1 Ki. 1:5; Psm. 49:11; Isa. 14:13.) Strife Forbidden. (Prov. 17:14; Phil. 2:3.)

Spiritual Surgery. (Rom. 6:6; 8:13; Col. 3:5.)

Questions

1. Why did Jesus send out his apostles in pairs? What instructions were given them?

2. Why did Jesus find it necessary to spend much time in seclusion?

3. Tell of the feeding of five thousand. Where did this take place?

4. Tell of Jesus' teaching on "The Bread of Life."

5. Where did Jesus retire for his second withdrawal? Tell of the healing of the Syro-Phoenician woman's daughter.

6. Tell of his third withdrawal. Of his fourth. Of his question about opinions concerning himself.

7. Explain what took place on the Mount of Transfiguration.

8. For what did Jesus rebuke his disciples? What did he say about children?

9. How often did Jesus say we should forgive an erring brother?

10. Did Jesus predict his own death? Tell of the different circumstances.

STORY 162

THE LATER JUDEAN MINISTRY IN JERUSALEM

Jesus in Jerusalem; great excitement; opposed by Pharisees. (Jno. 7:11-53.)
Frustration of Pharisees who accuse sinful woman. (Jno. 8:1-11.)
Sermon: Christ, the Light of the World. (Jno. 8:12-20.)
Exposure of the Pharisees; their increasing fury. (Jno. 8:21-59.)
Healing of a man blind from birth. (Jno. 9:1-41.)
Parable of the Good Shepherd. (Jno. 10:1-21.)
Mission and success of Seventy Evangelists. (Luke 10:1-24.)
Parable of the Good Samaritan. (Luke 10:25-37.)
Jesus in the home of Mary and Martha. (Luke 10:38-42.)

Je'sus had two very good reasons for refusing to go to Je-ru'sa-lem when urged by his brothers. His appearance in the capital among the throngs of pilgrims would have been a signal for the outburst of the bitter hatred which was smouldering in the hearts of the Jewish leaders. Furthermore, the time for the sacrificial offering of Christ in death was not yet at hand.

After a few days had passed, however, Je'sus went to Je-ru'sa-lem without the knowledge of the public in general. On his arrival he mingled with the crowds unrecognized, even though there was great excitement in the city over reports that the miracle-worker had proclaimed himself to be the promised Mes-si'ah. Everyone was asking where he was, and there were mixed opinions concerning the claims which were being made for him by his followers. The rulers, including Ca'ia-phas and his party, were unbelieving and hostile, and were chagrined by his failure to appear with the pilgrims from Gal'i-lee. Officers were then sent throughout the city to search for him.

When the Feast of Tab'er-na-cles was well under way, Je'sus suddenly appeared in the temple and spoke openly to the people, astonishing them both by the manner of his teaching and by the doctrines which he taught. He had not been trained as a Rabbi, but his words revealed deep knowledge of the Scriptures, and he spoke with such authority and conviction that the usual comment was, "Never man spake as this man." The common people heard him gladly, but among the ruling class only Nic-o-de'-mus was moved by his words.

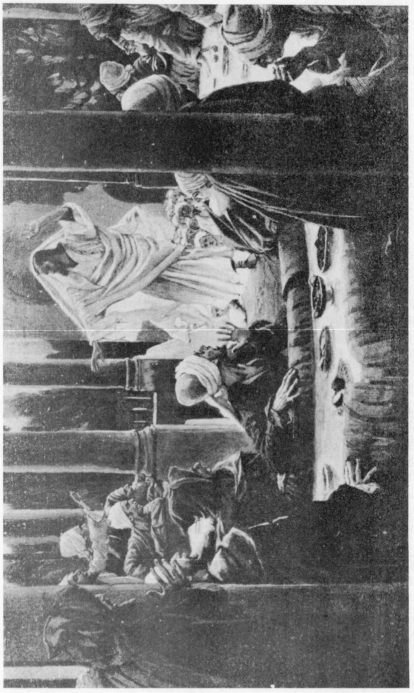

CHRIST REPROVING THE PHARISEES

Speaking in the temple, Je'sus described the Divine nature of his earthly ministry, and declared that he was acting as a messenger for his Father, from whom he had received the doctrines which he taught. Some of the people took sides with Je'sus, others became bitter enemies. New converts were won to his cause, but the chief priests and rulers of the San'he-drin were aroused to greater opposition. It was then that Je'sus announced that he would soon die at the hands of the Jewish rulers as a part of the Divine plan for human redemption. At that time, however, the officers who had been sent to arrest the Sav'ior were so greatly over-awed by his manner and teachings that it is said, "No man laid hands on him."

On the last day of the feast the entrance of the Is'ra-el-ites into the Promised Land was commemorated, and the priests carried pitchers of fresh water from the pool of Si-lo'am for the ceremonies. Drawing an illustration from this act, Je'sus said, "If any man thirst, let him come to me and drink."

A few days later, as Je'sus sat in the temple teaching the people, the scribes and Phar'i-sees sought to trap him. They brought before him a sinful woman whose conduct, according to the law of Mo'ses, demanded that she be stoned to death. Then they said, "Mo'ses in the law com-manded that such should be stoned: What sayest thou?" If he agreed that she should be stoned, then they could charge him with treason, for the Roman government had deprived the Jews of the right to inflict the death penalty. If he said that she should not be slain, then they could charge him with denying the law of Mo'ses.

Those who stood by thought that the Phar'i-sees had led Je'sus into a trap from which there was no escape, but they had not reckoned with the Divine wisdom of the Master. Facing the accusers he said, "He that is without sin among you, let him first cast a stone at her." Then, as Je'sus turned aside, the woman's accusers went out one by one. Addressing the woman, Je'sus said, "Hath no man condemned thee? Neither do I con-demn thee: go, and sin no more."

Je'sus continued his teachings in Je-ru'sa-lem for several days, and sharp disputes took place. When the Phar'i-sees challenged his claim that he was "the light of the world," he refuted them by truths often spoken be-fore: the witness of the Father upon him and his ministry, the testimony of the law and the prophets, and the evidence of the light imparted by him to benighted souls. To those who had believed on him he said, "If

THE GOOD SAMARITAN

ye continue in my word, then are ye my disciples indeed; and ye shall know the truth and the truth shall make you free."

Again the anger of the Phar'i-sees was aroused, and they boasted that they were A'bra-ham's seed and, therefore, slaves to no man. In reply the Master declared that the service of sin is slavery, and that, since they did not have the spirit of A'bra-ham, they were children rather of the wicked one. He then went on to tell them that before A'bra-ham ever lived he was in the bosom of his Father, and the Phar'i-sees became so enraged that they sought to stone him to death. But the hour for his death had not arrived, so he quietly slipped out of the temple and into the crowds.

As Je'sus mingled with the people, he met a man who had been blind from birth. The disciples asked, "Who did sin, this man, or his parents, that he was born blind?" It was commonly believed in those days that such afflictions as blindness were sent by the Lord in punishment for sin. The Sav'ior explained that neither the man nor his parents had sinned, but the blindness had been permitted so that the works of God might be revealed in the miracle about to take place. Je'sus then anointed the man's eyes with wet clay, and told him that his sight would be restored after he had washed in the pool of Si-lo'am. The cure took place exactly as the Lord had predicted, and a great sensation was caused among the man's neighbors.

The Phar'i-sees tried to discredit the miracle by saying that God would not permit healing on the Sab'bath, and that one who attempted such an unlawful act must be a sinner. Their arguments, however, were swept aside by the reply of the healed man, "Whether he be a sinner or no, I know not: one thing I know, that whereas I was blind, now I see." Then he outwitted the learned Phar'i-sees with this simple reasoning, "We know that God heareth not sinners: but if any man be a worshiper of God, and doeth his will, him he heareth. If this man were not of God, he could do nothing."

The continued criticism of the Phar'i-sees moved Je'sus to utter the beautiful Parable of the Good Shep'herd. The Phar'i-sees professed to be the true shepherds of the flock of God, yet they had rejected the ministry of the Good Shep'herd. Not satisfied with opposing the claims of the Mes-si'ah, the Phar'i-sees had sought to disturb his relations with those who accepted him as the Shep'herd of their souls. Je'sus reminded them in this parable that the only entrance to the heavenly fold was through him, and that he was the Good Shepherd for all who entered by faith.

Christ with Martha and Mary

He accused the scribes and Phar'i-sees of being cowardly hirelings who cared not for the people of God, but would seek their own safety when danger threatened Is'ra-el; then he said, "I am the good Shep'herd that giveth his life for the sheep."

In those sublime words Je'sus symbolizes His character as the Provider, Protector, Guide, and unfailing Companion of His people. Between the Good Shep'herd and His people there exist the tenderest relations—on the one side of unfathomable affection; and on the other of calm unlimited confidence. With the hand of the Shep'herd on all the sources of supply, none of His children can lack for temporal or spiritual good. He saves, protects, guides at the hazard of His own life.

There now remained only a few months for Je'sus to complete his earthly mission. Wishing to accomplish the greatest possible results in the brief time that was left, he sent out seventy evangelists to prepare the way for his visits in several parts of the country. The instructions which they received were similar to those which had been given to the twelve Apostles. They were most successful in their ministries, and brought back glowing reports to their Master.

As Je'sus was on his way to Beth'a-ny to visit Ma'ry and Mar'tha and their brother Laz'a-rus, he was approached by a young man who was a teacher of the law. Wishing to pit his learning against that of Je'sus, he asked which was the greatest of the Commandments. Je'sus replied that the greatest commandment is to love God with all the heart, and that the second commandment, which is like unto it, requires one to love his neighbor as himself. The entire law, he declared, is summed up in these two commandments. When the young man then asked, "Who is my neighbor?" Je'sus replied with the Parable of the Good Sa-mar'i-tan.

In this parable a traveler going down from Je-ru'sa-lem to Jer'i-cho fell among thieves, who robbed and beat him, and left him to die. A priest went by on the other side of the road, but did not trouble even to look at the wounded man. Then a Le'vite came along, but he, too, passed by without offering any help. Finally there came a Sa-mar'i-tan, a member of a despised half-pagan race, separated from the unfortunate traveler by both race and religion—but we are told, "He was moved with compassion, and came to the wounded man, and bound up his injuries, pouring on them oil and wine; and placing him on his own beast, he took him to an inn, and took care of him." The next day he showed further kindness by paying in advance for such care as the wounded man might need.

When Je′sus asked the self-righteous lawyer which of these men played the part of a neighbor, there was but one possible reply. Then the Master said, "Go thou, and do likewise." Once and for all Je′sus taught that Christian sympathy and aid must be extended to every race and creed, and that any person who needs help is our neighbor.

Living in the town of Beth′a-ny, a village about two miles from Je-ru′-sa-lem, was a family of two sisters and one brother. These people were in comfortable circumstances, and were intimate friends of Je′sus. On a visit in the home of this excellent family, Je′sus was graciously entertained by the two sisters. Mar′tha was much concerned with her domestic duties, while Ma′ry, who was more deeply religious, sat at the Master's feet for instruction. Mar′tha's complaint over her sister's failure to help her in preparing the meal led Je′sus to utter an important truth. He declared that the Bread of Life, as a necessary food for the soul, is more important than food for the body; and Ma′ry was praised for feeding her soul upon his teachings.

SUGGESTIONS FOR STUDY

Biblical Index to Helpful References

Jesus as a Rock of Offense. (Isa. 8:14; Rom. 9:32; 1 Pet. 2:8.)

The Hypocrisy of Christ's Rejectors. (Tit. 1:16; Rom. 2:23, 24.)

Overwhelming Power of Self-Guilt. (Acts 24:25; Rom. 2:1.)

Christ the Sinner's Friend. (Rom. 5:8; 1 Tim. 1:16.)

Christ the Light of the World. (Isa. 9:2; 42:6; Eph. 5:14; 1 Jno. 2:8.)

Christ's Qualifications as a Shepherd. (Isa. 40:11; Heb. 13:20; 1 Pet. 5:4.)

True Neighborliness of a Religious Kind. (Rom. 13:10; Rom. 15:1, 2; Jas. 2:8.)

Heartlessness of Religious Hypocrites. (Gen. 4:9; Jas. 2:16.)

The Spirit of True Human Compassion. (2 Chr. 28:15; Job 29:13; Acts 28:2.)

The Christian's Duty to Suffering Humanity. (Job 29:15, 16; Isa. 50:4.)

Duty and Privilege of Genuine Hospitality. (Rom. 12:13; Heb. 13:2; 1 Pet. 4:9.)

The Privileges of the Deeper Spiritual Life. (Psm. 1:2; Eph. 3:18, 19; Phil. 4:8.)

Questions

1. On his arrival in Jerusalem, what did Jesus do?

2. How were the people impressed as he spoke in the temple?

3. What did Jesus claim for himself as he addressed the people in the temple?

4. Tell of the efforts to trap Jesus by presenting a woman of ill-repute.

5. How did Jesus answer the question of the Pharisees about this woman?

6. What proof did Jesus give of his claim to be the light of the world?

7. When Jesus healed the blind man, how did the Pharisees discredit him?

8. Tell how the Jewish leaders rejected Christ as the Good Shepherd.

9. What supreme qualification has Jesus as the Good Shepherd?

10. Tell of the young man to whom Jesus spake the parable of the Good Samaritan.

11. According to this parable, who is our neighbor?

12. Tell of Jesus' visit in the home of Mary and Martha.

STORY 163

THE SAVIOR'S MINISTRY IN JUDEA

Repeats the Model Prayer for Disciples. (Luke 11:1-4.)
Parable of the Friend in Need. (Luke 11:5-13.)
Heals Dumb Maniac; Charged with Blasphemy. (Luke 11:14-36.)
Entertained by a Pharisee; Denounces Hypocrisy. (Luke 11:37-54.)
Parable of the Rich Fool. (Luke 12:1-21.)
Duty of Preparedness for His Return. (Luke 12:22-48.)
Foretells His approaching Death. (Luke 12:49-59.)
Parable of Barren Fig Tree. (Luke 13:1-9.)
Crippled Woman healed on the Sabbath. (Luke 13:10-17.)
Parables of Mustard Seed and Leaven restated. (Luke 13:18-21.)
Attacked by Pharisees at Feast of Dedication. (John 10:22-39.)

Following his visit in Beth'a-ny, Je'sus spent a few weeks teaching in Ju-de'a. The model prayer which he had taught his followers in the Sermon on the Mount was repeated, and was followed by the Parable of the Friend in Need. Here the temper of an evil-minded judge, who was swayed by the persistent pleas of a man in distress, is contrasted with the love of the Father toward all who pray in need.

Next came the miracle in which the healing of a dumb maniac brought another blasphemous accusation from the Phar'i-sees. Once again Je'sus was charged with casting out demons by the power of the chief of devils, but he refuted the charge with the same unanswerable logic which he had used on a former occasion.

While Je'sus was being entertained by a Phar'i-see, the discussion turned to the matter of eating without having performed certain ceremonial washings. Je'sus made it clear that to rely upon rites and ceremonies to cover up unrighteousness of heart is a serious error. The Phar'i-sees were denounced for their hypocrisy, their undue stress upon external forms of worship, and their narrow, conceited attitude. His disciples were later warned to remain faithful, and assured of God's personal interest and protection.

Je'sus then went on to warn his followers against the sin of covetousness by the Parable of the Rich Fool. He told the story of a rich man who became so completely absorbed in money-making and selfish pleasures that he never gave thought to preparing for the future life. Suddenly, in the midst of his prosperity, God said to him, "Thou fool; this night shall thy soul be required of thee: then whose shall these things be which thou hast provided?" Je'sus concluded the parable with this comment, "So is he that layeth up treasure for himself, and is not rich toward God."

Looking ahead to the time when he would return from his heavenly throne to reward his faithful servants, Je'sus solemnly warned his followers to prepare for that great day. These warnings were illustrated by the Parable of Wise and Unwise Stewards, and by the simile of the Goodman of the house who was robbed while in a state of unwatchfulness. There followed the story of an Oriental nobleman who had gone away without telling his servants when he would return; attention was called to the wisdom of the faithful servants who were prepared for the return of their master, and of the folly of those who were unwatchful and unprepared. This application was made more pointed by the urgent command: "Be ye therefore ready also: for the Son of man cometh at an hour when ye think not."

A DUMB MAN HEALED

While Je'sus was teaching the people the duty of repentance for sin, report was made of the massacre of a group of Gal'i-le-ans in the temple at Je-ru'sa-lem under orders of Pi'late. When it was suggested that the victims had suffered because of their wickedness, Je'sus declared, "Except ye repent, ye shall all likewise perish." Then he referred to an accident in which eighteen people had been killed by the falling of the tower of Si-lo'am, saying, "Think ye that they were sinners above all men that dwelt in Je-ru'sa-lem?" Again, he warned, "Nay, except ye repent, ye shall all likewise perish."

The Sav'ior rounded out his teachings on repentance with

the Parable of the Barren Fig Tree. The story was that a man planted a fig tree in good soil, had it well cultivated and dressed, but found it barren for three years in succession. When he ordered it cut down and burned, because it cumbered the ground, the keeper asked for one more year in which to cultivate it with even greater skill. The year of grace was granted, but without success; when no fruit was found, the tree was destroyed.

Je'sus then entered a synagogue and began to teach the people; suddenly there came before him a woman who had suffered from an incurable infirmity for eighteen years. Although she did not ask for help, Je'sus said to her, "Woman, thou art loosed from thine infirmity." The ruler of the synagogue was indignant because this act of mercy had been performed on the Sab'bath, and harshly reprimanded the Sav'ior. Je'sus said in reply, "If it is lawful for a man to loose his ox or donkey for watering on the Sab'bath, then should not this daughter of A'bra-ham be healed of her affliction on the Sab'bath?"

After this miracle Je'sus repeated the Parables of the Mustard Seed and The Leaven; then he went into Je-ru'sa-lem for the Feast of Ded-i-ca'tion. As he walked in the outer corridor of the temple, certain enemies demanded proof of his Mes-si-an'ic claims. The Jews were looking for an earthly ruler, so Je'sus answered his critics indirectly, saying: "The works that I do in my Father's name, they bear witness of me. But ye believe not, because ye are not of my sheep."

SUGGESTIONS FOR STUDY

Biblical Index to Helpful References

The Duty and Privilege of Prayerfulness. (Psm. 5:3; 55:17; Dan. 6:10.)

Excusing One's Sins by Blasphemy Against God. (Acts 13:45; Jas. 2:7.)

Hypocrisy Denounced. (Prov. 23:7; 1 Tim. 4:2; Tit. 1:16.)

The Sin of Trusting in Riches. (Psm. 52: 7; Prov. 18:11.)

Warnings Against Over-Anxious Care. (Psm. 127:2; Phil. 4:6.)

The Duty of Spiritual Strivings. (1 Cor. 12:31; Phil. 1:27.)

The Duty of Watchfulness. (1 Thess. 5:5, 6; Rev. 3:11; 16:15.)

The Fate of the Wicked. (Psm. 92:7; 112: 10; 2 Pet. 2:17.)

Questions

1. Where did Jesus labor for a few weeks after his visit with Mary and Martha?

2. Tell of his teachings regarding undue emphasis on ceremonialism.

3. In warning against covetousness, what parable did Jesus speak?

4. What parables did he use to emphasize the need of watchfulness?

5. Tell of the two examples of catastrophies used in teaching repentance.

6. What was the lesson taught by the parable of the Barren Fig Tree?

7. Tell of the healing of the woman of eighteen years' illness.

8. Why was Jesus able to escape his enemies at this time?

STORY 164

THE PEREAN MINISTRY OF HEALING AND TEACHING

Withdrawal beyond the Jordan.   (Jno. 10:40-42.)
Discussions concerning the Kingdom.   (Luke 13:20-35.)
In a Pharisee's home; a man healed of dropsy.   (Luke 14:1-6.)
Parable of the Wedding Feast.   (Luke 14:7-11.)
Parable of the Great Supper.   (Luke 14:15-24.)
Discourse on Counting the Cost.   (Luke 14:25-35.)
Three Parables defending the reception of Sinners.   (Luke 15.)
Parable of the Unjust Steward.   (Luke 16:1-13.)
Story of the Rich Man and Lazarus.   (Luke 16:14-31.)
Parable of the Unprofitable Servant.   (Luke 17:1-10.)

After the controversy with the Phar'i-sees during the Feast of Ded-i-ca'tion, Je'sus spent three months in the regions of Pe-re'a. Wherever he went, the people gathered to hear his teachings and to benefit from his miracles of healing. Much time appears to have been spent in private instruction of the disciples, for the time of his sacrificial death was drawing near. The record of four miracles which took place during this period has been preserved: the healing of a man with dropsy, the raising of Laz'a-rus from the tomb, the healing of ten lepers, and the restoration of sight to two blind men. The following parables were spoken during the ministry in Pe-re'a: The Wedding Guest, The Great Supper, The Lost Sheep, The Lost Coin, The Lost Son, The Unjust Steward, The Rich Man and Laz'a-rus, The Unprofitable Steward, Two Parables on Prayer, The Laborers in the Vineyard, and The Servants and the Pound.

The man who suffered from dropsy was healed when he dined on the Sab'bath with a group of Phar'i-sees. The Phar'i-sees had arranged for him to be present when they entertained the Lord, for they hoped to lure Je'sus into a violation of the Sab'bath. Suspecting the trap, Je'sus asked them, "Is it lawful to heal on the Sab'bath day?" This question completely disarmed the Phar'i-sees. If they said, "No," the people would blame them for interfering with the Lord's healing mission; if they agreed, then their whole scheme against Je'sus would fail. They were forced to remain silent, baffled by his wisdom; and Je'sus proceeded to heal the sick man. After the man was made well, Je'sus again routed his critics by reminding them of the common practice of mercy to animals on the Sab'bath.

The Parable of the Wedding Guest was spoken when Je'sus observed some of the guests at such a festival seeking out places of honor. True followers of the Lord should not seek worldly glory, but should be modest and unassuming under all circumstances.

In the Parable of the Great Supper, which was the next to be given, Je'sus compared the blessings of the gospel to a great feast with God as the host. The Jewish nation had been bidden to the feast by Mo'ses and the prophets, and John the Bap'tist and the Apostles had announced the hour for these heavenly enjoyments. Led by their rulers, however, the chosen people had refused both the original announcement and the later invitations. The vain excuses given by those who had rejected the gospel invitations were strikingly exposed, and Je'sus declared that Gen'tiles would enjoy the feast which had been prepared for the children of Is'ra-el.

Three of the most touching parables of Je'sus were spoken when the scribes and Phar'i-sees made the complaint, "This man receiveth sinners, and eateth with them." Je'sus did not deny the charge, but justified his conduct in the Parables of the Lost Sheep, the Lost Coin, and the Prodigal Son.

The first of these parables tells of a man who had a hundred sheep. When one of them was lost in the wilderness, he left the ninety-nine that were safe at home, and searched until he had found the lost sheep. Like this shepherd, Je'sus had left heaven and all the holy creatures of that celestial land safe in the care of God, and had

THE RETURN OF THE PRODIGAL

JESUS TEMPTED BY THE PHARISEES AND SADDUCEES

come to earth to "Seek and to save that which was lost."

Je'sus then related the story of a woman who lost one of her ten pieces of silver. She lighted a candle, and swept the house diligently until she found the lost coin.

What is probably the most loved of all the parables was then spoken to illustrate the tender, forgiving love of God toward sinners. A father had two sons. The younger son demanded his share of his father's estate, and soon squandered it in riotous living in a far country. His new friends proved false as soon as his money was gone, the memory of his reckless indulgences filled him with shame, and a famine which descended upon the land added to his misery. Reduced to hunger and nakedness, he was forced to work as a herder of swine; in his poverty and shame he was brought to realize the folly of what he had done. Then the wayward, but repentant young man decided to throw himself upon his father's mercy. Upon his arrival at his father's house he was welcomed with open arms, given full pardon, and made the guest of honor at a great feast.

The elder son, who was unduly proud of his own upright conduct, protested that his brother was unworthy of so kind a reception. To all his complaints, however, the father replied: "Son, thou art ever with me, and all that I have is thine. It was right for us to make merry and be glad: for this thy brother was dead, and is alive again; and was lost, and is found." In concluding these parables Je'sus said, "Likewise, I say unto thee, There is joy in the presence of the angels of God over one sinner that repenteth."

Sometime after delivering these three parables, Je'sus spoke to the disciples on the subject of stewardship. In this discourse he uttered the Parable of the Unjust Steward, telling the story of a dishonest man who used his position as a steward for his own gain. When he was told that the master was about to dismiss him, he gained the friendship of those who were indebted to the landlord by reducing their obligations. He was later praised by his master, not because he had acted with honor, but for his foresight and prudence.

Je'sus then rebuked the scornful Phar'i-sees by telling the story of the Rich Man and Laz'a-rus. The rich man is merely called "Dives" (the Latin word for "rich") and is represented as living in ease and luxury; while Laz'a-rus, a poor, suffering beggar, gratefully accepted crumbs from the rich man's table. Both of these men died, and their lot was reversed in the life beyond the grave. Angels led Laz'a-rus to a place of happiness, while Dives found himself in the torments of the unrighteous.

Seeing Laz'a-rus afar off in a state of perfect happiness, Dives implored A'bra-ham to send him with a drop of cold water, saying in his anguish, "For I am tormented in these flames." The plea was denied, and A'bra-ham declared that an impassable gulf separates the good from the wicked in the next life. When Dives asked that Laz'a-rus be sent back to this world to warn his five living brothers not to follow the example of proud, self-centered ease, he was told, "If they hear not Mo'ses and the prophets, neither will they be persuaded, though one rose from the dead."

The story of Dives and Laz'a-rus is followed by a series of conversations in which Je'sus instructed the disciples on various questions of service in his kingdom. He warned them of offenses, especially that of placing stumbling blocks in the way of weaker brethren. Directions were given concerning the duty of forgiveness, and stress was placed upon the need for peaceful fellowship. In this connection the Master spoke the Parable of the Dutiful Servant, a story in which a good servant refused to dine until he had done all that was necessary in preparing a meal for his master. This lesson taught the duty of all servants of the Lord to place the interests of His kingdom above all personal affairs.

SUGGESTIONS FOR STUDY

Biblical Index to Helpful References

Striving Earnestly in Religious Duties. (1 Cor. 9:25; Phil. 1:27; 3:14.)

Half-Heartedness in Religion of No Avail. (2 Ki. 10:21; Jas. 4:17.)

The Tragedy of Delay Until "Too Late." (Num. 14:40-45; 1 Sam. 15:24-26; Jer. 8: 20.)

Snares Laid for the Righteous. (1 Sam. 18:9; Psm. 35:7; 140:5; Hos. 5:1.)

Evil Men Put to Silence. (Job 5:16; Psm. 63:11; 1 Pet. 2:15.)

The Folly of Self-Exaltation. (Prov. 25: 6, 7; Isa. 14:13, 14; Obad. 4.)

Humbling of the Proud. (Psm. 18:27; Isa. 10:12; 14:11.)

Universal Provision of Gospel Privileges. (1 Tim. 2:4; Tit. 2:11, 12; 2 Pet. 3:9.)

Priority of God's Claims on Man. (Deut. 32:6; Ezek. 18:8.)

Priority of God's Claims on Man's Possessions. (Deut. 26:2; Neh. 10:35.)

Forethought and Prudence in Religion. (Prov. 22:3; 24:27; Hos. 14:9.)

Stewardship and Accountability. (1 Cor. 4:2; 1 Pet. 4:10.)

Questions

1. How long was the Later Perean Ministry?

2. Mention some of the important Kingdom Subjects discussed by Jesus during this period.

3. Name the notable parables spoken and explain the lesson of each one.

4. How did Jesus denounce the spirit of avarice?

5. Define the priority of God's claims as given in parables.

6. Explain the meaning of true service.

STORY 165

THE RAISING OF LAZARUS; PEREAN MINISTRY CONTINUED

Visit to Bethany; raising of Lazarus from the dead. (Jno. 11:1-53.)
Withdrawal to city near wilderness. (Jno. 11:54.)
Journey through Samaria, Galilee, Perea; ten lepers healed. (Luke 17:11-19.)
Discourse on the coming Kingdom. (Luke 17:20-37.)
Two Parables on Prayer. (Luke 18:1-14.)
Teachings concerning Divorce. (Matt. 19:13-15; Mark 10:1-12.)
Blessing little children. (Matt. 19:13-15; Mark 10:13-16; Luke 18:15-17.)
Question of the rich young ruler. (Matt. 19:16, 20:16; Mark 10:17-31; Luke 18:18-30.)
Parable of Laborers in the Vineyard; Jesus predicts his death; rebukes the ambition of James and John. (Matt. 20:17-28; Mark 10:32-45; Luke 18:31-34.)
Heals two blind men at Jericho. (Matt. 20:29-34; Mark 10:46-52; Luke 18:35-43.)
Zachaeus converted; Parable of the Pounds. (Luke 19:1-28.)

While Je'sus was engaged in his Pe-re'an ministry, the home of his dear friends in Beth'a-ny was visited by the angel of death. Laz'a-rus was stricken with a fatal disease, and Ma'ry and Mar'tha, his sisters, sent messengers to tell Je'sus of the illness. They did this in the belief that their brother would not die if the Sav'ior were present. Laz'a-rus died before the messengers could make their report, and then two days passed before Je'sus began his journey to the home of his friends. He then said to his disciples, "Our friend Laz'a-rus sleepeth; but I go, that I may awake him out of sleep."

Two more days passed before Je'sus and the disciples reached Beth'a-ny, and they were told upon arrival that Laz'a-rus had been in his tomb for four days. Mar'tha went out to meet Je'sus, saying, "Lord, if thou hadst been here, our brother had not died." There was no complaint intended in these words, for Mar'tha knew that Laz'a-rus had died before word of his illness had reached Je'sus. Even though her brother had been buried for four days, she proved her faith in the Lord's wonder-working powers by saying, "Whatsoever thou wilt ask of God, God will give it thee."

When Je'sus replied, "Thy brother shall rise again," Mar'tha thought that he was referring to the final resurrection of the dead, and mournfully resigned herself to the thought that Laz'a-rus would not rise again until the last day. Then Je'sus added the words which have comforted the hearts of millions at the time of bereavement:

"I am the resurrection, and the life: he that believeth on me, though he were dead, yet shall he live: and whosover liveth and believeth on me shall never die."

These words so strengthened the faith of Mar'tha that she hastened to bring her sister the good news that the Master had come. After Ma'ry had expressed her faith and love, falling down at the feet of Je'sus in reverence, He tenderly asked, "Where have ye laid him?" When Je'sus wept on his way to the tomb of Laz'a-rus, some of the Jews who opposed him said, "Could not this man, who opened the eyes of the blind, have caused that even this man should not have died?"

Upon reaching the sepulchre where Laz'a-rus was buried, Je'sus commanded his disciples to roll away the stone. He did this to convince all unbelievers that Laz'a-rus was really dead, for no one could deny that the body had begun to decay. After a brief prayer of thanksgiving, the Sav'ior cried out in a loud voice, "Laza-rus, come forth." The gospel record describes the miracle which followed in these words: "He that was dead came forth, bound hand and foot with graveclothes: and his face was bound about with a napkin." Je'sus then said to his disciples, "Loose him from his graveclothes, and let him go."

The miracle led many to accept Je'sus as the Mes-si'ah, but some hardened unbelievers who were present told the Phar'i-sees what he had done. A meeting of the Jewish San'he-drin—composed of scribes, Phar'i-sees, Sad-du-cees, and chief priests—was held to plot the death of Je'sus. Ca'ia-phas, the acting High Priest, declared that "it would be expedient that one man die for the people." These words, though spoken only as a suggestion that an innocent life be sacrificed in order to avoid trouble with the Roman authorities, was a striking prophecy of the spiritual purpose involved in Christ's death for the nation and for the world.

Je'sus then withdrew to a place called E'phra-im, some distance north of Je-ru'sa-lem on the border of the desert, where he and his disciples remained for some days before going into Sa-ma'ri-a and Gal'i-lee. During this period of retirement Je'sus passed through certain parts of Sa-ma'-ri-a and of Gal'i-lee, and made a brief visit to Jer'i-cho. In one of the villages through which he passed, ten lepers cried out to him for mercy. He healed them all, directing them to show themselves to the priests in proof that they were cured, as required in the Mo-sa'ic law. Only one of them returned to give thanks to the Sav'ior, and he was a Sa-mar'i-tan. In reply to the question of certain Phar'i-sees, Je'sus explained the spiritual nature of his kingdom, uttering many warnings of the judgments of God against the worldly-minded.

This discourse was followed by the Parable of the Importunate Widow and the Inconsiderate Judge, a story in which the persistent pleas of a widow finally led an unworthy judge to grant her request. After drawing from this parable the lesson and duty of importunate prayer, he added the story of a Phar'i-see and a publican who both went up into the temple to pray. The Phar'i-see thanked the Lord that he was not guilty of the sins of other men, and boasted of his righteousness; while the publican humbly confessed his sins and pleaded for mercy. The Sav'ior no doubt astonished some of his listeners by declaring that the publican went down to his house justified, while the Phar'i-see did not.

Turning to the question of marriage problems, Je'sus explained that the only Scriptural grounds for divorce is that of unfaithfulness to the marriage vow. The Phar'i-sees who had sought to entrap him by questions on this subject were routed by his revealing answers.

Next in the Scripture record comes the beautiful incident in which Je'sus taught the lesson of humility. Taking little children into his arms and blessing them, he said:

"Suffer little children to come unto me, and forbid them not: for of such is the kingdom of heaven."

Somewhere in the course of these travels Je'sus was approached by a rich young ruler, who inquired, "What good thing shall I do that I may have eternal life?" Je'sus reminded him of the Commandments, and the young man replied that he had faithfully observed them from his youth. The Sav'ior

LAZARUS

then said, "Yet lackest thou one thing: sell all that thou hast, and distribute unto the poor, and thou shalt have treasure in heaven: and come,
follow me." This test was more than the young man could meet, so he
went away sorrowful. In the lesson which was drawn from this incident,
Je'sus pointed out the great obstacles which those who are rich must overcome in attaining the Christian life.

The requirement which Je'sus exacted of this young man was very
unusual: the only recorded instance where a man was asked to give up
all his earthly possessions in order to become a disciple of the Sav'ior.

The reason for such a demand was that riches were enslaving the young
man's soul; though otherwise he was living a good life. So upright was
his character that the point is made in the story that "Jesus beholding him
loved him." The blessed Sav'ior looked with the most profound affection
at this lovable, ingenuous, humble-minded supplicant; while at the same
time He asked him for the most complete evidence of sincerity and surrender in his quest for God.

Mournfully the Master reflects on the power of earthly wealth to blunt
spiritual perception, and to prevent men from entering into the kingdom
of God. For the encouragement of those who must overcome such obstacles He said, "What is impossible with man is possible in the province
of Divine Grace."

The Parable of the Laborers in the Vineyard was delivered as a rebuke
to those who practice religion from a selfish motive. Those who engage
in the Lord's work in the hope of personal gain will be disappointed on
the day of reckoning, as will also be those who think that salvation can
be bought by gifts of time or money.

Je'sus then took counsel with his apostles, and again spoke plainly to
them of his approaching death at the hands of the chief priests and rulers
of the Jewish nation. The mother of John and James, who did not fully
grasp the spiritual nature of the Sav'ior's kingdom, asked that her sons
be permitted to sit on either side of Je'sus in heaven. When Je'sus asked
if they were able to share the cup of woe and death which should be his,
they replied, "We are able." They little knew the meaning of what
Je'sus had said, but he told them that they should suffer martyrdom for his
cause. Je'sus then denounced any self-seeking spirit that might exist
among his followers, and placed before them his own example in these
words:

"Even as the Son of man came not to be ministered unto, but to minis-

LAZARUS RAISED FROM THE DEAD

ter, and to give his life a ransom for many."

In Jer'i-cho two blind men pleaded with Je'sus for mercy. The name of one of them is given as Bar-ti-mae'us, and special note is made of the type of his appeal, for he addressed Je'sus as "Thou Son of Da'vid." Another important incident which took place in Jer'i-cho was the conversion of Zac-chae'us, who was so short in stature that he had to climb into a tree to see Je'sus as he passed by. Je'sus invited him to come down, saying, "Today I must abide at thy house." In proof of his full surrender to the Lord, Zac-chae'us proposed to return fourfold to every man whom he had defrauded in any way, and to give one half of his property for

THE RICH YOUNG MAN WHO WENT AWAY SORROWFUL

the care of the poor. The comment of the Sav'ior was, "This day is salvation come to this house."

Moved by the fact that many of his followers would expect him to set up an earthly kingdom during the Pass'o-ver Feast, Je'sus spoke the Parable of the Pounds. This was the story of a nobleman who went into a far country to receive a kingdom, leaving his affairs in the hands of his servants. When the master returned to reckon with the servants, it was found that one of them had gained ten pounds with the one which had been left in his keeping, and that another servant had gained five pounds in the same way. These servants were rewarded for their faithfulness and industry, one receiving authority over ten cities, the other being entrusted with five cities. One servant, however, had done nothing to increase the pound which he had received. When he tried to excuse his idleness by saying that he had been afraid of offending his stern, exacting master, he was told that he might at least have gained interest on the money by placing it in a bank. He was then deprived of the pound, which was given to the most able servant.

SUGGESTIONS FOR STUDY
Biblical Index to Helpful References

Christ's Friendships. (Jno. 13:23; 15:15.)

Christ's Wisdom. (Isa. 11:2; Col. 2:3.)

Divine Delays. (Psm. 13:1; 40:17.)

Faith Tested by Delays. (Gen. 15:2-5; Acts 12:5-7.)

The Lord's Sympathy for the Sorrowing. (Isa. 63:9; Heb. 4:15.)

The Sin of Busy-Bodying. (1 Tim. 5:13.)

Evil Plottings Against the Righteous. (Psm. 36:4; 37:7; Prov. 6:14.)

Warnings Against Unthankfulness. (Deut. 32:6; Rom. 1:21; 2 Tim. 3:2.)

Spiritual Nature of Christ's Kingdom.

(Rom. 14:7; 1 Cor. 4:20.)

Warnings Against Unreadiness for Death. (Eccl. 9:12; Rev. 1:7.)

Continuous Prayer Enjoined. (1 Chr. 16:11; Eph. 6:18; 1 Thess. 5:17.)

Duty of Child-Likeness. (1 Cor. 14:20; 1 Pet. 2:2.)

Sin a Universal Curse. (Psm. 53:3; Isa. 53:6; 64:6; Rom. 3:23.)

The Perils of Riches. (Deut. 8:13, 14; Prov. 28:20; 1 Tim. 6:9.)

Great Gain Through Lesser Loss. (Matt. 19:20; Phil. 3:8.)

Questions

1. Why did Mary and Martha send for Jesus?

2. How long did Jesus delay before going to the home of Mary and Martha?

3. What did he say about the death of Lazarus?

4. How did Martha receive Jesus? Mary? What did Jesus say to Martha?

5. In what way did Jesus display his grief and sympathy?

6. Tell of the raising of Lazarus.

7. How many lepers did Jesus heal on the roadside? How many gave thanks?

8. Tell of Jesus' attitude toward children.

9. Tell the story of the rich young ruler and its lessons.

10. Relate the parables of this story and their lessons.

PARABLE OF THE TEN VIRGINS

STORY 166

CLOSING MINISTRY IN JERUSALEM—
PASSION WEEK TRIUMPHAL ENTRY
ON SUNDAY; EVENTS ON MONDAY

A Sabbath Day of rest at Bethany. (Jno. 11:55-12:1, 9-11.)
Sunday—Triumphal Entry of Jerusalem; Weeping over the City. (Matt. 21:1-11; Mark 11:1-10; Luke 19:29-44; Jno. 12:12-19.)
Return to Bethany. (Mark 11:11.)
Monday—Return to Jerusalem; blighting of the barren fig tree. (Matt. 21:18-22; Mark 11:12-14.)
Second Cleansing of the Temple. (Matt. 21:10-17; Mark 11:12-19; Luke 19:45-48.)
Greeks seek to know Jesus. (Jno. 12:20-50.)

On his return to Je-ru'sa-lem after the Pe-re'an ministry, Je'sus reached the little town of Beth'an-y on the Sab'bath previous to his crucifixion on Fri'day. Here he paused for a day of rest in the home of his friends Ma'ry, Mar'tha, and Laz'a-rus. All roads leading to Je-ru'sa-lem were crowded with pilgrims going up for the Feast of the Pass'o-ver, and the chief topic of conversation was the fame of Je'sus. The great question on the lips of thousands was, "Will he come up to the Pass'o-ver?" The Jew'ish rulers, meanwhile, gave orders for his arrest on sight.

The news that Je'sus was in Beth'an-y spread rapidly, and hundreds of people went there. Some came to see Je'sus alone, while others wished to look upon Laz'a-rus, who had been raised from the dead a few weeks before. So great was the excitement caused by the raising of Laz'a-rus that the enemies of Je'sus threatened to have him slain.

The week leading up to the cruel execution of Jesus was crowded with momentous events. Sun'day was marked by the Triumphal Entry into Je-ru'sa-lem, the weeping of the Sav'ior over the approaching doom of the city, and the return to Beth'an-y. Leaving Beth'an-y, Je'sus and the disciples journeyed to Beth'pha-ge, where he sent two of the disciples to secure the animal on which he later rode through the streets of the capital city.

Mon'day was notable for three dramatic events: the cursing of the barren fig tree, the second cleansing of the temple, and the introduction

CHRIST TAKING LEAVE OF MARY

The Raising of Jairus' Daughter *by Johann Friedrich Overbeck*
MUSEUM AT STUTTGART : GERMANY

Christ's Triumphal Entry into Jerusalem *by Bernhard Plockhorst*
SYRACUSE MUSEUM OF FINE ARTS : SYRACUSE, NEW YORK

Christ in the Garden of Gethsemane *by Heinrich Hofmann*
RIVERSIDE CHURCH : NEW YORK

Birth "For God So Loved The World That I

"Gave His Only Begotten Son"

Crucifixion

Frank M. Donough

Peter's Repentance *by Ary Scheffer*
METROPOLITAN MUSEUM OF ART : NEW YORK

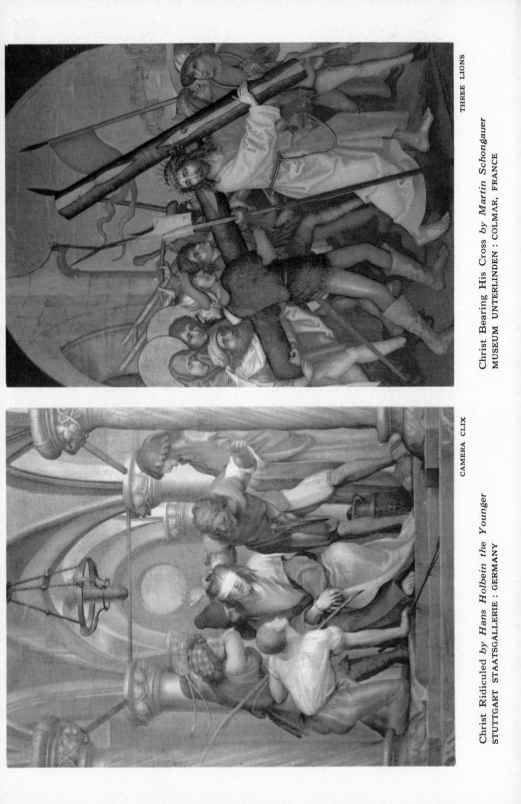

Christ Ridiculed *by Hans Holbein the Younger*
STUTTGART STAATSGALLERIE : GERMANY

Christ Bearing His Cross *by Martin Schongauer*
MUSEUM UNTERLINDEN : COLMAR, FRANCE

The Ascension *by Henrik Krock*
HELLIGAANDSHUSET CHURCH : COPENHAGEN

CAMERA CLIX

of certain Greeks. While on the way to Je-ru'sa-lem, Je'sus paused to gather fruit from a fig tree which was in full leafage. When he found that the tree was barren, he uttered a curse upon it. This was done, perhaps, as a symbol of the judgment of God upon the fruitlessness of the chief priests and rulers of the Jews.

Upon reaching the temple, Je'sus cleansed it for the second time in his ministry. The tables of the money-changers were overturned, and the traders who dealt in animals and doves for the temple sacrifices were driven out. Je'sus sternly denounced those who had profaned the temple, saying: "It is written, My house shall be called a house of prayer: but ye have made it a den of thieves."

The third event of the day took place when some Gentiles of Beth-sa'ida sought out their friends, Phil'ip and An'drew, saying, "We would see Jesus." When these two disciples brought their Greek friends to Je'sus, he was very happy, and said, "The hour is come that the Son of man should be glorified." Je'sus then likened himself to a grain of wheat, which must perish in the soil if a harvest of grain is to be reaped; and called the attention of his disciples to the sacrifices which would be required of them if they wished to honor God, and be honored by him.

SUGGESTIONS FOR STUDY

Biblical Index to Helpful References

Duty and Privilege of Christian Hospitality. (Rom. 12:1; Tit. 1:8; 1 Pet. 4:9.)

Cruel Hatreds for Jesus. (Lu. 6:11; 19:14; Jno. 15:18, 25.)

Palm Branches Used as Tokens of Triumphant Joy. (Lev. 23:40; Neh. 8:15.)

Jesus Proclaimed King. (Isa. 9:7; Jer. 23:5; Dan. 7:14.)

Humility of Christ's Appearance as King. (Zech. 9:9; Phil. 2:8.)

Popularity of Jesus. (Mk. 2:2; 3:10; 5:24; Lu. 5:1.)

Confounding of the Wicked. (Job 5:12; 12:17; Isa. 44:25; 45:16.)

God's Curse Against Unfruitfulness. (Isa. 5:1-7; Heb. 6:8.)

Magnetic Power of Jesus. (Songs 1:4; Hos. 11:4.)

Questions

1. Where did Jesus spend the Sabbath prior to his crucifixion?

2. Why did great multitudes throng the home of Mary, Martha and Lazarus?

3. Tell of the triumphal entry of Jesus into Jerusalem on Sunday.

4. Approaching the city for this entry, how did Jesus display his sympathy?

5. Why did Jesus blight a fig tree on the road?

6. What did Jesus on entering the temple?

7. Tell of certain Gentiles seeking an acquaintance with Jesus.

CHRIST'S TRIUMPHAL ENTRY INTO JERUSALEM

STORY 167

PASSION WEEK—EVENTS AND TEACHINGS ON TUESDAY
A DAY OF CONFLICTS AND TRIUMPHS

Returning to Jerusalem; observations over the blighted fig tree. (Matt. 21: 20-22; Mark 11:20-26.)

States authority for cleansing the temple. (Matt. 21:23-27; Mark 11:27-33; Luke 20:1-8.)

Parable of Two Sons. (Matt. 21:28-32.)

Parable of the Vineyard and Husbandmen. (Matt. 21:33-46; Luke 20:9-18.)

Parable of the Wedding Feast. (Matt. 22:1-14.)

Tribute to Caesar. (Matt. 22:15-22; Mark 12:13-17; Luke 20:19-26.)

Answers Sadducees concerning the Resurrection. (Matt. 22:23-33; Mark 12: 18-27; Luke 20:27-40.)

Answers lawyers question concerning the greatest Commandment. (Matt. 22: 34-40; Mark 12:28-34.)

Explains how he is both David's Son and David's Lord. (Matt. 22:41-46; Mark 12:35-37; Luke 20:41-44.)

Last public discourse in Temple; Arraignment of Pharisees. (Matt. 23:1-39; Mark 12:38-40; Luke 20:45-47.)

The Widow's offering; Olivet Discourses. (Mark 12:41-44; Luke 21:1-4.)

Future Disasters. (Matt. 24:1-28; Mark 13:1-23; Luke 21:5-26.)

Second Coming of Christ. (Matt. 24:27-51; Mark 13:24-37; Luke 21:27-36.)

Parable of the Ten Virgins. (Matt. 25:1-13.)

Parable of the Talents. (Matt. 25:14-30.)

The Last Great Judgment. (Matt. 25:31-42.)

Tues'day was a day of strenuous activity for the Sav'ior, not so much for the events which occurred, but because of his extensive teachings. On the way into the city he paused at the withered fig tree to make some observations on the subject of Faith. Upon entering the San'he-drin he was immediately questioned by members of the San'he-drin concerning his authority for cleansing the temple on the day before. In reply, Je'sus asked whether the ministry of John the Bap'tist was of God or of man. His enemies were baffled by this question: if they said, "Of God," they would have to admit the truth of John's testimony concerning Je'sus; if they said, "Of men," they would have angered the multitudes with whom John had been popular. His critics remained silent, and he declined to give any further answer.

Je'sus then delivered three parables which were evidently meant to apply to the religious leaders who had rejected him as the Mes-si'ah. The first was the story of a man who had two sons, who were asked to work in his vineyards. One son refused, but later obeyed; the other agreed to work, but then failed to keep his promise. Je'sus explained that the unworthy of Is'ra-el had led the people into conduct like that of the second son, while the first son was a symbol of those who had accepted his Mes-si-an'ic work.

The second parable dealt with a vineyard owner who placed his property in the hands of husbandmen. When the harvest season arrived, he sent his servants to receive the fruits of the vineyard, but the husbandmen abused the servants, refusing to give up the harvest. A second group of servants received the same ill treatment, and the owner's son, who was sent last of all, was slain by the wicked husbandmen. The meaning of this parable was perfectly clear to the enemies of Je'sus: the leaders of Is'ra-el had ill treated the servants of God under the law of Mo'ses and under the summons of the prophets, and were now plotting the murder of God's only begotten Son.

In the Parable of the Marriage Feast the kingdom of heaven was likened to a wedding banquet which had been scorned by the guests who were first invited. The ruler who gave the feast was forced to send out into the highways and by-paths of the world to find guests among the common people. When the banquet was ready, it was found that one of the guests had failed to provide himself with a wedding garment; this garment could have been had for the asking, so the thoughtless guest was cast forth into outer darkness. Again it was impossible for the Jew'ish leaders to miss the application of this story; they had scorned the Lord's invitation to the feast of salvation, and had failed to put on the garments of righteousness which are required in his kingdom.

The Phar'i-sees angrily sought to prevent the Lord from continuing his mission, but no man dared lay hands on him as yet. They united with the Her'od-i-ans, however, in a scheme to entrap him on the question of paying tribute to Cae'sar. With a Ro'man coin in hand, they asked Je'sus if it were lawful to pay tribute to Cae'sar; if he said, "Yes," they knew that the people would be enraged; while if he said, "No," they could accuse him of treason to Cae'sar. Je'sus then crushed their wicked plot by asking whose inscription was on the penny. When they were forced to admit that it was Cae'sar's, he said to them, "Render therefore unto Cae'sar the things which are Cae'sar's, and unto God the things which are God's."

The Sad'du-cees then joined in the concerted efforts of the religious leaders to ensnare Je'sus. They did not believe in the resurrection, so they asked Je'sus a very complicated question concerning a woman who was the widow of seven men. Their question was, "Whose wife will she be in the resurrection?" Je'sus then explained that in heaven all human relations are merged in the ties of one great spiritual household, and seized the opportunity for an instructive discourse on Immortality.

Je'sus then took the lead in his combat with the Phar'i-sees, asking them whose son they thought the Mes-si'ah to be. They were forced to answer, "The Son of Da'vid." Turning to one of the most striking of the Mes-si-an'ic Psalms, he explained how the Mes-si'ah is both the "Son of Da'vid" and "The Lord of Da'vid." In his earthly lineage he was a descendant of Da'vid, while in his Divine Sonship and redemptive grace he was the Lord of Da'vid.

The time had now come for his last public discourse in the temple. In these remarks he bitterly arraigned the Phar'i-sees for their hypocrisy, pronouncing upon them eight successive "woes." He charged them with laying heavy burdens upon the people without doing anything to help them; denounced them for oppressing widows and poor people while making long prayers, and for overlooking justice and mercy while giving scrupulous attention to tithing. For such sins he called them "whited sepulchers, full of uncleanness," and "A generation of vipers." Again he warned the nation of the calamities soon to descend upon Je-ru'sa-lem, and broadened his message to encompass the trials and troubles of future ages.

Before leaving the temple, Je'sus commented on the offerings being made by various people. The poor widow who cast two small coins into the treasury of the Lord's house was praised above those who had given great sums, for she had given "all her living."

On the way to Mount Ol'i-vet, Je'sus made a long address on a variety of subjects, including the destruction of Je-ru'sa-lem, the Second Coming of Christ, and the Final Judgment of Nations; these truths were illustrated by three of his most impressive parables. The first of the parables dealt with Ten Virgins who waited for the coming of the bridegroom; the five who brought an extra supply of oil in case of unexpected delay were called wise, while those who had neglected to take enough oil were called foolish. At midnight, when announcement was made that the bridegroom was coming, the Ten Virgins trimmed their lamps to go out to meet him. It was then that the foolish ones discovered their plight, and begged oil from those who had wisely brought an extra supply. This request could not be granted without endangering their own supply, so only the wise virgins went in to the marriage ceremony.

The second parable told of a man who went away on a journey, giving his servants a number of talents according to their several abilities, and instructing them to use them profitably until he returned. To one servant he gave five talents; to another, two; and to a third, one. The first two doubled their talents by industrious trading, and were highly praised when the master returned. The third servant, however, merely hid his talent in the earth, making no effort to use it for his master's profit; he was therefore denounced as a wicked and slothful servant.

In referring to the final judgment of all people and nations, Je'sus used the illustration of a shepherd separating the sheep from the goats. He reminded his hearers that in the last day those who believe shall be placed on his right hand, and welcomed to the everlasting abode of peace; while the unbelievers, who shall be placed on his left hand, shall be condemned to everlasting despair. He made it very clear that the final test of character will be determined on a basis of acts of mercy toward fallen members of the human race.

SUGGESTIONS FOR STUDY
Biblical Index to Helpful References

The Temple Appointed a Place of Worship. (Psm. 5:7; 138:2.)

Evil Men Put to Silence. (Psm. 63:11; 107:42.)

Unfaithful Servants in the Lord's Vineyard. (Isa. 56:10; Jer. 6:13-17; 12:10.)

Christ's Followers Required to Be Productive. (Phil. 1:11; Col. 1:10.)

Spiritual Feasts Prepared for Believers. (Isa. 25:6; Ezek. 34:14; Rev. 2:7, 17.)

God's Invitation to the Feast of Salvation. (Isa. 55:1; Ezek. 33:11.)

Rejectors of God's Call Cast Away. (Isa. 65:12; Jer. 7:13, 14; Hos. 9:17.)

Civic Duties to Be Faithfully Performed. (Rom. 13:1; Tit. 3:1; 1 Pet. 2:13, 14.)

Jesus the Son of David. (Rom. 1:3; 2 Tim. 2:8; Rev. 5:5.)

Foolish Questions to Be Avoided. (1 Tim. 1:14; 6:4; Tit. 3:9.)

Sacrificial Giving. (1 Ki. 17:13, 15; 2 Cor. 8:3, 4.)

Second Coming of Christ. (1 Thess. 5:2; Heb. 9:28.)

The Last Great Judgment. (Heb. 9:27; Jude 14, 15.)

Questions

1. For what was Tuesday of the Passion Week notable?

2. How did Jesus baffle the Pharisees when questioned about his authority?

3. Name and explain meaning of three parables spoken to Pharisees.

4. Give the answer of Jesus respecting tribute to Caesar.

5. Explain his answer to the Sadducees respecting the resurrection.

6. Tell of the arraignment of the Pharisees and Scribes.

7. Review the Olivet Discourse and explain the parables given.

8. What simile did Jesus use in describing the Last Great Judgment?

STORY 168

PASSION WEEK—EVENTS AND TEACHINGS ON WEDNESDAY AND THURSDAY ANOINTING BY MARY, THE PASSOVER AND THE LORD'S SUPPER

Wednesday
At Bethany; predicts his death in two days. (Matt. 26:1-5; Mark 14:1-2; Luke 22:1-2.)
Anointing by Mary in house of Simon. (Matt. 26:6-13; Mark 14:3-9; Jno. 12:2-8.)
Judas bargains with Sanhedrin. (Matt. 26:14-16; Mark 14:10-12; Luke 22:3-6.)

Thursday
Preparation for the Passover. (Matt. 26:17-19; Mark 14:12-16; Luke 22:7-13.)

Thursday night (Friday began at sunset)
Observes Passover with Disciples. (Matt. 26:20; Mark 14:17; Luke 24:16.)
Points out the traitor. (Matt. 26:21-25; Mark 14:18-21; Luke 22:21-23; Jno. 13:21-30.)
The Last Supper. (Matt. 26:26-29; Mark 14:22-25; Luke 22:17-20.)
Washes Disciple's Feet. (Luke 22:24-30; Jno. 13:1-17.)
Predicts Peter's Denial. (Matt. 26:33-35; Mark 14:29-31; Luke 22:31-34; Jno. 13:31-38.)
The Discourse in the Upper Room. (Jno. 14.)
The Discourse on the way to Gethsemane. (Jno. 15, 16.)
The Intercessory Prayer. (Jno. 17.)
In Gethsemane. (Matt. 26:36-45; Mark 14:32-42; Luke 22:39-46; Jno. 18:1.)
The Arrest of Jesus. (Matt. 26:47-56; Mark 14:43-52; Luke 22:47-53; Jno. 18:2-12.)
Before Annas and Caiaphas. (Matt. 26:57-68; Mark 14:53-65; Luke 22:54-71; Jno. 18:12-24.)
Peter's Denial. (Matt. 26:69-75; Mark 14:54, 66-72; Luke 22:54-62; Jno. 18:15-18.)
Judas' Remorse and Suicide. (Matt. 27:3-10.)

The events of that notable Tues'day, combined with the stirring teachings of the Sav'ior, increased the hatred of the rulers of the Jews toward him, and strengthened their determination to do away with him at the earliest possible moment. They plotted together, striving to find some way of taking him without causing a riot among the people. Meanwhile Je'sus withdrew to Beth'an-y, where he spent Wednes'day in retirement. He informed his disciples that within

THE LAST SUPPER

two days he would be given into the hands of his enemies, and crucified.

It was on Wednes'day evening that his friends in Beth'an-y invited him to a great supper in the house of Si'mon, a man whom the Lord had healed from leprosy. Mar'tha acted as hostess, Laz'a-rus was among the guests, and Ma'ry anointed the Sav'ior as he dined. The perfume which Ma'ry used in anointing him was very expensive, perhaps equal to a year's wages in any common employment. Ju'das complained that Ma'ry had been unduly extravagant, saying that the precious ointment should have been sold for the relief of the poor. He was not sincere in this suggestion, however; as treasurer of the little band, he no doubt wished to have the money placed in his greedy hands. Je'sus rebuked him for his fault-find ing, and declared that Ma'ry's gracious act would be remembered wher-ever his gospel should be spoken. The beauty of her loving deed fills the world today, and shall never be forgotten.

Ju'das made his first move for the betrayal of Je'sus on Wednes'day night. He went to the members of the San'he-drin, and agreed to betray Je'sus into their hands on the following night for thirty pieces of silver, which today would be worth less than seventeen dollars.

According to Jew'ish custom, Fri'day began at sunset on Thurs'day. The only notable event which belongs to Thurs'day, under this method of reckoning, was the preparation for the Pass'o-ver with his disciples. Je'sus sent Pe'ter and John to make ready for observing the Feast of the Pass'o-ver in the home of Ma'ry, the mother of John Mark.

The gathering of Je'sus and his apostles in the upper room was one of the most eventful moments of his entire life. First of all, he and the twelve apostles gathered around the table to observe the Pass'o-ver. While the sacred feast was in progress, Je'sus talked with them about his ap-proaching death, in which he should fulfill the spiritual meaning of the sacrifice made by his forefathers in E'gypt. Je'sus then declared that one of those present should betray him, and each of the disciples in turn solemnly asked, "Lord, is it I?" When he came to Ju'das he said, "Thou hast said," and bade him proceed at once with his plot.

Ju'das knew that the Sav'ior would retire to the Mount of Ol'ives later that night, and had already arranged with the San'he-drin to lead officers to a place where they might arrest his Master. Stunned by the news that Je'sus knew all about his plot, Ju'das hastened to report to the Jew'ish leaders for his part in the dreadful treachery of that night.

Je'sus then instituted the New Testament Pass'o-ver, commonly known

CHRIST IN GETHSEMANE

as The Lord's Supper. Taking bread which he had blessed, he broke it into enough pieces to serve the twelve apostles; as he gave a morsel of the consecrated bread to each of them he said, "Take, eat; this is my body." After this he took a cup filled with wine, blessed it, and said, "Drink all ye of it; for this is my blood of the new testament, which is shed for many for the remission of sins."

After the Supper was ended, Je'sus took a basin and some towels and washed the feet of his disciples. This act, usually performed by servants, was a symbol of the humility which should prevail among his followers.

Je'sus then told his disciples that, in addition to the treachery of Ju'das, the apostle Si'mon Pe'ter would deny him before sunrise. He explained to Pe'ter, however, that this testing would be a sifting by Sa'tan, and assured him that he had prayed for his faith to stand firm.

Before leaving the upper room for his retreat in the garden on the Mount of Ol'ives, Je'sus delivered that heart-touching discourse which begins with the words: "Let not your heart be troubled: ye believe in God, believe also in me." On his way to Geth-sem'a-ne he continued his intimate discourses with the disciples, stressing the promise of the coming of the Holy Spirit as the Comforter and Guide for his people.

It is impossible to give a satisfactory outline of these great discourses and the intercessory prayer which followed, for the Sav'ior was speaking with a fulness of power which no man can comprehend. The rich content of these passages can be understood only in part, and then only by those who are guided by the Holy Spirit. Let all devout readers, therefore, read over and over again the 14-17th chapters of John.

It must have been far into the night when Je'sus and his apostles reached the Gar'den of Ol'ives, which was later called Geth-sem'a-ne. Here Je'sus left eight of the apostles, taking only Pe'ter, James, and John into the secluded spot in which he prayed. The agonies which he suffered there—so great that he shed drops of blood—can be explained neither by the fear of death nor by the shame of crucifixion, but only by the weight of the sins of a guilty world. Three times he cried, "Father, if it be possible, let this cup pass from me; nevertheless, not as I will, but as thou wilt." Following each of these prayers he found the three most beloved disciples sleeping, and sorrowfully reproached them.

Soon the silence of that holy hour was broken by the tramping feet of the Ro'man soldiers who had been sent to help the Jew'ish authorities

CHRIST TAKEN CAPTIVE

in capturing their hated rival. The traitor betrayed his Lord with a kiss—not as the sign of true affection, but as a signal for the Sav'ior's arrest. Pe'ter drew a sword in a vain effort to protect his Master, and cut off the ear of a servant of the High Priest. Je'sus rebuked him for this deed, saying, "Put up thy sword; for all they that take the sword shall perish with the sword." He then healed the wound, declaring that he could have twelve legions of angels sent to his aid by praying to the Father. He asked for no help, however, and yielded to the officers without making any resistance.

Je'sus was first taken to the home of An'nas, a former High Priest who was still influential among the Jew'ish rulers. To the questions of An'nas the Sav'ior meekly replied, "Ask them who have heard me what I have taught them"; and, when brutally struck by an attendant, "If I have spoken evil, bear witness of the evil; but if well, why smitest thou me?"

After the mock examination by An'nas, Je'sus was led away to Ca'ia-phas, the acting High Priest, and was forced to undergo a mock trial before the Jew'ish San'he-drin. Two false witnesses testified that Je'sus had boasted that he could restore the temple within three days, should it be destroyed. The Sav'ior heard this charge of blasphemy in silence, and was then asked by the High Priest, "Art thou the Christ?" Admitting that he was the Mes-si'ah, Je'sus added, "Nevertheless I say unto you, Here-after shall ye see the Son of man sitting on the right hand of power, and coming in the clouds of heaven." These exalted words filled the High Priest with such rage that he rent his garments as a sign that he had heard blasphemy, and at once declared Je'sus worthy of death.

The examination of Je'sus at the midnight hour before An'nas, and the mock trial before Ca'ia-phas during the early hours of Friday, all demon-strate that they were merely a formal procedure to cover a foregone con-clusion and a sentence already framed by the intriguing and unscrupulous rulers of Je-ru'sa-lem.

The insincere questions asked, the unlawful smiting of an uncondemned prisoner, and the impunity with which Je'sus was condemned under the testimony of false witnesses, all show that these officers were acting as tools of the "prince of this world" in securing the death of the Son of God.

Meanwhile the disciples had scattered, only two of them daring to fol-low the Master in his trials before An'nas and Ca'ia-phas. While the Sav'ior was being insulted in the court of the San'he-drin, Pe'ter had been

CHRIST REJECTED

admitted to the courtyard. Here he was accused of being a disciple of Je'sus, first by the maid who opened the gate for him, then by some of the spectators who saw him warming himself by the fire in the courtyard, and finally by one of the servants who had been present when Je'sus was arrested. Each time Pe'ter vigorously denied that he was a disciple, and added to his shame by swearing that he did not even know Je'sus. The Master had previously warned him that he would deny Him three times before the crowing of the cock at dawn; immediately after the third denial the cock crew, and to this sign was added the kindly, yet reproachful look of the Master. Realizing how completely he had broken his faith, Pe'ter wept bitterly over his shameful conduct.

In the course of these events Ju'das was overwhelmed with remorse for his betrayal of innocent blood; returning to the Jew'ish rulers to confess his great wrong, he cast at their feet the thirty pieces of silver which had been the price of his treachery. Then, conscience stricken and in despair, he went out and hanged himself.

SUGGESTIONS FOR STUDY

Biblical Index to Helpful References

Christ's Predictions Concerning His Death. (Mark 8:31; Lu. 9:22; 12:50; 22:37; Jno. 3:14.)

Ministry of Good Women. (2 Ki. 4:10; Rom. 16:1, 2.)

Warnings Against Murmurings. (1 Cor. 10:10; Phil. 2:14.)

Warnings Against Misjudgment. (Rom. 14:13; 1 Cor. 4:5.)

The Everlasting Monument of Good Deeds. (Psm. 112:6; Prov. 10:7; 2 Tim. 1:5.)

Avaricious Traffic in Human Rights. (Gen. 37:28; 39:1; Joel 3:3; Amos 2:6.)

Betraying Innocent Men. (Jgs. 16:18; Psm. 41:9; 55:12-13; Mic. 7:6.)

Directions for Observing the Lord's Supper. (1 Cor. 11:18-34.)

The Danger of Over Self-Confidence. (Prov. 28:26; 1 Cor. 10:12.)

Christ our Mediator. (Isa. 59:16; 1 Tim. 2:5; Heb. 8:6; 9:15, 24; 12:24.)

The Intercession of Christ. (Isa. 53:12; Rom. 8:34; Heb. 7:25.)

The Indwelling Christ. (Gal. 2:20; Col. 1:27; Rev. 3:20.)

The Coming of the Holy Spirit. (Joel 2: 28; Acts 1:8.)

Believers Inseparable from Christ. (Rom. 8:38, 39.)

Jesus a Man of Sorrows. (Isa. 53:3.)

Questions

1. Describe the events of Wednesday in Jerusalem and in life of Jesus.

2. Who prepared a feast for Jesus on Wednesday night?

3. What notable incident took place at this feast?

4. For what purpose did Jesus and His apostles gather on Thursday night?

5. Who was pointed as the betrayer? What did he then do?

6. Following the Passover Feast, what institution did Jesus set up?

7. What warning did Jesus give to Peter?

8. Tell of the discourse given after the Supper? On way to Gethsemane. What took place in Gethsemane?

9. Tell of the arrest of Jesus. His mock trials before Annas. Before Caiaphas.

10. Tell of the denial of Peter. What became of Judas?

CHRIST BEFORE PILATE

STORY 169

THE ROMAN TRIAL; THE CRUCIFIXION OF THE SAVIOR

Jesus before Pilate. (Matt. 27:2, 11-18; Mark 15:1-14; Luke 23:1-5; Jno. 18:28-38.)

Jesus sent to Herod Antipas. (Luke 23:5-17.)

Barabas released; Jesus mocked. (Matt. 27:15-30; Mark 15:6-19; Luke 23: 13-25; Jno. 18:38-19-15.)

The march to the Cross. (Matt. 27:31-32; Mark 15:20-22; Luke 23:26-32; Jno. 19:17.)

The Crucifixion. (Matt. 27:33-35; 39-43; Mark 15:22-32; Luke 23:33-37; Jno. 19:17-25.)

The penitent Thief. (Luke 23:39-43.)

Death of Jesus. (Matt. 27:45-56; Mark 15:33-41; Luke 23:44-49; Jno. 19: 28-37.)

Burial of Jesus. (Matt. 27:57-66; Mark 15:42-47; Luke 23:50-56; Jno. 19: 38-42.)

The Jew'ish rulers were not permitted to inflict the death penalty, even for crimes against their religious laws, so it was necessary for them to make some political charge which would convince the Ro'man governor that Je'sus should be put to death. Early in the morning hours of Fri'day, Je'sus was brought before Pon'ti-us Pi'late, the Ro'man governor, and accused of undertaking to set up a Jew'ish kingdom in opposition to the rule of Cae'sar. When Pi'late heard the charge he asked Je'sus, "Art thou King of the Jews?" In his reply Je'sus explained the spiritual nature of his kingdom, and Pi'late, though he could not grasp the full meaning of the Sav'ior's work or personality, was convinced that Je'sus was not guilty of stirring up a political revolution. He frankly told the accusers that he "found no fault in him," but the people thronged the courtyard of the royal palace shouting, "Crucify him! Crucify him! We have no king but Cae'sar."

Still hoping to save Je'sus from the fury of his enemies, Pi'late offered to release a prisoner, for this was the custom at the annual Pass'o-ver. He placed before the people Bar-ab'bas and Je'sus, thinking that they would choose the gentle Naz'a-rene instead of a notorious criminal; but the people demanded that Bar-ab'bas be released, and that Je'sus be crucified. In an effort to avoid responsibility for the death of an innocent man, Pi'late sent Je'sus for examination before Her'od An'ti-pas, the ruler of

ECCE HOMO (BEHOLD THE MAN!)

Gal'i-lee and Syr'i-a. The wicked, superstitious king, who well knew the mighty works of the Son of God, refused to take any part in the proceedings.

As a final effort to appease the Jew'ish authorities, Pi'late delivered Je'sus to the soldiers for cruel scourging and mockery. They dressed him in the purple robes of a king, put a crown of thorns upon his head, and tormented him with blows and scornful salutations Pi'late then presented Je'sus before the people, hoping that they would be moved to mercy by the sad spectacle, but they insisted that he be crucified. When the Ro'man governor urged Je'sus to defend himself against the accusation of the Jews, saying, "I have power to release you, or to crucify you," Je'sus told him that his power to crucify or release was "given from above"; that he was an instrument for the working out of God's purpose in his death for the sins of the world.

After passing the sentence of death upon the Sav'ior, Pi'late turned him over to a group of Ro'man soldiers for crucifixion.

Bearing the cross upon which he was to die, Je'sus was led to the hill of Gol'go-tha, just outside the walls of the city. When he fell beneath the weight of the cross, they compelled Si'mon of Cy-re'ne, who later became a disciple, to bear it for him. Upon reaching the place of execution, Je'sus was nailed to the cross by his hands and feet, and the inscription: "This is Je'sus, the King of the Jews," written in He'brew, Greek, and Latin, was placed over his head. On either side of Christ were crucified two criminals, fulfilling the prophecy, "In his death he shall be numbered among transgressors."

As Je'sus hung on the cross in bitter agony, many of the onlookers taunted him, saying, "He saved others, himself he cannot save." Others said in ridicule, "If thou be the Christ, come down from the cross." Even the thieves who were crucified with him joined in these taunts, until one of them, realizing the innocence and power of the Sav'ior, cried to him for mercy. Some of those who had gathered around the cross, however, were loyal friends, Ma'ry, his mother, was there; Ma'ry Mag-da-le'ne and other devout women, as well as some of the apostles, were also present.

Even in the throes of death Je'sus was mindful of those for whom he was suffering. To his mother he said, "Woman, behold thy son!" The reference here was to the beloved disciple John, for to John he said, "Behold thy mother." To the penitent thief who cried to him for mercy he said, "Today shalt thou be with me in paradise." Speaking of those

CHRIST LEAVING THE PRAETORIUM

who were responsible for his cruel death, he prayed, "Father, forgive them; for they know not what they do."

In the agony of his sufferings Je'sus cried, "I thirst," and some of the soldiers gave him vinegar on a sponge. As the clouds of darkness caused by the weight of the sins of the entire world enshrouded the suffering Son of God, he cried out in anguish, "My God, my God, why hast thou forsaken me?" Then, as he triumphed over the powers of sin and darkness, he proclaimed his victory in the simple words, "It is finished." In final token of his sacrifice for the sins of the world, he prayed, "Father, into thy hands I commend my spirit."

When it was known that Je'sus was dead, Jo'seph of Ar-i-ma-thae'a, a wealthy man who had been a secret disciple, asked Pi'late for permission to bury the body of the Sav'ior in his own new tomb. Joined by Nic'o-de-mus, who brought spices for this purpose, they prepared the body for burial. The chief priests and Phar'i-sees, recalling the reports that Je'sus had said that he would arise on the third day, asked the Ro'man authorities to place guards at the tomb; other wise they feared that the disciples would steal the body and declare that he had risen. As a further precaution, the heavy stone which was placed at the mouth of the sepulchre was sealed with the official Ro'man seal.

SUGGESTIONS FOR STUDY

Biblical Index to Helpful References

The Awful Judgment Against False Witnesses. (Prov. 19:9; 24:28; 25:18.)

The Blamelessness of Christ. (Psm. 45:7; Jer. 23:5; Rev. 19:11.)

Innocent Sufferings of Christ. (Isa. 50:6; 53:3, 5; Heb. 2:10; 13:12; 1 Pet. 3:18.)

Reproaches Endured by Christ. (Psm. 69: 19-21.)

Deserted by Friends and Kinsmen. (Psm. 38:11, 12.)

Numbered Among Transgressors in His Death. (Isa. 53:12.)

Mocked by Spectators. (Psm. 22:7; 109: 25.)

Christ's Solitariness in Death. (Psm. 22:1; Heb. 5:7, 8.)

Commitment of His Soul to the Father. (Psm. 31:1-5.)

Buried with the Rich. (Isa. 53:9.)

Questions

1. Why was it necessary to secure the judgment of Pilate against Jesus?

2. What question did Pilate ask Jesus? What was the reply of Jesus?

3. Did Pilate find any fault in Jesus?

4. Tell of his efforts to secure his release. Could he have released him?

5. Tell of the scourgings and mockings of Jesus by the soldiers.

6. What was the final and determining charge of the Pharisees and elders?

7. Tell of the journey to the place of crucifixion.

8. Repeat in their proper order the seven sayings of Christ on the cross.

9. What miraculous events took place during his hours on the cross?

10. By whom was Jesus buried?

BEARING THE CROSS

STORY 170

THE RESURRECTION OF JESUS, HIS APPEARANCES, THE ASCENSION

A group of women visit the tomb. (Matt. 28:1-10; Mark 16:1-11; Luke 24:1-12; John 20:1-18.)
  The false report of the guards. (Matt. 28:11-15.)
  Appearance to two disciples on the road to Emmaus. (Mark 16:12-13; Luke 24:13-35.)
  Appearance on Sunday evening. (Mark 16:14; Luke 24:36-49; Jno. 20:19-23.)
  Appearance on second Sunday evening. (John 20:24-31.)
  Appearance to seven apostles at Sea of Galilee. (Jno. 21:1-14.)
  Peter's full restoration. (Jno. 21:15-21.)
  Appearance on mountain in Galilee. (Matt. 28:16-18.)
  The Great Commission. (Matt. 28:19-20; Mark 16:15-18; Acts 1:4-8.)
  The Ascension. (Mark 16:19-20; Luke 24:50-51; Acts 1:9-11.)

The body of Je'sus was taken down from the cross and placed in the tomb on Fri'day afternoon. The Jew'ish Sab'bath, which began at sunset on Fri'day and continued to sunset on Sat'ur-day, was a dark and hopeless period for his followers. Forgetting his promise to rise again on the third day, they gave up all hope when he perished on the cross. All day long their hearts turned to the sacred tomb where Ro'man guards kept watch over the body of their master. They gathered in small groups to discuss the tragedy, fearing that they, too, might be hunted down and slain.

Meanwhile a group of devout women, including Ma'ry Mag-da-le'ne, Ma'ry the mother of James, and Sa-lo'me, prepared mixed gums and fragrant spices which they meant to place in the wrappings about his body when the Sab'bath had passed. Early on Sun'day morning, just as the sun was breaking over the eastern hills of Pal'es-tine, they moved quietly to the little garden where tender hands had laid to rest the body of their blessed Master. They did not know that already angels had rolled away the great stone which sealed the tomb, and that the Sav'ior had risen. The Ro'man guards had been so terrified by the appearance of the angels that they fled into the city, where they were bribed to say that the disciples of Je'sus had overpowered them and stolen the body. Many people believed the false report, but soon the truth would be revealed to all.

THE CRUCIFIXION

Upon reaching the tomb, the women were startled to find the stone rolled away, and to see a young man clothed in a white robe sitting upon the stone. As they gazed in wonder at the empty tomb, the angel said, "Be not amazed, for Je'sus of Naz'a-reth, who was crucified and whom ye seek, has risen; he is not here, come see the place where they laid him." He then told them to carry the glorious news to the disciples, saying that the risen Lord would meet them in Gal'i-lee.

When the disciples heard the news, Pe'ter started toward the garden to see for himself, and was soon followed by John. Eagerly they ran over the road; John, being younger, reached the open tomb first. Overwhelmed at the sight which met his eyes, he stood in bewilderment; Pe'ter, however, rushed down into the tomb, where he saw the graveclothes folded and laid aside.

Ma'ry Mag-da-le'ne went to visit the tomb again, longing for a better understanding of the angelic message. This time she was met by two angels, who said to her, "Why do you weep?" She replied, "Because they have taken away my Lord, and I do not know where they have laid him." Then, turning her eyes from the tomb, she saw a stranger standing nearby. He also said to her, "Why do you weep? Whom do you seek?"

Thinking that the man who spoke to her might be the keeper of the garden, Ma'ry said to him, "Sir, if you have removed the body of my Lord, tell me where you have laid him, and I will take him away." Then the stranger tenderly said, "Ma'ry," and she cried out in joy, "Most excellent Master!" Je'sus said, "Do not touch me now, for I must first appear before my Father in heaven; but go to my disciples and tell them that I ascend to my Father and to their Father, and that I will return to see them."

As the other women went in search of the disciples, Je'sus suddenly stood before them, saying, "A joyous welcome to all of you!" He then commissioned them, as he had Ma'ry Mag-da-le'ne, to tell the disciples that he would meet them in Gal'i-lee.

Sometime later in the day Je'sus appeared to Pe'ter, but the words which passed between them were so sacred that no record of them has been preserved. No doubt the Sav'ior pardoned him for the shameful denial in the courtyard of Ca'ia-phas, for Pe'ter was deeply repentant.

Late that evening two of the disciples were walking along the road to Em'ma-us, a village about seven miles from Je-ru'sa-lem. They were discussing the various reports of what had happened during the past few

CHRIST BEING BORNE TO THE TOMB

days, when suddenly they were overtaken by one whom they thought was a stranger. He asked the reason for their sadness, and the disciple whose name was Cle′o-pas answered, "Even though you are a stranger in Je-ru′sa-lem, you ought to know the things which have happened there in recent days."

When asked what things he had in mind, Cle′o-pas said, "All the things concerning Je′sus of Naz′a-reth, a prophet mighty in word and in deed in the sight of God and all the people; but the chief priests and our rulers handed him over to the Ro′man authorities to be condemned to death, and they crucified him; and we had hoped that it should be he who should redeem our people Is′ra-el." The disciples went on to tell the stranger that some women had reported that the tomb was empty, and that angels had told them that he was alive.

Then the stranger spoke to them at length, asking why they were so slow to understand the teachings of the prophets concerning the promised Mes-si′ah, and telling them that they should know that it was necessary for Christ to suffer, and to die, and to rise again on the third day. "And beginning at Mo′ses and all the prophets, he interpreted to them in all the Scriptures the things concerning himself."

Upon reaching their destination, the two men urged their unknown companion to be their guest at dinner. As they partook of the meal there was something in the stranger's manner which opened their eyes to the fact that he was their Master. Then, to their great dismay, he suddenly vanished; and they said to one another, "Did not our heart burn within us, while he talked with us by the way, and while he opened to us the scriptures?" They hurried back to Je-ru′sa-lem to tell the disciples that they had seen the risen Lord.

On the night of that glorious first Eas′ter Sun′day a group of the disciples, including ten of the apostles, gathered to discuss the various happenings of the day. It was at this meeting that Si′mon Pe′ter reported seeing the risen Lord, and that the two disciples described how the Lord had appeared to them on the road to Em′ma-us. Thom′as, because of his doubting state of mind, was not present.

While the happy, yet wondering disciples were talking together, Je′sus suddenly appeared among them, saying, "Peace be with you." The disciples looked upon the scars in his hands and side, and were convinced that the Lord was really with them. They were told that they should presently go to all the nations with the gospel of repentance and the remission of

THE FIRST EASTER DAWN

sins, but that they should tarry in Je-ru'sa-lem until clothed with power from on high.

Just one week later he appeared to the disciples again, and this time Thom'as was present. He spoke to the doubting disciple with tender assurance, inviting him to thrust his hands into the scar in his side in proof that the One who was crucified was now alive again. Thom'as was convinced without this proof, and gladly confessed his renewed faith and love. Once more Je'sus commissioned his followers to preach the gospel to all the world, this time adding the significant words, "As the Father hath sent me into the world, even so send I you."

Sometime later Je'sus appeared to seven of the apostles on the shore of the Sea of Gal'i-lee. Pe'ter, Thom'as, Na-than'a-el, James and John, and two unnamed disciples had set out at Pe'ter's suggestion, on a fishing trip. All night they had toiled without taking any fish, and were greatly discouraged. Through the morning light they saw a man whom they did not recognize standing on the distant shore. He told them to cast their net on the right side of the boat for a draught of fishes, and to their amazement the net was soon full. It was then that the keen eye of John recognized the man on the shore as Je'sus, and that Pe'ter impetuously swam to shore to greet the Sav'ior. The other disciples rowed the boat to a safe landing, drawing with them the net with its great haul of fish. It was found that one hundred and fifty-three fish had been taken, yet the net was not broken.

After the disciples had enjoyed a meal with their Master, Je'sus engaged the apostle Pe'ter in a tender conversation. Three times he asked, "Pe'ter, lovest thou me?" Three times Pe'ter answered, "Yea, Lord; Thou knowest that I love thee," and each time Je'sus gave the solemn charge, "Feed my sheep; feed my lambs." There followed other words in which Je'sus seemed to foretell the probable martyrdom of Pe'ter, and to express great love for John. When Pe'ter asked concerning John, "Lord, what shall this man do?" Je'sus replied, "If I will that he tarry till I come, what is that to thee? Follow thou me."

On another occasion Je'sus appeared to his followers, apparently by appointment, on a mountain in Gal'i-lee. More than five thousand people gathered to hear his special instructions concerning the future work of his kingdom. Speaking to the great multitude, which included the eleven surviving disciples, Je'sus said: "All authority is given unto me in heaven and in earth. Go ye, therefore, into all the world and preach the gospel

THE ASCENSION

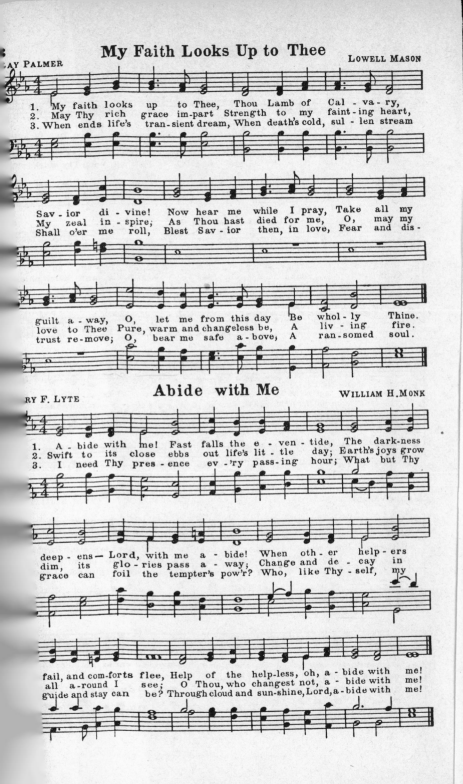

My Faith Looks Up to Thee

RAY PALMER   LOWELL MASON

1. My faith looks up to Thee, Thou Lamb of Cal - va - ry,
2. May Thy rich grace im - part Strength to my faint - ing heart,
3. When ends life's tran - sient dream, When death's cold, sul - len stream

Sav - ior di - vine! Now hear me while I pray, Take all my
My zeal in - spire; As Thou hast died for me, O, may my
Shall o'er me roll, Blest Sav - ior then, in love, Fear and dis -

guilt a - way, O, let me from this day Be whol - ly Thine.
love to Thee Pure, warm and change - less be, A liv - ing fire.
trust re - move; O, bear me safe a - bove, A ran - somed soul.

Abide with Me

HENRY F. LYTE   WILLIAM H. MONK

1. A - bide with me! Fast falls the e - ven - tide, The dark - ness
2. Swift to its close ebbs out life's lit - tle day; Earth's joys grow
3. I need Thy pres - ence ev - 'ry pass - ing hour; What but Thy

deep - ens — Lord, with me a - bide! When oth - er help - ers
dim, its glo - ries pass a - way; Change and de - cay in
grace can foil the tempt - er's pow'r? Who, like Thy - self, my

fail, and com - forts flee, Help of the help - less, oh, a - bide with me!
all a - round I see; O Thou, who chang - est not, a - bide with me!
guide and stay can be? Through cloud and sun - shine, Lord, a - bide with me!

to every creature, baptizing them in the name of the Father and of the Son and of the Holy Spirit; teaching them to observe all things whatsoever I have commanded you: and, behold, I am with you always, even unto the end of the age."

Je'sus also appeared to his half-brother James at some unspecified time prior to the ascension, but no details are given. James had not believed that Je'sus was the Mes-si'ah until the crucifixion, but he later became an ardent disciple and an able leader of the church in Je-ru'sa-lem.

The tenth and last appearance of Je'sus on earth took place forty days after the resurrection. Appearing to the eleven apostles, probably in Je-ru'sa-lem, he led them over the Mount of Ol'ives to a place near Beth'-an-y. Here he commissioned them to preach his gospel to the uttermost parts of the world, saying: "Tarry ye in Je-ru'sa-lem until ye shall be endued with power from on high. Then ye shall be my witnesses in Je-ru'sa-lem, in all Ju-de'a, in Sa-ma'ri-a, and to the uttermost parts of the world." Lifting up his hands to bless them, he began to rise into the air, and was gradually lost to their sight in the clouds of heaven.

SUGGESTIONS FOR STUDY

Biblical Index to Helpful References

Examples of True Constancy. (Ruth 1:16; 1 Sam. 20:17; Rom. 16:4; 2 Tim. 1:16.)

Reason for the Fear of the Keepers. (Isa. 2:19; 24:17; Heb. 10:27.)

Lying Devices and Bribery. (Prov. 17:23; Isa. 5:23.)

Resurrection of Christ Fundamental to His work of Redemption. (Acts 2:23, 24; 10:39-41; Rom. 4:25; 1 Cor. 15:4, 17.)

Resurrection of Christ a Guarantee of Our Resurrection. (1 Thess. 4:14; 2 Tim. 2:8; 1 Pet. 1:3; 3:18.)

Questions

1. How did the disciples spend the Sabbath after the crucifixion of Jesus?

2. Who were the first to visit the tomb of the third day?

3. What did they find? What did the angels tell them?

4. What had happened to the Roman Guards? What false report did they make?

5. Who was the first to see the risen Savior?

6. How many appearances did he make of that first Easter Day? Name them in their proper order.

7. Describe the appearances to the two disciples. To the gathered group.

8. When, where, and under what circumstances was his next appearance?

9. Tell of his appearance to seven fishermen. Of the conversation with Peter.

10. How many were present at his appearance on a mountain in Galilee?

11. To whom did he next appear?

12. Tell of his last appearance and commission to the apostles.

13. What promise was given by the angel as he ascended?

A COLLECTION OF
APPROPRIATE SONGS FOR HOME USE

Since "Beautiful Bible Stories" is a book for extensive use in the home, as well as general Bible study, this collection of popular and much-loved songs has been added as a supplement. You will find here the hymns and songs that have been sung in the church and in the home for generations, each one of them deeply spiritual and with divine messages of love, encouragement, and strength for every member of the family.

Gathered about the organ, as in the days of old, or assembled before the family altar, these songs will be sung with joy and spiritual exhilaration.

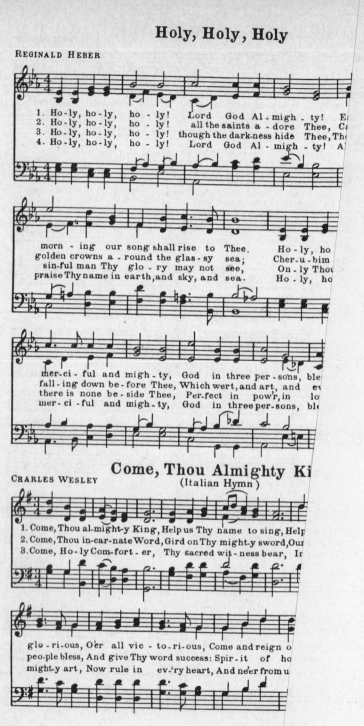

Holy, Holy, Holy

REGINALD HEBER

1. Ho-ly, ho-ly, ho-ly! Lord God Al-migh-ty! E
2. Ho-ly, ho-ly, ho-ly! all the saints a-dore Thee, Ca
3. Ho-ly, ho-ly, ho-ly! though the dark-ness hide Thee, The
4. Ho-ly, ho-ly, ho-ly! Lord God Al-migh-ty! A

morn - ing our song shall rise to Thee.   Ho-ly, ho
golden crowns a-round the glas-sy sea;   Cher-u-bim
sin-ful man Thy glo-ry may not see,   On-ly Thou
praise Thy name in earth, and sky, and sea.   Ho-ly, ho

mer-ci-ful and migh-ty, God in three per-sons, ble
fall-ing down be-fore Thee, Which wert, and art, and ev
there is none be-side Thee, Per-fect in pow'r, in lo
mer-ci-ful and migh-ty, God in three per-sons, ble

Come, Thou Almighty King
(Italian Hymn)

CHARLES WESLEY

1. Come, Thou al-might-y King, Help us Thy name to sing, Help
2. Come, Thou in-car-nate Word, Gird on Thy might-y sword, Our
3. Come, Ho-ly Com-fort-er, Thy sacred wit-ness bear, In

glo-ri-ous, O'er all vic-to-ri-ous, Come and reign o
peo-ple bless, And give Thy word success: Spir-it of ho
might-y art, Now rule in ev'ry heart, And ne'er from u

I Need Thee Every Hour

ANNIE S. HAWKS

ROBERT LOWRY

1. I need Thee ev-'ry hour, Most gra-cious Lord; No ten-der voice like
2. I need Thee ev-'ry hour, Stay Thou near by; Temp-ta-tions lose their
3. I need Thee ev-'ry hour, In joy or pain; Come quick-ly and a-
4. I need Thee ev-'ry hour, Most Ho-ly One; O make me Thine in-

CHORUS

Thine Can peace af-ford.
pow'r When Thou art nigh. I need Thee, O I need Thee; Ev-'ry hour I
bide, Or life is vain.
deed, Thou bless-ed Son!

need Thee; O bless me now, my Sav-ior, I come to Thee! A-men.

Blest Be the Tie That Binds

JOHN FAWCETT

HANS G. NAGELI

1. Blest be the tie that binds Our hearts in Christ-ian love;
2. Be-fore our Fa-ther's throne, We pour our ar-dent pray'rs;
3. We share our mu-tual woes, Our mu-tual bur-dens bear;
4. When we a-sun-der part, It gives us in-ward pain;

The fel-low-ship of kin-dred minds Is like to that a-bove.
Our fears, our hopes, our aims are one, Our com-forts and our cares.
And oft-en for each oth-er flows The sym-pa-thiz-ing tear.
But we shall still be joined in heart, And hope to meet a-gain.

I Love to Tell the Story

Katherine Hankey

Wm. G. Fischer

1. I love to tell the sto - ry; Of un - seen things a - bove, Of Je - sus and His glo - ry, Of Je - sus and His love. I love to tell the sto - ry, Be - cause I know 'tis true; It sat - is - fies my long - ings As noth - ing else can do.

2. I love to tell the sto - ry; More won - der - ful it seems Than all the gold - en fan - cies Of all our gold - en dreams. I love to tell the sto - ry, It did so much for me; And that is just the rea - son I tell it now to thee.

3. I love to tell the sto - ry; 'Tis pleas - ant to re - peat What seems, each time I tell it, More won - der - ful - ly sweet. I love to tell the sto - ry, For some have nev - er heard The mes - sage of sal - va - tion From God's own Ho - ly Word.

4. I love to tell the sto - ry; For those who know it best Seem hun - ger - ing and thirst - ing To hear it, like the rest. And when, in scenes of glo - ry, I sing the new, new song, 'Twill be the old, old sto - ry That I have loved so long.

CHORUS

I love to tell the sto - ry, 'Twill be my theme in glo - ry, To tell the old, old sto - ry Of Je - sus and His love.

Safe in the Arms of Jesus

FANNY J. CROSBY

WILLIAM H. DOANE

1. Safe in the arms of Je - sus, Safe on His gen-tle breast, There by His
2. Safe in the arms of Je - sus, Safe from cor-rod-ing care, Safe from the
3. Je - sus, my heart's dear ref - uge, Je - sus has died for me; Firm on the

love o'er-shad - ed, Sweet-ly my soul shall rest. Hark!'tis the voice of
world's temp-ta - tions, Sin can-not harm me there. Free from the blight of
Rock of A - ges, Ev - er my trust shall be. Here let me wait with

an - gels, Borne in a song to me, O - ver the fields of glo - ry,
sor - row, Free from my doubts and fears; On - ly a few more tri - als,
pa - tience, Wait till the night is o'er; Wait till I see the morn-ing

CHORUS

O - ver the jas - per sea.
On - ly a few more tears! Safe in the arms of Je - sus, Safe on His
Break on the gold-en shore.

gen-tle breast, There by His love o'er-shad - ed, Sweet-ly my soul shall rest.

9   Pass Me Not, O Gentle Savior

FANNY J. CROSBY   WILLIAM H. DOANE

1. Pass me not, O gen-tle Sav-ior, Hear my hum-ble cry; While on oth-ers
2. Let me at a throne of mer-cy Find a sweet re-lief; Kneel-ing there in
3. Trust-ing on-ly in Thy mer-it, Would I seek Thy face; Heal my wound-ed,
4. Thou the Spring of all my com-fort, More than life to me, Whom have I on

CHORUS

Thou art call-ing, Do not pass me by.
deep con-tri-tion, Help my un-be-lief.
bro-ken spir-it, Save me by Thy grace.   Sav-ior, Sav-ior, hear my
earth be-side Thee? Whom in heav'n, but Thee?

hum-ble cry, While on oth-ers Thou art call-ing, Do not pass me by.

10   Fling Out the Banner! Let It Float

GEORGE W. DOANE   JOHN B. CALKIN

1. Fling out the ban-ner! let it float Sky-ward and sea-ward, high and wide;
2. Fling out the ban-ner! heath-en lands Shall see from far the glo-rious sight,
3. Fling out the ban-ner! let it float Sky-ward and sea-ward, high and wide,

The sun that lights its shin-ing folds, The cross on which the Sav-ior died.
And na-tions, crowd-ing to be born, Bap-tize their spir-its in its light.
Our glo-ry, on-ly in the cross; Our on-ly hope, the Cru-ci-fied.

Jesus, Lover of My Soul

CHARLES WESLEY

SIMEON B. MARSH

1. { Je - sus lov - er of my soul, Let me to Thy bo - som fly
   { While the near - er wa - ters roll, While the tempest sill is high; }

2. { Oth - er ref - uge have I none, Hangs my help - less soul on Thee;
   { Leave, oh, leave me not a - lone, Still sup - port and com - fort me. }

3. { Thou, O Christ, art all I want, More than all in Thee I find;
   { Raise the fall - en, cheer the faint, Heal the sick and lead the blind. }

Hide me, O my Sav - ior, hide, Till the storm of life is past;
All my trust on Thee is stayed, All my help from Thee I bring;
Just and ho - ly is Thy name; I am all un - righteous - ness;

Safe in - to the ha - ven guide, Oh, re - ceive my soul at last.
Cov - er my de - fence - less head With the shad - ow of Thy wing.
Vile and full of sin I am, Thou art full of truth and grace.

Nearer, My God, to Thee

12

SARAH F. ADAMS

LOWELL MASON

Slowly

1. Near - er, my God, to Thee, Near - er to Thee! E'en tho' it be a cross
2. Tho' like the wan - der - er, The sun gone down, Dark - ness be o - ver me,
3. There let the way ap - pear Steps un - to heav'n; All that Thou sendest me
4. Or if on joy - ful wing Cleav - ing the sky, Sun, moon, and stars forgot,

D.S. Near - er, my God, to Thee,

Fine.

D.S.

That rais - eth me, Still all my song shall be, Near - er, my God, to Thee,
My rest a stone, Yet in my dreams I'd be, Near - er, my God, to Thee,
In mer - cy giv'n; An - gels to beck - on me, Near - er, my God, to Thee,
Up - ward I fly, Still all my song shall be, Near - er, my God, to Thee,

Near - er to Thee.

Lead, Kindly Light

JOHN HENRY NEWMAN

JOHN B. DYKES

1. Lead, kind-ly Light, a-mid th'en-cir-cling gloom, Lead Thou me on! The night is
2. I was not ev - er thus, nor pray'd that Thou Shouldst lead me on; I loved to
3. So long Thy pow'r hath blest me, sure it still Will lead me on O'er moor and

dark, and I am far from home; Lead Thou me on! Keep Thou my feet; I
choose and see my path; but now Lead Thou me on! I loved the gar - ish
fen, o'er crag and tor-rent, till The night is gone, And with the morn those

do not ask to see___ The dis-tant scene; one step e - nough for me.
day, and, spite of fears,___ Pride ruled my will. Re-mem-ber not past years!
an - gel fa - ces smile___ Which I have loved long since, and lost a - while.

In the Cross of Christ I Glory

JOHN BOWRING

ITHAMAR CONKEY

1. In the cross of Christ I glo - ry, Tow'r-ing o'er the wrecks of time;
2. When the woes of life o'er-take me, Hopes de-ceive, and fears an-noy,
3. When the sun of bliss is beam-ing Light and love up-on my way,
4. Bane and bless-ing, pain and pleas-ure, By the cross are sanc - ti - fied;

All the light of sa - cred sto - ry Gath-ers round its head sub-lime.
Nev-er shall the cross for - sake me; Lo! it glows with peace and joy.
From the cross the ra - diance stream-ing Adds more lus - ter to the day.
Peace is there, that knows no meas - ure, Joys that through all time a - bide. A - men.

God Be with You Till We Meet Again

15

JEREMIAH E. RANKIN

WILLIAM G. TOMER

1. God be with you till we meet a-gain, By His coun-sels guide, up-hold you,
2. God be with you till we meet a-gain, 'Neath His wings pro-tect-ing hide you,
3. God be with you till we meet a-gain, When life's per-ils thick con-found you,
4. God be with you till we meet a-gain, Keep love's ban-ner float-ing o'er you,

With His sheep se-cure-ly fold you, God be with you till we meet a-gain.
Dai-ly man-na still pro-vide you, God be with you till we meet a-gain
Put His arms un-fail-ing 'round you, God be with you till we meet a-gain.
Smite death's threat'ning wave before you, God be with you till we meet a-gain.

Till we meet, __ till we meet, Till we meet at Je-sus' feet;

Till we meet, till we meet, till we meet, Till we meet

Till we meet, __ till we meet, God be with you till we meet a-gain.

Till we meet, till we meet, till we meet,

Now the Day Is Over

16

SABINE BARING-GOULD

JOSEPH BARNBY

1. Now the day is o-ver, Night is drawing nigh, Shadows of the ev'ning Steal across the sky.
2. Jesus, give the weary Calm and sweet repose, With Thy tend'rest blessing, May our eyelids close.
3. When the morning wakens, Then may we arise Pure and fresh and sinless In Thy holy eyes.

17 Work, for the Night Is Coming

ANNIE L. WALKER-COGHILL

LOWELL MASON

1. Work, for the night is com - ing, Work thro' the morn-ing hours;
2. Work, for the night is com - ing, Work thro' the sun - ny noon;
3. Work, for the night is com - ing, Un - der the sun - set skies;

Fine.

Work, while the dew is spark - ling, Work 'mid spring-ing flow'rs;
Fill bright - est hours with la - bor, Rest comes sure and soon.
While their bright tints are glow - ing, Work, for day - light flies,

D.S. Work, for the night is com - ing, When man's work is done.
D.S. Work, for the night is com - ing, When man works no more.
D.S. Work while the night is dark'n - ing, When man's work is o'er.

cresc.

D.S.

Work, when the day grows bright - er, Work in the glow-ing sun;
Give ev - 'ry fly - ing min - ute, Some-thing to keep in store;
Work till the last beam fad - eth, Fad - eth to shine no more;

18 Softly Now the Light of Day

G. W. DOANE

CARL MARIA VON WEBER

1. Soft-ly now the light of day, Fades up - on my sight a - way;
2. Soon, for me, the light of day Shall for - ev - er pass a - way;

Free from care, from la - bor free, Lord, I would com - mune with Thee.
Then, from sin and sor - row free, Take me, Lord, to dwell with Thee.

Just As I Am

CHARLOTTE ELLIOTT   WM. B. BRADBURY

1. Just as I am, with-out one plea, But that Thy blood was shed for me, And
2. Just as I am, and wait-ing not To rid my soul of one dark blot, To
3. Just as I am, though toss'd a-bout With many a con-flict, many a doubt, Fight-
4. Just as I am, Thou wilt re-ceive, Wilt wel-come, par-don, cleanse, re-lieve; Be-

that Thou bidd'st me come to Thee, O Lamb of God, I come! I come!
Thee Whose blood can cleanse each spot, O Lamb of God, I come! I come!
ings and fears with-in, with-out, O Lamb of God, I come! I come!
cause Thy prom-ise I be-lieve, O Lamb of God, I come! I come! A-men.

Stand Up for Jesus

GEORGE DUFFIELD   GEORGE J. WEBB

1. Stand up, stand up for Je-sus, Ye sol-diers of the cross; Lift high His roy-al
2. Stand up, stand up for Je-sus, The trump-et call o-bey; Forth to the might-y
3. Stand up, stand up for Je-sus, Stand in His strength a-lone; The arm of flesh will
4. Stand up, stand up for Je-sus, The strife will not be long; This day the noise of

ban-ner, It must not suf-fer loss; From vic-t'ry un-to vic-t'ry, His ar-my
con-flict, In this His glorious day. Ye that are men, now serve Him, A-gainst un-
fail you, Ye dare not trust your own; Put on the gos-pel ar-mor, Each piece put
bat-tle, The next the vic-tor's song; To him that o-ver-com-eth, A crown of

shall He lead, Till ev-'ry foe is van-quish'd, And Christ is Lord in-deed.
num-ber'd foes; Let cour-age rise with dan-ger, And strength to strength op-pose.
on with pray'r; Where du-ty calls, or dan-ger, Be nev-er want-ing there.
life shall be; He with the King of glo-ry Shall reign e-ter-nal-ly. A-men.

Rock of Ages

A. M. TOPLADY

THOMAS HASTINGS

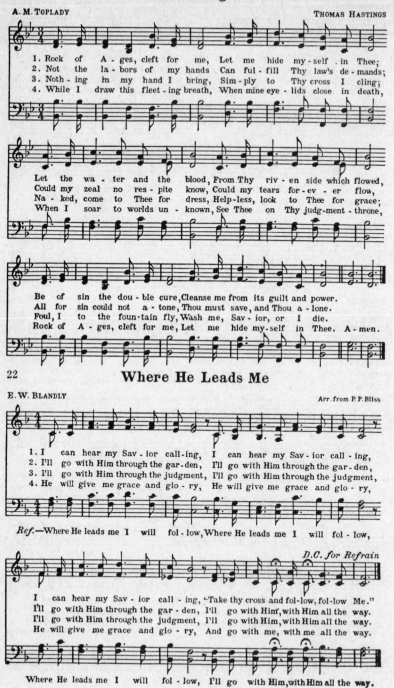

1. Rock of A - ges, cleft for me, Let me hide my - self in Thee;
2. Not the la - bors of my hands Can ful - fill Thy law's de - mands;
3. Noth - ing in my hand I bring, Sim - ply to Thy cross I cling;
4. While I draw this fleet - ing breath, When mine eye - lids close in death,

Let the wa - ter and the blood, From Thy riv - en side which flowed,
Could my zeal no res - pite know, Could my tears for - ev - er flow,
Na - ked, come to Thee for dress, Help - less, look to Thee for grace;
When I soar to worlds un - known, See Thee on Thy judg - ment - throne,

Be of sin the dou - ble cure, Cleanse me from its guilt and power.
All for sin could not a - tone, Thou must save, and Thou a - lone.
Foul, I to the foun - tain fly, Wash me, Sav - ior, or I die.
Rock of A - ges, cleft for me, Let me hide my - self in Thee. A - men.

22

Where He Leads Me

E. W. BLANDLY

Arr. from P. P. Bliss

1. I can hear my Sav - ior call - ing, I can hear my Sav - ior call - ing,
2. I'll go with Him through the gar - den, I'll go with Him through the gar - den,
3. I'll go with Him through the judgment, I'll go with Him through the judgment,
4. He will give me grace and glo - ry, He will give me grace and glo - ry,

Ref.—Where He leads me I will fol - low, Where He leads me I will fol - low,

D.C. for Refrain

I can hear my Sav - ior call - ing, "Take thy cross and fol - low, fol - low Me."
I'll go with Him through the gar - den, I'll go with Him, with Him all the way.
I'll go with Him through the judgment, I'll go with Him, with Him all the way.
He will give me grace and glo - ry, And go with me, with me all the way.

Where He leads me I will fol - low, I'll go with Him, with Him all the way.

Throw Out the Life-Line

E.S.U.

E. S. Ufford
Arr. by George C. Stebbins

1. Throw out the Life-Line a - cross the dark wave, There is a broth-er whom
2. Throw out the Life-Line with hand quick and strong: Why do you tar - ry, why
3. Throw out the Life-Line to dan-ger-fraught men, Sink-ing in an-guish where
4. Soon will the sea-son of res-cue be o'er, Soon will they drift to e -

some-one should save; Some-bod -y's broth - er! oh, who then, will dare To
lin - ger so long? See! he is sink-ing; oh, hast - en to - day— And
you've nev - er been: Winds of temp - ta - tion and bil - lows of woe Will
ter - ni - ty's shore, Haste then, my broth-er, no time for de - lay, But

CHORUS

throw out the Life-Line, his per - il to share?
out with the Life-Boat! a - way, then, a - way!
soon hurl them out where the dark wa - ters flow.   Throw out the Life - Line!
throw out the Life-Line and save them to - day.

Throw out the Life-Line! Some-one is drift - ing a - way; Throw out the

Life - Line! Throw out the Life-Line! Some-one is sink - ing to - day.

The First Noel

WORDS TRADITIONAL

AIR TRADITIONAL

1. The first No - el the an-gel did say Was to certain poor shepherds in fields as they lay
2. They look-ed up and saw a star Shining in the East beyond them far,
3. This star drew nigh to the north-west, O'er Beth - le-hem it took its rest,
4. Then en-ter'd in there Wise-men three, Full rev - 'rent - ly up - on their knee,

In fields where they lay keeping their sheep On a cold winter's night that was so deep.
And to the earth it gave great light, And so it con - tinued both day and night.
And there it did both stop and stay Right o - ver the place where Je - sus lay.
And of - fer'd there in His pres-ence, Their gold and myrrh and frank-incense.

CHORUS

No - el, No - el, No - el, No - el, Born is the King of Is - ra - el.

Silent Night

JOSEPH MÖHR

FRANZ GRÜBER

1. Si - lent night! Ho-ly night! All is calm, all is bright. Round yon virgin mother and Child!
2. Si - lent night! Ho-ly night! Shepherds quake at the sight! Glories stream from Heaven a-far,
3. Si - lent night! Ho-ly night! Son of God, love's pure light Radiant beams from Thy holy face,

Ho - ly Infant, so tender and mild, Sleep in heavenly peace, Sleep in heaven - ly peace.
Heav'nly hosts sing Al - le - lu - ia, Christ, the Savior, is born! Christ, the Savior, is born!
With the dawn of redeeming grace, Je - sus, Lord, at Thy birth, Je - sus, Lord, at Thy birth.

While Shepherds Watched Their Flocks

NAHUM TATE   ARR. FROM GEORGE F. HANDEL

1. While shepherds watched their flocks by night, All seated on the ground; The an-gel
2. "Fear not," said he,—for might-y dread Had seized their troubled minds, "Glad ti-dings
3. "To you in Da-vid's town this day, Is born of Da-vid's line, The Sav-ior,
4. The Heav'n-ly Babe you there shall find To hu-man view dis-played, All mean-ly
5. Thus spake the Ser-aph— and forth-with Ap-peared a shin-ing throng Of an-gels,
6. "All glo-ry be to God on high, And to the earth be peace; Good-will hence-

of the Lord came down, And glo-ry shone a-round, And glo-ry shone a-round.
of great joy I bring, To you and all man-kind, To you and all man-kind.
Who is Christ, the Lord, And this shall be the sign; And this shall be the sign;—
wrapped in swath-ing bands, And in a man-ger laid. And in a man-ger laid."
prais-ing God, who thus Ad-dressed their joy-ful song:— Ad-dressed their joy-ful song.
forth, from heav'n to me Be-gin and nev-er cease! Be-gin and nev-er cease!"

We Three Kings of Orient Are

J.H.H.   JOHN H. HOPKINS

1. We three kings of O-ri-ent are, Bear-ing gifts we trav-erse far
2. Born a babe on Beth-le-hem's plain, Gold we bring to crown Him a-gain;
3. Frank-in-cense to of-fer have I; In-cense owns a De-i-ty nigh.
4. Myrrh is mine; its bit-ter per-fume Breathes a life of gath-'ring gloom;
5. Glo-rious now be-hold Him rise, King and God and Sac-ri-fice;

Field and foun-tain, moor and moun-tain, Fol-low-ing yon-der Star.
King for-ev-er, ceas-ing nev-er, O-ver us all to reign.
Pray'r and prais-ing all men rais-ing, Wor-ship God on high.
Sorrowing, sigh-ing, bleed-ing, dy-ing, Sealed in the stone-cold tomb.
Heav'n sings "Hal-le-lu-jah!" "Hal-le-lu-jah!" earth re-plies.

CHORUS

Oh, star of won-der, star of might, Star with roy-al beau-ty bright,

West-ward lead-ing, still pro-ceed-ing, Guide us to the per-fect light.

Sun of My Soul

PETER RITTER
Arr. by William H. Monk

JOHN KEBLE

1. Sun of my soul! Thou Sav-ior dear, It is not night if Thou be near;
2. When the soft dews of kind-ly sleep My wea-ry eye-lids gen-tly steep,
3. A-bide with me from morn till eve, For with-out Thee I can-not live;
4. Come near and bless us when we wake, Ere through the world our way we take;

O may no earth-born cloud a-rise To hide Thee from Thy serv-ant's eyes.
Be my last thought, how sweet to rest For-ev-er on my Sav-ior's breast.
A-bide with me when night is nigh, For with-out Thee I dare not die.
Till, in the o-cean of Thy love, We lose our-selves in heav'n a-bove. A-men.

29

America, the Beautiful

(Tune "Materna")

KATHERINE LEE BATES

SAMUEL A. WARD

1. O beau-ti-ful for spacious skies, For amber waves of grain, For purple mountain
2. O beau-ti-ful for pil-grim feet Whose stern impassion'd stress A thorough-fare of
3. O beau-ti-ful for he-roes prov'd In lib-er-at-ing strife, Who more than self their
4. O beau-ti-ful for pa-triot dream That sees beyond the years Thine al-a-bas-ter

maj-es-ties A-bove the fruit-ed plain. A-mer-i-ca! A-mer-i-ca! God
freedom beat A-cross the wil-der-ness. A-mer-i-ca! A-mer-i-ca! God
coun-try loved, And mer-cy more than life. A-mer-i-ca! A-mer-i-ca! May
cit-ies gleam Un-dimmed by hu-man tears. A-mer-i-ca! A-mer-i-ca! God

shed His grace on thee, And crown thy good with brotherhood From sea to shining sea.
mend thine ev'ry flaw, Con-firm thy soul in self-control, Thy lib-er-ty in law.
God thy gold re-fine Till all success be no-ble-ness, And ev'ry gain di-vine.
shed His grace on thee, And crown thy good with brotherhood From sea to shining sea.